THE

COOKBOOK

VOLUME II

REVISED

THE

Gourmet

COOKBOOK

VOLUME II

REVISED

GOURMET

New York

COMPILED AND EDITED BY GOURMET, INC.

FIRST EDITION—5 PRINTINGS, 1957–1963
REVISED EDITION—FIRST PRINTING, 1965
SECOND PRINTING, 1969
THIRD PRINTING, 1971
FOURTH PRINTING, 1972
FIFTH PRINTING, 1974
SIXTH PRINTING, 1976
SEVENTH PRINTING, 1979

Published by
GOURMET BOOKS, INC.
777 THIRD AVENUE
NEW YORK, N.Y. 10017

Manufactured by Dai Nippon Printing Co., Ltd., Tokyo, Japan
ISBN: 0-933166-01-x

Introduction

Eight years ago, we had the pleasure of bringing forth Volume II of THE GOURMET COOKBOOK. *Its publication gave us the opportunity to put in book form a new selection of* GOURMET *recipes, to go further into pastry making* à la française, *outdoor cookery, and the accouterments of the grand buffet, and also to express our ideas on serving wines and spirits. Aside from a handful of basic preparations, none of the recipes in Volume II are found in Volume I. As previous owners of* THE GOURMET COOKBOOK *set know, each volume complements the other but is a complete and independent cookbook in itself.*

Now we are publishing, simultaneously, a new edition of THE GOURMET COOKBOOK, *Volumes I and II. Our reasons for doing so have been elaborated on in the introduction to Volume I, which we repeat here for the benefit of those who possess only this volume.*

This new edition of THE GOURMET COOKBOOK appears as GOURMET Magazine nears its silver anniversary. It is a time of pride for all of us who have labored together over the years in the cause of good living—a cause so beautifully served by the volume in your hands.

When I first decided to create a magazine devoted to good eating, my friends sought to dissuade me, saying there was not sufficient interest in this country to support such a publication. My answer was that if the interest was not there, we'd strive to bring it into being.

We did, and we succeeded. Twenty-five years ago many sophisticated people regarded this country as a gastronomic wasteland, and in many respects is was. While Americans appreciated many of the fine arts—painting and music, for example—few had respect for the art of gastronomy. Today there exists a new generation of gourmets—many thousands of Americans who have enriched and nourished their lives through the art of gastronomy, who have a deep appreciation of fine food and take pride and pleasure in preparing it. The interest in gastronomy has grown apace, and is reflected in the tremendous emergence of specialty foods and imported delicacies, the proliferation of truly fine restaurants, the increasing use of wines and knowledge of viticulture.

So many of these gourmets have been nurtured by GOURMET, the only American magazine devoted exclusively to good living as exemplified by fine food and drink. GOURMET has provided food for thought and inspiration—stories of the lore of gastronomy, reviews of restaurants, articles on the wine-growing regions of the world. It has articulated a philosophy whose basic tenet holds that good cooks make the most of what they have, but refuse to compromise with quality, and approach their art creatively and, above all, with joy—for enthusiasm is essential to achievement in any art. But most of all GOURMET has published recipes—several hundred a year—and it was from these that THE GOURMET COOKBOOK resulted . . . which immediately established itself as the greatest collection of recipes in the English language.

Why, it may be asked, in view of THE GOURMET COOKBOOK's enthusiastic acceptance in thousands of homes, and the continued growth of its sales, is this new edition necessary? Frankly, the answer is that recent technical refinements in the art of the book made us look critically at the original edition. When, a year or so back, we published GOURMET's MENU COOKBOOK, we had to recognize— as everyone else agreed—that it was GOURMET's most handsome book to date. The color photographs, in particular, were vastly superior to those in the first edition of THE GOURMET COOKBOOK. As we were determined to maintain the preeminence of this book, we decided to produce a new edition that would take full advantage of the new developments in photography and printing, and the photographs in this volume (there are ninety-five in full color) are entirely new.

And, since there is little that is human that cannot be improved, we also took the opportunity to make a few revisions in the text. These take into account suggestions that we have received over the years from owners of THE GOURMET COOKBOOK. We are confident that this handsome new edition will be even more useful in the kitchen than its celebrated predecessor.

If the photographs are all new, and some of the text is slightly modified, the cover design and vignettes are the same that the late . . . Henry Stahlhut executed for the original edition . . . (In Volume II, many drawings in the Stahlhut style have been supplied.)

As for the recipes, they, as before, come from every cuisine in the world—from the Orient where the Chinese were masters of the culinary art centuries before the Western world was even civilized; from Spain, Italy, Greece, South America, and Middle Europe; from France where evolved perhaps the greatest national cuisine the world has ever known; and from the United States, a rich hunting ground for remarkable regional specialties. Simple, intermediate, and complex recipes comprise the collection, some of them the masterpieces of the most celebrated chefs, others the creations of unknown cooks. But most have come down through the ages, and represent the cumulative wisdom of millions of cooks who practiced their craft with artistry and with love.

And now, as always, I wish you *bon appétit!* This classical salutation, in its various national forms—*buon appetito!*, *guten Appetit!*, *priyatnyi appetit!*, or, simply, good appetite!—is a hearty wish that all of you will enjoy your food and drink. It is a toast to your health, but also a hope that you will experience all the pleasures—gustatory, esthetic, emotional, and imaginative—that fine food and drink can afford. It is the summation of what GOURMET has always stood for.

Let this new edition of THE GOURMET COOKBOOK, like its predecessor, be dedicated to the art of gastronomy and to the continued appreciation of good eating in America.

Earle R. MacAusland
PUBLISHER

Contents

Color Photographs

Color Photographs

THE

COOKBOOK

VOLUME II

REVISED

Drinks

The most sacred rite of hospitality is the proffering of refreshments, and almost always this includes some form of alcoholic liquor.

To stimulate the appetite we offer here a goodly selection of apéritifs: to be served chilled from the bottle, poured over ice, or mixed into a simple cocktail. We have compiled a chart to help you decide which wines to serve with which foods; and we help you choose a beverage to accompany the after-dinner pleasantries.

For the rest, the long drinks, the punches, and the eggnogs, the coffees and the teas we leave you to choose the season.

Among the most popular of the apéritif flavored wines are Dubonnet, dry or sweet vermouth, Lillet, Amer Picon, Byrrh, St. Raphael, and the Italian specialty Campari bitters. Dry Madeira and Sherry are also apéritif— or appetizing—wines. Only foods of the nature of dry biscuits, cheese crackers, or olives should accompany the apéritif before a dinner with wine.

Apéritifs with Soda

For each drink put 3 or 4 ice cubes in a tall glass and half fill it with your favorite apéritif. Fill the glass with soda water, twist a strip of lemon peel over it, and drop in the peel.

These apéritifs lend themselves well to this recipe: Dubonnet, St. Raphael, Lillet, Byrrh, Pernod, and sweet or dry vermouth.

Amer Picon Cooler

For each drink put 3 or 4 ice cubes in a highball glass and pour over them 2 jiggers Amer Picon and 1/2 jigger grenadine. Stir well and fill the glass with soda water.

Americano Pour 2 jiggers sweet vermouth and 1 jigger Campari over ice cubes in a high-ball glass. Drop in a twist of lemon peel and fill the glass with soda water.

Byrrh Cassis Pour 2 jiggers Byrrh and 1 teaspoon *crème de cassis* over ice cubes in a highball glass. Fill the glass with soda water and blend.

For a shorter drink, combine the same ingredients in an Old Fashioned glass half full of ice.

Dubonnet On the Rocks Half fill an Old Fashioned glass with ice. Fill the glass with Dubonnet and add a strip of lemon peel, twisted.

Pernod Half fill a mixing glass with cracked ice and pour over it 1 part each of Pernod, dry vermouth, and sweet vermouth. Stir the mixture thoroughly and strain it into chilled cocktail glasses.

Picon Half fill a mixing glass with ice and pour over it 1 part each of Amer Picon and dry vermouth. Stir the mixture thoroughly and strain it into chilled cocktail glasses.

Picon Grenadine Half fill an Old Fashioned glass with cracked ice and pour over it 1 jigger Amer Picon and 1/2 jigger grenadine. Stir the mixture to blend it and fill the glass with soda water.

Vermouth Cassis Pour 2 jiggers dry vermouth and 2/3 jigger *crème de cassis* over ice cubes in a highball glass. Fill the glass with soda water and stir the mixture gently to blend it.

For a shorter drink, combine the same ingredients in an Old Fashioned glass half full of ice.

Vermouth Dubonnet Half fill a mixing glass with ice and pour over it 1 part each of dry vermouth and Dubonnet. Stir the mixture thoroughly and strain it into chilled cocktail glasses. Twist a strip of lemon peel over each drink and drop it in.

Vermouth Half and Half Half fill a mixing glass with ice and pour over it equal parts sweet and dry vermouth. Stir the mixture thoroughly and strain it into chilled cocktail glasses. Twist a strip of lemon peel over each drink and drop it in.

Half fill an Old Fashioned glass with ice. Fill the glass with either sweet or dry vermouth and add a strip of lemon peel, twisted.

Vermouth On the Rocks

Since hard liquors spoil the palate for fine wines, the knowledgeable gourmet generally reserves cocktails for occasions when food to inspire thirst and the drink to quench it are in order, and the meal, if any, that follows is not the concern of the host. The cocktails included here are those most likely to succeed with most hosts.

Cocktails

Half fill a cocktail shaker with cracked ice and pour over it 1 part Cherry Heering, 2 parts lime juice, and 8 parts gin. Shake the mixture vigorously and strain it into chilled cocktail glasses.

Admiral

Half fill a cocktail shaker with cracked ice and pour over it 1 part each of crème de cacao and heavy cream. Add 4 parts gin, shake the mixture vigorously, and strain it into chilled cocktail glasses.

Alexander

Half fill a cocktail shaker with cracked ice and pour over it 1 part each of lime juice and Cointreau and 2 parts apple brandy. Shake the mixture vigorously and strain it into chilled cocktail glasses.

Applecart

Half fill a cocktail shaker with cracked ice and add 1 part lemon or lime juice, 4 parts Bacardi light rum, and 1/2 teaspoon sugar and 3 dashes of grenadine for each drink. Shake the mixture vigorously and strain it into chilled cocktail glasses.

Bacardi

Half fill a cocktail shaker with cracked ice and pour over it 2 parts rum and 1 part each of applejack, lemon juice, triple sec, and pineapple juice. Shake the mixture vigorously and strain it into chilled cocktail glasses.

Banyan Tree

Half fill a cocktail shaker with cracked ice and pour over it 1 part each of white rum, brandy, and Cointreau or triple sec. Add the juice of 1/2 lemon for each drink, shake the mixture vigorously, and strain it into chilled cocktail glasses.

Between the Sheets

Half fill a mixing glass with cracked ice and pour over it 1 part lemon juice, 2 parts Curaçao, 8 parts brandy, and 1 dash of bitters for each drink. Shake the mixture vigorously and strain it into chilled cocktail glasses.

Brandy Cocktail

Bronx Half fill a cocktail shaker with cracked ice and pour over it 1 part each of orange juice and dry vermouth. Add 4 parts gin, shake the mixture thoroughly, and strain it into chilled cocktail glasses.

Champagne Cocktail In a chilled Champagne coupe, saturate a lump of sugar with Angostura bitters. Add a cube of ice and fill the glass with Champagne. Twist a strip of lemon peel over the glass and drop it in.

Chartreuse Champagne Cocktail In a chilled Champagne coupe put 1 lump of sugar, 2 drops of Angostura bitters, and 2 teaspoons Cognac. Let the mixture mellow for a while. Fill the coupe with well-chilled Champagne and carefully float on the wine 1 teaspoon green Chartreuse.

Maxim's Champagne Cocktail In a chilled Champagne coupe crush 1 lump of sugar and add 2 brandied cherries. Fill the glass with chilled Champagne.

Clover Club Half fill a cocktail shaker with very finely cracked ice and pour over it 1 part grenadine, 2 parts lemon juice, and 8 parts gin. Add the white of 1 egg for each 2 drinks, shake the mixture vigorously, and strain it into chilled cocktail glasses.

Cuban Tango Half fill a cocktail shaker with cracked ice and pour over it 1 part Curaçao, 2 parts each of pineapple and lime juice, and 8 parts white rum. Shake the mixture vigorously and strain it into chilled cocktail glasses. Twist a strip of lemon peel over each glass and drop it in.

Daiquiri Half fill a cocktail shaker with cracked ice and pour over it 1 part bar syrup, 2 parts lime juice, and 8 parts white rum. Shake the mixture vigorously and strain it into chilled cocktail glasses.

Dubonnet Cocktail Half fill a mixing glass with ice and pour over it 1 part each of Dubonnet and gin. Stir the mixture thoroughly and strain it into chilled cocktail glasses. Twist a strip of lemon peel over each glass and drop it in.

El Presidente Half fill a cocktail shaker with cracked ice and pour over it 1 part each of Curaçao and dry vermouth. Add 3 parts golden rum and 1 dash of grenadine. Shake the mixture vigorously and strain it into cocktail glasses.

The Flips Half fill a cocktail shaker with cracked ice, pour over it 1 teaspoon bar syrup and 1 jigger Port, Sherry, Cognac, or rum and drop in 1 egg. Shake the mixture vigorously and strain it into a cocktail glass. Sprinkle generously with freshly grated nutmeg.

Maxim's Champagne Cocktail

Frisco   Half fill a mixing glass with ice and pour over it 1 part Bénédictine and 4 parts bourbon. Stir the mixture thoroughly and strain it into chilled cocktail glasses. Twist a strip of lemon peel over each glass and drop it in.

Gibson   Half fill a mixing glass with ice and pour over it 1 part dry vermouth and 6 parts gin. Stir the mixture thoroughly and strain it into chilled cocktail glasses. Drop a cocktail onion into each drink.

Gin and Bitters   Rinse the inside of an Old Fashioned glass with Angostura bitters and pour out the excess. Add ice and 1 jigger gin. Optional: twist a strip of lemon peel over the glass and drop it in.

Irish Velvet   Half fill a cocktail shaker with ice and pour over it 1 part bar syrup, 2 parts lemon juice, and 6 parts Irish whiskey. Add 1 egg white for each 2 drinks, shake the mixture vigorously, and strain it into chilled cocktail glasses.

Jack Rose   Half fill a cocktail shaker with cracked ice and pour over it 1 part grenadine, 2 parts lime juice, and 8 parts apple brandy. Shake the mixture vigorously and strain it into chilled cocktail glasses.

Manhattan   Half fill a mixing glass with ice and pour over it 1 part sweet vermouth and 2 parts whiskey, and add a dash of bitters. Stir the mixture thoroughly and strain it into chilled cocktail glasses, each containing a cherry.

Dry Manhattan   Half fill a mixing glass with ice and add 1 part dry vermouth, 4 parts whiskey, and a dash of bitters. Stir the mixture thoroughly and strain it into chilled cocktail glasses. Twist a strip of lemon peel over each glass and drop it in.

Dry Martini   Half fill a mixing glass with ice and pour over it 1 part dry vermouth and 6 parts gin. Stir the mixture thoroughly and strain it into chilled cocktail glasses. A green olive, a strip of lemon peel, twisted over the glass, or both may be added to each cocktail.

Dry Martini on the Rocks   Half fill an Old Fashioned glass with ice and pour over it 1 part dry vermouth and 6 parts gin. Stir the mixture gently, twist a strip of lemon peel over the glass, and drop it in.

Half fill a mixing glass with ice and pour over it 1 part dry Sherry and 5 parts gin. Stir the mixture gently and strain it into chilled cocktail glasses. Twist a strip of lemon peel over each cocktail and drop it in. *Sherry Martini*

Half fill a mixing glass with ice and pour over it 1 part each of sweet and dry vermouth. Add 6 parts gin, stir the mixture thoroughly, and strain it into chilled cocktail glasses, each containing a green olive. *Sweet Martini*

Half fill a mixing glass with ice and pour over it 1 part dry vermouth and 6 parts vodka. Stir the mixture thoroughly and strain it into chilled cocktail glasses. A green olive may be added to each glass. *Vodka Martini*

In an Old Fashioned glass crush 1 lump of sugar with a dash of bitters and 1 teaspoon water. Half fill the glass with ice, add 1 jigger whiskey, and blend the mixture gently. Garnish with a cherry and a slice of orange, and twist a strip of lemon peel over the glass and drop it in. *Old Fashioned*

In an Old Fashioned glass crush 1 lump of sugar with a dash of bitters and 1 teaspoon water. Half fill the glass with ice, add 1 jigger Scotch whisky and blend the mixture gently. Garnish with a cherry and a slice of orange, twist a strip of lemon peel over the glass, and drop it in. *Scotch Old Fashioned*

In an Old Fashioned glass crush 1 lump of sugar with a dash of bitters and 1 teaspoon water. Half fill the glass with ice, add 1 jigger Canadian whiskey, and blend the mixture gently. Garnish with a cherry and a slice of orange, twist a strip of lemon peel over the glass, and drop it in. *Canadian Old Fashioned*

Half fill a cocktail shaker with cracked ice and pour over it 1/2 part bar syrup, 4 parts orange juice, and 8 parts gin. Shake the mixture vigorously and strain it into chilled cocktail glasses. *Orange Blossom*

Half fill a cocktail shaker with cracked ice and pour over it 1 part grenadine, 2 parts lemon juice, 2 parts apple brandy, 6 parts gin, and 1 egg white to each 2 drinks. Shake the mixture vigorously and strain it into chilled cocktail glasses. *Pink Lady*

Into a mixing glass half full of ice pour 1 1/2 parts vodka and 1/2 part each of white crème de menthe and Cognac. Stir the mixture thoroughly and strain it into a chilled cocktail glass. *Pump Room Special*

This is a Manhattan made with Scotch whisky. Half fill a mixing glass with ice and pour over it 1 part sweet vermouth, 2 parts Scotch whisky, *Rob Roy*

Screwdriver

and a dash of bitters. Stir the mixture thoroughly and strain it into chilled cocktail glasses, each containing a cherry.

Half fill a cocktail shaker with cracked ice and pour over it 1 part each of fresh lime juice and dark honey. Add 4 parts Barbados rum (or 2 parts each of Jamaica and Puerto Rican white rum), shake the mixture vigorously, and strain it into chilled cocktail glasses. *Rum Lime Cocktail*

Half fill a cocktail shaker with cracked ice and pour over it 1 part each of orange juice and white rum. Add 1 dash of grenadine for each drink, shake the mixture vigorously, and strain it into Champagne coupes. Garnish each drink with half an orange slice. *Rum Runner Cocktail*

Rinse the inside of an Old Fashioned glass with a dash of Pernod. Add 1 lump of sugar and moisten it with a dash each of Angostura and Peychaud's bitters. Add just enough water so that the sugar lump may be crushed and dissolved. Half fill the glass with ice and pour over it 1 jigger bourbon. Stir the mixture lightly, twist a strip of lemon peel over the glass, and drop it in. *Sazerac Cocktail*

Half fill an Old Fashioned glass with finely crushed ice and pour over it 1 jigger Scotch whisky. Twist a strip of lemon peel over each glass and drop it in. *Scotch Mist*

Half fill a cocktail shaker with cracked ice and pour over it 1 part each of orange juice and vodka. Shake the mixture vigorously and strain it into chilled cocktail glasses. *Screwdriver*

Half fill a cocktail shaker with cracked ice and pour over it 1 part bar syrup, 2 parts lime juice, 8 parts white rum, 3 dashes of grenadine, and 1 egg white for each 2 drinks. Shake the mixture vigorously and strain it into chilled cocktail glasses. *September Morn*

Half fill a cocktail shaker with cracked ice and pour over it 1 part each of Cointreau and lemon juice, and 2 parts brandy. Shake the mixture vigorously and strain it into chilled cocktail glasses. *Sidecar*

Sugar House
Special   Half fill a cocktail shaker with cracked ice and pour over it 3 parts white rum, 2 parts lemon juice, and maple syrup to taste. Shake the mixture vigorously and strain it into chilled cocktail glasses.

Sundowner   Half fill a cocktail shaker with cracked ice and pour over it 1 part each of lemon juice, orange juice, and Van der Hum. Add 6 parts brandy, shake the mixture vigorously, and strain it into chilled cocktail glasses.

Third Rail   Pour into a cocktail shaker half full of cracked ice 1 part each of dry vermouth, sweet vermouth, and orange juice. Add 6 parts golden rum, shake the mixture vigorously, and strain it into chilled cocktail glasses.

West End   Half fill a cocktail shaker with cracked ice and pour over it 1 jigger gin and 1/2 teaspoon each of cherry liqueur and orange juice. Shake the mixture vigorously, and strain it into a chilled Champagne coupe. Fill the glass with chilled Champagne and stir slightly to blend.

Whiskey Sour   Half fill a cocktail shaker with ice and pour over it 1 part bar syrup, 2 parts lemon juice, and 8 parts bourbon or rye whiskey. Shake the mixture vigorously, strain it into whiskey-sour glasses, and garnish with a cherry and a slice of orange.

Rum Sour   Half fill a cocktail shaker with ice and pour over it 1 part bar syrup, 2 parts lime juice, and 8 parts golden rum. Shake the mixture vigorously, strain it into whiskey-sour glasses, and garnish each drink with a cherry and a stick of pineapple.

Scotch Sour   Half fill a cocktail shaker with ice and pour over it 1 part bar syrup, 2 parts lemon juice, and 8 parts Scotch whisky. Shake the mixture vigorously, strain it into whiskey-sour glasses, and garnish with a cherry and a slice of lemon.

Brandy Sour   Half fill a cocktail shaker with ice and pour over it 1 part bar syrup, 2 parts lemon juice and 8 parts brandy. Shake the mixture vigorously, strain it into whiskey-sour glasses, and garnish each glass with a cherry.

White Lady   Half fill a cocktail shaker with cracked ice and pour over it 1 part Cointreau or triple sec, 2 parts lemon juice, and 8 parts gin. Add the white of 1 egg for each 2 drinks, shake the mixture vigorously, and strain it into chilled cocktail glasses.

Long drinks or coolers fit into the scheme of things at a cocktail party and also make odd-hour relaxation worthy of the name. Scotch and soda, gin and tonic, and bourbon and water contribute to civilized living, as do the mint julep and the various members of the Collins family. Long drinks are for leisure.

Half fill a Pilsner glass with very cold stout. Fill the glass very slowly with iced Champagne.

Black Velvet

Fill a large highball glass or a beer mug half full with ale, then fill the glass or mug to the top with ginger ale.

Shandygaff

Traditionally cobblers are wine coolers served in goblets. Fill a goblet with finely cracked ice and pour over it 2 jiggers Port, claret, Burgundy, Rhine wine, or Sauternes and add 1/2 jigger each of Cognac and Curaçao. Stir the mixture gently to blend well and garnish the drink with fruits and a sprig of fresh mint.
     Whiskey or rum may be substituted for the wine.

The Cobblers

Fill a silver mug or a glass goblet with finely shaved ice and stir until the outside of the mug is frosted. Pour in 2 teaspoons grenadine, the juice of 1/2 lemon, and 1 jigger liquor—Cognac, gin, rum, applejack, bourbon, or rye. Fill the mug with soda water and garnish with fruit and a cherry.

The Daisies

Half fill a cocktail shaker with ice and pour over it 1 teaspoon bar syrup, the juice of 1/2 lemon, and 1 jigger liquor. The liquor may be gin, vodka, applejack, bourbon, rye, rum or Irish or Scotch whisky. Shake the mixture thoroughly and strain it into a large highball glass over ice. Fill the glass with soda water and garnish with a cherry, orange or lemon slices, or what you will.
     The most familiar Collins is the Tom Collins, made with gin.

The Collinses

Half fill a cocktail shaker with cracked ice and pour over it the juice of 1 lemon, 1 teaspoon bar syrup, and 1 jigger liquor—gin, brandy, sloe gin, rum, applejack, rye, or bourbon. Shake the mixture vigorously and strain it into a highball glass containing ice cubes. Fill the glass with soda water and garnish it with a sprig of mint.

The Fizzes

The Rickeys Squeeze into a highball glass half full of ice the juice of 1/2 lime and drop in the shell. Add 1 jigger liquor—Cognac, rum, rye, bourbon, Scotch, gin, or sloe gin—and fill the glass with soda water.

The Slings Half fill a highball glass with cracked ice and pour over it 1 jigger liquor —gin, Cognac, Scotch, bourbon, or rye. Fill the glass with soda water and garnish it with a twist of lemon peel.

Empire Punch For each drink put 3 or 4 ice cubes in a tall glass and pour over the ice 1 teaspoon each of Bénédictine, Cointreau, and Cognac, and 2 jiggers claret. Blend the mixture gently and fill the glass with Champagne. Fresh whole strawberries or other fruit may be used to garnish the glass to your taste.

French "75" In a tall glass blend 1 jigger gin and 1/3 jigger lemon juice with 1 teaspoon confectioners' sugar. Half fill the glass with cracked ice and fill it with chilled Champagne.

Singapore Gin Sling Into a cocktail shaker half full of ice pour 1 teaspoon bar syrup, the juice of 1/2 lime, 1/2 jigger kirsch, 1 1/2 jiggers gin, and a dash of Angostura bitters. Shake the mixture vigorously and strain it into a highball glass. Add 2 or 3 ice cubes and fill the glass with soda water.

Ramos Gin Fizz Half fill a cocktail shaker with cracked ice and pour over it 1 teaspoon bar syrup, the juice of 1/2 lemon and 1/2 lime, 1/2 teaspoon orange flower water, 1 egg white, 1/2 jigger heavy cream, and 1 jigger gin. Shake the mixture for 5 minutes and strain it into a highball glass. Fill the glass with soda water.

Quinine or Tonic Highballs For each drink squeeze the juice of 1/4 lime over ice cubes in a highball glass and drop in the lime shell. Add 1 jigger liquor—gin or vodka—and fill the glass with quinine water.

Moscow Mule Pour 1 jigger vodka and the juice of 1/2 lime over ice cubes in a copper mug, silver goblet, or highball glass and fill the container with ginger beer. Stir the drink gently and garnish with a slice of lime.

Gourmet's Mint Julep The traditional mint julep cannot be successfully prepared either in quantity or ahead of time. Each must be made when needed. In a chilled glass or, preferably, a silver julep mug, put 3 or 4 leaves of fresh mint and 1 teaspoon each of sugar and water. Bruise the mint leaves gently with a wooden muddler and stir the mixture until the sugar is dissolved. Pack the glass to the brim with very finely crushed ice. Pour in 1 jigger bourbon and stir briskly until a frost appears on the outside of the container, then fill it with bourbon to the brim. Sprinkle a sprig of mint lightly with confectioners' sugar, cut the stem short, and set the mint in the ice to garnish the drink.

Squeeze into a mixing glass half full of ice the juice of 1/2 lime and drop in the shell. Add 1 jigger Demerara or Jamaica rum, 1 teaspoon grenadine, and a dash of Curaçao. Blend the mixture well and pour it into a highball glass with the ice. Fill the glass with soda water and garnish it with a stick of fresh pineapple and a cherry.   *Planter's Punch*

Pour 1 jigger golden rum and the juice of 1/2 lime over ice cubes in a large highball glass. Fill with cola and blend the drink gently.   *Cuba Libre*

Half fill a mixing glass with ice and pour over it 1 jigger Jamaica rum, 1 jigger each of Puerto Rican golden rum and white rum, 1 jigger pineapple juice, 1 jigger papaya juice, the juice of 1 lime, and 1 teaspoon bar syrup. Shake the mixture vigorously and pour it with the ice into a very tall highball glass. Garnish with a pineapple stick and a cherry and float 1 teaspoon Demerara rum on the top.   *Zombie*

Put 3 or 4 ice cubes in a tall glass and half fill the glass with Rhine, Moselle, or any other white wine. Fill the glass to the top with chilled soda water.   *Spritzer*

For each drink put 1 teaspoon bar syrup and the juice of 1 lemon in a tall glass. Add 2 jiggers claret and blend the mixture thoroughly. Put 3 or 4 ice cubes into the glass and fill it to the top with chilled soda water.   *Claret Lemonade*

Half fill a highball glass with crushed ice and pour over it 2 jiggers claret, 2 jiggers pineapple juice, a dash of lemon juice, and 1 teaspoon bar syrup. Blend the mixture thoroughly and fill the glass with soda water.   *Sangria*

After Dinner
Drinks

Although the trend in these times is for the gentlemen to withdraw from the dining room with the ladies, the tray of beverages offered with the demi-tasse still includes a selection of the liqueurs and fruit cordials that were once considered a feminine prerogative, as well as of the allegedly more masculine brandies. The choice is a bewildering one: apricot, anisette, Bénédictine, blackberry, Chartreuse, Cherry Heering, Cointreau, the crèmes —of fruit and of violette, cacao, café, menthe—Drambuie, kümmel, peach, Southern Comfort, Strega, tea, triple sec, Vieille Cure. Fruit brandies, Cognac, Armagnac, and the Greek Metaxa and the heavy-bodied Port and sweeter Madeiras also belong to the pleasant hour after dinner.

B. & B.   Half fill a liqueur glass with Bénédictine and fill it to the top with brandy.

D. & S.   Half fill a liqueur glass with Drambuie and fill it to the top with Scotch.

Angel's Dream   Fill a liqueur glass three-quarters full with apricot liqueur and then almost to the brim with heavy cream.

Angel's Kiss   Fill a liqueur glass three-quarters full with crème de cacao and top with heavy cream.

Occasionally this drink is made in four layers, with crème Yvette and prunelle between the crème de cacao and the cream.

Gourmet's Pousse-Café   In the glass especially designed for this drink, pour 2 teaspoons each of the following liqueurs in the order given: grenadine (red), crème de cacao (brown), maraschino (white), orange Curaçao (orange), crème de menthe (green), parfait amour (violet), and Cognac (amber). Add the liqueurs very slowly and carefully and they will not run together. A rainbow effect will be achieved.

Grasshopper   Half fill a cocktail glass with cracked ice and pour over it 1 part each of green crème de menthe, white crème de cacao, and cream. Shake the mixture thoroughly and strain it into chilled Champagne coupes.

Crème de Menthe Frappé   Lightly pack a Champagne coupe with shaved ice. Fill the coupe with green crème de menthe and serve it with a short straw.

In a mixing glass without ice, combine 2 parts Cognac and 1 part Drambuie. Blend the mixture thoroughly and serve it in liqueur glasses at room temperature. *Lanai Cordial*

Half fill a cocktail shaker with cracked ice and pour over it 1 part each of white crème de menthe and Cognac. Shake the mixture and strain it into cocktail glasses. *Stinger*

Half fill a cocktail shaker with cracked ice and pour over it 1 part lime juice, 2 parts white crème de menthe, and 6 parts Cognac. Shake the mixture vigorously and strain it into chilled cocktail glasses. *Dry Stinger*

In a mixing glass without ice, combine 1 part each of Cordial Médoc, Cognac, and Cointreau. Put an ice cube in each Champagne coupe, cover it with the liqueur mixture, and fill the glasses with chilled champagne. *Toscanini*

Half fill a cocktail shaker with cracked ice and pour over it 1 part each of apricot brandy, peach brandy, and fresh lime juice. Shake the mixture vigorously and strain it into chilled cocktail glasses. *Willard Hotel*

The following punch and eggnog recipes will produce 25 generous servings. Whether or not this amount will serve 25 persons depends on the duration of the party and the thirst of the guests.

Combine 1 1/2 fifths rye whiskey, 1 1/2 fifths claret, 6 cups strong black tea, 1 1/2 pints dark Jamaica rum, 3/4 pint gin, 3/4 pint Cognac, 3 ounces Bénédictine, 3 cups orange juice, and 1 1/2 cups lemon juice. Let the mixture stand 2 hours to develop full flavor and pour it over a large block of ice in a punch bowl. If a sweeter punch is desired add bar syrup to taste. *Artillery Punch*

In a large pitcher blend 1 cup each of bar syrup and Curaçao, 2 cups each of lemon juice and orange juice, 1 jigger grenadine, and 2 bottles Cognac. Allow the mixture to ripen for several hours. To serve, pour it over a large block of ice in a punch bowl and slowly add 2 bottles chilled Champagne, stirring the punch gently. *Brandy Punch*

In a pitcher combine 3 cups each of lemon juice and orange juice, 1 1/2 cups each of Curaçao and bar syrup, 1/4 cup grenadine, and 1 bottle Cognac *Brandy Champagne Punch* and let the mixture stand for 1 hour or more to ripen. To serve, pour the mixture over a large block of ice in a punch bowl and slowly blend in 2 bottles chilled Champagne.

Bubbly on the Block Blend together in a crock or bowl 1 pint vodka and 1/2 pint Triple Sec. Add 1 small unpeeled cucumber seeded and cut into strips and allow the mixture to ripen for at least 1 hour. To serve, pour the cucumber-liquor mixture over a large block of ice in a punch bowl and gently stir in 5 bottles chilled Champagne.

Claret Cup In a large pitcher put 8 slices of pineapple, cut in pieces, 8 small ripe peaches halved, 8 peach stones, 4 oranges, sliced, 2 lemons, sliced, 1/4 cup sugar, and several strips of cucumber rind. Add 1/2 cup each of Cognac and maraschino liqueur and allow the mixture to mellow for 4 hours. After another hour or at serving time, remove the peach stones and the cucumber rind and pour the mixture over a large block of ice in a punch bowl. Blend in 4 bottles claret and 2 quarts soda water. Garnish the bowl with mint sprigs.

Claret and Sauternes Punch In a pitcher blend 1 cup bar syrup, the juice of 6 lemons, and 1 cup each of Cointreau and Cognac. Pour the mixture over a large block of ice in a punch bowl and add to it 2 bottles each of chilled claret and Sauternes. Blend the punch while pouring in 2 quarts soda water and garnish it with thin slices of lemon and sprigs of fresh mint.

Dragoon Punch In a large punch bowl, without ice, combine 3 pints each of porter and ale, 1 cup each of Cognac, dry Sherry, and bar syrup, and 3 lemons, thinly sliced. To serve, put a large block of ice into a punch bowl and slowly add 2 bottles chilled Champagne.

East India Punch In a pitcher put the thinly cut rind of 4 lemons, cover with 3 cups Cognac, and let the mixture stand for 3 hours. To serve, strain the Cognac over a block of ice in a punch bowl, add 3 pints white Port, 2 cups bar syrup, 1 1/2 cups fresh lime juice, 2 quarts soda water, 1/2 cup arrack, and 5 or 6 sprigs of syringa, and taste the punch for sweetness.

Fish House Punch In a large bowl dissolve 1 1/2 cups sugar in 3 cups water. Add 3 cups lemon juice and 4 more cups water and stir thoroughly. Add 1 bottle Jamaica rum, 1 bottle Puerto Rican golden rum, and 1/2 cup peach brandy. Let the mixture stand for 3 hours to ripen, stirring it occasionally, pour it over a block of ice in a punch bowl and blend gently.

Golden Punch In a large pitcher combine 4 cups lemon juice, 3 cups orange juice, 1 cup grenadine, and 2 cups each of Curaçao and Cognac, and sweeten to taste with bar syrup. Let the mixture stand for 1 hour or more to ripen. To serve, pour the liquid over a large block of ice in a punch bowl and blend in 2 bottles white rum.

Peel, core, and slice 3 small, ripe pineapples. Put the slices in a bowl and sprinkle them with 2 cups fine granulated sugar. Cover, allow the fruit to marinate for 1 hour or more, and add 2 cups Cognac, 1 cup strained lemon juice, 3/4 cup *eau de vie de framboise*, 1/2 cup peach brandy, and 1/4 cup maraschino liqueur. Blend the mixture gently, cover, and allow to stand overnight to ripen. To serve, pour the mixture over a large block of ice in a punch bowl and slowly add 5 bottles chilled Champagne. Garnish the bowl with fresh raspberries, sprigs of fresh mint, thinly sliced lemons and oranges, and other fruits to taste.

Gourmet's Champagne Punch

In a crock or glass jar put 6 bunches *Waldmeister*, or woodruff, sprinkle them with 1 cup fine granulated sugar, and let them stand for 1 hour. Add 1/2 pint Cognac and 1 bottle Moselle, cover the mixture and let it stand in a 'cool place overnight. To serve, strain the mixture over a block of ice in a punch bowl and blend in 3 bottles Moselle and 2 bottles Champagne.

May Wine Bowl

Slice 8 oranges very thinly into a bowl or crock, sprinkle them with 1 cup fine granulated sugar, and add 1 bottle Moselle. Cover the bowl and let the fruit marinate in the wine for 1 hour or more. Pour the mixture over a large block of ice in a punch bowl and add 1 bottle chilled sparkling Moselle and 4 bottles chilled Champagne.

Moselle Cup

Peel and slice 6 ripe peaches into a small bowl or crock. Sprinkle the fruit with 1 cup fine granulated sugar and pour over it 1/2 bottle Rhine wine. Cover the bowl and let the fruit marinate in the wine overnight. To serve, pour the marinated fruit over a block of ice in a punch bowl and add 5 bottles Rhine wine. Serve one or two slices of peach in each glass.

Peach Bowle

Sliced fresh apricots, nectarines, or pineapple, or whole strawberries may be used in this recipe.

In a large pitcher combine 1/2 cup each of Cognac, Curaçao, and maraschino liqueur, 3 lemons, thinly sliced, 4 oranges, thinly sliced, and 1 pint

Penthouse Champagne Punch

raspberries. To serve, put a punch bowl on a bed of ice (no ice goes into the bowl), pour in the liqueur-fruit mixture, and gently stir in 6 bottles chilled Champagne.

Pink Champagne Bowl In a mixing bowl sprinkle 1 quart fresh, firm strawberries with 1/2 cup sugar. Add 1 bottle Sauternes and 1 cup Cognac and let the fruit marinate in the refrigerator for at least 1 hour. To serve, pour the strawberry mixture over a block of ice in a punch bowl, slowly add 4 bottles pink Champagne, and blend the punch gently.

Regent Punch In a large crock combine 1 fifth each of whiskey and golden rum, 3 cups strong tea, the juice of 6 oranges and 6 lemons, and 2 cups sugar. Blend the mixture thoroughly and let it ripen for several hours. To serve, pour it over a large block of ice in a punch bowl and gently stir in 2 bottles Champagne.

Rhenish Punch Combine in a pitcher 3/4 cup each of peach liqueur and Bénédictine, 3 oranges and 2 lemons, thinly sliced, and 3 sprigs of mint. Allow the mixture to stand for at least 2 hours. Pour it over a large block of ice in a punch bowl and add to it 2 cups washed and hulled strawberries. Add 6 bottles very cold Rhine wine and stir the mixture gently but thoroughly.

Rhine Wine Cooler Put a large block of ice in a punch bowl and pour over it 3/4 cup Falernum, the juice of 12 limes, 2 cups very dry Sherry, 1 1/2 cups Cognac, 1 1/2 cups strong tea, and 4 bottles Rhine or Moselle wine. Garnish the bowl with thin slices of peeled cucumber.

Rhine Wine Punch In a large bowl combine 1/2 pint each of bar syrup, dry Sherry, Cognac, and strong black tea. Add 2 cups fresh lemon juice and 3 bottles Rhine wine and blend the mixture thoroughly. Add the peel from a small cucumber but remove it after it has marinated for about 10 minutes. To serve, pour the mixture over a block of ice in a punch bowl and slowly blend in 1 quart soda water.

Rhine Wine and Pineapple Cut a fresh, ripe pineapple into 1-inch cubes, cover them in a crock or in a glass jar with 1 bottle Rhine wine, and let the mixture stand for several hours. To serve, pour the mixture over a large block of ice in a punch bowl, add 3 bottles chilled Rhine wine, 1 bottle chilled Champagne or sparkling Moselle, and 1 pint Jamaica rum. Blend the mixture gently.

St. Cecelia Society Punch Slice thinly 6 limes or 4 lemons and 1 ripe pineapple and marinate the fruit overnight in a covered crock with 1/2 bottle Cognac. At noon on the following day add 1 cup Jamaica rum, 3 cups green tea infusion, 1/2 bottle peach brandy, and 2 cups sugar. Blend the mixture thoroughly and pour it over a block of ice in a punch bowl. Stir in gently 3 bottles Champagne and 1 quart soda water.

Slice 4 peeled peaches and 2 peeled apricots into a bowl and add 2 cups Cognac or to cover. Allow the fruit to marinate 1 hour or longer. Put the fruit through a fine sieve, crack the fruit stones, add them to the bowl and marinate the mixture for 1 hour longer. Strain it over a block of ice in a punch bowl. Add 4 bottles chilled Sauternes and 2 bottles soda water and stir the punch gently. *Sauternes Punch*

In a large bowl blend together 1 cup brown sugar, 1 pint fresh lime juice, and 1 quart pineapple juice. Let the mixture ripen for at least 3 hours. To serve, pour it over a large block of ice in a punch bowl and add 4 bottles golden rum. Stir the punch thoroughly. *Stirrup Cup*

In a pitcher blend 3 bottles dry white wine, 3 jiggers maraschino liqueur, 3 jiggers Cognac, the thinly peeled rind of 2 lemons, and bar syrup to taste. To serve, pour the mixture over a block of ice in a punch bowl and blend in 2 quarts chilled soda water. Garnish the punch with peeled cucumber slices and fruits. *White Wine Cup*

Hot drinks—punches and toddies and their ilk—are cold weather favorites. *Hot Punches*

In a saucepan combine 3 fifths Calvados or applejack, 4 large twists of lemon peel, and 3 cups sugar. Heat the mixture but do not let it boil. When the sugar has dissolved pour the mixture into a warmed silver punch bowl, ignite it, and while it burns, slowly add 2 quarts boiling water. *Country Flamer*

In a saucepan heat, but do not boil, 4 bottles claret or another red wine, 2 quarts water, 1/2 teaspoon Angostura bitters, 1 teaspoon allspice, a 2-inch stick of cinnamon, 12 whole cloves, and 1/2 cup sugar. Swirl hot water in a silver punch bowl, pour off the water, and strain the wine into the bowl. *Mulled Wine*

In a large saucepan heat, but do not boil, 4 bottles hard cider, 1/2 teaspoon *Mulled Cider*

Angostura bitters, 1 teaspoon allspice, a 2-inch stick of cinnamon, 12 whole cloves, and 1/2 cup each of sugar and golden rum. Swirl hot water in a silver punch bowl, pour it off, and strain the hot cider mixture into the bowl.

Wassail Bowl   In a large saucepan combine 2 cups water, 2 teaspoons ground ginger, 1 teaspoon freshly grated nutmeg, a 2-inch stick of cinnamon, 6-whole cloves, 6 allspice berries, 4 coriander seeds, and 4 cardamom seeds. Bring the mixture to a boil and simmer it for 10 minutes. Add 2 quarts ale and 2 bottles Sherry or Madeira, and stir in 4 cups sugar. Heat the brew but do not let it boil. Beat 12 egg yolks until they are pale in color and fold in 12 egg whites beaten until stiff. Gradually strain half the ale and Sherry mixture over the eggs. Turn the brew into a warmed silver punch bowl. Bring the remaining ale and Sherry to the boiling point and strain it into the egg mixture. Add 1 cup Cognac and 12 roasted lady apples and serve hot. The apples may be served with the punch.

Grog   For each drink put the juice of 1/2 lemon, 1 lump of sugar, a slice of lemon studded with 3 cloves, a strip of orange rind, and 1 jigger golden rum in a glass or mug. Fill the glass with boiling water and stir with a stick of cinnamon.

Hot Buttered Rum   For each drink scald a china mug or an Old Fashioned glass and in it put 1 teaspoon maple sugar, 1 slice of lemon studded with 6 whole cloves, a 1-inch stick of cinnamon, and a pinch of nutmeg. Pour in 1 jigger golden rum, fill the mug with boiling water, drop in a generous teaspoon of unsalted butter. Carefully float a teaspoon of rum, warmed and ignited, on top.

Hot Buttered Rum and Cider   For each drink put into a silver or pewter cup a 2-inch strip of orange peel, 1 to 2 teaspoons brown sugar, and 1/2 jigger rum. Ignite the spirit and let the flame die. Add 1 jigger golden rum, 1 generous teaspoon unsalted butter, a small piece of cinnamon stick, and 3 pinches each of powdered cloves and allspice. Fill the mug to the top with scalding hot cider and stir vigorously.

Tom and Jerry   For each drink beat 1 egg yolk until it is pale and light. Add 1 teaspoon maple sugar, 1/2 teaspoon allspice, and 1 jigger white or golden rum, and beat the mixture until it is smooth and thick. Blend in 1 stiffly beaten egg white and 1/2 jigger brandy. Pour the mixture into a warmed Tom and Jerry mug, fill it with hot milk or boiling water, and sprinkle generously with grated nutmeg.

Into a glass put 1 teaspoon lemon juice, 1/4 cup rum, and a slice of lemon peel. Fill the glass with hot tea, stir with a cinnamon stick, and serve immediately.

For each drink put 2 teaspoons sugar, 2 whole cloves, a small piece of cinnamon stick, 6 or 8 raisins, and 1 jigger Cognac in a silver bowl. Ignite the mixture and stir it gently until the flame dies. Blend in 1/2 jigger dry Sherry for each portion and serve the *glögg* in metal cups.

Glögg I

In separate saucepans heat but do not boil 3 bottles claret and 3 bottles aquavit. To the claret add 2 oranges, each stuck with 16 whole cloves, and 20 cardamom seeds. Put 24 lumps of sugar in a silver punch bowl and over them pour about 2 cups of the hot aquavit. Ignite the aquavit and while it is burning pour in the rest of the aquavit and the hot wine, which will extinguish the flame. Put a few blanched almonds and a sprinkling of seeded raisins in each serving mug, fill with the *glögg*, and serve hot.

Glögg II

No holiday reception is complete without its creamy eggnog.

Beat 12 egg yolks until they are thick and pale in color. Add 2 cups sugar and continue to beat the mixture until the yolks are thick and light in color. Chill the mixture. To serve, pour the egg mixture into a punch bowl and slowly stir in 1 fifth Cognac, 1 fifth golden rum, and 1 cup peach brandy. Add 6 cups chilled milk, 3 cups chilled heavy cream, and 12 stiffly beaten egg whites.

Baltimore Eggnog

Beat 12 egg yolks until they are light. Add gradually 1 1/2 cups fine granulated sugar and continue to beat until the yolks are thick and light in color. Pour the mixture into a punch bowl set on a bed of crushed ice Whip in 1 quart milk and 1 quart heavy cream and add very slowly 1 1/2 quarts bourbon and 1 pint Cognac, stirring constantly. Fold in 12 egg whites, stiffly beaten, and sprinkle the surface of the punch with 1/8 cup Jamaica rum and grated nutmeg to taste.

Gourmet's Eggnog

Beat 12 egg yolks until they are thick and pale in color. Add 2 cups fine granulated sugar and continue to beat the mixture until the sugar is dissolved.

Kentucky Eggnog

Chill the mixture for 2 hours. To serve, pour the batter into a punch bowl and slowly blend in 2 fifths bourbon, and 1 cup each of golden rum and Cognac. Add 2 cups chilled milk and 6 cups chilled heavy cream and fold in 12 egg whites stiffly beaten. Sprinkle the eggnog generously with grated nutmeg.

Southern Eggnog Beat 18 egg yolks until they are light. Add gradually 2 cups fine granulated sugar and continue to beat until the yolks are thick and light in color. Slowly stir in 2 fifths bourbon and 1/2 cup Jamaica rum. Add 2 cups chilled light cream. Whip 6 cups heavy cream and blend it lightly into the mixture. Fold in 18 egg whites, very stiffly beaten. Pour the eggnog into a punch bowl and sprinkle each serving with grated nutmeg.

Williamsburg Eggnog Beat 18 egg yolks until they are thick and pale in color. Add 2 1/2 cups fine granulated sugar and continue to beat the mixture until the sugar is dissolved. Very slowly add 1 fifth Cognac and set the mixture aside. Beat 18 egg whites with 1/2 cup sugar until they are very light. To the egg yolk mixture add 1 quart each of milk and heavy cream and pour it into a punch bowl. Pour in 2 fifths more Cognac slowly and blend thoroughly. Fold in the egg whites and sprinkle the mixture generously with grated nutmeg.

Coffee has a natural affinity for spirits.

Café Royal Frappé Half fill a cocktail shaker with finely shaved ice. Add 2 parts chilled double-strength coffee and 1 part Cognac. Shake the mixture vigorously and pour it into chilled Champagne coupes. Serve with short straws.

Café au Cacao Frappé Half fill a cocktail shaker with finely shaved ice and add equal parts of chilled double-strength coffee and crème de cacao. Shake the mixture vigorously and pour it into chilled Champagne coupes. Serve with short straws.

Café Diable Preheat a silver bowl and a ladle with hot water. Pour into the bowl 2 cups warm Cognac and add 6 lumps of sugar, 4 cloves, and the rind of 1/2 lemon and 1/2 orange. Dip up a ladleful of the Cognac, put in it 2 more lumps of sugar, and ignite the spirit. Lower the flaming ladle into the bowl and very slowly pour in 2 cups strong black coffee, all the while dipping up ladlefuls of the coffee-Cognac mixture and pouring it back until all the spirit is ablaze. When the flame dies, serve the *café diable* in demitasse cups.

Float 1 tablespoon Cognac on a cup of hot coffee. Place a cube of sugar in a teaspoon and fill the spoon with warm brandy. Hold the spoon just above the coffee; the heat will warm the brandy so that it may be ignited. Lower the ignited brandy gently into the coffee. Swish the spoon back and forth in the cup until the flame dies.

Café Royale

Lacking an espresso machine—there are several designed for home use—one may prepare this rich brew in a drip pot or a *machinetta*. The proportions: 1 cup dark-roast, pulverized coffee to 2 cups water. This makes about 6 small cups. A dash of any of the following may be added to the hot espresso: Fernet Branca bitters, anisette, Cognac, Strega, rum, white crème de menthe, kümmel, Cointreau, Grapa, or Curaçao.

Caffè Espresso

If coffee must face dilution with ice, it should be doubly strong; use 2 tablespoons coffee, instead of 1, to 6 ounches, or 3/4 cup, water. Chill freshly brewed, double-strength coffee in an enamel, glass, or pottery jug for not more than 3 hours. Serve it over ice cubes in tall glasses; sugar and cream should be added to taste.

Iced Coffee

Fill a tall glass with ice and add 3 dashes of Angostura bitters. Fill the glass three-fourths full with cooled double-strength coffee and fill to the top with club soda or seltzer. Stir and serve.

Angostura Iced Coffee

Pour 3 cups hot double-strength coffee over 4 cloves, 4 allspice berries, and a 1-inch stick of cinnamon. Let the infusion stand for about 1 hour. Strain the coffee over ice in tall glasses and serve it with cream and sugar.

Spiced Iced Coffee

Beat 6 eggs until they are light and foamy, add a scant 1/2 cup sugar and continue to beat until the sugar is dissolved. Add 3 cups freshly made and cooled coffee and 1 tablespoon brandy or more to taste, stirring gently to blend the mixture. Chill thoroughly and serve in earthenware mugs. Sprinkle the top of each drink lightly with nutmeg.

Brandied Iced Coffee

Melt 1 ounce semisweet chocolate over boiling water and add to it 1/4 cup sugar, 1/8 teaspoon salt, and 1 3/4 cups boiling water. Simmer the mixture, stirring constantly, for 5 minutes. Add 1/2 cup each of milk and light cream and reheat the mixture without boiling. Add 1 teaspoon vanilla and 2 cups hot, freshly made coffee. Beat the mixture well and chill it.

Chocolate Coffee à la Russe

Tea plays an important part in the preparation of many punches. There are, in addition, some non-alcoholic tea drinks that should be recorded here.

Spiced Tea   Put 1 teaspoon whole cloves and a 1-inch stick of cinnamon in a cheesecloth bag. Put 3 tablespoons black tea in another cheesecloth bag and close both bags securely with kitchen thread. Bring 3 quarts water to a boil and steep the tea and spice bags in it for 5 minutes. Remove the bags. Heat together the juice of 1 1/2 lemons and 3 oranges with 1 cup sugar and add this to the tea. Makes about 20 servings.

Minted Orange Tea   Pour 3 cups boiling water over 2 tablespoons tea and brew for 5 minutes. Stir, strain, and add to the tea 1/3 cup lemon juice, 1/2 cup orange juice, and sugar to taste. Chill. To serve, add 1 pint ginger ale, and pour the mixture over ice cubes into tall glasses. Decorate each glass with a sprig of mint and an orange slice. Makes 6 servings.

Hot Tea Punch   Pour 6 cups boiling water over 6 teaspoons tea leaves and let stand. In a saucepan combine 1/2 cup each of water and sugar, a 2-inch stick of cinnamon, 1 teaspoon grated lemon rind, and 1 1/3 teaspoons grated orange rind. Bring to a boil and boil for five minutes. Remove the cinnamon stick, add 1/4 cup orange juice and 2 tablespoons pineapple juice, and strain the tea into the fruit mixture. Serve very hot. Makes 6 to 8 servings.

Wine Service

"DRINK no longer water." These words precede the frequently cited saintly admonition "Use a little wine for thy stomach's sake," and we quote them to our purpose because we are persuaded that those who drink no longer water—at their meals, at least—will discover for themselves the wisdom of Saint Paul's advice.

The theory that good wine enhances the pleasure of a good dinner is an ancient one, often proved and well documented. Traditionally the drinking of wine has been surrounded with a rather discouraging aura of rite and formula; discouraging because in the effort to avoid choosing the "wrong" wine, the timid may not choose at all. Any wine that pleases the drinker's taste is the right wine for him. Any wine that to the drinker seems harmonious with the food it accompanies is the right wine, for him, for that food.

Yet over the centuries, certain formulae have evolved that are worth recording because they represent the cumulative experience and preferences of many wine lovers of many tastes. Learning enough about wines to make exceptions to these rules is the happy privilege of the novice. The chart that follows is a summation of the rules.

The ritual of wine service, once forbiddingly complicated, has happily been reduced to a handful of necessary and logical strictures. The custom of serving a different wine, or even two, with each course, has gone the way of the lengthy, ponderous dinner that gave it birth. Even the most formal of modern dinners does not demand more than three wines, and usually one wine, chosen to complement the main course, not to overwhelm it, is enough. If there is to be more than one wine, subordinate the lesser wines to the important, climactic wine that will accompany the *pièce de réstistance*. Protocol and good sense suggest white wines or rosés before reds, light before heavy, dry before sweet. If the main dish was cooked in wine, it is often logical to drink with it more of the same wine.

White wines and rosés are served chilled, red wines at room temperature, but it behooves the steam-heated American to remember that European room temperature, on which this rule is based, is likely to be closer to 65° F. than to 80° F.! The only red wines that may profitably be chilled are Beaujolais—a very light, fruity red—and the Swiss Dôle.

Red wine should rest, upright, for a day or two before it is served. For longer storage, it should lie on its side in a fairly cool place at even temperature. Careless handling will disturb the sediment that falls to the bottom. Remove the foil from only the mouth of the bottle, wipe the neck clean, and carefully draw the cork, forcing the corkscrew to the bottom of, but not through, the cork. Examine the cork: a shrunken, dry cork can mean spoiled wine. The cork should smell of wine, not of cork. Red wine should stand, uncorked, for an hour or two at room temperature so that it can "breathe." During this breathing space, the sediment will settle to the bottom of the bottle, and the wine may be carefully poured off the sediment into the decanter from which it will be served.

The more expansive ménage may boast an assortment of wine glasses, each of them especially designed to enhance the drinker's enjoyment of a particular wine, but for practical purposes a clear, large, stemmed, tulip-shaped glass will serve for any table wine except Champagne. And even this rule cries to be broken!

Fill the glass one-third full with red wine, never more than half full with white. There should be, as the old saying goes, room for the drinker's nose.

Leftover wine will not keep; it can be used for cooking for a day or two; after that, if it is allowed to rest, it will obligingly make itself available for use as a basis for salad vinegar.

Speaking of salads: salads do not go with wine. Salad dressings and other acidulous sauces do not go with wine—nor do citrus fruits, tomatoes, any vegetables served as a separate course, or asparagus or artichokes at any time. With curry, *smörgåsbord*, and barbecued meats and with pungent, strongly salted, brined meats and fish, drink heavy, stout-hearted wines or beer. With cheese rabbits, drink beer.

Since the question most asked, in this day when the wine merchant replaces the wine cellar for most gourmets, is generally something like "What wine shall I serve with *foie gras?*"—or with *filet de boeuf* or with sole—we have endeavored to answer this kind of question by the use of two simple, co-ordinating devices. On the pages that follow you will find a chart. We have, for convenience's sake, divided all wines commonly obtainable in this country into types. The types appear as headings at the top of the chart. The best-known examples of these types—and their American approximations—are named on the pages following the chart.

Champagne is not listed on the chart because it may properly and pleasantly be served with any course, or indeed at any time. Except for dessert, when Extra Dry—actually a moderately sweet wine—or Dry, which is quite sweet, is preferable, choose Brut or English Market Brut, which are, respectively, dry and still dryer.

For each general grouping of dishes, we have indicated in the chart with the figure 1 the type of wine we prefer to serve. The figure 2 is our second, or alternate, choice. The wines marked 3 are, in our opinion, also suitable, and there are among them wines to please any palate and purse. We have deliberately avoided naming vintages. The wine lover's best friend is his supplier, an honest wine merchant will sell you the best wine you can afford.

The further one goes into the subject of choosing wine, the more one's prejudices show. Frankly and unashamedly prejudiced are the judgments that follow.

THE WINE SAMPLER

Note: The Footnote to the Wine Sampler (page 47) lists equivalent American wines that are marketed under varietal names.

Legend:
1 — PREFERRED WINE
2 — ALTERNATE CHOICE
3 — OTHER SUITABLE WINES

	WHITE WINES and ROSÉS													RED WINES							
	Bordeaux (DRY)	Bordeaux (SWEET)	Burgundy	Rhône	Loire	Alsatian	German (DRY)	German (SWEET)	Italian (DRY)	Italian (SWEET)	Swiss	Chilean	Rosé (ALL REGIONS)	Bordeaux (LIGHT)	Bordeaux (HEAVY)	Burgundy (LIGHT)	Burgundy (HEAVY)	Rhône	Italian	Swiss	Chilean
Hors-d'Oeuvre																					
SEAFOOD	3	3		1	3	2			3		3	3	3								
MEAT, COLD													1	2		3			3	3	3
PÂTÉ			3		3	3	3						3	1		2			3	3	3
Fish																					
BLAND VARIETIES	3	1	3	3	3	2			3		3	3	3								
FULL-FLAVORED VARIETIES	3	2	1	3	3	3			3		3	3	3								
Shellfish																					
ALL VARIETIES	3	1			2	3	3		3		3	3									
Poultry																					
CHICKEN	3	2	3	3	3	3			3		3	3	3	1		3			3	3	3
CHICKEN, WHITE SAUCES	3	3	3	3	3	1			3		3	3	2								
OTHER POULTRY		2	3			3							3			1					
Beef																					
OVEN ROASTS, STEAKS														3	3	3	1	2	3		3
BRAISED, STEWS														3	1	2	3	3	3		3
SMOKED, SPICED														3	2	3	3	1	3		3
Lamb																					
ALL PREPARATIONS													3	1		2			3	3	3
Mutton																					
ALL PREPARATIONS													3		1	2			3	3	3
Veal																					
ALL PREPARATIONS			3			3	3						3	2		1			3	3	3
Pork, Ham																					
ALL PREPARATIONS		2	3		3	1							3								

Fish — BLAND VARIETIES: Bass, Cod, Eel, Flounder, Frogs' Legs, Haddock, Halibut, Herring, Pike, Red Snapper, Sturgeon, Swordfish, Trout, Weakfish, Whitefish.

FULL-FLAVORED VARIETIES: Mackerel, Octopus, Pompano, Salmon, Shad, Shad Roe, Smelts, Squid, Snails, Turtle, Smoked Fish.

Poultry — CHICKEN: Miscellaneous preparations, Livers.

OTHER POULTRY: Duck, Turkey, Guinea Hen, Squab, Pigeon, Rock Cornish Game Hen, Goose.

Legend:

1 — PREFERRED WINE
2 — ALTERNATE CHOICE
3 — OTHER SUITABLE WINES

Note: The Footnote to the Wine Sampler (page 47) lists equivalent American wines that are marketed under varietal names.

Columns 2–14 = **WHITE WINES and ROSÉS**; Columns 15–22 = **RED WINES**

	Bordeaux (DRY)	Bordeaux (SWEET)	Burgundy	Rhône	Loire	Alsatian	German (DRY)	German (SWEET)	Italian (DRY)	Italian (SWEET)	Swiss	Chilean	Rosé (ALL REGIONS)	Bordeaux (LIGHT)	Bordeaux (HEAVY)	Burgundy (LIGHT)	Burgundy (HEAVY)	Rhône	Italian	Swiss	Chilean
Innards and Such — MISCELLANEOUS (Brains, Haggis, Heart, Kidneys, Liver, Oxtail.)														1	2				3		3
SAUSAGE						2	3		3		3	3	3	1		3			3	3	3
TONGUE							3							2				1			
SWEETBREADS	3		1		3	2	3		3	3	3										
TRIPE							3						1	2		3			3	3	3
Game — FEATHERED (Wild Duck, Wild Goose, Wild Turkey, Partridge, Pigeon, Pheasant, Quail, Grouse, Woodcock.)															3		1	2			
FURRED (Venison, Bear, Buffalo, Boar, Rabbit and Hare, Squirrel, Miscellaneous Small Game.)															3		1	2			
Eggs — MISCELLANEOUS														1	2				3	3	3
FISH OMELETTES	1		3		3	2	3		3	3											
Cheese — UNCOOKED														1	2				3	3	3
FONDUES	3					2	3		3		1	3									
SOUFFLÉS														1	2				3	3	3
Aspics — LIGHT MEAT and POULTRY, SMOKED MEAT, EGGS	3		3			3	3		3		3	3	1	2		3			3	3	3
DARK MEAT and POULTRY, GAME, GAME BIRDS													1	3		2			3	3	3
FISH					3	3	2				3	3	1								
Pasta — WITH MEAT, CHEESE, BUTTER SAUCES														2		3			1	3	3
WITH FISH SAUCES	2		3	3	3				1		3	3									
Curries (Mild Only) — MEAT, POULTRY																		3			
FISH				3																	
Barbecues (Except Fish)																		3			
Desserts — ALL		1			3			2		3											

Wine

Footnote to the Wine Sampler

IMPORTED   AMERICAN EQUIVALENTS (1)   *White Wines*

BORDEAUX DRY

IMPORTED	AMERICAN EQUIVALENTS
Graves	Sauvignon Blanc
Barsac (drier)	Dry Semillon

BORDEAUX SWEET

Sauternes	Sweet Semillon
Barsac (sweet)	

BURGUNDY

Chablis (2)	Pinot Chardonnay
Pouilly-Fuissé	Pinot Blanc
Clos Blanc de Vougeot	Folle Blanche
Corton Charlemagne	
Meursault	
Montrachet	

RHÔNE

Hermitage Blanc
Châteauneuf-du-Pape Blanc

LOIRE

Pouilly-Fumé
Muscadet
Sancerre
Quincy
Anjou (3)
Vouvray (3)

ALSATIAN

Sylvaner	Traminer
Riesling	Sylvaner
Traminer	
Gewürztraminer	

(1) American wines marketed under European wine names are not listed.
(2) Chablis is the lightest and driest of these wines, which represent their sections' best.
(3) The sweeter varieties of these wines are suitable only for dessert.

FOOTNOTE TO THE WINE SAMPLER

	IMPORTED		AMERICAN EQUIVALENTS
White Wines		GERMAN DRY	
	Rhine (4)		Johannisberg Riesling
	Moselle (4)		Grey Riesling
	Franconian		
	Palatinate (4)		
		GERMAN SWEET	
	Rhine (5)		
	Moselle (5)		
	Palatinate (5)		
		ITALIAN DRY	
	Soave		
	Orvieto Secco		
		ITALIAN SWEET	
	Orvieto Abbocato		
	Lacrima Christi (still)		
	Est! Est!! Est!!!		
	Asti (still)		
		SWISS	
	Neuchâtel		
	Fendant		
	Johannisberg		
		CHILEAN	
	Riesling		
	Undurraga Rhin		
		AUSTRIAN DRY	
	Kremser (6)		
	Gumpoldskirchner (6)		
	Grinzinger (6)		
		HUNGARIAN DRY	
	Badacsony		
		HUNGARIAN SWEET	
	Tokay—3, 4, or 5 Puttonys		
		SPANISH	
	Rioja (7)		

(4) German wine labels often indicate the ripeness of the grapes. Almost all wines labeled Auslese and Spätlese—two degrees of ripeness—are relatively dry, as are wines that bear no such indication.
(5) German wines labeled Beerenauslese or Trockenbeerenauslese are made from very ripe grapes and are very sweet.
(6) These light and flavorful wines may be used wherever Alsatian or German dry wines are suggested.
(7) The white Rioja has been compared to Graves, and may be used accordingly.

IMPORTED	AMERICAN EQUIVALENTS	
		Red Wines
	BORDEAUX LIGHT	
Médoc	Cabernet	
Graves	Sauvignon (8)	
	BORDEAUX HEAVY	
Saint Emilion	Cabernet	
Pomerol	Sauvignon (8)	
	BURGUNDY LIGHT	
Beaujolais	Gamay (8)	
Volnay	Zinfandel	
Pommard		
	BURGUNDY HEAVY	
Fixin (9)	Gamay (8)	
Chambertin	Pinot Noir	
Clos de Vougeot		
Romanée Conti		
Nuits-Saint-Georges		
Corton		
Beaune		
	RHÔNE	
Châteauneuf-du-Pape		
Hermitage		
Côte Rôtie		
	ITALIAN	
Chianti	Barbera	
Valpolicella	Grignolino	
Bardolino		
Barolo		
	SWISS	
Dôle		
	CHILEAN	
Burgundy		
	SPANISH	
Rioja (10)		

FRENCH: Alsace, Provence, Anjou, Tavel *Rosés*
ITALIAN: Chiaretto del Garda
PORTUGUESE: Rosé
AMERICAN: Grenache Rosé, Gamay Rosé, Grignolino

(8) Both the Cabernet Sauvignon and the Gamay grape produce both light and heavy wines.
(9) These Burgundies are arranged in order from least heavy to heaviest.
(10) The red Rioja is comparable to a light red Bordeaux.

49

Hors-d'Oeuvre

Included in this chapter are the closely related hors-d'oeuvre of France, the *smörgåsbord* of Sweden, and the antipasto of Italy. All these are intended to excite the taste buds, but never, never to satisfy the appetite.

Hors-d'oeuvre is served even in the most modestly situated French families, and may, in this case, consist frugally of odds and ends of yesterday's meat, fish, and vegetables, flavorfully sauced and spiced and attractively presented in small dishes or in sectional trays. A more elaborate hors-d'oeuvre course—and this is not to be confused with the canapés and other finger foods that are served with cocktails—may include *pâté de foie gras*, sausages, sardines, eggs, seafood and other delicacies, as well as any of the preparations for which recipes are given in this section, selected for compatibility of flavors and textures.

The basic components of *smörgåsbord* are *smor*, *ost*, and *sill*, butter, cheese, and herring, and this formula holds true whether this array of appetizers is called *smörgåsbord*, or *smørrebrød*, as it is in Denmark, or *koldt bord*, as it is in Norway, or *voileipäpöytä*, as it is in Finland. In Norway and in Denmark, the various kinds of fish, meat, and cheese are sometimes piled high on open-faced sandwiches, which must then be eaten with knife and fork. A *smörgåsbord*, which we may fairly regard as typical of the four, is likely to include herring in several guises, anchovies in some simple preparation or as they come from the can, smoked, brined, and wined fish, smoked eel, a variety of sausages, pâtés, and cold meats, aspics of fish and meat, vegetable salads, and such simple hot additions to the feast as boiled potatoes and meatballs. Scandinavian hardtack and the hearty, dark breads of the northland are always provided; the usual beverages are beer and ice-cold aquavit.

Although *smörgåsbord* is supposedly an appetizer or hors-d'oeuvre course, it frequently serves as a lavish buffet meal. For the uninitiate, a word of advice is in order; it is perfectly proper to return to the *smörgåsbord* three times or more. On the first trip, fill your plate with the various kinds of fish, which should be eaten with bread and butter. On the second trip, try the meats and salads; on the third, the hot dishes and cheese.

Antipasto, which means, literally, before the pasta, has won universal acceptance. And rightly so, since this assortment of flavors, textures, and colors will please any gourmet's taste.

Fish, meat, vegetables, and sometimes cheese and eggs form the basis of antipasto. Canned anchovies, sardines, mussels, and tuna fish—all packed in oil—pimientos, artichoke hearts, chick-peas, mushrooms, pickled or in oil, olives, black and green, *prosciutto*, salami and other sausages are all welcome, as are such fresh raw vegetables as lettuce, tomatoes, radishes, peppers, scallions, celery, and fennel. Any of these may be combined with any homemade hors-d'oeuvre preparation, so long as the combination pleases eye and palate and offers an appetizing variety.

The vegetable preparations that follow may be served individually as the first course of a formal meal or as a salad-cum-relish or as part of an assortment of hors-d'oeuvre.

Vegetables Vinaigrette

THE vegetables should never be overcooked, but should be simmered until barely tender in salted water and drained. When they are cool, moisten generously with *sauce vinaigrette* and marinate in the sauce for at least 30 minutes before serving. Place them in a cold serving dish and sprinkle with chopped parsley.

Cooked asparagus, cauliflower flowerets, celery or fennel hearts, beets, broccoli, leeks, raw mushrooms, cucumbers, and lentils and beans of many kinds lend themselves to this treatment.

Sauce Vinaigrette

MAKE a well-seasoned French dressing as follows: Mix together 2 tablespoons vinegar, 6 tablespoons olive oil, 1 teaspoon each of salt and dry mustard, freshly ground black pepper to taste, and 1 split garlic clove. Before using the dressing, remove the garlic clove and mix the dressing well.

For hot or cold vegetables, add to the dressing 1 teaspoon each of chopped parsley, tarragon, chives, and chervil and 1 hard-cooked egg, finely chopped. If desired, add 1 teaspoon chopped capers or pickles. Blend well.

Vegetables à la Grecque

COMBINE in a saucepan 1/4 cup olive oil, the juice of 1 lemon or 1 1/2 tablespoons wine vinegar, 1/2 teaspoon salt, 1 garlic clove, 4 peppercorns, and a *bouquet garni* consisting of 2 stalks each of parsley and chervil, 1 stalk each of tarragon and thyme, and 1 bay leaf. Add prepared vegetables such as small artichokes, celery hearts, cauliflower flowerets, asparagus stalks, sliced carrots, small white onions, juilenne of eggplant, sliced cucumber and zucchini, or mushroom caps. Add enough boiling water to cover the vegetables and simmer until they are just barely tender. Drain the vegetables and arrange them in a serving dish.

Strain the sauce, and simmer it over low heat until it is reduced by half. Pour the sauce over the vegetables. Cool and chill before serving.

Antipasto Salad

IN a large saucepan heat 3/4 cup olive oil until it smokes. Add 2 cups each of celery stalks, cut into 1/2-inch lengths, and chopped onions, 1 cup each of diced mushrooms, fresh tomato, peeled and chopped, cauliflower flowerets, blanched in boiling water for 1 minute, and diced green pepper, 1/2 cup chopped garlic, 1 1/2 cups tomato paste, 2 cups dry white wine, 2 teaspoons salt, 1/2 teaspoon freshly ground black pepper, and a *bouquet garni* of parsley, celery, and bay leaves tied together. Cook the mixture for about 15 minutes. The vegetables should not be allowed to get too soft. Add 1/2 cup each of sliced green olives, sliced ripe olives, and diced pimiento, 2 cups raw tuna fish or fresh salmon, cut into small pieces, 6 anchovy filets, chopped, and 1 teaspoon anchovy paste, and continue to cook for 5 minutes. Correct the seasoning and chill the ingredients for 24 hours.

Serve the antipasto on individual plates on a bed of lettuce leaves and garnish each plate with 1/4 hard-cooked egg, a slice of tomato, a thin slice of salami, and an anchovy filet.

Fonds d'Artichauts
ARTICHOKE BOTTOMS

REMOVE the stems from 12 small artichokes, trim the bottoms neatly with a sharp knife, and rub the exposed cut surface of the vegetable with lemon juice to prevent it from darkening. With a very sharp knife trim the leaves so that only 1/8 to 1/2 inch of the green is left around the artichokes.

In a saucepan combine 6 cups water with a paste made from 1 tablespoon flour, 2 tablespoons salt, and the juice of 1 large lemon or 3 tablespoons vinegar. Bring the water to a boil, add the artichokes, and cook them for 30 to 45 minutes. Remove the artichokes and turn them upside down to drain. Separate the leaves and remove the center choke. Chill the hearts well and fill them with various savory mixtures.

FILL cooked and cooled artichoke hearts with cooked mussels and shrimps bound with mayonnaise. Sprinkle them with finely chopped parsley and place on top of each a large cooked shrimp.

Fonds d'Artichauts à la Dieppoise

DICE the meat of a cooked lobster and combine it with 3 tablespoons mayonnaise, the juice of 1/2 lemon, and 1/2 teaspoon Worcestershire sauce. Use this mixture to fill the centers of small cooked artichokes. Garnish each with a small cooked crayfish in its shell.

Fonds d'Artichauts Glacés à la Mazarin

MASH 1/2 cup cooked tuna with a fork, combine the fish with 2 tablespoons mayonnaise, the juice of 1/2 lemon, and 1/2 teaspoon Worcestershire sauce. Use this mixture to fill the centers of small cooked artichokes. Sprinkle the tuna mixture with hard-cooked egg yolks and parsley, both finely chopped.

Fonds d'Artichauts au Thon

PUT an avocado half, chilled and peeled, on an individual plate on a bed of watercress. Fill the avocado cavity with fresh crab meat and sprinkle the crab meat with a little lemon juice. Cover avocado and filling with a hard-cooked egg pressed through a sieve and sprinkle with finely chopped parsley or chives. Serve chilled, with French dressing or mayonnaise.

Avocado Stuffed with Crab Meat

COMBINE sliced cooked beets and very thin raw onion rings, and sprinkle with a little marjoram, a grating of nutmeg, and a few slivers of garlic. Serve with French dressing made with tarragon vinegar.

Beet and Onion Ring Salad

MIX 4 cups white beans, cooked until tender, cooled, and drained, with 1 large onion, chopped, 1/4 cup finely chopped parsley, 3 tablespoons each of olive oil and vinegar or lemon juice, and salt and pepper to taste. Serve on lettuce leaves and garnish with cucumber wedges and olives.

White Bean Salad

53

Beet Salad

Cream Mustard

WASH 6 medium beets and bake them in a moderately hot oven (375° F.) for about 40 minutes, or until they are tender. Peel the beets, cool them, and cut them in julienne. Add 1/2 cup chopped scallions and toss the salad with French dressing or with cream mustard made by mixing together 1/2 cup heavy cream, 1 teaspoon prepared mustard, a few drops of lemon juice, and a little salt and pepper.

Red Cabbage for Hors-d'Oeuvre

CLEAN a red cabbage, quarter it, and remove the hard core. Shred the quarters and put the shreds in a bowl with 1 tablespoon salt. Leave the cabbage in a cold place for 24 hours, turning it over from time to time. Squeeze out all the water. Add 1 garlic clove, 1 bay leaf, 8 peppercorns, and 2 tablespoons vinegar and let the cabbage stand for a few hours to pickle.

Celery Stuffed with Roquefort Cheese

CREAM together 1/2 cup each of Roquefort cheese and soft butter and blend in 1/4 cup finely chopped watercress. Force the mixture through a pastry bag to fill the center of chilled celery stalks. Chill before serving.

Celery Stuffed with Pâté de Foie Gras

CREAM 1 cup *pâté de foie gras* with 1 tablespoon soft sweet butter. Force the mixture through a pastry bag to fill the center of chilled celery stalks. Use a pastry tube to put a narrow ribbon of anchovy butter along the edges.

Celery Victor Gourmet

REMOVE the tough outer stalks from a bunch of celery, trim the roots, and cut off most of the leafy tops. Split the cleaned hearts lengthwise into 3 or 4 pieces, depending on their size. Put the celery in a saucepan with boiling hot chicken or turkey stock to cover and add 2 sprigs of parsley, a few slices each of carrot and onion, and salt to taste. Simmer the celery slowly until it is just tender, drain it well, and lay it in a shallow dish to cool.

Mix together 1 1/2 cups olive oil, 1/2 cup white-wine vinegar, a pinch of chervil, and salt and freshly ground pepper to taste. Pour this sauce over the cooled celery and chill the platter until serving time. Garnish the celery with strips of washed anchovy filets arranged crosswise and with bands of pimiento. Sprinkle with chopped parsley.

Celery Victor Gourmet

Celeriac Salad COOK 3 peeled celeriacs in boiling salted water until they are tender. Cool them, and cut them in julienne. Add 1 onion, chopped, and 2 tablespoons chopped parsley, toss carefully with French dressing, and marinate the salad in the refrigerator for 2 hours. Garnish with mayonnaise.

Cucumbers with Dill SLICE cucumbers thinly. If they are garden fresh, do not peel them. Sprinkle the slices with salt, weigh them down with a heavy china plate, and let them stand for 2 hours. Rinse the slices in cold water, drain them, and put them in a glass or china bowl.

For every two cucumbers combine 1/2 cup vinegar, 2 tablespoons each of water and sugar, 1 tablespoon chopped fresh dill, and a dash of pepper. Pour the dressing over the cucumbers and chill them for 1 to 2 hours before serving.

Cucumbers in Cream PEEL 2 cucumbers and slice them thinly. Sprinkle them with salt and pepper and pour over them 1/4 cup vinegar. Beat 1 cup heavy cream until it is thickened but not stiff, pour it over the cucumbers, mix lightly, and chill thoroughly.

Cucumber Salad PEEL cucumbers, slice them thinly, and soak the slices for 1 hour in salted ice-cold water. Drain the slices, press the water from them, and serve them with a tart French dressing.

Stuffed Cucumber Rings CHOOSE uniform cucumbers and remove their centers with an apple corer. Stuff the cavities with cream cheese mixed with finely chopped nutmeats, parsley, chives, and a little paprika. Chill the cucumbers in the refrigerator until the stuffing is firm and slice the cucumbers very thinly. Arrange the slices on a bed of finely shredded lettuce, romaine, or watercress and top them with a little mayonnaise.

Eggplant Sicilian PEEL and dice 2 medium eggplant. In a skillet sauté the cubes in 1/2 cup hot olive oil for about 8 minutes, or until they are soft and lightly browned. Remove the eggplant to a saucepan and set it aside.

To the oil remaining in the skillet add 2 onions, sliced, and sauté them for about 3 minutes, or until they are golden, adding a little more oil if necessary. Add 2 1/2 cups cooked Italian plum tomatoes and 1 cup diced celery and simmer the mixture for 15 minutes, or until the celery is tender.

Add 1/4 cup capers and 1 tablespoon pine nuts, and add the mixture to the eggplant.

In a small saucepan heat 1/4 cup wine vinegar and 2 tablespoons sugar, stirring until the sugar is dissolved. Stir the vinegar into the eggplant mixture and add salt and pepper to taste. Bring the mixture to a boil, cover the saucepan, and simmer the mixture over very low heat for 20 minutes, stirring occasionally. Cool the mixture, turn it into a serving bowl, and chill it before serving.

WASH and trim a large, perfect eggplant. Quarter it, and make several small incisions in the flesh with a sharp paring knife. Dip the quarters in olive oil and arrange them on a large, flat baking pan, cut side up. Bake them in a very hot oven (450° F.) for 20 minutes, or until they are tender.

Crush 4 garlic cloves and brown them lightly in olive oil. Add 2 large cans Italian-style tomatoes and simmer the mixture for 1 1/2 hours. Remove the sauce from the heat and season it to taste with orégano, salt, and pepper. Pour the sauce over the eggplant, sprinkle with capers, and serve hot or cold.

Eggplant Provençale

TRIM and discard the stem ends from 2 quarts fiddleheads and wash the ferns well. Put in a saucepan the juice of 1 lemon, 3 cups water, 1/2 cup salad oil, 3 tablespoons vinegar, 1 teaspoon salt, 2 stalks of celery, chopped, 1 stalk of fennel, chopped, 5 coriander seeds, and a few peppercorns. Bring the mixture to a boil, add the fiddleheads, and cook them slowly for 15 to 25 minutes. Serve cool.

Fiddleheads

SOAK 1 pound *garbanzos* overnight in cold water. In the morning bring the water to a boil and simmer the beans until they are tender. Drain them and grind them to a fine paste. Sauté 1 cup chopped onions in 3 tablespoons olive oil until the onion is tender. Add 2 tablespoons each of parsley and *pinones*, or pine nuts, stir the mixture into the *garbanzo* paste, and mix thoroughly. Serve cold, sprinkled with sesame-seed oil.

Garbanzo Appetizer

COVER 2 cups lentils with 5 cups cold water and add 2 teaspoons salt. Bring the water slowly to a boil, and simmer the lentils for about 30 minutes, or until they are tender. Drain them thoroughly and chill them. Sprinkle with

Lentil Salad

chopped parsley, a little minced garlic, and some chopped scallions. Toss carefully with French dressing and serve the salad cold.

Cheese Stuffed Mushrooms

CREAM together equal amounts Roquefort cheese and soft butter and moisten the mixture with a little Cognac. Clean and remove the stems from perfect fresh mushrooms and fill the cavities with the cheese mixture, pressed through a pastry bag. Sprinkle with parsley and chill.

Stuffed Raw Mushrooms

CREAM together 1/2 cup each of Roquefort and Camembert cheese. Blend into the mixture 1/2 cup ground walnut meats, 1 teaspoon Worcestershire sauce, and 1/2 teaspoon curry powder. Clean and stem 12 large mushrooms. Force the cheese mixture through a pastry bag into the mushroom caps. Serve cold.

Chinese Mushroom Hors-d'Oeuvre

WASH 9 ounces dried black mushrooms, cover them with boiling water, and let them stand in a covered bowl for about 30 minutes. Drain the mushrooms and remove the stems, reserving them for another use. Put the caps in a casserole and add 6 cups unsalted chicken broth. Cover the casserole tightly and cook the caps in a very slow oven (275° F.) for 2 hours.

Heat 1/3 cup lard in a saucepan, pour in the mushrooms and broth, and add 6 tablespoons soy sauce and 2 teaspoons sugar. Cook the mixture for about 3 minutes. Serve chilled. Add 3/4 teaspoon sesame-seed oil just before serving, if desired.

Champignons Marinés

MARINATED MUSHROOMS

CLEAN 12 large mushroom caps. Slice them, arrange them in an hors-d'oeuvre dish and pour over them the juice of 2 lemons and 1/4 cup olive oil. Sprinkle them lightly with salt and black pepper. Marinate the mushrooms for 2 hours before serving.

Mushrooms for Hors-d'Oeuvre

USE small buttom mushrooms, if possible. Clean them and remove the stems. If large mushrooms must be used, cut them into large dice. For each pound of mushrooms put in a saucepan 3 tablespoons olive oil, 2 tablespoons lemon juice, and 1 tablespoon each of chopped shallots and onion. Add the mushrooms, cover the saucepan, and simmer them for 10 to 12 minutes. Cool the mushrooms, turn them into a serving dish with some of the cooking liquid, and sprinkle them with chopped parsley. The liquid may be thickened with a little mayonnaise or heavy cream seasoned with prepared mustard.

CLEAN 1 pound mushrooms and cut off the stems close to the caps. Quarter the caps, and reserve the stems for other uses. Sauté the caps gently with 3 tablespoons grated onion in 3 tablespoons olive oil for 5 minutes. Sprinkle the caps with salt and pepper, pour over them 2 tablespoons Cognac and 1 tablespoon lemon juice, and chill them for several hours, stirring occasionally.

Mushroom Cocktail

Just before serving, toss the mushrooms lightly with 1 cup sour cream and garnish with finely chopped parsley or chives.

DRAIN the liquid from a jar of large ripe olives. Crush the olives gently until they burst and return them to the jar. Add 3 garlic cloves, crushed, fill the jar with olive oil, and let it stand for 2 days before serving.

Garlic Olives

DRAIN a pint jar of ripe olives, reserving the liquid. To the jar add a small red chili pepper, 2 garlic cloves, crushed, several sprays of fresh dill, and 3 tablespoons olive oil. Fill the jar with the reserved liquid and let the olives marinate for 2 days.

Spiced Ripe Olives

DRAIN a large jar of large green olives and crush them until they burst. Put them in a deep dish and add 3 garlic cloves, crushed, 2 red chili peppers, 2 sprays of fresh dill, and 1 bay leaf. Pour over the olives 1/4 cup each of olive oil and vinegar and let the olives marinate for 2 hours before serving, stirring them occasionally so that all of them are well coated with the dressing.

Green Olives with Garlic and Herbs

COOK 2 whole canned pimientos with 2 tablespoons tomato purée and salt and cayenne to taste over low heat for about 10 minutes and force the mixture through a fine sieve. While the purée is still hot, stir in 1 tablespoon gelatin, softened in 1/4 cup cold water. Blend the mixture until all the gelatin is dissolved and put it in the refrigerator to set. When the purée begins to set, use it to fill pitted olives, forcing it from a pastry bag with a fancy tube. Serve the olives on a bed of parsley or shredded lettuce.

Olives à la Sicilienne

Spiced Onions   CLEAN 1 pound small white onions or spring scallions and put them in a saucepan with 1 cup each of white-wine vinegar, sugar, and seedless white raisins, a little grated nutmeg and cinnamon, a few peppercorns, and 1/2 teaspoon paprika. Bring the mixture to a boil and simmer it until it reaches a jamlike consistency. Serve cold.

Oignons à la Monégasque   PEEL 1 pound very small white onions and put them in a saucepan with 1 1/2 cups cold water, 1/2 cup each of white-wine vinegar and seedless raisins, 3 tablespoons each of olive oil and tomato paste, 1/4 teaspoon thyme, 1 bay leaf, a sprig of parsley, and salt and freshly ground pepper. Cover the saucepan and simmer the mixture over low heat for about 1 1/2 hours, or until the onions are tender and the sauce is thick and greatly reduced. Arrange the onions in a flat serving dish, pour the sauce over them, and serve chilled.

Poivrons Grillés
GRILLED PEPPERS   SELECT 3 or 4 sweet green, yellow, or red peppers, cut them in three or four sections, and remove the seeds. Coat the sections on both sides with olive oil, and let them stand for 1 hour. Wipe them, grill them lightly on both sides, and slice them. Cool the slices and pour over them French dressing flavored with 1 teaspoon chopped onion and 1/2 teaspoon dry mustard.

Peperoni Ripieni
STUFFED PEPPERS   CUT a slice from the top of 6 green or red peppers and remove the seeds. Stuff each pepper with a mixture made by combining 3 cups fresh bread crumbs with 6 anchovy filets, washed and chopped, 1/2 cup chopped, stoned ripe olives, and 2 tablespoons chopped capers. Put the peppers in an oiled baking pan, pour 1 tablespoon olive oil on each, and bake them in a moderate oven (350° F.) for 35 to 40 minutes. Top each pepper with a few capers. Serve hot or cold.

Tomatoes Stuffed with Smoked Salmon   COMBINE 1/2 cup ground smoked salmon with 1 tablespoon each of anchovy butter, grated onion, lemon juice and finely minced parsley. Remove the center part of the tops of 12 Italian plum tomatoes and carefully scoop out pulp, seeds, and juice. Season the hollowed-out tomatoes with salt and pepper to taste. Stuff them with the salmon mixture, and serve cold on a bed of salad greens.

Stuffed Peppers

Tomatoes Stuffed with Crab Meat

COMBINE 3/4 cup flaked cooked crab meat, 2 tablespoons mayonnaise, and 1 teaspoon each of Worcestershire, grated onion, and finely chopped parsley. Remove the center part of the tops of 12 Italian plum tomatoes and carefully scoop out pulp, seeds, and juice. Season the cases with salt and pepper. Stuff them with the crab-meat mixture and sprinkle with finely chopped egg yolks.

Tomatoes Vinaigrette

PEEL ripe tomatoes and slice them thinly. Sprinkle the slices with very finely chopped onion, scallions, including some of the green tops, or shallots, plenty of finely chopped parsley, and freshly ground black pepper. Pour vinaigrette sauce over the tomatoes and marinate them in the refrigerator for about 1 hour before serving.

Belgian Tomato Salad

SLICE thinly 1 large Spanish onion. Spread the rings on the bottom of a large high-sided bowl. Cover the onion rings with 6 large tomatoes, peeled and cut in thick slices. Sprinkle the onions and the tomatoes with 1/2 teaspoon sugar, 3/4 teaspoon salt, a dash of freshly ground pepper, 1 well-rounded tablespoon each of chopped chives, basil and dill, and 1 teaspoon celery seeds. Cover the bowl and chill the salad well.

Cold fish and shellfish, piquantly spiced, are admittedly the most effective of all spurs to appetite and thirst.

Ceviche

CHOP 5 pounds raw fresh fish, free of skin and bones, into very small pieces, and put the fish into a deep glass or china dish. Add 3 onions, finely minced, 2 cups lime juice, and 1 tablespoon olive oil, stirring the mixture constantly with a wooden spoon and taking care that the mixture is covered with lime juice at all times. Add hot yellow peppers, minced, to taste. Cover the dish. The *ceviche* may be stored in the refrigerator for 2 or 3 days.

Escabèche of Fish

USE small whole fish, such as smelts, fresh anchovies, or fresh sardines, or cut fish filets into small pieces about the size of smelts. Clean the fish and roll them in flour. Fry them in hot deep fat (370° F.) for 2 to

3 minutes until they are golden brown, drain them on absorbent paper, and put them in a deep earthenware dish.

Sauté 1 carrot and 1 onion, both sliced, and 5 or 6 garlic cloves in 1/2 cup olive oil until the onion begins to turn golden. Add 1 cup vinegar, 1/2 cup water, 1 teaspoon salt, a little pepper, a little thyme, 1 bay leaf, and 1 pimiento, chopped. Bring the liquid to a boil and simmer the mixture for 10 to 15 minutes. Pour the marinade over the fish and marinate them for 24 hours before serving.

RINSE and dry 12 anchovy filets and chop them finely. Arrange them in a circle on a small plate. Arrange a circle of finely chopped onion within the anchovy ring and slip a raw egg yolk into the center. Garnish with finely chopped parsley.

Anchovy "Eye"

DRAIN the oil from a large can of anchovy filets into a bowl and arrange the filets in an oblong serving dish. Mix the oil with enough finely chopped parsley to make a thick paste and add 2 or 3 shallots, finely chopped, and 1 tablespoon tarragon vinegar. Pour the sauce over the filets and marinate them for about 1 hour before serving.

Marinated Anchovies

TRIM slices of day-old white bread and cut each slice into 2 triangles. Toast the triangles and arrange one or two on individual plates. Put a generous tablespoon of fresh caviar on each triangle, garnish with lemon wedges, and serve with a side dish of sour cream.

Caviar with Sour Cream

CUT 2 eels, skinned and cleaned, into pieces 1 to 1 1/2 inches long. Sauté 1 small onion, chopped, in 1 tablespoon oil until the onion begins to turn golden. Add the eel pieces, 2 cups white wine, or enough to cover the fish, 1 tablespoon each of paprika and chopped shallot or onion, a little thyme, 1 bay leaf, 1 stalk of celery, minced, 3 sprigs of parsley, a little salt, and 6 to 8 peppercorns. Bring the mixture to a boil, cover the pan, and simmer the mixture for about 18 minutes, or until the fish is tender. Strain the liquid, add 1 teaspoon gelatin softened in cold water, and stir until the gelatin is dissolved. Cool the fish, split the pieces, and remove

Jellied Eels

Marinated Crabs

the bones. Arrange the filets in a serving dish, pour the gelatin mixture over them, and chill them. Sprinkle with paprika just before serving.

PUT a rack in the bottom of a steamer and put into the kettle 3 cups vinegar, 2 tablespoons each of salt and dry mustard, and 1 teaspoon each of black pepper, red pepper, and Tabasco. Bring the liquid to a boil, put in the kettle 24 well-washed live hard-shelled crabs, and cover the kettle tightly. Bring the liquid to a boil and steam the crabs for 20 minutes.

Cool the crabs, remove the top shells and aprons, and discard the spongy substance and the intestines. Crack the claws and split the bodies in half.

Make a French dressing by combining 1 1/2 cups olive oil with 1/2 cup of the vinegar from the kettle. Add salt, pepper, and lemon juice to taste and pour the dressing over the crabs. Marinate them in the refrigerator for several hours. Serve cold in the shell. To eat, pick the meat from the shell with a lobster pick or with a two-tined fork. Use the French dressing in which the crabs were marinated as a dip, or serve them with any suitable sauce.

Marinated Crabs

DICE some filets of smoked herring. Slice thinly an equal amount of cooked potatoes and dice an equal amount of peeled and cored sour apples. Combine the herring, potatoes, and apples in a bowl with 1 tablespoon chopped parsley, 1 teaspoon each of chopped chives and mixed chopped chervil and tarragon, and, if available, a little fennel. Moisten with French dressing and serve in a *ravier*, or hors-d'oeuvre dish.

Herring Canadienne

CLEAN 1 large salt herring, remove the head, and soak the fish overnight in cold water. In the morning, drain, skin, and filet the fish and cut it crosswise into thin slices. Arrange the slices side by side in a shallow dish and pour over them 1/4 cup sugar dissolved in 1/2 cup white-wine vinegar and 2 tablespoons water. Add to the liquid 2 tablespoons chopped onion, 1 bay leaf, 6 allspice and 6 white peppercorns, crushed, and 3 sprays of fresh dill. Let the herring marinate for several hours or overnight before serving. Garnish with sliced onion rings.

Inlagd Sur Sill
PICKLED HERRING

SOAK in cold water for at least 24 hours 12 salt herring, changing the water 3 or 4 times. Carefully remove the heads, tails, and skins, halve the herring lengthwise, and remove the dorsal bones. Reserve the roe. Arrange a layer

Marinated Herring in Sour Cream

of 6 halved herring in a flat, deep earthenware dish and spread over them 2 onions, thinly sliced. Slice a small lemon very thinly, seed it, and arrange the slices on the onion rings. Scatter over this 12 whole peppercorns. Repeat the procedure until all the herring halves have been used.

Put the herring roe through a sieve, stir in an equal amount of white wine or tarragon vinegar, and add enough sour cream to make sufficient quantity to cover the herring halves. Cover the dish lightly and marinate the herring for at least 24 hours.

Maquereaux Marinés
MARINATED MACKEREL

SPRINKLE 6 fresh mackerel generously with salt on both sides and put them in the refrigerator for 6 hours or overnight. Rinse the mackerel, dry them, and put them in a flameproof casserole on a bed of finely chopped onions and carrots. Add 2 sprays of parsley, a sprig of thyme, 1/2 bay leaf, 2 cloves, and a little freshly ground black pepper. Add enough white wine and vinegar in equal amounts to reach the top of the fish and cover with more finely chopped carrots and onions.

Top with a round of buttered paper, set the casserole over low heat, and bring the liquid to a boil. Cover the casserole tightly and simmer the mackerel for 15 minutes. Cool them in the liquid and serve chilled.

Mussels for Hors-d'Oeuvre

SCRUB and wash mussels thoroughly and scrape off the beards. Steam the mussels in a small amount of water for a few minutes until the shells open. Remove the mussels from the shells and chill them thoroughly. Serve with mayonnaise mixed with mustard and a little cream.

Moules à la Tartare

COAT cooked mussels with tartar mayonnaise and serve surrounded by lemon wedges.

Mussels in Piquant Sauce

SCRUB and wash thoroughly in salt water 2 pounds mussels and scrape off the beards. Dry the mussels. Brown 1 garlic clove in 2 tablespoons olive oil, remove the garlic, and add the mussels in their shells and 5 anchovy filets, chopped. Add 3/4 cup each of dry white wine and vinegar, cover the kettle, and steam the mussels until they open. Put them in an earthenware casserole and sprinkle them with 1 tablespoon chopped parsley and a dash of cayenne. Reduce the cooking liquor over medium heat by half. Pour the liquor over the mussels and marinate them for 3 days.

CUT unpeeled cucumbers into inch-long pieces and remove enough of the seedy center from each piece to form baskets large enough to hold an oyster. Poach oysters in their own liquor for a few minutes and drain them. Cool them and trim the edges. Cook the liquor until it is reduced to almost nothing and mix with a little chili sauce. Roll the oysters in the sauce, put them in the baskets, and sprinkle with chopped parsley.

Cucumbers Stuffed with Oysters

MAKE a court bouillon of 2 quarts water, 1/4 cup onions, sliced, 1 garlic clove, 1 bay leaf, 2 stalks of celery with the leaves, 1 1/2 tablespoons salt, and 1/8 teaspoon cayenne. Simmer the court bouillon for 15 minutes and add 2 pounds raw shrimps, washed and drained, and 1/2 lemon, sliced. Simmer the shrimps for 4 minutes and let them cool in the court bouillon. Chill, shell, and devein the shrimps.

Marinated Shrimps

Rub a mixing bowl with garlic and in it combine 1/2 cup finely chopped celery and 1 scallion, finely chopped, 6 tablespoons olive oil, 3 tablespoons lemon juice, 2 tablespoons each of chili sauce, tomato ketchup, and horse-radish, 1 tablespoon each of prepared mustard and chopped chives, 3/4 teaspoon salt, and 1/4 teaspoon each of paprika and Tabasco.

Marinate the prepared shrimps in this sauce for 12 hours and serve chilled.

CLEAN well in three changes of water 2 pounds unshelled small shrimps. In a 4-quart kettle bring 2 quarts water to a boil. Add 2 scallions, trimmed, 1 slice of fresh ginger, and 2 tablespoons each of Sherry and salt and bring the liquid again to a boil. Add the cleaned shrimps, lower the heat, and simmer the shrimps for about 5 minutes for very small shrimps, or for 6 or 7 minutes if the shrimps are somewhat larger. Leave them in the liquid and cool them to room temperature before chilling.

Spiced Shrimps

Shrimps prepared in this manner, left in the liquid, covered and refrigerated, can be kept for as long as one week. Serve the shrimps without removing the shells. To serve as a seafood cocktail, drain, and remove the shells.

Shrimp Bowl COOK 4 pounds large shrimps, shelled and deveined, in court bouillon, and drain them. Marinate them for 2 hours in the refrigerator in 3/4 cup tarragon vinegar, 2 bay leaves, 12 peppercorns, and 6 sprigs each of dill and parsley. Hang the shrimps on the edge of a bowl filled with Russian dressing for dipping.

Shrimp Cocktail ARRANGE cooked shrimps, shelled and deveined, on a bed of shredded lettuce in a cocktail glass surrounded by crushed ice and serve with rémoulade or ravigote sauce.

Prawn Sambal IN a skillet heat 1 tablespoon peanut oil and add 1 hot red pepper, seeded and chopped, 2 tablespoons peanut butter, 1 small onion, chopped, and 1/2 teaspoon salt. Add 8 to 10 shelled prawns, 2 tablespoons water and 1 teaspoon sugar and cook the prawns for about 10 minutes, or until they are pink and firm. Serve cold as a condiment with curried dishes.

Smoked Sturgeon SERVE paper-thin slices of smoked sturgeon with lemon wedges and with freshly ground black pepper.

Hot fish or shellfish preparations for hors-d'oeuvre may also serve as the fish course at a formal meal.

Coquilles of Crab Meat MIX together 1/2 cup mayonnaise, 2 egg yolks, and 2 tablespoons chopped chives. Combine this with 1 1/2 pounds cooked lump crab meat, mixing carefully, and season with salt and pepper. Pile the mixture in 6 crab shells or *coquilles*, mounding it high in the center. Spread each shell lightly with mayonnaise and garnish with thin strips of anchovy filets and slices of stuffed green olives. Bake the shells in a moderate oven (350° F.) for about 15 minutes, or until the mixture is heated through.

Clams Nantais IN a saucepan cook 6 tablespoons chopped mushrooms, 4 tablespoons chopped shallots, and 1 tablespoon minced garlic in 3 tablespoons butter until the shallots are transparent. Add 24 large raw clams, chopped, and their juice, cover, and simmer the mixture for 15 minutes. Remove the saucepan from the heat and stir in 1 tablespoon chopped chives, 1 beaten egg, and about 3 cups fresh white-bread crumbs, or enough to thicken the mixture.

Pile clams *nantais* in clam shells or ramekins, dot with butter, and bake the shells in a moderate oven (350° F.) for 10 minutes.

Chinese Lobster Roll

MAKE a thin pancake batter by beating 2 eggs with 1 cup sifted flour, 1/2 teaspoon salt, and about 1 cup water. Brush a small, hot skillet or crêpe pan with peanut oil. Pour into the pan about 2 tablespoons batter, or just enough to coat the pan, tipping it to spread the batter evenly. Cook the pancake only on one side. It will brown on the bottom in about 1 minute. Flip it out onto a kitchen towel. Repeat this process until almost all of the batter is used; save a little to seal the rolls.

To prepare the filling, cook 2 tablespoons each of shredded carrot and celery in boiling water for 3 to 4 minutes. Drain and cool the vegetables and combine them with 1 tablespoon chopped green onion, 1/2 cup each of minced cooked pork and minced cooked lobster meat, and 1 tablespoon chopped green onion. Season with 2 teaspoons peanut oil, 1 teaspoon sugar, and salt and pepper to taste. Put a spoonful of this mixture on the browned side of each pancake. Roll the pancakes and tuck in the ends. Seal the rolls with the reserved batter. Chill them until serving time. Brown them on all sides in hot oil and drain them well.

Chinese Mustard

Serve the rolls with soy sauce and with dry mustard mixed to a paste with flat beer.

Anchovies au Gratin

PEEL and thinly slice 4 medium potatoes. Butter a small casserole and put half the potato slices in the bottom. Cover the potatoes with 2 onions, sliced and sautéed in 2 tablespoons butter until golden, top the onions with 20 anchovy filets, and finish with the remaining potatoes. Pour in a little oil from the anchovy tin and dot with 2 tablespoons butter. Bake the casserole in a hot oven (400° F.) for 10 minutes and add 3/4 cup heavy cream. Bake the casserole for another 10 minutes and add another 3/4 cup heavy cream. Bake the casserole for 10 minutes longer, lower the heat to slow (300° F.), and bake it for 30 minutes longer, or until the potatoes are tender. Serve very hot from the casserole.

Snails with Garlic Butter

FOR 24 snails prepare this butter: Cream 1/3 pound butter and add to it 1/2 tablespoon finely chopped parsley, 1 teaspoon each of finely chopped shallots and salt, 2 garlic cloves, crushed, and pepper to taste. Put a little of the butter in each of 24 shells, put a snail in each shell, and cover it with a little of the remaining butter. Pour 2 tablespoons white wine into a flat baking dish, arrange the shells in the dish, and sprinkle them with fine bread crumbs. Bake the snails in a very hot oven (450° F.) or put the dish under the broiler until the crumbs are golden brown. Serve immediately.

Escargots au Vin Rouge
SNAILS IN RED WINE

PARBOIL 1/4 cup fat salt pork, diced, for 5 minutes and drain it. Melt 1 table-spoon butter in a heavy pan or casserole and in it sauté the pork dice until they are golden brown. Add 1 1/2 cups red wine, 12 small white onions, 1 large garlic clove, crushed, and a *bouquet garni* made by tying together 3 sprigs of parsley, 1 stalk of celery, 1/2 bay leaf, and a little thyme. Bring the liquid to a boil, cover the casserole and cook the mixture slowly for about 1 hour. Add 24 canned snails and heat them for 5 minutes. Discard the herbs and thicken the sauce by swirling in *beurre manié* made by creaming together 1 tablespoon butter and 1/2 tablespoon flour. Add 1 tablespoon brandy and sprinkle the snails with chopped parsley.

Meat hors-d'oeuvre run the gamut from the simplest tartare steak to the most elaborate pâtés in haute cuisine.

Sweet Marinated Beef Slices

SLICE 1 pound cooked sirloin steak in julienne. Add 1 onion, sliced, and salt and pepper to taste. Sprinkle 1 tablespoon lemon juice over the meat mixture and add 1 cup sour cream. Combine the mixture thoroughly and serve on leaves of lettuce.

Tartare Steak

MIX together 1 pound freshly ground raw sirloin or tenderloin steak, 1/2 cup finely chopped onions or scallions, 1 egg yolk, salt, freshly ground black pepper, and capers. Form the meat into patties and make a small indentation in each. Into each indentation place the yolk of a raw egg. Serve on individual plates garnished with chopped onion, capers, and a little chopped parsley.

Fresh Calves' Tongues

IN a saucepan combine 2 tablespoons flour, 2 to 3 tablespoons vinegar, and the juice of 1 lemon. Add 2 quarts water, 1 tablespoon salt, and 4 calves' tongues. Bring the water to a boil and cook the tongues for about 1 hour, or until they are tender. Cool the tongues in the liquor, cut them into thin slices, and arrange the slices in a bowl. Spread sliced or chopped sour pickles and chopped hard-cooked eggs over the tongue. Moisten with French dressing and sprinkle with chopped parsley and chives.

REMOVE the skin or fell and any fat from a 2-pound boned leg of veal. Make several incisions in the meat and insert 2 anchovy filets, cut into small pieces. Roll up the meat and secure the roll with string. Put the meat in a kettle and cover it with boiling water. Add an onion stuck with 2 whole cloves, 1 bay leaf, 1 stalk of celery with the green top, 1 carrot, scraped and cut into quarters, a few sprigs of parsley, and a little salt. Cover the pan and simmer the meat for 1 1/2 hours. Remove the meat from the broth and cool it thoroughly.

Pound 1/2 cup tuna fish, packed in oil, with 2 anchovy filets, and add gradually a generous 1/2 cup olive oil, working the oil into the fish to make a light paste. Thin the sauce with the juice of 2 lemons and add 1/4 cup drained capers.

Slice the cold veal thinly, arrange the slices in a shallow terrine, and pour the tuna sauce over them. Let the meat marinate overnight in a cold place before serving it in the terrine, garnished with slices of lemon.

Vitello Tonnato
VEAL WITH TUNA FISH SAUCE

CUT a chilled honeydew or Persian melon into wedges, discard the seeds, and cut away the rind. Serve each wedge on an individual plate with 2 very thin slices of *prosciutto* and garnish with a slice of lime. Fresh figs or any other variety of melon may be served with this Italian ham.

Prosciutto and Fruit

GRIND 1 pound larding fat and 1/2 pound each of filet of veal and lean pork through the finest blade of a food chopper, add 2 lightly beaten eggs, and mix well. Season the paste with salt, pepper, and spices to taste. Stir in 1/4 cup warmed and ignited Cognac and force the mixture through a fine sieve. Turn it into a buttered mold lined with thin slices of larding pork and bake the pâté in a moderate oven (350° F.) for 1 1/2 to 2 hours. Serve cold, in thin slices.

Pâté chez Madeleine

IN a saucepan in 1/4 cup butter sauté 1/3 cup minced green onion and 1 tablespoon finely chopped fresh tarragon or 1/2 teaspoon dried tarragon.

Tarragon Pâté

Add 1 pound chicken livers, cut in small pieces, and cook them for 1 minute, or until the red juices cease to flow. Force the mixture through a fine sieve or purée it in a blender. Beat 2 eggs with 1/3 cup cream and 1/2 teaspoon salt and combine them with the liver purée. Turn the pâté into a small earthenware casserole, cover it with buttered paper, and bake it for 1 hour in a slow oven (300° F.). Cool and chill before serving, as a spread or in slices.

Cold Meat Pâté PUT through the finest blade of a food chopper 1 pound each of calf's liver and sausage meat, 1/2 pound each of cooked ham and tongue, 1/4 pound liver sausage, and 1 small onion. Blend the mixture and season it highly with salt, cayenne, a pinch of thyme, and 1 teaspoon chopped parsley. Butter a mold or loaf pan. Line the mold with 4 or 5 thin strips of bacon and fill it with half the ground meat mixture. Set on the meat 2 hard-cooked eggs, end to end, and cover the eggs with the remaining meat mixture. Lay 2 small bay leaves on top and cover the pâté with buttered paper. Cook it, in a pan of water, in a moderate oven (350° F.) for 1 1/4 to 1 1/2 hours. Remove the buttered paper and the bay leaves, cover the pâté with a cloth, and place a weight on it. Chill it well. Turn the pâté out of the mold and serve it sliced.

Rillettes of Pork IN a heavy saucepan combine 2 pounds fat pork and 1 1/2 pounds fresh lean pork, both finely diced, 1 1/2 teaspoons salt, a little pepper, a pinch of poultry seasoning, 1 bay leaf, and 1 cup boiling water. Cook the mixture slowly, stirring occasionally until the water is cooked away and the meat and fat are brown. Drain in a colander, saving the fat that drains out. Discard the bay leaf from the meat and grind the meat very finely. Gradually stir in all but about 1 cup of the hot fat, pack the mixture into small jars, and pour the remaining fat over it. Store the jars in the refrigerator until ready to serve.

Chicken Liver Spread SIMMER 2 pounds chicken livers in a little stock until they are cooked through and grind them with 4 hard-cooked eggs, using the medium blade of a food chopper. Chop coarsely 2 medium onions and brown them very lightly in about 1/4 cup rendered chicken fat. Combine all the ingredients well to make a thick, cohesive paste and add salt and black pepper to taste. Serve on freshly made toast, in a lettuce cup, or as a cocktail spread.

Rillettes of Pork

Terrine de
Chevreuil

IN a bowl combine 1 1/4 pounds venison and 1/4 pound each of lean ham and salt pork, all diced. Season the meat with pepper and a little cinnamon, ginger, and cloves. Add 1/4 cup brandy and let the meat marinate in the refrigerator for 3 to 4 hours. Put twice through the finest blade of a food chopper 1/2 pound each of venison and fresh fat pork and 1/4 pound each of veal and fresh lean pork. Mix the ground meat with 2 teaspoons crushed peppercorns, 1 teaspoon powdered ginger, 1/4 teaspoon each of cinnamon and cloves, and a pinch of salt. Stir in 1/4 cup brandy and mix the ground mixture with the marinated meat and 2 eggs, well beaten. Turn the mixture into a deep, oval earthenware baking dish or terrine lined with thin strips of bacon. Cover the dish, set it in a shallow pan of hot water, and bake it in a moderate oven (350° F.) for about 1 1/2 hours, or until the fat that rises to the top is very clear. Remove the dish from the oven, set a pan or plate directly on the pâté and weight this down with a heavy weight. Let the pâté stand under the pressure until it is completely cold.

Eggs for hors-d'oeuvre are often also eggs for luncheon and supper. Many such are given in the chapter devoted to eggs, most of them among the poached-egg preparations. The eggs for hors-d'oeuvre that follow require the use of a knife and fork and are intended to be served as a first course, alone or as part of an assortment of appetizers, and therein they differ from the stuffed eggs of the cocktail party.

Cold Eggs
World's Fair

HALVE lengthwise hard-cooked eggs and remove the yolks. Press the yolks through a fine sieve and mix in an equal amount avocado purée and chopped cooked ham. Add a little mayonnaise and season to taste with salt and pepper. Arrange thin slices of smoked tongue on a serving dish, arrange the egg whites on top, and fill the whites with the stuffing. Coat the stuffed eggs with aspic and sprinkle them with a mixture of finely chopped parsley, chives, tarragon, and chervil.

Oeufs
Mollets for
Hors-d'Oeuvre

COOK fresh eggs in simmering water for 5 to 6 minutes, chill them quickly under cold running water, and remove the shells. The yolks should be soft and the whites firm. In a serving dish arrange slices of cooked ham or tongue or sliced fresh tomatoes or cooked artichoke bottoms, or chopped cooked vegetables mixed with mayonnaise. Arrange the eggs on top, coat them with aspic, and decorate with parboiled tarragon leaves or with chopped mixed tarragon and chervil.

HALVE lengthwise 6 hard-cooked eggs and put them in a serving dish, yolk side down. Cover them with a sauce made by combining 1 cup mayonnaise, 3 tablespoons chili sauce, and 1 tablespoon each of chopped onion, chives, parsley, and green olives. Chill before serving.

Eggs à la Russe

HALVE lengthwise 6 hard-cooked eggs. Remove the yolks and mash them to a paste with 1 tablespoon anchovy purée and a little mayonnaise. Season the mixture with a drop of Tabasco and form it into small balls. Roll the balls in finely chopped dill and arrange 3 balls in each egg white. Place each egg white on a thin slice of tomato sprinkled with salt and pepper, cross 2 thin strips of anchovy filets over the balls, and sprinkle with paprika.

Anchovy Egg Appetizer

The essential difference between the hors-d'oeuvre that serve as a first course and the hors-d'oeuvre that accompany a cocktail is simply a matter of cutlery. The guest who must balance a glass in one hand appreciates the convenience of appetizers that he can hold in the other hand and dispose of in one or two bites.

HARD cook 6 fresh eggs, turning them four or five times during the cooking to help set the yolks at dead center. Cool them quickly by plunging them into cold water. Halve the eggs lengthwise and carefully remove the yolks. Or cut off the narrow end, split the eggs crosswise, and cut a small slice from the other tip so that the halves will stand upright. Stuff and garnish them as follows:

Stuffed Eggs

Mash the egg yolks to a paste and combine them with 2 tablespoons each of *pâté de foie gras* and sweet butter, 1 teaspoon lemon juice, and 1/2 teaspoon salt. Anchovy paste may be added to taste. Force the mixture through a pastry bag into the egg whites and garnish with green pepper.

Mash the egg yolks and combine them with 1 tablespoon butter, 1/2 teaspoon each of Worcestershire sauce, salt, grated onion, and finely chopped

Stuffed Eggs

chives, and 1/4 teaspoon each of white pepper and dry mustard. Force the mixture through a pastry bag into the egg whites. Surround the fillings with ribbons of caviar.

Force the egg yolks through a sieve. Fill the hollows with caviar and garnish the edge with the sieved egg yolk.

Press the yolks through a fine sieve and mix in a purée of cooked fish or shellfish, a little mayonnaise, and some finely chopped parsley. Fill the egg whites and arrange them in a serving dish. Coat the stuffed eggs with aspic and sprinkle with finely chopped tarragon.

Mash the egg yolks to a paste and combine them with 2 tablespoons butter and 8 cooked, shelled, and deveined chopped shrimps. Season the paste with 1 teaspoon each of grated onion and Worcestershire sauce, 1/2 teaspoon salt, and a dash of Tabasco. Force the mixture through a pastry bag into the egg whites and garnish with tiny shrimps.

Remove the yolks and use them to garnish another dish. Combine 1 cup cooked cubed white meat of chicken with 1/2 cup blanched and toasted almonds, 3 tablespoons mayonnaise made with tarragon vinegar, and 1 teaspoon chopped tarragon. Force the mixture through a pastry bag into the egg whites. Garnish with shredded almonds.

Eggs with Caviar

HALVE lengthwise hard-cooked eggs and remove the yolks. Fill the hollows with caviar and garnish the edges with the egg yolks, finely chopped and mixed with finely chopped parsley.

Pickled Eggs

SIMMER 2 tablespoons sugar, 1 teaspoon each of mixed pickling spices and salt, and 1/2 teaspoon celery seeds in 2 cups vinegar and 1 cup water. Cool the liquid and strain it over 1 dozen shelled hard-cooked eggs. Add 1 garlic clove, chopped, and marinate the eggs, covered, in the refrigerator for 2 to 3 days. A little beet juice may be added for color.

The do-it-yourself craze has encompassed food service at the cocktail hour; these savory dips and spreads may be offered with an appropriate

variety of crackers, breads, or chips. The same mixtures are also used for prepared canapés of every sort, and even for tea sandwiches.

Anchovy Spread CHOP finely 12 anchovy filets and mix them with 1 cup soft cream cheese, 2 tablespoons chopped chives, and 1 tablespoon chopped fresh dill.

Avocado Cheese Dip PEEL and mash the pulp of 1 or 2 avocados. To 1 cup of the avocado purée add 1/4 cup mashed blue-veined cheese such as Langlois, Danish blue, or Roquefort, and 2 tablespoons sour cream. Stir in 1 tablespoon lemon juice and enough olive oil to make a smooth consistency. Season to taste with salt and pepper.

Chicken Piquant COMBINE 2 cups ground cooked white meat of chicken, 2 leaves of fresh tarragon, chopped, and 1 tablespoon each of chopped parsley, chives, and sweet gherkins. Add enough mayonnaise to bind the mixture and add salt and pepper to taste.

Salpicon à la Reine COMBINE 1 cup ground cooked white meat of chicken, 1/2 cup chopped cooked mushrooms, and 1/4 cup chopped blanched almonds. Stir in enough mayonnaise to bind the mixture and season to taste with salt, pepper, and nutmeg.

Egg and Swiss Cheese Spread FORCE the yolks of 6 hard-cooked eggs through a fine sieve and mix in 1 cup grated Swiss cheese. Add 1 teaspoon prepared mustard and stir in just enough mayonnaise to bind the ingredients to a smooth paste. Season to taste with salt.

Baba Gannoj
EGGPLANT APPETIZER BAKE an unpeeled eggplant in a moderate oven (350° F.) until it partially collapses and is very soft. Let it cool a little, open it, and remove the pulp. Beat the pulp until it is the consistency of a smooth paste, and add 1 teaspoon very finely chopped garlic, and salt, pepper, olive oil, and lemon juice to taste. Chill well before serving as a spread.

Ham Olive Spread COMBINE 1 cup ground cooked or smoked tongue and 1/2 cup each of chopped olives and Brazil nuts. Add enough mayonnaise to bind the mixture and season to taste with salt.

CHOP finely 2 cups cooked crab meat, lobster, or shrimps, and mix in 1 cup finely diced celery, 1 chopped hard-cooked egg, 2 tablespoons chopped parsley, enough mayonnaise to bind the mixture, and salt to taste.

Seafood Spread

DRAIN and mash a large can of tuna thoroughly. Add 1 cup chopped olives, 1 tablespoon grated onion, 1 teaspoon lemon juice, and enough mayonnaise to moisten the mixture.

Tuna Olive Spread

GRATE 2 pounds Cheddar cheese into a mixing bowl. Gradually add 1 cup softened butter and mash the mixture with a fork until it is well blended. Season with 1/4 teaspoon powdered mace and cayenne to taste and stir in 1/2 cup Port. Press the cheese into small pots, cover it with butter that has been melted and poured of the milky sediment at the bottom of the pan, and store the jars in a cool, dry place.

Cheddar with Port

GRATE 1/2 pound Cheddar cheese and mix it with 1 garlic clove, minced, 1 tablespoon Worcestershire sauce, 1/2 teaspoon dry mustard, and a dash of cayenne. Stir in gradually about 1/2 cup beer, or enough to make a paste of spreading consistency.

Cheddar with Beer

FORCE through a fine sieve or whip in a blender 1 cup cottage cheese, 1/4 cup milk, and 2 garlic cloves, crushed. Add a generous amount of salt and, if necessary, a little more milk to make a spread or a dip soft enough to pick up on potato chips.

Garlic Cheese

COMBINE 3 tablespoons chutney, 2 tablespoons each of chopped preserved ginger and grated fresh coconut, 1/2 teaspoon curry powder, and 1 cup soft cream cheese.

Curried Cream Cheese

CREAM 3 ounces cream cheese with 2 or 3 tablespoons sour cream. Stir in 1/2 cup finely chopped watercress leaves and 1 teaspoon freshly grated horseradish.

Horseradish Cream Cheese

Cream Cheese and Capers

CREAM 3 ounces cream cheese with 1 tablespoon heavy cream and 1 teaspoon juice from a bottle of capers. Stir in 1 tablespoon capers and salt and pepper to taste.

Roquefort Dip

COMBINE cottage cheese and Roquefort cheese in any desired proportion; 3 parts cottage cheese to 1 part Roquefort is a popular blend. Cream well and add enough heavy cream or sour cream to make a mixture of the desired spreading or dipping consistency. A little grated onion may be added, to taste.

Cucumber and Pot Cheese Spread

COMBINE 1/2 pound cottage or pot cheese with 1 cucumber, peeled, seeded, and diced, and 1 tablespoon chopped chives. Season to taste with salt and freshly ground black pepper and a dash of cayenne.

Crab Meat and Cheese

IN a bowl combine 1/2 cup cream cheese with 1/3 cup sour cream. Add 1 tablespoon each of capers and chopped chives and 1/2 teaspoon curry powder, and season the mixture with salt and pepper to taste. In another bowl shred or chop 1 cup cooked crab meat very finely. Combine the cheese mixture and the crab meat and blend well. Serve as a spread with toasted crackers.

Sour Cream Olive Dunk

MIX 2 cups sour cream, 3/4 cup finely chopped ripe olives, 1 tablespoon grated onion, and salt and pepper to taste. Use as a dip for raw vegetables, crackers, or potato chips.

Sour Cream Vegetable Dip

TO 2 cups sour cream add 1 cup chopped peeled cucumber, 1/4 cup each of finely chopped chives, parsley, and thinly sliced radishes, and salt and pepper to taste.

Tomato and Cream Cheese

PEEL and halve a large ripe tomato and press the pulp through a fine sieve to remove the seeds. Combine the purée with 3 ounces cream cheese. Stir in 1 garlic clove, minced, and season the spread with salt and pepper to taste.

Here is another popular pattern for hors-d'oeuvre: slices of smoked meat and fish spread with various fillings and rolled into cigarettes or cornucopias.

CUT thin slices of smoked salmon into triangles. Roll them into cornucopia shapes, fill them with caviar and sprinkle the cornucopias with lemon juice and freshly ground black pepper. Arrange them dial fashion on a platter and put a rosette of sweet butter in the open end of each. Chill before serving.

Smoked Salmon Cornucopias

CUT thin slices of smoked salmon into inch-wide strips. Spread each strip with caviar and roll it up. Skewer the rolls and chill them for at least 1 hour before serving.

Salmon and Caviar Rolls

BLEND 1 cup cream cheese with 2 tablespoons prepared horseradish and chill the mixture. Spread it on thin slices of dried beef, roll them into cornucopia shapes, and garnish the open end of each with a rosette of sweet butter and a spray of watercress.

Dried Beef Cornucopias

SLICE salami paper thin and halve each slice. Twist the half slices into cornucopia shapes, fill a pastry bag fitted with a small, decorative tube with cream cheese seasoned to taste with horseradish, and force the cheese into the cornucopias. Chill them for at least 30 minutes before serving.

Salami Cornucopias

SPREAD thin slices of ham with watercress butter and arrange sprigs of watercress stem to stem, so that the leaves stick out at each end when the ham is rolled.

Cream together equal amounts sweet butter and finely chopped watercress leaves. Season the butter to taste with anchovy paste.

Ham Rolls

Watercress Butter

Another popular cold hors-d'oeuvre is the ball on a stick, made of any tasty preparation firm enough to roll into a ball about 1/2 inch in diameter and spear on a disposable cocktail pick or skewer. The balls should be made well in advance and chilled before serving.

Curried
Chicken Balls

POUND 1/2 cup cooked white chicken meat to a paste in a mortar. Add curry powder and salt and pepper to taste and form the mixture into small balls. Roll the balls in finely chopped parsley and spear each with a wooden pick.

Piquants

MIX 1 generous teaspoon each of drained prepared horseradish, dill pickle, capers, and blanched almonds, all finely chopped, and 1 teaspoon each of minced parsley and chives. Blend well with 3/4 cup cream cheese. Chill the mixture, shape it into small balls the size of a walnut, and roll the balls in finely chopped parsley and nutmeats. Spear each one with a cocktail pick.

Cream Cheese
and
Curry Balls

COMBINE 1 cup cream cheese, 1 tablespoon finely chopped chutney, and 1 teaspoon curry powder. Shape the mixture into small balls and roll the balls in freshly grated coconut.

Olive Cheese
Balls

CREAM together 1 cup cream cheese, 1/2 cup chopped black olives, and 1 tablespoon butter. Form the mixture into small balls the size of marbles and roll the balls in finely chopped walnut meats.

Hot morsels are always welcome at the cocktail party. Any well-seasoned, savory croquette mixture may be shaped into bite-sized morsels and deep-fried to pass with cocktails, as may miniature kebabs.

Petites
Croquettes
de Volaille
COCKTAIL CHICKEN
CROQUETTES

COMBINE 1 cup ground cooked white meat of chicken with 1/2 cup sliced mushrooms, sautéed in butter until tender, 2 tablespoons finely chopped truffles, 1 tablespoon Sherry, and salt and pepper to taste. Bind the mixture with about 1 cup thick béchamel sauce and chill thoroughly.

Form the mixture into tiny balls about the size of marbles. Roll them in flour, dip them in beaten egg, and roll them in dry bread crumbs. Fry the croquettes a few at a time in hot deep fat (380° F.) until they are delicately browned. Drain them on absorbent paper and pierce each with a cocktail skewer.

Crab Meat
Bouchées

MELT 2 1/2 tablespoons butter in a saucepan, stir in 3 tablespoons flour, and gradually add 1/2 cup chicken stock, stirring constantly. Cook the mixture for a few minutes, stirring, and slowly add 1/2 cup heavy cream, blending it into the mixture thoroughly. Remove the saucepan from the heat and add 2 cups cooked crab meat, 3 tablespoons sautéed chopped mushrooms, 2 teaspoons chopped parsley, 1/2 teaspoon each of chopped tarragon and salt. Spread the mixture on a platter to cool, form it into small balls, and brown the balls in hot deep fat (380° F.). Pierce the *bouchées* with wooden picks and serve them hot to accompany cocktails. The *bouchées* may be reheated in the oven at serving time.

Walnut Chedder Balls

COMBINE 1 cup grated Cheddar, 2 tablespoons flour, 1/2 teaspoon each of salt and chili powder, 1/4 teaspoon orégano, and 1 egg white, stiffly beaten. Form the mixture into balls, roll the balls in coarsely chopped walnuts, and chill them thoroughly. Just before serving, sauté the balls in butter or fry them in hot deep fat (380° F.).

Olive Ripiene

COMBINE 1/2 cup each of ground cooked chicken meat and ham. Bind the mixture with 1 egg yolk and season it to taste with freshly grated Parmesan cheese, salt, cayenne, and nutmeg. Remove the pits from large firm olives and fill the cavities with the chicken-ham mixture. Roll the stuffed olives in flour, in beaten egg yolk, and in fine bread crumbs. Fry the olives in hot deep fat (370° F.) until they are golden and drain them on absorbent paper.

Fritto Bolognese

COOK in butter, with a pinch of salt and pepper, 4 chicken livers and an equal quantity of diced parboiled sweetbreads until the chicken livers are just firm. Dice the livers. Cut an equal amount of cooked tongue, Gruyère cheese, and 1 truffle into dice of the same size as the other ingredients.

Thread the five ingredients onto 24 wooden picks with the pieces of sweetbread and truffle in the middle. Spread them with a mixture of chopped herbs and grated Parmesan bound to a paste with beaten egg, so that the dice are completely masked. Dip the picks in beaten egg and fine bread crumbs and fry them in hot deep fat (365° F.). Serve them on a napkin with sprigs of fried parsley and slices of lemon.

Bollos

SOAK 1 pound black-eyed peas overnight. In the morning, remove the husks by rubbing the peas between the hands until they are loose. Put the peas in water again and the husks will rise to the top. Pour off the husks and put the peas through the finest blade of a food chopper, together with 2 garlic cloves and 2 small red peppers. Grind a second time, if necessary, to reduce the peas, garlic, and peppers to a very fine paste. Save the drippings from the grinder and stir them into the paste along with 1 teaspoon salt. Stir the mixture over low heat until it becomes creamy. If the mixture is too dry, add a little water. Drop it by spoonfuls into hot deep fat (375° F.) and fry the· *bollos* until they are brown on all sides.

Bocadillo de Apio

MIX grated *apio* or celeriac to a paste with a little butter and season it with salt and pepper. Form it into balls, dip the balls in egg and bread crumbs, and fry them in hot deep fat (365° F.).

Miniature Shish Kebabs

CUT 1 pound lean lamb into small cubes and put the meat in a bowl with 2 tablespoons olive oil, the juice of 1 lemon, 1 garlic clove, and salt and pepper. Marinate the lamb in this mixture for 1 hour, stirring occasionally. Arrange the lamb on small brochettes with a slice each of onion, tomato, and green pepper between the cubes. Cook the filled skewers under the broiler heat, turning them to brown on all sides and basting frequently with melted butter.

Skewered Chicken

CUT cooked chicken into large dice, and sauté briefly in butter as many medium-sized mushrooms as there are dice of chicken. Alternate on a small skewer a mushroom, a piece of chicken, and a piece of truffle until the skewer is filled finishing with a piece of chicken. Roll the skewers in thick, lukewarm Villeroi sauce, coat them *à l'anglaise*, and cook them in hot deep fat (380° F.) until they are golden brown. Drain them on absorbent paper and serve on the skewers. These may be accompanied by *sauce suprême* or tomato sauce, if desired.

Skewered Sweetbreads

FOLLOW the recipe for skewered chicken, substituting cooked diced sweetbreads for the chicken and omitting the truffles. Serve with *sauce suprême* or tomato sauce.

Anchovy Sardines

PUT an anchovy filet inside each sardine. Dip the sardines in beaten egg, roll them in fine, dry bread crumbs, and fry them in hot deep fat (380° F.) until they are golden. Drain on absorbent paper.

Mix 5 tablespoons arrowroot with 1/4 cup cool chicken stock. In a sauce-pan bring 1/2 cup chicken stock to a boil, add the arrowroot, and heat the mixture, stirring, until it thickens. Add 1/3 cup light cream and season with salt to taste. Pour the liquid quickly into a shallow tray, cool it, and chill it until it is set. Cut the jelly into 1-inch cubes, roll them in fine dry bread crumbs, and fry them in hot deep fat (385° F.) for a few seconds, to brown the crumbs.

Cha Hsueh Yi

FRIED CHICKEN
JELLY CUBES

A canapé (literally meaning a couch or sofa) is basically an appetizer pre-sented on a small piece of bread or toast, or thin pastry baked in the form of a small boat or some other special mold. The number and variety of such offerings can be endless, and the construction of an original canapé is a challenge for the artist-cook. Bearing in mind the general procedures and hints on technique that follow, the cook can give imagination free rein.

Canapés

    Canapé bases should be firm: certain breads, like the thinly sliced dark pumpernickel, will stand up under even a moist filling; others should be toasted. The shape of the canapé is a matter of taste—squares, ovals, diamonds, triangles, all lend interest.

Canapé Bases

    Canapé butters, which consist of butter creamed and seasoned to taste with, for example, garlic, anchovy paste, herbs, or mustard, serve a dual purpose. They help to insulate the bread base and they add their own delightful flavors.

Canapé Butters

    The usual decorations for canapés include truffles, pimiento, black and green olives, pickles, hard-cooked egg, capers, radishes, and parsley. A set of truffle cutters, to sculpture tiny flower, leaf, and geometric shapes from any of these, is a useful tool. The other essential instrument for the creator of decorative canapés is a pastry bag and an assortment of small tubes through which various savory mixtures may be piped.

*Canapé
Decorations*

    Mimosa, a mixture of chopped hard-cooked eggs—yolk and white—and an equal quantity of very finely chopped parsley, is a popular garnish for hors-d'oeuvre.

Mimosa Garnish

    Facile fingers can quickly learn to twist thin slices of smoked meats and fish into cornets or flowerlike cups, and create carrot and celery curls, radish roses, and cucumber and lemon whorls.

    We have described enough canapés to serve as a starting point for the building of a canapé repertoire.

Aspic
Canapés

SPREAD thin slices of white or whole wheat bread cut the length of the loaf with soft butter and spread over the butter a very thin layer of good mustard. Cover the bread with paper-thin slices of ham or tongue, sliced turkey breast, or smoked salmon. Brush the surface with cool, but still liquid aspic and chill the bread until the aspic is set. Cut each slice of bread into triangles, squares or strips and decorate each canapé with small cutouts of truffle slices and egg white cut to resemble flowers. Brush each canapé with aspic and chill the canapés again until the aspic is set. Give each canapé a final thin coating of aspic and, while the aspic is still liquid, pipe a tiny edging of creamed butter around the edges.

Canapés
Admiral

COVER one-third of a square of toast with a slice of smoked sturgeon, the second third with smoked salmon, and the remaining third with caviar. Garnish the edges of the canapé with mimosa.

Canapés
Cardinal

SPREAD toast with Russian dressing and top it with a thin slice of ripe tomato. Garnish with half a cooked, shelled, and deveined shrimp.

Canapés
Diplomat

COVER rounds of toast with thinly sliced Westphalian ham. Garnish with a cross of anchovy filets and arrange slices of pimiento-stuffed olive between the filets. Dip the edges in mimosa.

Canapés
Favorite

COVER small toast shapes with a slice of Swiss cheese and one of tongue, and make a border of finely chopped sour pickles.

Canapés
Olga

COVER half of each square of toast with a slice of smoked sturgeon and the other half with a slice of smoked salmon. Spread a generous covering of caviar on the sturgeon and anchovy paste on the salmon. Dip the edges of the canapé in mimosa.

Canapés
du Maine

TOSS 2 cups chopped cooked lobster with 1/2 cup mayonnaise, 1 tablespoon chili sauce, 1 teaspoon finely chopped chives and a little tarragon, finely chopped, and salt and pepper to taste. Spread the mixture on toast squares, put a slice of lobster-claw meat in the center, and dip the edges of the squares in mimosa.

COVER toast with alternating rows of skinned and boned sardines and sliced spring onions. Decorate with a cutout of pimiento.

Canapés Portugaise

SPREAD squares of toast with anchovy paste and cover the paste with alternating strips of anchovy filets and pimiento. Garnish with slices of green olive.

Canapés Seville

SPREAD small rounds of crisp toast with butter creamed with anchovy paste to taste. Put a tiny heart of artichoke in the center and pipe around it a decorative border of cream cheese, whipped until it is light and fluffy with a little milk and seasoned with salt and pepper.

Artichoke Canapés

PRESS 2 hard-cooked eggs and 6 anchovy filets through a potato ricer and stir in 2 tablespoons mayonnaise. Cut bread into diamond shapes. Return the egg mixture to the ricer and press it over the bread. Garnish each diamond with sliced stuffed olives.

Anchovy Diamonds

SPREAD crescents of crisp toast with black caviar. Sprinkle one end of each crescent with sieved egg white, the other with sieved egg yolk. Put a curled anchovy filet in the center.

Caviar Crescents

BLEND 1/2 pound grated Swiss cheese with 1/2 cup soft butter, and add enough cream to make a thick paste. Add 1/2 cup Swiss cheese cut into tiny cubes and 1/2 cup chopped blanched pistachio nuts.

Pistachio Cheese Rolls

Trim the ends from 4 hard French rolls and remove the soft insides. Stuff the shells with the cheese-nut mixture and chill the rolls for several hours. To serve, cut the rolls crosswise in thin slices.

Mediterranean Loaf   SCOOP out a long loaf of French or Italian bread lengthwise to make a long hollow tube with a 1/2-inch crust. Combine the crumb with 4 tomatoes, peeled, seeded, and chopped, 4 green onions, including the green parts, thinly sliced, 1/2 cup each of ripe olives and olives stuffed with pimiento, both chopped, 2 generous tablespoons finely chopped parsley, a few capers, 1/2 teaspoon crushed dried mint leaves, and a pinch of thyme. A tablespoon of any grated cheese may also be added. Add enough olive oil—about 2 tablespoons—to moisten the mixture, a dash of lemon juice, and salt and black pepper to taste. Stuff the loaf firmly with this mixture, wrap it in aluminum foil, and chill it for 24 hours before serving. Cut the loaf very carefully in 1/2-inch slices and serve it as a cocktail appetizer.

These hot canapés can be prepared in advance and conveniently finished under the broiler or in the oven as they are needed to replenish plates and trays.

Anchovy and Cheese Rolls   REMOVE the crusts from a day-old loaf of bread and with a sharp knife slice the bread as thinly as possible. Flatten each slice by pressing it with the side of a cleaver. Spread each slice with softened cream cheese and put an anchovy filet lengthwise in the center. Roll each slice lengthwise and arrange the rolls on a baking sheet. Just before serving, toast the rolls in a very hot oven (450° F.).

Anchovy Garlic Canapé   POUND 16 anchovy filets in a mortar with 3 garlic cloves, chopped. Add 2 tablespoons bread crumbs soaked in water and pressed as dry as possible in a towel, a little ground pepper, and 1 teaspoon anchovy oil. Work the mixture to a smooth paste and season it with a few drops of wine vinegar. Spread the paste on slices of French bread brushed with olive oil and broil the slices. Serve very hot.

Hot Shrimp Canapés   CHOP 1 pound poached, shelled, and deveined shrimps finely and stir in 2 scallions, minced, and 3 to 4 tablespoons mayonnaise, or enough to make a thick mixture. Spread the mixture thickly on rounds of toast, piling it

Mediterranean Loaf

high in the center. Sprinkle with grated Parmesan cheese and broil the canapés for about 5 minutes, or until the toppings sizzle.

Canapés à la Provençale — SAUTÉ 1/4 cup finely chopped onions lightly in 2 tablespoons butter. Add 3 tomatoes, peeled, seeded, chopped, and drained, salt and pepper to taste, and 1/4 teaspoon minced garlic. Cook the mixture very slowly until it is reduced to a thick paste. Stir in 1/2 tablespoon minced parsley.

Sauté rounds of bread in butter until they are lightly brown on both sides. Spread them with the tomato paste and arrange on each 4 pitted black olives that have been simmered in boiling water for 2 minutes. On the olives lay a filet of anchovy. Sprinkle the canapés with dry bread crumbs sautéed in butter until they are golden. Bake them in a hot oven (400° F.) for 3 to 4 minutes.

Canapés aux Sardines — BUTTER narrow rectangles of toast and arrange a sardine on each. Mask the sardine with a little tomato sauce, sprinkle with lemon juice, and bake the canapés in a hot oven (400° F.) for about 6 minutes.

Canapés aux Oeufs Durs — CUT toast into rectangles and spread each piece with chopped hard-cooked egg mixed to a paste with béchamel sauce. Top each with 2 slices of hard-cooked egg, sprinkle with fine dry bread crumbs sautéed in butter until they are golden, and brown them under the broiler.

Hot Cheese Canapés — INTO 2 cups hot thick béchamel sauce stir 1 pound grated Gruyère cheese, 1/2 cup dry white wine, 1 garlic clove, finely chopped, 1 egg, lightly beaten, and a little salt, pepper, and nutmeg. Toast rounds of bread on one side. Spread the untoasted side with the cheese mixture, leaving a 1/4-inch border all around so that the cheese will not run over the sides. Arrange the canapés, cheese side up, on a baking sheet and brown them in a very hot oven (450° F.) or under the broiler.

Canapés Ecossaise — REMOVE skin and bones from cooked smoked herring and chop the meat coarsely. To each cup of fish add 2/3 cup thick béchamel sauce, 1 tablespoon grated Parmesan cheese, and pepper to taste. Heap the mixture on rounds of toast, sprinkle lightly with grated Parmesan, and brown quickly under the broiler. Serve hot.

MIX 6 hard-cooked eggs, diced, with 1/2 cup Mornay sauce. Spread the mixture on squares of toast, sprinkle thickly with grated Cheddar and lightly with paprika, and brown the canapés under the broiler. Serve hot.

Canapés Américaine

TOAST 6 thin slices of bread on one side and halve them. Cover the toasted side of 6 of the pieces with a thick slice of mozzarella and 2 anchovy filets. Sprinkle with a little orégano and freshly ground black pepper and cover with the other half slices, toasted side down.

Neapolitan Appetizers

In a skillet heat 1/4 cup olive oil or butter and in it sauté the sandwiches on both sides until the cheese is melted and the bread is golden.

CUT a loaf of firm white bread lengthwise into inch-thick slices. With a cookie cutter cut out 1/2-inch rounds. Hollow out each round, leaving a shell about 1/8 inch thick. Spread the rims and cups of the shells with soft butter and bake them on a baking sheet in a hot oven (400° F.) for about 12 minutes, or until the *croûtes* are golden brown and crisp.

Croûtes

Sauté chopped cooked cauliflower in hot butter for 2 to 3 minutes, stirring constantly, and fill tiny *croûtes*. Mask the filling with sauce Mornay, sprinkle it with grated cheese, and brown it under the broiler.

Croûtes du Barry

Grind cooked white meat of chicken several times through the finest blade of a food chopper, bind it with velouté sauce and season it to taste with salt, pepper, and nutmeg. Fill *croûtes* with the mixture and put a thin slice of truffle on the filling. Sprinkle with finely chopped parsley.

Croûtes Ambassadrice

Sauté 1/2 pound chopped mushrooms in butter with a little lemon juice for about 3 minutes, or until the mushrooms are lightly browned. Cool and combine the mushrooms with 4 hard-cooked eggs, chopped. Mix in lightly 1/4 cup chopped truffles and moisten the mixture with béchamel sauce. Fill *croûtes* with the mixture and top each *croûte* with a curled anchovy filet. Sprinkle the anchovy with fine bread crumbs, dot with butter, and put the *croûtes* under the broiler until the crumbs are browned.

Croûtes Brillat-Savarin

Combine 1 cup finely chopped cooked lobster meat with 1/4 cup chopped truffles. Bind the mixture with béchamel sauce and stir in 1 tablespoon

Croûtes Cardinal

lobster butter. Fill *croûtes* with the mixture. Sprinkle with fine bread crumbs, dot with shellfish butter, and brown the crumbs under the broiler. Before serving, garnish each *croûte* with a thin slice of truffle and one of cooked lobster meat.

Croûtes au Fromage Fill shallow *croûtes* with shredded Gruyère cheese seasoned with paprika and freshly grated nutmeg. Sprinkle with grated Parmesan cheese and melted butter and brown under the broiler.

Puff paste—it is de rigueur *and very practical to use the scraps left from a grand* gâteau *for this purpose—makes hot cocktail appetizers of unsurpassed lightness and crispness. They take many forms—pies, turnovers, sticks, boats, shells—and accomodate themselves to many fillings. If preference or convenience dictates, any unsweetened pie dough may take the place of puff paste. Our puff paste recipes are presented in their classical form; the imaginative reader will discover for himself the endless permutations and combinations which are possible.*

Petits Pâtés à l'Indienne
CURRIED CHICKEN PIES
ROLL out puff paste into a thin sheet and cut it into 2-inch rounds with a fluted cutter. Combine 1 cup ground cooked chicken meat with 1/2 cup curry sauce and 1 tablespoon chutney and put 1 teaspoon of the mixture in the center of half the rounds. Moisten the edges of the pastry, place another round on top, and press the edges firmly together. Brush with beaten egg and bake the pies in a very hot oven (450° F.) for 10 to 15 minutes, or until they are brown.

Petits Pâtés à la Strasbourgeoise
GOOSE LIVER PIES
PUT 1 teaspoon *purée de foie gras* in the center of half the rounds of puff paste, above, and top with a thin slice of truffle. Cover the pies and bake as indicated above.

Anchovy Turnovers ROLL out puff paste 1/8 inch thick and cut it into rounds 3 inches in diameter. Put a curled anchovy on each round and dot it with garlic-butter. Moisten the edges of the rounds, fold them in half, and crimp the edges with the tines of a fork. Brush the turnovers with beaten egg and bake them in a very hot oven (450° F.) for 10 to 15 minutes.

ROLL out puff paste 3/8 inch thick and cut it into bands 3 inches wide. Brush the bands with 1 egg, lightly beaten with 1 teaspoon water. At 3/4 inch intervals apply a thin strip of any savory *farce* or filling. Cover this with a second band of puff paste and seal the bands between the strips of filling by pressing with the fingers. Brush again with the beaten egg. The egg seals the *allumettes* and gives them an attractive gloss. With a sharp knife or a pastry wheel, cut the bands into strips 3/4 inch wide, each containing the *farce*. Bake the *allumettes* on a baking sheet in a hot oven (400° F.) for 12 to 15 minutes.

Allumettes

Blend 1/2 cup cooked tuna fish, finely mashed, 2 teaspoons anchovy paste, and 3 tablespoons *béchamel maigre*. Proceed as indicated in the recipe for *allumettes*, topping each strip of filling with an anchovy filet. As a variation, sardines may be substituted for the anchovies.

*Allumettes
aux Anchois*

Combine 1/4 pound cooked white meat of chicken, cut into small cubes, 2 tablespoons each of sautéed mushrooms and truffles, coarsely chopped, and 3 tablespoons béchamel sauce. Use to fill *allumettes*.

*Allumettes
à la Reine*

Prepare a *farce* for *allumettes* by combining 1/2 cup thick spinach purée, 2 tablespoons béchamel sauce, and 1 tablespoon grated Parmesan cheese.

*Allumettes
Florentine*

Prepare a *farce* for *allumettes* by combining 1/2 cup purée of cooked pike and 3 tablespoons shellfish butter made with crayfish. Top each strip of filling with a crayfish tail and a slice of truffle before applying the covering pastry.

*Allumettes
Grimod
de la Reynière*

Combine 1/4 pound *foie gras* with 2 tablespoons truffles, coarsely chopped, and 1 tablespoon *glace de viande*, or 1 to 2 teaspoons meat glaze, to taste. Use to fill *allumettes*.

*Allumettes
Lucullus*

Tiny open tarts filled with savory mixtures, browned in the oven, and served hot are called *tartelettes* or *barquettes* depending upon their shapes. The round one are *tartelettes* and the ovals, *barquettes*. Roll out puff paste or flaky pie dough very thinly and cut it into the right size and shape for the special little molds, either fluted or plain. Fit the cutouts into the molds and press the dough firmly against the bottom and sides. Prick

*Tartelettes and
Barquettes*

the dough, cover it with wax paper, and fill the molds with rice or dried beans to prevent buckling and shrinking. Bake in a moderately hot oven (375°–400° F.) for 12 to 15 minutes. Remove the rice or beans and the wax paper. Unmold the pastry shells and fill them as desired.

Barquettes de Homard Remove the meat from a cooked lobster weighing about 1 1/2 pounds. Chop the meat finely and sauté it gently in 2 tablespoons butter with 1 tablespoon each of chopped onion and parsley, until the onion is transparent. Stir in 1/2 cup warm cream mixed with 2 egg yolks and 1/4 cup Cognac. Spoon the mixture into baked puff paste *barquettes*, boat-shaped tart shells. Sprinkle the *barquettes* with grated Parmesan and buttered crumbs, and brown the topping under the broiler. Serve at once.

Mussels Poulette en Barquettes Steam 18 to 20 thoroughly scrubbed and washed mussels with 2 finely chopped shallots or 1 small white onion and 1/2 cup white wine for 6 to 8 minutes, or until the shells open. Remove the mussels from their shells, draining all the liquor from them into the wine in the pan. Cook the liquor until it is reduced to about one-third and thicken it with *beurre manié*, made by creaming together 2 tablespoons butter and 1 tablespoon flour. Add 1 tablespoon chopped parsley and 4 or 5 cooked mushrooms, thinly sliced, combine the sauce and mussels, and turn the filling into baked *barquettes*. Sprinkle with fine bread crumbs, dot with butter, and brown in a very hot oven (450° F.)

Barquettes de Crevettes Put 1 or 2 shrimps, cooked in court bouillon, shelled, and deveined, in each *barquette*. Mask them with Mornay sauce, sprinkle with grated Parmesan cheese, and put them under the broiler to brown.

Barquettes d'Huîtres Bourguignonne Poach small oysters in their own liquor for a few minutes and drain them well. Put them in pastry shells and cover them with *escargot* butter, made by creaming butter with finely chopped shallots and garlic. Sprinkle with fine crumbs made from water crackers and brown the topping in a very hot oven (450° F.) or under the broiler.

Barquettes d'Huîtres Monselet Combine 3/4 cup rich béchamel sauce with 1/2 cup cooked artichoke hearts and truffles, both coarsely chopped. Spoon some of the mixture into each *barquette*, sprinkle with Parmesan cheese and dot with bits of butter. Brown the topping quickly under the broiler and top each *barquette* with a fried oyster.

Mix 1 cup cooked ham, finely chopped, with 2 tablespoons prepared mustard, 3 white onions, finely chopped, and a pinch of cayenne. Fold in 1 cup heavy cream, whipped until stiff, and pile the mixture into baked tart shells. Sprinkle the tarts lightly with paprika and very finely chopped parsley.

Tartelettes
au Jambon

Mix together equal amounts finely diced cooked mushrooms and truffles and add enough hot cream sauce to bind the mixture. Fill baked tart shells with the mixture, sprinkle the tops with fine bread crumbs sautéed in butter until golden brown, and put a small slice of sweetbread sautéed in butter on top of each. Bake the tartlets in a hot oven (400° F.) for 2 to 3 minutes, or until they are very hot.

Tartelettes Rachel
SWEETBREAD
TARTLETS

Wash, dry, and thinly slice 1 pound mushrooms and sauté them gently with 3 tablespoons minced shallots or scallions in 1/4 cup butter for 5 minutes. Add 3 tablespoons flour and cook, stirring, for 2 minutes longer. Add gradually 1 cup hot chicken stock and cook, stirring, until the sauce is smooth and thick. Stir in 1 cup heavy cream and 2 tablespoons Sherry, season to taste with salt and pepper, and bring to a boil.

Mushroom Tarts

Turn the mushroom mixture into baked tart shells, and bake the tarts in a moderately hot oven (375° F.) for 12 minutes.

Bouchées *are bite-sized patty shells or cases made of puff paste. They are* vol-au-vent *in miniature.*

ROLL out puff paste 1/4 inch thick on a lightly floured board and cut it into small circles with a fluted cookie cutter. Cut the center from half the circles to make rings. Brush the edges of the whole circles with water and press a ring on top of each. Lay the rounds on a baking sheet lined with heavy paper, brush them with beaten egg and replace the tiny cutouts lightly in each ring. Chill the *bouchées* for 20 minutes, then bake them in a very hot oven (450° F.) for 10 minutes, or until they are well puffed. Reduce the oven temperature to moderately hot (375° F.) and bake the *bouchées* until they are lightly browned.

Petites
Bouchées

Bouchées
aux Huîtres

Fill very small patty shells made of puff paste with poached oysters, drained, and bound with *sauce normande.*

Bouchées
à la Dieppoise

Fill *bouchées* with cooked mussels and shrimps, coarsely chopped, and bound with a little white-wine cream sauce.

Bouchées
à la Varenne

Fill *bouchées* with cooked sweetbreads chopped and bound with velouté sauce. Garnish with truffles and small asparagus tips.

Brioche
Containers for
Hors-d'Oeuvre

Bake tiny brioches à tête *and cool them. Remove the heads and set them aside. Hollow out the brioches, being careful not to break through the outer crust. Dry the brioche shells for 3 to 4 minutes in a moderate oven (350° F.), fill them, and replace the top. Just before serving, heat the filled brioches in the oven.*

The fillings for croûtes *are well adapted for use with these shells, as are other savory mixtures.*

Petits Beignets
HORS-D'OEUVRE
FRITTERS

Beignets *are edible trifles dipped in fritter batter—*pâte à frire*—and cooked in hot deep fat at 375°, the temperature at which a 1-inch cube of bread will brown in 60 seconds. Anything will make a* beignet, *and tiny* beignets *can make a success of a tray of hot hors-d'oeuvre.*

Pâte à Frire
FRITTER BATTER
FOR
HORS-D'OEUVRE

Sift 1/2 cup flour and a pinch of salt into a bowl and stir in 1 egg, beaten, and 1 tablespoon melted butter. Add gradually 1/2 cup flat beer, stirring only until the mixture is smooth, and let the batter rest for an hour in a warm place. Just before using, fold in 1 egg white, beaten until stiff.

Artichoke
Fritters

Quarter cooked artichoke bottoms. Sprinkle them with a little olive oil, lemon juice, salt, and pepper and let them marinate for 30 minutes. Dip the pieces in fritter batter for hors-d'oeuvre and fry them, a few at a time, in hot deep fat (375° F.). Drain them on absorbent paper, sprinkle with salt, and arrange them in a pyramid on a heated serving plate.

Sweetbread
Fritters

Cut 1 large parboiled sweetbread into 1-inch squares. Marinate the squares for 30 minutes in a mixture of 3 tablespoons oil, 1 tablespoon lemon juice,

1 teaspoon chopped parsley, and salt and pepper. Dip the squares in fritter batter for hors-d'oeuvre and fry them in hot deep fat (375° F.).

The cocktail puff, made of pâte à chou, *cream puff paste, may be filled with almost any savory mixture; it looks and tastes far more complicated and luxurious than it actually is. Half the recipe for* pâté à chou *will make about 35 tiny puffs, or* choux.

Cocktail Puffs

Make small cocktail puffs. Split each puff and fill one half with cream cheese, whipped until fluffy with milk and seasoned with salt and pepper. Put a tiny heart of artichoke on the cheese and cover with the other half.

Artichoke Puffs

Put 1 cup cooked crab meat 3 times through a food chopper. Add 1/4 cup mushrooms, sautéed in a little butter and finely chopped, and salt and pepper to taste. Blend well and fill cocktail puffs.

Crab Puffs

Whip cream cheese with cream to make a fluffy mixture. Add chopped chives and salt and pepper. Blend well and use to fill cocktail puffs.

Chive Cheese Puffs

Combine 1/2 pound cottage cheese, 6 ounces cream cheese, and 1/3 cup sour cream and rub the mixture through a fine sieve. Season with salt and stir in 3 tablespoons minced chives, a dash of cayenne, and 1 scant teaspoon celery salt or curry powder. Fold in 1/2 cup heavy cream, whipped. Slit cocktail puffs on the side and fill them with the mixture, forcing it through a pastry bag. Chill before serving.

Choux au Fromage

Combine 1 cup finely ground cooked, shelled, and deveined shrimps and 2 tablespoons minced truffles. Stir in enough béchamel sauce to bring the mixture to the desired consistency. Stir in 2 tablespoons shrimp butter and add salt and cayenne to taste. Fill tiny *choux* with the mixture and serve cold.

Choux à la Nantua

Combine 1 cup mashed ripe avocado, 1 tablespoon lime or lemon juice, and 1 1/2 teaspoons grated onion. Season to taste with salt and cayenne. Slit tiny *choux* on the side and fill with the mixture. Chill before serving.

Choux Méxicaine

Cut the tops from small puffs. Fill the puffs with caviar and decorate them with a border of mimosa. Replace the tops so that the filling shows.

Choux au Caviar Mimosa

97

Choux
au Vert-Pré

Combine 1/3 cup each of hot purée of freshly cooked green beans, of peas, and of asparagus. Stir in 1 tablespoon chopped chervil and enough cream sauce to bind the purée. Correct the seasoning with salt and pepper. Fill cocktail puffs with the mixture and heat them in a slow oven (300° F.) before serving.

When chou *paste—lightened or not with an extra egg white—is fried, it becomes a* beignet soufflé, *a most versatile preparation that may appear at every course from hors-d'oeuvre to dessert. The* beignet soufflé *for hors-d'oeuvre is made without sugar, is tastefully spiced and seasoned, and serves as a vehicle for cheese, meat, fish, or poultry.*

Beignets
Soufflés

IN a saucepan bring to a boil 1/2 cup water, 1/4 cup butter, and 1/4 teaspoon salt. When the butter is melted and the water boiling rapidly, add all at once 1/2 cup sifted flour, raise the saucepan over the heat, and stir briskly with a wooden spoon until the paste comes away from the sides of the pan and forms a smooth ball. Remove the pan from the heat. Add 2 eggs, one at a time, beating thoroughly after each addition until the batter is smooth and shiny. Fold in 1 egg white.

Drop the batter by teaspoonfuls into hot deep fat (365° F.) and fry a few beignets at a time until they take on a light golden color. Raise the heat to 375° F. and fry the *beignets* until they are brown. Dry them on absorbent paper. Serve immediately.

Cheese Beignets

Add to the batter for hors-d'oeuvre *beignets soufflés* 1/4 cup grated Parmesan cheese, and fry the *beignets* as indicated.

Ham Beignets

Add 1/2 cup chopped ham and 1/8 cup chopped truffles to the batter for *beignets soufflés* and fry as indicated.

Paprika
Beignets

Add 6 tablespoons onion, finely chopped and sautéed in butter to a pale golden brown, to the batter for hors-d'oeuvre *beignets soufflés*. Add 1/2 teaspoon or more paprika, to taste. Form the seasoned paste into nuggets the size of a hazelnut and fry them a few at a time in hot deep fat (375° F.). Drain the paprika *beignets* on absorbent paper and sprinkle them with salt. Serve hot.

The simplest appetizers are often the most suitable, sometimes the most satisfactory in every way. To accompany the predinner apéritif, *whether it is a glass of Sherry or Madeira or a Martini, nuts or cheese crackers are enough and not too much.*

SIFT together 2 cups flour and 1 teaspoon each of double-action baking powder and salt. With a pastry blender cut in 3/4 cup butter. Add 1 egg and 1 tablespoon milk, to make a dough that can be handled. Chill the dough for 1 hour. Grate 1/2 pound Cheddar, Parmesan, or Edam cheese. Roll out the chilled dough on a lightly floured board into a rectangle 1/4 inch thick. Sprinkle half the dough with half the grated cheese and cover it with the rest of the dough. Press the edges together to seal in the cheese. Fold the dough in half again and roll it out to its original size. Repeat the process. Cut the dough into finger sticks and bake the sticks on a baking sheet in a hot oven (450° F.) for about 10 minutes, until they are delicately browned. Store in a tightly covered metal container.

Cheese Sticks

THIS cheese dough may be shaped into squares, diamonds, crescents or rounds, and sprinkled with paprika, cayenne, caraway seeds, or celery salt, to make an assortment to please the eye and the palate.

Or scraps of puff paste may be rolled out, cut into sticks or *allumettes*, and layered with grated cheese and seasonings.

Cheese Crackers

BLANCH 2 cups almonds. Beat 1 egg white slightly, add the prepared almonds, and stir them until they are entirely coated with the egg. Spread the nuts on a large pan. Sprinkle them with salt and bake them in a moderately hot oven (375° F.) until they are heated through. Keep the oven door open during the baking time and stir the almonds often to prevent burning.

Glazed Salted Almonds

SHELL almonds and blanch or not according to preference. Fry them in a frying basket in hot deep fat or oil (325° F.) for 5 to 6 minutes. When the nut is broken, the center should be pale brown. Be careful not to over-fry or the nuts will be bitter. Drain the nuts on absorbent paper and sprinkle them with salt while they are still hot.

Deep Fried Almonds

Assorted Nuts

HEAT 1/4 cup butter in a frying pan and add 1 cup blanched dry almonds. Stir constantly with a wooden spoon until the nuts are lightly golden. Remove them immediately from the heat and continue to stir for a few minutes, or until further browning of the nuts ceases. Add salt and a pinch of saffron, red pepper, or ginger for a variety of flavors.

Sautéed Almonds

HEAT 1/2 cup butter or olive oil in a saucepan. Add 1 pound shelled hazelnuts and cook, stirring with a wooden spoon, until the nuts are a golden brown. Remove the pan from the heat and continue to stir for a few minutes; the color of the nuts will deepen. Sprinkle lightly with 1 to 2 tablespoons coarse salt.

Toasted Hazelnuts

SAUTÉ 2 dozen Brazil nuts to a light golden brown in 2 tablespoons melted butter, remove the pan from the heat and salt the nuts lightly. Wrap each nut in 1/2 slice raw lean bacon and secure it with a wooden pick, if necessary. Broil the nut rolls until the bacon is crisp, turning them often.

Brazil Nuts in Bacon

PEEL and cut very small eggplant into paper-thin slices and drop the slices at once into hot deep fat (375° F.). Fry the chips until they are golden. Drain them on absorbent paper and sprinkle with salt.

Eggplant Chips

WRAP large stuffed olives each in 1/2 slice of lean bacon and fasten the bacon with a wooden pick. Set the olives under the broiler, turning them occasionally, until the bacon is crisp. Drain on absorbent paper.

Broiled Olives

SEPARATE the seeds of a pumpkin from the yellow fibers to which they cling, but do not wash them. Spread the seeds in a shallow baking pan and sprinkle them with salt. Coat the seeds with melted butter and brown them lightly in a very slow oven (250° F.).

Salted Pumpkin Seeds

SIFT 2 cups flour with 1/2 teaspoon salt onto a pastry board and make a well in the center. Dissolve 1/2 cake compressed yeast or 1/2 package granular yeast in 1/2 cup water at temperature given on page 573 and turn it into the well. Work the flour gradually into the liquid and knead the mixture for several minutes. Add 1 tablespoon olive oil, knead the dough for 15 minutes, until it is smooth, and shape it into a ball.

Pizza Dough

Cover it with a cloth and let it rise for 1 hour in a warm place. Punch it down and roll or stretch it over the back of the hands into a large circle, slightly thicker at the edges than in the middle.

Pizza with Parmesan

Lay the dough in an oiled 12-inch pie pan and spread it thickly with tomato sauce. Sprinkle it generously with orégano, basil, and salt and pepper, and lightly with crushed hot pepper. Sprinkle it with 1/2 cup grated Parmesan cheese and with 2 tablespoons olive oil.

Bake the pizza at once in a very hot oven (450° F.) for about 25 minutes, until the crust is browned and blistered and the cheese browned. Serve it immediately, piping hot and cut in wedges.

Chicken Liver Pizza

SAUTÉ a crushed garlic clove in 3 tablespoons olive oil for a few minutes, but do not let it brown. Discard the garlic and in the oil brown 1 pound chicken livers. Chop the livers coarsely. Add to the pan 1 cup tomato sauce or tomato purée seasoned with basil and orégano, to taste. Spread this savory mixture on thinly rolled pizza dough, and bake the pizza at once in a very hot oven (450° F.) until the dough browns and blisters.

Pissaladière
TOMATO AND
OLIVE TART

LINE a 12-inch pie tin with basic pie dough, rolled out 1/4 inch thick, and chill it.

In a saucepan heat 2 tablespoons olive oil, add 6 large ripe tomatoes, peeled, seeded, and chopped, and cook until the excess moisture is cooked away, mashing the tomatoes occasionally to form a thick paste. Sauté 3 Spanish onions, sliced, in 3 tablespoons butter until the onions are transparent and golden. Sprinkle the pie dough with freshly grated Parmesan cheese and add the onions. Sprinkle the onions with rosemary and cover with the tomato paste. Arrange anchovies in a latticework on top and place a ripe olive in the center of each latticework square. Brush the olives with olive oil and bake the tart in a moderately hot oven (375° F.) for about 25 minutes, or until the crust is golden. Brush with olive oil again before serving.

Song of the Soup Kettle

Most soups begin with stock or bouillon. In usage, the names are interchangeable and the preparations—strong extracts of meat, fish, or fowl—so alike that no harm is done by the confusion of nomenclature. Consommé is a stock or bouillon that has been transmuted to a liquid of crystal clarity.

Brown Stock

SPREAD 3 to 4 pounds beef bones and 2 pounds veal bones, both cut in rather small pieces, in a roasting pan and strew over them 1 large carrot and 1 large onion, both peeled and sliced. Put the pan in a hot oven (400° F.) for 30 to 40 minutes, or until the bones and vegetables are a good brown. Transfer them to a large soup kettle and add 5 quarts water.

Discard the fat from the pan in which the bones were browned, add some water, and bring it to a boil, scraping in the brown bits clinging to the pan. Pour the liquid into the soup kettle. Add a handful of celery stalks and tops, 1 or 2 leeks, 1 onion, 1 carrot, several sprays of parsley, 1 table-spoon salt, and 6 peppercorns. Add any trimmings from beef or veal, raw or cooked, that may be on hand and, if possible, the carcass of a roast chicken. Bring the liquid slowly to a boil, remove the scum as it accumulates on the surface, and simmer the liquid for at least 3 hours. There should be 3 or more quarts of liquid at the end of the cooking.

Remove the bones and vegetables carefully from the kettle and ladle the stock through cheesecloth, working carefully to avoid stirring up the small particles. Pour the stock into jars, cool it as quickly as possible, and remove the fat from the surface. A fine layer of sediment may settle in the jar, and in removing the stock be careful not to disturb this as it will cloud the liquid. The stock will keep for 4 or 5 days in the refrigerator, and may be used for soups or sauces as desired.

White Stock PARBOIL 2 pounds veal bones, cut in rather small pieces, until the scum rises, and drain them. Put the bones in a kettle with 5 quarts cold water, 2 teaspoons salt, a handful of celery stalks and tops, 1 leek, 1 onion, 1 carrot, several sprigs of parsley, and 6 peppercorns. Add any available veal trimmings or chicken bones, bring the liquid to a boil, and remove the scum as it accumulates on the surface. Simmer the stock for at least 3 hours, cool it, and remove the fat from the surface. Strain the stock through several thicknesses of cheesecloth. It will keep for 4 or 5 days in the refrigerator, and may be used for soups or sauces as desired.

Chicken PUT a 4-pound chicken in a large soup kettle with 1 veal knuckle, 4 chicken
Bouillon feet, cleaned and skinned, 3 quarts water, 2 teaspoons salt, and 6 pepper-
or Stock corns. Bring the water slowly to a boil and simmer it for 1 hour, skimming frequently. Add 3 small leeks, 2 carrots, and 2 stalks of celery, all cut into small pieces, and 1 onion stuck with 3 cloves. Add 1 garlic clove, 1/2 bay leaf, and a pinch of thyme and simmer the bouillon for 1 hour longer. Correct the seasoning and strain the bouillon through a fine sieve. Cool it, remove the fat from the surface, and reheat. It will keep for 4 or 5 days in the refrigerator.

Chicken REMOVE the fat from cool chicken bouillon. Add salt to taste. To clarify
Consommé the bouillon break up together the white and shell of 1 egg for each quart of bouillon. Add this to 1 cup of the bouillon, beat it until it is frothy, and add it to the bouillon. Bring the bouillon slowly to a boil, stirring constantly. Boil it for 3 to 4 minutes, still stirring, then lower the heat and barely simmer it for 20 minutes longer. Skim the bouillon and strain it through 2 thicknesses of cheesecloth. The consommé should be absolutely clear. Serve it hot or chilled to a jelly.

Beef Bouillon PUT into a large soup kettle 1 pound veal knuckle, 1 1/2 pounds lean brisket, 1 beef knuckle, 4 chicken feet, cleaned and skinned, 2 leeks, 1 large onion stuck with 2 cloves, 2 stalks of celery with the leaves, 3 sprigs of parsley, and 6 peppercorns. Add 3 quarts cold water and bring it slowly to a boil, removing the scum as it accumulates on the surface. Simmer the bouillon gently for 1 hour, add 2 teaspoons salt, and simmer for 1 hour longer, or until the meat is tender. Correct the seasoning and strain the bouillon through a fine sieve. Cool it, remove the fat from the surface, and reheat. It will keep in the refrigerator for 4 or 5 days.

COMBINE 3 quarts beef bouillon with 1 1/2 pounds very lean, coarsely chopped beef. To clarify the bouillon, break up together the whites and shells of 2 eggs, add them to 1 cup of the stock, and beat the mixture until it is frothy. Add it to the bouillon. Bring the bouillon slowly to a boil, stirring constantly, lower the heat, and simmer the consommé for 1 hour. The solid matter will settle to the bottom of the kettle. Ladle out the consommé and strain it through several thicknesses of cheesecloth.

Beef Consommé

The perfection of consommé is enhanced by judicious additions and refinements.

Reduce 2 quarts clarified consommé over high heat by half. Stir in 2 teaspoons Cognac, taste for seasoning, and serve steaming hot.

Double Consommé

Garnish each consommé cup with 3 or 4 very thin slices of avocado, pour over them boiling chicken consommé, and sprinkle with chopped chives.

Consommé with Avocado

To 1 beaten egg add 3 tablespoons raw spinach and 1 tablespoon chopped blanched almonds. Season the mixture with salt and bake it like a pancake on a lightly buttered griddle, turning it to brown both sides. Cut the pancake into narrow strips and put the strips into 6 consommé cups. Fill with hot chicken consommé.

Consommé Florentine

Bring to a boil 1 quart consommé, add gradually 1/2 cup vermicelli, and simmer it for 10 minutes. Just before serving add 2 truffles cut into small julienne.

Consommé Vermicelli

Reduce 2 cups tomato purée over high heat by half, and add it to 1 quart hot chicken consommé. If necessary, a little beet juice may be added to

Consommé Madrilène

Jellied Madrilène

intensify the color of the consommé if the tomato is not quite red enough.

If the madrilène is to be served jellied, stir in 1 tablespoon gelatin softened in 1/4 cup beet juice. Cool the madrilène and chill it until the gelatin sets.

Madrilène au Fumet de Concombre

Add the peelings from 1 or 2 cucumbers to 1 quart boiling consommé madrilène and keep the soup hot over boiling water for 30 minutes or more. To serve, remove the peel and add a little cucumber cut in dice or small olive shapes and poached for a few minutes in lightly salted water or stock.

Consommé au Madère

To 1 quart chicken consommé add 1 cup Madeira, bring the soup to a boil, and serve it very hot.

Celery Consommé

Bring 1 quart beef consommé to a boil. Put a large bunch of celery in the soup and keep the soup over boiling water for 30 minutes or more. When the celery flavor has penetrated sufficiently, remove the stalks and serve the consommé garnished with julienne of the cooked celery.

Consommé Windsor

Bring 1 quart beef consommé to a boil. Mix in a bowl 2 eggs, 1/4 teaspoon flour, and 1 tablespoon heavy cream. Strain the mixture through a fine sieve into the boiling consommé, stirring constantly. Set the soup where it will keep warm, but do not let it boil.

Consommé Stracciatella

Combine 2 eggs, 3 tablespoons warm chicken broth, 2 tablespoons grated Parmesan, and 1 1/2 tablespoons flour and beat for about 5 minutes.

Bring 1 quart chicken bouillon to a boil and add the egg mixture slowly, stirring constantly. Simmer the soup for 5 minutes, stirring, and serve in bouillon cups with a sprinkling of finely chopped chervil.

Consommé Bavette

Cook 2 cups *bavette*, or medium macaroni, in 5 cups beef consommé. Add the egg-and-cheese mixture as for *consommé stracciatella* and season with fresh marjoram.

Consommé Princesse

Bring 1 quart chicken consommé to a boil. Garnish 6 bouillon cups with 1 teaspoon each of cooked barley and asparagus tips and add 2 or 3 pieces of *royale princesse*. Pour the hot consommé over the garnishings and sprinkle with a little finely chopped chervil.

Clear Tomato Soup

SIMMER together for 1 hour 5 cups beef bouillon, 1/2 cup Sherry, 2 beaten egg whites, 4 large ripe tomatoes, chopped, 3/4 pound ground shin of beef, 1 celeriac, 2 leeks, and 1 carrot, all chopped, salt and pepper to taste, and 1 teaspoon sugar. Strain the soup through a fine cloth. Just before serving, add 1/2 cup Madeira.

SIMMER together for 45 minutes in 3 cups water, 2 stalks of celery, 1 carrot, 1 onion, and 3/4 pound mushrooms, all finely diced. Strain the broth and add 1 quart rich chicken bouillon. Season to taste with salt, coarsely ground pepper, and paprika. To serve, add 1 tablespoon dry Sherry to each cup of hot soup.

Clear Mushroom Soup

A strong consommé should jell naturally: if necessary, softened and dissolved gelatin may be added at will.

BRING 4 cups beef consommé to a boil and stir in 2 tablespoons gelatin, softened in 1/2 cup water, and 1 teaspoon sugar. Add 1 cup dry red wine such as a Bordeaux or a California Cabernet and correct the seasoning with salt and pepper. Add a dash of lemon juice and chill the soup until it sets. Whip the jelly lightly with a fork and serve in cups, garnished with finely chopped sweet onion and parsley.

Jellied Wine Consommé

COMBINE 2 cups each of avocado purée, sour cream, and jellied chicken consommé. Beat the mixture with a fork, season it with lemon juice, salt, and chili powder to taste, and serve it very cold.

Jellied Avocado Soup

Most so-called vegetable soups actually begin with a meat stock.

IN a deep saucepan melt 2 tablespoons butter. Add 2 carrots, 1 white turnip, and 2 leeks, all thinly sliced, 1/4 head Savoy cabbage, shredded, and 1/2 cup water. Cover the pan and braise the vegetables over low heat until they are tender. Add 2 quarts chicken stock, bring the stock to a boil, and skim off all the fat. Add 1/2 cup fresh peas, and 1/2 cup each of green beans and celery, cut in small pieces. Simmer the soup for about 20 minutes, or until the vegetables are tender. Add 1/2 cup each of shredded sorrel and shredded lettuce, bring the soup to a boil again,

Potage Paysanne
COUNTRY STYLE SOUP

and correct the seasoning with salt. A little cooked rice, barley, or vermicelli may also be added.

Okra Chowder WASH and stem 4 cups okra and slice it thinly. In a stainless steel or enamel saucepan sauté 1 onion, finely chopped, in 2 tablespoons butter. Add 3 tomatoes, peeled, seeded, and chopped, 1 sprig of thyme, 1 bay leaf, 1 table-spoon chopped parsley, and 1 hot red pepper pod. Cover the saucepan and cook the mixture gently for 5 minutes. Add 6 cups chicken stock and bring the soup to a boil. Add the okra and simmer the soup gently for about 30 minutes. Taste occasionally and remove the hot pepper when it has sufficiently flavored the soup.

Onion Soup Gratinée MELT 3 tablespoons butter in a large saucepan and in it sauté very slowly 4 large onions, thinly sliced, until they are soft and golden but not brown. Add 1 teaspoon flour and cook the onions a minute or two longer. Add 2 quarts brown stock. Simmer the stock for 10 minutes and season with salt and pepper. Pour the soup into an earthenware casserole or into individual casseroles and top it with slices of crusty bread. Sprinkle the bread with grated Parmesan cheese and put the casserole in a very hot oven (450° F.) until the cheese is melted and browned.

Ciorba De Ceapa

RUMANIAN ONION SOUP

SAUTÉ 5 large onions, minced, in 3 tablespoons butter. Add 5 cups beef bouillon, a pinch of dried lovage or a few dried celery leaves, and 1 large potato, thinly sliced. Simmer the mixture, covered, for 30 minutes. Rub the soup through a sieve or purée it in a blender, and add 1 cup dry white wine, 1 tablespoon vinegar, and 2 teaspoons sugar. Bring the purée to a boil, lower the heat, and simmer the soup for 5 minutes longer. Add 1 cup cream, 1 tablespoon minced parsley, and salt and pepper. Reheat the soup, but do not let it boil. Serve in a heated tureen.

Polish Borsch SIMMER 2 quarts beef bouillon with 1 large onion, chopped, for 2 hours. Strain the stock and remove the fat. Wash, chop, and soak in hot water 4 large dried mushrooms, add them to the hot soup, and boil it for 15 minutes.

Okra Chowder

Toss 1 teaspoon sugar with 3 cups grated beets, 2 cups shredded cabbage, 1 cup diced carrots, and 1 teaspoon chopped parsley. Let the mixture stand until the sugar is dissolved. Add the mixture to the soup and continue to boil for 25 to 30 minutes, until the vegetables are tender. Strain out the vegetables and add 1 cup sour cream and 1 teaspoon lemon juice to the soup. Reheat without boiling and add salt if necessary. Serve a mealy, freshly boiled potato in each soup plate.

Soupe Chiffonnade

SHRED a head of lettuce finely and put it in a saucepan with 1 cup young peas, 4 scallions, finely chopped, 6 tarragon leaves, 2 fresh mint leaves, and 1 tablespoon finely chopped chervil. Add 5 cups chicken consommé and season with salt and freshly ground black pepper. Simmer gently, covered, for 15 minutes.

Potage Princesse Anne

IN a saucepan sauté 2 small onions, finely chopped, in 1/4 cup butter until the onion is transparent. Add 6 tomatoes, chopped, and cook the mixture briskly for 3 to 4 minutes. Add 1 teaspoon tomato paste, 1 bay leaf, 1 garlic clove, crushed, and 6 peppercorns. Cover and cook gently for 10 minutes, stirring occasionally. Press the mixture through a fine sieve and add the purée to 6 cups chicken stock. Bring the soup to a boil, add 1/4 cup cooked rice, and simmer for 15 minutes. Correct the seasoning and just before serving add the shredded pulp of 1 tomato and 2 teaspoons each of chopped parsley and mint.

Egg yolks and/or cream thicken and enrich soups simultaneously.

Durchgetriebene Hirnsuppe

CREAM OF CALF'S BRAIN SOUP

SAUTÉ 1 onion, sliced, in 3 tablespoons butter until it is lightly browned. Stir in 2 to 3 tablespoons flour, add gradually 6 cups chicken stock, and cook, stirring, until the soup is smooth and slightly thickened. Cook gently for 20 minutes.

Clean one calf's brain. Discard the outer skin, wash the brain well under cold running water, and cut it into large pieces. Add the pieces to the soup. Simmer it for 10 minutes longer, and press it through a fine sieve. Stir in 3 egg yolks, lightly beaten with 1/2 cup heavy cream, and reheat the soup, stirring constantly and being careful not to let it boil. Serve with croutons browned in butter, and with grated Parmesan cheese and finely chopped chives.

SCALD 1 cup milk and stir in the freshly grated meat of 2 coconuts. When the mixture is cool, strain it through a napkin, then wring the napkin hard to force through all the liquid. Discard the pulp. To the coconut milk add 3 cups clear chicken bouillon and 2 well-beaten egg yolks and mix thoroughly. Heat the soup, but do not let it boil. Adjust the seasoning. Sprinkle each serving generously with chopped, roasted almonds.

Colombian Coconut Soup

BEAT 3 egg yolks well with 1/2 cup cream and stir this into 6 cups cold brown stock. Heat the soup slowly, stirring, until it reaches the boiling point, but do not let it boil. Serve with a slice of toasted Italian bread on each serving, and pass grated Parmesan cheese separately.

Venetian Soup

SHRED finely 1 cup almonds. Pour over the almonds, in the cup, enough warm milk to fill the cup. Let the almonds soak in the milk for 30 minutes, drain them, and reserve the almond milk. Bake the shredded almonds on a pie plate in a moderate oven (350° F.) until they are golden brown, stirring frequently to prevent their burning. Add the almond milk to 1 quart chicken consommé and bring it almost to a boil. Stir in 2 egg yolks mixed with 1/2 cup heavy cream and a little of the hot soup. Continue to stir the soup for 2 minutes but do not let it boil. Garnish each serving with some of the shredded toasted almonds.

Chicken Soup Margot

SIMMER 1 cup minced ripe olives and 1 garlic clove in 3 cups chicken stock for 20 minutes. Discard the garlic and stir in 1 cup hot heavy cream mixed with 2 egg yolks, well beaten. Season to taste with salt and pepper.

Cream of Olive Soup

IN a saucepan melt 1/4 cup butter and in it sauté 12 scallions, including the tender part of the green stalks, chopped, and 1 garlic clove, chopped, until the scallions are soft but not brown. Stir in 3 tablespoons flour and add gradually 3 cups hot chicken stock, stirring constantly. Cook, stirring, until the soup is thickened, then rub it through a fine sieve. Return the soup to the heat, add 2 cups minced mushrooms, and cook for 5 minutes. Stir in 1 cup heavy cream and 1 tablespoon chopped parsley.

Mushroom Scallion Soup

SAUTÉ 2 cups chopped scallions, including the green parts, and 1 garlic clove in 3 tablespoons butter over low heat until they are tender but not brown. Stir in 2 tablespoons flour and add gradually, stirring constantly, 4 cups

Spring Scallion Soup

hot chicken bouillon. Simmer gently for 30 minutes and strain the soup through a fine sieve. Just before serving, stir in 1 egg yolk lightly beaten with 1/4 cup cream and a little of the hot soup. Garnish each portion with 1 tablespoon whipped cream and sprinkle with finely chopped chives.

Crème Crécy
CREAM OF CARROT
SOUP

MELT 2 tablespoons butter in a saucepan, add 4 or 5 carrots and 1 onion, all chopped, and 1 teaspoon salt. Cook slowly for 15 minutes, stirring occasionally. Add 1/2 cup rice and 1 quart chicken bouillon and cook slowly for about 45 minutes, or until the carrots are done. Strain the soup through a fine sieve and add 2 cups more bouillon. Bring it to a boil and add 1 cup milk and 1 tablespoon butter.

Cucumber and Chervil Soup

MELT 1/4 cup butter in a saucepan, add 2 scallions, chopped, and cook them gently until they are soft but not brown. Add 3 1/2 cucumbers, peeled and sliced, 1 cup water, and a little salt and pepper and simmer the slices for 15 minutes, or until they are soft. Stir in 3 tablespoons flour, mixed to a paste with a little cold water, and 3 cups hot chicken consommé. Stir the mixture over the heat until it comes to a boil. Rub it through a fine sieve and return the soup to the saucepan. Correct the seasoning to taste, add 1/2 cucumber, peeled and minced, 1 cup cream, and 1/2 cup finely chopped chervil. Reheat and serve.

Crème Georgette

COOK 1 celery root, peeled and quartered, in boiling salted water for 12 minutes and drain it. Peel and dice finely 2 potatoes. In a saucepan melt 3 tablespoons butter, stir in 2 tablespoons flour, and add gradually 6 cups beef bouillon, stirring constantly. Add the celery root and potatoes and 2 tomatoes, peeled and quartered, and simmer the soup for 1 hour. Press it through a fine sieve and bring the purée to a boil. Add 1/2 cup milk and correct the seasoning. Stir in off the heat 2 tablespoons butter and 1/2 cup heavy cream.

Belgian Herb Soup

MELT 2 tablespoons butter in a heavy skillet. Add 3/4 cup each of shredded lettuce and watercress, 1/3 cup spring onion tops, chopped, 1/4 cup shredded spinach, 2 tablespoons chopped parsley, and 1/2 teaspoon each of chopped sweet basil and portulaca leaves. Cover closely, and cook the mixture gently for 10 to 15 minutes, stirring from time to time. Add 6 cups chicken bouillon and simmer the mixture slowly for about 30 minutes. Add salt and pepper to taste and 1/3 cup cream, if desired. Sprinkle with chopped chives.

MIX together 1/2 pound ground venison, 1/2 cup rice, 1/4 cup each of chopped onion and parsley, and salt and pepper to taste. Form the mixture into small balls the size of filberts, drop them into 2 quarts simmering chicken broth, and poach them for about 1 hour.

Arkayagan Abour
ROYAL SOUP
ARMENIAN

In a soup tureen beat 3 eggs lightly with the juice of 2 lemons and 1/2 cup of the hot soup. Remove the soup from the stove and pour the broth very gradually into the lemon-egg mixture, beating constantly. Add the poached venison balls and serve immediately.

There is no end to the variety of cream soups that may begin with the versatile cream of chicken base.

MELT 1/4 cup butter in a saucepan, stir in 1/2 cup flour—rice flour is traditionally used—and cook the *roux*, stirring constantly, until it starts to turn golden. Add 2 quarts chicken broth and cook, stirring, until the soup base is smooth. Add 1 onion, 1 stalk of celery, and 2 leeks, all chopped, 2 sprigs of parsley, and a little salt if necessary, and simmer the soup for 30 minutes, removing the scum as it accumulates on the surface. Strain the base through a fine sieve.

Cream of Chicken Soup Base

Use this soup as a base for the variations that follow and for other variations, *ad libitum.*

Mix 2 egg yolks with 1 cup cream and a little hot cream of chicken base, stir the mixture into 1 quart chicken base, and bring the soup almost to a boil. Correct the seasoning with salt and add 1 more cup cream and enough chicken stock to give the desired consistency.

Crème de Volaille
CREAM OF
CHICKEN SOUP

Cook 1 pound washed spinach in a little boiling salted water, drain it, and rub it through a fine sieve. Combine the purée with 1 1/2 quarts cream of chicken base, bring the soup to a boil, and cook it for a few minutes. Stir in 2 egg yolks mixed with 1 cup cream and a little of the hot soup and cook,

Crème Florentine
CREAM OF
SPINACH SOUP

stirring, for about 3 minutes, being careful that the soup does not boil or it will curdle. Correct the seasoning with salt and strain the soup through a fine sieve.

Crème Favorite
CREAM OF
GREEN BEAN SOUP

Add 1 1/2 cups green beans, cut in small pieces, to 1 1/2 quarts cream of chicken base and cook until the beans are soft. Rub the soup through a sieve and finish it with egg yolks and cream as in *crème florentine*.

Crème Forestière
CREAM OF
MUSHROOM SOUP

Melt 1 tablespoon butter in a saucepan, add 1 onion, chopped, and cook the onion until it starts to turn golden. Add 1/2 pound finely chopped mushrooms and cook until most of the moisture is cooked away. Add 1 1/2 quarts cream of chicken base and cook the soup for 1 hour longer. Rub it through a fine sieve and finish with egg yolks and cream as in *crème florentine*.

Crème Béatrice

Add 1/2 cup finely diced cooked chicken to *crème forestière*.

Crème Du Barry
CREAM OF
CAULIFLOWER SOUP

Break a small cauliflower into pieces, parboil it for a few minutes in salted water, and drain. Cook the cauliflower in 1 1/2 quarts cream of chicken base until it is soft and rub the soup through a sieve. Bring the soup back to a boil and add stock or milk to give the desired consistency. Finish with egg yolks and cream as in *crème florentine*.

Crème Boston
CREAM OF
CELERY SOUP

Clean and cut up enough celery stalks or roots to make 1 1/2 cups. Parboil the celery in salted water for a few minutes, drain it, and add it to 1 1/2 quarts cream of chicken base. Cook until the celery is soft and rub the soup through a fine sieve. Finish the soup with egg yolks and cream as in *crème florentine*.

Crème Marie Stuart
CREAM OF
VEGETABLE SOUP

Cut 1 cup mixed carrots, turnips, celery, and leeks into fine dice and cook the vegetables in 1 tablespoon butter with 1/2 cup chicken stock until they are tender. Cook enough whole barley to make 1 cup. Add the vegetables and barley to 1 1/2 quarts cream of chicken base.

Crème de Tomates
CREAM OF
TOMATO SOUP

Add to 2 quarts cream of chicken base 6 large tomatoes, 4 cups Italian tomato purée, 1 garlic clove, 8 white peppercorns, and 1 tablespoon sugar. Cook the soup for 2 hours, skimming it as necessary. Press the soup through a fine sieve or purée it in a blender. To serve, add 1 cup cream and 1 table-spoon sweet butter. Thin the soup to the desired consistency with milk.

When cooked rice is added to *crème de tomates* its name is *crème portugaise*. *Crème Portugaise*

Melt 1 tablespoon butter in a saucepan, add 1/2 cup shredded sorrel, and cook it until most of the moisture is cooked away. Combine with 1 quart cream of tomato soup. *Crème Rose Marie*

Cook 2 tablespoons pearl tapioca in 2 cups chicken stock until it is clear and add the thickened stock to 1 quart cream of tomato soup. *Crème Américaine*

Cold soups are most welcome in warm weather, but their refreshing quality earns them a place on year-round menus.

CHOP finely the leaves of a large bunch of parsley. Add the parsley to 3 cups chicken consommé, bring to a boil, and simmer for 20 minutes. Strain the soup and stir in 2 cups cream mixed with 2 egg yolks. Stir the soup over low heat for about 3 minutes, or until it is slightly thickened, being careful not to let it boil. Correct the seasoning with salt and cayenne, cool the soup, and chill it. Serve in bouillon cups. Garnish each portion with a spoonful of salted whipped cream and a large sprig of parsley. *Iced Cream of Parsley Soup*

IN a saucepan combine 3 teaspoons curry powder and 6 cups chicken stock. Bring it to a boil and simmer it for 8 minutes. Stir 2 egg yolks, beaten, into 1/2 cup hot heavy cream and stir the mixture gradually into the hot soup. Remove the pan immediately from the heat and cool and chill the soup. *Iced Curry Soup*

Beat the cold soup well with a rotary beater and pour it over 3 or 4 thin slices of avocado in each plate. Garnish with julienne strips of tart green apple.

STIR 2 cups mashed avocado into 2 cups hot chicken stock and press the mixture through a fine sieve. Stir in 1 1/2 cups heavy cream, 1/2 cup dry white wine, and 1 teaspoon lemon juice. Season the soup to taste with salt, pepper, and cayenne. Chill it, and serve generously sprinkled with finely chopped dill. *Iced Cream of Avocado Soup*

Borsch PEEL and grate coarsely 8 young beets. Simmer the beets in 4 cups water for 20 minutes, or until they are tender. Stir in the juice of 1 lemon and add sugar, salt, and pepper to taste. Continue to cook the borsch for 5 minutes longer and strain out and discard the beets. Chill the borsch and serve it with a dollop of sour cream in each cup.

Gazpacho RUB a glass bowl with a cut garlic clove and put in it 6 large ripe tomatoes and 2 cucumbers, both peeled, seeded, and finely chopped, and 1/2 cup each of minced red or green sweet pepper and onion. Pour over the vegetables 2 cups fresh tomato juice, 1/3 cup olive oil, and 3 tablespoons lemon juice. Season the *gazpacho* to taste with salt, pepper, and a dash of Tabasco and chill it thoroughly. Serve *gazpacho* in individual chilled glass bowls. Add an ice cube to each and sprinkle the soup generously with chopped parsley.

Iced Cucumber Soup IN a saucepan put 3 cucumbers, peeled and thinly sliced, 1/2 cup chopped green onions, 1/2 teaspoon salt, and a sprinkling of pepper. Add 1 cup water, bring the liquid to a boil, and simmer it until the cucumbers are soft. Stir in 2 tablespoons flour, mixed to a smooth paste with a little cold water, and 2 cups chicken stock. Stir the soup until it comes to a boil, and simmer it for 10 minutes. Add a pinch of cayenne and more salt if needed and strain the soup through a fine sieve, pressing through as much of the vegetable pulp as possible. Add 1 tablespoon chopped chervil and stir the soup over ice until it is cold. Stir in 1/2 cup heavy cream and chill until ready to serve. Garnish each serving with a thin slice of scored cucumber.

Iced Cucumber Beet Soup CHOP finely 1 garlic clove with 1/2 teaspoon salt and mix thoroughly with 2 cups finely chopped cucumber and 1 cup chopped cooked beets. Add 4 cups sour cream and 1 cup milk, 2 teaspoons each of chopped parsley and chives, and salt and pepper to taste. Chill and serve with a few thin slices of unpeeled cucumber and an ice cube in each soup plate.

Crème d'Asperges Glacée
ICED CREAM OF
ASPARAGUS SOUP
CUT the tips off 2 pounds fresh asparagus and set them aside. Snap off the tough white ends and discard them. Wash the stalks, slice them into 2-inch pieces, and put them in a saucepan with 1 bunch of scallions, thinly sliced, and 1/4 cup water. Cover the pan and cook the vegetables very slowly until they are tender. Add 1/4 cup flour and blend well. Pour in 2 cups chicken stock and stir the mixture until it reaches the boiling point. Remove the pan from the heat and rub the soup through a fine sieve. Add salt and

white pepper to taste and set the soup aside to cool. Add 1 cup heavy cream and blend well. Garnish the soup with the reserved asparagus tips, cooked until tender and chilled, and serve it very cold.

Iced Tomato Soup

IN a saucepan put 6 large ripe tomatoes, coarsely chopped, 1 onion, finely chopped, 1/4 cup water, 1/2 teaspoon salt, and a sprinkling of pepper. Bring the liquid to a boil and cook briskly for 5 minutes. Stir in 2 tablespoons tomato paste and 2 tablespoons flour mixed to a paste with a little cold water. Stir in 2 cups hot chicken stock and continue to stir until the soup comes to a boil. Press the soup through a fine sieve, forcing through as much of the vegetable pulp as possible. Stir the soup over ice until it is cold. Stir in 1 cup heavy cream and correct the seasoning with salt. Garnish each portion with thin slices of peeled tomato sprinkled with finely chopped dill.

Crème de Cresson Glacée
ICED CREAM OF
WATERCRESS SOUP

IN a saucepan melt 2 tablespoons butter and in it sauté until golden 3 leeks and 1 onion, sliced. Add 3 to 4 potatoes, sliced, 3 cups chicken stock, and 1 teaspoon salt. Bring the stock to a boil and simmer the vegetables for 35 to 40 minutes, or until they are tender. Rub the soup through a fine sieve or purée it in a blender. Add 1 cup milk, bring the soup to a boil, stirring constantly, and stir in 1 cup heavy cream. Cook 1 bunch of watercress in boiling water for a few minutes. Drain the leaves thoroughly and force them through a fine sieve. Stir the watercress purée into the soup. Chill well and garnish with watercress.

The truly great soups of every national cuisine are those that serve as a meal-in-a-bowl.

Petite Marmite Henri IV

PARBOIL for 10 minutes 1 pound lean beef brisket, 1 oxtail, and the legs and neck of a chicken, all cut into pieces. Drain the meat, rinse it in cold water and turn it into a *marmite*—a deep clay casserole—or a soup kettle. Add 2 to 3 quarts brown stock and 1 tablespoon salt. Bring the stock to a boil, skim it, and cook it gently for 2 hours, removing the scum as it accumulates on the surface.

Parboil 2 carrots, sliced, 1 turnip, cut in small pieces, and 2 leeks and 2 stalks of celery, cut in inch pieces. Brown 2 small onions in butter, sprinkling them with a little sugar to give them color. Add the vegetables to the *marmite* and cook the soup for 2 hours longer, skimming from time to time. Correct the seasoning with salt. Keep the soup hot, but not boiling, and remove all fat from the surface. Serve the soup very hot, with small thin slices of crusty rolls and a bowl of grated Parmesan or Gruyère cheese.

Pot au Feu PARBOIL for 10 minutes in water to cover 1 pound lean beef from the rump or the shoulder, 1 pound plate beef, and 1 medium oxtail, cut in pieces. Drain the meat and transfer it to a deep soup kettle. Add 3 quarts stock and simmer it over low heat for 1 1/2 to 2 hours, skimming as needed. Parboil a small fowl or a few chicken legs for a few minutes and add them to the soup kettle. Clean and cut in olive-shapes enough carrots to make 2/3 cup, turnips to make 1/2 cup, and enough leeks, using the white part only, in 1/2- to 3/4-inch pieces, to make 2/3 cup. Add the vegetables to the kettle. Bring the soup to a boil again and simmer it over low heat for 1 1/2 hours longer, or until the meat is tender, skimming as needed. Correct the seasoning with salt. Remove the meat and chicken, put the soup where it will keep hot without boiling, and remove the fat from the surface.

Serve the broth with small rounds of toast spread with poached marrow and sprinkled with finely chopped parsley. Or serve the *pot au feu* in deep soup plates, giving each person some broth, meat, and vegetables. Traditional accompaniments are coarse salt, sour pickles, horseradish or mustard, and crusty French bread.

Poached Marrow To poach marrow: Remove the marrow from the bones without breaking it. Cut the marrow into 1/2-inch slices, put the slices in cold water, and bring the water to the boiling point but do not let it boil. Add a little cold water to reduce the temperature and keep the marrow in a warm place until ready to serve.

Canja Soup HAVE the butcher cut up a stewing chicken and reserve the fat. Render the chicken fat in a Dutch oven with 2 garlic cloves and with a skimmer remove and discard the cracklings and the garlic. There should be about 3 table-spoons fat.

Season the chicken with salt and freshly ground pepper and brown it lightly in the Dutch oven. Add 1 onion, finely chopped, and 1/4 cup water and cook the mixture gently, tightly covered, until the onion is quite soft. Add 1/2 cup well-washed rice and 1/4 cup finely chopped uncooked smoked ham. Cover tightly and cook gently until the rice has absorbed all the liquid, stirring occasionally.

Add 8 cups briskly boiling water, 1/4 teaspoon marjoram, 2 celery stalks with leaves, 3 sprigs of parsley, and 4 bay leaves. Simmer the chicken very slowly, tightly covered, until it falls from the bones. Discard bones and herbs. Trim the pieces of chicken to spoon size and return them to the soup with 2 tablespoons dry Sherry.

Serve *canja* steaming hot, with thick chunks of French bread rubbed with garlic, buttered, and toasted on the buttered side only.

PUT 1 1/2 pounds each of veal shin bone and beef shin bone in a roasting pan, spread over the bones 1 large onion, peeled and sliced, and brown the bones well in a hot oven (400° F.) for 30 to 40 minutes. Parboil an oxtail, cut into small pieces, for 5 minutes and drain. Put the browned bones in a large soup kettle, add 4 quarts brown stock, and bring the stock to a boil. Skim well. Tie the oxtail in a cheesecloth bag and add it to the pot with 1 pound chopped lean beef, 1 large carrot, 3 leeks, 2 stalks of celery, 2 tomatoes, 1 garlic clove, 1 bay leaf, 2 tablespoons salt, 1/2 teaspoon thyme, and 6 peppercorns. Bring the liquid again to a boil and skim it until the scum ceases to rise. Cover the kettle and simmer the soup for 4 to 5 hours. Remove the oxtail and discard the cheesecloth bag.

Queue à la Parisienne
PARISIAN OXTAIL SOUP

Fit a piece of muslin into a large strainer and put in the muslin 1/2 teaspoon each of rosemary, summer savory, sage, and basil. Strain the soup over the herbs, return it to the heat, and bring to a boil. Correct the seasoning with salt and add the oxtail, small balls of cooked carrots and turnips, and 1/2 cup dry Sherry. This soup may be slightly thickened with cornstarch mixed with Sherry.

HAVE the butcher cut, clean, and bone a calf's head. Soak the head in a kettle in cold water to cover for about 2 hours and drain it well. Boil for 30 minutes 2 quarts water with 2 whole onions, each studded with 3 whole cloves, a handful of green celery tops, 2 carrots, 1 large leek, 12 whole peppercorns, 3 sprigs of parsley, and a little salt.

Mock Turtle Soup

Simmer the drained calf's head and the bones in this court bouillon for

Ukrainian Borsch

2 hours, or until the meat is tender, and remove the head to a plate. Boil the stock rapidly until it is reduced to 1 quart and strain it.

Melt 1/4 cup butter, add 1/2 cup flour and stir the *roux* over low heat until the flour is lightly browned. Add 2 cups brown stock and bring the mixture to a boil, stirring constantly. Add the strained court bouillon, 1 cup strained stewed tomatoes, 1 cup meat from the head, cut in dice, and the juice of 1/2 lemon. Heat well and at the last moment add a little Cognac or Madeira.

SHELL 3 pounds green peas and cook them until they are tender in a little boiling salted water. Drain and press the peas through a fine sieve. Add 1 quart commercial green turtle soup to the pea purée and heat the mixture to the boiling point. Add 1/2 cup Sherry and season to taste with salt and freshly ground pepper.

Ladle the soup into 6 individual earthenware casseroles, making sure that each serving includes a piece or two of turtle meat. Whip 1/2 cup heavy cream and put a generous tablespoon on each serving. Put the casseroles under the broiler for 2 to 3 minutes, or until the cream is lightly browned. Serve immediately.

Boula
GREEN TURTLE
AND PEA SOUP

IN a soup kettle put 1 1/2 pounds lean beaf, 1 pound lean fresh pork, 1/2 pound smoked pork, and 10 cups cold water. Bring the water slowly to a boil, skim carefully, and add 1 bay leaf, 8 peppercorns, 1 garlic clove, a few sprigs of parsley, 1 carrot, 1 stalk of celery, and 2 leeks. Simmer the soup, covered, for 1 1/2 hours.

Cook 8 beets, unpeeled, in salted water for about 40 minutes, or until they are tender, peel, and cut each beet into 8 segments. Peel and grate a raw beet and soak it in 1/4 cup cold water.

Remove the meat from the soup and strain the soup into a saucepan. Add the cooked beets, 1 cup shredded cabbage, 2 onions and 3 potatoes, all peeled and quartered, 6 tomatoes, peeled, quartered, and seeded, 1 1/2 tablespoons tomato purée, 1 tablespoon vinegar, 1 teaspoon sugar, and the meat. Bring the soup to a boil and simmer it for 40 minutes. Add 1/2 cup cooked navy beans and 4 frankfurters, thickly sliced, and continue to simmer for 20 minutes longer.

Thicken the soup with 1 tablespoon flour mixed to a paste with 1 tablespoon butter, add the liquid strained from the grated raw beet, and correct the seasoning with salt. Cut the meat into thick slices and put it in a heated soup tureen. Pour the soup over the meat and serve very hot as a main dish.

Ukrainian Borsch

Magerítsa
GREEK EASTER
SOUP

WASH 1 1/2 pounds heart and lung of lamb, cut into pieces, and put the meat in a saucepan with 1 quart water. Bring the water to a boil and simmer it for 25 minutes, removing the scum as it accumulates until the broth is clear. Remove the meat and chop it finely.

Melt 6 tablespoons butter in a skillet and in it sauté the meat and 2 large scallions and 4 sprays of dill leaves, all finely chopped, for about 15 minutes, stirring occasionally.

Strain the broth and add to it enough water to make 2 quarts liquid. Season with salt and pepper to taste, add the meat mixture, and simmer the soup gently for about 1 hour. Remove it from the heat to cool a little.

Avgolemono
Sauce

Beat together 3 eggs, 6 tablespoons lemon juice, and 1 tablespoon water. In Greek cookery this mixture is called *avgolemono* sauce. Pour the hot soup over the egg mixture, stirring vigorously, and serve immediately.

Crème
de Volaille
à la Reine
CREAM OF CHICKEN
SOUP IN THE
QUEEN'S MANNER

COOK a 3-pound chicken until it is tender in 6 cups water with a few sprigs of parsley, a sprig of thyme, 2 stalks of celery with the leaves, 1 onion, sliced, 1/2 carrot, slivered, 1 slice of lemon peel, 6 peppercorns, and salt to taste. Cut part of the breast meat into very small dice for garnish. Grind the rest of the meat, white and dark, in a mortar or put it through the finest blade of a food chopper.

Strain the broth into a saucepan; there should be at least 1 quart. Add 1/2 cup rice and cook it until it is soft. Add the ground chicken meat, simmer the mixture for 30 minutes, and force it through a fine sieve or purée it in a blender. Heat the soup and stir in the yolks of 2 eggs lightly beaten with 1 cup heavy cream and a little of the hot soup. Cook the soup, stirring without letting it boil, for 3 minutes. Correct the seasoning and serve. Garnish each portion with a little of the diced white chicken meat.

Game soups are less a luxury than one might suppose. The trimmings, leftovers, and carcasses of roasted game are used in soups more often than the whole bird or choice cuts of the animal.

Pheasant Soup
Amandine

INTO a large soup kettle put the cracked bones, scraps of meat, and the skin left over from a brace of roasted pheasant, a *bouquet garni* composed of 12 sprigs of parsley, 4 sprigs of green celery tops, 2 large bay leaves, and 1 sprig of thyme, 2 whole cloves, 8 peppercorns, bruised, 1 sprig of marjoram, 2 small carrots, 2 onions, and 1 small white turnip, all quartered, 2 leeks, halved and carefully washed, and 1 1/2 teaspoons salt.

Cover the ingredients with 2 quarts water mixed with 2 cups dry white wine and bring the liquid very slowly to the boiling point. Lower the heat and simmer the soup gently for 2 hours, with the lid of the kettle tilted slightly. Strain the soup into another kettle to cool.

Skim off all the fat that has accumulated on the surface, heat the stock to the boiling point, and strain it through a fine cloth. Bring it again to the boiling point and boil it until the liquid is reduced to 1 1/2 quarts. To serve, stir in 6 tablespoons toasted ground almonds, ladle the soup into cups, and sprinkle each serving with a little paprika.

The carcasses of guinea hen, squab, or partridge may be used in place of the pheasant.

Game Bird Soup Amandine

IN a heavy kettle put the cut up carcasses and leftover meat of 2 roast rabbits with 2 onions and 2 carrots, both sliced, 2 or 3 stalks of celery, a *bouquet garni* composed of 6 sprigs of parsley, 2 sprigs of thyme, 1 bay leaf, and 8 cups brown stock. Bring the soup to a boil and simmer it for 1 1/4 hours, removing the scum as it accumulates on the surface. Remove the pieces of rabbit and detach any bits of meat from the bones. Put the meat through the finest blade of a food chopper and grind it in a mortar with 1 tablespoon cooked rice. Add the paste and 1/2 cup Port to the soup, season it lightly with cayenne, and strain it through a fine sieve, forcing through as much of the meat and vegetables as possible. Reheat the soup, but do not boil it. Serve with croutons.

Potage Saint-Hubert

RABBIT SOUP

Most heartily satisfying and most economical of all soups are those made with dried beans.

SOAK 1 pound white beans overnight in cold water to cover. Drain the beans and put them in a soup kettle with a ham bone that still has some meat on it and 3 quarts water. Bring the water to a boil and simmer the mixture for about 2 hours. Stir in 1 cup cooked mashed potatoes and add 3 onions, 1 small bunch of celery including the tops, and 2 garlic cloves, all finely chopped, and 1/4 cup chopped parsley. Simmer the soup for 1 hour longer, until the beans are thoroughly cooked. Remove the ham bone from the kettle, dice the meat on it, and return the meat to the soup.

U.S. Senate Soup

Garbanzo Soup

SOAK 1/2 pound *garbanzos* or dried chick-peas overnight in water to cover with 1 tablespoon salt. In the morning drain the beans and put them in a kettle with 1 beef bone and 1 ham bone. Add 2 quarts water, bring the water to a boil, and simmer the beans for 45 minutes.

Sauté 4 strips of bacon and 1 onion, finely chopped, until the bacon is crisp and the onion is golden, and add them to the soup pot with 1 pound small potatoes, peeled, a pinch of saffron, and salt to taste and cook the soup for about 30 minutes longer, or until the potatoes are done. Remove the beef and ham bones. Garnish with slices of *chorizo*, or any other garlicky sausage, sautéed in butter, and serve hot.

Garbure Basque

SOAK 1 1/2 cups small dried Lima beans overnight in water to cover. Drain the beans and put them in a soup kettle with a ham bone, 4 medium potatoes and 4 carrots, all sliced, 4 small turnips, diced, 1/4 head of cabbage, shredded, and enough lightly salted water just to cover. Bring the water to a boil and simmer the beans for 3 hours. To serve, ladle the soup into individual flameproof casseroles, sprinkle them with grated cheese, and put them under the broiler until the cheese is melted. Serve with croutons.

Pasta e Fagioli

SOAK 1 cup white navy beans overnight in water to cover. Drain the beans.

In a kettle cook 1 1/2 cups chopped onions and 1 tablespoon finely chopped garlic in 3 tablespoons olive oil over moderate heat, stirring often, for 5 minutes, or until the vegetables are softened. Add 1 1/4 pounds oxtails, 4 cups water, 1 cup beef stock, 1 tablespoon chopped parsley, 1 3/4 teaspoon salt, 1 1/2 teaspoon rosemary, and the beans. Bring the liquid to a boil, cover the mixture, and simmer it for 1 hour, or until the beans are almost tender.

Remove the oxtails and add to the soup 1 cup peeled and chopped Italian tomatoes and 1/3 cup tomato paste. Simmer the mixture for 10 minutes.

Cook 1 cup pasta shells in boiling salted water for 15 minutes, drain them, and add them to the soup. Add salt and pepper to taste and serve hot.

Excellent soups may be made without the assistance of meat, fish, or fowl.

Beer Soup

BRING to a boil 1 quart beer with 1/2 cup sugar, stirring just long enough to dissolve the sugar. Beat together 4 egg yolks, 3 tablespoons sour cream, and a little of the hot beer, and return the mixture gradually to the beer.

Pasta e Fagioli

Add salt, pepper, and a pinch of cinnamon, stir the soup for a few seconds over the heat, and pour it at once into soup plates, each containing a slice of toasted French bread.

Cheddar Soup   MELT 2 tablespoons butter in the top of a double boiler and stir in 2 tablespoons flour. Gradually stir in 3 cups hot milk, add a garlic clove, and cook the mixture over boiling water for 20 minutes. Discard the garlic, stir in 1 cup each of dry white wine and grated Cheddar cheese, salt, pepper, and a pinch of nutmeg. Cook gently, stirring constantly, until the cheese is melted. Beat 2 egg yolks lightly with 2 tablespoons heavy cream, stir the yolks gradually into the soup, and cook, stirring, for 3 minutes longer. Sprinkle the soup with a little grated Cheddar.

Spring Soup   MELT 3 tablespoons butter in a large saucepan. Add 3 leeks, cleaned and chopped, and 1 onion, chopped, and sauté the vegetables until they begin to take on color. Add 2 potatoes, 1 sliced carrot, 1/2 tablespoon salt, and 2 quarts water. Bring the liquid to a boil and boil it for about 15 minutes. Add 1/4 cup rice and the tender upper parts of 12 stalks of asparagus, cut in pieces, and cook the soup for 25 minutes longer. Add 1 pound fresh, washed spinach, coarsely chopped, and cook the soup for 10 to 15 minutes longer. Add salt and pepper to taste, and finish the soup with 1/2 cup cream.

Cream of Corn Soup   SCRAPE from the cob and put through a food chopper 2 1/2 cups cooked fresh corn kernels. Sauté 1/2 onion, chopped, in 3 tablespoons butter until the onion is tender and transparent. Add 3 tablespoons flour and cook, stirring constantly, for 5 minutes. Add the corn, 2 1/2 cups milk, 1/2 cup cream, 1 1/2 teaspoons salt, and a dash each of freshly ground pepper and nutmeg. Heat the soup to the boiling point and serve it sprinkled with chopped chives.

Potage Saint-Germain   COVER 2 cups split peas with water, soak them for about 1 hour, and drain them. Put the peas in a large saucepan with 4 cups fresh water and 1 teaspoon salt. Bring the water to a boil, skim, and cook the peas slowly, covered. In another saucepan cook 1/2 cup finely chopped salt pork in 1 tablespoon butter for a few minutes. Add 1 medium onion, chopped, and cook the onion until it is soft and just starting to turn golden. Add 1 medium carrot and the green part of 2 leeks, both chopped, 1 cup chopped spinach or green lettuce, a small piece of bay leaf, and a pinch of thyme. Cook these for a few minutes longer, add the peas, and continue cooking for about 1 hour, or until the peas are very soft. Rub the soup through a fine sieve and add 1 cup water. Bring the soup back to a boil, correct the seasoning with salt, and add 1 teaspoon sugar and 1 or 2 tablespoons butter.

For a richer soup, add 1/2 cup heavy cream. If fresh peas are available cook 1 cup (or use both pods and peas of very tiny new ones) in water until they are very soft, rub them through a sieve, and add the purée to the pea soup.

COMBINE 3 cups *potage Saint-Germain* and 3 cups cream of tomato soup. Add 2 cups vegetables cut in julienne and cooked in 2 tablespoons butter with 1/2 cup stock until they are tender.

Potage Mongole

CLEAN 4 leeks well, remove the coarse green tops, and chop the white parts finely. (If leeks are not available, substitute 2 onions for the 4 leeks.) Melt 2 tablespoons butter in a large saucepan, add the finely chopped leeks and 1 onion, finely chopped, and sauté the vegetables slowly, stirring occasionally with a wooden spoon, until they are soft but not browned. Peel and dice 4 large potatoes and add them to the leeks and onion with 4 cups water and 1 teaspoon salt. Bring the water to a boil and cook the soup slowly for 30 to 35 minutes, or until the potatoes are very soft. Rub the soup through a fine sieve and return it to the saucepan. Bring the soup back to a boil and add 3 cups hot milk and 1 tablespoon butter. Correct the seasoning with salt. Serve with croutons. For a richer soup, mix 2 egg yolks with 1 cup heavy cream and a little of the hot soup and stir the mixture into the hot soup. Bring it almost to a boil, stirring constantly, but do not let it boil.

Potage Parmentier

Clean and trim 2 bunches of watercress and cook it for a few minutes in boiling salted water. Drain the watercress well and rub it through a fine sieve. Combine it with 1 1/2 quarts *potage Parmentier* and bring to a boil. Stir in 1 cup heavy cream.

Crème Cressonière
CREAM OF
WATERCRESS

Add to *potage Parmentier* 1 cup chervil, finely chopped.

Cream of Chervil

The seafood soups that, by virtue of their greater solid content, are more chowder or stew than soup will be found elsewhere. Here we list some of the popular creams and bisques in which puréed or finely chopped shellfish play an essential role.

**Fish Velouté
Base for
Shellfish
Bisques**

PUT the bones and trimmings of 6 whitings, or other white-fleshed fish, in a pan with 2 quarts water, 1 cup white wine, 1 carrot and 1 onion, sliced, half a bay leaf, a little thyme, 2 sprigs of parsley, and 8 pepper-corns. Bring the liquid to a boil and simmer it for 30 minutes, skimming as necessary. In another pan melt 1/4 cup butter and stir in 3/4 cup flour—rice flour is traditionally used. Cook the *roux*, stirring, until it begins to turn golden. Strain the fish stock into the *roux*, stirring constantly and cook, stirring, until the *velouté* is thick and smooth. Cook it for 20 minutes longer, stirring occasionally and skimming as necessary. Strain the *velouté* through a fine sieve.

Oyster Bisque

POACH 2 dozen freshly opened oysters in their own liquor for 20 minutes. Drain the oysters, reserving the liquor, and chop them finely or purée them in a blender. Strain the liquor and add it to the oyster purée along with 2 quarts fish *velouté* base. Reheat the bisque to the boiling point without letting it boil and strain it through a fine sieve. Correct the seasoning with salt.

Clam Bisque

SCRUB and shuck 3 dozen hard-shelled clams and reserve the liquor. Chop the clams. Brown 2 tablespoons butter lightly in a saucepan and in it sauté the chopped clams for 2 minutes. Add the clam liquor, 1/2 cup white wine, and 2 quarts fish *velouté* base. Cook the bisque, stirring occasionally, for 20 minutes, and strain it through a fine sieve. Reheat the bisque to the boiling point without letting it boil, and swirl in 1/4 cup butter. Season to taste with salt and a little cayenne pepper.

**Bisque
de Crevettes**
SHRIMP BISQUE

MAKE a *mirepoix* by cooking 1/2 carrot and 1/2 onion, both finely chopped, in 2 tablespoons butter with 2 sprigs of parsley, a little thyme, and 1/2 bay leaf. Add 1 cup white wine, and poach 24 shrimps in it for 8 minutes. Shell and devein half the shrimps, dice the meat, and reserve it to use as a garnish. Crush the shells and the remaining shrimps in a mortar, or put them through a food chopper. Combine this purée with 2 quarts fish *velouté* base, the *mirepoix*, and the liquid in which the shrimps were poached, bring the mixture to a boil, and simmer it for 20 minutes. Strain the soup through a fine sieve, and if it seems too thick, add a little milk. Strain it again, through several thicknesses of cheesecloth. To serve, bring the bisque to the boiling point and finish it with 2 tablespoons butter, 3 tablespoons cream, and 2 tablespoons brandy, Sherry, or Madeira. Garnish with the reserved shrimps.

SPLIT a lobster down the back and cut it crosswise into several pieces, using a heavy knife. Discard the intestinal vein. Put the lobster in a saucepan with 1/4 cup brandy and 2 quarts fish *velouté* base. Bring the soup to a boil and simmer it for 20 minutes. Remove the lobster and take the meat from the shells. Crush the shells in a mortar, or put them through a food chopper, and return them to the pan with the soup. If the soup seems too thick, add a little milk. Cook the soup for 25 minutes and strain it through a fine sieve. Add 1 cup cream and salt to taste and strain the soup again through several thicknesses of cheesecloth. To serve, bring the soup to the boiling point and add 2 tablespoons Sherry. Serve a few small cubes of lobster meat with each portion; the rest of the lobster meat may be used for another purpose.

Bisque de Homard
LOBSTER BISQUE

MELT 1/4 cup lard in a saucepan, add 2 slices of fresh ginger and 1 scallion, trimmed and finely chopped, and sauté these for about 1 minute. Add 1/2 cup shredded crab meat, 1 tablespoon Sherry, and 1/4 teaspoon salt and cook the mixture for 1 minute. Add 4 cups chicken stock and bring it to a boil. Discard the ginger.

Combine 2 beaten egg whites with 1/4 cup light cream, 2 tablespoons chicken stock, and 1 1/2 teaspoons cornstarch and gradually add this to the crab-meat mixture. Cook for 2 minutes. Serves 4.

Cream of Crab Soup
HSIEH FUNG KENG

Fine garnishes make fine soups . . .

SIFT 1 1/2 cups flour and a little salt onto a board and make a well in the center. Break 2 eggs into the well and gradually work the eggs into the flour. Knead the dough until it is smooth and elastic, adding a little more flour if necessary to make a firm dough. Roll it out as thinly as possible on a lightly floured board and let it dry until it is no longer sticky, but

Noodle Dough

Noodles for Soup   still flexible. Fold the dough up several times and cut it into very narrow strips. Toss the strips lightly on the board and let them dry thoroughly before cooking them. Cook the noodles for 5 minutes in boiling water or soup, or store them in a covered jar for later use.

Derelye   ROLL out dough for noodles thinly on a lightly floured board and cut it into 1 1/2-inch squares. Combine 1 cup ground cooked beef with 1 egg, 1 teaspoon salt, a pinch of pepper, and 1/2 tablespoon onion juice. Put a generous teaspoon of the filling on each square, fold the squares into triangles, and press the edges together firmly. Drop the *derelye* into boiling broth and cook them for about 15 minutes. Serve in hot soup.

Kreplach   ROLL out noodle dough thinly on a lightly floured board and cut it into 1 1/2-inch squares. Combine 1 1/2 cups ground cooked chicken, 1 egg, 1 tablespoon minced parsley, and 1 teaspoon onion juice. Put half a teaspoon of the filling in the center of each square, fold the squares in half, and pinch the edges together securely. Cook the *kreplach* in boiling salted water for about 15 minutes, or until they are cooked through. Serve in clear soup.

     Kreplach may be filled with a mixture of 1/2 cup sautéed chicken livers, 2 chopped hard-cooked eggs, 1 tablespoon minced parsley, a pinch each of marjoram and thyme, and salt and pepper to taste.

Cappelletti   COMBINE 3 slices of *prosciutto* or other ham, finely chopped, 1/2 cup ground cooked chicken, 1/4 cup chopped roast pork, 1 egg, beaten, 2 teaspoons grated Parmesan cheese. 1/4 teaspoon salt, and a dash each of pepper and nutmeg.

     Roll out noodle dough thinly on a lightly floured board and cut it into 2 1/2-inch circles. Put a teaspoon of the filling in the center of each circle, fold the dough over, seal it, and bring the ends together, shaping each turnover into a little cap. Add the *cappelletti* to 6 cups boiling chicken broth and simmer them for about 15 minutes.

Tortellini   ROLL out noodle dough thinly on a lightly floured board and cut it into 2 1/2-inch circles. Sauté 1 chicken breast in 2 tablespoons butter until it is cooked through and put it through a food chopper. Blend in 2/3 cup ricotta cheese, 2 tablespoons grated Parmesan cheese, 2 egg yolks, 1 egg white, 1/8 teaspoon each of nutmeg and grated lemon rind, and salt and pepper. Put 1 teaspoon filling in the center of each circle of dough. Fold the circle in half and press the edges firmly together. Cook the *tortellini* in 2 quarts chicken broth for about 15 minutes.

BEAT 3 eggs with 2 tablespoons olive oil and 1 teaspoon salt and stir the mixture into 2 cups flour to make a firm dough. Form the dough into pencil-thin rolls between the palms of the hands, flatten them slightly on a lightly floured board, and cut them into 1/2-inch pieces. Bake them on a baking sheet in a moderately hot oven (375° F.) for 10 minutes, or until they are lightly browned, stirring occasionally so that they will brown evenly on all sides. Sprinkle a few *mandlen* into each serving of hot broth.

Mandlen
SOUP NUTS

BEAT 2 eggs with 2 tablespoons cold water. Stir in 1/4 teaspoon salt, 1 tablespoon chopped parsley, and about 1/2 cup matzo meal, or enough to make a soft dough. Chill the dough for several hours, then shape it into small balls. Drop the balls into boiling water, cover the pan, and cook the balls for 20 minutes. Drain the balls and serve in hot soup.

Knaidlach
MATZO BALLS

MELT 1/3 cup butter in a saucepan over low heat. Stir in 1 cup flour and 1/2 teaspoon salt and add gradually 1 3/4 cups cold water, stirring until the dough is thick and smooth. Remove the pan from the heat and add 3 eggs, one at a time, beating after each addition. Drop the batter from a teaspoon into 6 cups boiling broth, cover, and simmer for 10 minutes. Divide the *Nockerln* among 6 soup plates, pour the hot broth over them, and garnish each serving with parsley. Serve with grated Parmesan.

Schwamm-Nockerln
SPONGE NOCKERLN

IN a saucepan sauté 1 tablespoon chopped onion in 2 tablespoons butter until it is golden. Stir in 2 cups whole wheat bread crumbs soaked in water and squeezed dry and 1 teaspoon salt. Remove the saucepan from the heat and cool the mixture. Stir in 2 eggs, 1/2 cup cracker crumbs, 1 teaspoon chopped parsley, and a pinch each of paprika, nutmeg, and ginger and mix well. Shape the mixture into balls and cook them in simmering broth for 15 minutes.

Bread Dumplings

DROP *pâte à chou* in tiny mounds the size of peas on a buttered baking sheet and bake until browned. Or bake slightly larger *choux*, slit them and fill with very finely minced chicken bound with cream sauce.

Petites Profiteroles

131

Croutons   CUT crusty French rolls lengthwise and remove the soft crumb. Cut the crusts into 1-inch pieces and dry them in a very slow oven (250° F.). They may first be spread with melted butter.

Slice crusty French rolls from 1/8 to 1/4 inch thick, brush the slices with butter, and toast them in the oven.

Slice crusty French rolls 1/4 inch thick. Sprinkle the slices with grated Parmesan cheese and melted butter and brown them in the oven.

Cut bread 1/4 inch thick, discard the crusts, and cut the bread into 1/4-inch cubes. Sauté the cubes in butter until golden or sprinkle them with melted butter and brown in the oven. Croutons may be cut in any desired shape.

Cheese Toast   SLICE small French rolls 1/2 inch thick and spread the slices with 1 egg yolk mixed to a paste with 1 teaspoon sweet butter, 1 tablespoon grated Parmesan cheese, and a dash of cayenne. Toast the slices under the broiler or in a hot oven (400° F.) until they are golden. Serve in consommé or pass separately.

Soup Macaroons   COMBINE 1 egg yolk, well beaten, 1/4 cup grated blanched almonds, and 2 tablespoons cracker crumbs. Fold in 2 egg whites, stiffly beaten. Drop small portions of the batter into hot deep fat (370° F.) and fry the macaroons until they are lightly browned. With a skimmer, remove the macaroons to absorbent paper. Add a spoonful of the macaroons to each serving of hot chicken broth.

Spätzli   SIFT 3 cups flour into a bowl, make a depression in the center, and break into it 3 eggs. Add 3/4 teaspoon salt, 1/4 teaspoon each of black pepper and nutmeg, and 1 cup water, or enough to make a medium batter. Beat the batter only until it is smooth. Pour it into a colander with large holes and let the *Spätzli* fall directly into a pot of boiling soup. Stir gently so that the *Spätzli* do not stick together. When the *Spätzli* rise to the surface they are cooked.

Rivels   SIFT together into a mixing bowl 1 cup sifted flour, 1/2 teaspoon baking
FARMER'S RICE   powder, and 1/4 teaspoon salt. Add 1 unbeaten egg and mix thoroughly, until tiny particles are formed. It may be necessary to add a little more

flour if the egg was a large one. Drop the particles of dough into boiling soup and cook for 15 minutes.

Royale
Princesse

BEAT 2 eggs until they are light and add gradually 1 cup chicken consommé, 1 tablespoon each of cooked asparagus purée and fresh pea purée, and salt and pepper to taste. Mix the custard well and bake it in a moderate oven (350° F.) for about 20 minutes, or until it is set. Cool the custard and cut it into fancy shapes. *Royale* may be seasoned simply with salt and pepper, or with a little curry, and the vegetables omitted.

Diablotins
Garbure

CUT carrot, turnip, celery, leek, and a little cabbage into small pieces and braise the vegetables in butter with a little consommé until they are soft. Rub the vegetables through a fine sieve to make a purée and add an equal quantity of purée of peas. Slice crusty French rolls 1/2 inch thick and spread the slices with the purée, mounding it up in the center. Sprinkle with grated Parmesan cheese and a little butter and brown under the broiler. Pass with consommé.

Garniture
Julienne

CUT vegetables into fine strips. For each cup of vegetables melt about 1 tablespoon butter in a saucepan. Add the vegetables and 2 or 3 tablespoons consommé. Place on the vegetables a round piece of buttered or wax paper with a tiny hole in the center, cover the pan, and braise the vegetables slowly until they are tender.

Garniture
Célestine

COMBINE 2 tablespoons flour, 1 egg, 1/2 cup milk or chicken stock, and 1/2 teaspoon chopped parsley or chervil. Pour the batter by spoonfuls onto a buttered skillet to make small thin pancakes. Brown the cakes lightly on both sides, cut them into fine julienne or squares, and add to hot consommé when serving.

$\mathscr{F}$ish and Shellfish

The gourmet believes that the shortest road to variety in cuisine is substitution; and this faith is nowhere more justified than in fish cookery. Fish differ principally in fat content: the fat, full-flavored fish such as salmon, mackerel, shad, and trout exchange recipes profitably, as do the lean varieties such as haddock, pike, and perch.

Shellfish and crustaceans are here, too, with emphasis on how to cook so as to retain a just-caught flavor. Recipes for mussels, oysters, and clams are fairly interchangeable.

It should be a pleasure, not a penance, to abstain from flesh!

In haute cuisine *seafood cookery begins with court bouillon.*

White Wine Court Bouillon for Fish
BRING to a boil 1 quart each of water and dry white wine, 1 tablespoon salt, 2 small carrots and 2 medium onions, thinly sliced, 12 bruised peppercorns, 2 cloves, and a *bouquet garni* composed of 2 large bay leaves, 4 green celery tops, 6 sprigs of parsley, and 1 sprig of thyme. Simmer the liquid for 30 minutes.

Court Bouillon for Shellfish
PUT 2 quarts water in a large kettle and add 1 onion, 1 carrot, and 3 stalks of celery, all chopped, 1 bay leaf, 2 sprigs of parsley, 6 peppercorns, 1 tablespoon salt, and 2 cloves. Bring the water to a boil, add 2 tablespoons white vinegar, and simmer the court bouillon, covered, for 30 minutes.

Court Bouillon

All the basic cookery methods apply to fish, and within the bounds of taste and judgment, any of these basic methods may apply to any fish.

Poached Fish   MELT 1 tablespoon butter in a large shallow pan and sprinkle it with 1 tablespoon finely chopped shallot or onion. Arrange seasoned fish filets on this and add about 1 cup mixed wine, water, and fish stock in any desired proportion barely to cover the fish. Add some mushrooms and cover the fish with a circle of buttered paper with a small hole in it to allow the steam to escape. Cover the pan and simmer the fish, or poach it in a moderate oven (350° F.), for about 10 minutes, or until the flesh is translucent and flakes readily at the touch of a fork. Be careful not to overcook the fish. Remove the cooked filets to a heated serving dish and reduce the sauce by two-thirds. Add 1 cup cream sauce and adjust the seasoning. Finish the sauce with 1/4 cup hot heavy cream or with 3 tablespoons butter. Pour the sauce over the fish and serve it immediately.

Filets of firm-fleshed fish such as sea bass, striped bass, pompano, red snapper, and Spanish mackerel are especially adapted to poaching, as are filets of sole and flounder.

Boiled Whole Fish   WRAP a 5- to 6-pound fish in cheesecloth. Lay the fish on a rack in a fish kettle and add strained court bouillon to cover. Bring the court bouillon to a boil and simmer the fish for 40 to 50 minutes, or about 10 to 12 minutes per pound. The fish is done when the flesh can be lifted cleanly from the bones with a fork. The fish may be allowed to cool in the cooking liquid. In this case, the cooking time should be reduced by a few minutes. To serve, carefully remove the cheesecloth and lay the fish on a napkin on a heated platter. The napkin will absorb any excess liquid. Carefully lift off the top skin and cut away any dark flesh. Serve hot, with hollandaise sauce or any fish sauce, or chill and serve with mayonnaise. This recipe may be used for halibut, salmon, striped bass, and cod.

Broiled Fish   BROILING is a particulary successful method with oily fish like mackerel, bluefish, and shad. The fish may be left whole; or it may be split open, with the bones removed or not, and laid flat on the broiler; or the fish may be cut into slices or into steaks or filets. The broiling oven and pan should be preheated before the fish is put in, so that the hot oven and the hot pan will cook the under side of the fish while the broiler browns the top side and it will not be necessary to turn the fish and risk breaking it.

Season the fish with salt and pepper and brush it generously with oil or butter. Broil it on a preheated pan 3 or 4 inches from the heat. Broiling time depends upon the thickness of the fish. Baste the fish with butter as it cooks, and serve it with maître d'hôtel butter. Be careful not to overcook the fish and thus dry it out.

IN a large baking dish put 1 sliced onion, 1 sliced carrot, some mushroom *Braised Fish* stems and peelings, a sprig of parsley, a bay leaf, a pinch of thyme, 1 cup fish stock or water, and 1/2 cup wine. Lay the cleaned and scaled fish on the vegetables and season it with salt and pepper. Cover the pan and cook the fish in a moderately hot oven (375° F.) for 30 minutes to 1 hour, depending upon the size of the fish. Transfer the fish to a heated serving dish and remove and discard the skin. Cook the liquid until it is reduced by two-thirds. Thicken the sauce with 1 cup thick cream sauce or with *beurre manié* made by kneading 2 tablespoons butter with 1 tablespoon flour. Strain the sauce over the fish on the platter.

The less fatty fish, such as cod, carp, snapper, and halibut, are well suited to braising.

DIP in milk and in flour seasoned with salt small whole fish, fish filets, *Fish Sauté* or slices of large fish. In a large skillet, heat 1/4 inch oil and brown the fish *Meunière* on both sides, shaking the pan constantly. Remove the fish to a heated serving dish and sprinkle it with pepper, lemon juice, and chopped parsley. Garnish each piece of fish with a slice of lemon. Pour off the oil in which the fish was browned and in the same pan melt 1 tablespoon butter for each serving. Cook the butter until it is a rich hazelnut brown and pour it over the fish.

Any fish may be sautéed but this simple method of cookery is a favorite for the fisherman's catch, since it best makes the most of the delicate, unfortunately elusive, flavor of freshly caught fish.

BEAT 2 eggs with 1/4 cup milk, 2 tablespoons salad oil, and 1 teaspoon salt. *Fried Fish* Wipe dry small whole fish, fish filets, or slices of large fish, dip them in *à l'Anglaise* flour, in the egg mixture, and in fine dry bread crumbs. The excess egg mixture should be allowed to drain off before the final dipping. Fry the fish in hot deep fat 360° F. to 380° F., depending upon the size of the fish. Small fish should be fried at the higher temperature. Drain on absorbent paper and serve with tartar sauce or any desired sauce.

Baked Fish

INTO a warm bowl sift 1 cup flour and a pinch of salt. Make a well in the center and add 1 tablespoon salad oil, 3/4 cup warm water, and 1 egg yolk. Mix the ingredients together thoroughly but quickly. The batter will be thick. Cover the bowl and let the batter stand in a warm place for 3 to 4 hours. Fold in 1 egg white, stiffly beaten. Dip the fish into the batter, drain off the surplus, and fry the fish in hot deep fat at 360° F. to 380° F., depending upon the size of the fish. Small pieces of fish should be fried at the higher temperature. Drain on absorbent paper and serve with any desired sauce.

Batter Fried Fish

DIP well-cleaned and carefully scaled fish in flour seasoned with a little salt. Put a 1/4-inch layer of salad oil or freshly rendered pork fat in a shallow baking dish and put the dish in a very hot oven (450° F.). When the fat is hot, lay the fish in it and bake it for 10 to 20 minutes; the size and thickness of the fish determines the cooking time, and the fish is done when it flakes easily with a fork, loses its translucence, and can be cleanly lifted away from the bones. Baste the fish frequently with the oil in the pan. If the fish is large, it is wise to bake it in a dish that can be brought to the table. Pour off the cooking fat and serve the fish with maître d'hôtel butter.

Fat fish such as shad, bluefish, and mackerel are suitable for baking.

Baked Fish

PREPARE duxelles sauce as follows: Cook 1/2 pound finely chopped mushrooms in 2 tablespoons butter with 1 teaspoon chopped shallot or onion, 1/2 teaspoon salt, and 1 teaspoon chopped parsley until the moisture is cooked away. Add 1 cup thick cream sauce and blend well.

Brush 6 medium fish filets generously with butter, season them with salt, and broil them on a preheated baking sheet for 5 or 6 minutes, until they are golden brown. For the papillotes, or paper cases, trim 12 pieces of white parchment or aluminum foil, about 8 1/2 by 11 inches, into modified heart shapes. Put a spoonful of duxelles on each of 6 paper hearts, put a broiled filet on the sauce, and cover the fish with more duxelles. Cover with the remaining paper hearts and seal by folding over 1 inch of the edges all the way around and crimping them together. Bake the papillotes in a hot oven (400° F.) for 5 to 6 minutes. To serve, put each papillote on a serving plate and cut around the sides and bottom of the case. Roll the flap back. The fish should be eaten directly from the paper.

Fish Filets en Papillote

POUND or put through the finest blade of a food chopper 1 pound raw fish flesh with 1/2 teaspoon salt and a little pepper and nutmeg. Gradually add the whites of 2 eggs, pounding the fish vigorously in a mortar. Rub the

Mousseline Forcemeat of Fish

mixture through a fine sieve and put it in a bowl over cracked ice. With a wooden spoon gradually work in about 2 cups heavy cream.

Any fish or shellfish can be made into a *mousseline* forcemeat.

Quenelles de Poisson

SHAPE *mousseline* forcemeat into small ovals by heaping a teaspoon or a tablespoon with the mixture and, with another spoon the same size, round off the top. Dip the second spoon into warm water and gently slide the quenelle off the first spoon into a shallow, well-buttered pan. Carefully add salted water or fish stock barely to cover the quenelles, bring the liquid gently to a boil and poach the quenelles over very low heat for 8 to 10 minutes, or until they are firm. Remove them with a perforated spoon and drain them on a towel. Serve them on a heated platter with any fish sauce. The platter may be garnished with cooked shrimps, oysters, or mussels.

In many of the recipes that follow, other similar fish may be substituted for the variety indicated.

Bar Rayé de Mer au Gratin

FILETS OF STRIPED BASS AU GRATIN

REMOVE and set aside the stems from 8 medium mushrooms. Clean the caps and cook them for about 5 minutes in water to cover with 4 or 5 drops of lemon juice. Leave the mushroom caps in the cooking liquor.

In a small saucepan melt 1 tablespoon butter and in it sauté 1 tablespoon chopped shallot or onion until it is transparent, but not brown. Clean 6 medium or 12 small mushrooms, combine them with the reserved stems of the cooked mushrooms, and chop all together finely. Add the chopped mushrooms to the butter and shallots and cook the mixture slowly until almost all the moisture from the mushrooms is cooked away. Add 1 teaspoon chopped parsley and 1/2 cup brown sauce and cook the sauce for a few minutes until it is thoroughly combined.

Spread the bottom of an ovenproof serving dish with about half the sauce and on it arrange the boned and skinned filets of 3 small striped bass. Sprinkle the filets with a little salt and pepper. Drain the mushroom caps, arrange them on the filets, and cover with the remaining sauce. Sprinkle with fine bread crumbs, 1 tablespoon melted butter, and about 1/3 cup white wine and put the dish in a hot oven (425° F.) for 12 to 15 minutes, or until the top is brown and the fish is cooked. Sprinkle with a few drops of lemon juice and 1 teaspoon chopped parsley and serve in the baking dish.

SPREAD 1 1/2 tablespoons butter in a shallow pan and sprinkle over it 3 shallots, finely chopped, and 1 teaspoon finely chopped parsley. Season 6 filets of sea bass with salt and a little white pepper and arrange them in the pan. Add 1 cup fish stock and about 1/3 cup white wine. Bring the liquid to a boil, cover the pan, and simmer the bass slowly for 10 to 12 minutes. Add 12 freshly shucked oysters and cook them for 2 or 3 minutes. Remove the filets and oysters to a heated serving dish and put with them 12 cooked shrimps and 12 cooked mushrooms. Arrange small cooked potato balls around the fish.

Filets of Sea Bass Pershing

Cook the liquid remaining in the pan until it is reduced by about half. Thicken it with 3 tablespoons cream sauce and add 1 1/2 tablespoons butter. When the butter is just melted, fold in 3 tablespoons cream, whipped. Correct the seasoning and pour the sauce over the fish and its garniture of oysters, shrimps, and mushrooms. Glaze the sauce quickly under the broiler.

IN a skillet put 3 to 4 pounds bass cut into inch-thick steaks. Add 1 cup water, 3 tablespoons peanut oil, 1/4 cup green onions, finely chopped, 3 tablespoons each of soy sauce and dry white wine, and 1 tablespoon preserved ginger chopped. Cover the skillet and bring the liquid quickly to a boil. Lower the heat and simmer the fish for about 15 minutes, or until the flesh flakes readily with a fork.

Sea Bass Chinoise

In a saucepan cook 1 pound bean sprouts in 2 tablespoons peanut oil and 1 tablespoon soy sauce for 5 minutes. Add 1/2 cup of the sauce from the skillet in which the fish was cooked and simmer the sprouts for 5 minutes longer. Arrange them on a heated serving dish, lay the fish steaks on top of them, and cover the fish with the remaining sauce. Serve with fluffy boiled rice and peas.

CLEAN and scale a 3-pound bass and cut it into thick slices. Melt 1/4 cup butter in a skillet, stir in 2 tablespoons flour, and cook, stirring, for 3 minutes. Add gradually 2 cups dark beer and cook the sauce, stirring, until it is smooth and thickened. Add 1 tablespoon brown sugar, 1 teaspoon salt, 6 peppercorns, and 2 cloves. Add the fish slices and simmer them for about 15 minutes, or until the fish flakes easily, turning the pieces once during the cooking.

Bass in Beer

Arrange the fish on a heated serving platter, stir 1 tablespoon lemon juice into the sauce, and strain it over the fish.

*Broiled
Butterfish*

CLEAN 6 butterfish and wipe them with a damp cloth. Sprinkle them with salt and pepper, brush them with butter, and broil them about 3 inches from the heat for 5 minutes, or until they are golden brown, basting them several times with melted butter. Turn the fish and brown the other side, basting with butter.

Transfer the fish to a heated platter and spread them with 6 tablespoons soft butter mixed with 3 teaspoons each of grated lemon rind and chopped parsley, 1 teaspoon each of chopped sweet basil and chervil, and a pinch of chives. Garnish with lemon wedges.

*Codfish
with Oysters
Cape Cod*

COOK 12 freshly shucked oysters in their own liquor over low heat until the edges begin to curl. Drain them and reserve the liquor.

Wash 6 codfish steaks quickly in cold water, put them into a well-buttered casserole, and spread them with 3 tablespoons finely chopped onion. Pour over the steaks 1/2 cup dry white wine and the oyster liquor. Bake the fish in a moderate oven (350° F.) for 15 minutes, or until it flakes easily with a fork. Transfer the steaks to a heated serving dish and keep them warm.

In a saucepan melt 3 tablespoons butter and blend in 2 tablespoons flour. Add the stock from the casserole, stirring constantly. Season with salt and pepper to taste, and cook the sauce until it is smooth and thick. Add the cooked oysters and heat them thoroughly. Pour the sauce over the steaks and sprinkle them with 2 tablespoons finely chopped parsley and 1 teaspoon lemon juice.

*Codfish
Carcassonne*

WASH 6 codfish steaks in cold salted water, and drain and dry them well. Melt 1 tablespoon butter in a large saucepan, put the steaks in the pan, and spread them with 2 medium onions, finely chopped, and 2 tablespoons chopped parsley. Add 1/2 cup water to the pan and simmer the steaks gently for 15 minutes, or until the water has cooked away.

In another saucepan put 1 tablespoon each of finely chopped walnuts, hazelnuts, and almonds, and shake them over low heat for 3 minutes. Add 2 tablespoons bread crumbs and continue to shake the pan over the heat for 3 minutes longer, or until the crumbs are brown. Add 1 cup white-wine court bouillon, stir well, and bring the sauce to a boil.

Cover the bottom of a heated serving dish with croutons browned in butter on both sides, lay the fish steaks on the croutons, pour the sauce over all, and garnish the platter with parsley or watercress.

Wash and dry 6 slices of fresh codfish, each about 3/4-inch thick. Combine 4 egg yolks, 5 tablespoons cornstarch, 2 tablespoons dry Sherry, and 1/2 teaspoon salt. Coat the filets with this mixture and roll them in 1/2 cup fine dry bread crumbs. Fry them in hot deep fat (365° F.) for 5 to 7 minutes, drain them, and just before serving, pour over them this sweet-sour sauce: In a saucepan heat 1/4 cup lard and add 1/2 cup chicken stock, 1/4 cup sugar, 6 tablespoons cider vinegar, 2 tablespoons each of minced fresh ginger and tomato ketchup, and 1 1/3 tablespoons cornstarch mixed with 1/3 cup cold water. Stir the sauce over the heat until it is hot and well blended.

Chinese Fried Codfish

Skin an eel weighing about 2 1/2 pounds, split it open and clean it thoroughly. Remove the backbone, taking care not to pierce the meat, and wipe the eel with a damp cloth. Brush it on all sides with beaten egg and put it in a buttered baking dish. Sprinkle it with salt and pepper to taste, the juice of 1/2 lemon, and 1/4 cup fine dry bread crumbs. Dot it with 2 tablespoons butter and bake it in a moderately hot oven (375° F.) for about 40 minutes, basting frequently and adding a little hot water if needed. Serve the eel hot or cold with lemon wedges or with tartar sauce.

Ugnstekt ål
BAKED EEL

In a saucepan in 2/3 cup olive oil sauté 2 small onions, finely chopped, and 4 garlic cloves with the grated rind of 1/2 lemon and 1/4 teaspoon sage until the garlic is golden. Discard the garlic. To the pan add 4 pounds cleaned, skinned eels, cut into 3-inch pieces, and cook the pieces for 5 minutes, turning them from time to time. Mix 1/4 cup tomato paste with 1 cup water and add this and 1 cup dry white wine to the pan. Cook the pieces slowly for 10 minutes. Season them with salt and pepper to taste and simmer the sauce for about 8 minutes longer, or until it is very thick.

Anguille alla Marinara
EELS MARINARA

Skin, clean, and cut into 3-inch pieces a 2 1/2-pound eel and simmer it for about 20 minutes in white-wine court bouillon for fish. Cool the eel in the liquid and drain and dry the pieces thoroughly. Dip them in oil or

Grilled Eel with Tartar Sauce

melted butter, roll them in fine bread crumbs, and sprinkle them with butter or oil. Broil the pieces slowly, turning them to brown on both sides. Serve with fried parsley and tartar sauce.

Marinated Eel SKIN and clean an eel weighing about 2 1/2 pounds and lay it in a circle on the bottom of a large kettle. Add 1 garlic clove, sliced, 1/2 teaspoon each of salt and pepper, 3 bay leaves, and 1 cup each of wine vinegar and olive oil. Cover the kettle tightly and cook the eel gently for 20 to 30 minutes, or until it is tender. Remove it to a serving dish, strain the pan juices over it, and chill it thoroughly before serving.

Anguilla
alla Romana
EEL STEWED
WITH PEAS

SKIN, clean, and cut into 3-inch lengths an eel weighing about 2 1/2 pounds. In a saucepan brown lightly in 1/4 cup olive oil 6 scallions, chopped, and 1 garlic clove, minced. Add the pieces of eel, sprinkle them with salt and pepper, and sauté them until the liquid from them has evaporated and the meat is brown on all sides. Add 3 cups freshly shelled peas, 3/4 cup dry white wine, 1/4 cup warm water or stock, and 1 1/2 tablespoons tomato sauce and cook the pieces for about 15 minutes longer, or until the peas are tender, adding a little more water if needed. Serve hot, garnished with lemon wedges and parsley.

Eel Stew
Normandy

DICE 3 onions, 2 carrots, and 3 stalks of celery, and put the vegetables in a saucepan. Cut 2 pounds skinned eel into 2-inch lengths and lay the pieces on the vegetables. Sprinkle the fish with 1 teaspoon salt and add 2 cups cider and a *bouquet garni* composed of 2 sprigs each of parsley and tarragon, tied together. Bring the cider to the boiling point, lower the heat, and simmer the stew until the eel is tender, about 25 minutes. Transfer the pieces of eel to a heated platter and keep them hot. Reduce the eel stock to about 1 cup and strain it.

In the top of a double boiler melt 3 tablespoons butter, blend in 3 tablespoons flour and cook the *roux* for 5 minutes. Add the reduced stock gradually and cook, stirring constantly until the sauce thickens. Cook slowly for 5 minutes longer. Beat 2 egg yolks with 1/2 cup cream, add a little of the hot sauce, and return the mixture to the double boiler. Over hot water, heat the sauce well, but do not let it boil. Correct the seasoning and pour the sauce over the eel. Surround the stew with cooked chopped sorrel and garnish the platter with small buttered boiled white onions and croutons browned in butter.

IN a saucepan sauté 2 tablespoons green pepper and 1 small onion, both finely chopped, in 1/4 cup butter until the onion takes on color. Remove the saucepan from the heat and add 3 cups picked-over crab meat, 1 teaspoon parsley, salt and pepper to taste, and a pinch of garlic.

Clean, split without separating, and remove the backbone from six 1-pound flounders. Stuff the fish with the crab-meat mixture, fasten the halves together with skewers, and arrange the stuffed fish on a buttered baking sheet. Sprinkle them with salt and pepper and broil them slowly, basting frequently with a mixture of lemon juice and butter, until they are golden brown, first on one side and then on the other.

Garnish the serving platter with parsley and lemon wedges and serve hollandaise sauce separately.

SOAK 18 pairs of medium-sized frogs' legs in milk for 1 to 2 hours. Wipe them dry, roll them in flour, dip them in beaten egg, and roll them in fine bread crumbs. Sauté the legs in 1/4 cup each of olive oil and butter for about 5 minutes, or until they are nicely browned. Arrange the frogs' legs on a hot platter. To the juices in the pan add salt and pepper to taste, 1/4 teaspoon dry mustard, and a generous dash each of Worcestershire sauce and whiskey. Heat the sauce well, blending thoroughly, and pour it over the frogs' legs.

WASH 18 pairs of medium-sized frogs' legs in cold water, wipe them dry, and put them in a bowl. Sprinkle them with salt and pepper, pour over them the juice of 2 lemons and marinate them for 30 minutes, turning them occasionally to expose all sides to the liquid.

Dry the frogs' legs again thoroughly. Brush them with oil and broil them 2 inches from the broiler for 4 to 5 minutes on each side, or until they are golden brown. Be careful not to overcook. Arrange them on a heated serving dish and pour over them a little maître d'hôtel butter. Sprinkle them with chopped parsley.

*Frogs' Legs
Vinaigrette*

POACH 18 pairs of medium-sized frogs' legs for 5 minutes in half white wine and half water to cover, seasoned with salt and pepper to taste. Chill them, drain them, and serve them on lettuce leaves with a highly seasoned vinaigrette sauce. Garnish the platter with quarters of hard-cooked eggs, and with green olives and pickles.

*Chinese
Frogs' Legs*
SEN CHAO TIEN CHI

SOAK 3 ounces dried mushrooms in hot water for 30 minutes, wash them, discard the stems, and cut the tops into small squares. Trim 2 scallions and cut them into 1-inch lengths; cut 1/2 green pepper into diamond-shaped pieces about 1 inch by 1 1/2 inches; and slice 3 ounces water chestnuts 1/8 inch thick.

Wipe 9 pairs of medium-sized frogs' legs with a damp cloth and cut each pair into 4 pieces. In a skillet in 5 tablespoons lard sauté 2 garlic cloves, crushed, 2 slices of fresh ginger, and the frogs' legs for 2 minutes. Add the scallions, 1 tablespoon Sherry, and a dash of white pepper and cook for 3 minutes longer. Remove the frogs' legs and vegetables, leaving the oil in the pan.

In the same skillet sauté for 2 minutes the prepared green pepper, mushrooms, and water chestnuts. Skim out the vegetables. To the juices in the pan add 1/4 cup chicken stock, 1/3 teaspoon sugar, a pinch of salt, and 1 teaspoon cornstarch mixed with 2 tablespoons cold water. Cook, stirring, until the sauce is smooth and well blended, add the frogs' legs and the vegetables, and cook over high heat for 1 1/2 minutes. Serves four.

*Frogs' Legs
Osborn*

SEASON 18 pairs of medium-sized frogs' legs with salt and pepper and sauté them in 1/2 cup butter over high heat until they are golden brown on all sides. Transfer the frogs' legs to a heated casserole and add to the butter in the skillet 1 tablespoon finely chopped onion, 1 green pepper, cut into thin julienne, 6 tomatoes, peeled and cut into eighths, and 1 cup finely chopped mushrooms. Cook the vegetables for 5 minutes, stirring constantly, and add them to the frogs' legs in the casserole. Pour over them 1 1/2 cups hot brown sauce, cover the casserole, and bake the legs in a hot oven (400° F.) for about 15 minutes, or until they are tender. Serve in the casserole, plentifully sprinkled with chopped parsley.

Haddock Filet
TSAO LIU YU PIEN

SOAK 3 ounces dried mushrooms in boiling water for 30 minutes, rinse them, discard the stems, and quarter each top. Cut a haddock filet, weighing 3/4 pound, into pieces 2 inches square by 1/4 inch thick and sprinkle the pieces with 1/2 teaspoon cornstarch.

In a skillet in 1/2 cup lard sauté 1 slice of fresh ginger and 1 garlic clove for 1 minute. Add the haddock pieces, sauté them for 1 1/2 minutes, and remove them to a warm place.

In the same skillet put 2 scallions, trimmed and cut into 1-inch lengths, 1/3 cup Sauternes, 1/2 cup bamboo shoots, sliced, the quartered mushrooms, 3 tablespoons vinegar, and salt and pepper and cook the mixture for 2 minutes. Add 1/2 teaspoon cornstarch mixed with 2 tablespoons cold water, add the haddock, and cook for 2 minutes longer. Serves four.

SOAK 2 pounds finnan haddie in 2 cups each of water and milk for 2 hours. Simmer the fish gently in the same liquid for 15 minutes. Drain the fish, reserving the liquid, and flake it.

Sauté 1 green pepper and 8 small onions, chopped, in 1/2 cup butter until the onion is transparent. Stir in 1/2 cup flour and slowly add 2 1/2 cups cream, stirring constantly, and 2 cups of the reserved liquid. Cook the sauce, still stirring, until it is smooth and thick. Add the flaked fish and a little white pepper to taste and turn the fish and sauce into a baking dish. Cover with crumbs, dot with butter, and bake in a hot oven (400° F.) until the crumbs are browned.

Finnan Haddie au Gratin

SPRINKLE 6 filets of chicken halibut with salt, pepper, a little cayenne, and lemon juice. Roll the filets and secure the rolls with toothpicks. Arrange the *paupiettes* in a buttered baking dish, pour over them 3 cups fish *fumet* made with white wine, and poach them in a moderate oven (350° F.) for about 20 minutes, or until the flesh flakes easily. Arrange the *paupiettes* in a ring on a heated serving platter and put 2 dozen oysters, fried in hot deep fat, in the center of the ring.

Cover the fish with white-wine cream sauce made by reducing the cooking liquor, or 3 cups fish stock, by half and stirring in 1 cup fish *velouté* and 1/2 cup heavy cream. Finish with 2 tablespoons sweet butter. Correct the seasoning, add a few drops of lemon juice, and strain.

Garnish the platter with small tomatoes stuffed with cooked crab meat mixed with a little of the hot sauce, and bread triangles sautéed in butter.

Paupiettes de Flétan Jacqueline
PAUPIETTES OF HALIBUT

White Wine Cream Sauce

IN a mixing bowl combine 6 medium potatoes, thinly sliced, 6 anchovy filets, finely chopped, 1/2 garlic clove, minced, 1/2 cup olive oil, 1 tablespoon chopped parsley, 1/2 teaspoon salt, and a generous grinding of pepper.

Baked Halibut Steaks

Curried Halibut Steaks

Put half the mixture into a well-buttered casserole, lay 6 halibut steaks cut about an inch thick on it, and cover the fish with the rest of the mixture. Bake the fish in a hot oven (400° F.) for 35 minutes, or until the potatoes are tender.

Broiled
Halibut
with Vermouth

ARRANGE 6 slices of halibut, cut 1 inch thick, in a shallow flameproof casserole. Melt 1/2 cup butter in 1/2 cup heated vermouth and pour the mixture over the halibut. Sprinkle the fish with salt and pepper and broil it a few inches from the heat for about 20 minutes, or until done, basting frequently. Remove the casserole from the broiler, sprinkle the fish with bread crumbs mixed with an equal amount of grated cheese, and broil the topping for 2 to 3 minutes, or until it is browned. Serve from the casserole.

Curried
Halibut Steaks

WASH and dry 6 halibut steaks, and put them in a shallow saucepan with enough water barely to cover. Add 1 bay leaf, 1 onion, halved, 1 carrot cut in several pieces, 1 stalk of celery, 1/4 teaspoon salt, and 6 peppercorns. Cover the pan and bring the liquid just to a boil. Lower the heat and simmer the fish gently for 10 minutes. Strain the stock.

In a saucepan in 1/4 cup butter sauté 1 small onion, 1/2 green pepper, and 1 stalk of celery, all finely chopped. Add 3 tablespoons flour and 3/4 teaspoon curry powder and blend well. Add 1 cup of the strained fish stock and stir the sauce over low heat for 5 minutes. Add 1 cup dry white wine, 2 drops Tabasco sauce, and 2 tablespoons chopped parsley. Add salt and pepper to taste and bring the sauce to a boil, stirring constantly.

Remove the skin and the bones from the halibut steaks, arrange the filets on a heated serving dish, and cover them with the hot sauce.

Stuffed
Halibut Steaks
en Casserole

BRUSH 2 halibut steaks, each weighing 1 1/2 pounds, with melted butter and sprinkle them with salt and pepper. Lay one steak in a buttered casserole and spread it with this filling: Combine 1 cup soft bread crumbs, 1 onion, chopped and sautéed in butter until transparent, 1 cup cooked crab meat, 2 eggs, beaten, 1 tablespoon finely chopped parsley, and salt, pepper, and cayenne to taste. Blend the mixture thoroughly and moisten it with 2 tablespoons Sherry. Set the second steak over the filling and sprinkle it with the juice of half a lemon. Add 1 cup heavy cream and dot the fish with butter. Bake the fish in a hot oven (400 ° F.) for 35 to 40 minutes, or until the flesh flakes easily. If the top begins to brown too much, cover the casserole with a piece of buttered paper. Serve the fish from the casserole.

Fisherman's Herring Omelet

CLEAN 6 small fresh herring, split them, and remove as many of the small bones as possible. Cut off and discard the heads and tails, and cut the filets in half. Wash and dry the pieces well and dredge them in seasoned flour. Brown them on both sides in 1/3 cup butter, in a skillet large enough to hold the fish in a single layer. When the flesh flakes readily at the touch of a fork, the fish is cooked. Beat 2 egg yolks lightly with 1/2 cup milk, 1/4 cup chopped chives, and 1 tablespoon each of finely chopped parsley, grated onion, and prepared mustard. Add salt, pepper, and a dash each of nutmeg, thyme, and marjoram, to taste. The mixture should be very highly seasoned. Fold in 2 egg whites, stiffly beaten, and pour the mixture over the fish in the skillet. Cover the skillet and cook the omelet over low heat until it sets and is puffy. Invert the omelet on a heated platter and serve it with fried potatoes.

Broiled Deviled Fresh Herring

CLEAN, scale, and remove the heads from 6 fresh herring, each weighing about 1 pound. Wash the fish quickly in cold water and dry them well. Rub each fish with mixed salt, cayenne, nutmeg, and mace, and with prepared mustard flavored with tarragon. Roll the fish in sieved dry bread crumbs and broil them on both sides, very slowly, 5 or 6 inches from the heat. Serve on a heated platter. Garnish with parsley sprigs and lemon wedges, and pour a little maître d'hôtel butter over the fish. Mackerel may be substituted in this recipe with very good results.

Pickled Herring

SKIN and bone 12 fat salt herring and soak them overnight in water to cover. Tie 1 tablespoon pickling spices securely in a cheesecloth bag. Bring to a boil 1/2 cup each of water and brown sugar and add the bag of spices. Boil the mixture for 5 minutes and cool it. Add 1 1/2 cups white vinegar. Cut the herring into bite-sized pieces and put a layer in the bottom of a crock. Fill the crock with alternate layers of herring and thinly sliced onions and lemons. Cover all with the vinegar mixture and chill the herring for 48 hours before serving. It will keep indefinitely. Serve it with sour cream, if desired.

SPLIT kippers without breaking the back skin and place them, skin side down, in a buttered pan. Brush them generously with melted butter and sprinkle with lemon juice and a little freshly ground pepper. Broil the kippers for about 10 minutes, or until they flake with a fork.

Broiled
Kippers

SEASON 6 small cleaned pike with salt and pepper, dip them in flour, and brown them on both sides in 6 tablespoons melted butter. Pour over the fish a small liqueur glass of warmed brandy and ignite the spirit. When the flame dies, add salt and pepper to taste and 1 cup heavy cream. Bring the sauce to a boil, remove the pike to a heated serving dish, and strain the sauce over them. Sprinkle with slivered toasted almonds.

Brochet
à la Crème
PIKE IN CREAM

HAVE a 3-pound pompano boned and dressed. Stuff it with a forcemeat made by combining 2 cups finely minced cooked shrimps, 1 egg, lightly beaten, 1/2 cup heavy cream, 2 tablespoons each of Sherry and chopped mushrooms, and salt and pepper to taste. Sew the opening and put the fish in a buttered pan. Sprinkle it with salt and pepper, pour over it 1/2 cup cream, and bake it in a moderate oven (350° F.) for about 30 minutes, or until the flesh flakes easily.

Baked
Pompano

POACH 6 pompano filets in salted water for 5 minutes. Cook 2 cups crab meat in 1/4 cup butter and 2 tablespoons white wine for 5 minutes. Sauté 2 onions and 2 truffles, both finely chopped, and 1 cup chopped mushrooms in 2 tablespoons butter until the onion is lightly browned. Stir in 1 tablespoon flour and add gradually, stirring constantly, 2 cups hot fish stock made by simmering the heads, bones, and trimmings of the pompano in seasoned water. Cook the sauce until it is reduced by about one-fourth and add 1/4 cup white wine and salt and pepper to taste. Remove the sauce from the heat and stir in 2 egg yolks lightly beaten with a little of the hot sauce.

Pompano
en Papillote
New Orleans

Divide the crab meat in 6. Put one portion on half of each filet and fold the other half over the filling. Put each filet on a square of parchment or aluminum foil well brushed with olive oil, and dress them liberally with the sauce, within the fold as well as outside. Fold the paper over the fish and secure it tightly so that no juice can escape. Bake the papillotes on an oiled baking sheet in a very hot oven (450° F.) for 10 minutes. Serve the filets *en papillote*, to be opened at the table.

Filets of Pompano Florida

CUT the peel of 2 oranges in fine julienne, put it in a saucepan with water to cover, and parboil it. Drain. Melt 2 tablespoons butter in a shallow pan and add 1 teaspoon finely chopped shallots or onion. Season 6 filets of pompano, or other firm-fleshed fish, lightly with salt and arrange them in the pan. Add 1/2 cup fish stock or water and the juice of 2 oranges and 1/2 lemon and spread the julienne on top of the fish.

Cut a circle of paper the size of the pan, make a small hole in the center, butter the paper, and lay it, butter side down, on the fish. Cover the pan. Bring the liquid to a boil and cook the fish for 10 to 12 minutes. Remove it to a heated serving dish. Cook the liquid in the pan until it is reduced by half and add 1 cup Newburg sauce. Bring it to a boil and add 1/2 cup Sherry or Madeira. Strain the sauce over the fish, replacing any orange peel that falls off.

Planked Pompano

WIPE a 3- to 4-pound dressed pompano with a damp cloth and sprinkle it inside and out with salt and pepper. Lay the pompano on an oiled and heated oak plank and bake it in a moderate oven (350° F.) for about 35 minutes, or until the flesh flakes easily from the bones, basting often with a mixture of equal amounts melted butter and white wine.

Decorate the plank with a border of duchess potatoes forced through a pastry bag, brush the potatoes with lightly beaten egg, and return the plank to a hot oven (425° F.) until the potatoes are lightly browned. Arrange buttered cooked vegetables, such as green beans, peas, or asparagus tips, on the plank and garnish it attractively with lemon wedges, parsley, and broiled tomato halves.

Planked Salmon

Salmon may be treated in the same way.

Stuffed Red Snapper

WASH and clean a 4- to 5-pound red snapper. Season it inside and out with salt and pepper, rub it with butter, and sprinkle it lightly with flour. Combine 1 cup each of dry fine bread crumbs, raw shrimps, shelled, deveined, and chopped, chopped oysters, and scallions—green and white chopped together—and 1/2 cup chopped celery. Add 2 tablespoons melted butter and use this mixture to stuff the fish. Skewer or sew the opening and lay the fish on a buttered baking dish.

Score the fish to prevent it from buckling and lay a few strips of bacon on it. Bake the fish for about 45 minutes in a moderate oven (350° F.), until it flakes readily at the touch of a fork. Baste it often with the pan juices.

IN a fish kettle large enough to hold a 6-pound salmon, put 2 quarts water, 1 bottle dry white wine, 1 onion, sliced, 1/2 carrot, sliced, 1 tablespoon salt, 6 crushed peppercorns, and a *bouquet garni* consisting of 1 bay leaf and 1 sprig each of parsley, thyme, and celery tops. Bring the court bouillon to a boil and simmer it for 20 minutes. Let it cool slightly, then lower the salmon wrapped in cheesecloth onto the rack. Simmer the salmon gently in the court bouillon for 1 hour, or until the flesh flakes easily and is no longer translucent. Remove the fish, unwrap it, and carefully remove the skin. Arrange the salmon on a heated platter. Garnish the platter with slices of lemon, cucumber strips, and parsley sprigs. Serve with *sauce mousseline*.

Saumon Poché Mousseline
POACHED SALMON, MOUSSELINE SAUCE

SAUTÉ 1 cup finely chopped onions in 1/4 cup butter until they are transparent. Remove the onions from the pan and add 1/4 cup butter. Sprinkle 6 individual salmon steaks with flour, a generous amount of curry powder, and salt and pepper. Sauté the steaks on both sides in the butter until the flesh flakes at the touch of a fork. Remove the steaks to a heated platter and keep them warm. Return the onions to the pan and heat them. Add 2 tablespoons curry powder, mix well, and gradually stir in 2 cups sour cream. Heat the sauce but do not let it boil. Pour the curry sauce over the steaks and serve immediately.

Curried Salmon Steaks

SKIN and bone fresh salmon and slice it into strips 1 1/2 inches by 8 inches and no thicker than 1/2 inch. Two pounds of filets will make 8 servings. Butter 8 custard cups and coil the salmon filets around the insides of the cups.

Cook 3/4 cup sliced fresh mushrooms in 1/4 cup butter and 1 teaspoon onion juice for 5 minutes in the top of a double boiler. Add 1/4 cup flour, 1/2 cup light cream, 1/4 teaspoon salt, 1/8 teaspoon pepper, and a

Baked Rolled Salmon Filets

few grains each of cayenne and mace. Over hot water, cook the sauce until it is thick but not boiling, stirring constantly. Divide the mixture among the custard cups. Any scraps of fish may be used to garnish the filled cups. Bake them in a moderately hot oven (375° F.) for 25 minutes.

Drain off any juice and unmold the rolls on a heatproof dish. Sprinkle with buttered bread crumbs and top each with a small perfect mushroom cap that has been dipped in melted butter or olive oil. Broil the rolls until the mushroom caps are cooked and the crumbs browned. Garnish with parsley and lemon wedges. Serves 8.

Salmon Slices Baked in Cream

WIPE dry 3 large slices of salmon, halve each slice, and sprinkle with salt and pepper. Arrange the slices in a buttered baking dish and add enough cream barely to cover them. Add 1/2 bay leaf, 2 cloves, 3 slices of onion, 4 sprigs of parsley, and a sprig of thyme, and bake the slices in a hot oven (400° F.) for about 25 minutes, basting occasionally to keep the top of the slices from drying out. Arrange the salmon on a heated serving platter and keep it hot.

In a saucepan melt 1/4 cup butter and stir in 1/4 cup flour. Stir in gradually 2 cups of the hot cream in which the fish slices were baked and cook the sauce, stirring constantly, until it is smooth and thickened. Season the sauce with salt, pepper, and a little lemon juice and simmer it for 10 minutes. Pour the sauce over the fish and sprinkle generously with finely chopped parsley. Garnish the platter with lemon wedges, slices of cucumber, and halved hard-cooked eggs.

Broiled Shad

SPLIT a 3-pound boned shad, brush it generously with melted butter or olive oil, and sprinkle it with salt and paprika. Arrange the fish, skin side down, on an oiled broiler pan and broil it 4 or 5 inches from the heat for 15 to 20 minutes, or until it is golden brown and the flesh flakes easily with a fork. Sprinkle frequently with melted butter or olive oil. Put the shad on a heated serving platter and spread it with 2 tablespoons soft butter kneaded with 1 teaspoon each of finely chopped parsley and chervil and 1/2 teaspoon finely chopped chives. Serve with watercress and lemon wedges.

Alose Tourangelle
STUFFED SHAD
TOURANGELLE

CLEAN and stuff a boned shad weighing about 3 pounds with this forcemeat: Soak 3/4 cup soft bread crumbs in milk for 10 minutes, drain them, and press out the excess moisture. Add 3 tablespoons melted butter, 2 onions, chopped and sautéed in butter until they are golden, 1 tablespoon each of chopped parsley and chervil, 1 teaspoon each of chopped tarragon and chives, and a pair of shad roes poached for 3 minutes in salted water to cover, and mix thoroughly.

Simmer 1/2 pound each of sorrel leaves and young beet tops, finely shredded, and the white parts of 4 leeks, finely chopped, in a little salted water for 10 minutes and drain. Spread the vegetables in the bottom of a baking dish, set the shad on top, and pour over it 2 cups dry white wine. Sprinkle lightly with salt and pepper, cover with buttered paper, and bake the shad in a slow oven (300° F.) for about 1 hour.

Put the shad on a heated serving platter. Reduce the cooking liquid by half, stir in 1/4 cup heavy cream, and pour the sauce over the fish.

STUFF a 3-pound shad with this forcemeat: Put 1 pound pickerel or pike and 1/2 pound mackerel, both free of bones, through the finest blade of a food chopper. Stir in 4 mushrooms, thinly sliced and cooked in 2 tablespoons butter until soft, 2 tablespoons chopped parsley, and salt, pepper, nutmeg, and cayenne to taste. Bind the mixture with about 1 cup thick *sauce béchamel maigre* and force it through a fine sieve or purée it in a blender.

Skewer or sew the opening with kitchen thread. Make several bias gashes in the back of the fish, put it in a buttered baking dish, and cover the gashes with strips of salt pork. Roast the shad in a moderate oven (350° F.) for 30 to 40 minutes, basting frequently with melted butter.

Discard the salt pork, arrange the fish on a heated serving platter, and serve with *sauce Rubens*, prepared as follows: Shell and devein 1/4 pound shrimps, reserving the shells. With the meat make a shrimp paste: Pound the flesh in a mortar with 1/3 cup heavy cream and force the paste through a fine sieve. The shells are used for shrimp butter. Pound the shells with 2 tablespoons butter and rub as much of the butter as possible through a fine sieve.

Cook 1/3 cup finely chopped carrots, 1/4 cup finely chopped onions, and 1 tablespoon minced parsley in 1 tablespoon butter with a bay leaf and a sprig of thyme for 10 minutes. Add 1 1/2 cups fish *fumet* and 1 cup dry white wine, bring the liquid to a boil, and simmer for 25 minutes. Add the coral from a lobster, cook the sauce 5 minutes longer, and strain it through a fine sieve.

Skim the sauce and return it to the heat, and continue to cook it until it is reduced to 1 cup. Add 1 tablespoon Madeira and stir in 2 egg yolks

Alose
Farcie Rubens
BAKED
STUFFED SHAD

Sauce Rubens

beaten with a little of the hot sauce. Cook it for 2 minutes over low heat but do not let it boil. Stir in 1/3 cup butter, the shrimp butter, the shrimp paste, and a pinch of paprika.

Iekan Bandang Panggang

SPICED BAKED SHAD

MIX 1/2 teaspoon salt with 1/8 teaspoon pepper and 1 or 2 garlic cloves, minced, and rub the mixture into a boned 3-pound shad. Combine 1/2 cup melted butter, 1/4 cup soy sauce, 3 tablespoons lemon or lime juice, and 2 ground fresh hot red chili peppers. Bake the fish in a hot oven (400° F.) for about 30 minutes, basting it frequently with the soy-butter mixture. Arrange the fish on a heated platter and pour the remaining sauce over it. Garnish with parsley sprigs and slices of lemon.

Broiled Shad Roe

Beurre Noir
BLACK BUTTER

SPRINKLE 3 shad roes with salt and pepper and broil them on a buttered rack 4 inches from the heat for about 5 minutes, or until they are pale gold, basting with melted butter. Turn and broil the other side until lightly brown, basting several times with melted butter. Serve very hot with *beurre noir*, made as follows: In a small saucepan melt 1/2 cup butter and cook until it turns brown. Stir in 1 tablespoon vinegar and season with freshly ground black pepper and salt to taste. A little finely chopped parsley or a few capers may be added at the last minute.

If desired, serve the roe with baked potatoes and bacon, and garnish with lemon wedges.

Poached Shad Roe

IN a large skillet melt 1 cup butter over low heat. Dip 3 shad roes in flour and put them in the pan. Turn the roes so that both sides will be bathed in the melted butter, cover the skillet, and cook the roes very gently for 10 minutes. Turn them, cover with a generous layer of finely chopped parsley, and continue to poach them in the butter for 10 minutes longer. Season the roes with salt, freshly ground pepper, and lemon juice. Arrange them on a heated serving platter, pour over them the pan juices, and garnish with watercress.

Shad Roe Mousse

PREPARE a *mousseline* forcemeat with 1 pound raw halibut. Sauté 1 pair of shad roes slowly in 1/4 cup butter for 12 to 15 minutes. Remove and

Broiled Shad Roe

discard the veins and skin and mash the roe thoroughly. Combine the cooked roe with the forcemeat, work in 1 cup cream and taste the mixture for seasoning. Turn the forcemeat into a buttered mold and cover the mold with buttered wax paper. Set the mold in a pan of hot water and bake the mousse in a moderate oven (350° F.) for about 30 minutes, or until a skewer inserted in the center comes out clean. Unmold the mousse onto a heated platter and serve it with any desired fish sauce based on béchamel sauce for fish. Serves 4.

Broiled Smelts   SPLIT and clean as many smelts as are desired, allowing 3 to 5 for each serving. Roll them in melted butter and in fine bread crumbs. Arrange the fish on a hot, buttered pan and broil them, basting them frequently with butter, for about 5 minutes, or until the flesh flakes easily from the bones when tested with a small pointed knife. Serve with lemon wedges.

Paupiettes   CRUSH 1 pound tomatoes, peeled and seeded, season them with salt and
of Sole   pepper, and cook them slowly over low heat, stirring frequently, until they
Prosper   are reduced to a paste.
Montagné   Spread 12 small filets of sole with a little of the tomato paste, roll them, and secure them with toothpicks. Place the *paupiettes* in a generously buttered flameproof casserole just large enough to hold them and add dry white wine to cover. Put 1 teaspoon butter on each filet and cover the casserole with buttered paper. Bring the wine to a boil over moderate heat and poach the filets in a moderate oven (350° F.) for 10 minutes.

In a saucepan sauté 1 tablespoon chopped shallots in 2 tablespoons butter until the shallots are transparent. Stir in 1/2 cup Cognac, the wine in which the filets were poached, and 1 tablespoon of the tomato paste. Cook until the liquid is reduced by half, add 2 cups heavy cream, and bring to a boil. Simmer the sauce gently for about 10 minutes, or until it thickens. Stir in, bit by bit, 1/4 cup butter, correct the seasoning, and strain. Keep the sauce warm over hot water.

Hollow out 6 small tomatoes and cook them gently in butter until they are soft but not mushy. Fill the hollows with mushrooms, minced, sautéed in butter until tender, and bound with a little of the sauce.

Spread a warm serving platter with a thin layer of the tomato paste and arrange the *paupiettes* in the center. Place the stuffed tomatoes around the fish and pour the sauce over the fish. Sprinkle with finely chopped parsley and garnish with lemon wedges.

POACH 6 filets of sole for about 10 minutes in 1 1/2 cups each of white wine and fish stock to which have been added a little salt and pepper, 3 tablespoons sweet butter, and 2 shallots, finely chopped. Remove the filets to a flameproof serving dish and cook the liquid until it is reduced by two-thirds. Add 3 tablespoons béchamel sauce for fish and another 3 tablespoons sweet butter. Stir until the butter is melted and strain the sauce through a fine sieve.

    Arrange around the fish filets 2 dozen mussels and the same number of shrimps, cooked in fish stock and drained, and 2 dozen mushroom caps, cooked until tender in 2 tablespoons butter and the juice of 1 lemon. Fold 2 tablespoons whipped cream into the sauce, pour it over the filets, and glaze the sauce very briefly under the broiler.

Filets of Sole Marguery

MELT 2 tablespoons butter in a large shallow pan and sprinkle with 1 tablespoon finely chopped shallot or onion. Season 6 filets of sole with salt and arrange them side by side in the pan. Peel, seed, and chop coarsely 4 tomatoes and spread them over the fish. Add 1/2 cup tomato juice, 1 garlic clove, and 1 tablespoon chopped parsley. Cover the fish with a circle of buttered paper with a tiny hole in the center, bring the liquid to a boil, cover the pan, and simmer the fish for 10 to 12 minutes, depending upon the thickness of the filets. Discard the garlic and transfer the filets to a heated serving dish. Reduce the sauce rapidly over high heat by one-third. Thicken it with *beurre manié* made by kneading together 2 tablespoons butter and 1 teaspoon flour. Stir the sauce until it is well blended, correct the seasoning with salt and pepper, and finish by swirling in 1 tablespoon sweet butter. Pour the sauce over the filets and sprinkle the fish with chopped parsley. Other filets may also be prepared by this recipe.

Filets of Sole Dugléré

FOLLOW the recipe for filets of sole Dugléré, adding 1/2 pound sliced mushrooms with the tomatoes, and thicken the sauce with 1/2 cup cream sauce.

Filets of Sole Portugaise

CUT 4 to 6 filets of sole in finger strips. Dip the strips in milk and in flour seasoned with a little salt. In a skillet in 3 tablespoons butter sauté the strips until they are golden brown, turning them as required. Cook 1 cup potatoes, cut in very small julienne, in butter until they are well browned

Filets of Sole Murat

Filets of Sole à la Normande

and tender, and sauté 6 cooked artichoke bottoms, each cut into 6 pieces, in butter. Mix the vegetables with the fish and arrange on a heated serving platter. Or the fish can be put in the center and the potatoes and artichokes arranged alternately around it. Parboiled and sautéed celeriac may be used instead of artichokes. Add 1 to 2 tablespoons butter to the pan, cook it until it is hazelnut brown, and pour over all. Sprinkle with a few drops of lemon juice and a little finely chopped parsley.

STEAM 12 mussels, thoroughly scrubbed and washed, in 1/4 cup water until the shells open, and drain them, reserving the liquor. Cook 12 mushrooms in 2 tablespoons water for about 5 minutes, or until they are tender, and drain them. Combine the mushroom liquor and the mussel stock and reserve the liquid. Poach one dozen freshly shucked oysters in their own juice until the edges curl.

Filets of Sole à la Normande

Put 12 small or 6 large filets of sole into a buttered saucepan with 1 teaspoon chopped shallots and 1 1/2 cups dry white wine. Bring the wine to a boil and poach the filets very gently for 10 minutes. Remove them to a heated serving dish and surround them with the mussels removed from their shells, the oysters, the mushrooms, and 2 dozen cooked, shelled, and deveined shrimps. Strain *sauce normande* over the fish and garnish with slices of truffle, 1 dozen small smelts or gudgeons, breaded and sautéed in butter until they are brown, and 12 crescent-shaped croutons.

In a saucepan mix 2 tablespoons butter and 1 tablespoon flour, and cook, stirring, until the *roux* is golden. Stir in gradually 1 1/2 cups of the reserved liquid and continue to stir until the sauce is slightly thickened. Boil it for 5 minutes. Combine 2 egg yolks with 1/2 cup cream and a little of the hot sauce and stir them into the sauce. Bring the sauce almost to a boil, stirring constantly, but do not let it boil, or it will curdle.

Sauce Normande

Cook the wine in which the filets were poached until it is reduced to almost nothing and stir this glaze into the hot sauce. Finish the sauce with 1/4 cup sweet butter and correct the seasoning with salt.

POUND or put through the finest blade of a food chopper 1 1/2 pounds raw fish such as pike, cod, or halibut with 3/4 teaspoon salt and a little freshly ground white pepper. Gradually add the whites of 3 eggs, working vigorously with a pestle or wooden spoon. Rub the mixture through a fine

Filets of Sole Joinville

sieve and put it in a bowl over cracked ice. Gradually work in 3 cups heavy cream. Poach 2 quenelles made of the forcemeat and turn the remainder into a buttered ring mold. Cover the top with a piece of buttered heavy paper. Place the mold in a pan containing about 1 inch of hot water and bake it in a moderate oven (350° F.) for 30 minutes, or until the forcemeat is firm to the touch.

Fold 12 small filets of sole in half and poach them very gently in *fumet de poisson* to cover for 10 minutes.

Unmold the fish mousse on a heated serving platter and decorate it with truffle slices. Drain the folded filets, arrange them in a circle around the mousse, pour a little *sauce Joinville* over them, and put a slice of truffle on each.

Fill the center of the mousse with *garniture Joinville*. Thrust into it a skewer threaded with a whole truffle and the quenelles. In a circle around this skewer arrange alternately cooked turned mushrooms and cooked, shelled, and deveined shrimps. Set 2 decorative attelets in the garniture. Serve *sauce Joinville* separately.

Garniture Joinville   Chop 1 pound cooked shelled shrimps and 1/2 pound mushrooms, sautéed in butter until tender. Add 2 truffles, diced, and bind the mixture with 1 cup *sauce Joinville*.

Sauce Joinville   To *sauce normande* add 3 tablespoons each of lobster and shrimp butter.

Paupiettes of English Sole George VI   SPREAD 6 filets of English sole with a mixture of *mousseline* fish forcemeat and artichoke purée—2 parts forcemeat to 1 part purée. Roll up each filet and secure it with wooden picks. Melt 2 tablespoons butter in a shallow pan large enough to hold the *paupiettes* and sprinkle the bottom with 1 tablespoon finely chopped shallots. Arrange the *paupiettes* on end in the pan and add 2 cups Chablis. Cover the fish with a circle of buttered wax paper with a very small hole in the center. Bring the wine to a boil, cover the pan, and poach the fish for 10 to 12 minutes, or until the flesh flakes easily. Put the fish carefully on absorbent paper to drain thoroughly.

Sauté 6 cooked artichoke bottoms in butter and arrange them in a circle on a warm serving dish. Fill the small hollow of each artichoke with diced truffles and set a *paupiette* on top.

Cook the liquid in which the fish was poached until it is reduced by half. Add 2 cups Mornay sauce, mix well with a wire whisk, and fold in 2 tablespoons whipped cream. Pour the sauce over the fish and glaze under the broiler. Put a slice of truffle on each of the *paupiettes* and 6 bouquets each of 4 or 5 cooked asparagus tips between them.

SAUTÉ 1 1/2 cups mushrooms, finely chopped, in 1/4 cup butter. Add 1/2 cup each of chives, parsley, and onion, all chopped, and cook the vegetables until they are tender. Season the mixture with salt and white pepper to taste, and spread it evenly on 8 filets of sole. Roll the filets and skewer them with wooden picks. Beat 2 eggs with 3/4 cup milk and season lightly with salt. Dip each fish roll into the batter and then in fine dry crumbs. Let the coating dry briefly. Brown the rolls lightly in melted butter on all sides; the fish is done when it flakes readily with a fork. Remove the fish to a flameproof serving platter.

Paupiettes de Soles

To the butter in which the fish was cooked, add 3 tablespoons flour. Cook the *roux* for a few minutes, stirring in all the brown bits, and add 1 cup white wine. Cook, still stirring, until the sauce is smooth and somewhat reduced. Stir in 1 cup cream and heat well. Pour the sauce around the fish, sprinkle all with grated Parmesan, and brown the cheese under the broiler.

POACH 6 filets of sole in equal amounts fish stock and white wine to cover for 10 minutes and arrange them on a heated serving platter. Reduce the cooking liquid by half its original quantity and stir it into hot *sauce cardinal.* Surround the filets with slices of cooked lobster tail, strain the sauce over the fish, and garnish with slices of truffle.

Filets of Sole Cardinal

Flavor 2 cups hot fish *velouté* with a little truffle juice and tint it pink with 3 tablespoons lobster butter.

Sauce Cardinal for Fish

Wash the octopus or squid thoroughly. Cut the body—the cylindrical coat or envelope of flesh—remove the tooth and translucent pen, flip the body inside out, and rip out the insides, being careful not to puncture the ink sac. The octopus or squid should be young, and the skin will slip off easily. If it is stubborn, slash it with a knife and remove. The head of the octopus and the squid are usually discarded.

To Prepare Octopus and Squid

CLEAN, skin, and wash a young octopus. Season a large kettle of boiling water with salt, a few peppercorns, 3 slices of lemon, 6 sprigs of parsley, and 3 sprigs of thyme. Drop the octopus slowly into the boiling water so that the tentacles will spread, and boil it rapidly for 5 to 10 minutes, de-

Fried Octopus

pending on the size of the fish. Remove the octopus from the water to drain and cool.

Cut the octopus into 2- to 3-inch pieces, dip the pieces into beaten egg, dredge them in flour, and fry them in hot deep fat (370° F.) for 3 to 4 minutes, or until they are golden brown. Drain the pieces of octopus on absorbent paper and sprinkle them with salt and freshly ground black pepper.

Insalata di Calamari
SQUID SALAD

CLEAN, wash, and cut 2 pounds squid into 2-inch pieces. Drop the pieces into boiling salted water and simmer them for about 30 minutes, or until they are tender. Drain the squid and sprinkle with salt and pepper.

Combine 1/4 cup olive oil, the juice of 1 lime or lemon, 1 teaspoon chopped mint, and 1 garlic clove, minced, pour the mixture over the squid, and chill it for several hours. Serve the marinated squid on a bed of lettuce, garnished with slices of ripe tomato and lemon wedges.

Calmaretti alla Genovese
SMALL SQUID
GENOA

CLEAN, skin, and wash 3 pounds small squid and cut them into serving pieces. Sauté 2 onions, chopped, in 6 tablespoons olive oil until they are lightly browned. Add 1/2 pound mushrooms, sliced, 2 tablespoons chopped parsley, 1/2 teaspoon rosemary, and 1 garlic clove, chopped, and cook the mixture for 5 minutes. Add the squid, 1 cup water, and 1/4 cup tomato purée, cover, and cook the squid gently for about 40 minutes, or until they are tender.

Chinese Stir-Fried Squid

CLEAN, skin, and wash 12 small squid. Cut off the tentacles and dice them. Slit open the bodies, cut them into 1 1/2-inch squares, and cut a few length-wise and crosswise slashes on each square.

Heat 1/4 cup oil or lard over high heat. Add the squid, 2 scallions, cut into 1-inch pieces, and 3 slices of fresh ginger, chopped, and stir for 1 minute. Add 2 tablespoons each of soy sauce and Sherry and stir for 2 minutes longer. Transfer the squid to a heated serving dish and to the pan juices add 1 teaspoon cornstarch mixed with 2 tablespoons water. Stir the gravy over moderate heat until it becomes translucent and pour it over the squid.

Italian Stuffed Squid

CLEAN, skin, and wash 12 small squid. Cut off the tentacles and chop them very finely. Combine the chopped pieces with 1 garlic clove, minced, 1/3 pound mushrooms, chopped, 4 slices of bread, crumbled, 1 tablespoon chopped parsley, 3/4 teaspoon salt, 1/2 teaspoon pepper, 1/4 teaspoon oré-gano, and 6 tablespoons olive oil. Stuff the squid bodies with the mixture and sew the openings. Arrange the squid in a buttered casserole, pour over them 6 tablespoons olive oil, and sprinkle lightly with salt, pepper, and chopped parsley. Bake the stuffed squid in a moderately hot oven (375° F.) for 45 minutes. Serve with lemon wedges.

WASH and dry 6 slices of swordfish, cut about an inch thick, and season them generously on both sides with salt, black pepper, and paprika. Spread one side of the steaks with butter and broil them, buttered side up, in a preheated broiler about 2 inches from the heat. Cook the steaks for 3 minutes, turn them, spread the uncooked side with butter, and broil them for 4 minutes longer. Arrange the steaks on a heated serving dish and keep them warm.

Swordfish Royale

In a small saucepan melt 3 tablespoons butter. Add 8 green olives, chopped, and heat them well. Pour the sauce over the fish in the serving dish and serve hot.

HEAT 1/4 cup olive oil in a casserole and in it brown a 1 1/2- to 2-pound swordfish steak on both sides. Sprinkle the fish with salt and pepper and add to the casserole 1 medium onion, chopped, 1/2 green pepper, seeded and diced, 4 tomatoes, peeled, seeded, and chopped, 6 or 8 fresh mushrooms, sliced, and 1 garlic clove, chopped, and cook for 10 minutes. Add 1/2 cup white wine or the juice of 1 lemon, a *bouquet garni* composed of 3 sprigs of parsley, 1 bay leaf, 1 stalk of celery, and a pinch of thyme, and enough fish stock or water to cover the fish. Cover the casserole and bake the fish for 35 to 40 minutes in a moderate oven (350° F.), or cook it on top of the stove over low heat until the fish is done and flakes readily at the touch of a fork.

Swordfish Provençale

Transfer the fish to a serving dish and keep it warm. Discard the *bouquet garni* and reduce the liquid by half. Blend in 1 tablespoon flour kneaded with 2 tablespoons butter, bring the sauce to a boil, correct the seasoning, and pour it over the fish or around it. Garnish the serving platter with 2 tablespoons diced pimientos and 1 tablespoon capers.

CLEAN 6 medium-sized trout, remove the filets from each side, and use the bones to make fish stock. Spread each filet with a thin layer of *mousseline* forcemeat made with 1/2 pound of fish, mixed with 1/2 cup finely chopped

Trout Mandone

truffles. Reassemble the fish, putting two filets together with the forcemeat in the middle. Tie the filets together with string. Arrange the fish in a buttered casserole on a bed of finely chopped carrots, onions, and shallots. Add a *bouquet garni* of several sprigs of parsley, 1 sprig of thyme, and 1 bay leaf, 6 peppercorns, and a few mushroom peelings. Add enough fish stock and white wine in equal amounts to half cover the trout. Bring the liquid to a boil, cover the pan with buttered paper, and poach the trout in a moderate oven (325° F.) for 15 to 20 minutes, being careful that the liquid barely simmers and does not actually come to a boil. The trout is cooked when it flakes readily with a fork.

Arrange the trout on a heated serving platter. Strain the liquid from the casserole into a saucepan and cook it rapidly until it is reduced to 1/4 cup. Stir the reduced liquid into 2 cups brown sauce, bring the sauce to a boil, and pour it over the trout.

Truites à la Bourbonnaise

TROUT BOURBONNAIS

CLEAN 6 brook trout, each weighing about 1/2 pound. Cut off the fins, slit the fish on both sides of the backbones, and remove them. Prepare *mousseline* forcemeat with 1/2 pound fish, 1 egg white, and 1 cup cream. Prepare a duxelles as follows: In a saucepan put 1 cup finely chopped mushrooms, 1 tablespoon butter, and 1 teaspoon chopped shallots or onion, and cook very slowly, stirring frequently, until most of the moisture is cooked away and the mixture is like a heavy paste. Add 2 tablespoons tomato sauce and 2 teaspoons chopped parsley to the duxelles and season with salt and pepper. Cool.

Combine the duxelles and the forcemeat. Divide this stuffing into six parts and stuff the trout. Season the fish with salt and pepper, roll each one in well-buttered parchment, and tie with string. Arrange the fish in a deep saucepan side by side and add enough red wine barely to cover. Cover the pan, bring the wine to a boil, and poach the fish on top of the stove or in a hot oven (400° F.) for about 18 to 20 minutes. Remove the trout to a warm serving dish and continue to cook the liquid in the pan until it is reduced by one-third. Add 1 1/2 cups heavy cream and cook the sauce until it is slightly thickened. Remove the pan from the heat and stir in 3 egg yolks, beaten with a little of the hot sauce, 3 tablespoons butter, and salt to taste. Discard the strings and paper from the trout and remove the skins. Put a few small cooked mushrooms on the fish, and pour the sauce over it.

CLEAN 6 fresh trout and roll them in flour. Salt and pepper them and brown them in butter on both sides. Remove the cooked trout to a heated dish and add to the butter in the pan 3 tablespoons finely chopped onion and 1 garlic clove. Sauté the onion until it is tender and golden, discard the garlic, and stir in 3/4 cup heavy cream, 2 tablespoons tomato paste, and 1/2 teaspoon powdered saffron. Heat thoroughly, add salt and pepper to taste, and pour the sauce over the trout.

Trout Barbizon

CAREFULLY slit 6 trout each weighing about 3/4 pound on both sides of the backbones and remove them. Fill each trout with this stuffing: Scrape the flesh from the bones and add it to 6 small filets of sole, finely chopped. Put the combined fish flesh in a mortar and grind it to a smooth paste. Work in about 1 1/2 cups heavy cream and stir in 1 tablespoon chopped shallot, sautéed for 1 minute in butter, 2 tablespoons chopped truffle, and salt and pepper to taste. Sew up the openings.

Truites Farcies Dédé
STUFFED TROUT

Wrap the fish in flaky pie dough, keeping the shape of the fish. Decorate with small crescents of dough to simulate fish scales and brush with 1 egg yolk beaten with a little milk. Bake the trout in a moderate oven (350° F.) for 40 minutes.

In a saucepan beat 2 egg yolks with 1 tablespoon cold water, the juice of half a lemon, and salt and pepper. Stir with a whisk over hot water, adding, bit by bit, 2 tablespoons butter until the sauce is creamy. Remove the sauce from the heat and whisk in 1/4 cup hot fish stock made by cooking the bones of the trout and the sole in water flavored with salt, pepper, white wine, parsley, thyme, and 1 bay leaf. Serve the sauce separately.

In a large skillet sauté 2 onions, thinly sliced, in 3 tablespoons butter until the onions are lightly browned. Add 1 cup each of white wine, water, and fish stock, salt and pepper to taste, 1 bay leaf, and 4 cloves. Bring the liquid to a boil and cook it for 10 minutes. Put 6 cleaned trout carefully in the pan, turn down the heat so that the water just simmers, and poach the fish for 10 to 12 minutes, basting often.

Trout Mollau

Sauté 1/2 cup fine bread crumbs in 6 tablespoons butter until they are golden. Arrange the trout on a heated serving platter. Spoon over each trout 1 tablespoon of the bouillon in which they were poached and pour the crumbs and butter over them.

*Salmon
Trout
Admiral*

CLEAN a salmon trout weighing from 3 to 4 pounds and trim off the fins. If the fish is too long for the serving dish, remove the head and tail; otherwise leave them on. Wash, dry, and peel 12 to 15 medium mushrooms. Put the mushrooms in a saucepan with 1/2 cup water, a little salt, and the juice of half a lemon. Bring the liquid to a boil, simmer the mushrooms for 8 to 10 minutes, and set them aside.

Spread 1 tablespoon soft butter in a shallow pan. Sprinkle the butter with 1 tablespoon finely chopped shallots and set the fish on the shallots. Sprinkle the fish with salt and pepper and add the peelings and stems of the mushrooms and 1 cup each of white wine and fish stock. Bring the liquid to a boil, put on top of the fish a piece of wax paper the size of the pan with a tiny hole cut in the center for the steam to escape, cover the pan, and cook the fish slowly over low heat or in a hot oven (400° F.) for 35 to 40 minutes.

While the trout is cooking, poach 12 to 18 shrimps, make 12 small fish quenelles, and bake 12 crescent-shaped croutons of puff paste or sauté lozenge-shaped pieces of bread in butter until they are golden.

Remove the fish from the kettle, trim off the skin, and cut away the layer of dark flesh. Arrange the fish on a heated serving platter and keep it warm.

Reduce the liquor remaining in the pan by half, or to about 1 cup. In another pan melt 1 1/2 tablespoons butter, add 1 teaspoon flour, and cook the *roux*, stirring, until it just starts to turn golden. Stir in the reduced cooking liquor and cook the sauce, stirring, until it is smooth and well blended. Add 1 cup cream, bring to a boil, and correct the seasoning with salt. Add a few drops of lemon juice and strain the sauce through a very fine sieve.

Arrange the mushrooms and shrimps on the trout, mask with the sauce, and garnish with the quenelles and croutons. Sprinkle the quenelles with chopped truffles and the fish with chopped parsley.

*Turtle Steaks
in White Wine*

POUND 1 1/2 pounds very thin turtle steaks with the edge of a plate. Dredge the steaks with seasoned flour and brown them lightly and quickly in butter. Add 1/2 cup white wine and 1 tablespoon paprika, cover the pan and simmer the steaks for 1 hour, or until they are very tender. Transfer the turtle to a heated platter. To the pan juices add 1 cup sour cream and cook the sauce, stirring, until it is very hot. Do not let it boil. Pour the sauce over the turtle steaks and sprinkle them with paprika and chopped parsley.

PUT a layer of bacon slices in the bottom of a shallow pie plate. Put thin slices of cooked turtle meat over the bacon and cover with more bacon slices. Cover all with rich tart dough and bake the pie in a moderate oven (350° F.) for about 1 hour.

Remove the pie from the oven, make a small hole in the top, and pour in a mixture of 3/4 cup hot brown sauce and 1/4 cup Sherry. Serve at once.

Turtle Pie

POUND in a mortar 3 shallots and 1 small garlic clove, all chopped, 2 teaspoons chopped parsley, and 1 teaspoon each of chopped chervil and chopped chives until well blended. Add 2 tablespoons butter and the juice of 1/2 lemon. Work all together again and press through a fine sieve.

Slit open a 3-pound weakfish, remove the backbone and lay the fish, skin side down, in a shallow buttered baking dish. Season the fish with salt and pepper and spread it with the green butter. Bake the fish in a moderate oven (350° F.) for about 30 minutes, basting often with the butter.

Weakfish Veneziana

SKIN and bone 2 pounds fresh salmon or halibut. Cover the trimmings with boiling salted water and simmer the stock for 30 minutes.

Put the fish through the medium blade of a food chopper. Add 1 tablespoon each of cornstarch, flour, and salt. Grind twice more. Add 1 beaten egg and 1/8 teaspoon each of pepper and nutmeg. With a potato masher work in gradually 2 cups milk. Shape the mixture into balls the size of a walnut and simmer them in the stock until they are cooked through.

Fish Balls

It is not true that fish twice cooked is fish spoiled. Many recipes that follow are proof that fish twice cooked is fish improved.

COMBINE 1 cup freshly mashed potato with 1 cup cooked fish, such as haddock, sole, or cod, free of skin and bones. Stir in 2 eggs or 3 egg yolks, slightly beaten, and cool the mixture. Add salt and pepper to taste. Shape it into cakes, coat them *à l'anglaise*, and fry them in hot deep fat (385° F.) until they are golden brown.

Fish Cakes

CUT 1 1/2 pounds cooked fish into pieces. Put 2 tablespoons water, 1 tablespoon butter, and a little salt in a shallow pan, add the fish, and cook it

Creamed Fish au Gratin

169

over low heat until the water is cooked away. Make a border of duchess potatoes around a flat ovenproof serving dish, using a pastry bag. Spread 1 cup Mornay sauce in the center of the dish, put the hot fish on the sauce, and cover the fish with another cup of sauce. Sprinkle the sauce with grated Parmesan cheese and a little melted butter. Brush the potatoes with melted butter and brown them in a hot oven (450° F.) or under the broiler.

Deviled Fish   Cut 1 1/2 pounds leftover cooked fish or shellfish into pieces. Put 2 tablespoons water, 1 tablespoon butter, and a little salt in a shallow pan, add the fish, and cook it over low heat until the water is cooked away. Prepare 2 cups Mornay sauce. In a saucepan melt 2 tablespoons butter, add 1 1/2 teaspoons English mustard, and stir in 1 1/2 cups of the sauce. Combine the sauce and the fish and season with salt and pepper. Fill scallop shells with the mixture. Fold 2 tablespoons whipped cream into the remaining 1/2 cup of Mornay sauce, spread it over the fish in the shells, and sprinkle with grated Parmesan. Brown the topping under the broiler.

Fish Loaf   Combine 3 cups flaked cooked salmon, tuna, or any white-fleshed fish, with 3/4 cup fine bread crumbs, 6 tablespoons soft butter, 3 eggs, slightly beaten, 1 1/2 tablespoons minced parsley, a pinch of thyme, and salt and pepper to taste. Blend thoroughly, adding a little hot milk if the mixture needs moistening.

Put the mixture in a buttered mold, put the mold in a pan in 1 inch of hot water, and bake it in a moderately hot oven (375° F.) for 1 hour. Serve the loaf hot with shrimp sauce or any sauce based on *béchamel maigre*.

Hot Kedgeree   Cut into pieces 1 pound or more leftover fish such as salmon, cod, haddock, or halibut. Put 2 tablespoons water, 1 tablespoon butter, and a little salt in a shallow pan, add the fish, and cook it over low heat until the water is cooked away. Prepare rice pilaff as follows: In a saucepan melt 2 tablespoons butter, add 2 tablespoons finely chopped onion, and cook the onion until it is soft but not brown. Mix in 1 cup rice and add 2 cups boiling water and a little salt. Cook the rice, tightly covered, over low heat for 20 to 25 minutes, or until the rice has absorbed all the water. Turn the rice into a hot pan, add 1 tablespoon butter, and toss gently with a fork without crushing the grains. Mix 1 tablespoon curry powder into 4 cups béchamel sauce for fish. Add the fish and 2 hard-cooked eggs, chopped, and mix lightly. Spread half the rice in a hot serving dish and cover with half the fish mixture.

Put the remaining rice over the fish and top with the remaining fish. Sprinkle with 2 sieved hard-cooked egg yolks. Serve at once.

Salmon Croquettes

MELT 3 tablespoons butter in a saucepan over low heat. Stir in 3 tablespoons flour, add gradually 1 cup hot milk, and cook the sauce, stirring constantly, until it is smooth and thick. Add 2 cups minced cooked salmon, 1 tablespoon each of chopped parsley and onion, and salt and cayenne to taste. Cook the mixture over low heat for 10 minutes, stirring occasionally. Beat 1 egg lightly with 2 tablespoons heavy cream and stir it into the croquette mixture. Cook, stirring, for 1 minute, remove the pan from the heat, and add 1 teaspoon lemon juice.

Cool the mixture in a buttered shallow dish and shape it into croquettes. Roll the croquettes in fine bread crumbs, in 1 egg lightly beaten with 2 tablespoons water, and again in bread crumbs. Fry them, a few at a time, in hot deep fat (385° F.) until they are delicately browned.

Soufflé de Poisson

DISCARD the skin and bones from 2 cups leftover cooked fish and chop the flesh very finely. Heat the fish in 1 tablespoon butter and force it through a fine sieve to make a purée. Add the fish purée to 1 cup well-seasoned, thick béchamel sauce for fish. Beat 4 egg yolks and combine them with the fish-and-sauce mixture. Heat all together just to the boiling point, stirring briskly, but do not let the mixture boil. Cool the mixture to luke-warm. Beat 5 egg whites until they are stiff but not dry. Fold into the mixture thoroughly and carefully one-fourth of the beaten egg whites and add the remaining egg whites, cutting them in lightly and completely by raising and folding the mixture over and over. Pour the batter into a buttered and floured mold and bake the soufflé in a moderate oven (350° F.) for 25 to 30 minutes.

Salmon Sauté Florentine

COAT 4 salmon steaks lightly with flour and sauté them in 1/4 cup heated butter until they are nicely browned on each side. Season the steaks to taste with salt and pepper. Cook 3 cups chopped spinach in the water that clings to the leaves with 1 garlic clove, chopped, 1 teaspoon tarragon, and a little lemon juice for several minutes or until the spinach is tender. Serve the salmon steaks on the spinach and surround them with slices of sautéed potatoes mixed with sautéed sliced mushrooms.

Shellfish

The clam is a native American and the subject of endless interregional disputes, all of which are happily settled when chowder is temporarily forgotten, as here, and the clam is used in other native-born recipes and as a substitute for mussels in recipes from haute cuisine.

Clams Marinière

SCRUB well 6 dozen clams. Put them in a large kettle with 1 cup white wine, 1/4 cup butter, 1 large onion, 1 tablespoon chopped parsley, 1 bay leaf, and a pinch of thyme. Cover the kettle and cook the clams over high heat for 6 to 8 minutes, or until the shells open. Discard any clams that do not open. Pile the clams on individual serving dishes. Strain the sauce through a fine sieve, taste it for seasoning, reheat it, and add 1 tablespoon butter and 1 tablespoon finely chopped parsley. Pour the sauce over the clams and serve immediately.

Panned Clams

MELT 3/4 pound butter in a saucepan or chafing dish and add 1 1/2 quarts freshly shucked and drained whole clams. Cook the clams just long enough to heat them through. Add 3 teaspoons Worcestershire sauce and salt, pepper, and paprika to taste. Serve on buttered toast.

Chafing Dish Clams

SHUCK and chop enough freshly opened clams to measure 2 cups. Melt 2 tablespoons butter in the top of a chafing dish, and add the clams and 3 tablespoons Sherry. Cook for a minute or two and stir in 1 cup cream blended with 4 egg yolks. Heat through without boiling, stirring, add 1 tablespoon chopped chives, and serve on toast.

Clam Quiche

RESERVE 1 cup liquor from freshly shucked clams. Wash the clams and chop them finely to make 1 cup. Line a 9-inch plate with basic pie dough. Sauté 6 slices of bacon until crisp and drain them on absorbent paper. In the bacon fat sauté until soft but not brown 3 tablespoons minced onion. Beat 4 eggs lightly and add to them the reserved clam juice with 1 cup cream.

Season to taste with salt and pepper. Crumble the bacon and sprinkle the pie crust with the sautéed onion, the bacon, and the chopped clams. Add the custard mixture and bake the *quiche* in a moderately hot oven (375° F.) for 40 minutes, or until the custard is set and a knife inserted near the center comes out clean.

SAUTÉ 1 large onion and 2 stalks of celery, both finely chopped, in 1/4 cup butter until the vegetables are golden. Put 20 freshly shucked clams through a food chopper and add them to the vegetable mixture. Add salt and pepper and 1 cup cream and bring the mixture to a boil. Remove the pan from the heat and stir in 4 beaten egg yolks and 1/3 cup minced chives. Fill individual ramekins with the clams, sprinkle with buttered bread crumbs and bake in a hot oven (400° F.) until the topping is golden brown.

Deviled Clams

MELT 6 tablespoons butter in a large heavy skillet and in it sauté until transparent 1 small onion, finely minced. Add 2 cups finely diced cooked potatoes and 2 cups chopped clams. Add salt and freshly ground black pepper to taste. Spread the mixture evenly over the bottom of the skillet and cook over low heat for 10 minutes. Pour 1/2 cup cream over the clams and continue cooking until the hash is nicely browned on the bottom, about 30 minutes. Fold the hash with a spatula and slide it onto a heated platter. Garnish with lemon wedges and chopped parsley.

Clam Hash

PUT 18 well-scrubbed large clams in a kettle with just enough water to cover the bottom. Cover the kettle and steam the clams over high heat until the shells open. Discard any clams that do not open. Remove the clams from the shells and discard the tough necks. Chop the clams finely and mix them with 3 tablespoons finely chopped mushrooms, sautéed in butter for 1 minute, 2 tablespoons each of finely chopped shallots or scallions and bread crumbs, 1 1/2 tablespoons minced chives, and 1 teaspoon minced parsley or chervil. Stir in 1 teaspoon Sherry and just enough dry white wine to moisten the mixture. Heap the mixture into the clam shells, sprinkle with buttered bread crumbs, a dash of paprika if desired, and bake the shells in a moderate oven (350° F.) for about 15 minutes, or until the crumbs are golden.

Stuffed Clams Normande

SAUTÉ 2 garlic cloves in 3/4 cup olive oil until they are lightly brown. Discard the garlic and to the olive oil add 3 anchovy filets, chopped, 2

Clam Soup

tablespoons minced parsley, and 3/4 cup dry red wine. Cook the mixture for 5 minutes and add 4 teaspoons tomato paste, 3/4 cup warm water, and 3/4 teaspoon each of salt and freshly ground pepper and cook 4 minutes more.

Add 5 dozen well-scrubbed littleneck clams in their shells and cook them for about 5 minutes, or until the shells open. Put 2 slices of toasted Italian bread in each soup plate and pour the clam broth over them. Serve the clams separately in soup plates.

Clam Fritters Mix 2 cups finely chopped clams with 2 well-beaten egg yolks, 1 cup cracker crumbs, 1 tablespoon finely minced parsley, salt and pepper to taste, a pinch of cayenne, and enough clam juice to make a heavy batter. Fold in 3 stiffly beaten egg whites. Drop the batter by spoonfuls into hot deep fat (370° F.) and cook the fritters until they are brown on all sides, turning them once.

Clams COMBINE in a bowl the crumbled crusts from 4 slices of stale bread, 1 or
Origanata 2 garlic cloves, finely chopped, 1 heaping tablespoon parsley, finely chopped, a generous pinch of orégano, and salt and pepper to taste. Mix thoroughly and blend in enough olive oil to moisten the mixture.

Open 25 or 30 clams, leaving them on the half shell. Put 1 teaspoon of the bread crumb mixture on each clam. Put the clams in a shallow baking pan on a bed of rock salt or crumbled aluminum foil and brown them under the broiler for 5 minutes.

Cleaning *When boiled crabs are cool enough to handle, crack the claws and legs*
Crabs *and remove the meat. Break off the "apron," or segment that folds under the body from the rear, wedge a strong knife into the opening, and force the shells apart. Discard the gills and sand bag and remove the meat. Eighteen average-sized crabs will yield about 1 1/2 pounds crab meat, or enough to make six to eight main-dish servings.*

Boiled Crabs PLUNGE live crabs into rapidly boiling water seasoned with a dash of vinegar, salt, and cayenne, or into a court bouillon made by simmering a *bouquet garni* of 1 stalk of celery, 1 sprig each of tarragon and thyme, 4 sprigs of parsley, and half a bay leaf in half water and half dry white wine for 30 minutes. Simmer the crabs for 15 minutes.

MAKE a sauce by combining 1 1/2 cups light cream, 1/4 cup each of butter and A-1 sauce, 3 scant tablespoons mustard, 3/4 teaspoon sugar, and salt and pepper to taste, and 1 1/2 cups hollandaise sauce. Heat the sauce, stirring constantly, and add the juice of 1 lemon. Add 1 1/2 pounds lump crab meat, heat well, and serve on wild rice.

Crab Meat Andrew

BROWN 1 pound crab meat very lightly in 1/4 cup butter. Blanch and split 3/4 cup almonds and sauté them until golden in 3 tablespoons butter. Add the almonds to the crab meat along with 1/3 cup cream and 3 tablespoons finely chopped parsley. Season the mixture with salt and white pepper to taste, bring it to a boil, and cook it for 2 minutes. Serve on freshly made toast.

Sautéed Crab Meat in Cream

IN a saucepan sauté 1/2 cup chopped onion in 1/4 cup butter until it is soft. Combine the onion and butter with 1 pound crab meat, 1 cup soft bread crumbs, soaked in water and squeezed dry, 1 egg, beaten, 1/2 cup finely chopped celery, 1 teaspoon finely chopped parsley, 1/2 teaspoon mixed dried thyme, sage, and marjoram, and salt and pepper to taste. Mix all together lightly but thoroughly. Pile the mixture into 6 crab shells. Dot with butter and bake the shells in a very hot oven (450° F.) for 15 to 20 minutes, or until they are golden brown.

Stuffed Crabs

MELT 2 tablespoons butter in a saucepan, add 1 pound crab meat, and warm it over very low heat. Add 1 1/2 teaspoons English mustard mixed to a thin paste with a little water. Prepare about 1 1/2 cups Mornay sauce and add 1 cup to the crab meat with 1/2 teaspoon salt and a little freshly ground pepper. Fill individual baking shells with the mixture. Add 2 tablespoons whipped cream to the remaining Mornay sauce and spread the filled shells with it. Sprinkle with a little grated Parmesan cheese and brown the topping under the broiler or in a hot oven (450° F).

Deviled Crab Meat Mornay

COMBINE 1 medium green pepper and 1 pimiento, both finely diced, 2 teaspoons each of dry English mustard and salt, 1/2 teaspoon white pepper, 2 eggs, and 1 cup thick mayonnaise. Turn the mixture into 3 pounds lump crab meat and mix gently. Heap the crab meat loosely into 8 crab shells,

Crab Meat Imperial

coat it lightly with mayonnaise, and sprinkle with paprika. Bake the shells in a moderate oven (350° F.) for 15 minutes. Serve at once, or let the crab meat cool, chill it, and serve cold. Serves 8.

Crab Meat Dewey

SAUTÉ 1/2 cup sliced mushrooms and 2 tablespoons each of chopped red and green pepper in 2 tablespoons butter for about 10 minutes, or until the vegetables are tender.

Sauté 1 pound lump crab meat in 1/4 cup butter until it is thoroughly heated. Sprinkle the crab meat with salt and a little cayenne, pour over it 1/4 cup warmed brandy, and ignite the spirit. When the flame dies, add 1 cup heavy cream and a *bouquet garni* composed of 3 sprigs of parsley, 1 sprig of thyme, and 1/2 bay leaf. Cook, covered, over boiling water for 10 minutes.

Add the flesh from 6 cooked frogs' legs and 1/2 cup oyster crabs and cook for 10 minutes longer. Stir in the vegetables. Serve crab meat Dewey from a chafing dish or turn the mixture into individual shells or ramekins and glaze the tops under the broiler.

Crab Meat and Shrimps Creole

MELT 2 tablespoons butter or heat 2 tablespoons salad oil in a saucepan, add 1 onion, chopped, and cook it until it is golden. Add 5 or 6 mushrooms, chopped or sliced, 1/2 cup each of chopped celery and chopped green pepper, and 1/4 cup chopped pimiento and cook the mixture for a few minutes. Add 3 cups freshly stewed or canned tomatoes, bring the mixture to a boil, and simmer it for about 1 hour. Mix 1 tablespoon cornstarch with 2 tablespoons cold water and add it to the mixture. Cook the mixture, stirring until it thickens. Correct the seasoning with salt and add a little freshly ground pepper and 1 tablespoon chopped parsley.

Add 2 pounds shrimps, cooked in court bouillon, shelled, and deveined, and 2 pounds picked-over crab meat. Bring again to the boiling point. The mixture may be kept hot over boiling water. Serves 12.

King Crab Salad

ON a salad plate arrange a bed of shredded lettuce and on it lay a slice of tomato. On the tomato put an artichoke heart stuffed with a mixture of cold cooked asparagus tips, cut green beans, cauliflower buds, and green peas.

Arrange 2 chilled King crab legs on the vegetables and garnish the arrangement with strips of red and green peppers. Around the artichoke and tomato sprinkle finely chopped hard-cooked egg, and serve the salad with Thousand Island dressing. Serves 1.

Crab Meat Dewey

Baltimore Crab Cakes BEAT 1 egg and combine it with 1 1/2 cups soft white bread crumbs. Brown in butter 1 small onion and 1 small green pepper, both minced, and 2 tablespoons finely chopped celery and add it to the egg mixture, with 1 pound flaked crab meat, 1/2 teaspoon salt, 1/4 teaspoon dried thyme, and a few dashes of cayenne. Mix well, and stir in 2 tablespoons mayonnaise and 2 teaspoons minced parsley. Chill the mixture for 1 hour, form it into small cakes, and fry them in hot deep fat (375° F.). Drain on absorbent paper and serve with tartar sauce.

Crab Meat Soufflé MELT 1/4 cup butter, stir in 3 tablespoons flour, and add gradually 1 cup hot milk, stirring constantly until the sauce is smooth and thickened. Stir in 4 egg yolks, lightly beaten, 1 cup shredded cooked crab meat, 1 tablespoon lemon juice, a pinch each of nutmeg and cayenne, and salt and pepper to taste, and cool. Fold in 6 egg whites, stiffly beaten, and turn the mixture into a buttered soufflé dish. Bake the soufflé in a moderate oven (350° F.) for 35 to 40 minutes and serve immediately with a light white-wine sauce.

Cleaning Soft Shelled Crabs *Use scissors to trim the soft shell. Cut off the head, about one-fourth inch behind the eyes. Squeeze gently to force out the green bubble behind the eyes. The fluid in the bubble has a disagreeable flavor. Lift the soft shell where it comes to a point at each side and cut off the white gills. Peel back the apron and cut it off. There is very little waste. Dip the crabs in cold salted water, dry them on a towel, and prepare them in any of the following ways. Serve 2 or 3 to each person.*

Sautéed Soft Shelled Crabs CLEAN, wash, and dry 12 soft-shelled crabs. In a large skillet melt 1/2 cup butter. Sprinkle the crabs with salt and pepper, dredge them in flour, and sauté them, 6 at a time, back side down, in the hot butter for 5 minutes. Turn the crabs and sauté them for 3 minutes longer. Transfer them to a heated platter and sprinkle with lemon juice. Pour the pan juices over them.

Soft Shelled Crabs Sautéed à la Diable SAUTÉ 12 cleaned, washed, and dried soft-shelled crabs that have been dredged in 1 cup fine dry bread crumbs mixed with 2 teaspoons chili powder. Remove the crabs to a heated serving platter and add to the pan juices 2 teaspoons tarragon vinegar, 1 tablespoon finely chopped parsley, and a dash of Worcestershire sauce. Pour the mixture over the crabs and serve garnished with lemon wedges.

SAUTÉ 12 cleaned, washed, and dried soft-shelled crabs and transfer them to a heated serving platter. Add 3/4 cup shredded blanched almonds to the pan juices and sauté them, stirring, until golden. Pour almonds and pan juices over the crabs and serve garnished with lemon wedges and sprigs of parsley.

Soft Shelled Crabs Sautéed Amandine

CLEAN, wash, and dry 12 soft-shelled crabs and soak them in 2 cups lightly salted milk for 15 minutes. Drain and dry the crabs, roll them lightly in flour, and arrange them on a shallow, buttered baking pan, tucking the claws close to the bodies. Put 1 teaspoon soft butter on each crab and sprinkle them with lemon juice. Broil the crabs under the broiler for about 10 minutes, or until they are a delicate brown, turn them, and broil them for 5 minutes longer.

Broiled Soft Shelled Crabs

Transfer the crabs to a serving platter and sprinkle them with freshly ground pepper. Pour over the crabs a little melted butter, sprinkle them with chopped parsley, and serve garnished with lemon wedges.

CLEAN, wash, and dry 12 soft-shelled crabs. Sprinkle the crabs with salt, dip them into 2 eggs beaten with 1/4 cup water and roll them in 1/2 cup cornmeal mixed with 1/4 cup flour and 1/2 teaspoon pepper or in fine dry bread crumbs. Fry the crabs two at a time in hot deep fat or oil (360° F.) for 3 minutes, or until they are golden brown.

Deep Fried Soft Shelled Crabs

Arrange the crabs on a warm serving platter, garnish with watercress, and serve with tartar mayonnaise.

The crayfish is a fresh-water shellfish that is equally popular in France, where it is called écrevisse, *in Sweden, where they call it* kräftor *and consume enormous quantities boiled with dill and washed down with aquavit, and in Louisiana, where the natives say* crawfish.

Wash the crayfish in cold water and tear off the tiny wing in the center of the tail. This loosens and brings with it the small black intestine.

Cleaning Crayfish

Shrimps in Garlic Sauce

IN a kettle combine 1 gallon water, 1 cup dry white wine, 1 onion, thinly sliced, 1 garlic clove, crushed, 1 stalk of celery, 12 allspice berries, 6 whole cloves, 3 bay leaves, 1 teaspoon caraway seeds, 1 sprig of thyme, 1/2 teaspoon cayenne pepper, and enough salt to make the liquid quite salty. Simmer for 30 minutes. Wash 4 dozen crayfish well and soak them for 10 to 15 minutes in a brine made of 1 gallon water and 1/2 cup salt. Drain the crayfish, add them to the court bouillon together with 2 lemons, thinly sliced, and boil them for about 20 minutes. Cool them in the liquid and, just before serving, arrange them on a bed of cracked ice and garnish with parsley.

Boiled Crayfish

Or the crayfish may be boiled in salted water with 6 large heads of fresh dill.

SAUTÉ quickly 3 pounds washed, cleaned, and dried crayfish tails in 1/2 cup olive oil for about 5 minutes, shaking the pan over high heat. The bottom of the skillet should be covered with oil to a depth of about 1/4 inch. Season the tails with salt and pepper and remove them to a heated serving platter. Add to the oil remaining in the pan 4 garlic cloves, very finely minced, and 1/2 cup finely chopped parsley. Shake the pan over the heat for a few seconds and pour the sauce over the crayfish. Serve immediately. Shrimps or prawns may be substituted for the crayfish in this recipe. The dish is very like the famous Italian *scampi*.

Ecrevisses Provençale
CRAYFISH IN GARLIC SAUCE

Shrimps in Garlic Sauce

WASH and clean 4 dozen live crayfish. Pour into a large pot 1 cup each of dry white wine, tarragon vinegar, and beef stock, and 1/2 cup Champagne. Add 1/4 cup fresh pork fat, cut in small cubes, 2 small carrots, scraped and diced, 4 medium onions, peeled and chopped, 1 dozen small shallots, peeled and chopped, 2 small garlic cloves, crushed, 1 teaspoon grated orange rind, 1 generous tablespoon coarse salt, 1 teaspoon whole peppercorns, gently bruised but not crushed, a tiny pinch each of nutmeg, cloves, freshly ground white pepper, and cayenne, and a *bouquet garni* composed of 3 sprigs of parsley, 1 sprig each of thyme and tarragon, and 1 bay leaf, tied together.

Ecrevisses Cardinal de M. Le Prieur
CRAYFISH PRIOR

Cook the court bouillon until it is reduced by half and add the drained crayfish. Cook them in the liquid until they are a bright cardinal red, and simmer for 10 minutes longer. Put the crayfish in a heated soup tureen. Reduce the court bouillon further and pour it over the crayfish.

MIX to a paste 3/4 cup each of cream cheese and Roquefort cheese and 1/2 cup olive oil and stir in 1 truffle and 2 pimientos, both chopped. Spread

Crayfish Sarapico

half the paste in the center of a large sheet of aluminum foil and cover it with 1/2 pound shelled crayfish meat. Cover the crayfish with the remaining paste and top with another 1/2 pound crayfish meat. Garnish with 4 cooked shrimps, shelled and deveined, 2 slices of lemon, a little chopped parsley, and 4 thin slices of American cheese. Add 1/4 cup Champagne, the juice of 1 lemon, and a pinch of salt. Close the aluminum foil securely and bake in a moderate oven (350° F.) for 30 minutes. Serves 4.

Ecrevisses à la Bordelaise　WASH and clean 4 dozen crayfish. Melt 2 tablespoons butter in a saucepan and add 1 carrot and 1 onion, both finely diced, 1 tablespoon chopped shallots or onion, 2 sprigs of parsley, 1 garlic clove, crushed, a little thyme, and 1 small bay leaf, crumbled. Cook the vegetables very slowly for about 15 minutes, or until they are soft. Add 4 tomatoes, peeled, seeded, and chopped, 1/2 teaspoon salt, and the crayfish, and cook the mixture over high heat, shaking the pan constantly, until the crayfish turn red. Add 1/4 cup warmed Cognac and ignite the spirit. When the flame dies, add 2 cups white wine, and cook the mixture over high heat for 12 minutes longer. Remove the crayfish to a heated deep serving dish. Cook the liquid until it is reduced by half and thicken it by swirling in *beurre manié* made by creaming 3 tablespoons butter with 1 teaspoon flour. Correct the seasoning with salt and add a little freshly ground pepper. Pour the sauce over the crayfish and sprinkle with chopped parsley.

The lobster, unlike its near relative the spiny lobster or crayfish, is a denizen of cold Northern waters on both sides of the Atlantic. Those who may have tender scruples about cooking a live lobster—the only way a lobster should be cooked—may purchase lobster meat frozen or canned or the frozen tails of South African rock lobster. One presumes, naturally, that lobster thus purchased was in the first instance cooked alive. A lobster that weighs about two and a half pounds will yield about two cups of meat; heavier lobsters yield proportionately more meat, lighter, proportionately less.

Homard aux Fines Herbes　POACH 6 1 1/2-pound lobsters in court bouillon for 12 to 15 minutes. Remove the lobsters from the liquid and halve them lengthwise. Reduce the court bouillon by three-fourths.

In a saucepan melt 3 tablespoons butter and stir in, off the heat, 3 tablespoons flour. Stir in gradually 3/4 cup of the hot, reduced court bouillon, 1 1/2 cups heavy cream, and 1/2 cup dry white wine and cook the sauce, stirring constantly, until it is smooth and slightly thickened. Cook it over low heat, stirring occasionally, for 10 minutes, then stir in 3 egg yolks lightly beaten with a little of the hot sauce. Be careful not to let the sauce boil after the egg yolks are added. Stir in 1 teaspoon each of chopped parsley, chervil, and tarragon, and correct the seasoning with salt and pepper.

Arrange the halved lobsters on a heated platter, cover them with the sauce, and garnish the plate with parsley.

PLUNGE a 2 1/2- to 3-pound lobster into boiling water, and boil it for 20 to 25 minutes. Remove the lobster to drain and cool. Cut off the claws and legs so that only the body of the lobster is left. Hold the lobster with its top side up, and, using kitchen shears, cut an oval opening in the top of the shell from the base of the head to the tail. Remove all the meat from the body and claws.

Baked Lobster Savannah

Cut the lobster meat into cubes and put in it a buttered baking dish with 1 tablespoon butter and 1/4 teaspoon salt. Bake the lobster in a moderately hot oven (375° F.) for 20 minutes. Drain off the liquid.

Prepare 1 cup cream sauce, enrich it with 2 egg yolks, and add 2 tablespoons Sherry, or to taste. To the sauce add the lobster meat, 1/2 cup chopped fresh mushrooms, and 1/4 cup diced green pepper. Cook the mixture over medium heat, stirring constantly, for 15 minutes. Remove the pan from the heat and stir in 1 pimiento, sliced, 1 teaspoon paprika, and salt and pepper to taste.

Pile the filling into the lobster shell and sprinkle it with a mixture of 1/4 cup each of fresh bread crumbs and grated Parmesan cheese. Set the lobster on a shallow pan and bake it in a moderately hot oven (375° F.) for 15 minutes, or until the topping is golden. Arrange the lobster on a heated serving dish, sprinkle it with several tablespoons of Sherry, and garnish it with lemon wedges. Serves 2.

CRACK the claws and cut the tails of 5 pounds live lobsters into thick slices. Reserve the rest for another use. Cook the lobster in 6 tablespoons butter melted with 3 tablespoons oil, turning the pieces often until the shells are red on all sides. Add 1 small carrot, grated, 2 shallots, 1 onion and 1 garlic clove, all finely chopped, and a *bouquet garni* of thyme, parsley, and 1 bay leaf. When the vegetables are slightly soft, add 2 tablespoons tomato paste, 1 tablespoon *glace de viande*, a pinch each of saffron and curry powder, a good pinch of cayenne, and 2 cups dry white wine. Add salt and pepper,

Lobster à l'Américaine Brittany

cover the pan, and simmer the mixture for about 30 minutes. Pour 1/4 cup warmed brandy over the surface and ignite the spirit. When the flame dies, stir in 1/4 cup heavy cream. Serve in a deep dish and sprinkle with finely chopped parsley, chives, and tarragon.

Gratin de Homard à la Nantua

POACH 3 pounds live lobsters for 15 minutes in just enough salted water to cover. Drain them and put them in a saucepan over low heat with 1/4 cup melted butter. Turn the lobsters in the butter for a few minutes. Add 1/2 cup each of dry white wine and mushroom liquor, made by simmering 1/2 cup sliced mushrooms for a few minutes in water barely to cover with salt and a little lemon juice. Cover, bring the liquid to a boil, and simmer it for 5 to 6 minutes. Drain the lobsters, reserving the liquid, and remove the meat from the shells. Slice the meat and arrange it in a heated shallow baking dish with the cooked mushrooms and 1 truffle, thinly sliced.

In a saucepan over low heat combine 1 tablespoon butter and 1 1/2 tablespoons flour. Add gradually the lobster liquid slightly reduced, 1 cup cream, and 2 tablespoons lobster butter. Simmer the sauce for 3 minutes and pour it over the lobster. Sprinkle with a little grated Swiss cheese, and delicately brown the top under the broiler. Serves 2.

Nova Scotia Lobster Bluenose

SIMMER together for 10 minutes over very low heat 1 quart cooked lobster meat, cut in small pieces, and 1/4 cup sweet butter, stirring frequently. Mix in 1/2 cup cider vinegar and season with 1 teaspoon sugar and a dash each of white pepper, cayenne, nutmeg, and salt to taste. Simmer the mixture for 5 minutes more, without letting it come to a boil. Stir in 1 cup hot heavy cream. Serve on freshly made toast.

Soufflé de Homard Plaza-Athénée

REMOVE the claws and tails from 5 pounds of lobster, and with a large heavy knife divide each of the body sections into three or four pieces. In a large saucepan make the following vegetable mirepoix: Melt 2 tablespoons butter, add 1 medium carrot, finely diced, 2 tablespoons finely chopped onion, and 1 tablespoon chopped chives. Cook the mirepoix over very low heat until the vegetables are soft but not brown. Add 1 tablespoon chopped parsley and remove the pan from the heat.

Sprinkle the cut-up lobsters with salt and pepper. In a large shallow pan, cook them until they are red in 1/2 cup very hot salad oil. Put the lobster pieces in the saucepan with the mirepoix and sprinkle them with 1 teaspoon paprika. Mix all together and add 1 cup heavy cream, 1/2 cup dry white wine, and 2 tablespoons Cognac. Bring the sauce to a boil and cook the lobsters for 18 to 20 minutes. Remove them from the pan, carefully separate the meat from the shells, and cut the meat into slices 1/4 inch thick. Over high heat reduce the liquid remaining in the pan by about half. Add 1 cup cream sauce and 3 tablespoons each of heavy cream and dry Sherry. Strain the sauce and combine half of it with the lobster meat. Butter two 1-quart molds or straight-sided soufflé dishes and divide the lobster mixture between them. Set the rest of the sauce aside to keep warm, stirring it from time to time.

Prepare a cheese soufflé mixture as follows: Melt 2 tablespoons butter in a saucepan, add 1/4 cup flour, and cook the *roux* until it starts to turn golden. Stir in 3/4 cup hot milk and cook the sauce for about 5 minutes, or until it is very thick, stirring constantly. Add 1/2 teaspoon salt and a little cayenne. Beat 5 egg yolks well, combine them with the first mixture, and heat all together just to the boiling point, stirring briskly. Do not let the sauce boil. Add 3/4 cup grated Parmesan or dry Swiss cheese. Beat 5 egg whites until they are stiff but not dry. Fold into the mixture thoroughly and carefully one-fourth of the beaten egg whites and add the remaining egg whites, cutting them in lightly and completely by raising and folding the mixture over and over.

Spoon the cheese soufflé mixture over the lobster-and-sauce mixture in the molds. Bake the soufflés in a moderate oven (350° F.) for 18 to 20 minutes, or until they are puffed and golden brown. To serve, put some of the top of the soufflé on one side of each plate and some of the lobster mixture from the bottom on the other side. Pass the reserved lobster sauce separately.

In a mixing bowl combine 1 1/2 cups lobster meat, 2 tablespoons each of finely chopped parsley and dry vermouth, and salt and pepper to taste. Line a 9-inch flan ring with any unsweetened pastry and chill it for about 1 hour. Brush the surface of the pastry with white of egg and fill it with the lobster. Beat lightly 5 eggs, 1 1/2 cups milk, and a pinch of cayenne, and pour the custard over the lobster. Dust the *quiche* lightly with paprika and bake it in a very hot oven (450° F.) for 10 minutes. Lower the heat to moderate (350° F.) and bake the *quiche* for about 20 minutes longer,

Lobster Quiche

or until the custard is set and a knife inserted near the center comes out clean. Serve warm.

Crab Meat Quiche   Substitute crab meat for the lobster meat to make a crab-meat *quiche.*

Chausson de   IN a heavy saucepan melt 3 tablespoons butter and in it sauté 1 small onion,
Homard   finely chopped, until the onion turns golden. Add 6 shallots, finely chopped,
à l'Américaine   5 ripe tomatoes, peeled, seeded, and chopped, 1 garlic clove, chopped, 3 tablespoons chopped parsley, 1 tablespoon chopped fresh tarragon, 1 teaspoon fresh thyme, and half a bay leaf, and simmer the mixture over low heat for 1 hour. Stir in 3 tablespoons tomato purée and keep the mixture hot.

Split 5 pounds live lobsters, discard the intestinal tracts, and reserve the coral and liver. Cut the tails into sections and remove and crack the claws. In a skillet sauté the lobster in 1/2 cup olive oil until the shells are red, turning the pieces constantly with a large spoon. Put the lobster in the sauce, add 1 1/2 cups dry white wine, 1/4 cup Cognac, and a pinch of cayenne. Cover the skillet and simmer the lobsters for 20 to 25 minutes. Pick out the meat and discard the shells.

Roll out puff paste into a circle 1/3 inch thick on a lightly floured board. Arrange the lobster meat on half the circle and pour a little sauce over the meat. Fold the puff paste over the lobster meat, pinch the edges firmly together, and brush with 1 egg, beaten. Bake the turnover in a very hot oven (450° F.) for 15 minutes, lower the oven temperature to moderate (350° F.), and bake the turnovers for about 20 minutes longer.

Stir into the remaining sauce the lobster coral and liver and bring the sauce to a boil. Add salt and pepper and stir in 2/3 cup heavy cream and 1 tablespoon each of butter and chopped parsley. To serve, cut the *chausson* into strips and pass the sauce separately.

Lobster Strudel   REMOVE all the meat from a large boiled lobster and chop it finely. Add 1 cup each of chopped cooked shrimps and flaked cooked fish, such as cod or sole or flounder, and 4 medium mushrooms, finely diced and gently sautéed for about 5 minutes in 2 tablespoons butter.

In a saucepan melt 1/4 cup butter, stir in 3 tablespoons flour, and add gradually 1 cup hot milk, stirring constantly. Cook the sauce, stirring, until it is smooth and thick. Stir in 1/4 cup grated cheese and 2 tablespoons heavy cream and season the sauce with a little mustard, salt, and pepper.

Make strudel dough and brush it with melted butter. Sprinkle the fish filling on half the dough and spoon the sauce over the filling by the tablespoonfuls. Roll the strudel, brush it generously with melted butter, and bake it in a moderately hot oven (375° F.) for about 45 minutes, or until browned, basting frequently with butter.

CHOP 1 pound cooked lobster meat finely, add salt and pepper to taste, and beat in very gradually 3/4 cup heavy cream. Fold in 2 stiffly beaten egg whites and turn the cream into a buttered fish mold decorated with truffles cut in fancy shapes. Put the mold in a shallow pan of hot water and bake it in a moderate oven (350° F.) for 20 minutes, until it is firm. Unmold the mousse onto a warmed platter, garnish it with lemon wedges and parsley, and serve it with lobster sauce flavored with Sherry.

Lobster Mousse

If mussels were as rare as sturgeon, they would perhaps be more greatly sought after; but their very numbers have deprived them of the public regard, at least in our own country and at least until recent years. Mussels are still to be had for the gathering along our shores, and in cities with foreign populations they may be purchased for a pittance at the fishmonger's. Mussels are not unlike clams in flavor; they are frequently more tender than clams. They tend to secrete sand in the crevices of their blue-back, pearly shells, so that they demand scrupulous washing and scrubbing.

SCRUB 3 quarts of mussels with a stiff brush and wash them thoroughly in several changes of cold water and scrape off the beards. Discard any with open shells. Put them in a kettle with 1/4 cup water and a little parsley and freshly ground pepper. Cover the kettle tightly and cook the mussels over high heat for 4 to 5 minutes, or until the shells open. Turn them into a covered dish and keep them warm.

Strain the broth and let the sand settle to the bottom. Pour the cleared broth carefully into a sauce bowl and serve separately.

*Moules
au Naturel*
STEAMED MUSSELS

SCRUB thoroughly with a stiff brush in a large quantity of water the desired number of very fresh mussels and scrape off the beards. Put the mussels in a kettle and for each quart of mussels add 1 quart of water, 1 small chopped onion, 2 sprigs of parsley, a little thyme, 1/2 bay leaf, 6 peppercorns and a scant 1/2 cup dry white wine. Cover the kettle and cook the mussels over

*Mussels for
Garnishing*

high heat about 6 to 8 minutes or until the shells open wide. Remove the mussels from their shells and return them to the liquor. The liquor may be strained and used in the sauce for the fish dish that the mussels are to garnish.

Mussel Soup   SCRUB 4 dozen mussels with a stiff brush and scrape off the beards. In a large kettle heat 3/4 cup olive oil with 2 garlic cloves, 3 tablespoons tomato purée, and 3/4 teaspoon salt. Add also a little piece of hot red pepper, if desired. Add the mussels, cover the kettle, and cook the mussels rapidly until they open. Add 3/4 teaspoon orégano. Cut a long Italian loaf into inch-thick slices, toast the bread, and rub it well with garlic. Put 2 slices of garlic toast in each soup plate and serve the soup hot.

Moules   SCRUB 3 quarts of mussels with a stiff brush, wash them several times in
à la Crème   cold water, and scrape off the beards. Melt 3 tablespoons butter in a kettle.
CREAMED MUSSELS   Add 1/2 cup thinly sliced carrots and a *bouquet garni* composed of parsley, thyme, chervil, and tarragon, and cook the mixture slowly for about 20 minutes, until the carrots are tender. Add the mussels, cover the kettle tightly, and cook them over high heat for 4 to 5 minutes, or until the mussel shells open. Discard one shell from each mussel and keep the mussels warm in a covered dish.

Cook 1 1/2 cups chopped mushrooms in 2 tablespoons melted butter until they are tender. Stir in 1/4 cup flour and cook, stirring, for a few minutes without letting the flour brown. Strain the mussel broth through a double thickness of cheesecloth, add it gradually, and cook for 5 minutes. Correct the seasoning and finish the sauce with another 2 tablespoons butter and 3/4 cup heavy cream. A trickle of lemon juice or vinegar may be added.

Arrange the mussels on a heated platter and serve them coated with the sauce.

Moules   COOK large mussels, scrubbed, thoroughly washed, and the beards removed,
à la Villeroi   in a little water in a covered kettle over high heat for 4 to 5 minutes, or
FRIED MUSSELS   until the shells open. Remove the mussels from their shells, dry them well on a cloth, and dip them in *sauce Villeroi*, made with the cooking liquor of the mussels. Chill the coated mussels thoroughly and dip them in 2 eggs that have been lightly beaten with a little salt and pepper and 2 teaspoons oil. Coat the dipped mussels with flour or fine bread crumbs, dip them again in the egg mixture, and give them a final coating of bread crumbs. Fry the mussels in hot butter or oil until they are nicely browned on both sides.

STEAM open 3 quarts mussels in a kettle with 1 garlic clove, minced. Set aside 18 large mussels and remove the rest from their shells. Keep them all warm.

Crush 4 anchovies with 3 tablespoons butter in a mortar and force the mixture through a fine sieve. Sauté 1 onion and 1 garlic clove, chopped very finely, in 2 tablespoons butter until the onion is transparent. Add the anchovy butter and 1/2 cup each of tomato purée and grated bread crumbs moistened with a little milk and well drained. Add salt, pepper, and paprika to taste, stir in enough carefully strained liquid from the mussels to bring the mixture to the consistency of a rather thin sauce, and cook it slowly for 15 minutes. Stir in the yolks of 2 eggs beaten lightly with 1/2 cup cream and a little of the hot sauce. Add the mussels and 1 1/2 tablespoons butter and stir for 2 minutes, or until the mussels are heated through, being careful not to let the sauce boil.

Serve the mussels in a heated serving dish surrounded by the reserved mussels in their shells.

Suçarelle
de Moules
MUSSEL SUÇARELLE

DROP a live hard-shelled crab into 2 quarts rapidly boiling court bouillon and simmer it for 15 minutes. When it is cool enough to handle, pick out the meat and force it through a fine sieve.

Steam open 3 quarts well-scrubbed mussels, discard the shells, and put the mussels in a casserole to keep warm.

Melt 3 tablespoons butter in a saucepan. Stir in 2 tablespoons flour and cook the *roux*, stirring, for a few minutes without letting it brown. Stir in the crab purée, 1/2 cup heavy cream, and 1/4 cup each of grated Gruyère and Parmesan cheese. Mix thoroughly and moisten the purée with enough mussel liquor to give it the consistency of a thick sauce.

Cover the mussels in the casserole with the sauce and sprinkle with 1 tablespoon dry bread crumbs mixed with 1/2 tablespoon each of grated Gruyère and Parmesan. Bake the mussels in a moderate oven (350° F.) for 15 minutes, or until the crumbs are lightly browned. Individual casseroles or scallop shells may be used instead of the large casserole.

Moules
au Gratin
MUSSELS
WITH CHEESE

HOLD an oyster firmly, cupside down, on a towel on the table. Insert the tip of the oyster knife—a sturdy, blunt-tipped blade—near the pointed edge

How to Shuck
an Oyster

of the oyster. Twist the knife to get enough leverage to force the shells apart. Slide the knife close to the upper shell and cut the muscle. Then slide the knife close to the lower shell to cut that connection.

Oysters on the Half Shell   Serve the oysters in the deep shell. Lemon wedges and freshly ground black pepper are the usual seasonings.

Fried Oysters   DRY raw oysters well, dip them in flour, and coat in beaten egg and in fresh bread crumbs. Fry them in hot deep fat (385° F.) until they are brown, not more than 1 to 2 minutes. Drain on absorbent paper.

Roast Oysters   SCRUB and rinse under cold running water 3 dozen oysters in their shells. Put the oysters on a baking sheet and roast them in a very hot oven (450° F.) for about 15 minutes, or until the shells begin to open. Serve in the shells with plenty of hot melted butter on the side.

Oysters Eleanore   ARRANGE 3 dozen oysters in their deep shells on a tray of coarse salt and bake them in a hot oven (400° F.) for 2 minutes. Spread each with 1/2 teaspoon chili sauce. Combine 1 cup Mornay sauce with 2 tablespoons whipped cream. Spread the sauce over the oysters and return them to the oven or broiler to brown.

Oysters Bordelaise   ARRANGE 3 dozen oysters in their deep shells on a bed of rock salt in a baking dish, and pour over the oysters a mixture of 1 teaspoon salt, 1/2 teaspoon paprika, 2 tablespoons finely chopped shallots or scallions, and 1/2 cup dry red wine. Sprinkle the oysters with bread crumbs and bake them in a hot oven (425° F.) for 3 to 5 minutes, or until they are hot and plump.

Oysters Delmonico   DICE 4 slices of lean bacon and fry the dice until it is crisp in a small skillet over low heat. In a saucepan melt 2 tablespoons butter, add 10 shallots, finely chopped, and 3 small red and 3 green peppers, cut in small squares. Sauté the vegetables for about 5 minutes or until they are tender. Season to taste with salt and a dash of cayenne. Drain 3 dozen freshly opened oysters and arrange them on the half shell. Cover the oysters with the bacon and vegetable mixture, sprinkle them with lemon juice, and top them with buttered bread crumbs. Set the oysters in a pan of rock salt and bake them in a moderately hot oven (375° F.) for 8 to 10 minutes.

OPEN 3 dozen fresh oysters. Set the deep shells on a bed of rock salt in a baking pan and strain the liquor through a sieve lined with flannel wrung out of cold water. There should be about 1 cup of liquor.

*Oysters
Bercy*

In a small saucepan bring to a boil the strained oyster liquor and 1 cup dry white wine with 1 tablespoon finely chopped shallots and 4 sprigs of parsley. Reduce the liquid by half over high heat and strain it through a fine sieve into another saucepan. Stir in 2 tablespoons sweet butter, 1 1/2 teaspoons lemon juice, and salt and pepper to taste. Poach the oyster in the sauce for about 1 minute or until the edges begin to curl and lift them out with a skimmer.

Beat 2 egg yolks with a little of the hot sauce, stir the mixture into the sauce, and cook, stirring constantly, until the sauce thickens, being careful not to let it boil.

Put 1 teaspoon of the sauce in the deep half of each oyster shell. Arrange an oyster on the sauce and cover the oyster with a generous teaspoon of the sauce. Sprinkle the sauce with fine dry bread crumbs, dot with butter, and brown quickly under the broiler. Serve immediately.

MAKE a *salpicon* as follows: Grind finely 3/4 cup cooked, shelled, and deveined shrimps, 1/2 cup each of flaked cooked crab meat and cooked boned sole or flounder and force the mixture through a fine sieve. Moisten it with 1/2 cup béchamel sauce and season to taste with salt and pepper.

*Oysters
Nantua*

Shuck 3 dozen oysters and poach them in their own liquor until the edges curl slightly. Spread a little *salpicon* in the deeper shells of the oysters, put 1 oyster in each shell, and sprinkle it with a few drops of brandy. Cover the oysters smoothly with sauce Nantua and brown the sauce under the broiler. Top each oyster with a thin slice of truffle.

GENTLY sauté in 1/4 cup butter 1 shredded green pepper and 1 medium-sized onion, thinly sliced. After 2 or 3 minutes, add 1 pound small whole mushrooms and salt and pepper to taste, and cook these slowly for 4 min-

*Gratin of
Oysters and
Mushrooms*

utes more. In the top of a double boiler melt 1/4 cup butter and stir in 1/4 cup flour. Add slowly, stirring constantly, 1 1/2 cups heavy cream, 1 cup thin cream, 2 tablespoons grated Parmesan cheese, and a pinch each of nutmeg and paprika. Cook the sauce, stirring, for 6 minutes, or until it is thick. Add to the sauce the sautéed vegetables and 3 cups freshly shucked oysters. Add 1/3 cup dry white wine, pour the mixture into a baking dish, and sprinkle it with bread crumbs. Brown the crumbs quickly under the broiler and serve the dish immediately.

Deviled Oysters

POACH 1 quart oysters in their liquor until the edges curl. Remove the oysters with a skimmer and stir into the liquor 1 cup cracker crumbs, 1/2 cup finely chopped celery, 1/4 cup minced onion browned very lightly in 2 tablespoons olive oil, 2 tablespoons each of Worcestershire sauce, finely chopped parsley, and ketchup, 4 dashes of Tabasco, the juice of half a lemon, and salt and pepper to taste. Add the oysters and turn the mixture into a buttered casserole. Sprinkle with fine dry bread crumbs, dot with butter, and bake the casserole in a hot oven (425° F.) for about 15 minutes, or until the oysters are sizzling hot.

Scalloped Oysters

HAVE ready 2 cups freshly shucked oysters and their liquor. Mix together 1 cup cracker crumbs and 1/2 cup each of bread crumbs, and melted butter. Put a thin layer of this mixture in the bottom of a well-buttered baking dish and cover it with 1 cup of the oysters and some liquor. Sprinkle the oysters with salt, pepper, and a few grains of cayenne. Add another layer of the crumb mixture and the remaining oysters and repeat the seasoning. Finish with the rest of the crumbs, sprinkle with 1/4 cup Sherry, and dot thickly with bits of butter. Set the dish in a moderately hot oven (375° F.) for 15 minutes. Serves 4.

Chafing Dish Oysters Virginia

MELT 3 tablespoons butter in the top pan, or blazer, of a chafing dish over direct heat. Add 3 tablespoons flour and cook, stirring, for about 5 minutes, without letting the flour brown. Add gradually 1 cup each of hot chicken stock and hot cream and continue to cook, stirring constantly, until the sauce is thick and smooth. Put the blazer over hot water and add 1/4 cup dry Sherry, 1 cup cooked ham, cut into 1/2-inch cubes, and 2 cups oysters, heated in their own liquor and drained. Heat the mixture thoroughly

Deviled Oysters

without letting it boil and adjust the seasoning with white pepper and a little salt. Serve on freshly made toast or in patty shells.

Only the muscle of the scallop is eaten, and in this country only the muscle is sold at the fish market. Bay scallops are tiny and choice; the larger sea scallops may be sliced.

French Fried Scallops

RINSE scallops to remove any sand and dry them well. Dip them in milk and then in flour. Shake off the surplus flour and cook the scallops in hot deep fat (390° F.) for 2 to 3 minutes, or until they are golden brown. They will rise to the surface when done. Drain the scallops on absorbent paper and sprinkle them with a little salt. Serve with tartar mayonnaise. Fried parsley and broiled bacon are often served with them.

The scallops may be sautéed in a generous amount of butter.

To Prepare Scallops

WASH and drain 2 pounds (1 quart) scallops (the French *coquilles Saint-Jacques*) and put them in a saucepan with 2 cups dry white wine, or enough barely to cover. Bring the wine slowly to a boil and simmer the scallops for 10 minutes. Strain and reserve the liquor, and slice the scallops if they are large. Then proceed as indicated in any of the following recipes.

Coquilles Saint-Jacques à la Paimpolaise
SCALLOPS PAIMPOL

Heat 2 tablespoons each of butter and olive oil in a saucepan and in it sauté 1 medium-sized onion, 2 shallots or 2 green onions, and 1/2 pound mushrooms, all finely chopped. When the onion is lightly browned, add a little salt, pepper, and nutmeg and stir the mixture over high heat until the moisture has evaporated. Spread this duxelles on the bottom and sides of scallop shells, real or ceramic, or ramekins and set them aside. Cook 2 pounds scallops.

Sauté 2 shallots, finely chopped, in 2 tablespoons butter for 5 minutes but do not let them brown. Stir in 3 tablespoons flour and continue to stir until the mixture is smooth. Then add the hot scallop liquor and cook, stirring constantly, until the sauce is thickened. Add the scallops, 1 tablespoon finely chopped parsley, 2 tablespoons Sherry, a pinch of cayenne, and salt to taste. Let the mixture cook gently for 5 minutes. Lift the scallops out of the sauce and arrange them in the shells on top of the duxelles, mounding them attractively in the center. Add 2 tablespons each of lemon juice and whipped cream to the sauce and spread it evenly over the scallops in the shells. Sprinkle with bread crumbs, dot with butter, and bake in a hot oven (450° F.) for about 8 minutes, or until the tops are golden brown.

Scallops Normande

Cook 2 pounds bay scallops and reserve the cooking broth. Simmer 1/4 pound mushrooms, sliced, in 1 tablespoon butter and 2 tablespoons water for 10 minutes. Drain and add the juices to the scallop stock. Reduce the broth by half.

Melt 3 tablespoons butter in a saucepan, stir in 2 tablespoons flour, and add gradually the hot wine broth. Continue to stir until the sauce is smooth and thickened, add salt and pepper to taste, and finish with 2 tablespoons cream and 1 tablespoon butter. Remove the sauce from the heat and stir in 1 truffle, chopped. Put a little of the sauce in the bottom of scallop shells or ramekins. Fill the shells with alternate layers of scallops and mushrooms and cover with more of the wine sauce. Pipe a border of duchess potatoes around each shell, using a pastry bag fitted with a fluted tube. Brush the potato with a little beaten egg and set the prepared shells under the broiler for a few moments to glaze.

Coquilles Saint-Jacques au Cari
CURRIED SCALLOPS

Cook 2 pounds scallops as above. Melt 3 tablespoons butter in a saucepan, stir in 3 tablespoons flour and 1/4 teaspoon curry powder, and add gradually the hot scallop liquor. Continue to stir until the sauce is smooth and thickened, add the scallops and salt to taste, and stir in 1/4 cup heavy cream.

Fill scallop shells with this mixture and sprinkle with parsley.

Scallops Mornay

WASH and drain 2 pounds (1 quart) scallops and put them in a saucepan with 2 shallots, chopped, 2 tablespoons butter, and 2 cups dry white wine. Bring the liquid to a boil and simmer the scallops gently for about 8 minutes. Remove them, strain and save the cooking liquor, and slice them.

Simmer the scallop liquor until it is reduced by three-fourths. Stir in 1 1/2 cups thick Mornay sauce, blend thoroughly, strain the sauce through a fine sieve, and mix it with the scallops. Add salt and pepper to taste and 1 tablespoon finely chopped parsley and fill scallop shells or ramekins with the mixture.

Fold 1/4 cup whipped cream into 1/2 cup Mornay sauce and coat the tops of the filled shells. Sprinkle with grated Parmesan cheese and brown the coquilles in a very hot oven (450° F.) or under the broiler.

Bay Scallops in Wine Sauce

WASH and drain 3 pints bay scallops and put them in a saucepan with a little salt, 6 peppercorns, 3 cups dry white wine, and a *bouquet garni* composed of 4 sprigs of parsley, 2 sprigs of fresh thyme, and 1 bay leaf. Bring the wine to a boil and simmer the scallops for 10 minutes, or until they are tender. Strain and reserve the wine broth.

Cook 1 pound mushrooms, thinly sliced, and 12 shallots, minced, in 1/4 cup water and 2 teaspoons lemon juice with 2 tablespoons finely chopped parsley and 1/4 cup butter for 10 minutes. Drain the vegetables and add the liquor to the wine broth.

Melt 6 tablespoons butter in a saucepan, add 6 tablespoons flour, and stir the *roux* until it is well blended. Add gradually the combined hot liquors from the scallops and the mushrooms and cook the sauce, stirring constantly, until it is thick and smooth. Remove the pan from the heat and stir in 3 egg yolks beaten with 1/2 cup warm heavy cream. Correct the seasoning and stir in the scallops and vegetables. Keep the mixture hot over simmering water.

Serve in individual flaky pastry shells or timbales. Serves 12.

Scallop and Crab Meat Casserole

SAUTÉ 2 pounds small bay scallops and 1 pound lump crab meat in 2 tablespoons butter until the seafood is heated through. Sprinkle it with salt and pepper, pour over it 2 tablespoons warmed Cognac, and ignite the spirit. When the flame dies, turn the seafood and juice into a casserole and sprinkle it with 1/2 cup shredded sweet peppers. In a saucepan melt 1/4 cup butter and stir in 1/4 cup flour. Stir in gradually 1 cup dry white wine and cook, stirring, until the sauce is very thick and smooth. Stir in gradually 2 cups hot cream and 1/4 cup Sherry and season the sauce to taste with salt, cayenne, and a pinch of nutmeg. Pour the sauce into the casserole and set it aside.

Just before serving time, cover the casserole and bake it in a moderate oven (350° F.) for 30 minutes. Serves 8 to 10.

Most shrimp fanciers have never seen a shrimp with its head on; the head, along with other inedible parts of the crustacean, is cut away and discarded as soon as possible after the shrimp is caught. Cook shrimps in a well-seasoned court bouillon or in hot butter or oil until they turn bright pink; overcooking spoils their texture. Or shell and devein the shrimp before its brief cooking; there are arguments for both procedures.

WASH, shell, and devein 2 pounds shrimps and sauté them slowly in a generous amount of butter until they are bright pink. Season with salt, white pepper, and a little curry. Serve on buttered white rice.

Sautéed Shrimps

SHELL and devein 2 pounds raw shrimps and halve them. Cut each half in two, wash thoroughly, and dry on absorbent paper. Toss the shrimps well with 2 beaten egg whites, to prevent the shrimps from overcooking in the hot oil. Heat 1/2 cup lard or salad oil in a skillet and add 2 garlic cloves, 2 scallions, trimmed, and the prepared shrimps. Sauté them for about 2 minutes, stirring and adding 2 tablespoons Sherry and a pinch of salt, until the shrimps turn pink. Drain them.

Sautéed Shrimps with Water Chestnuts

In another skillet heat a little salad oil and in it sauté for 2 minutes 2 dozen water chestnuts, peeled and sliced 1/8 inch thick. Combine 1 cup chicken broth, 2 teaspoons cornstarch, 1 teaspoon sugar, and 1/2 teaspoon salt and stir this into the water chestnuts. Cook, stirring, until the liquid thickens, add the cooked shrimps and heat them for about a minute. Serve immediately.

SHELL 1 pound small raw shrimps, leaving the tails intact. Wash them well and dry them on absorbent paper. In a skillet heat to the smoking point 1/4 cup lard or shortening and add 2 scallions, trimmed and cut into 1-inch lengths, and 1 slice of fresh ginger and 1 garlic clove, both mashed to a pulp. Add the shrimps and sauté them for 2 to 3 minutes over high heat, stirring. Stir in 2 tablespoons dry Sherry and 1/4 cup diced sweet pickles and cook the shrimps for another minute. Remove them and the vegetables to a warm place.

Phoenix Tail Shrimp Sauté

To the liquid in the skillet add 3 tablespoons soy sauce, 1/3 teaspoon sugar, and 1 1/2 teaspoons cornstarch stirred to a paste with 1 tablespoon cold water. Cook, stirring constantly, until the mixture is smooth and thick. Add the shrimps and vegetables and cook for 1/2 minute, or until heated through. Serves four.

IN a kettle combine 2 quarts water, 1 crushed garlic clove, 1 teaspoon vinegar, 1 tablespoon salt, 1 bay leaf, and 3 peppercorns. Bring the liquid to a boil and add 3 pounds shrimps. Simmer them, covered, for 10 minutes. Let the shrimps stand in the court bouillon for 20 minutes more. Shell, devein, and wash the shrimps. Strain the court bouillon and reserve 2 cups.

Shrimps in Dill

Heat the reserved stock and thicken it with 1/4 cup flour mixed to a paste with a little cold stock. Cook the sauce, stirring, until it is smooth.

In a separate saucepan put 1 cup dry white wine and 6 minced scallions. Reduce the wine to 1/2 cup, add the thickened sauce, and bring the mixture to a boil, stirring constantly. Strain the sauce and add 1/2 cup finely chopped dill. Season to taste with salt and Sherry. Pour the sauce over the prepared shrimps and serve at once.

Shrimps
New Orleans

MELT 1/4 cup butter in a shallow pan and in it cook until soft 1/4 cup chopped onions. Add 2 pounds cooked, shelled, and deveined shrimps and toss them in the hot butter for a few minutes. Add 1/2 cup Madeira. In another pan melt 2 tablespoons butter and in it sauté 1 cup mushrooms, sliced. Add 1 green pepper and 1 pimiento, both diced, 6 tomatoes, peeled, seeded, and chopped, and 1 cup tomato sauce. Cook the vegetables for a few minutes, until they are barely tender, and add the shrimps. Mix well together, heat thoroughly, and serve in a rice ring.

Shrimps André

COOK 2 pounds jumbo shrimps in court bouillon for shellfish until they are bright pink. Shell and devein the shrimps and split them in half without separating the halves. Sauté 6 shallots and 12 mushrooms, both finely sliced, in 1/4 cup melted butter. Add 1 garlic clove, finely chopped, 2 tablespoons lemon juice, 2 tablespoons dry Sherry, a little meat extract, and 2 tablespoons finely chopped parsley. Heat the sauce well and add the shrimps. Cook, stirring, until the shrimps are heated through. Serve on croutons browned in butter with a garlic clove.

Penang
Shrimp Curry

POACH 2 pounds shrimps in boiling salted water for about 10 minutes, or until they turn bright pink. Reserve 1 quart of the liquid in which they were cooked, shell and devein the shrimps, and set them aside.

In a large saucepan combine 1 onion, 2 shallots, 1 stalk of celery, 1 carrot, 1 apple, 1 green pepper, 1 chili pepper, and 1 tomato, all chopped, and 1 garlic clove, minced. Add 1 sprig each of parsley and thyme, 1 bay leaf, 2 whole cloves, 2 sprigs of mint, 1/2 teaspoon each of chopped basil and salt, freshly ground black pepper to taste, 1/4 teaspoon each of marjoram, nutmeg, and cayenne, 1 tablespoon curry powder, and the grated rind of 1 lime. Add the reserved liquid and bring to a boil. Stir in bit by bit 2 tablespoons flour mixed to a smooth paste with 2 tablespoons butter and simmer the mixture for 1 hour. Strain the liquid into another saucepan, add the cooked shrimps, and simmer them for 10 minutes. Serve in a ring of cooked rice.

PUT 1/2 pound cooked lobster meat through the finest blade of a food chopper. Mix the ground lobster with 1 tablespoon each of minced water chestnuts and bamboo shoots, 1/2 teaspoon salt, and a dash of pepper.

    In a heavy skillet sauté 1 crushed garlic clove in 1/4 cup hot oil over medium heat for 3 minutes. Discard the garlic and add to the skillet the lobster mixture, 1 cup chicken stock, and 1 1/2 pounds shrimps, shelled and deveined. Cover the skillet and cook the shrimps over medium heat for 10 minutes. Stir in 1 egg lightly beaten with a little of the hot pan juice and stir the mixture over low heat for 2 minutes. Stir in 1 tablespoon cornstarch mixed with 1/4 cup water and continue to cook, stirring constantly, for 2 minutes longer. Add 2 tablespoons finely chopped scallions and serve immediately with hot fluffy rice. Serves 3.

Foo Young Har Kow
SHRIMPS WITH LOBSTER SAUCE

SOAK 3 slices of stale bread cut 1/2 inch thick in 1 cup milk. Mash the bread with a fork and mix in 2 cups freshly cooked, shelled, and deveined shrimps, 2 tablespoons butter, 1 teaspoon Worcestershire sauce, 1/2 teaspoon freshly ground peppercorns, a good dash each of mace and nutmeg to taste, and 3 tablespoons Sherry. Mix the ingredients thoroughly, add salt to taste, and turn the mixture into a buttered baking dish. Top with 1 cup tiny cubes of bread lightly browned in butter and bake in a moderate oven (350° F.) for 15 to 20 minutes. Serve at once. Should the top brown too fast, cover it with buttered paper.

Scalloped Shrimps Norfolk

COMBINE 5 eggs, 3 cups milk, 1 cup pineapple juice, 1 tablespoon sugar, and 1 teaspoon each of salt and baking powder. Beat the mixture well and add gradually 2 cups flour, beating until the batter is well blended. Shell and devein 3 pounds large raw shrimps, leaving the tails intact. Wipe the shrimps with a damp cloth, slit them down the back without separating the halves and press them flat, like a butterfly. Dip the prepared shrimps in the batter and then in shredded coconut, and fry them in hot deep fat (375° F.) for 3 minutes.

Hawaiian Fried Shrimps

WASH 3 pounds raw shrimps and put them in a saucepan with just enough beer to cover. Bring the beer to a boil, add a pinch of rosemary and a bay leaf, and cover the pan. Simmer the shrimps for about 8 minutes, until

Shrimps in Beer

they are bright pink, shell and devein them, and transfer them to a dish to keep warm. Reduce the stock by half.

Melt 2 tablespoons butter, stir in 2 tablespoons flour, and add the reduced beer stock. Cook the sauce, stirring constantly, for about 2 minutes. Add 1 cup cream and 2 teaspoons chopped parsley and heat the sauce to the boiling point, stirring it constantly. Stir in 1/2 teaspoon paprika. Return the shrimps to the sauce and heat it without boiling.

Mousse of Shrimps Nantua

MAKE a *mousseline* forcemeat with 1 pound raw shrimps, peeled and deveined.

Turn the forcemeat into a buttered ring mold, cover the top with a piece of buttered heavy paper, set the mold in a pan in about 1 inch hot water and bake it in a moderate oven (350° F.) for 30 minutes, or until it is firm to the touch.

Lightly flour 1 pound bay scallops, sprinkle them with salt and pepper and sauté them quickly in 1 tablespoon each of olive oil and butter until they are golden.

Unmold the shrimp mousse on a warm serving platter, garnish the center with the scallops and pour over ring and filling *sauce Nantua.*

Bouillabaisse, matelote, cioppino, *chowder—every country that has an ocean in its backyard makes fish stews of one kind or another, most of them savory mixtures of several kinds of fish.*

Oyster Bar Oyster Stew

IN a deep saucepan heat for each serving 2 tablespoons butter with a dash each of paprika, celery salt, and Worcestershire sauce. When the butter is bubbling, add 7 freshly opened oysters and 1/2 cup oyster liquor. Simmer the oysters in the liquor until the edges curl, add 1 cup milk or 1/2 cup each of milk and cream, and bring the liquid to the boiling point. Pour the stew into a soup bowl and top with a little paprika and 1 teaspoon butter.

Chesapeake Oyster Stew

STRAIN the liquor from 1 1/2 pints freshly shucked large oysters. Melt 5 tablespoons butter in a large skillet or in the top pan of a chafing dish, add the oyster liquor, and heat the liquid slowly. When it begins to bubble, add 1 cup each of finely chopped onion and finely chopped celery, including the leaves, and half a small apple, finely chopped. Cook slowly, stirring constantly, until the onion and celery are soft, but not browned. Add 1 cup cream, heat well, and add the oysters. Continue to cook slowly, without letting the liquid boil, until the oysters are hot. If the stew needs thinning, add 1/2 cup milk. Serves two.

SIMMER 5 pounds live lobsters in boiling water for 15 to 20 minutes. Cool the lobsters a little in the liquid and then twist off the large claws, crack them with a nutcracker, and pick out the meat, keeping the pieces as large as possible. Cut the lobsters lengthwise from head to tail. Discard the intestinal veins and the small sacs near the base of the head, and remove the meat. Cut the meat into thin slices and put it in a large saucepan. Sprinkle the lobster meat with freshly ground black pepper and a pinch of dry mustard and pour over it 2 cups each of cream and milk. To serve, bring the soup to a simmer, correct the seasoning with salt, and stir in 1/2 cup Sherry and 3 tablespoons butter. Serve the stew in a warmed soup tureen and ladle it into heated soup plates.

Lobster Stew Gourmet

BOIL 1 onion, sliced, and 2 tablespoons fat salt pork in water to cover for 10 minutes. Strain the stock and add it to 4 cups potato dice cooked in boiling water for 5 minutes. Chop finely the hard portions of 1 quart freshly shucked clams and add the chopped clams, the strained clam liquor, and 2 cups boiling water to the potatoes. Cook the potatoes until they are nearly tender. Add 1 cup stewed, strained tomatoes, 1 cup each of hot milk and cream, a pinch of baking soda, and salt and pepper to taste. Continue to cook until the potatoes are done. Add the soft parts of the clams and 2 tablespoons butter and heat well. Serve the chowder with pilot crackers.

Rhode Island Clam Chowder

IN a saucepan sauté 1 onion, finely chopped, in 1/4 cup butter until the onion is transparent. Add 6 ripe tomatoes, peeled, seeded, and finely chopped, and stew the tomatoes, covered, over very low heat for 5 minutes. Add 5 cups chicken consommé and 3 leaves of thyme and bring the consommé to a boil. Add the kernels cut from 3 ears of corn, 1 pound lump crab meat, and a dash of Tabasco, cover, and simmer the chowder gently for

Crab Meat Chowder

5 minutes. Correct the seasoning with salt and freshly ground pepper, turn the soup into a tureen, and sprinkle with finely chopped parsley or chervil. Serve immediately.

Abalone
Chowder

BROWN lightly 4 slices of bacon, diced, and pour off all but about 2 tablespoons of the bacon drippings. To the bacon dice add the meat of 6 abalones, which has been pounded and cut into small cubes. Trimmed abalone meat bought at the market is already pounded. Add 1 large raw potato, peeled and diced, 1 medium onion, finely chopped, and 1 small garlic clove, crushed. Sauté the mixture until it is golden brown. Add 1 1/2 cups hot water, cover the pan, and simmer the mixture until the abalone and potato are tender. Add 3 cups hot milk, 1 tablespoon butter, and salt and pepper to taste. Stir the chowder well and serve it hot.

Shrimp,
Oyster,
and Squash
Chowder

IN a saucepan scald 4 cups milk. Add 3/4 cup finely diced celery, 1 carrot and 3 onions, both sliced paper-thin, 3 tablespoons diced green pepper, and salt and pepper to taste. Cover the saucepan and cook the vegetables over boiling water for about 30 minutes, or until they are tender.

Halve and remove the seeds from 2 acorn squash and bake the squash, skin side down, in a pan containing 1 inch of boiling water in a moderate oven (350° F.) for about 45 minutes, or until it is tender. Spoon the flesh from the shells, press it through a fine sieve, and stir it into the soup. Add 1 cup shrimps, shelled and deveined, and cook the mixture for 5 minutes longer. Add 1 cup freshly shucked oysters and a generous lump of butter and serve as soon as the edges of the oysters curl.

Codfish
Chowder
Biscayne

TRIM a 4-pound codfish and put the trimmings into a saucepan with 1 1/2 quarts cold water, 2 large tomatoes, coarsely chopped, 1 bay leaf, 10 peppercorns, 2 cloves, and 10 sprigs of parsley. Heat gently to the boiling point and simmer for 25 minutes. Strain the stock through a fine sieve and add all but 1 cup of the codfish meat, boned and cut into small pieces, 2 tablespoons each of finely chopped onion and celery, and salt to taste.

Bring the mixture to a boil and simmer gently for 20 minutes, stirring frequently to prevent scorching. Add 2 cups diced raw potatoes and simmer for 10 minutes longer. Combine 2 tablespoons butter and 1 1/2 tablespoons flour into a smooth paste and stir it gradually into the chowder along with 1 cup cream.

Put the cup of codfish meat, free from bones, through the finest blade of a food chopper and combine it with 1 egg, slightly beaten, 2 tablespoons fine bread crumbs, a pinch of mace, 1 tablespoon finely chopped chives and parsley, a dash of cayenne, and 1 teaspoon salt. Shape this mixture into about 18 small balls. Bring the chowder to a brisk boil, add the fish balls, cover the pan, and simmer the chowder for 10 minutes. Five minutes before serving, add 1 cup raw shrimps, shelled and deveined, and cook them until they are pink. Serve with finger-shaped pieces of toast rubbed with garlic and buttered.

SOAK 1/2 pound salt codfish for 24 hours in water to cover, changing the water several times, then flake the fish.

Salt Codfish Chowder

In a saucepan sauté 2 tablespoons finely chopped salt pork until it is lightly browned. Add 1 tablespoon chopped onion and continue to sauté until the onion is golden. Add 3 cups cooked diced potatoes and enough water just to cover the vegetables. Bring the water to a boil and simmer the vegetables until they are tender. Add 4 cups milk and the flaked fish and bring the soup again to a boil. Just before serving add 8 crumbled soda crackers.

PUT the trimmings—the head and backbone—of a 4-pound fileted red snapper in a soup kettle with 1 pound inexpensive fish and cover it with 2 cups each of cold water and dry white wine. Add a *bouquet garni* composed of 2 bay leaves, 2 sprigs of celery tops, 10 sprigs of parsley, 1 sprig of thyme, and 3 cloves, all tied together. Add also 1 carrot and 1 onion, sliced, 1 garlic clove, 1 leek, quartered lengthwise, and 2 slices of lemon. Bring the mixture to a boil, season with salt and pepper to taste, and simmer it very gently for 30 minutes. Strain the stock through a fine sieve, discarding the bones, vegetables, and *bouquet garni*, and keep it hot.

Red Snapper Chowder

Cut the red snapper filets into small pieces, sprinkle with a little salt and pepper, and add to fish stock. Bring the stock again to a boil and simmer gently for 10 minutes. Add 2 cups potato cubes, 1 cup each of carrot cubes, and chopped onions, and 1/2 cup turnip cubes. Cook the chowder gently for 20 minutes longer, or until the vegetables are tender.

Cream together 3 tablespoons butter and 2 tablespoons flour, add the *beurre manié*, bit by bit, to the chowder and cook for 5 minutes longer. Correct the seasoning and when ready to serve, stir in 1 1/2 cups hot cream mixed with the lightly beaten yolks of 3 eggs.

Nassau Chowder

POACH 2 pounds lake trout filets in a mixture of half water and half white wine to cover, until the flesh flakes easily. Remove the filets and flake the flesh into small pieces.

Cook 1 small onion, thinly sliced, in 3 tablespoons butter with a piece of bay leaf and a sprinkling of freshly ground black pepper until the onion is soft but not brown. Add 1 cup of the poaching liquid, the flaked trout filets, and 3 cups light cream and heat the liquid to the boiling point. When ready to serve, stir in 1 tablespoon butter and garnish each portion with finely chopped chives.

Lake Trout Stew

SCALE, clean, and filet 3 pounds striped bass and 1 pound halibut. Put the heads, skin, and bones in a soup kettle, put the filets on top, and add 3 cups water. Bring the liquid to a boil and simmer the fish for about 15 minutes, or until the broth reduces to 2 cups. Strain the broth and cut the filets into 1 1/2-inch squares. Put the squares in a buttered saucepan and sprinkle them with salt and freshly ground black pepper. On top of the fish put 4 potatoes, peeled and diced, and a layer of thinly sliced Bermuda onions and 6 small white onions, thinly sliced. Add 4 cups stewed tomatoes, the strained fish broth, and 1 teaspoon mixed pickling spice, bring the liquid to a boil, and simmer the chowder for 30 minutes, or until the onions and potatoes are tender. Correct the seasoning with salt, and stir in 1 cup Sherry and the juice of 1 lime. Just before serving add 1/4 cup butter and serve the chowder as soon as the butter is melted.

Nassau Chowder

SKIN and clean an eel weighing about 2 pounds. Cut the meat into 3-inch sections and put them in a casserole over a bed of mixed sliced onions and shallots, a garlic clove, chopped, a sprinkling of pepper, and a *bouquet garni* composed of 2 sprigs of parsley, 1 bay leaf, and a sprig each of thyme and tarragon. Cover the casserole and cook the stew over low heat for about 10 minutes, or until the onions are transparent and the eel is heated through. Pour over the meat 1/4 cup warmed Cognac and ignite it. When the flame dies, add red wine to cover the eel, a little salt, and simmer the stew gently for 20 minutes.

Put the eel in another casserole with 12 small whole onions and 12 mushroom caps, both cooked in butter until tender, and keep the casserole warm.

Reduce the cooking liquor to less than half its original quantity. Thicken the sauce with a *beurre manié* made by mixing 3 tablespoons butter and 1 tablespoon flour to a paste. Correct the seasoning and simmer the sauce for 10 minutes. As the wine cooks, the sauce will become lighter in color.

Matelote d'Anguille Bourguignonne
EEL STEW
WITH BURGUNDY

Add a little meat extract to make the sauce brown and strain it over the eel. Garnish the stew with 6 crayfish, cooked in court bouillon, and triangles of bread, fried until golden in hot oil.

Pesang Isda

PHILIPPINE
FISH STEW

CLEAN and filet a white-fleshed fish, weighing about 3 pounds, and cut it into serving pieces. Put the fish in the soup kettle with 2 tablespoons each of butter and grated fresh gingerroot, 1 teaspoon salt, and 12 peppercorns. Add 3 cups water, bring the water to a boil, and simmer the fish for about 6 minutes, or until the flesh flakes easily.

In a skillet sauté 1 onion and 1 garlic clove, both chopped, in 2 tablespoons butter until the onion is golden. Add 3 tomatoes, chopped, and 2 cups water and simmer the vegetables until they are tender. Strain the tomato sauce into the soup, reheat to the boiling point, and serve very hot, garnished with chopped scallions.

Matelote à la Bourbonnaise

CUT 4 pounds assorted fresh-water fish, such as perch and carp, including always 1 eel, into 1-inch slices. Put the slices in a deep saucepan, add red wine to cover, the stems and peelings of 1/2 pound mushrooms, 1 onion, sliced, 3 sprigs of parsley, 1 stalk of celery, 1 bay leaf, 2 garlic cloves, 1 teaspoon salt, and a little thyme. Bring the liquid to a boil, add 2 to 3 tablespoons warmed Cognac, and ignite the spirit. When the flame dies, cover the pan, and simmer the stew for 15 to 18 minutes.

Remove the fish to a serving dish, strain the liquid into another pan, and stir in bit by bit *beurre manié* made by kneading 3 tablespoons butter with 2 1/2 tablespoons flour. Bring the liquid again to a boil, stirring constantly, and cook, stirring, until it is smooth and as thick as cream. Correct the seasoning with salt and a little freshly ground pepper.

To serve, arrange on the fish 12 to 15 small white cooked onions and 1/2 pound mushrooms, simmered in water with a little lemon juice for 5 minutes. Pour the sauce over all and garnish with 1/2 pound cooked, shelled, and deveined shrimps and slices of French bread sautéed in butter.

Cacciucco Leghorn

IN a soup kettle sauté 2 garlic cloves, chopped, 1 tiny red pepper, and 3 onions, chopped, in 3/4 cup olive oil until the onions are delicately colored.

Add 3/4 pound shrimps, shelled, deveined, and chopped, and 3/4 pound squid, skinned, cleaned, and cut into small pieces. Cook the mixture, covered, over low heat for 30 minutes, or until the squid is tender. Add 3/4 cup dry red wine and cook the soup until the wine is reduced to one-quarter the original amount. Add 3 tablespoons tomato paste, 6 cups water, and salt to taste and cook for 5 minutes. Add 1 1/2 pounds cod filets and 3/4 pound each of scallops and halibut, all cut into small pieces, and cook the soup for 15 minutes longer.

Put a slice of Italian bread, toasted and rubbed with a cut garlic clove in each serving dish and pour the soup over it.

SAUTÉ lightly 1 garlic clove and 1 small onion, both minced, in 1/3 cup olive oil. Add 1/2 cup celery and 1/2 carrot, both minced, 1 bay leaf, and 1/4 cup chopped parsley and simmer the vegetables gently for 10 minutes. Add 1 cup dry white wine and simmer them for 10 minutes more. Skin, filet, and cut into serving pieces 5 pounds mixed fish, using whiting, flounder, bass, or any other white fish. Add the fish, 1 cup each of water and cooked Italian plum tomatoes, and salt and pepper to taste and continue cooking for 15 minutes more, or until the fish is cooked. Correct the seasoning and serve the chowder from a tureen with toasted Italian bread as an accompaniment.

*Fish Chowder
Pesaro*

SCALD 1 dozen hard-shelled crabs. Clean them, cut off the claws, crack and remove the outside shell, and cut the bodies into quarters. Season them with salt and pepper.

In a soup kettle in 2 tablespoons butter, cook the pieces, covered, and put in the crabs. Cover for 5 minutes. Add 6 large fresh tomatoes, peeled and quartered, 1 large onion, chopped, 1 sprig of thyme, and 1 sprig of parsley and cook the mixture, stirring, for 5 minutes. Add 2 pints okra, finely sliced, 1 beef bone, 1 bay leaf, and 2 quarts boiling water.

Simmer the soup gently for 30 minutes. Add 1/2 red pepper, free of seeds, and simmer for another 30 minutes. To serve, remove the beef bone, season to taste with cayenne and salt, and pour the gumbo into a heated soup tureen.

*Gumbo
aux Crabes*

Most fish sauces begin, logically enough, with fish stock. These are capable of infinite variation. The purpose of a fish sauce, as of any sauce, is to enhance the flavor of the food it graces, not disguise it.

Fumet de Poisson

FISH STOCK
FOR SAUCES

PUT 2 pounds chopped raw fish bones and trimmings in a buttered pan with 1 onion, minced, a few sprigs of parsley, and 10 peppercorns. Add 1 quart each of white wine and water and season with a pinch of salt. Bring the liquid to a boil and simmer it for 25 minutes. Strain the stock before using it.

Fish Velouté

IN a saucepan melt 2 tablespoons butter. Stir in 2 tablespoons flour and cook the *roux* slowly until it turns golden. Gradually stir in 2 cups warm fish stock and cook, stirring, until the sauce is smooth and thickened. Cook the sauce for 15 to 20 minutes longer, correct the seasoning with salt to taste, and strain.

Sauce Béchamel Maigre

BÉCHAMEL SAUCE
FOR FISH

IN a saucepan in 1/4 cup butter sauté over low heat 1/2 onion, minced finely, until it is soft but not at all browned. Stir in 1/4 cup flour and cook it slowly for a few minutes without letting it take on color. Add gradually 3 cups each of scalded milk and fish stock, stirring vigorously with a wire whip. Add 1/2 teaspoon salt, 5 white peppercorns, a sprig of parsley, and a pinch of freshly grated nutmeg. Cook slowly, stirring frequently, for about 30 minutes, or until the liquid is reduced by one-third and the sauce has the consistency of heavy cream. Strain the sauce through a fine seive and dot the surface with tiny flecks of butter. The butter will melt and prevent a film from forming.

Shrimp or Lobster Sauce

TO 1 cup béchamel sauce for fish add 1/2 cup fish stock and 1/4 cup cream. Reduce the sauce a little over high heat and stir in 1 tablespoon butter and 1/3 cup hot cooked shrimps or lobster cut into pieces. Serve with poached fish, fish puddings, and with elaborate hot preparations involving *mousseline* of fish.

To 2 cups hot *sauce béchamel maigre* add 3 egg yolks beaten with a little hot cream. Cook the sauce, stirring, until it just reaches the boiling point, and stir in over the heat 2 generous tablespoons grated Parmesan or Swiss cheese.

Mornay Sauce for Fish

To 1 cup hot béchamel sauce add 1/4 cup scalded heavy cream. Blend the mixture well and strain it through a fine sieve or cheesecloth into a saucepan. Heat without boiling, add salt and pepper to taste, and stir in 2 tablespoons each of crayfish butter and finely chopped cooked crayfish tails, or use shrimp or lobster butter and chopped shrimps or lobster. The chopped shellfish may be omitted.

Sauce Nantua

To 1 cup béchamel sauce for fish add 1/4 cup capers, washed, drained, and coarsely chopped, 1 tablespoon butter, and 1 1/2 teaspoons lemon juice. Use for poached fish.

Caper Cream Sauce

Blend 1 teaspoon dry mustard to a smooth paste with 1 tablespoon water and stir the paste into 1 cup hot béchamel sauce for fish. Serve with hot or cold poached or sautéed fish.

Mustard Sauce

Reduce 3 cups fish *velouté* to 2 cups, cool it slightly, and beat in 2 lightly beaten egg yolks. Heat the sauce again, stirring, until it just reaches the boiling point. Cool the sauce to lukewarm and use it to coat fish and shellfish for frying. When the *Villeroi* is made with stock other than fish stock, it may be used to coat other foods for frying.

Sauce Villeroi for Fish

Sauce Villeroi

Heat 2 tablespoons butter in a saucepan, blend with 1 tablespoon flour, and gradually add 1 cup hot cream, stirring constantly until the sauce is thick and smooth. Do not boil. Season with salt and cayenne to taste and pour the sauce slowly over 2 well-beaten egg yolks, stirring constantly. Set the pan over boiling water and cook, stirring, for 3 minutes. Flavor with 2 tablespoons dry Sherry.

Newburg Sauce

Bercy Sauce for Fish

IN a saucepan melt 2 tablespoons butter and in it sauté 1 tablespoon finely chopped shallots or scallions until they are transparent. Then add 1/4 cup each of dry white wine and fish *fumet* and cook until the liquid is reduced by half. Stir in 1/2 cup fish *velouté* and finish the sauce with 1 tablespoon each of butter and very finely chopped parsley.

Fines Herbes Sauce for Fish

IN a saucepan melt 2 tablespoons butter. Add 1 shallot or 2 scallions, finely chopped, and 1/3 cup dry white wine and simmer the sauce until the shallot or scallions are transparent. Add 1 teaspoon each of chopped parsley and chervil and salt and pepper to taste.

Shellfish Butter

CRAYFISH, SHRIMP, OR LOBSTER BUTTER

DRY in the oven for a short time the shells from 1 pound shrimps or crayfish or from a large lobster. Pound the shells in a mortar until they are broken up as finely as possible. Melt 1/4 pound butter slowly over simmering water. Add 2 tablespoons water and the pulverized shells and cook for 10 to 12 minutes, without letting the butter boil. Strain off the liquid. Add a little boiling water to the shells and strain this off. Pour the combined liquids through cheesecloth into a bowl of ice water and chill the butter until it hardens. Skim off the butter and pack it into a jar. Cover the jar and store it in the refrigerator. Use to enrich and flavor sauces for fish and seafood.

Tartar Sauce

MASH and pound to a paste 2 hard-cooked egg yolks. Add salt and freshly ground black pepper to taste. Beat in slowly 1 cup olive oil, adding the oil in a constant thin stream. Finish the sauce with 1 teaspoon tarragon vinegar and a pinch of minced chives pounded with 1 generous teaspoon mayonnaise. For fried and sautéed fish.

Tartar Mayonnaise

TO 1 cup homemade mayonnaise add 1 teaspoon each of parsley, shallots, fresh tarragon leaves, sweet gherkins, and green olives, all finely chopped. Season with salt, freshly ground pepper, and about 1 teaspoon prepared mustard, to taste. For fried and sautéed fish.

Sauce Verte

GREEN MAYONNAISE

FOLD into 2 cups mayonnaise, 2 tablespoons parsley, and 1 tablespoon each of chives and tarragon leaves, 1 teaspoon each of chervil and dill, all finely chopped. Chill the mayonnaise for about 2 hours before serving with cold fish and shellfish.

Poultry

Among the many virtues of chicken, in the eyes of the gourmet, is its adaptability; having no intensely individual flavor of its own, it accommodates itself to every possible method of cookery and to almost every possible sauce.

The elderly hen that lends its ripe, full flavor—and its tough and sinewy flesh—to the soup kettle is not specified here for other uses, except where the stock produced by long simmering is an important part of the completed dish. Generally we recommend for so-called stews or for casserole preparations a plump roasting chicken that weighs in at 4 to 6 tender pounds, a youngster under 2 1/2 pounds for the broiler, and fryers—under 3 1/2 pounds—for most other uses.

How to Bone a Chicken

SINGE a chicken and remove head and feet. Cut off the neck and all but the first joint of the wings but keep the skin of the neck as long as possible. Using a sharp-pointed boning knife, cut a straight line down the back beginning at the neck through both skin and flesh. Now begin to scrape and cut the flesh from the backbone right down to the shoulder blade, being careful not to pierce the skin. At the leg and wing joints, cut through the joints. Proceed in the same manner on the other side; the meat will be free from the carcass, and the entire carcass with the entrails in place may be lifted out, leaving the fleshy part of the bird and the skin intact. Scrape the flesh from the thigh bone, cut through the leg joint, and pull out the thigh bone. Continue to scrape the flesh from the leg and wing bones and draw them out of the flesh. Wash the skin and flesh in cold running water and dry it.

Sautéed Chicken

CLEAN and singe 2 chickens each weighing about 3 pounds. Remove the legs and second joints in one piece and loosen the skin at the end of the legs and push it back so that the bone protrudes. This prevents the drying of the thin layer of meat at the end of the bone. Lay the chicken skin side down on a board and with the dull edge of a large knife crack through the cartilage between the leg and the second joint. Remove the second-joint bone by pulling it out at the exposed end. Make an incision down the underside of the leg. The whole piece will then lie flat in the pan, and so cook more evenly. Cut off the wings. Cut off the breast meat in three pieces, one from each side and one from the front. Dry each piece of chicken thoroughly and season it with salt and pepper. You may dredge the pieces in flour, but shake off the surplus or it will scorch.

Clarified Butter

The best fat for sautéing is salad oil or clarified butter—butter that has been melted and poured off the milky sediment at the bottom of the pan. (If oil is used, it must be poured off when the chicken is almost cooked and butter added to make the sauce.)

Heat 2 or 3 tablespoons clarified butter in a heavy metal skillet and cook the pieces of chicken slowly over low heat, skin side down, until the skin is brown. Turn the pieces and cook them, partially covered, until they are tender. The juices that follow a fork or skewer inserted at the thickest part of the second joint should show no trace of pink. The breast meat will take less time to cook than the dark portions, and may be removed to a heated serving platter earlier.

Sautéed chicken may be served as it is in the above recipe, or in any of the following ways.

Poulet Sauté Bordelaise

Remove the cooked chicken to a heated platter. To the juices in the pan add 1 tablespoon chopped shallots or onion, 1 teaspoon flour, and a generous 1/3 cup red wine, and cook, stirring, until the sauce is slightly thickened. Return the chicken to the pan and simmer all together for a minute or two. Arrange the chicken on a heated serving dish and pour the sauce over it.

Garnish the dish with French fried onion rings, fried parsley, artichoke bottoms sautéed in butter, and potatoes *rissolé.*

Arrange the cooked chicken on a heated platter. To the juices in the pan add 1 tablespoon finely chopped shallots or onion and 1 teaspoon flour. Stir in 1/4 cup each of wine and chicken broth and 3 tablespoons tomato sauce. Cook the sauce for a few minutes, stirring, until it thickens slightly. Add salt and pepper to taste. Strain the sauce around the chicken on the platter and sprinkle with chopped parsley.

Poulet Sauté Bercy

Prepare sautéed chicken Bercy. Sauté 1 1/2 pounds cooked and drained spinach in 2 tablespoons butter for a few minutes. Make a bed of the spinach on a serving platter and arrange the sautéed chicken on it. Garnish the chicken with cooked sliced mushrooms or with pieces of *foie gras* and truffle slices. Pour the sauce over all.

Poulet Sauté Florentine

In a saucepan combine 2 cups shelled peas, 8 small spring onions, 1/2 cup diced carrots, 5 or 6 leaves of lettuce, shredded, 1/4 cup water, 1/4 teaspoon salt, 1 tablespoon sugar, 3 tablespoons butter, and a *bouquet garni* made by tying together 3 sprigs each of parsley and chervil. Cover the pan and cook the vegetables until they are tender and most of the water has cooked away. Discard the *bouquet garni.*
Prepare sautéed chicken Bercy. Return the chicken to the pan with half the sauce, add the vegetables, and simmer together for 10 minutes. Arrange the chicken on a serving platter with the vegetables around it and sprinkle with chopped parsley. Serve the rest of the sauce separately.

Poulet Sauté Printanière

Wash 1 pound morels, making sure to wash every bit of sand from the crevices. Cook them in a saucepan with 1/4 cup water, 2 tablespoons butter, 1 teaspoon lemon juice, and a little salt for about 10 minutes, or until almost all the water has evaporated.
Prepare sautéed chicken and remove it to a heated platter.
To the juices in the pan add 1 tablespoon chopped shallots or onion, 1 garlic clove, crushed, and 1 teaspoon flour. Chop the morels and add them and their juice, 1/4 cup tomato sauce, and 2 or 3 tablespoons stock. Stir well and cook for 5 minutes longer. Correct the seasoning with salt and freshly ground pepper and add 1 tablespoon chopped parsley. Return

Poulet Sauté aux Morilles

the chicken to the pan and simmer it for 10 minutes. Arrange the chicken on a heated serving platter and pour over it the sauce and morels.

If the recipe requires that the chicken be partially cooked, and cooked further with additional ingredients, it need only be browned on both sides.

Poulet Sauté à la Française

Parboil 4 carrots and 4 onions, both thinly sliced, for 5 to 10 minutes in a little water sweetened with 1 teaspoon sugar. Drain the vegetables and add them to the browned chicken in the pan. Add 1 tablespoon chopped parsley and 1 cup cream, cover the pan and cook the chicken very slowly for 25 to 30 minutes. Remove it to a heated serving dish. Thicken the sauce with 2 tablespoons cream sauce and add 1 tablespoon brandy and salt and pepper to taste. Pour sauce and vegetables over the chicken.

Poulet Sauté Chasseur

To the browned chicken in the pan add 1/4 pound mushrooms, sliced, and cook the mushrooms until they are tender. Remove the chicken from the pan. To the mushrooms add 2 tablespoons butter, 1 tablespoon chopped shallot and 1 teaspoon flour and cook, stirring, until the flour is golden. Stir in 1/4 cup white wine and continue to cook until the wine is reduced by half. Add 3/4 cup cooked tomatoes and cook the sauce for 5 minutes longer. Return the chicken to the sauce and simmer all together for 15 to 20 minutes, or until the chicken is done. Arrange the chicken on a heated serving dish. Add 1 teaspoon finely chopped mixed *fines herbes* and salt to taste. Pour the sauce over the chicken.

Sautéed Chicken Portugaise

To the browned chicken in the pan add 1 tablespoon chopped shallots or onion and cook it slowly for a few minutes. Add 1 teaspoon flour, 1 garlic clove, crushed, 1/2 cup each of stock and cooked tomatoes, and 1/4 cup white wine. Simmer the chicken for 25 to 30 minutes and correct the seasoning with salt and pepper. Transfer it to another pan and strain the sauce over it. Add 4 or 5 fresh tomatoes, peeled, seeded, and chopped, and cook the chicken for 10 to 15 minutes more. Arrange it on a heated serving platter, pour the sauce over it, and sprinkle with chopped parsley.

Sautéed Chicken Gloria Swanson

To the browned chicken add 10 mushrooms and cook them for 5 minutes. Stir in 1 teaspoon chopped shallots or onion and 1 tablespoon flour and cook the mixture for a few minutes longer. Add 1/2 cup cream, 1/4 cup white wine, and a *bouquet garni* composed of 3 sprigs of parsley, a bay leaf, and a sprig of thyme, and cook the chicken slowly, partly covered, for about 25 to 30 minutes, until it is done. Add salt to taste. Discard the *bouquet garni*.

Stir into the sauce 2 egg yolks, lightly beaten with 1/2 cup warm cream. Stir the sauce, off the heat, so that it will not curdle. Arrange the chicken on a heated serving dish and pour the sauce over it. Garnish with 4 tomatoes, halved, sautéed in butter, and sprinkled with parsley, and with small molds of rice pilaff topped with slices of truffle.

QUARTER a 3-pound chicken. Sprinkle the pieces lightly with flour and brown them in clarified butter over moderate heat. As the chicken browns, sprinkle it very lightly with equal amounts rosemary, thyme, tarragon, and sage. Lower the heat and cook the chicken until it is tender.

Four Herb Chicken

Remove the chicken to a heated serving platter, skim off the fat from the pan, and to the juices remaining add 1/3 cup dry white wine, Anjou or Burgundy. Simmer the wine until the sauce thickens slightly, pour it over the chicken, and serve immediately. Serves 4.

BROWN a 3-pound chicken, cut in pieces, in olive oil and butter until it is tender. Season it with salt, pepper, and finely chopped shallots. Discard the excess fat in the skillet and pour over the chicken 1/4 cup each of white wine, Sherry, and chicken consommé. Simmer the liquid for a few minutes. Just before serving, add 2 egg yolks beaten with a little warm thick cream, stirring constantly to prevent curdling. Add minced chives and parsley to the sauce, and a pinch of nutmeg if desired. Serves 4.

Chicken Raphael Weill

BROWN two 2-pound chickens, cut in pieces, in clarified butter.

Chicken Financière

In a saucepan melt 1/4 cup butter. Remove the pan from the heat, add 2 tablespoons flour, and blend the *roux* until it is smooth. Stir in 1 cup chicken consommé and cook the sauce over moderate heat for 10 minutes, stirring constantly. Add 2 sautéed chicken livers, cubed, 12 mushrooms, cubed, 12 green olives, stoned, a dash of cayenne, and salt and pepper, and cook the mixture over low heat for 30 minutes.

Add the browned chicken and 1 cup Sherry and cook the chicken slowly for 30 minutes, or until it is tender. Arrange it on a heated platter, pour the sauce over it, and garnish with slices of truffle and with cockscombs.

CUT a 4-pound chicken into serving pieces and roll the pieces in flour. Brown the chicken on all sides in 1/2 cup clarified butter. Season with salt, white pepper, and nutmeg to taste.

Chicken Jerusalem

Add 1 pound sliced mushrooms. Cut 6 tender artichoke bottoms into quarters and add them to the chicken. Moisten the mixture with 1/2 cup Sherry, cover the saucepan, and simmer the chicken for 25 minutes, or until it is tender. Stir in 2 cups hot heavy cream. Sprinkle the top with finely chopped parsley before serving.

Gallina con Salsa de Almendras
CHICKEN IN ALMOND SAUCE

CUT a 4- to 5-pound roasting chicken into serving pieces, sprinkle the pieces with salt and pepper, and brown them in 6 tablespoons oil. Add 1 onion, minced, a crushed garlic clove, if desired, 1 cup chicken broth, 1/2 cup each of cubed smoked ham and Sherry, and the juice of 1 sour orange or 1 lemon. Cover and cook slowly.

Blanch 3/4 cup almonds. Grind them in a mortar until they are reduced to a paste. When the chicken is almost done, add the almond paste and continue to cook until the chicken is tender.

Ajam Boomboo Roedjak
SPICED CHICKEN

CUT into serving pieces 2 chickens each weighing 1 1/2 to 2 pounds. Sauté the pieces in clarified butter or peanut oil until they are light brown. Put together through a food chopper 7 medium onions, 1 garlic clove, 3 whole hot red peppers, seeded, 5 Brazil nuts, 1 teaspoon anchovy paste, 2 lemon sections or 1 large lime, 1 tablespoon brown sugar, and a pinch of salt. Sauté the mixture in 2 tablespoons butter until it is golden brown. Add to it 1/2 coconut, grated, 1/4 cup coconut milk, 1 bay leaf and the juice of 1 lime. Add the chicken to the seasonings and, if necessary, add a little water. Simmer the mixture until the sauce is thick and the chicken is tender.

Poulet à la Vallée d'Auge

CUT two 2-pound chickens into serving pieces, season them with salt and pepper, and brown them lightly on all sides in a large skillet in 1/2 cup clarified butter. Lower the heat and cook the pieces for 15 minutes longer, turning them often. Add 1/4 cup warmed Calvados or applejack, ignite the spirit, and shake the pan until the flame dies. Add 5 or 6 shallots, finely chopped, 1 tablespoon chopped parsley, 1 sprig of thyme or 1/4 teaspoon dried thyme, and 1/2 cup cider or white wine. Blend the sauce well, cover the pan, and cook the chicken until it is tender. Arrange it on a heated platter. Add 1/2 cup heavy cream to the liquid in the pan and heat the sauce without boiling it. Pour the sauce over the chicken just before serving.

Poulet à la Vallée d'Auge

Poularde
Flambée

QUARTER two 2-pound chickens and sauté them gently in a large skillet in 6 tablespoons clarified butter for 2 to 3 minutes on each side. Add 6 shallots, chopped, 12 mushroom caps, quartered, and 1 tablespoon chopped fresh tarragon and continue to sauté the pieces for 5 minutes, turning them frequently so that they will cook evenly but will not brown. Pour 1/2 cup warmed Cognac over the chicken and ignite the spirit. When the flame dies, add 3/4 cup dry white wine and a *bouquet garni* composed of 1 leek, split, 4 sprigs of parsley, and 1 stalk of celery with the leaves. Add salt and pepper to taste, cover the skillet, and cook the chicken over low heat for about 25 minutes, or until it is tender.

Arrange the chicken on a heated platter and stir 1 1/2 cups hot heavy cream into the juices in the skillet. Stir in small bits of *beurre manié* (equal amounts of flour and butter kneaded to a smooth paste) until the sauce is the right consistency. Strain the sauce over the chicken and serve with rice.

Chicken cooked en casserole *is an ideal choice for the host-cum-cook. Whether it completes its progress toward tender mellowness in the oven or over direct heat, it demands a minimum of last-minute attention, and most casserole recipes may be prepared well ahead of time and reheated just before serving.*

Coq au Vin
Rouge

CHICKEN IN
RED WINE

CUT two 2-pound chickens into serving pieces. Wipe the pieces with a damp cloth and rub them with salt, black pepper, paprika, and a little nutmeg. Dredge them in flour. In a large shallow earthenware casserole brown 1/2 pound salt pork cut in finger-size strips. Add 24 whole small white onions, peeled, and brown them lightly. Add the chicken pieces and brown them on all sides, turning them frequently.

Discard the fat from the casserole. Pour over the chicken 3 tablespoons warmed brandy, and ignite the spirit. When the flame dies, pour in 1 bottle of heated red Burgundy and add 1 large lump of sugar, 2 mashed garlic cloves, 12 whole small mushrooms, and a *bouquet garni* consisting of 2 sprigs of green celery top, 1 sprig of thyme, 6 or 7 sprigs of fresh parsley, 2 sprigs of rosemary, and 1 large bay leaf. Cover the casserole and cook the chicken in a moderately hot oven (375° F.) for about 45 minutes, or until it is tender.

Remove the *bouquet garni* and serve the chicken in the casserole. If the sauce seems too thin, thicken it with 1 tablespoon *beurre manié*, and simmer it for about 10 minutes, or until it thickens.

HAVE the butcher bone and quarter two 2-pound chickens. Melt 2 tablespoons each of butter and oil in a heavy skillet and in it sauté the chicken until the pieces are golden on all sides. Transfer the chicken to a heavy casserole. In the skillet sauté until golden 1 carrot and 1 onion, both finely chopped. Add the vegetables to the casserole with the chicken. Season well with salt, pepper, a pinch of cloves, a *bouquet garni* composed of a sprig of thyme, a bay leaf, a stalk of celery, and a sprig of parsley, and 2 garlic cloves. Add 1 bottle of warmed white Burgundy, cover the casserole, and cook the chicken over high heat for 30 minutes. Maintain the level of liquid by adding chicken or veal stock as necessary.

Transfer the chicken to a heated platter and keep it warm. Add to the sauce in the casserole 1/4 cup *beurre manié* made by kneading together 2 tablespoons each of butter and flour, and cook the sauce until it is thickened, stirring it constantly with a wire whip. Strain the sauce and pour it over the chicken. Add 10 or 12 small, cooked white onions and 12 mushrooms, cooked for 5 minutes in a little butter and lemon juice. Garnish the platter with heart-shaped croutons and serve the chicken immediately.

Coq au Vin Blanc
CHICKEN IN WHITE WINE

CUT the wing tips from three 2 1/2-pound broilers and cook them in water to cover, with the giblets, necks, and feet for 1 hour. Season the broth with salt and pepper to taste and strain it.

Sauté the chickens' livers in butter and chop them finely with 3/4 cup chopped parsley and 1/3 cup butter. Season this mixture to taste with salt and pepper and use it to stuff the birds. Brown the birds on all sides in 1/3 cup butter in a Dutch oven. Add about a half inch of broth to the pot and cover it closely. Cook the chickens very slowly for about 45 minutes, or until they are tender, basting them from time to time with the broth and adding more broth as necessary. Remove the chickens to a heated serving dish and reduce the sauce over high heat. Add 1 tablespoon butter kneaded with 1 tablespoon flour and cook for a few minutes longer. Stir in 1 cup cream and heat the sauce just to the boiling point. Strain it and serve it in a sauceboat.

Poulet au Persil
PARSLEY CHICKEN

CLEAN and truss a large roasting chicken and brown it on all sides in a heavy roasting pan in 5 tablespoons butter. Sprinkle the chicken with salt and pepper and surround it with 3 carrots, 6 small onions, and 12 mushroom stems, all chopped, and add a *bouquet garni* composed of 1 leek, split,

Poularde au Cognac

Madras Chicken Curry

4 sprigs of parsley, and 1 sprig of tarragon. Cover the chicken and roast it in a moderate oven (375° F.) for 1 hour, or until it is tender, basting frequently.

Transfer the chicken to a large casserole. Discard the vegetables from the roasting pan and skim the fat from the surface of the pan juices. To the juices remaining in the pan add 1/4 cup butter, 18 mushroom caps, 2 truffles, sliced, and 1/4 cup each of Cognac and Port. Bring the sauce to a boil, stirring constantly. Add 1 1/2 cups heavy cream and cook the sauce, stirring, until it almost reaches a boil. Stir in 4 egg yolks lightly beaten with 1/2 cup cream and a little of the hot sauce and continue to stir over very low heat for 3 minutes, or until the sauce is thickened, being careful that it does not boil. Correct the seasoning, pour the sauce over the chicken, and serve from the casserole.

HALVE a 2- to 2 1/2-pound broiler, season it with salt and pepper, and brown it on all sides in butter. Arrange the chicken in a baking dish and pour over it a mixture of 1/2 pint sour cream, 1/4 pound crumbled Roquefort cheese, and 1 garlic clove, forced through a press. Cover the dish and bake the chicken in a moderate oven (350° F.) for about 45 minutes, or until the bird is thoroughly cooked. Serves 2.

Chicken Elizabeth à l'Épicure

CUT the meat of a 2 1/2- to 3-pound chicken into pieces about 1 inch square and not more than 1/2 inch thick. Dust the chicken pieces with flour and sauté them in 3 tablespoons butter until they are lightly browned on all sides. Remove the meat to a platter and keep it warm. To the butter remaining in the pan add 3 onions and 1 garlic clove, both minced, and sauté them until they are golden.

In a saucepan melt 2 teaspoons butter, add 1 1/2 tablespoons curry powder, and stir until the mixture is smooth. Stir in gradually 2 cups hot chicken stock. Add 2 tablespoons chutney, chopped, 1/2 cup seedless raisins, 2 tart apples, peeled and sliced, and 1/2 teaspoon each of powdered ginger and salt. Cover and simmer for 30 minutes.

Chop 1/4 cup blanched almonds and sauté them lightly in 1 teaspoon butter. Pound them in a mortar to a smooth paste. Stir the almond paste gradually into 1/2 cup hot cream and cook the cream over low heat for 5 minutes. Add this almond cream to the sauce, along with the sautéed onions and garlic and the chicken, and simmer the mixture uncovered, for about 15

Madras Chicken Curry

minutes, or until the sauce is thickened. Add the juice of 1/2 lemon and serve with cooked rice. If the sauce seems too thick, add a little hot chicken stock.

Serve with suitable accompaniments.

Mexican Chicken

DISJOINT a 4- to 6-pound roasting chicken and sprinkle the pieces with salt and pepper. In a large skillet sauté the chicken in 3 tablespoons butter until the pieces are browned on all sides. Add 12 blanched almonds, 1/2 cup seeded raisins, 1 cup chopped pineapple, 1/8 teaspoon each of ground cinnamon and cloves, and 2 cups orange juice. Cover the skillet tightly and simmer the chicken for 45 minutes, or until it is tender.

Stir in 1 tablespoon flour mixed to a smooth paste with 2 tablespoons cold water. Cook, stirring constantly, until the sauce is thickened. Simmer the sauce for 10 minutes longer.

Arrange the chicken on a warmed serving platter and pour a little of the sauce over it. Garnish the platter with half-moon slices of avocado and serve the rest of the sauce separately.

Chicken with Rosemary

CLEAN a 2 1/2-pound chicken and cut it into serving pieces. Sprinkle the pieces lightly with flour and brown them in 1/4 cup butter over high heat. Soak 1 tablespoon rosemary in 2 cups white wine. Transfer the chicken to a casserole and pour the wine over it. Add 2 thinly sliced onions and salt and pepper to taste. Cover the casserole and bake the chicken in a moderately slow oven (325° F.) until it is tender. Serves 4.

Smothered Chicken au Gratin

QUARTER two 2 1/2-pound chickens. Brush the pieces with butter and dredge them with salt, pepper, and flour. Melt 6 tablespoons butter or chicken fat in a heavy skillet and in it sauté the chicken pieces until they are well browned on all sides. Cover the skillet and cook the chicken for about 10 minutes.

Boil 1 pound broad egg noodles in salted water until they are tender. Drain the noodles, put them in a buttered casserole, and arrange the chicken on top.

Stir into the fat remaining in the skillet 1 tablespoon flour. Stir in gradually 2 cups hot cream and cook the sauce, stirring, until it is slightly thickened, scraping all the brown bits from the bottom of the pan. Pour the sauce over the chicken in the casserole, sprinkle generously with bread crumbs, and dot with butter. Bake the chicken in a moderate oven (350° F.) for about 20 minutes, or until the sauce starts to bubble through the layer of crumbs and the chicken is thoroughly cooked.

CUT into serving pieces two 3-pound chickens. Sauté 2 large onions, chopped, in 1 tablespoon fat in a heavy saucepan. Add half a green pepper, shredded, and 2 tablespoons or more sweet Hungarian paprika, and mix well. Add the chicken, lightly sprinkled with salt, and 1 small, ripe tomato, peeled, seeded, and chopped. Pour in 1 cup chicken stock and cover the pan. Cook the chicken slowly, turning it from time to time, until it is tender. Adjust the seasoning with salt and pepper to taste. Transfer the chicken to a warmed platter. Add a little more chicken stock to the pan and bring it to a boil, scraping the brown bits from the bottom and sides of the pan. Add 1 cup sour cream, if desired, heat the sauce, and pour it over the chicken on the platter. Serve with buttered noodles.

Chicken Paprikás

CLEAN and disjoint a 3-pound frying chicken and rub the pieces with a mixture of 2 tablespoons each of soy sauce and olive oil. In a deep skillet heat 1 quart oil to 390° F., or until a cube of bread browns in 30 seconds. Lower the chicken pieces gently into the hot fat and fry them for about 6 minutes, or until they are golden on both sides.

Chicken Cantonese

Drain all the fat from the pan and add to the chicken 2 tablespoons soy sauce mixed with 1/4 cup water, 2 tablespoons chopped scallions, and a dash of white wine. Cover the pan tightly and cook the chicken over low heat for about 20 minutes, or until it is tender.

Arrange the chicken on a warmed serving platter and to the juices in the pan add 1 cup chicken stock. Bring the stock to a boil, stir in 1/2 tablespoon cornstarch mixed with 1/4 cup water, and cook, stirring, until the sauce is smooth and thickened. Pour the sauce over the chicken, sprinkle with cashews, if desired, and serve with boiled rice. Serves 4.

CUT a 2 1/2-pound frying chicken into serving pieces and brown the pieces on all sides in a casserole in 1/2 cup hot olive oil. Remove the chicken and to the juices in the casserole add 2 garlic cloves, 1 onion, and 1 green pepper, all chopped, and sauté them until the onion is golden. Add 1 bay leaf and 1 cup whole cooked tomatoes. Return the chicken to the casserole and add 1 quart chicken broth. When the broth boils add 1 tablespoon salt, 1/2 teaspoon powdered saffron, and 1 cup rice. Cover the casserole and bake it in a moderate oven (350° F.) for 20 minutes, or until the rice is tender. Garnish with strips of pimiento, 1/2 cup cooked green peas, 4 cooked asparagus tips, and chopped parsley. Serves 4.

Arroz con Pollo Valenciana

*Paella
Valenciana*

CUT a 3- to 3 1/2-pound chicken into serving pieces and sauté the pieces in 1/2 cup butter with 1 crushed garlic clove until they are golden brown on all sides. Remove the pieces and set them aside. In the juices remaining in the pan sauté 2 cups rice until it is golden. Add 1/2 teaspoon saffron and 4 cups hot chicken stock and bring the liquid to a boil. Season with salt and pepper.

Butter the bottom and sides of a deep casserole or Dutch oven. Put half the pieces of chicken in the casserole, and cover the chicken with 1 *chorizo*, the highly seasoned Spanish sausage, sliced, and 1/2 cup diced pimientos. Add almost all the rice and top with the remaining pieces of chicken. Add 1 more *chorizo*, 1/2 cup diced pimientos, and the remaining rice. Bake the casserole, uncovered, in a moderate oven (350° F.) for 30 minutes, adding a little chicken stock from time to time as needed. Add 1 lobster, cut into pieces, and cook for 15 minutes longer. Add 12 cleaned mussels, 18 shelled and deveined shrimps, and cook the *paella* for 10 minutes longer. Garnish with strips of pimiento and serve from the casserole with garlic bread and a tossed green salad.

If desired, steamed clams may be used in the *paella* in place of, or in addition to, the mussels.

*Chicken
Pilaff*

CLEAN and wipe dry a 4 1/2- to 5-pound stewing fowl. Put it in a kettle with cold water to cover and add an onion, a *bouquet garni* composed of 2 stalks of celery, 1 sprig of thyme, and 2 sprigs of parsley, and salt. Simmer the bird gently for 2 1/2 hours. When the chicken is tender remove it from the stock and cut the meat from the bones in large pieces. Return the bones to the stock, add 1 cup water, and continue cooking.

In a saucepan sauté 4 stalks of celery, cut in small pieces, and 2 onions, thinly sliced, in 2 tablespoons olive oil until the vegetables are transparent. Remove the onions and celery and reserve them. Add enough olive oil to the pan to make 2 tablespoons. Stir in 2 cups raw rice and cook the rice, stirring constantly, until it is gilded. Strain the chicken broth and skim off the fat. There should be 4 cups broth in all. Add 3 cups of the broth to the rice. Steep 1/2 teaspoon saffron in the remaining cup of broth and add it to the rice. Add salt and pepper to taste and cook the rice over very low heat for 10 minutes. Turn the partly cooked rice into a casserole and add the chicken meat, 1 cup raisins, 1 cup blanched and slivered almonds, and the celery and onions. Bake the casserole in a moderately slow oven

(325° F.) until the rice is tender, adding a little water or stock if it becomes too dry. Serve with a tossed green salad.

CUT two 2 1/2-pound broilers into serving pieces and roll the pieces in flour. Melt 1/4 cup butter in a skillet and in it sauté the chicken pieces until they are lightly browned on all sides. Transfer the pieces to a buttered casserole and add 1 cup chicken stock. Cover the casserole and bake the pieces in a moderate oven (350° F.) for 45 minutes, or until they are tender. Add 1 cup warm heavy cream and 3 dozen freshly shucked oysters. Correct the seasoning with salt and pepper and bake the casserole for 10 minutes longer. Serve from the casserole.

Chicken and Oyster Casserole

CUT a 4-pound chicken into serving pieces and put them in a flameproof casserole with 1 pound lean pork cut into strips 1 inch wide and 2 inches long. Add 1 teaspoon peppercorns, crushed, 3 garlic cloves, crushed, 4 tomatoes, peeled, seeded and chopped, 1/4 cup cider vinegar, 1/2 cup whole stuffed olives, 2 teaspoons salt, 1 small bay leaf, and 2 cups water. Let the meat stand in this marinade for 1 hour.

Adobo
CHICKEN AND PORK

Cover the casserole, set it over low heat, and simmer the meat for 2 to 2 1/2 hours, shaking the pot from time to time. Keep the casserole covered and the heat as low as possible without stopping the cooking process. The liquid should be almost absorbed and the chicken and pork very tender. Serve with rice.

CLEAN and singe a 3- to 3 1/2-pound chicken and cut the breast and wing sections into 4 pieces and the legs and second joints into 4 pieces, removing the bones from the legs and second joints. Clean and slice 8 to 12 mushrooms. Mash the yolks of 4 hard-cooked eggs, force them through a fine sieve into a bowl, and stir in gradually 1 cup chicken stock. Add 1 onion, finely chopped, 1 teaspoon finely chopped parsley, 1/2 teaspoon salt, a little pepper, 1/2 teaspoon Worcestershire sauce, and 1/4 cup white wine or 1 tablespoon vinegar. Add the chicken and toss the pieces until they are well coated.

English Chicken Pie à la Ritz

In each of four individual casseroles put 1 piece each of white and dark meat. Divide the mushrooms evenly among the casseroles and lay

2 pieces of broiled bacon on top. Add 1 cup chicken broth to each casserole. Roll out either puff paste or pie pastry about 1/4 inch thick and cut it into rounds to fit the tops of the casseroles. Cover the casseroles, fitting on the pastry securely. Brush the tops with an egg beaten with a little milk and prick them to allow the steam to escape. Bake the casseroles in a moderately hot oven (375 to 400° F.) for 1 hour, or until the crust is brown and the chicken is done. Serves 4.

Wild Rice Stuffing HAVE the butcher remove all but the leg bones of 6 squab chickens. Wash 1 cup wild rice in several changes of cold water, discarding any kernels that float to the top of the water. Cover the rice generously with cold water and add 1 teaspoon salt. Bring the rice to a boil and cook it, uncovered, for about 30 minutes, or until it is tender but not mushy. Drain the rice in a colander. Sauté 3 hearts of celery and 3 medium onions, both finely chopped, in 6 tablespoons butter until the onions are transparent. Add the butter and vegetables to the rice; add salt and pepper to taste, and mix lightly. Stuff the birds with this wild rice stuffing and tie or sew them securely, restoring the original shape as nearly as possible.

Boned Squab
Chickens
en Casserole In a large flameproof casserole melt 1/4 cup butter and in it sauté 3 carrots and 3 onions, both thinly sliced, until they are golden. Add the birds and brown them on all sides. Add 2 cups chicken stock, cover the casserole, and cook the chickens in a moderate oven (350° F.) for about 45 minutes, or until they are tender. Drain the juice into a saucepan. Pour over the birds 1/3 cup warmed Cognac and ignite the spirit. When the flame dies, thicken the juice by stirring in, bit by bit, *beurre manié*, made by mixing equal amounts of soft butter and flour to a smooth paste. About 1 tablespoon each of flour and butter should be sufficient, for the sauce should not be too thick. Return the sauce to the casserole.

Roast
Chicken CLEAN and singe a plump young roasting chicken. (A 4-pound roasting chicken will generally feed four people; roast 2 smaller ones for six.) Season the chicken with salt inside and out and stuff it or not, as desired.
To Truss
a Chicken Truss the legs and wings close to the body in this manner: Thread a six- or eight-inch kitchen needle with strong white thread. Pierce the second joint,

or thigh, and push the needle through the body and the other second joint. Pierce through the chicken again, pushing the needle back through the leg, the body, and the other leg. Go back again through the wing, the body, and the other wing, and tie the ends of the thread across the back (so that it will not mar the breast). Run another thread through the folded-back wing tips and tie the ends.

Set the chicken on its side in a roasting pan, spread over it 2 table-spoons butter, and add 1/4 cup water to the pan. Roast the chicken in a hot oven (400° F.) for about 10 minutes and turn it on its other side. When it begins to take on a golden color reduce the heat to moderately hot (375° F.) and continue to cook it, turning it and basting it every 15 minutes and adding more water as necessary. There should be just enough water to keep the juice in the pan from scorching. Cook the chicken for 1 to 1 1/2 hours or until it is done, turning the bird on its back for the last 15 minutes to brown the breast. To test, pierce the second point with a two-tined kitchen fork or a metal skewer; if the juice that comes out is clear and colorless, the bird is done; if it has a pink tinge, more cooking is needed.

Pan Gravy

Remove the chicken from the pan. Add 1/2 cup water or chicken stock to the pan and cook the gravy over moderate heat for a few minutes, stirring in all the brown bits. Correct the seasoning with salt and swirl in 1 tablespoon butter. Remove the pan gravy from the heat before the butter has completely melted.

Roast Chicken with Prunes

GARNISH a roast chicken with prunes prepared as follows: Soak 12 extra-large prunes in warm water for 2 hours. Drain and dry them, and remove the pits. Wrap each prune in a strip of lean bacon and broil them two inches from the heat until the bacon is crisp. Turn them once or twice.

Roast Truffled Birds

To prepare a stuffed, truffled bird for roasting so that the skin does not appear to have been cut, follow this method: Remove all the pin feathers, being careful not to tear the skin. Cut off the head, leaving on as much neck as possible; slit the skin at the back of the neck and remove neck and crop. Now, working very carefully with a sharp knife, cut the wishbone away from the breast meat. Use this neck aperture to clean out the bird. To detach the end of the intestinal tract, cut as small an opening as possible under the bird's tail. Make sure the bird is cleanly drawn and wipe the inside thoroughly with a damp cloth. Pack the prepared stuffing loosely into the cavity, reserving 1 or 2 cups to fill the crop cavity. Carefully loosen the skin over the breasts and slide under the skin on each side 6 slices of truffle that have been soaked in Madeira. Fill the crop cavity, bring the neck skin over the back of the bird, and sew the skin neatly in place.

Truss the bird, sprinkle it with a very little flour, and cover the breast with thin slices of fat salt pork. Wrap the bird loosely in buttered paper and refrigerate it for a few hours, so that the *parfum aux truffes* permeates the flesh. Remove the bird from the refrigerator an hour or so before roasting time and proceed in the usual way.

When the bird is done, remove the paper and the fat pork. If necessary, the bird may be returned to the oven for further browning. Serve with *sauce périgourdine*.

Truffled Chicken

INSERT 1 thinly sliced white Italian truffle under the skin of the breast of a plump roasting chicken and rub the bird with salt and pepper. Put another sliced white truffle inside the bird and truss it. Wrap the bird in foil and refrigerate it for 24 hours. Pour 1/4 cup melted butter over the bird and roast in a slow oven (300° F.), basting frequently, for 1 1/4 hours. Season the chicken with salt, add 1/2 cup dry Marsala to the pan juices, and continue cooking for another 1 1/4 hours, basting frequently, until the bird is tender and cooked through.

Poulet Rôti en Casserole
ROAST CHICKEN IN CASSEROLE

CLEAN and singe a plump 4-pound chicken and truss the legs and wings close to the body. Season it with salt inside and out and put a garlic clove in the cavity. Set the chicken on its side in a casserole large enough to accommodate the bird and vegetables. Add a little good fat and cook the chicken over low heat until the bird is brown on one side. Turn it to brown the other side and continue to cook for about 30 minutes, turning and basting the chicken with the fat. Pour off the fat and reserve it. Put 12 small white onions and 2 tablespoons butter around the bird and cook the onions until they are brown. Add 4 potatoes, peeled and cut into wedges, and 2 more tablespoons butter and cook the casserole, partly covered, until the potatoes are brown. Add 1/4 pound diced salt pork, blanched and sautéed until brown in the reserved fat, 1/4 pound mushroom caps, browned in a little fat, and 1/2 cup chicken stock or water and cook the casserole for 20 to 30 minutes longer, or until the chicken is done. Remove the chicken, carve it, and arrange it on a warmed serving platter. Arrange the vegetables

Roast Chicken in Casserole

around it and sprinkle with chopped parsley. Serve the gravy from the casserole separately. Serves 4.

Roast Broilers

RUB 3 broilers with soft butter and sprinkle them with salt, pepper, paprika, and flour. Into the cavity of each bird put 1/4 cup butter and 1 tablespoon chopped chives. Truss the legs and wings close to the bodies and roast the broilers in a very hot oven (500° F.) for 15 minutes. Lower the temperature to hot (400° F.) and continue to roast the birds for about 30 minutes, or until they are done, basting frequently. Serve with the pan juices and sprinkle with chopped chives.

Baked Broilers

SPLIT 3 broilers, season them with salt and pepper, and arrange them skin side up in a buttered baking pan. Sprinkle the birds with flour, put 1 teaspoon butter on each half, and pour over them 1 cup heavy cream. Put the birds in the refrigerator overnight.

The next day brown the birds in a hot oven (400° F.) for 15 minutes. Reduce the temperature to moderate (350° F.), cover the pan, and bake the birds for 30 minutes longer, or until they are done, adding a little more cream if necessary.

Poussin Montmorency

SQUAB CHICKEN IN PORT AND CHERRY SAUCE

HAVE the butcher bone a squab chicken weighing about 1 1/4 to 1 1/2 pounds. Wipe it with a damp cloth and spread it out, skin side down, on a board. Season with salt and freshly ground black pepper and fill the center with a mixture of *foie gras* and chopped truffles. Roll the chicken into shape and secure it with skewers.

Bake the stuffed *poussin* in a shallow pan with 1/4 cup sweet butter in a moderately hot oven (375° F.) for about 35 minutes, basting frequently. Remove the chicken from the pan and keep it hot in a warm casserole.

To the juices in the pan add 1/2 cup Port and reduce the liquid by half. Add 10 to 15 pitted black cherries and cook for 5 minutes. Thicken the sauce with *beurre manié*—1 teaspoon flour and 1 tablespoon butter kneaded together—or with 1/2 teaspoon cornstarch blended with 1 table-spoon cold water. Pour the sauce around the chicken in the casserole and pour over it 1/4 cup browned butter. Serve hot, with wild rice or noodles. Serves 2.

If roasted birds differ at all, they differ because of their stuffings. Great variety is possible, and should be compulsory. Count on 3/4 cup stuffing mixture to each pound of the bird's dressed weight and fill the cavity loosely, since stuffings expand when they cook.

SAUTÉ 10 shallots, finely chopped, in 1/2 cup butter and when they are lightly colored add 1/4 pound smoked ham, finely ground, 1/4 cup chopped parsley, 1 teaspoon salt, and 1/2 teaspoon each of thyme and freshly ground pepper. Blend the mixture with 4 cups zwieback crumbs or toasted bread crumbs, 2 whole eggs, 1/4 cup Madeira, and 2/3 cup blanched almonds. Mix thoroughly and taste for seasoning.

Almond Stuffing

COOK 1/2 cup wild rice or 3/4 cup white rice in boiling salted water for 30 to 45 minutes and drain. This will make about 1 1/2 cups cooked rice. Heat 2 tablespoons butter in a saucepan and add the rice. Mix well and season with salt and pepper. In another pan, plump 2 tablespoons raisins in a little butter and stir them lightly into the rice. Slice about 12 cooked apricot halves, fresh or dried. Add the apricots to the rice with 2 or 3 tablespoons beef gravy and 3 tablespoons chicken *velouté*. Mix all the ingredients lightly.

Apricot Stuffing

MELT 1 cup butter or any good fat in a saucepan. Add 1 cup chopped onions and cook them until they turn golden. Add 2 cups fresh bread crumbs, firmly packed, 1 tablespoon chopped parsley, 1/2 teaspoon thyme, a little rosemary, if desired, and salt and pepper to taste. Cool the mixture and add 2 stalks of celery, cut in small pieces and stewed in a little water until tender, and a little liquor from the oysters.

Oyster Stuffing

Drain 12 freshly shucked oysters. Roll them in flour, in beaten egg mixed with a very little salad oil, and then in cracker crumbs. Sauté them in hot butter or oil for 1 minute on each side. The oysters should be golden-brown but still juicy inside. Stuff the bird with alternate layers of the bread mixture and of oysters.

English Stuffing

COOK 1 pound sausage meat long enough to extract most of its fat. Discard all but 3 tablespoons of the sausage fat and in the remaining fat brown 2 chopped large onions. Remove the pan from the heat and stir in 1/4 pound poultry livers, finely chopped, and 1 large slice of bread soaked in milk, squeezed dry, and crumbled. Add 1/2 teaspoon salt, 1/4 cup apple brandy, Madeira, or Sherry, 12 coarsely chopped cooked chestnuts, a small pinch of dried thyme, 1 teaspoon minced parsley, and 1 egg. Add the sausage meat and mix well. Especially for goose.

Breton Stuffing

SAUTÉ 2 cups each of chopped onions and thinly sliced celery in 3/4 pound melted butter until the onions are golden. Toss the vegetables and butter with 9 cups stale bread crumbs in a large mixing bowl. Add 2 teaspoons salt and 1 teaspoon each of thyme, marjoram, and sage, and mix thoroughly. If a small amount of the mixture rolled between the fingers does not stick together, add a little turkey stock.

Chestnut Stuffing

Slit the shells of 3 pounds chestnuts and simmer the nuts in water to cover for 5 minutes. Working very quickly, while the nuts are still hot, remove and discard the shells and skins. Put the nuts in fresh boiling water and cook them gently for about 20 to 30 minutes, or until they are tender. Put the chestnuts through the finest blade of a food chopper and blend them thoroughly with the bread. Especially for turkey.

IN a large saucepan melt 1/2 pound butter, add 3 onions, chopped, and cook the onions slowly until they are golden brown. Add 1 1/4 pounds white bread crumbs, 1/2 teaspoon salt, 1/4 teaspoon thyme, a little freshly ground pepper, 1 1/2 teaspoons finely chopped parsley, and sage to taste. Mix the ingredients together and cook them slowly until the mixture is well combined. Cool before using. This is an all-purpose stuffing. Makes enough to stuff a 6-pound bird.

English Stuffing

CANNED truffles come peeled or unpeeled. If necessary, peel them as thinly as possible, removing the rough skin very carefully. Put the peelings of 9 truffles through the finest blade of a food chopper with 2 pounds *panne*, or pork leaf fat, and 1/2 pound goose liver or goose liver pâté. Or as a variation, use 1 1/2 pounds *panne* and 1/4 pound each of lean veal, and goose liver, all finely ground. Add 2 eggs, lightly beaten, season the mixture with 1 teaspoon salt, and rub it through a fine sieve. Add 6 of the peeled truffles, cutting them in half if they are large, 1/2 bay leaf, finely crushed, and a pinch of thyme. Moisten the stuffing with the juice from

Farce Truffée
TRUFFLE STUFFING

233

the can of truffles (about 1/2 cup) and 1/4 cup each of brandy and Madeira or Sherry.

Store the *farce* in the refrigerator for 24 hours before using it; this recipe makes enough to stuff a large bird. Slice the remaining 3 truffles thinly, sprinkle them with Madeira or Sherry and a little truffle juice from the can, and lay them on the bird's breast. During the roasting, their flavor will permeate the bird.

Pecan Wild Rice Stuffing

WASH 1 1/2 cups wild rice thoroughly in cold water and boil the rice in boiling salted water for 20 minutes, stirring constantly. Drain the rice, return it to the pot, and shake it dry over low heat. In a skillet, render 3 tablespoons cubed salt pork. Add 3 tablespoons chopped onion and continue to cook, stirring, until the onions are lightly browned. In another skillet sauté 1/2 pound chopped mushrooms in 1/3 cup butter for 3 minutes. Add the mushrooms and the onions and pork cracklings to the rice along with 1 1/2 tablespoons minced parsley, 1 teaspoon marjoram, 1/2 teaspoon poultry seasoning, and 1/4 cup coarsely chopped pecans. This makes sufficient dressing to stuff 6 squabs or 1 large capon.

Wild Rice and Chicken Liver Stuffing

COOK 1 cup wild rice and toss it with 1/2 cup chicken livers sautéed in butter and diced. Add 1/4 cup brown sauce, gravy from a roast, or velouté sauce to bind the mixture, and use it to stuff poultry for roasting.

Poule Bouillie au Riz

BOILED FOWL WITH RICE

CLEAN and singe a 4- to 5-pound fowl and truss the wings and legs close to the body. Put it in a deep pan and cover with water. Bring the water to a boil and skim well. Add 1 tablespoon salt, 2 carrots, 2 onions, one of them studded with a clove, 2 leeks, and a faggot made by tying together 2 stalks of celery, 4 sprigs of parsley, 1 small bay leaf, and a sprig of thyme. Cook the fowl slowly for 2 hours, or until it is tender. Half an hour before the fowl is done, prepare the rice as follows: Melt 2 tablespoons butter in a pan, add 1 tablespoon chopped onion, and cook until the onion is soft. Add 1 cup rice and shake the pan over the heat until the grains are coated with butter. Add 2 cups of the boiling chicken broth in which the fowl is cooking, cover closely, and cook in a moderate oven (350° F.) or on top of the stove over very low heat for 20 to 25 minutes, or until the liquid has been absorbed by the rice. Add 1 tablespoon soft butter and toss it through the rice with a fork to avoid mashing the grains.

While the rice is cooking, prepare the following sauce: Melt 2 tablespoons butter in a saucepan and stir in 1 1/2 tablespoons flour. Stir in gradually 1 1/2 cups chicken broth and cook, stirring constantly, until the sauce is smooth and thick. Correct the seasoning, add a little nutmeg, and cook the sauce gently for 10 minutes longer. Mix 1 egg yolk with 1/4 cup cream and a little of the hot sauce and stir the mixture into the sauce. Add a few drops of lemon juice and cook the sauce for 2 or 3 minutes, but do not let it boil.

Make a bed of the rice on a heated serving platter, carve the fowl, and arrange it on the rice. Slice the carrots and arrange them around the bird. Pour half the sauce over the fowl and rice, and serve the rest separately.

A tender young chicken may be cooked for about 30 minutes and served in the same way.

COOK a tender 4-pound fowl as for *poule bouillie* and serve it with a sauce-boat of the following sauce: In a saucepan melt 2 tablespoons butter, stir in 1 1/2 tablespoons flour and cook the *roux* over low heat for 3 minutes. Stir in gradually 2 cups of the hot stock from the chicken and cook the sauce, stirring, until it is smooth and thickened. Simmer the sauce for 10 minutes and stir in 2 tablespoons capers.

Poached Chicken with Caper Sauce

PUT a 5-pound fowl in water to cover, along with 1 large onion and 1/2 stalk of celery, and simmer the bird for 2 1/2 to 3 hours, or until the meat falls from the bones. Discard the bones, skin, and vegetables. Skim the broth and keep the chicken hot.

Sift 2 cups sifted flour with 1 teaspoon salt and 1 teaspoon baking powder. Mix into the dry ingredients 2 teaspoons shortening and add enough sweet milk to make a manageable dough. Roll out the dough on a lightly floured board, cut it into strips 1 1/2 by 3 inches, and let the strips dry while the chicken broth is brought again to a boil. Drop one strip at a time into the broth, never letting the liquid stop boiling. As the dumplings cook, draw them over to the edge, leaving room in the center for the next addition. Cook the dumplings for about 10 minutes, or until they are done. Serve meat and dumplings with some of the broth, on a deep platter.

Chicken and Dumplings

That ineffable delicacy, the breast of chicken, or suprêmes de volaille, *is further refined by removing from the tender white flesh, before cooking,*

To Prepare Chicken Breasts

235

the skin, wing tips, and all bones except those of the wing. The suprêmes *may be cooked* à brun, *which is to say that they are browned, or they may be cooked* à blanc, *which means that they are not allowed to take on any color as they cook. In either case they are prepared for cooking by skinning and boning as described here. In the following recipes 'chicken breast' refers to the entire breast portion of one chicken.*

Suprêmes de Volaille à Brun
BROWNED BREAST OF CHICKEN

BONE 3 chicken breasts, skin them, halve them, and remove the wing tips but not the main wing bones. Season the breasts with salt and pepper and dredge them lightly with flour. Melt 6 tablespoons clarified butter in a heavy skillet over moderate heat and sauté the breasts, turning them frequently, until they are brown and cooked through, about 20 minutes.

Chicken Breasts à l'Indienne

Follow the directions for *suprêmes de volaille à brun*. Arrange the cooked chicken breasts in a crown on a heated platter. Fill the center of the crown with fluffy boiled rice and spoon curry sauce over the breasts.

Suprêmes de Volaille Archiduc
CHICKEN BREASTS ARCHDUKE

Follow the directions for *suprêmes de volaille à brun*, adding a pinch of thyme to the seasonings. Sauté the chicken breasts until they are lightly browned but not cooked through. Over the sautéed chicken breast pour 1/4 cup warmed brandy and ignite the spirit. When the flame dies add 1 1/2 cups heavy cream, cover the pan, and simmer the breasts slowly over low heat for 10 to 15 minutes, turning them once. Stir in 1 teaspoon paprika and correct the seasoning of the sauce with salt. Arrange the breasts on a heated platter, surround them with toast points, and garnish the platter with cooked asparagus tips. Strain the sauce over the chicken and asparagus and sprinkle with 2 tablespoons finely chopped truffles.

Chicken Breasts Gloria

In the pan in which 3 prepared chicken breasts were sautéed *à brun* heat 2 tablespoons butter and sauté 6 generous slices of ham. Put the ham on a warm serving platter and lay the chicken breasts on the ham.

In the same pan heat 12 whole apricots, pits removed, or 18 to 24 halves. Add 1/4 cup warmed brandy and ignite the spirit. When the flame dies, stir in 1/2 cup apricot juice. Arrange the apricots around the chicken breasts. Make a sauce in the pan by adding a little meat extract and swirling in 1 tablespoon butter. Pour the sauce over the chicken and ham.

Chicken Breasts Amandine

Sauté 3 prepared chicken breasts *à brun*. Pour 1/4 cup warmed Sherry or brandy over the chicken and set the breasts aside. To the juice in the pan add 2 tablespoons butter and 1 tablespoon finely chopped shallots or scallions. Cook for 1 minute, add 1/2 cup split, blanched almonds, and cook slowly until the almonds begin to brown. Stir in 1 teaspoon tomato paste, 1 teaspoon meat glaze, and 3 tablespoons flour. Add gradually, stirring constantly, 2 cups chicken stock and 1/2 cup white wine and bring to a boil. Season the sauce to taste with salt and pepper, and return the breasts to the sauce. Add 2 sprigs of fresh tarragon, cover, and simmer the chicken slowly for 25 minutes. Arrange the breasts on a serving dish, pour the sauce over them, and sprinkle with 1/2 cup almonds, blanched, slivered, and browned in butter.

Sauté 3 prepared breasts of chicken *à brun*. Three minutes before the chicken is cooked, add 6 large mushroom caps. In another heavy skillet, quickly sauté 6 thin slices of *prosciutto* in 2 tablespoons butter, until the ham is hot. Place small rounds of buttered toast in 6 individual heated casseroles, cover each toast round with a slice of ham and a chicken breast, and top with a mushroom cap.

Suprêmes de Volaille Eugénie

Combine the butter from the two skillets, add 3/4 cup each of Sherry and scalded light cream and boil for 1 minute, stirring. Season to taste with salt and white pepper. Strain the sauce over the chicken, ham, and mushrooms, cover each casserole with a glass bell and put them in a moderate oven (350° F.) to steam for 3 to 4 minutes. Serve the casseroles covered with the bells, which are removed at the table.

Sauté 3 prepared chicken breasts *à brun*. Arrange the breasts on a warmed serving platter and put a slice of goose liver, sautéed in butter for 1 minute on each side, on each breast. Arrange 3 slices of truffle on each slice of goose liver. In a saucepan combine 1 1/2 cups brown sauce and 1 tablespoon *glace de viande* or about 1 teaspoon meat extract. Add 1 truffle, chopped, 2 tablespoons truffle juice, and 1/2 cup cooked cockscombs, simmer for 10 minutes, and stir in 2 tablespoons Madeira. Pour the sauce around the chicken breasts.

Chicken Breasts Lucullus

BONE 3 chicken breasts, skin them, halve them, and remove the wing tips but not the main wing bones. Season the breasts with salt and pepper and brush them with melted butter. Put them in a buttered baking dish, sprinkle them with the juice of half a lemon and cover the dish. Bake in a very hot oven (450° F.) for 8 to 10 minutes, or until the meat is done, but not at all colored.

Suprêmes de Volaille à Blanc
BAKED CHICKEN BREASTS

Chicken Breasts with Mushrooms

Follow the directions for *suprêmes de volaille à blanc*. In a covered sauce-pan cook 12 mushroom caps slowly in 3 tablespoons butter until the caps are tender. Arrange the breasts on a heated serving platter and garnish them with the mushrooms. Combine the butter in which the breasts were cooked, the mushroom juice, and 1 1/2 cups *sauce suprême* and spoon the sauce over the breasts.

Suprêmes de Volaille à la Florentine

Follow the directions for *suprêmes de volaille à blanc*. Arrange the cooked chicken breasts on a bed of spinach in a flameproof serving dish, cover them with Mornay sauce, and sprinkle them with grated Parmesan cheese. Dot with bits of butter and put the dish under the broiler to brown the sauce.

Chicken Breasts Tarragon

PUT 3 prepared chicken breasts in a saucepan with 1 small carrot and 1 onion, both thinly sliced, 3 sprigs of tarragon, and 1/2 cup white wine. Add enough water or chicken stock barely to cover, bring the liquid to a boil, and simmer the breasts, covered, for 25 minutes. Arrange them on a warm serving platter. Strain the liquid and reduce it over high heat to 2 cups. In a saucepan melt 3 tablespoons butter, stir in 3 tablespoons flour, and add gradually the hot reduced liquid. Cook the sauce, stirring, until it is smooth and thickened. Season to taste with salt and pepper, stir in bit by bit 2 tablespoons butter, and simmer the sauce for 6 minutes. Add 1 table-spoon chopped tarragon leaves and stir in 1 egg yolk lightly beaten with 3 tablespoons heavy cream and a little of the hot sauce. Pour the sauce over the chicken and garnish with blanched tarragon leaves.

Suprêmes de Volaille Panés

BREADED CHICKEN BREASTS

IN a mixing bowl, combine 2 slightly beaten eggs, 2 teaspoons salad oil, 1/2 teaspoon salt, and a pinch of white pepper. Season 3 prepared chicken breasts with salt and pepper, dredge them lightly with flour, and dip them into the egg and into fresh bread crumbs. Sauté them rapidly in 6 table-spoons melted butter until they are browned evenly on both sides.

Suprêmes de Volaille Koriniloff

CHICKEN BREASTS KORNILOV

POUND 3 prepared chicken breasts with the flat side of a cleaver until they are very thin. In a saucepan sauté 8 mushrooms, sliced, in 3 tablespoons butter, add 3/4 cup thick béchamel sauce and 3 tablespoons purée of *foie gras* and stir. Put 2 tablespoons of this mixture on each chicken filet. Combine 1 slightly beaten egg with 1 teaspoon water and brush this onto the borders of the filets. Fold the meat over the filling to form 6 cutlets of even shape. Dip the cutlets into the egg mixture, roll them in fresh bread crumbs, and fry them in hot deep fat (370° F.) until they are delicately browned.

Chicken Breasts Virginia

PUT 3 prepared chicken breasts between 2 sheets of wax paper and flatten them slightly with the flat side of a cleaver. Cut 6 thin slices of smoked ham the same shape as the chicken breasts. Beat 4 eggs lightly, dip the ham slices into the beaten eggs, and lay the slices on the chicken. The egg will hold the two together. Dip the paired chicken and ham slices into the egg mixture and roll them in fine bread crumbs. Place them in a large skillet and sauté them in 1/4 cup butter until lightly browned. Transfer the sautéed chicken to a baking dish, pour over it butter from the skillet, and bake in a moderate oven (375° F.) for about 10 minutes. Arrange the chicken on a heated serving platter, put a medallion of *foie gras* on each breast, and pour the pan juices over them. Garnish the platter with watercress.

Suprêmes de Volaille Pojarski
CHICKEN CUTLETS

SOAK 1 cup fresh bread crumbs in 1/2 cup milk for 15 minutes. Drain and press the crumbs to remove the excess liquid and combine them with 3 cups ground raw breast meat of chicken, 1/2 cup butter, and 1/4 cup heavy cream. Season the mixture with 1 teaspoon salt and 1/2 teaspoon white pepper, and form it into 6 portions shaped to resemble breasts of chicken. Flour the cutlets lightly and sauté them gently in clarified butter until they are nicely browned on both sides and cooked through.

Chicken Breasts in Champagne

PUT 3 prepared chicken breasts in a saucepan with 12 small pork sausages, 3 shallots, finely chopped, and 3 truffles, sliced. Add 1 1/2 cups Champagne and about 3/4 cup chicken stock or enough barely to cover the chicken breasts. Bring the liquid to a boil and simmer the breasts for 25 to 30 minutes, or until they are tender. Remove the chicken and sausages to a hot platter. Beat 3 egg yolks with 1/4 cup cream and a little of the hot liquid, and stir the egg mixture into the broth. Cook the sauce over very low heat for 3 minutes, stirring constantly, until it is thickened. Be careful not to let it boil. Stir in 1 tablespoon butter and a dash of lemon juice and pour the sauce over the chicken.

*Chicken
Queen
Elizabeth*

TRIM the skin from 3 chicken breasts and separate them. Separate the top filet section of each breast from the smaller one lying beneath. Flatten each filet a little with a small mallet or the broad side of a heavy knife. The smaller filet, which is thicker, should be flattened until it spreads to the same size as the upper one. Cut 6 thin slices from a well-flavored cooked ham and 6 slices of Swiss cheese the same size as the filets and sandwich the filets with 1 slice each of ham and cheese. Moisten the edges of the filets with beaten egg to hold them together securely. Roll the breasts in flour, and shake off the excess.

Melt 3 tablespoons butter in a shallow pan large enough to hold the filets side by side. Sauté the filets in the butter for 10 to 12 minutes, or until they are golden brown on one side. Turn and sauté them for 5 to 6 minutes, or until they are done. Put them on a serving platter and keep them warm until ready to serve.

To the butter in the pan, add 1/2 pound small mushrooms, caps and stems, 1 teaspoon chopped shallots, and 1/3 cup dry white wine, and cook the liquid until it is reduced by half. Peel 4 or 5 firm tomatoes, cut them in half, and squeeze them gently to remove the seeds and juice. Chop the tomatoes coarsely and add them to the pan with the mushrooms. Cook briskly until most of the liquid is cooked away, but do not let the tomatoes become mushy. Add 1 cup sweet cream and continue to cook until the cream is reduced by half. Add 1 cup cream sauce and correct the seasoning with salt. Pour the sauce over the chicken and sprinkle with finely chopped parsley. Garnish the platter with small molds of rice and top each rice mold with a slice of truffle.

*Chicken
Momi*

PUT through the finest blade of a food chopper 1/4 pound each of veal, lean pork, and beef, 3 slices of white bread soaked in cream and pressed, and 1/2 medium-sized onion. Season with 2 tablespoons soy sauce, 1/2 teaspoon ground ginger, and a pinch each of cayenne and monosodium glutamate. Chop 10 water chestnuts coarsely and mix them with the forcemeat. Bone carefully 4 whole chicken breasts that weigh 1/2 pound each. Fold the stuffing into the breasts. Salt the breasts lightly and arrange them on a baking pan lightly sprinkled with oil. Bake the chicken in a moderate oven (350° F.) for 35 minutes, or until it is tender.

Split two small pineapples lengthwise, remove and discard the cores, and slice the flesh into chunks. Cut each cooked stuffed breast into 4 slices and reshape it on top of the pineapple in the shell. Spread the chicken breasts with 1 teaspoon honey and with some of the juices from the baking pan. Sprinkle with sesame seeds and put the shells into a hot oven to brown the seeds. Serves 8.

Chicken Queen Elizabeth

Chinese
Almond
Chicken

IN a skillet sauté 1 cup finely sliced raw breast of chicken in 2 tablespoons peanut or olive oil until golden. Add 1 cup each of diced bamboo shoots and celery, 1/2 cup each of diced Chinese chard and water chestnuts, 1/4 cup blanched almonds, 1 to 2 tablespoons soy sauce, 1 teaspoon monosodium glutamate, and 1 1/2 cups hot chicken broth. Mix the ingredients, cover, and steam for 5 minutes. Remove the lid and thicken the sauce slightly with 2 tablespoons cornstarch mixed with 3 tablespoons cold water. Simmer for a few minutes to cook the starch, stirring well. Serve very hot. Serves 2.

Breast of
Chicken with
Walnuts
HU TAO CHI TING

FRY 1/4 cup walnut halves in deep fat (365° F.) for 1 1/2 minutes. Drain them and keep them warm.

Melt 1/2 cup lard in a skillet and in it brown lightly for about 1 minute 1 cup chicken breast, diced and coated with 1/2 teaspoon cornstarch mixed with 1 egg white. Remove the chicken to a warm place.

In the same skillet sauté 3 mushrooms, cut into 1/2-inch dice, for 1/2 minute and add, stirring constantly, 5 tablespoons chicken stock, 1 tablespoon dry Sherry, 1/3 teaspoon sugar, 1/2 teaspoon cornstarch stirred to a paste with 2 tablespoons cold water, and salt and pepper to taste. Cook the sauce, stirring, until it is smooth. Add the nuts and chicken and heat for 1 to 2 minutes. Serves 2.

Chicken Livers
with Apples

WASH and dry carefully 1 1/2 pounds chicken livers and dredge them lightly with flour mixed with salt and paprika. Brown the livers in melted butter, turning them to cook both sides, and keep them warm on a serving dish.

In a small pan cook in butter 3 small Spanish onions, cut into rings, and spread them over the livers. In another pan sauté in butter 12 thick rings of tart green apples, peeled and cored. Sprinkle the apple rings with sugar to glaze them and arrange them on top of the livers and onions. This recipe may be prepared in a chafing dish.

Chicken Livers
with
Mushrooms

BROWN 1 1/2 pounds chicken livers in 1/4 cup melted butter. Transfer the livers to a heated serving dish and keep them warm. To the pan add 1 tablespoon butter and 1 1/2 pounds sliced mushrooms, caps and stems together. Cook the mushrooms gently for about 5 minutes. Stir in 1/4 cup flour and add gradually 1 1/2 cups chicken stock and 3/4 cup dry white wine. Cook, stirring constantly, until the sauce thickens, and finish it with

1 tablespoon lemon juice. Return the chicken livers to the sauce, heat them through, and serve hot.

MARINATE 1 1/2 pounds chicken livers in a little soy sauce and brown them lightly in 1/3 cup peanut oil. Add to the pan 1 cup pineapple chunks and 3/4 cup blanched, coarsely shredded almonds, and stir the mixture over the heat for a few minutes. Stir 3 tablespoons cornstarch to a paste with 1/3 cup wine vinegar and add the paste to 1 2/3 cups pineapple juice with 1/2 teaspoon salt and 1/3 cup sugar, more or less to taste. Cook the sauce until it is clear and thick and pour it over the livers, pineapple, and almonds. Serve hot, with rice.

Chinese Chicken Livers

IN the top pan of a chafing dish, over direct heat, sauté 1 onion, finely chopped, in 2 tablespoons butter until it is golden, Add 1 tablespoon mixed parsley and sweet marjoram and 1 1/2 pounds cut-up chicken livers. Sear the livers for a few minutes over high heat, stirring, then put the pan over hot water and stir in 1 cup sour cream. Simmer the mixture for 3 minutes, add 1/4 cup beef stock, and simmer the mixture for 3 minutes longer. Add salt and pepper to taste and sprinkle with finely chopped parsley. Serve hot, with rice.

Chicken Livers Paysanne

BROWN quickly in 1/4 cup butter 1 1/2 pounds chicken livers. Transfer the chicken livers to a plate to keep warm. Add 1 tablespoon butter to the pan and stir in 3 tablespoons flour. Cook the *roux* for a minute or two and stir in 1 2/3 cups hot cream. Cook the sauce, stirring constantly, until it is thick and smooth. Add 1/3 cup Sherry and salt and pepper to taste. Return the chicken livers to the sauce and heat them through. Serve on freshly made buttered toast.

Chicken Livers in Cream

DREDGE 1 1/2 pounds chicken livers lightly in flour and sauté them for a few minutes in the top pan of a chafing dish over direct heat in 1/4 cup butter. Remove the livers to a plate to keep warm. Put the pan over hot water and into the juices stir 2 tablespoons flour. Add gradually 1/2 cup Madeira or Sherry and 1 cup chicken broth and cook, stirring, until the sauce is smooth and thickened. Add salt and pepper to taste.

Return the chicken livers to the chafing dish, cover it, and cook the chicken livers for about 10 minutes, or until the sauce is very hot and the livers are heated through.

Chicken Livers in Madeira

Poached Boned Capon

Combine 1 cup freshly grated coconut with 1 cup milk, bring the liquid to a boil and remove it from the heat immediately. Let the mixture stand for 15 minutes. Drain off the liquid, pressing the milk from the grated coconut, and discard the pulp.

Melt 1/4 cup butter in a saucepan and add to it 1 onion, chopped, 3 garlic cloves, finely minced, and 2 finely chopped hot red peppers. Sauté the mixture for 5 minutes, stirring occasionally. Add 1 1/2 pounds coarsely chopped chicken livers and sauté them for 5 minutes. Add the coconut milk, 1/4 cup ground roasted almonds, 2 tablespoons each of grated lemon rind and orange juice, 1 tablespoon each of lemon juice and plum jam, and 1 teaspoon each of sugar and salt. Cook the mixture over low heat for 10 minutes, stirring frequently. Serve hot, with boiled rice.

Sambal
Goreng Ati
CHICKEN LIVER
SAMBAL

The capon may be substituted for a chicken of roasting weight and size in any recipe; its characteristically fat and succulent flesh makes it a sought-after luxury.

Bone a capon according to the directions given for boning a chicken.

Spread the capon out flat on a cloth, skin side down, and make a forcemeat as follows: Put 1 pound lean raw pork through the finest blade of a food chopper and pound it in a mortar to a smooth paste. Stir in 4 eggs, beaten, 6 tablespoons minced parsley, and 1/4 cup each of pistachio nuts and pine nuts. Mix thoroughly and cover the flesh of the capon with the forcemeat. Arrange lengthwise on top 1/2 pound smoked tongue, cut into filets about 4 inches long and 1 inch thick, and cover the tongue with a layer of 1/2 pound sliced *prosciutto*. Roll the capon lengthwise into a firm roll and wrap the cloth securely around it. Tie the cloth tightly at both ends and at intervals between so that the roll will hold its shape during the cooking.

Put the capon into a large pan with 2 quarts water, 2 cups white wine, the bones from the capon, 2 onions, each stuck with 2 cloves, 2 carrots, sliced, 1 garlic clove, 2 teaspoons salt, 8 peppercorns, and a *bouquet garni*. Bring the liquid slowly to a boil, reduce the heat so that the liquid barely simmers, and poach the capon for about 2 hours, or until it is tender.

Remove the roll from the stock, unwrap, and slice it with a sharp knife. Sprinkle the roll with finely chopped parsley and garnish with cherry tomatoes dipped in coarse salt.

Cappone
Lesso
POACHED
BONED CAPON

Capon with
Gold Sauce

RUB a 6-pound capon with salt and pepper and brown it in a heavy kettle in 3 tablespoons butter. Add 1 large onion and 1 carrot, both sliced, and when the onion begins to color, add 2 cups boiling water or chicken stock, 1 stalk of celery with the leaves, 3 sprays of parsley, and 1 bay leaf. Cover the kettle and simmer the capon for about 1 1/2 hours, or until it is tender.

In a small saucepan melt 1 tablespoon butter and in it sauté 3 shallots, finely chopped, until the shallots are tender. Stir in 1 tablespoon flour and cook the *roux* over low heat for a few minutes. Add gradually 1 1/2 cups of the broth in which the capon was simmered and cook, stirring, until the sauce is smooth and thickened. Add 1 tablespoon finely chopped celery and cook for 10 minutes. Add 6 tablespoons cream sauce and bring again to a boil. Remove the sauce from the heat and stir in 2 egg yolks beaten with 2 tablespoons heavy cream and a little of the hot sauce. Return the sauce to the heat and cook, stirring vigorously, for 2 minutes, being careful not to let it boil. Correct the seasoning with salt and pepper and add 1 table-spoon lemon juice.

Carve the capon and arrange the pieces on a hot platter. Pour the sauce over the bird and serve with hot fluffy boiled rice.

Capon
Edward VII

CLEAN a capon weighing from 5 to 6 pounds, and prepare the following stuffing: Mix together lightly 3 cups cooked rice, 6 to 8 cubes of goose liver, sautéed quickly in butter, and 2 or 3 truffles, diced. Add 2 tablespoons *glace de viande*, or about 2 teaspoons meat glaze, and 2 or 3 tablespoons *sauce suprême* or *velouté*. Mix well, stuff the capon, and sew up the vent. Poach the capon in chicken stock to cover for 50 to 60 minutes, or until it is tender when tested with a fork. Set the capon on a warm serving dish and garnish with creamed cucumbers. Add 1 tablespoon diced pimiento to 2 cups *velouté au currie* and serve the sauce separately.

A 5-pound chicken is enough for 6, but a duckling of the same weight serves only 3 persons. Proceed accordingly.

Roast Duckling

TRIM the wing tips and cut off the neck of a 4- to 5-pound duckling. Wash it thoroughly, inside and out, with cold water and dry it carefully. Rub the cavity with lemon juice and in it put a few celery leaves and 1 onion, sliced. Place the duckling, breast side up, on a rack in a shallow baking pan. Cook the bird in a moderately slow oven (325° F.) for 30 minutes. Drain the fat from the pan and add 1 1/2 cups dry white wine. Baste the duckling and continue cooking it for 1 1/2 hours, basting it with the pan juices every 20 minutes. If a very crisp skin is desired, brush the duckling with 1 tablespoon honey about 15 minutes before taking it from the oven and do not baste it again.

ROAST a duckling, remove it to a hot serving platter, and keep it warm. Skim the excess fat from the juices in the roasting pan.

    In a heavy saucepan combine 1/2 cup sugar and 1 tablespoon wine vinegar. Cook the mixture over medium heat until the sugar melts and begins to caramelize. Add the juice of 2 oranges, 1/2 cup Grand Marnier, and the grated rind of 1 orange, stir well and cook for 5 minutes. Combine this mixture with the juices in the roasting pan and add 1/4 cup orange peel cut in julienne strips, cooked in a little water for 5 minutes and drained. Correct the seasoning and pour the sauce over the duckling on the serving platter.

Caneton au Grand Marnier
DUCKLING IN GRAND MARNIER SAUCE

ROAST a duckling, remove it from the pan, and keep it warm. Skim off all the fat in the roasting pan and add to the juices remaining 2 tablespoons butter, the grated rind of 1 orange, 1/2 cup raw sliced mushrooms, and 1 small garlic clove, crushed. Bring the mixture to a boil and simmer it gently for about 2 minutes. Remove the pan from the heat and blend in 1 tablespoon arrowroot. Stir in 1/4 cup each of dry Sherry and Cognac and 1/2 cup each of Cointreau and orange juice. Return the pan to the heat and cook, stirring, until the mixture is smooth and thick. Add 1 tablespoon each of currant jelly and finely chopped truffles. Remove and discard the garlic and season the sauce to taste with salt and pepper. Cut the duckling into quarters and heat the pieces well in the sauce. Arrange the pieces on a serving platter and mask them with the sauce. Garnish the platter with sautéed mushroom caps and slices of orange.

Duckling with Cointreau Sauce

CLEAN and trim a plump duckling for roasting. Season it with a little salt and roast it in a hot oven (450° F.) for about 15 to 20 minutes, or until the skin is golden brown. Remove the duck and pour off all but 1 tablespoon of the fat from the pan. Stir in 1 tablespoon butter and add 1 table-

Spring Duckling with Apricots

247

spoon flour, stirring. Cook the *roux* until it is golden brown. Stir in gradually 1 cup stock or water and 1/4 cup white wine and cook the sauce, stirring briskly, until it is smooth and thickened. Return the duckling to the pan, cover it, and roast it in a moderate oven (350° F.) for 1 to 1 1/2 hours, or until it is done.

While the duckling is cooking, peel the rind of 1 or 2 oranges (the thinnest layer of outside skin minus the white part) and cut it into fine julienne. Boil the strips in water to cover for 2 or 3 minutes and drain. Remove the duckling from the pan, skim off all the fat, and cook the sauce until it is reduced to about 1 cup. Cook 1 tablespoon sugar and 1 tablespoon water in a small pan to a light caramel color. Strain the reduced sauce into this syrup and stir the mixture over the heat until it is well combined. Add the julienne of orange peel, 1/4 cup juice of stewed fresh apricots, and salt. Carve the duck and arrange it on a warm serving platter. Garnish the platter with 18 heated apricot halves, alternating with segments of orange, and pour the sauce over the duckling.

Duckling with Port

PUT 24 fresh figs in a jar and add enough dry Port to cover them. Seal the jar and marinate the figs in the wine for 24 hours. Prepare a duckling as for roasting and bake it in an earthenware baking dish in a moderately slow oven (325° F.) for 30 minutes. Drain the fat from the baking dish. Add the wine in which the figs were marinated, reserving the figs. Return the duckling to the oven and continue to cook it for 1 hour, basting it frequently with the wine. Surround the duckling with the marinated figs and return it to the oven for 30 minutes longer. Arrange the duckling on a heated serving dish and surround it with the hot figs. Skim the excess fat from the pan juices and pour the sauce over the duck. Serve with buttered brown rice and new peas.

Peking Duck

SELECT a duck that is not too fat. Scald it in boiling water 3 or 4 times and dry it thoroughly. Mix together 1 generous tablespoon brown sugar, 1 tablespoon each of soy sauce and leek or chives, very finely chopped, 2 teaspoons Sherry, 1 generous teaspoon salt, 1 teaspoon each of monosodium glutamate and cinnamon, 1/8 teaspoon freshly ground black pepper, a pinch each of cloves and ground aniseed, and 3 garlic cloves, crushed. Cook these ingredients over low heat for 2 or 3 minutes, then stuff the duck with the mixture. Sew the neck opening and the abdominal cavity securely.

Rub the duck well with a mixture of 2 tablespoons each of soy sauce and honey and 1 tablespoon white wine. Roast the bird in a very hot oven (500° F.) for 2 or 3 minutes, uncovered, then baste it with the soy sauce-honey mixture, reduce the temperature to hot (425° F.), and cover the roasting pan tightly. Roast the duck for about 45 minutes. Uncover, baste, and continue to roast for about 15 minutes longer, turning and basting the duck frequently so that it becomes evenly brown and crisp. To serve, cut the duck into bits, bones and all, with poultry shears.

Szechwan
Duck

RUB a 5- to 6-pound duck inside and out with salt and put in the cavity 2 slices of fresh ginger, 2 scallions, 2 tablespoons dry Sherry, and 6 to 8 aniseeds. Sew the openings and steam the bird in a covered steamer for 1 1/2 to 2 hours, or until the leg meat is tender when tested with a fork.

Remove the duck from the steamer to a rack to drain for half an hour. Rub the duck thoroughly with a mixture of 1/2 cup soy sauce and 6 tablespoons brown sugar and fry it in hot deep fat (380° F.) for 5 to 7 minutes, or until the skin is light chocolate in color.

Ginger Duck
with Pineapple

CUT a tender duck into serving pieces and marinate the pieces for several hours in 1/4 cup soy sauce with 1 tablespoon chopped fresh ginger and 2 garlic cloves, minced. Sauté the duck in 1/4 cup butter until the pieces are brown on both sides and transfer them to an ovenproof casserole. Add the juice from a small can of pineapple rings, the marinade, and 1/2 cup mushroom slices, sautéed until golden in butter. Cook, covered, in a moderate oven (350° F.) or over low heat for about 1 hour, or until the duck is tender. Sauté the pineapple slices in butter until lightly browned on both sides and serve them with the duck.

Caneton
en Chemise
DUCK WITH
ROUENNAISE

BONE a 5- to 6-pound duck and stuff it with *rouennaise* to which 1 egg has been added. Roll up the duck securely in a napkin, tying both ends with soft string. Plunge the duck into a kettle of boiling stock, return the stock to the boil, and simmer the duck for about 1 hour, or until it is tender. Remove it from the kettle, discarding the napkin, and put it on a heatproof platter with a little of the stock. Brush the duck with butter and brown it in a hot oven (400° F.) or under the broiler. Arrange the duck on a serving platter and garnish the top with slices of orange. Put slices of lemon around the platter. Slice through the duck and stuffing, and serve the slices with *sauce rouennaise*.

*Chinese
Almond Duck*

IN a skillet brown lightly 1 cup finely sliced raw breast of duck in 2 tablespoons peanut oil. Add 1 cup each of diced bamboo shoots, celery, and *bok choy* (Chinese cabbage), 1/2 cup sliced water chestnuts, 1/4 cup blanched almonds, 1 tablespoon soy sauce, 1 teaspoon monosodium glutamate, and 1 1/2 cups stock. Cover the skillet tightly and simmer the meat and vegetables for 10 minutes. Just before serving stir in 2 tablespoons cornstarch blended with 3 tablespoons cold water and continue to cook and stir until the sauce is thickened and clear.

*Canard
Montmorency*

DUCK WITH
CHERRIES

LINE a heavy casserole with slices of salt pork and place a trussed duck of 4 to 5 pounds on top. Add to the casserole 2 carrots, finely minced, 2 onions, and 2 stalks of celery hearts, finely chopped, all cooked in a little butter for 10 minutes. Rinse out the pan in which the vegetables were cooked with 2 tablespoons Madeira and add it to the casserole, along with 3 cups white wine, a spray of thyme, and a little salt and pepper. Cover the casserole and bake the duck in a moderately slow oven (325° F.) for about 1 1/2 hours, or until it is tender.

Untruss the bird and place it on a warm serving platter. Skim off the fat from the casserole and strain the liquid through a fine sieve into another saucepan. Add 1 cup brown stock and simmer the mixture until it reduces a little. Correct the seasoning, add 1 cup preserved Montmorency cherries, and continue to simmer until the cherries are heated through. Arrange the cherries around the duck, pour over it half the sauce, and serve the rest separately.

*Caneton
aux Ananas*

DUCKLING WITH
PINEAPPLE

ROAST a duckling according to the directions above and remove it to a hot serving dish. Sauté 8 slices of pineapple and 6 slices of orange lightly in 2 tablespoons butter. Cut the pineapple slices in half and arrange them, with pieces of orange, around the duckling and in attractive shapes on its breast. Keep the duckling warm in a very slow oven (250° F.).

Skim the excess fat from the liquid in the roasting pan and set the pan over high heat. Add 1/3 cup pineapple juice and reduce the mixture rapidly. Add 1/2 cup white wine, 1 tablespoon wine vinegar, and 2 teaspoons meat glaze, blend well, and cook the sauce just to the boiling point. Remove the pan from the heat and add 2 tablespoons butter and salt and pepper to taste.

Decorate the duckling platter with pineapple leaves, if you wish, and at the table, pour 1/3 cup warmed triple sec over the duckling and ignite the spirit. When the flame dies, carve the duckling. Pass the sauce separately.

Duckling en Casserole

CLEAN a young duck weighing from 4 1/2 to 5 pounds and cut it into serving pieces. Roll the pieces in flour and brown them in a skillet in 1/4 cup butter. When they are nicely browned on all sides, place them in a casserole and sprinkle them with salt and pepper. Add the duck giblets, chopped, 1/2 cup white wine, 2 tablespoons chopped parsley, 1 small onion, finely chopped, 1/2 bay leaf, and a pinch of thyme. Cover the casserole and bake the duck in a moderate oven (350° F.) for about 1 1/4 hours, or until it is tender. Stir in 1/4 cup heavy cream and serve very hot in the casserole. Serve the duck with young white turnips, peeled, sliced, cooked in a little water until just tender, and tossed in melted butter.

Pompadour de Caneton à la Mirabeau
DUCKLING AND
OLIVE TIMBALE

IN a heavy kettle put 2 carrots, sliced, 3 onions, sliced, 2 stalks of celery with the leaves, chopped, 1 garlic clove, 1/2 bay leaf, 1 pinch thyme, and 6 peppercorns. On this bed of vegetables lay a duckling weighing from 4 1/2 to 5 pounds, cleaned, singed, and rubbed inside and out with salt. Cover the kettle tightly and let the duck and the vegetables braise slowly for about 1 hour, or until the duck is tender. Remove the duck, let it cool, discard the skin, and cut the meat from the bones.

Remove the fat from the cooled liquid in the bottom of the kettle and stir into the pan juices 1 1/2 tablespoons flour. Then stir in 1 1/2 cups chicken stock and 1/4 cup Madeira. Season the sauce with salt and pepper to taste, simmer for 10 minutes, and strain.

Make a veal forcemeat in this way: Soak 4 slices of bread in a little chicken stock. Mix together 1 pound ground veal, 1 egg, 1 teaspoon finely chopped shallots, 1 tablespoon finely chopped parsley, 1/4 cup each of melted butter and heavy cream. Add the bread and salt and pepper to taste, and work this mixture into a smooth paste.

Use part of this forcemeat to stuff the centers of 1 pound large, pitted green olives. Poach the stuffed olives in boiling water for 5 minutes in order to cook the *farce*, drain them, and let them cool.

Butter a timbale mold or deep cake tin. Cut in half as many olives as are needed to line the inside walls of the mold and apply the halves to the bottom and sides so that the walls are completely covered. Or you may cut 3 thick slices from the center of the olive for lining. Over the olives spread a layer of the forcemeat, pressing it firmly against them. Keep your hand moistened with water so that the forcemeat does not stick to the fingers and thus pull the olives away from the mold. Place the pieces of duck meat and the remaining olives in the timbale, pour over this 2 tablespoons of the sauce, and close the timbale with a layer of the forcemeat.

Put the timbale in a large pan containing enough hot water to come three-fourths of the way up the side of the mold. Cover the mold with buttered paper and let the water boil gently for 3/4 hour. Unmold the *pompadour* on a large, round, heated platter and garnish it with warmed pimiento-stuffed olives, duck meat, and mushrooms, if desired. Serve the sauce in a heated sauceboat.

Duck with Braised Cabbage

QUARTER 2 large or 4 small heads of cabbage and remove the hard center core. Clean the quarters under running water. Put the cabbage into boiling water, parboil it for 5 to 10 minutes, and plunge it in a large pan of cold water. After 2 or 3 minutes, transfer it to a colander to drain.

Parboil 1/2 pound fat salt pork to remove some of the salt and drain it.

In a roasting pan put 2 carrots, 1 or 2 onions, 2 garlic cloves, and a faggot made by tying together 2 stalks of celery, 3 sprigs of parsley, a bay leaf, and a little thyme. Add any poultry bones, wing tips, or necks, on hand. Add the salt pork and a garlic sausage and place the well-drained cabbage on top. Season with freshly ground pepper and a little salt and pour on enough white stock or water to cover well. Cover the pan with a lid that has a steam vent in it, bring the liquid to a boil, and put the pan in a hot oven (400° F.). Or cook it gently on top of the stove for 1 hour. Small potatoes may be added during the last 30 minutes.

Carve a roasted duck in slices, and lay the slices on the cabbage to reheat. This improves the flavor of the vegetable. To serve, arrange the cabbage with the slices of duck, garlic sausage, and carrot on a large serving dish. The liquor drained from the cabbage can be served as soup.

Anitra in Agrodolce

DUCKLING IN SOUR-SWEET SAUCE

SLICE 2 large onions very thin and sauté them in 2 tablespoons butter until they are transparent. Dredge a 4- to 5-pound duckling in seasoned flour and put it in a large saucepan. Add the sautéed onions and a pinch of cloves. Brown the duckling well on all sides and pour over it 3 cups chicken stock. Cover the pan and simmer the duckling for about 1 hour, or until it is tender.

Put the duckling on a serving dish and keep it warm in a slow oven. Skim off as much fat as possible from the roasting pan and reduce the remaining liquid over high heat to about 1 1/2 cups. Add 2 tablespoons each of chopped fresh mint, wine vinegar, and sugar lightly caramelized with 1 tablespoon water. Blend the mixture well and cook it over low heat until it just begins to thicken. Serve the sauce separately.

CLEAN 3 plump young ducklings. Rub them inside and out with brandy or lemon juice and with mixed salt and pepper. Roast the birds for 17 minutes in a hot oven (425° F.).

*Caneton
à la Presse*
PRESSED DUCKLING

Place the roast ducklings on a heated platter, cover them with a hood and bring them to the table, where a duck press and hot chafing dish are ready. Carve off the 6 breasts and put them in the chafing dish with the juice drained from the ducklings during the carving. Cover the chafing dish and turn up the heat.

Put the duck carcasses in the well of the press. Make a smooth sauce from the juice of 2 lemons, 1/3 teaspoon cayenne, 2/3 teaspoon celery salt, 6 tablespoons melted sweet butter, 1 cup warm red wine, and 4 tablespoons *pâté de foie gras*. Pour the sauce into the press. Turn the pressure wheel and force the sauce and blood through the press into a heated dish. Return this blended sauce to the press and force it through twice more. Stir in 2 tablespoons Cognac and pour the sauce over the breasts in the chafing dish. Heat the sauce but do not let it boil.

BRING to a boil 5 quarts water with 4 pounds rock salt, 1 cup sugar, 10 tablespoons saltpeter, and 6 bay leaves, crumbled, 1 tablespoon crushed peppercorns, and 6 cloves, all three spices tied in a cheesecloth bag. Stir until the salt, sugar, and saltpeter are dissolved, remove the bag, and cool the marinade.

*Smoked Duck
Aviz*

Truss a plump duck for roasting and submerge it in the marinade for 5 to 6 days. At the end of the marinating period, wipe the duck dry and smoke it for 6 to 7 days over olive wood chips or olive tree twigs. The temperature in the smokehouse or barrel should be maintained at approximately 100° F. The smoked duck will keep for a considerable time. Store it in the refrigerator.

To cook: Put the duck in a deep pot and cover it with equal parts of water and dry white wine. Bring the liquid to a boil and simmer the duck for 15 minutes. Remove the duck and cool it completely.

Slice the breasts paper thin and serve with fresh figs or slices of melon. It may also be served with buttered brown bread, a squeeze of lemon, and a sprinkling of freshly ground pepper. The thighs may be thinly sliced and served in the same manner and a fine stock may be made from the carcass.

Caneton Rechauffé au Madère

CHAFING DISH DUCKLING WITH MADEIRA

DICE 2 cups roast duckling. In the blazer of a chafing dish over direct heat sauté the duck liver in 1 tablespoon butter for 5 minutes, or until it is cooked through. Mash the liver with a fork and add to it the juice of 1/2 lemon, 1/4 cup butter, 1/2 cup Madeira, 1 tablespoon minced parsley, 1/2 teaspoon salt, a dash of cayenne and 1/4 cup fat-free juices from the pan in which the duckling was roasted. Heat the sauce thoroughly, add the diced duckling, and heat it thoroughly. Serves 2.

There was a time when turkey appeared on the table only on holidays—and occasionally spoiled a festive dinner by proving to be something less than tender. The modern turkey is an every-weekend bird, and although it has thus been deprived of its special significance, it is always tender, always plump-breasted, and always lavish of white meat. Progress has its points. There are several schools of thought about the proper method of roasting a turkey; some cooks sear the bird at high temperature, others use a uniformly low temperature throughout; some cover or wrap in brown paper or in aluminum foil; others leave off the cover and baste generously. Whatever the method, the aim is the same: a browned, crisp-skinned bird cooked until the juices that follow a fork that pierces the flesh at the joint of the thigh run clear, with no tint of pink, and the drumstick moves easily and readily twists out of the joint.

Chicken Liver Stuffing

CHOP the turkey liver with 12 chicken livers and mix this with 2 onions, diced, and 1 cup sliced mushrooms, both sautéed in butter or turkey fat, 2 quarts stale bread crumbs, 1/4 cup finely chopped parsley, about 2 teaspoons mixed thyme and marjoram, and salt and pepper to taste.

Old Fashioned Roast Tom Turkey

Stuff a 12- to 15- pound turkey loosely, put a crust of stale bread in the bird's vent, and truss the legs and wings close to the body. Butter the turkey well and place it, breast down, on a rack in a roasting pan. Roast the bird in a very hot oven (500° F.) for 20 minutes. Add to the pan 1 cup chicken stock, 8 peppercorns, 1 teaspoon salt, and a *bouquet garni* of 1 stalk of celery, 4 sprigs of parsley, and a spray of thyme, reduce the oven temperature to moderate (350° F.), and continue to roast, basting frequently with the pan juices, until the bird is done, about 18 minutes per pound. Turn the bird breast up for the last hour to brown the breast.

Transfer the turkey to a heated platter. Skim of all but 2 tablespoons of fat from the liquid in the pan and discard the *bouquet garni*. Stir 2 tablespoons flour into the pan juices and cook the gravy on top of the stove, stirring in all the brown bits from the bottom and sides of the pan. Stir in 2 cups hot beef stock and cook the gravy for 5 minutes, stirring constantly. Correct the seasoning and strain the gravy through a fine sieve.

To make the forcemeat, put 2 pounds fresh pork fat, 1/2 pound raw poultry livers, and the peelings from 1 1/2 pounds truffles through the finest blade of a food chopper. Blend the mixture in a mortar with salt, pepper, and a pinch of thyme until it is reduced to a smooth paste and press it through a fine sieve. Put one quarter of the paste into a saucepan with the truffles, quartered or left whole if they are small. Season with salt, pepper, thyme, and powdered bay leaf and stir over low heat for 10 minutes. Stir the hot forcemeat into the rest of the forcemeat stuffing, add 1/4 cup Cognac, and mix well. When the forcemeat is cool, stuff the turkey and sew up the opening.

Dindonne au Truffé
TRUFFLED TURKEY

Sprinkle 12 large slices of truffle with salt, pepper, and Cognac. Loosen the skin from the breast of a 10- to 12-pound turkey by slipping the fingers under the skin, and lay 4 of the truffle slices over the breast meat on each side. Loosen the skin from the legs in the same way and insert 2 truffle slices over the leg meat on each side. Truss the turkey and refrigerate it for 2 days so that the flavor of the truffles will permeate the bird.

Traditionally, *la dinde truffé* is roasted on a spit. To roast it in the oven, lard the breast with strips of fat pork and wrap the turkey completely in buttered heavy paper. Roast the bird in an open roasting pan in a moderate oven (350° F.) for 2 1/2 to 3 hours. Unwrap the turkey during the last 30 minutes of roasting to brown it. Serve with either the pan gravy or with *sauce Périgueux* to which the pan juices are added.

HAVE the butcher bone a 10- to 14-pound turkey. Spread the boned turkey out on a board, skin side down, and spread it with a layer of veal forcemeat made by mixing together thoroughly 2 pounds finely chopped veal, 2 beaten eggs, 1 tablespoon chopped parsley, 1 teaspoon salt, and 1/2 tea-

Poupeton de Dindonneau
STUFFED
TURKEY ROLL

spoon white pepper. Sprinkle with the turkey liver, diced, and 2 large truffles, finely chopped.

Simmer 1 large pair prepared sweetbreads for 15 minutes in salted water mixed with the juice of 1 lemon. Drain the cooked sweetbreads and plunge them into cold water. Remove the tubes and membranes gently, being careful not to tear the tissue, and cut the sweetbreads into small cubes. Sprinkle the cubes over the forcemeat. Roll the turkey jelly-roll fashion into a *poupeton*, wrap the roll in cheesecloth, and tie the roll securely at both ends and in the middle.

Sauté in butter for a few minutes 3 carrots, sliced, and 2 large onions, sliced, and put them into a braising kettle large enough to hold the turkey. Cover the vegetables with 3 slices of boiled ham and lay the turkey roll on the ham. Cover the kettle tightly and cook the turkey roll over direct heat for 15 minutes, turning it several times. Add 1 cup Madeira and 1 cup chicken consommé and bake the turkey in a moderate oven (350° F.) in the tightly covered braising kettle for 3 1/2 hours, or until it is very tender.

Arrange the *poupeton* on a large heated platter. Strain the vegetables through a fine sieve along with the juices from the kettle, forcing through as much of the vegetable pulp as possible. If the gravy is too thick, it may be thinned with a little chicken consommé. Serve with the gravy poured over the turkey.

Pavo Relleno à la Catalana
STUFFED TURKEY CATALAN

SIMMER the neck, wing tips, and all the giblets, except the liver, of a 15-pound turkey in lightly salted water to cover. Sprinkle the inside of the turkey with salt and pepper.

In a skillet melt 1/2 cup butter and in it sauté 1/2 pound chopped lean ham and the turkey liver, diced, until the meat is lightly browned. Add 8 pork sausages, sliced, 1/2 pound each of soaked dried prunes and peaches, 1 pound cooked shelled chestnuts, and 3/4 cup pine nuts, all chopped. Add 1/2 cup Sherry, salt and pepper to taste, and a *bouquet garni* of several sprigs of parsley, 1 bay leaf, 1 sprig of thyme, and 1 stalk of celery with the leaves. Cover the skillet and simmer the stuffing for 20 minutes. Discard the *bouquet garni* and stir in 2 truffles, diced. Stuff and truss the turkey and store in the refrigerator overnight.

Next day, brush the turkey generously with melted butter and put it breast side down on a rack in an open roasting pan. Roast it in a moderate oven (350° F.) for 3 1/2 to 4 hours, or until it is done, basting it frequently with a mixture of 1 cup each of chicken stock and Sherry. Put the turkey on a heated serving platter. Skim the fat from the roasting pan and strain the remaining pan juices into a heated sauceboat.

Stuffed Turkey Catalan

Braised
Stuffed Turkey

FOR a 10- to 12-pound turkey, make a *risotto* as follows: Melt 3 table-spoons butter in an earthenware casserole. Cook 1 onion, finely chopped, in the butter for a minute or two, stirring constantly. Add 1 cup well-washed rice and stir until every grain of rice is covered with butter. Add 3 cups rich beef or chicken stock, cover the casserole, and simmer gently until the liquid is all but absorbed and the rice is still slightly underdone. Add 1/2 pound cooked lean ham, cut into dice, and salt and pepper to taste. Stuff the turkey with this mixture and truss it.

In a braising kettle put 1/2 cup each of carrot, celery, and onion, all minced and a *bouquet garni* of several sprigs of parsley and thyme and 1 bay leaf, tied together. Add 1 cup beef or chicken stock and lay the stuffed turkey on the vegetables. Cover the kettle and braise the bird in a moderately hot oven (375° F.) for 3 hours, or until it is quite tender. Transfer the turkey to a heated serving platter.

Reduce the juices in the kettle rapidly and add 1/4 cup Port, scraping the kettle to incorporate the brown bits. Add 2 cups heavy cream and bring the sauce to the boiling point. Strain it through a fine sieve, add salt and pepper to taste, and serve in a heated sauceboat.

Turkey
Casserole

CUT a small plump turkey into serving pieces and remove the skin and bones. Roll the filets in flour and sauté them in a skillet in 5 tablespoons butter until they are golden brown on all sides. Sprinkle the meat with salt and freshly ground black pepper and transfer it to an ovenproof casserole. To the juices remaining in the pan add 1 onion, finely chopped, and sauté the onion until it is transparent. Add 1/2 cup Sherry to the skillet, stir in all the brown bits from the sides and bottom of the pan, and pour onion and liquid over the turkey. Add enough chicken stock just to cover the meat, cover the casserole, and bake in a moderate oven (350° F.) for about 1 hour, or until the turkey is tender. Add 1 cup freshly cooked peas and 1 dozen small cooked white onions and keep the casserole hot until ready to serve.

Mexican
Turkey
MOLE
DE GUAJOLOTE

PREPARE a turkey for cooking and parboil it in water barely to cover until it is just tender. Cut it into neat joints and sauté it in 1/2 cup lard or other fat until it is nicely brown. Put the pieces in a casserole and keep them warm.

Grind 2 sweet peppers, seeded, 1 1/2 teaspoons aniseeds, 2 tablespoons sesame seeds, 6 garlic cloves, 3/4 cup almonds, 3 tortillas (purchasable in tins), and 6 large fresh tomatoes, seeded, and mix them all into a paste. Add to the paste a pinch of ground cloves, 1/4 teaspoon ground cinnamon, 1 teaspoon salt, 1/8 teaspoon pepper, 1/2 teaspoon powdered coriander, 2 ounces grated bitter chocolate, and 2 tablespoons chili powder. Mix the spices in thoroughly.

Add another 1/2 cup fat to the skillet and in it stir the paste until it is very hot. Cover the turkey pieces in the casserole with 2 cups stock and put the paste on top. Cover the casserole and let the *mole* simmer very slowly for 2 1/2 hours, stirring occasionally to prevent sticking. Serve with steamed rice. This turkey gains flavor in the reheating the second day.

Three small birds that resemble game but are not strictly game are the guinea hen, the Rock Cornish game hen, and the squab. They require special preparation and are especially appreciated for their qualities of delicacy and succulence.

REMOVE the breasts from 3 guinea hens, each weighing from 2 to 2 1/4 pounds. Discard the skin, cut each breast into two portions, and sprinkle with salt and pepper.

In a large skillet melt 1/4 cup butter and in it sauté the breasts until they are delicately browned on both sides. Continue to cook the breasts over low heat for about 20 minutes, or until the meat is tender, shaking the pan frequently. Arrange the breasts on a heated serving platter and keep them warm.

Add 2 tablespoons butter to the pan juices and in it sauté 2 small onions, minced, over low heat until they are soft but not browned, stirring constantly. Add 1/2 cup dry white wine, stir well, and let the liquid reduce to almost nothing, stirring occasionally. Stir in 1 cup hot sour cream and simmer the sauce gently for 5 minutes. Strain the sauce through a fine sieve and season to taste with salt and pepper. Add 1 teaspoon lemon juice and

Breast of Guinea Hen Smitane

259

pour the sauce over the breasts. Arrange 1 large mushroom cap, sautéed in butter, on each breast and sprinkle with finely chopped truffles.

Suprêmes de Pintade Périgourdine

BREASTS OF GUINEA HEN PERIGOURDINE

A 2-pound guinea hen will serve 2. Clean the bird, season it with salt, and spread it with butter. Roast the hen in a hot oven (425° F.) for 40 to 45 minutes, basting it frequently. Carve off the legs, then remove the breasts. Reserve the legs and carcass for making *salmis* the following day.

Make a sauce in the roasting pan as follows: Pour off the fat from the pan and add to the pan 1/3 cup Sherry, 1 to 2 tablespoons liquid from a can of truffles, 1 cup brown sauce, and 2 teaspoons meat extract. Cook the sauce slowly for about 10 minutes, stirring in all the brown crustiness around the edge of the pan. Strain. Add 2 to 4 tablespoons diced truffles and 2 tablespoons Sherry or Madeira. Correct the seasoning and bring the sauce to a boil. Remove the skin from the breasts of the guinea hens and trim the breasts to give them a neat, natural shape. Arrange the breasts on a warm serving dish and pour the sauce over them. Lay on each a heated slice of goose liver or *pâté de foie gras* and garnish the platter with sautéed mushrooms.

Pintades en Cocotte

CASSEROLE OF GUINEA HENS

CLEAN 3 guinea hens weighing about 2 pounds each. Wrap them in paper-thin slices of larding pork and truss them. In a heavy casserole melt 1/4 cup butter and in it brown the guinea hens on all sides. Cover the casserole and simmer the birds over low heat for 15 minutes.

Wash 1/8 pound lean salt pork, dry it, cut it into narrow strips, and brown it in 1 tablespoon butter.

Remove the guinea hens from the casserole and stir into the pan juices 3 tablespoons flour. Add gradually 3/4 cup Madeira and 1 1/4 cups chicken stock and continue to cook and stir until the sauce is thickened. Add 2 teaspoons tomato paste and the strips of salt pork. Return the guinea hens to the casserole, cover, and continue to cook for 20 minutes longer. Untruss the guinea hens, discard the larding pork, and serve the birds in the casserole.

Guinea Hen Chimay

Noodle Stuffing

CLEAN a tender guinea hen weighing about 4 pounds and prepare the following stuffing: Cook enough medium noodles to make 3 cups and drain them well. In a skillet heat 3 tablespoons butter until it is hazelnut brown. Add the noodles, sprinkle with a little salt and pepper, and toss the noodles in the butter. Add 6 pieces of goose liver, sautéed briefly in butter, and 2 tablespoons each of *glace de viande* and velouté sauce. Mix well, stuff the bird, and sew up the vent. Spread the guinea hen with butter and set it on its side in a roasting pan. Roast the bird in a hot oven (425° F.) until it is brown on one side, turn, and brown the other side. Reduce the oven temperature to hot (400° F.) and continue to roast the bird for 1 3/4 hours, or until it is tender, turning it occasionally and basting it frequently.

Place the guinea hen on a warm serving platter. Pour the fat from the pan and add to the pan juices 6 tablespoons Madeira, 1/2 cup chicken stock, and 1 to 2 teaspoons meat extract. Cook, stirring in all the brown bits from the sides and bottom of the pan, and serve the sauce with the guinea hen.

PIT 4 cups black cherries and tie the pits in a cheesecloth bag. Put cherries and pits in a saucepan with 1/2 cup each of kirsch and water. Bring the liquid to a boil and simmer the cherries gently for several minutes until they are tender.

Pintadeaux aux Cerises

BABY GUINEA HENS WITH CHERRIES

Clean and split 6 small guinea hens and season them with salt and pepper. In 2 large skillets melt enough butter to generously cover the bottom of the pans and arrange the birds skin side down on it. Cook the birds until the skin is golden brown. Turn them and cook them on the other side, partly covered, for about 20 to 25 minutes, or until they are tender. Arrange the guinea hens on a serving dish. Discard the bag of pits and pour cherries and juice into the pan in which the birds were sautéed. Bring to a boil, stirring, and pour sauce and cherries over the birds. Sprinkle with 3 tablespoons warmed Cognac and ignite the spirit. Serve the birds flaming.

SAUTÉ 3 shallots, minced, in 3 tablespoons butter until they are soft. Add 3 slices of bacon, diced, and cook the bacon until it is crisp. Add 2 table-spoons chopped parsley and remove the pan from the heat. Stir in 1 1/2 cups fine bread crumbs, 1/2 teaspoon poultry seasoning, and salt to taste.

Rock Cornish Game Hens en Couronne

Stuff the cavities of 6 Rock Cornish game hens with the mixture, truss the birds loosely, and arrange them in a shallow buttered roasting pan. Sprinkle them with salt and pepper and rub the breasts and sides generously with soft butter. Roast the birds in a very hot oven (450° F.) for about 15 minutes, or until they are golden, basting frequently. Lower the oven temperature to moderate (350° F.), and continue to roast the birds for 30 minutes longer.

Arrange the birds on a heated platter in a circle, legs up, around a socle, or support, of bread.

To the juices in the roasting pan add 1/2 cup chicken both and 1/4 cup dry white wine and simmer the sauce for a few minutes, stirring in all the brown bits from the pan. Stir in 1 teaspoon cornstarch dissolved in a little consommé of wine and cook the sauce until it is clear and slightly thickened. Garnish the platter with watercress, with browned potato balls in sautéed mushroom caps, and with cooked artichoke hearts stuffed with chestnut purée. Serve the sauce separately.

Rock Cornish Game Hens Stuffed with Brown Rice

WIPE 6 Rock Cornish game hens inside and out with a damp cloth. Sprinkle them lightly inside with salt and pepper. Make a stuffing of brown rice cooked and seasoned as follows: Wash 1 cup brown rice in several changes of cold water and put it in a heavy saucepan with 3 cups cold water and 1 teaspoon salt. Bring the water to a rolling boil, cover the saucepan tightly, and turn the heat down as low as possible. Let the rice cook, without stirring or removing the saucepan cover, for 20 minutes, or until it is barely done. Test by rubbing a kernel between thumb and finger. Drain off any water that may remain in the pan, stir in 1/4 cup melted butter, and set the rice aside to cool.

In a skillet melt 3 tablespoons butter and in it cook 1/2 cup each of finely chopped onion and celery for about 5 minutes, or until they are lightly browned. Combine the vegetables and rice, add 3 tablespoons finely chopped parsley, and season the stuffing to taste with salt and freshly ground black pepper.

Stuff the body cavities of the game birds and close the openings with skewers. In the bottom of a roasting pan put 1 onion and 1 carrot, both thinly sliced. Arrange the birds side by side on the vegetables and pour over them 1/2 cup melted butter. Roast the birds in a very hot oven (450° F.) for 40 minutes, basting frequently.

Arrange the birds on a warm serving dish and garnish them with watercress. Remove the vegetables from the roasting pan, put the pan over high heat, stir in 1 cup hot chicken broth, and cook the gravy for 2 minutes. Serve it separately.

Rock Cornish Game Hens Normandy

PUT a few slices of tart apple in the cavities of 6 Rock Cornish game hens. Truss the birds loosely and brown them lightly on all sides in 1/2 cup butter. Pour over the birds 1/4 cup warmed Calvados or applejack, ignite the spirit, and shake the pan until the flame dies. Transfer the birds and the pan juices to a casserole and add 5 or 6 shallots, finely chopped, 1 tablespoon chopped parsley, 1 sprig of thyme, and 1/2 cup cider or white wine. Cover the casserole and cook the birds in a moderate oven (350° F.) for 40 to 50 minutes, or until they are tender.

Arrange the birds on a heated platter and stir bit by bit into the juices in the casserole 1 teaspoon flour mixed to a paste with 2 teaspoons soft butter. Stir in gradually 1/2 cup hot heavy cream, cook the sauce until it is slightly thickened, and pour it over the birds.

CLEAN six 1-pound Rock Cornish game hens. Put 1 small onion, minced, and 1 tablespoon each of chopped parsley and butter in each bird, sprinkle them with salt and pepper, and tie the legs and wings close to the bodies. In a heavy skillet melt 2 tablespoons butter and in it brown the birds delicately on all sides. Transfer the birds to a large well-buttered casserole and sprinkle them with 1/4 pound of salt pork, finely diced. Cover the casserole and cook the birds in a moderately slow oven (325° F.) for 30 minutes.

Rock Cornish Game Hens en Cocotte

Brown lightly in butter, in separate skillets, 18 small white onions and 18 thin strips of carrot. Add the browned vegetables to the casserole and pour over the chickens 1 cup chicken stock, 1/4 cup Sherry or Madeira and 3 tablespoons dry white wine or Champagne. Correct the seasoning with salt and pepper and cook, covered, for about 30 minutes longer. Scoop out about 30 small potato balls from large potatoes with a French potato-ball cutter. Sauté them in a little hot olive oil until they are delicately browned and thoroughly cooked. Set them aside. To serve, add the potatoes to the casserole and garnish with sprigs of parsley. Serve the birds from the casserole.

SAUTÉ 1/2 pound sausage meat for 5 minutes, stirring it with a fork. Drain off the fat and then add the chopped livers of 6 Rock Cornish game hens sautéed in 2 tablespoons butter, 1 cup toasted bread crumbs, 1 tablespoon chopped parsley, and a pinch each of thyme and freshly ground black pepper. Use this mixture to stuff the birds. Truss them lightly and arrange them in a roasting pan. Sprinkle the birds with salt and pepper, and cover the breasts with thin slices of bacon. Add 1/2 cup each of chicken stock and Port and roast the birds in a hot oven (400° F.) for 35 to 40 minutes, basting several times with the pan juices.

Rock Cornish Game Hens au Porto

Discard the bacon and arrange the birds on a warm serving platter. Skim off the excess fat from the pan juices. Add 1 teaspoon flour kneaded with an equal amount butter and stir in 1/2 cup hot heavy cream. Pour the sauce over the birds or serve it separately.

Poached Rock Cornish Game Hens with Truffle Sauce

INTO a large soup kettle put 2 veal bones, the giblets from 6 Rock Cornish game hens, and 2 quarts water. Bring the water to a boil, add 2 carrots, cut into strips, 2 onions, each stuck with a clove, 1 stalk of celery including the leaves, 3 sprigs of parsley, 2 teaspoons salt, 6 peppercorns, and a sprig of thyme, and simmer for about 1 hour, or until the broth is reduced by one-third.

Put the birds, breast side down, in the broth, cover the kettle, and poach the birds gently for 30 to 35 minutes, or until they are done. Drain the birds and arrange them on a warm serving platter.

Cook gently 1/2 cup chopped truffles in 2 tablespoons butter for 2 to 3 minutes. Season with salt and pepper, add 1 tablespoon warmed brandy, and ignite the spirit. Combine 1 cup each of hot heavy cream and béchamel sauce. Bring the sauce to a boil and stir in the truffles and 2 tablespoons butter. Pour the sauce over the birds and garnish the platter with cooked artichoke hearts covered with a slice of *foie gras*, and mounds of glazed tiny carrots and buttered peas.

Boned Rock Cornish Game Hens

HAVE the butcher bone 6 Rock Cornish game hens. In a saucepan sauté the livers in about 2 tablespoons butter for 2 minutes. Chop the livers and add them to 1 cup finely ground cooked ham. Add 1 1/2 cups fresh bread crumbs, 2 tablespoons grated onion, and salt and pepper to taste, and mix well. Stir in 1 cup shelled pistachio nuts.

Use about 1/2 cup of the stuffing for each bird. Roll the bird around the stuffing, reshaping it carefully to resemble its original form, and tie securely. Melt 1/2 cup butter in a roasting pan and add 2 carrots and 1 onion, both finely chopped. Rub the birds with soft butter, sprinkle them with salt and pepper, and arrange them in the pan. Cook them in a hot oven (400° F.) for 15 minutes, or until they are browned, basting them frequently with a mixture of half white wine and half chicken stock. Reduce the oven temperature to slow (300° F.) and continue to cook the birds for about 30 minutes, or until they are done. Transfer the birds to a warm serving platter. Add 1/4 cup Madeira or Sherry to the pan juices and boil the sauce vigorously for a minute or two, stirring in all the brown crustiness. Strain it over the birds and garnish the platter with a wreath of watercress or sprays of parsley.

CLEAN and singe 6 plump young squabs. Peel and seed 4 dozen muscat grapes. Mix half the grapes with 1/2 cup fine, dry bread crumbs, moisten with 1 tablespoon brandy, and season with salt and pepper. Divide the grape mixture among the 6 birds and stuff the cavities. Arrange the squabs in a buttered baking pan and sprinkle with salt and pepper. Pour a little brandy over them and let them mellow for 1 hour before roasting.

Add 1/4 cup each of Port and water to the pan and roast the birds in a hot oven (425° F.) for 30 to 35 minutes, basting often. Arrange the squabs on a warm serving platter and add 1/2 cup Port and the remaining grapes to the juices in the roasting pan. Stir in 1/2 tablespoon flour mixed to a paste with 1 tablespoon butter and bring the sauce to a boil, stirring constantly. Correct the seasoning and pour the pan gravy over the squabs. Garnish with watercress.

CLEAN and singe 6 small squabs. Truss them to hold the legs close to the bodies and sprinkle with salt and pepper.

Parboil 1 cup diced fat salt pork. Drain and sauté the dice in 1/4 cup butter. Remove them and keep them in a warm place. Add 12 to 18 small onions, peeled, to the fat in the pan and cook them until they are lightly browned. Remove the onions and put them with the pork. Sauté the squabs in the hot fat remaining in the pan, turning them frequently to brown evenly. Remove the squabs to a warm place.

Drain all but 3 tablespoons fat from the pan and stir in 1 tablespoon flour. Cook the *roux* until it is golden and add gradually 1 cup chicken stock, stirring constantly. Continue to stir until the sauce thickens and comes to a boil. Put the squabs, diced pork, and onions in the pan with a *bouquet garni* of several sprigs of parsley, 2 stalks of celery with the leaves, 2 sprigs of fresh thyme, and 1/2 bay leaf. Bring the sauce to a boil, cover the pan, and cook the mixture over moderate heat for 30 minutes. Add 1 cup pitted, blanched green olives and cook the mixture for 10 to 15 minutes. Remove the squabs to a heated serving dish. Discard the *bouquet garni* and pour the sauce around the birds on the platter. Garnish with parsley and triangles of hot buttered toast.

Squabs
with Peas

PROCEED as for squabs with olives, but omit the olives and add 2 cups new peas and salt to taste to the sauce about 20 minutes before the cooking is completed.

Squab Pie
Bourguignonne

CLEAN, singe, and split 3 fine plump squabs. Brown them in 1/4 cup butter, sprinkle with salt and pepper, and cook them, covered, for about 12 minutes. Pour over them 6 tablespoons warmed brandy and ignite it. When the flame dies, add 12 small white onions, peeled, and 3/4 cup each of diced lean ham and Burgundy and cook for 4 minutes longer.

Put the pieces of squab in a large, buttered baking dish, add 3 tablespoons finely chopped carrot, and the squab livers, chopped, and pour the pan juices with the ham and onions over them. Add 3/4 cup chicken consommé and cover the casserole with flaky pastry dough brushed with egg yolk. Bake the pie in a hot oven (425° F) for about 10 minutes, reduce the temperature to moderate (350° F.), and bake for about 35 minutes longer, or until the crust is golden. Serve hot from the baking dish.

Squabs
under Glass

IN a large skillet sauté in butter 3 plump squabs, cleaned, singed, and split, until they are brown on both sides. Sprinkle them with salt and pepper, cover, and cook until tender. Cook 6 mushrooms caps in butter with a little lemon juice until they are tender.

Dress each half squab on a hot slice of broiled lean ham on an individual glass bell dish and garnish with a mushroom cap. To the butter and juices in the skillet add 1/2 cup Sherry and 1 cup heavy cream. Thicken with a little flour mixed to a paste with an equal amount of soft butter, boil for a minute or so, and season with salt and pepper. Pour the sauce over the squabs and garnish each serving with cooked fresh green peas, cooked asparagus, or thinly sliced cooked carrots. Cover each dish with a glass bell and heat the dishes in a slow oven (300° F.) for about 10 minutes. Serve sizzling hot, covered with the bell, which imprisons the flavor and aroma until the last possible minute.

Squabs Sautéed
in White Wine

SINGE, clean, and split 6 small squabs. Melt 8 tablespoons butter in a large skillet and in it lightly brown the squab halves on both sides over high heat. Sprinkle them with salt and pepper and add 3 tablespoons chopped shallots and 3/4 cup dry white wine. Reduce the heat, cover the skillet, and let the squabs simmer gently for 15 minutes.

Add 3 tablespoons finely chopped parsley, 1 tablespoon finely chopped tarragon, and another 1/2 cup wine, and cook, uncovered, for 5 minutes longer.

Set each half squab on a triangle of crisp toast on a heated serving platter, spoon a little of the pan sauce over each, and serve with a garnish of artichoke hearts cooked in butter.

AFTER the first 15 minutes of cooking, as above, add to the skillet another 1/2 cup white wine, the squab livers and a chicken liver, cut in small pieces, 2 cloves, and a small can of *cèpes*, and cook for 10 minutes. Serve with fluffy rice and buttered peas.

Squabs Royale

IN a casserole brown 6 squabs in 1/4 cup butter. Sprinkle them with salt, cover the casserole, and cook the squabs in a moderate oven (350° F.) for about 30 minutes, or until they are tender and cooked through.

Pare, core, and quarter 6 tart apples. Add 1/2 cup water and 2 table-spoons butter, cover, and cook the apples over moderate heat until they are tender. Force the apples through a fine sieve and sweeten the purée very lightly with a little sugar. Spread a layer of the applesauce on a warm serving platter, arrange the birds on the applesauce, and pour over each bird 2 tablespoons warm heavy cream.

Pigeonneaux à la Normande
SQUABS
WITH APPLES

IN a saucepan melt 1/2 cup butter with 1 tablespoon oil. Add 4 tablespoons finely chopped celery, 3 tablespoons grated carrot, and salt and pepper to taste. Stir in 1/3 cup red wine and cook the sauce for 2 to 3 minutes. Add 2 cups cooked wild rice and cook the mixture, stirring, until it is well blended. Stuff 6 squabs with the mixture, truss the birds, and rub them with soft butter. Cover the bottom of a flameproof baking dish with a layer of carrots, split lengthwise and quartered. Arrange the birds breast side down on the carrots and roast them in a very hot oven (450° F.), basting occasionally with red wine, for about 10 minutes, or until they are tender. Pour 1/2 cup heated whiskey over the squabs and ignite the spirit. When the flames have subsided, remove the squabs to a heated platter and keep them warm.

Add 1 cup red wine to the baking dish and cook the sauce, stirring in all the brown bits, over moderate heat until the wine is reduced by half. Strain the sauce, pour it over the birds, and serve immediately.

Squabs en Casserole

Casserole of Stuffed Squabs

WASH 1 pound wild rice in four or five waters until it is thoroughly clean. Soak it overnight in cold water and drain it.

Sauté 1 onion, finely chopped, and the livers of 12 squabs in 1/4 cup butter until the onion is tender but not brown and stir the mixture into the wild rice with 2 cups shelled pistachio nuts and 1 cup shredded cooked ham. Season the stuffing with salt and pepper.

Bone the 12 squabs and fill them with the wild rice stuffing. Tie and sew them securely, reshaping them as neatly as possible.

In a casserole large enough to hold all the birds, melt 6 tablespoons butter. Add 4 carrots and 4 onions, both finely chopped, and the squabs and brown the squabs lightly on all sides. Sprinkle them with salt and pepper, pour over them 1/2 cup warmed Cognac and ignite it. When the flame dies, add 2 cups chicken stock, 1/2 cup white wine, and a *bouquet garni* of 4 sprigs of parsley, 1 stalk of celery with the leaves, and 2 sprigs of thyme. Cover the casserole tightly and cook the birds in a moderate oven (350° F.) for 45 minutes. Thicken the sauce if necessary with a little *beurre manié*, flour rubbed to a paste with an equal amount of butter, and serve the squabs in the casserole. Serves 12.

The liver of the goose ranks as one of the three greatest gourmet delicacies—the others, of course, are truffles and caviar. As for the goose itself, it comes too seldom to the tables of American gourmets. Save every drop of the molten gold that oozes from the roasting bird; goose fat is a genuine treasure for cooking and flavoring.

IN a large saucepan sauté 1/2 cup chopped onion in 1/2 cup butter until the onion is transparent. Add 4 cups each of peeled diced apples and cooked chopped chestnuts, 1 cup parboiled seedless raisins, drained and dried, the chopped liver of the goose, and 2 cooked potatoes, diced. Continue to sauté until the apples are soft and the mixture is lightly browned. Remove the pan from the stove and stir in 1 1/2 teaspoons salt, 1/4 teaspoon black pepper, 1/4 cup chopped parsley, and 1/2 teaspoon each of powdered mace, sage, nutmeg, and cloves.

Wipe a tender goose and rub the cavity with salt. Stuff the goose with

*Pigeonneaux
Farcis en
Casserole*
CASSEROLE OF
STUFFED SQUABS

*Gebratene
Gans*
ROAST GOOSE
WITH APPLE
STUFFING

the apple-chestnut stuffing, sew up the vent, and rub the bird with salt. Turn the skin of the neck backward and secure it with a small skewer. Twist the wings back and run a skewer through the thighs and body. Prick well with a 2-tined fork. Place the goose on a rack in a roasting pan and roast in a hot oven (400° F.) for 20 minutes. Reduce the heat to moderate and continue to roast, allowing 20 minutes per pound, undressed weight. Baste the goose frequently with a little water or white wine and pour off most of the fat as it accumulates in the pan.

Put the goose giblets and neck in a saucepan with 1 small onion, a few celery leaves, 1/2 teaspoon salt, and pepper to taste. Cover with cold water and simmer the mixture gently for 1 hour. Strain the broth, reserving it for the gravy, and chop the giblets.

When the goose is done, arrange it on a heated platter and remove the skewers and thread. Skim off most of the fat from the roasting pan and stir in 1 tablespoon flour. Gradually add the giblet broth and a little water, if necessary, to make 1 1/2 cups liquid in all, stirring constantly and scraping the bottom and sides of the pan to remove all the brown bits. Add the chopped giblets and simmer for 5 minutes. Pour the gravy into a sauce-boat and serve it separately.

Oie Farcie aux Marrons
GOOSE STUFFED WITH CHESTNUTS

WITH a sharp knife, slit the shells of 2 pounds chestnuts on the convex side. Put them in a saucepan with water to cover and bring it to a boil. Remove the pan from the heat and, without draining them, take the chestnuts from the saucepan, one by one, and remove the shell and inner skins while the nuts are still hot. Cook them in chicken stock with a stalk of celery for about 30 minutes, or until they are just tender. Season 1 pound fresh sausage meat with a pinch of poultry seasoning and 2 tablespoons brandy, add the chestnuts, and mix lightly. Stuff a goose with this forcemeat and sew up the vent. Truss the bird, brush it with melted goose fat, and roast it in the usual way, with 1/2 cup water in the pan. As the water evaporates, add more and remove the accumulating fat.

Garnish the goose with watercress on a heated platter. Remove the fat from the pan juices, add 1/2 cup chicken stock, and cook, stirring in all the brown crustiness that has formed around the pan. Serve the gravy separately.

Roast Goose with Stewed Apples

CLEAN a young goose weighing about 10 pounds and rub it inside and out with salt.

Place the goose in a roasting pan, add 4 cups water, 1/2 onion, sliced, and 6 crushed peppercorns, and roast in a moderate oven (350° F.) for

20 minutes per pound, basting frequently. When the water is reduced by half, add 1/2 cup butter and continue to baste occasionally until the goose is golden and the skin is crisp.

Place the goose on a warm serving platter, remove the excess fat from the pan, and stir 2 tablespoons flour into the juices remaining in the pan. Stir in 2 cups hot stock and simmer, stirring, for 5 minutes, or until the gravy is smooth and lightly thickened. Serve the gravy with the goose, and serve also a dish of apples stewed as follows: Wash, peel, and core 2 pounds apples. Cut the fruit into thick slices and sauté the slices in 2 tablespoons butter for 3 minutes. Sprinkle the fruit with 1/2 cup sugar, add 1/2 cup each of water and white wine, a small piece of lemon peel, and 1 tablespoon lemon juice, and cook the apples over low heat, covered, until they are just tender.

COOK 10 medium potatoes in salted water until tender. Dice the potatoes and reserve the potato water to baste the goose. Sauté 1 cup chopped onions and 1/2 cup chopped celery in 1 tablespoon goose fat or butter until the onions are transparent. Add the vegetables to the potatoes and stir in 4 slices of bread, cubed, 1/2 pound salt pork, ground, 1 teaspoon each of poultry seasoning and salt, and 1/4 teaspoon pepper.

Rub a 12-pound goose inside and out with salt and pepper. Stuff the goose with the potato stuffing and sew up the vent. Roast the goose in a moderate oven (375° F.) for about 3 hours, basting frequently with potato water.

Goose with Potato Stuffing

CLEAN a young goose weighing about 10 pounds. Wipe it with a damp cloth, tie the neck with heavy string, and rub the goose inside and out with salt and pepper.

Stuff the goose with 4 tart apples, peeled, cored, and quartered, and 16 large dried prunes, halved, and sew up the vent. Place the goose in a roasting pan, breast side up, and roast it in a hot oven (400° F.) for about 2 1/2 hours, or until the goose is tender, basting it frequently with the fat in the pan and a little hot water, as needed.

Gaasesteg med Aebler or Svesker
DANISH GOOSE WITH FRUIT

CLEAN a young goose weighing about 8 pounds and wipe it dry inside and out. In a saucepan sauté a mashed garlic clove in 1 teaspoon olive oil until it is brown. Discard the garlic, add half an onion, finely chopped, and

Chinese Roast Goose

271

sauté for 2 minutes. Add 1/4 cup chopped celery, 1/2 teaspoon cinnamon, a few aniseeds, 3/4 cup soy sauce, 1 tablespoon sugar, and 2 cups water and bring to a boil.

Tie the goose neck with string, pour the sauce inside the goose, and sew up the vent securely so that the sauce will not bubble out. Rub the bird with salt and place it on a rack, breast up, in a roasting pan. Roast the goose in a hot oven (400° F.) for 20 minutes, lower the temperature to moderately hot (375° F.) and roast the bird for 20 minutes per pound, basting frequently with a mixture of 2 cups boiling water, 1/2 cup honey, 1/4 cup vinegar, and 1 tablespoon soy sauce.

When the goose is done, open the vent, let the sauce drain into the roasting pan, and place the goose on a warm serving platter. Thicken the sauce with a little cornstarch mixed to a paste with cold water, cook it for a few minutes, and serve it separately.

Oie
à l'instar
de Visé

GOOSE WITH
GARLIC CREAM
SAUCE

SUBMERGE a goose, cleaned and singed, in salted water in a large heavy kettle and bring the water to a boil. Remove the scum, add 3 onions and 1 carrot, both coarsely sliced, a head of garlic, 8 peppercorns, and a *bouquet garni* of parsley, celery stalks with the leaves, thyme, and tarragon. Simmer the goose gently until tender, cut it into serving portions, and sauté the pieces gently in melted butter until they are lightly browned on both sides.

Heat 4 cups milk to the simmering point with 15 garlic cloves. Stir in 5 egg yolks lightly beaten with 1/2 cup warm heavy cream and a little of the hot milk and continue to stir for 2 or 3 minutes until the sauce is thickened, being careful not to let it boil. Add salt to taste and strain the sauce.

Arrange the pieces of goose on a warm serving platter. Pour over them the melted butter in which they were browned and mask with the sauce.

Goose
Giblets
Ménagère

SEASON the wing tips, neck, gizzard, and heart of a goose with salt. Melt 2 tablespoons goose fat in a saucepan, add the pieces of goose, and cook them on all sides until they are golden brown. Drain any excess fat from the pan and add 1 tablespoon chopped onion, 1 teaspoon chopped shallots, 1 garlic clove, crushed, and 2 tablespoons flour. Mix well and cook until the flour is golden brown. Add 1 cup red or white wine (and 1/2 cup tomato juice, if desired) and enough water to cover the pieces of goose. Bring to a boil, mix well, and add a *bouquet garni* composed of 4 sprigs of parsley, 1 stalk of celery, a little thyme, and a small bay leaf.

In another pan parboil 2 cups chopped celery or knob celery and 3 carrots cut in pieces for 8 to 10 minutes and drain. Sauté 12 small onions in butter or goose fat until golden. Add the vegetables to the stew. Add also 2 to 3 cups potatoes cut in pieces.

Cook the stew for 45 to 60 minutes longer, or until the meat is tender. Remove the *bouquet garni* and, if desired, add 24 cooked shelled chestnuts, heating them for a few minutes in the stew. Correct the seasoning and add a little freshly ground pepper. Put the stew in a heated serving dish and garnish with broiled small sausages and chopped parsley.

Escalopes de Foie Gras à la Monselet

HEAT 6 slices of cooked goose liver in butter. Fill 6 cooked artichoke bottoms with julienne strips of truffle, heated in butter and bound with a little cream sauce. Arrange the artichoke bottoms in a circle on a warm serving platter, lay a slice of *foie gras* on each, and garnish the liver with a thin slice of truffle. Fill the center of the platter with tiny potato balls browned in butter. Bring to a boil 1/2 cup brown sauce and stir in 1 teaspoon meat extract and 2 tablespoons juice from the can of truffles. Pour a ribbon of the sauce around the artichokes.

When les restes, *what we less delicately call leftovers, are of chicken, they become the base of some exquisite preparations. Naturally, the* restes *of other birds may be substituted for the chicken.*

Niu Moa Ai
CHICKEN AND VEGETABLES IN A COCONUT

SAW the tops off 6 small fresh coconuts and scrape out half the coconut meat. Sauté 4 strips of bacon, diced, until the bacon is crisp and golden. Add 3 onions, thinly sliced, 6 tomatoes, chopped, 1 garlic clove, finely chopped, 1 green pepper, chopped, and salt and pepper to taste and simmer the vegetables until they are tender. Press the vegetables through a fine sieve and add 1/4 cup of the shredded coconut meat, 1 cup raw corn kernels, and 2 cups diced meat from a plump cooked chicken. Divide the mixture among the 6 coconut shells, replace the coconut tops, and seal the tops with a stiff paste of flour and water. Put the coconut casseroles in a baking pan containing 1 inch of water and bake them in a hot oven (400° F.) for 1 hour, basting them every 10 minutes with the water.

Chicken Hash Saint-Germain

COMBINE 2 cups finely diced white meat of chicken or turkey with 1 cup cream and cook until the cream is reduced by half. Add 1/2 cup cream sauce and a little salt. Force enough cooked green peas through a sieve to make 2 cups purée, and stir the purée over low heat until the surplus moisture is cooked away. Stir in 2 egg yolks. Make a border of this purée around a serving dish and fill the center with the chicken hash. Spread the chicken with 1/2 cup Mornay sauce mixed with 1 tablespoon whipped cream and glaze it under the broiler. Serves 4.

Coquilles de Volaille à la Parisienne

STIR 2 egg yolks, beaten lightly with 3 tablespoons cream, into 2 cups velouté sauce, and add 2 tablespoons butter. Cook 12 small mushrooms for 5 minutes in a little water with a few drops of lemon juice and 1 teaspoon butter. Cut enough cooked chicken into small slices to make 2 cups. Put 1 tablespoon sauce in each *coquille* or scallop shell, add 5 or 6 slices of chicken, 2 mushrooms, and 2 slices of truffle. Add 2 tablespoons whipped cream to the remaining sauce and divide it among the *coquilles*, covering the chicken, mushrooms, and truffle slices with it. Place the *coquilles* on a baking sheet and brown the sauce in a very hot oven (450° F.) or under the broiler.

Minced Chicken with Noodles

COOK 5 mushrooms, sliced, in 2 tablespoons sweet butter until tender. Add a cooked chicken breast, minced, and 1/4 cup Sherry and cook until the wine is reduced to almost nothing. Stir in 1 cup cream sauce and salt and pepper to taste.

Cook some fine noodles and put them in a *gratin* dish with the chicken and mushrooms in the middle. Mask with Mornay sauce, sprinkle with grated cheese, and brown in a hot oven (400° F.). Serves 2.

Coconut Milk

GRATE the meat of a small coconut into a bowl and add 1 cup hot milk. In 15 minutes squeeze the coconut through cheesecloth, reserving the coconut milk. Repeat with another cup of hot milk.

Chicken Hawaii

In the top of a double boiler heat 3 tablespoons olive oil or butter and in it sauté 1 onion, chopped, 2 tablespoons chopped fresh gingerroot, and 1 garlic clove, mashed, until the onion is golden. Stir in 3 tablespoons flour mixed with 1/2 teaspoon cinnamon and 2 teaspoons each of curry powder and sugar and continue to cook gently, stirring constantly, for 5 minutes. Stir in gradually the 2 cups coconut milk and cook, stirring, until the sauce is thickened. Place the pan over boiling water and cook the sauce for 45 minutes. Add the cooked meat of a tender young chicken, cut in 2-inch pieces, and salt to taste. Serve with cooked rice and small dishes of quartered limes, the grated coconut, chutney, pickled pineapple cubes, chopped crisp bacon, and chopped hard-cooked eggs.

SAUTÉ 3 tablespoons chopped onions in 2 tablespoons butter until they are golden. Add 1 tablespoon finely chopped shallots, 1 garlic clove, crushed, and 1 1/2 cups sliced mushrooms. Cook slowly until the mushrooms are soft. Sprinkle the mushrooms with 1 tablespoon flour, mix well, and add 1/3 cup white or red wine, 2 cups stock or gravy or cooked tomatoes, and 3 fresh tomatoes, peeled, seeded, and chopped. Cook, stirring constantly, until the sauce is thickened and continue to cook for about 10 to 15 minutes. Add 3 cups diced cooked chicken and bring the sauce back to the boil, but do not boil. Correct the seasoning with salt and add a little pepper. Place the *capilotade* in a serving dish, sprinkle it with chopped parsley, and garnish it with croutons.

Capilotade de Volaille
CHICKEN RAGOUT

COOK 1/2 pound mushrooms for 5 minutes in water to cover. Add 1/4 cup of the mushroom stock to 2 cups hot cream sauce and stir in 2 egg yolks beaten with 2 tablespoons sweet cream.
    Combine 2 cups diced cooked white meat of chicken with the mushrooms, 1 truffle, and 1 cup cooked sweetbreads, all cut into uniform dice. Add 1/4 cup Madeira and heat the mixture thoroughly. Add the hot sauce and keep the mixture hot over hot water. Serve in puff paste patty shells.

Bouchées à la Reine

SAUTÉ 1/2 pound mushrooms and 1 green pepper, coarsely chopped, in 1/2 cup butter for 5 minutes, or until they are soft. Stir in 2 pimientos, sliced, and 2 cups diced cooked chicken. Add 1/2 cup Sherry and cook until the wine has been absorbed. Add 2 cups cream and simmer for 5 minutes. Thicken the sauce with 2 egg yolks and finish with 1 tablespoon butter. Season with nutmeg and salt and white pepper to taste. Turn the chicken into a serving dish, add 1 tablespoon Sherry, and sprinkle with 1 cup toasted slivered almonds. Serves 4.

Almond Chicken

IN the top pan of a chafing dish over hot water, melt 2 tablespoons butter. Add 2 tablespoons finely chopped scallions and cook until the scallions are soft and golden. Add 2 cups cooked chicken, cut into 2-inch pieces, 1/2 cup sliced water chestnuts, 1 teaspoon slivered fresh ginger, and 1 cup sour cream. Heat thoroughly. Serves 4.

Chicken Marka

275

*Chicken
à l'Indienne*

PREPARE a curry sauce as follows: In a saucepan cook 2 tablespoons chopped onion in 1 tablespoon butter until the onion is soft but not brown. Add 1 small bay leaf, a little thyme, and 1 to 2 tablespoons curry powder, according to taste, mix well, and stir in 1/4 cup white stock. Bring the sauce to a boil, add 1 1/2 cups *velouté* and cook over low heat for 10 to 15 minutes. Strain the sauce through a fine sieve, add 1/2 cup cream, and return to the boil. Heat 3 cups cooked sliced chicken in a little stock, add the curry sauce, and bring to the boil. Serve with rice or *Kasha*.

*Soufflé
à la Reine*

CHICKEN SOUFFLÉ

CHOP very finely 1 1/2 to 2 cups cooked chicken, using all white meat, or a mixture of white meat and the more tender parts of the dark meat. The meat may be rubbed through a sieve; it should be as fine as a purée.

Melt 2 tablespoons butter in a saucepan, add 3 tablespoons flour, and cook the *roux* until it starts to turn golden. Stir in 1 cup hot milk, combining it with a whip. Return the pan to the heat and cook the sauce for about 5 minutes, or until it is very thick, stirring it constantly with the whip. Season the sauce with grated nutmeg.

Add the chopped chicken and 4 egg yolks, beaten until light and warmed with a little of the hot sauce. Correct the seasoning with salt. Beat 5 egg whites until they are stiff but not dry. Fold into the mixture thoroughly and carefully one-fourth of the beaten egg whites and add the remaining egg whites, cutting them in lightly and completely by raising and folding the mixture over and over. Pour the batter into a buttered and lightly floured mold and bake the soufflé in a moderate oven (350° F.) for 25 to 30 minutes.

*Chicken Soufflé
Virginia*

SUBSTITUTE 1/2 cup very finely chopped, richly flavored Virginia ham for the same amount of chicken in the recipe for *soufflé à la reine*.

Turkey Pilaff

SAUTÉ 1 large onion, chopped, in 1/4 pound melted butter until it is golden. Add diced cooked giblets from a turkey and 2 cups raw rice, and season with 3/4 teaspoon thyme and salt and pepper to taste. Continue to cook, stirring, until the rice turns golden. Add 2 cups cooked turkey, diced, and 3 1/2 cups turkey broth, cover the pan, and simmer the pilaff for 20 minutes, or until the rice is tender and all the liquid is absorbed. Toss the rice lightly with 2/3 cup chopped walnuts and serve hot.

Chicken à l'Indienne

Sliced Turkey with Paprika Sauce

MELT 1 tablespoon butter in a saucepan, add 1 tablespoon finely chopped onion, and cook until golden. Add 2 tablespoons paprika and mix well. Add 1 cup sweet cream gradually, mixing well, and cook, stirring, for about 10 minutes. Add 1 cup cream sauce or 6 tablespoons *velouté* to thicken the sauce. Correct the seasoning with salt.

Arrange 2 cups sliced cooked turkey in the blazer of a chafing dish over boiling water and pour the hot sauce over it. Serve with boiled rice. Serves 4.

Sauce Diable

ADD 4 shallots, chopped, and 8 peppercorns, crushed, to 1 cup dry white wine or vinegar and cook the mixture until it is reduced to a thick paste. Add 2 cups *sauce espagñole*, 1 teaspoon Worcestershire sauce, and 1/2 teaspoon chopped parsley.

Deviled Turkey Breast

Dip 6 thick slices of cold cooked turkey breast in 1/2 cup melted butter and then in this *sauce diable*, and roll the meat in fine bread crumbs. Broil the slices under moderate heat until they are brown, turning them once. Serve with more *sauce diable*.

Curried Turkey Wings

SAUTÉ 2 onions, chopped, in 3 tablespoons butter until they are golden; add 1 unpeeled apple and 1 green pepper, both finely chopped, and cook until they are tender. Stir in 2 cups turkey broth and season with 2 tablespoons curry powder. Cook the sauce slowly for 30 minutes. Add the cooked wings and drumsticks or other oddments of roasted turkey and heat the meat thoroughly. Add 1 cup thickened turkey gravy made with the drippings in the roasting pan and 1 cup white seedless grapes, and season to taste, adding more curry if necessary. Serve with wild rice.

Waterzooi de Dinde

REMOVE the stringy fibers and slice very thin enough celery hearts to make 2 cups. Wash and slice the white parts of 3 medium leeks and 1/2 pound mushrooms. In a heavy casserole melt 2 tablespoons butter with 1 tablespoon oil. Put the sliced vegetables in the casserole with a large sprig of parsley in the center. On this bed lay a trussed tender young turkey weighing 4 to 4 1/2 pounds. Add salt, white pepper, a few lumps of butter, and 1/2 cup dry white wine. Cover the casserole closely and braise the turkey over very low heat for 1 1/4 hours, or until it is tender. Protect the dish with an asbestos mat or plaque and do not let the vegetables brown.

When the turkey is done, remove it, carve it into serving pieces, and keep them hot in a deep serving dish. Beat 4 egg yolks with 1 cup heavy cream and add it to the vegetables and juices in the casserole, stirring well. Season with salt to taste reheat the mixture just until it thickens, without letting it boil. Pour it over the chicken and serve at once.

WASH 1 cup wild rice in several changes of lukewarm water and soak it in cold water for 1 1/2 hours. Drain the rice and put it in a mixing bowl. Toss the rice with 2 cups cooked turkey, diced, and 1/2 pound sliced sautéed mushrooms, and add 1 1/2 cups each of heavy cream and turkey stock. Add 2 tablespoons chives, finely chopped, and salt and pepper to taste. Turn the turkey mixture into a well-buttered casserole, adjust the cover, and bake it for 1 hour in a moderate oven (350° F.). Add 1 cup turkey stock and continue to bake for 35 minutes longer, or until the rice is tender. Sprinkle the casserole with 1/2 cup grated Parmesan, dot it with 1 tablespoon butter, and brown the topping lightly under the broiler.

Turkey and Wild Rice Casserole

PUT 1 pint freshly opened oysters and their juices in a saucepan with 1 cup water, bring the water slowly to a boil, and simmer the oysters for about 2 minutes, or until the edges curl. Drain the oysters and chop them coarsely. Reserve the liquid.

In a skillet, slowly blend 3 tablespoons flour with 3 tablespoons melted butter, add 1 cup of the oyster liquid, and stir constantly until the mixture comes to a boil. Slowly add 1 cup light cream, season with salt and pepper to taste, and simmer the sauce for a few moments longer. Add 3 cups cooked turkey, diced, and simmer the mixture over low heat for 3 minutes. Add the oysters and heat all together for 2 minutes longer.

Serve the hash on a hot platter garnished with triangles of toast.

Turkey and Oyster Hash

CHILL cooked but still crisp bean sprouts and combine them with one-third their volume the shredded cooked white turkey meat. Prepare a Chinese mustard dressing by shaking 1/2 cup salad oil, 2 tablespoons sesame seed oil, 1/4 cup each of wine vinegar and soy sauce, 2/3 teaspoon salt, and 2 teaspoons sugar with 2 tablespoons dry mustard. Let the dressing stand to mellow for several hours. Toss the salad lightly with the mustard dressing and serve it at once.

Turkey Salad with Bean Sprouts

$\mathcal{M}eats$

The first prerequisite for good roast beef is an honest butcher. We deny that there is any validity to Brillat-Savarin's assertion that one must be born knowing how to roast meat; given a good piece of meat, anyone can produce a fine, juicy roast. Beef can be roasted on a spit; it can be seared in a hot oven and finished at reduced heat, or it can be cooked at a uniformly low temperature. A meat thermometer will temporarily take the place of experience in judging the state of doneness of roasted meat.

The directions for prime ribs of beef apply equally well to other roasts; adjust cooking time according to weight. A rolled boneless roast requires 5 to 10 minutes longer per pound.

Roast Prime Ribs of Beef   SPREAD a rib roast of beef generously with rendered beef suet. Put it in a roasting pan, curved side up. Brown the beef in a very hot oven (450° F.) for about 20 minutes, reduce the heat to moderate (350° F.), and continue to roast, basting frequently. Allow about 10 to 12 minutes, in addition to the searing time, per pound for rare, 15 minutes for medium, and 18 minutes for well-done roasts, or use a meat thermometer. In cooking a large roast, add a few tablespoons water to the pan to prevent the fat from burning. Remove the meat to a warm platter to rest for about 20 minutes before carving.

To make the gravy, pour off the fat from the pan, add about 1 cup stock or water, and cook the gravy over moderate heat, stirring in all the brown crustiness in the pan. Correct the seasoning with salt and swirl in 1 tablespoon butter. Remove the gravy from the heat before the butter has completely melted. Add to the gravy the juice that runs on the platter when the roast is carved. Serve with Yorkshire pudding made as follows: Sift together into a bowl 2 cups sifted flour and 1 teaspoon salt. Slowly stir in 2 cups milk or 1 cup each of light cream and milk, beating vigorously until smooth. Add 4 eggs, one at a time, beating for a minute with a beater after each addition. Cover the bowl with a towel and chill the batter for at least 2 hours. About 30 minutes before the roast is done, spoon 8 tablespoons fat drippings from the roast into a shallow pan and put it in the oven until the drippings are sizzling hot. Beat the chilled batter vigorously a few times and pour it about 1/2 inch deep into the pan. Bake the pudding in a very hot oven (450° F.) for about 15 minutes. When it has risen, reduce the temperature to moderate (350° F.) and bake it for 10 to 15 minutes longer, or until it is light, crisp, and brown.

Yorkshire Pudding

THE filet of beef is a roughly pyramidal piece of beef cut from under the loin of the steer, near the kidney. The filet is often cut into steaks, to make the chateaubriand, the tournedos, and the filets mignons; but it may be roasted or braised. It makes a particularly elegant entrée, hot or cold. Trim the filet, removing the skin and any sinews. Lard it with strips of larding fat, since it is lean by nature, or wrap it in sheets of suet. The filet of beef may be browned in a heavy pan and cooked, covered, over direct heat; or it may be braised; or it may be roasted, in a very hot oven (450° F.) or on the spit. In any case, it should be rare, and the cooking time should not exceed 35 minutes for even the largest filet. The filet may be served *au jus*, but it is usually—and fittingly—more elaborately sauced and garnished.

Filet of Beef

ROAST a filet of beef in a moderate oven (350° F.), basting it with 1 cup white wine and white stock in equal parts. While the meat cooks, melt 2 table-spoons butter in a saucepan, stir in 1 tablespoon flour and cook the *roux*, stirring, until it begins to turn golden. Add the pan juices from the roast and cook and stir the sauce until it is smooth. Add a little more stock if necessary to make a fairly thin sauce. Add 1 cup pitted, drained olives, heat the olives

Filet of Beef with Olives

well, and adjust the seasoning with pepper and a very little salt, since olives are salty. Arrange the filet on a heated platter, surround it with the olives, and pour the sauce over the meat. Serve hot.

Filet de Boeuf Fourré Perigourdine
STUFFED FILET OF BEEF

TRIM a filet of beef, reserving the narrow end and the wide end for another purpose; the roast should consist only of the heart of the filet. With a knife-sharpening steel, perforate the roast from end to end. Fill the opening thus formed with a mixture of *foie gras* and truffles. Lard the roast with small strips of larding fat and tie well, being careful to enclose the stuffing firmly. Roast the meat in the usual way and serve it *au jus*, or with *sauce périgueux*. Garnish the platter with fluted mushrooms, sautéed lightly in butter, with whole truffles, and with mounds of duchess potatoes forced through a pastry bag fitted with a fancy tube.

Filet of Beef Marchand de Vin

TRIM and roast a filet of beef in the usual manner. While the meat is cooking, peel and chop 4 shallots and sauté them lightly in 1/4 cup butter. Add 1/2 cup claret and reduce the liquid by half. Add 1 cup brown sauce and 1 tablespoon *glace de viande* or about 1 teaspoon meat extract. Simmer the sauce for a few minutes and finish it with 1 tablespoon butter and a generous dash of lemon juice.

Arrange the filet on a heated platter, pour the sauce over the meat, and garnish the platter with stuffed mushrooms, stuffed cooked artichoke bottoms, grilled small tomatoes, and cooked asparagus tips.

Filet of Beef Smitane

TRIM a filet of beef and rub it with salt, pepper, and butter. In a roasting pan melt a little suet or beef fat and put the filet in the pan. Add 1 tablespoon grated lemon rind, 2 tablespoons each of chopped parsley and onion, and 1/4 cup chopped carrots and roast the meat in a moderate oven (350° F.) for 25 to 35 minutes, or until it is done to taste. The meat should be rare.

Keep the meat warm on a heated platter.

Pour off all but 2 tablespoons of the fat in the pan and stir into the remaining fat 1 tablespoon flour. Cook, stirring, until the *roux* is brown. Stir in gradually 1 cup warm sour cream and cook, stirring vigorously, until the sauce is hot, smooth, and thickened. Strain the sauce over the meat and garnish the platter with watercress.

Filet of Beef Wellington

TRIM a good-sized filet of beef, smear it generously with butter, and sprinkle it with salt and pepper. Put it in a flat pan with scraps of celery, onion, and parsley, 1 bay leaf, and a pinch of rosemary and roast it in a very hot oven (450° F.) for about 25 minutes. Remove it and let it cool.

When the filet is cold, spread it with a substantial layer of *pâté de foie gras* and wrap it in pie pastry, rolled about 1/8 inch thick. Trim the edges of the pastry, moisten them with a little cold water, and press firmly together. Bake the rolled filet on a baking sheet in a hot oven (450° F.) for about 15 minutes, or until the crust is delicately browned. For a shiny crust, brush the surface with beaten egg yolk before baking.

Add 1 cup veal stock, 1/4 cup *pâté de foie gras*, and 1 large truffle, chopped, to the roasting pan. Simmer the sauce for 15 minutes and serve it separately.

TRIM a filet of beef and lard it generously with strips of fat pork. Melt 2 tablespoons butter in a roasting pan and in it cook until they are soft 2 carrots, 2 onions, and 2 stalks of celery, chopped, with several sprigs of parsley and 1 bay leaf. Sprinkle the filet with salt and pepper and with melted butter. Roast it in a very hot oven (450° F.) for about 25 minutes, basting it once with melted butter. Brush it with *glace de viande* or meat extract, and arrange it on a heated serving platter.

Filet of Beef Moderne

Cut cooked carrots and turnips into uniform sticks. Butter 8 small molds and put a slice of truffle in the bottom of each. Line the bottom half of the sides of 4 of the molds with carrots standing upright and the top half with turnips; reverse the order for the remaining molds. Spread the vegetables with a little veal forcemeat to hold them in place. Fill the molds with well-seasoned purée of cabbage, carefully drained of excess moisture. Put the filled molds in a flat pan in simmering water reaching about halfway up their sides and cook them for 10 minutes.

Unmold the vegetables and use them to garnish the filet on the platter, alternating them with hearts of lettuce that have been braised for a few minutes with butter and a *mirepoix* of chopped vegetables. Garnish the ends of the platter with large *mousselines* of veal.

Add 1 cup brown stock to the juices in the roasting pan, simmer the liquid for 10 minutes, and strain it. Skim off the fat and thicken the sauce with a little arrowroot or flour. Pour a little of the sauce around the meat and serve the rest separately.

MAKE a thick paste of rock salt and water and plaster it thickly over a large roast of beef until the whole roast is encased in a crust of salt. Roast the

Beef Roasted in Rock Salt

meat in a moderately slow oven (325° F.) for about 22 minutes per pound for a 6- to 8-pound roast. Take the roast from the oven and immediately remove the crust of rock salt with a hammer. Serve with Yorkshire pudding.

Beef may be pot-roasted, or it may be braised, over direct heat or in the oven. This long slow gentle cooking by either method produces tender, flavorful meat that is always well done and served in its own rich gravy. The wine or vinegar added to the braising liquid acts as a natural tenderizer.

Pot Roast in Beer

LARD a 4- to 5-pound pot roast of beef with strips of fat and put it in an enamel or earthenware bowl. Sprinkle it with 2 tablespoons sugar and 1 tablespoon salt, and add 1/2 teaspoon cloves, 6 peppercorns, a dash of cayenne, and 1 onion and 1 carrot, both sliced. Pour 1 1/2 cups beer and 1/2 cup olive oil over the meat and put it in the refrigerator to marinate for several hours or overnight, turning it several times in the marinade.

Melt 2 tablespoons butter in a heavy kettle and in it brown the meat well on all sides. Add 1/2 cup of the marinade, cover tightly, and cook the meat over low heat for about 3 hours, or until it is tender, adding more marinade as needed.

Marinated Pot Roast

HAVE the butcher lard and tie a 4-pound piece of top round. Rub the meat with salt and pepper and put it in a large earthenware crock or bowl. Heat but do not boil 3 cups each of wine vinegar and water with 1 onion, sliced, 1 bay leaf, 1 teaspoon peppercorns, 2 tablespoons sugar, and 2 cloves. Pour the hot mixture over the beef and let it cool. Cover the bowl and put it in the refrigerator for 24 to 36 hours, turning the meat occasionally.

When the meat is ready, place a heavy kettle over high heat and in it melt 2 tablespoons lard. Dredge the beef with 2 tablespoons flour and sear it in the hot lard, browning it on all sides. Pour in the marinade, reduce the heat, cover the kettle tightly, and simmer the meat for 2 to 3 hours, or until it is tender and the marinade has cooked down. Remove the beef and keep it warm.

Taste the gravy in the pan. If it is too sour, add a little water; if not sour enough, add vinegar to taste. Crumble in 5 or 6 small gingersnaps and stir until the gravy has thickened. Strain it into a gravy bowl and serve it separately with the beef.

Ragout with Dumplings

CUT 1/4 pound salt pork into small strips and roll them in a mixture of salt, pepper, ground cloves, and nutmeg. Cut deep gashes in a 4-pound rump of beef and lard it with the spiced strips of pork. Line the bottom of a stew kettle with 3/4 pound sliced salt pork. Add a lemon wedge, 2 carrots, cut into strips, and 1 bay leaf. Put the larded roast on the pork slices and pour over it 2 cups red wine and enough good beef stock to cover the meat by half. Cover the kettle and simmer the meat for about 3 hours, or until it is tender. Discard the carrots, bay leaf, and lemon.

Remove the meat to a heated platter and thicken the gravy in the pot with 1 tablespoon flour kneaded with 1 tablespoon butter. Bring the gravy to a boil, drop in dumpling dough, cover tightly, and let the dumplings steam for 15 minutes. Surround the meat with the dumplings, stir into the gravy 1/2 cup sour cream, and serve the gravy separately.

Steaks

THE broiled steak on the favorite American menu of steak, French fries, salad, and apple pie is likely to be either porterhouse or sirloin; and very good both are. Have them cut reasonably thick, from 1 1/2 inches to 2 inches or even 3. Trim off most of the outside fat and cut several diagonal gashes in the remaining fat to keep the meat flat. Remove the steak from the refrigerator an hour or more before cooking it. Season it with salt and pepper before or after broiling, as desired. The meat may be rubbed with a garlic clove and brushed with oil or with butter. Sirloin and porterhouse may be sautéed in oil or in butter; they should be seared quickly and then cooked over reduced heat to the desired degree of doneness. A thin steak is best sautéed. Steak may be cooked on a hot skillet with little fat, or none at all if a generous sprinkling of salt is applied to the hot pan. A ball of maître d'hôtel butter melting on the hot meat makes an attractive sauce.

Filets Mignons

THE filets mignons, usually about 1 to 1 1/2 inches thick, are cut from the small end of a filet of beef. Flatten them with the flat side of a knife, spread them with softened butter, and coat them with dried bread crumbs, pressing the crumbs firmly against the meat. Sprinkle the breading with melted butter and broil the filets mignons briefly on both sides. Serve a sauce separately, using any of the sauces and garnishings suggested for other steaks. The filets mignons may also be sautéed in a generous amount of butter, in this case, the butter may be used as a sauce.

Filet Mignon Capuchina

BROIL a portion of filet mignon to the desired state of doneness.

Sauté half a Spanish onion, chopped, and 4 chopped chicken livers in 1/2 cup butter until the onion is tender. Add 1/2 cup dry red wine, a large mushroom cap, sliced, and 1/2 teaspoon salt, and simmer slowly for 5 minutes. Spread half the sauce in a bag made of parchment paper or aluminum foil, lay the steak on the sauce, and spread it with the remaining sauce. Add 6 toasted almonds and 1 teaspoon chopped parsley, close and seal the bag, and bake the package in a very hot oven (500° F.) for 3 minutes.

Tournedos   THE tournedos lie next to the filets mignons at the narrow end of the filet of beef; they are cut fairly thick and are usually quickly sautéed in butter or in a mixture of butter and oil, although they may be liberally spread with butter and broiled to the medium-rare stage. The various preparations of tournedos are named for their garnishings.

Tournedos Algérienne   SEASON the tournedos with salt and paprika and sauté them in butter. Arrange them on round croutons also sautéed in butter and garnish with small egg tomatoes, sautéed until just tender in butter, and with potato croquettes. To the butter remaining in the pan add a little white wine, cook for a moment, scraping in all the brown bits which adhere to the pan, and pour the sauce over the tournedos.

Tournedos Beaugency   BROIL 6 tournedos in the usual way and arrange them on a serving platter on round croutons cut the same size as the tournedos and sautéed in butter. Fill small artichoke bottoms with béarnaise sauce and use them to garnish the platter. Garnish also with potatoes cut in small balls and sautéed in butter until they are golden and with watercress.

Tournedos Bordelaise   SEASON the tournedos with salt and pepper, spread them with butter, and broil them. Arrange on each tournedos a slice of poached beef marrow and sprinkle the marrow with minced parsley. Serve with a side dish of bordelaise sauce.

Tournedos Chasseur   SAUTÉ 6 tournedos in butter and arrange them in a ring on a round serving platter. To the pan in which the steak was cooked, add 1/2 pound mushrooms, chopped, and a minced shallot, and cook, stirring, for a few minutes. Add

1 cup dry white wine and cook, stirring in all the brown bits, until the sauce is reduced by half. Add to the sauce 1 tablespoon each of *glace de viande* and butter, cook it for 2 minutes, and finish it with 1 teaspoon mixed chopped parsley, chervil, and tarragon. Pour the sauce over the tournedos.

SAUTÉ the tournedos and arrange them on individual serving dishes. Garnish each dish with 2 tiny hearts of artichoke, stuffed with freshly cooked, buttered peas, and with small potato balls browned in butter. To the pan in which the steaks were sautéed, add 1/2 cup each of dry white wine and white stock and cook the sauce over high heat, stirring in the brown bits which adhere to the pan, until it is reduced by half. Pour the sauce over the meat.

Tournedos
à la Clamart

SAUTÉ 6 tournedos in butter with a few drops of olive oil and arrange them in a crown on a warmed serving platter. Top each with several slices of truffle heated in a little butter. Serve with *sauce Foyot*—1 cup béarnaise mixed with 2 teaspoons *glace de viande*.

Tournedos
Impériale

SAUTÉ in butter 6 tournedos and arrange them on a warm serving platter. Sauté 6 slices of goose liver for 1 minute on each side and lay them on the steaks. Toss 1/4 cup each of truffles and mushrooms, both cut in julienne strips, in a little butter. Add 1 cup brown sauce and 1 tablespoon *glace de viande*, and bring the sauce to a boil. Simmer it for 10 minutes, stirring from time to time, and finish with 2 tablespoons Madeira. Pour the sauce over the meat and serve at once.

Tournedos
La Vallière

THE chateaubriand is cut from the thickest part of the filet of beef; it is perhaps the most succulent and flavorful, certainly the most tender, of all beefsteaks. Season the steak and broil it quickly at first, then reduce the heat so that the steak will cook lightly at the center before the outside surface chars. Or sauté it in butter or butter and oil, again taking into consideration the thickness of the cut. *Pommes soufflés* traditionally accompany the chateaubriand, but it may be served with any steak garniture and sauce.

Chateaubriands

SAUTÉ a chateaubriand in a generous amount of butter, and 10 minutes before it is done, add to the pan 1/2 pound mushroom caps. Remove meat and mushrooms to a serving platter. To the pan add 1/2 cup each of dry white wine and *demi-glace* sauce, and cook, stirring in the brown bits, until

Chateaubriand
aux
Champignons

Entrecôte à la Tyrolienne

the sauce is reduced by half. Strain the sauce through a fine sieve, swirl in 1 tablespoon butter, and pour it over meat and mushrooms.

THE entrecôte is the rib steak; it may be cut thick or thin, and in France it is generally boned before broiling.

Entrecôtes

BROIL the entrecôte to taste and garnish it with mounds of shoestring potatoes and with bouquets of watercress. Serve with maître d'hôtel butter.

Entrecôte au Vert-Pré

BROIL a rib steak and arrange it on a serving dish. Cover the meat with 2 large onions, cut into rings and sautéed in butter until just translucent. Surround the meat with stewed tomatoes and sprinkle all with minced parsley.

Entrecôte à la Tyrolienne

COOK steak over an open fire, grill it under a broiler, or pan-broil it to the desired doneness. Put it on an oak plank that has been oiled thoroughly with olive oil, butter, or other fat and heated in the oven. Arrange around the steak such cooked vegetables as broiled tomatoes, glazed onions, or buttered peas or string beans. Decorate the plank with duchess potatoes and brown the entire ensemble under the boiler. Decorate with sprays of parsley or watercress.

Planked Steak

HAVE a piece of sirloin steak cut 2 1/2 to 3 inches thick and large enough to serve six. Insert a sharp knife in the center of one side and slice horizontally to within an inch or two of the edges of the steak to make a pocket.

Stuff the pocket with 18 to 20 small raw oysters, seasoned with salt and pepper. Sew the edges of the opening together. Broil the steak in a preheated broiling oven for about 12 to 15 minutes on each side. For well-done meat, transfer the steak to a hot pan, spread it with 2 tablespoons butter, and continue to cook for a few minutes longer under a medium heat, basting with the butter. Serve with maître d'hôtel butter and the juices in the pan.

Carpetbag Steak

PRESS coarsely ground black pepper or crushed peppercorns into both sides of a 2-inch-thick steak. Sprinkle both sides lightly with coarse salt.

In a large skillet heat 1/4 cup butter with 1/4 cup olive oil over high

Steak au Poivre

heat. Sear the steak on both sides and then cook it from 5 to 7 minutes on each side, depending on the degree of rareness desired. Transfer the meat to a heated serving platter.

Heat 1/3 cup each of dry white wine and veal stock with the pan juices in the skillet. Add 1/4 cup Cognac. Swirl the pan over the heat for a moment and pour the pan juices over the steak.

Steak Diane — IN a heavy skillet melt 2 tablespoons butter and in it sauté gently 1 tablespoon chopped shallot until the shallot is golden. Put in the skillet 2 portions of sirloin steak, pounded and trimmed, and sear them on both sides. Add 1 tablespoon each of chopped chives and parsley, Worcestershire sauce, and A-1 sauce, and 1 more tablespoon butter and mix well over the heat. Sprinkle the steaks with salt and pepper and continue to sauté them until done to taste. Serves 2.

It is not always the less tender cuts of beef that go into the stewpot. Some of the most famous dishes of this type begin with sirloin, filet of beef, or another choice cut.

Beef Stroganoff with Mushrooms — CUT 2 pounds tender beef into narrow strips 1/2 inch thick and 2 inches long, season generously with salt and pepper, and let the meat stand for 2 hours in a cool place or in the refrigerator.

Make a *roux* by blending 2 tablespoons butter with 1 tablespoon flour over low heat until the mixture bubbles and is smooth. Gradually stir in 2 cups beef stock and cook the mixture until it begins to thicken. Boil it for 2 minutes and stir in 2 teaspoons prepared mustard and 1/4 cup sour cream, stirring constantly. Simmer very gently, without boiling.

Brown the pieces of meat in 3 tablespoons butter. In a separate pan sauté lightly in butter 3 cups mushrooms and 1 onion, both thinly sliced. Add the meat, mushrooms, and onion to the sour cream sauce. Cover the saucepan and put it over hot water for 20 minutes. Serve the Stroganoff hot with green noodles.

Beef with Green Peppers — IN a preheated, heavy 10-inch skillet heat 1/3 cup salad oil, 1 teaspoon salt, and a little pepper to taste. Cut 1 1/2 pounds lean filet of beef, tenderloin, top round, or sirloin across the grain into thin strips. Brown the strips in the hot oil over high heat, stirring constantly. Add 6 tablespoons finely minced onion or scallions, 1 garlic clove, finely chopped, 4 green peppers, finely diced, and 1 1/2 cups celery, sliced diagonally into 1/4-inch pieces, and cook, stirring, for a few minutes longer. Add 1 1/2 cups beef stock, cover the pan tightly and cook over moderate heat for about 10 minutes, or until the meat and vegetables are tender. Add 2 tablespoons cornstarch mixed to a paste with 1/4 cup water and 1 tablespoon soy sauce. Cook for a few minutes more, stirring constantly, until the liquid thickens and the mixture is very hot. Serve immediately with fluffy white rice.

IN a skillet or in the top pan of a chafing dish directly over the heat combine 1/4 cup olive oil with 1 garlic clove, crushed, 1 teaspoon each of salt and finely chopped green gingerroot, and 1/2 teaspoon pepper. Add 1 pound flank steak, cut into thin diagonal slices, and brown the meat lightly for a minute or two. Add 1/4 cup soy sauce and 1/2 teaspoon sugar, cover the skillet, and cook the beef for 2 minutes longer. Remove the meat and keep it warm. To the pan juices add 2 cups bean sprouts, 2 tomatoes, peeled, seeded, and coarsely chopped, and 2 green peppers, seeded and cut into strips, cover, and cook briskly for 3 minutes. Add the meat and stir in 1 tablespoon cornstarch blended with 1/4 cup cold water. Cook, stirring, until the sauce is thickened, turn into a warm serving dish, and sprinkle with 2 or 3 scallions, cut into 1-inch pieces. Serves 4.

Chinese Pepper Steak

CUT 5 pounds chuck beef into large cubes. Roll the cubes in flour and brown them on all sides in a skillet over high heat in 1/4 cup each of butter and olive oil. Sprinkle the meat with salt and pepper, pour over it 1/4 cup warmed Cognac, and ignite the spirit. When the flame dies, transfer the meat to a casserole.

To the skillet add 1/2 pound bacon, diced, 4 garlic cloves, 2 carrots, 2 leeks, and 4 medium onions, all coarsely chopped, and 2 tablespoons chopped parsley and cook, stirring, until the bacon is crisp and the vegetables are lightly browned. Transfer the vegetable mixture to the casserole and add 2 bay leaves, 1 teaspoon thyme, 1 bottle of Burgundy, and enough water to just cover the meat. Cook the beef in a moderate oven (350° F.) for 1 1/2 to 2 hours. Stir in bit by bit 1 tablespoon flour mixed to a paste with 1 tablespoon butter and cook the meat for 2 to 3 hours longer.

Brown 2 pounds small onions in butter with a sprinkling of sugar. Add a little red wine, cover, and cook for about 15 minutes, or until the onions are almost tender.

Sauté 1 pound mushroom caps in a little butter and olive oil until

Boeuf Bourguignonne
BEEF BURGUNDY
STYLE

they are lightly browned on one side. Sprinkle them with lemon juice, and turn them to brown the other side. Keep them warm, but do not cover.

To serve, add the onions to the casserole, arrange the mushroom caps on top and sprinkle with finely chopped parsley. Serves 12.

Stefato
GREEK BEEF STEW

CUT 1 1/2 pounds lean beef in 1-inch cubes and brown the cubes on all sides in a skillet in 1/4 cup butter. Transfer the meat to a casserole. In the skillet sauté until golden 8 small onions. Transfer the onions to the casserole. To the skillet add 3/4 cup tomato paste and 2 cups water. Bring the sauce to a boil and pour it over the meat and onions. Cover the casserole and simmer the stew over moderate heat for 1 1/2 hours. Add 2 carrots, sliced, 2 potatoes, cut in cubes, salt and pepper to taste and 1 teaspoon cinnamon. Cover the casserole and cook for 30 to 35 minutes longer, until meat and vegetables are tender. Serves 4.

Gypsy Goulash

HAVE the butcher cut 2 pounds lean, tender beef in strips 1/4 inch thick and 1/4 inch wide. Brown the strips with 6 thinly sliced onions in 3 tablespoons lard. Blend in 1 teaspoon salt and 1 tablespoon each of flour and paprika. Add 2 cups red wine and 1 cup sour cream. Turn the mixture into a casserole, cover it and bake the goulash in a moderate oven (375° F.) for 1 1/2 hours, or until the meat is tender. Just before serving add 3/4 cup more sour cream and reheat the mixture without letting it boil. Serve with buttered noodles.

English Beef Stew

CUT 3 pounds off the top of the rump into slices about 1/8 inch thick and sprinkle the slices with salt and pepper. In a large skillet sauté the slices in hot beef fat or butter until they are golden brown on both sides. Arrange the slices side by side in a casserole.

To the juices in the skillet add 1 cup each of brown sauce and brown stock. If no brown sauce is on hand, use 1 cup tomato juice or sauce and 1 teaspoon beef extract. Bring the sauce to a boil, correct the seasoning, and add 1/4 teaspoon Worcestershire sauce. Pour the sauce over the meat.

Parboil 2 cups carrots, diced, for 5 minutes. Drain them and add them to the casserole. Add 1 cup small white onions, browned in butter, and a faggot of 4 sprigs of parsley, 1 small bay leaf, a little thyme, and 1 stalk of celery. Cover the casserole and cook the meat in a hot oven (400° F.) for 1 1/2 to 2 hours, or until is tender. Remove the casserole from the oven,

Greek Beef Stew

let it stand for 10 minutes, and carefully remove the fat that rises to the surface. Discard the faggot.

Arrange the slices of meat in a ring on a warmed serving platter, put the vegetables in the center, and pour the sauce over all. Sprinkle with 1 cup cooked green peas.

Chili Con Carne

BROWN 2 pounds stewing mutton or beef and 1 pound fresh pork, cut into small cubes, 1 onion, chopped, and 4 garlic cloves, chopped, in 2 tablespoons lard or drippings. Cover the pan and cook for about 20 minutes. Stir in 3 tablespoons sweet chili powder mixed with 1 tablespoon flour and a little water. Rub 1 quart ripe tomatoes or 1 large can tomatoes through a sieve, add them along with 3 bay leaves, 1 teaspoon each of orégano, salt, and cuminseed, and cook slowly for about 2 hours. Add 2 cups pitted ripe olives, sliced, and cook for another 30 minutes. Correct the seasoning and serve with boiled red beans.

Braciola

POUND a thin slice of round steak weighing about 1 1/2 pounds until it is smooth and almost transparent. Cover it with wafer-thin slices of *prosciutto* and young celery leaves and season it with salt and pepper. Roll up the beef like a jelly roll and tie it securely.

Brown a garlic clove in 3 tablespoons olive oil. Discard the garlic, add 2 tablespoons butter, and in it brown the roll of meat with a bouquet of 4 green onions and 1 carrot cut into lengthwise strips. Add 1/4 pound dried mushrooms soaked in 1 cup hot water for 30 minutes, the mushroom liquor, and 3 cups strained tomatoes and simmer the mixture for 1 1/2 hours, or until the sauce is dark and thick and the meat very tender.

Paupiettes de Boeuf Braisées Bourbonnaise

BEEF ROLLS
BOURBONNAISE

SLICE a 2- to 2 1/2-pound piece of lean rump of beef into 12 or 15 pieces and flatten each slice with a wooden mallet. Season the slices with a little salt and pepper and spread the center of each with the following stuffing: Season 1 pound each of ground lean pork and ground fat pork with 1/2 teaspoon poultry seasoning mixed with a little salt. Add a generous 1/4 cup Madeira or Sherry and mix thoroughly. Roll up each slice, wrap it with a thin slice of larding pork, and tie it with a string.

In a shallow casserole melt 1 tablespoon butter. Spread over the butter 1 onion and 1 carrot, both sliced, and arrange the rolls of beef side by side on top of the vegetables. Add 1 garlic clove and a faggot made of 1 stalk of celery, 4 sprigs of parsley, 1 bay leaf, and a pinch of thyme. Spread a little melted butter over the beef rolls, put the casserole in a moderately hot oven (375° F.), and cook the rolls until they have taken on a little color. Sprinkle 1 tablespoon flour over the vegetables around the meat and add 2 cups red or white wine. If the liquid does not come to the top of the meat, add stock or water. Bring the liquid to a boil, cover the casserole, and braise the meat for 1 1/2 to 2 hours, basting from time to time. If the liquid is reduced too much, add a little stock or water. Just before serving, uncover the pan, discard the larding pork, and cook the rolls a few minutes longer. Remove them to a serving dish. Discard the faggot, correct the seasoning of the sauce, and pour it over the rolls. Garnish the platter with 1 pound cooked mushrooms and 16 small glazed white onions.

The existence of beef trimmings has inspired many a cook to sprightly inventions on the theme of ground beef.

WASH 1 cup rice and cook it in 4 cups boiling salted water for about 20 minutes, or until it is tender.

Arancini

SICILIAN RICE
AND MEATBALLS

Heat 2 tablespoons olive oil in a saucepan. Add 1/4 pound chopped beef, 2 chicken livers, minced, and 1 garlic clove and 1/2 small onion, both finely chopped, and stir until the meat is browned. Add 1/4 pound mushrooms, sliced, and cook for 1 minute. Add 2 tablespoons tomato paste and 1 cup warm water and cook for 30 minutes. Add salt and pepper.

Drain the rice, add 1/2 cup butter and 3 tablespoons grated Parmesan, and cool a little. Add 2 egg yolks and the gravy drained from the meat mixture, reserving the meat and mushrooms. Mix the rice well and form it into little balls, putting inside each ball some of the meat mixture. Dip the balls into beaten egg, roll them in fine dry bread crumbs, and fry them, a few at a time, in 1 cup hot olive oil until they are golden.

HALVE 6 medium tomatoes. Heat 1/3 cup oil in a large skillet and put the tomatoes, cut side down, in the skillet. Pierce each tomato with a fork, cook for 5 minutes, and turn. Sprinkle with a mixture of 1 tablespoon chopped parsley and 1 garlic clove, chopped, and salt and pepper. Lower the heat and cook the tomatoes until tender.

Minced Beef with Provençal Tomatoes

In a skillet heat 1/3 cup olive oil and sauté 4 onions, chopped, until they are golden. Add 2 pounds freshly ground beef, stir, and sprinkle with 4 teaspoons flour. Stir until the flour disappears and stir in 1 1/2 cups bouillon. Add salt and pepper and cook for 15 minutes.

Put the beef in a shallow heatproof platter and arrange the tomatoes on top. Pour the cooking juices from the tomato skillet over all and heat for 10 minutes in a hot oven (400° F.).

Swedish Meatballs

MIX together thoroughly 1 pound ground beef, 1/2 pound each of ground veal and pork, 1 cup bread crumbs soaked in 2 cups milk, 2 eggs, 6 tablespoons finely chopped onion sautéed until golden in 2 tablespoons butter, 1/2 teaspoon pepper, and salt to taste. Shape the mixture into tiny balls and sauté them in 4 to 6 tablespoons butter until they are brown, shaking the pan continuously to keep the balls from flattening.

Swedish Meatballs

Turn the meat into a deep casserole or chafing dish and keep it warm. To the juices in the pan, add 2 tablespoons flour. Stir in 2 cups heavy cream and cook the sauce over low heat, stirring constantly, for 10 minutes. Season the sauce to taste with salt, pepper, and nutmeg or caraway and pour it over the meatballs.

COMBINE 1/2 pound sausage meat with 1 pound ground round steak, 1 egg, beaten, 1 teaspoon salt, and 1/4 cup minced onion. Form the meat into small balls and sauté them in a skillet in hot bacon fat until they are brown on all sides. Remove the meatballs and discard all but 2 tablespoons of the fat in the pan. In this sauté lightly a garlic clove. Discard the garlic and stir into the fat 2 tablespoons flour. Cook, stirring, until the flour is lightly browned, add gradually 1 1/2 cups beer, and continue to cook, stirring constantly, until the sauce is smooth and thickened. Stir in 1/2 cup tomato paste and add 1/2 teaspoon crushed dill seeds and the meatballs. Cover the skillet and cook the meatballs over low heat for 10 minutes. Add 1 cup stuffed green olives, cook for 2 minutes longer, and serve with cooked noodles.

Savory Meatballs

COMBINE 1 1/2 pounds finely ground raw beef, 1/4 pound finely chopped fat pork, and 1/4 cup butter. Add 1 cup soft bread crumbs soaked in water and squeezed nearly dry, 3 whole eggs, salt and a dash of pepper, and 2 teaspoons lemon juice, and mix thoroughly.

Königsberger Klops
GERMAN BALLS

Shape the mixture into small dumplings, about the size of a golf ball, roll them in flour, and poach them in simmering stock or salted water for 15 minutes.

In a saucepan melt 2 tablespoons butter, stir in 2 tablespoons flour, and add gradually 2 cups stock. Bring the sauce to a boil, stirring constantly, and simmer for 5 minutes. Add 1/4 cup dry white wine, 1 tablespoon lemon juice, and salt and pepper to taste and simmer for 5 minutes longer.

Put the meatballs in a heated casserole or serving dish and pour the sauce over them. Serve with sauerkraut.

*Spezzatino
Bolognese*

BOLOGNESE
RAGOUT

IN a saucepan sauté 1/4 pound salt pork, chopped, with 1 onion and 1 carrot, both sliced, 1 stalk of celery, chopped, and 1 clove, until the onion and pork are lightly browned. Add 3/4 pound chopped beef and 1/4 pound each of pork and veal, both chopped, and brown the meat, stirring, over low heat. Add 1 1/4 cups brown stock and simmer the ragout slowly until the stock evaporates. Add 1 teaspoon tomato paste, salt and pepper, and enough water to cover the meat. Cover the pan and cook the ragout slowly for 1 hour. Add 1/4 pound mushrooms and 2 chicken livers, both chopped, and cook for 15 minutes longer.

Just before serving, stir into the *spezzatino* 1/2 cup heavy cream and 1 truffle, thinly sliced. Serve on rice or noodles.

Boeuf Bouilli

BOILED BEEF

PUT a 3-pound piece of beef bottom round in a large kettle with 6 quarts water, 2 tablespoons salt, and 1 teaspoon bruised peppercorns. Bring the liquid to a boil and skim the scum as it rises to the surface. When the broth is clear, add 3 leeks, washed, split, and tied with thread, 2 carrots, 1 onion stuck with 3 cloves, half a parsnip and 1 turnip, and a *bouquet garni* consisting of several sprigs of parsley and thyme and a bay leaf, tied together. Simmer the meat for 4 hours, or until it is very tender. Arrange the meat on a heated serving platter and surround it with the cooked vegetables, or with freshly cooked vegetables. Serve with tomato sauce, horseradish sauce, or any suitable piquant sauce.

The strained bouillon may be poured over rounds of toast in individual soup plates and a few slices of the meat and some the vegetables put in each plate.

Boiled beef and roast beef are as much liked cold as hot, but both can be reheated and served in various guises.

*Cold Beef
à la Parisienne*

SLICE 1 pound cold boiled beef and overlap the slices in an oblong serving dish. Garnish the sides of the dish with sliced cooked potatoes, sliced tomatoes, cooked green beans, carrots cut in julienne, and sliced or quartered hard-cooked eggs. Arrange very thin slices of onion on top of the meat and sprinkle with chopped parsley. To 1/2 cup vignaigrette sauce, add 1 teaspoon each of chopped chives and tarragon, and pour the sauce over the meat and vegetables.

Piquant Beef

SLICE leftover cooked beef about 1/4 inch thick. Arrange the slices on a platter, season them with a little salt and pepper, and sprinkle with finely chopped parsley and a few drops of vinegar. Let the meat stand for 15 minutes to absorb the seasonings. Dip the slices in flour, coat them with 1 egg beaten with 2 tablespoons milk and 1 tablespoon salad oil, and dip them in fine bread crumbs. Sauté the slices in 3 tablespoons butter until they are brown on both sides. Serve with a piquant sauce such as tartar sauce or tomato sauce.

Boeuf Bouilli
Sauté à la
Moutarde
SLICED BOILED
BEEF WITH
MUSTARD

CUT leftover boiled beef into thin slices. Spread both sides of each slice with prepared mustard and coat thoroughly with fresh bread crumbs. Sprinkle the slices with a little melted butter and sauté them in hot butter until they are brown on both sides. Arrange the slices on a flat dish, sprinkle them with salt and pepper, a few drops of vinegar, and some chopped parsley, and let them stand about 15 minutes to absorb the vinegar.

Dip the meat in flour, then in an egg beaten with 1/4 cup milk, 1 tablespoon oil, and 1/4 teaspoon salt. Roll the slices in fine dry crumbs and sauté them in butter or good fat until brown on both sides. Serve with tomato sauce.

Boeuf Moreno

IN a saucepan melt 2 tablespoons butter and stir in 2 tablespoons flour, stirring until the *roux* is smooth. Add 3/4 cup beef stock and stir it into the *roux* to make a smooth mixture. Add 4 tablespoons mixed finely chopped parsley and finely chopped green onion or chives. Simmer the mixture for 20 minutes and season to taste with salt and freshly ground pepper.

In a shallow flameproof casserole melt 2 tablespoons butter and add 2 tablespoons finely chopped green pepper or pimiento and 1/2 cup sliced mushrooms, caps and stems, or pitted olives. Heat the vegetables thoroughly, but do not let them brown. Add 1 pound 2-inch-thick leftover steak or roast beef that has been cut in thin strips, and heat the meat thoroughly.

Add 1 cup sour cream slowly to the parsley and onion mixture and stir in 3 tablespoons brandy or whiskey. Pour the cream mixture over the meat in the casserole and serve immediately with hot fluffy rice or noodles cooked *al dente*.

Paprika Beef IN a shallow pan heat 3 to 4 tablespoons butter and in it brown lightly 3 cups diced, leftover cooked beef. Remove the meat to a platter, add 1/2 cup chopped onions to the butter remaining in the pan, and cook them until they are golden. Stir in 2 tablespoons paprika mixed with 1/2 cup cream and cook for 5 minutes. Add 1/2 cup cream sauce or béchamel sauce and the meat and bring just to a boil. Serve with noodles.

Beef Fermière IN a saucepan melt 2 tablespoons butter and in it sauté 1 cup chopped onions until they are golden. Stir in 1 tablespoon flour and cook until the butter and the flour are combined. Stir in gradually 1 cup stock, 1/2 cup cooked tomatoes, 1/2 teaspoon salt and a little pepper. Cook, stirring, until the sauce comes to a boil and continue to cook, stirring occasionally, for 20 to 25 minutes. Add 3 sliced sour pickles and, for a sharper sauce, 1/2 teaspoon dry mustard mixed with a little vinegar and 1 teaspoon grated horseradish. Do not let the sauce boil after adding the pickles. Slice thinly 1 pound leftover cooked beef and overlap the slices in a shallow heatproof serving dish. Pour the sauce over the meat, sprinkle with bread crumbs and a little melted butter, and brown in a hot oven (450° F.) or under the broiler. Garnish the dish with slices of boiled potatoes or sautéed eggplant.

Emincé de Boeuf aux Marrons
BEEF HASH WITH CHESTNUTS
IN a saucepan melt 1 tablespoon butter and in it sauté 2 tablespoons chopped onion until golden. Add 1 tablespoon flour and continue to cook until the flour turns golden. Stir in gradually 1 1/2 cups stock and 3 tablespoons tomato purée or tomato sauce and cook slowly for 20 to 25 minutes, stirring occasionally and skimming as necessary. Add 1 tablespoon chopped parsley and 1 pound diced, leftover cooked beef, mix gently, and bring just to a boil. Add 10 shelled cooked chestnuts, coarsely chopped. Correct the seasoning with salt and add a little pepper. Turn into a heated serving dish and garnish with whole chestnuts.

Beef Bonne Femme IN a saucepan sauté lightly 2 tablespoons chopped onion in 1 tablespoon melted butter. Add 1 tablespoon flour and continue to cook until the flour begins to turn golden. Add gradually 1 1/2 cups stock and 3 tablespoons tomato purée and cook slowly for 20 to 25 minutes, stirring occasionally and skimming as necessary. Add 1 tablespoon chopped parsley. Stir in gently about 1 pound leftover cooked beef, finely diced, and bring the sauce just to a boil.

Peel, quarter, and boil 3 or 4 large potatoes in salted water until done.

Paprika Beef

Drain, dry them over the heat, and put them through a food mill or sieve into a pan. Beat in 1 to 2 tablespoons soft butter with a wooden spoon. Add about 1/2 cup hot milk, little by little, or enough to make the potatoes creamy, and correct the seasoning with salt. Put the sauced beef in a flame-proof shallow serving dish and cover it with mashed potatoes. Sprinkle the potatoes with 3 tablespoons grated Parmesan cheese or Swiss cheese, 1/2 tablespoon fine bread crumbs, and a little melted butter, and brown the topping in a very hot oven (450° F.) or under the broiler.

Roasted and broiled lamb, like beef, tastes best when it is underdone and slightly pink.

Roast Saddle of Lamb

Pan Gravy

SPRINKLE a saddle of lamb with salt and put it in a roasting pan with 1/2 cup water. Roast the saddle in a hot oven (400° F.) for 1 hour, basting frequently. Remove the meat from the pan and discard the fat. To the pan add 2 cups stock or water and stir to dissolve all the browned juices in the pan. Thicken the gravy with 2 tablespoons *beurre manié* made by kneading equal parts of butter and flour. Set the pan gravy aside to be reheated and served with the cooked meat and vegetables.

Toss 8 potatoes, peeled and sliced, with 1/2 cup chopped onion, 1 tablespoon chopped parsley, 1 teaspoon salt, and a little pepper. Spread the seasoned potatoes in the roasting pan and add enough boiling water barely to cover the vegetables. Dot with 1 tablespoon butter and bring the liquid to a boil.

Set the partially roasted saddle of lamb on top of the vegetables, return the roasting pan to the oven and continue to roast the meat for 45 minutes, allowing about 15 minutes to the pound in all. Arrange the lamb on a serving platter, surround it with the potatoes and serve the pan gravy separately.

Roast Leg of Lamb Bûcheronne

RUB a 6- to 7-pound leg of lamb generously with garlic or insert slivers of garlic into tiny slits cut in the meat. Sprinkle the meat with salt and roast it in a moderately hot oven (375° F.) for about 2 hours. Remove the meat from the pan to a heated serving platter and make the pan gravy.

While the meat is roasting, prepare the following garnish: Drain 2 large cans of *cèpes* and sauté them in 1/2 cup very hot oil until they are golden brown. Drain the *cèpes* and transfer them to another pan con-

taining 3 tablespoons butter. Season them with salt and pepper and add
1 tablespoon chopped shallots, 1 garlic clove, crushed, 1 tablespoon chopped
parsley, and 2 tablespoons fresh bread crumbs. Cook for a few minutes
until the crumbs are brown, shaking the pan to combine the ingredients
as they cook. Peel 5 or 6 medium potatoes and cut them into slices the
size of a silver dollar. Parboil the slices for 2 minutes and drain. Heat
3 or 4 tablespoons butter in a skillet, add the potatoes, and cook in a hot
oven (450° F.) or over moderate heat until they are golden brown, turning
them from time to time. Season with salt. Slice the lamb and arrange the
slices on a warmed serving platter. Arrange the potatoes and the *cèpes*
alternately around the meat and sprinkle the potatoes with chopped parsley.
Serve pan gravy separately in a heated sauceboat.

TRIM the skin and fat from a leg of lamb. Spread about 1/2 cup mixed
sliced carrots and sliced onions in a roasting pan and add a sprig of parsley,
a bay leaf, and a cracked bone of mutton. Put the leg of lamb on the vegetables and roast the meat in a moderately hot oven (375° F.) until the
meat is well browned. Add 1 1/2 to 2 cups boiling water to prevent burning
and cover the pan with a piece of buttered paper. Reduce the heat to
moderately slow (325° F.) and cook the meat for 5 hours longer, or until
it is ready to fall apart, adding more water as needed. Remove the leg to a
heated serving dish.

*Gigot
d'Agneau
à la Cuillère*

LEG OF LAMB
SERVED WITH A
SPOON

   Strain the liquid in the pan and thicken it with arrowroot or cornstarch mixed with a little water or Sherry. Strain the gravy through a fine
sieve. Serve the meat with a spoon instead of carving it.

TRIM the skin and surplus fat from a 6- to 8-pound leg of mutton and
season the meat with salt. In the bottom of a kettle large enough to hold
the leg put 2 tablespoons fat and spread over it 3 onions and 3 carrots,
both sliced. Add a faggot of stalks of celery, 4 sprigs of parsley, 1 bay
leaf, and a little thyme. Sprinkle the vegetables with 1 tablespoon flour,
cover them with cracked bones, and put the leg on top. Cook the meat
in a moderately hot oven (375° F.) until it is brown all over, turning it
frequently.

*Braised Leg of
Young Mutton*

   Add 1 1/2 to 2 cups water or stock and 2 or 3 tomatoes, chopped, or
1 cup canned tomatoes. Cover with a piece of buttered or wax paper, cut
to fit the pan, with a small hole in the center for the steam to escape.
Cover the kettle, reduce the oven temperature to moderately slow (325° F.),
and braise the meat for 3 to 3 1/2 hours, basting it from time to time.
During the cooking add more water or stock if needed. Remove the meat

Broiled Rack of Lamb

from the kettle, strain the gravy, and skim all the fat from the surface. Correct the seasoning with salt. If the gravy is too thin, reduce it a little.

FOLLOW the recipe for braised leg of mutton. Parboil 12 white turnips, cut in quarters, and 18 small white onions for 5 minutes and glaze them in butter until lightly browned. Add the vegetables to the gravy about 15 minutes before the meat is done. Remove the lamb and vegetables from the kettle, thicken the gravy if necessary, and strain it. Slice the lamb and serve with the vegetables and gravy.

Braised Leg of Young Mutton with Turnips

IN a heavy kettle brown a small leg of lamb on all sides over high heat in 1 tablespoon lard. Add 1/2 teaspoon salt, 3/4 teaspoon freshly ground pepper, 1 garlic clove, 1 teaspoon rosemary, and 1 sage leaf, and continue browning the meat a little longer, turning it often. Sprinkle the lamb with 1 1/2 teaspoons flour and press it into the meat with a wooden spoon. Add 1/2 cup each of wine vinegar and water, cover the kettle, and cook the meat over low heat for 1 1/2 hours, or until it is tender, adding a little water or stock from time to time during the cooking. When the meat is done, mix 2 anchovy filets, chopped, with 1 teaspoon water, add them to the gravy, and cook the gravy for 1 minute longer.

Roman Lamb

CAREFULLY remove the meat from each side of a saddle of lamb, cutting it out in lengthwise pieces. Trim away sinews. Cut each piece crosswise into 4 or 6 slices and sauté the slices in butter or broil them for 3 to 5 minutes on each side. The meat should still be pink when it is served. Put a slice of sautéed goose liver on each piece of meat and on the goose liver put a slice of truffle.

Noisette d'Agneau Montpensier
KERNEL OF LAMB MONTPENSIER

HAVE the butcher clean the ends of the rib bones of a 6- to 8-chop rack of lamb. Dot the meat with butter and brown it under the broiler. Turn it once to brown both sides. This process takes about 30 minutes, and the bone ends should be well charred.

Parboil a dozen small white onions for 5 minutes in salted water to cover. Drain the onions well and gild them lightly in 2 tablespoons melted butter. Add 1/4 pound mushrooms, sliced, and cook these together for 3 minutes. Stir in 2 cups *sauce espagnole*. Arrange the meat on a heated serving platter, spoon the hot vegetable sauce over the meat, and garnish the platter with alternating mounds of baby Lima beans, peas, and whole

Carré d'Agneau à la Boulangère
BROILED RACK OF LAMB

young green beans, all cooked separately until barely tender and seasoned with butter, salt, and pepper. Cover the charred bone ends with paper frills and serve the rack at once. Serve 3.

Lamb Chops Bermuda

SEASON 6 thick lamb chops with salt and pepper and sauté them in butter on both sides until they are golden brown. Drain off the fat. Add 6 onions, sliced, and 2 cups stock or water and cook the chops gently for 25 to 30 minutes. Add 12 Bermuda potatoes, sliced, and 2 teaspoons chopped parsley. Correct the seasoning and cook the potatoes for 30 to 35 minutes, or until they are done.

Lamb Chops Louise

FOLLOW the recipe for lamb chops Bermuda and about 10 minutes before the cooking is finished, add 6 tomatoes, peeled, halved, and free of seedy pulp.

Côtelettes d'Agneau Ménagère

LAMB CHOPS FAMILY STYLE

SEASON 6 thick shoulder lamb chops with salt and pepper and sauté them in butter on both sides until they are golden brown. Put them in a large saucepan with 2 leeks, chopped, 3 potatoes, sliced, 1 large onion, sliced, a garlic clove, crushed, 1 quart white stock or water, 1 teaspoon salt, and a little pepper. Cook for 25 to 30 minutes.

Remove the chops to another pan and cover them with the following vegetables: 3 new carrots, sliced and parboiled for a few minutes, 2 onions, sliced, 1 to 2 cups green beans, cut in pieces, 3 potatoes, sliced, 3 stalks of celery, chopped, 1 to 2 cups fresh peas, and 2 small white turnips, sliced and parboiled for a few minutes. Rub the cooking liquid from the first pan through a fine sieve into a bowl and skim off the fat. Correct the seasoning with salt and pour the liquid over the meat and vegetables. Add 1 teaspoon chopped parsley and cook for 35 minutes longer, or until the vegetables are done.

Côtelettes d'Agneau Panées

BREADED LAMB CHOPS

WIPE 6 lamb chops 1 1/2 inches thick with a damp cloth, sprinkle them with salt and pepper, and roll them in flour. Dip them in 1 egg lightly beaten with 1 tablespoon olive oil and roll them in fine dry bread crumbs. Sauté the chops in butter for about 6 minutes on each side. Put paper frills over the bone ends and arrange the chops in a crown on a warm serving platter. Circle the chops with 6 cooked artichoke bottoms filled with buttered wild rice and topped with turned mushrooms sprinkled with a little minced parsley. Garnish the platter with watercress.

IN a heavy kettle brown 2 pounds lamb, diced, 3 slices of lean bacon, minced, and 1 onion, chopped, in 2 tablespoons lard or butter. Sprinkle the meat with salt and pepper and 3 tablespoons flour and mix well. Add 1/2 cup dry white wine and cook until the wine is reduced by half. Add water barely to cover the meat, cover the kettle, and simmer the lamb for 45 minutes, or until it is tender.

With a fork mix lightly 3 egg yolks with 1 tablespoon lemon juice and a little of the hot liquid in the kettle. Add to the yolks 2 tablespoons chopped parsley and 1/2 teaspoon marjoram. Remove the kettle from the heat and stir in the egg mixture. Cover the kettle and let the stew stand for 5 minutes before serving.

Agnello Brodettato
BRAISED LAMB

CUT 3 pounds boneless shoulder of young lamb into small uniform chunks and sauté the pieces in 1/4 cup butter until lightly browned. Sprinkle with salt and pepper and continue to cook over low heat for 15 to 20 minutes, stirring occasionally. In another pan sauté 1 cup small white onions in 3 tablespoons butter until almost tender. Add 1/2 pound small mushroom caps and cook for 3 minutes longer. Turn the onions and mushrooms into a casserole and add the lamb. Rinse the pan in which the lamb was cooked with 1/2 cup Madeira or Sherry and add the liquid to 3/4 cup hot velouté sauce. Add 1/2 cup heavy cream to the sauce, bring to a boil, and simmer for 10 minutes. Season to taste with salt and pepper and strain the sauce into the casserole. Cover the casserole and bake it in a moderately slow oven (325° F.) for 35 to 40 minutes.

Blanquette of Baby Lamb

CUT 3 pounds lamb shoulder into rather large pieces. Put the meat in a saucepan, cover it with water, and parboil it for 5 to 6 minutes. Remove the lamb from the pan, discard the water, and rinse the meat in fresh cold water. Clean the pan and return the meat to it. Add 2 quarts water, 3 onions, 3 or 4 potatoes, 4 leeks, 4 stalks of celery, all chopped, 1 garlic clove, 1 tablespoon salt, and 4 or 5 peppercorns. Bring the water to a boil and cook the ingredients gently for 1 hour. Remove the meat to another pan. Skim the fat from the broth, strain, rubbing through the sieve as much of the vegetables as possible, and correct the seasoning.

Prepare 18 small white onions, 24 small potato balls, 18 small white turnips, and 24 slices of carrot. Put all the vegetables on top of the meat.

Ritz Lamb Stew

Sprinkle with 1 tablespoon chopped parsley and add the strained broth. Bring the broth to a boil and cook for 45 minutes or until the meat is done. A few cooked green peas or string beans may be added just before serving. For a sharper flavor add 1 teaspoon of Worcestershire sauce to the gravy.

Lamb Shanks in Red Wine

ROLL 6 lamb shanks in flour, sprinkle them with salt, pepper, and powdered orégano, and brown them in a heavy kettle in 3 tablespoons butter and 1 tablespoon olive oil with 1 split garlic clove. Pour over the shanks 2 tablespoons warmed brandy, ignite it, and when the flame dies, transfer the contents of the kettle to a heavy casserole. Add 3 cups each of dry red wine and water, 1/2 cup each of diced carrots and chopped celery, and 1 cup chopped onion, 1 bay leaf, and a pinch of thyme, cover the casserole, and bake it in a moderate oven (350° F.) for 2 hours.

Remove the fat from the sauce and thicken the sauce with *beurre manié*, 1 tablespoon flour mixed to a paste with 1 tablespoon butter. Stir in 1 teaspoon *glace de viande* or a very little meat extract, correct the seasoning with salt and pepper, and add a little lemon juice.

Kibbe
LAMB LOAF

WASH 1 cup *burghul*, or cracked wheat, and soak it in cold water for 1 hour. Put 1 pound lean lamb and 1 onion twice through a food chopper. Add salt to taste. Drain the soaked *burghul* and combine it with the meat. Add a little cold water if necessary to make the mixture malleable. Put the *kibbe* through the food chopper again.

Spread half the *kibbe* in a buttered baking pan and smooth it with a knife dipped in cold water. Cover it with 1/2 pound fat lamb, ground, seasoned with 1 onion, and browned in butter with 1/4 cup shelled pine nuts. Cover this layer with the rest of the *kibbe* and cut the loaf into diamond shapes. Dot the surfaces of the loaf generously with butter and bake it in a moderately hot oven (375° F.) until it has a rich golden-brown crust.

Groundnut Chop

CUT 3 cups cooked lamb into 1/2-inch cubes. Heat 2 tablespoons olive oil in a skillet and add, stirring vigorously, 2/3 cup peanut butter, 2 3/4 cups water, 2 teaspoons salt, 1/4 teaspoon black pepper, 1/2 teaspoon paprika, and 1/4 teaspoon nutmeg. Add the meat, cover the pan, and cook gently for 6 to 7 minutes, stirring from time to time. Season the meat to taste and serve it in a ring of dry cooked rice with side dishes of chutney, freshly grated coconut, fresh hot pepper, and any other desired relish.

Our American veal does not have the mother-of-pearl whiteness of the milk-fed veal of Europe, but when it is thoroughly cooked it is just as tender and nearly as delicious.

TIE up a saddle of veal securely with string and put it in a roasting pan on a bed of sliced onions and carrots. Season it with salt and spread with 2 tablespoons butter. Add some veal bones and a *bouquet garni* of 4 sprigs of parsley, 3 stalks of celery, a little thyme, and a piece of bay leaf. Put the pan, uncovered, in a moderately hot oven (400° F.) and roast the veal, basting frequently, until the onions and carrots are brown. Add 2 cups water, cover the meat with buttered paper cut to fit the inside of the pan, and cover the pan. Reduce the oven temperature to moderately hot (375° F.) and continue to cook the veal for 3 to 3 1/2 hours, or until the meat detaches easily from the bones, adding more water or veal stock if needed. Remove the meat, add enough water or veal stock to the drippings in the pan to make 3 or 4 cups light veal gravy, thickening it with a little arrowroot or cornstarch, and set it aside.

Selle de Veau Maintenon
SADDLE OF VEAL

Cut 30 or 40 slices of *foie gras* about 1/8 inch thick, and the same number of truffle slices of the same thickness. Put the truffle and *foie gras* trimmings through a fine strainer and add them to 2 cups *purée Soubise*.

With a very sharp knife cut down both sides of the center bone of the saddle of veal, leaving 1/2 inch of meat uncut at each end. Remove the filets from both sides, leaving intact the meat at the ends, and cut the filets into slices 1/4 inch thick. Spread a little onion purée on the uncut ends of the saddle and lay on the purée a piece of truffle and *foie gras* and a slice of the filet. Continue to reconstruct the saddle in this manner, using about 15 to 20 slices each of truffle and *foie gras* on each side. Spread the re-formed saddle with purée, then with alternate slices of the goose liver and truffles, and finally with another coating of the purée. Cover it with Mornay sauce and sprinkle with grated Parmesan.

Set the platter on a pan that contains a little warm water and reheat the veal in a moderate oven (350° F.) until the sauce is golden brown. Garnish with small glazed carrots, artichoke bottoms stuffed with tiny peas, hearts of braised celery, small potatoes *rissolé*, asparagus tips, and green beans. Serve the gravy separately.

Veal Roast with Anchovies and Garlic

HAVE the butcher bone, roll, and tie a piece of veal rump weighing about 6 pounds. Into the folds of the roll slip 3 garlic cloves, cut into thin slivers. Roll 5 anchovy filets in chopped basil and insert these in the folds. Put the veal in a deep dish and cover it with 2 1/2 cups white wine. Let the meat stand in the wine for 24 hours, turning it from time to time to insure that it is evenly marinated. Arrange the meat on a rack in a roasting pan and roast it in a moderately slow oven (325° F.) for about 2 hours, basting it from time to time with the wine. Transfer the cooked meat to a heated platter.

To the juices in the roasting pan add 3 tablespoons cornstarch mixed to a paste with a little cold water. Cook the gravy, stirring in the brown bits that cling to the pan, for a few minutes, until it is clear and quite thick. Add 1 cup hot cream and 3 tablespoons capers, washed and dried. Heat the sauce again, without boiling it, and adjust the seasoning, if necessary, with salt. Serve the sauce separately.

Poitrine de Veau Farcie
STUFFED BREAST OF VEAL

HAVE the butcher bone a 4-pound breast of veal. Rub the meat well with a cut garlic clove and season it with salt and pepper.

Work 2 unbeaten egg whites and 1 1/2 cups cream into 1 pound ground raw veal. Season this forcemeat with salt and pepper to taste. Spread the forcemeat on the boned breast and cover it with 1/4 pound cooked ham, cut into julienne strips. Roll up the meat, cover the roll with strips of bacon, and secure the roll by tying it at intervals along its length with kitchen twine. Put the meat on a rack in a roasting pan and roast it in a moderate oven (350° F.) for about 2 hours, basting it often with 1 cup dry white wine.

Serve the roast with the following tomato sauce: Melt 1 1/2 tablespoons butter and add 1 tablespoon flour. Remove the pan from the heat and stir in 2 tablespoons tomato paste. Add 1 1/2 cups water and stir the sauce over moderate heat until it comes to a boil. Add salt, pepper, a little crushed garlic, and 3 or 4 tomatoes, peeled and sliced. Simmer the tomatoes for

15 minutes and finish the sauce with 1 1/2 tablespoons butter and the pan juices from the roast.

CUT a pocket in a breast of veal weighing about 4 pounds.

Sauté 3 tablespoons minced onion and 1/2 pound sausage meat in 1/4 cup drippings or fat until well browned. Drain off the fat and put onions and sausage in a large mixing bowl. Add 3 cups finely chopped cooked spinach, 1 cup bread crumbs, 4 eggs, 2 teaspoons salt, and 1/4 teaspoon pepper, and mix well.

Season the veal, outside and inside the pocket, with salt and pepper and stuff the pocket with the spinach forcemeat. Skewer or sew the end of the pocket and put the veal, fat side up, in an open roasting pan. Roast it in a moderately slow oven (325° F.) for about 2 1/2 hours. Transfer the veal to a heated platter, remove the skewers or thread, and garnish with parsley.

SEASON a 3- to 4-pound loin of veal, with the kidney, with 1 teaspoon salt and a little pepper and sprinkle it with flour. In an earthenware casserole brown the veal in 3 tablespoons hot butter. Remove the meat to a plate. Add to the casserole 18 to 24 small white onions and 6 to 8 carrots, cut in pieces. Sprinkle the vegetables with 1 tablespoon sugar and cook until they are brown. Add 1 garlic clove, crushed.

Return the meat to the casserole and add 1/2 cup white wine, 3 tomatoes, peeled, seeded, and chopped, or 2 tablespoons tomato sauce, 1/2 cup stock or water, and a *bouquet garni* composed of 1 stalk of celery, 4 sprigs of parsley, 1 small bay leaf, and a little thyme. Bring the liquid to a boil, cover the casserole, and simmer for 1 1/2 hours. Add 2 cups fresh peas and 6 green leaves of lettuce, finely chopped, and simmer for 45 minutes to 1 hour longer, adding a little more stock or water if needed. There should be just enough gravy to sauce the meat and vegetables. Remove the meat to a serving dish. Discard the *bouquet garni* and serve the vegetables and gravy from the casserole.

LARD a rolled, boned veal roast, weighing about 5 pounds, with strips of fat pork, batons of ham, and pieces of truffle. Brown the meat in butter and braise it with a *mirepoix* in a covered kettle for about 2 hours, or until it is tender, basting it from time to time and turning it frequently. The meat may be braised over low heat or in a moderate oven (350° F.). Remove the cover and glaze the surface of the meat briefly in a very hot oven (450° F.).

Carve enough slices for the first serving and arrange the meat at one end of a large serving platter.

Line a buttered mold with cooked carrot and turnip sticks, following the procedure described in the recipe for *filet de boeuf moderne*, and fill the mold well with the same vegetables, bound with the forcemeat. Unmold in a puff paste shell bordered with duchess potatoes and browned under the broiler. Put this shell at the end of the platter opposite the meat.

Complete the garniture with château potatoes sprinkled with parsley, and with small puff-paste shells filled with *purée Soubise* topped with truffle slices and with buttered green peas.

Veal and Tomato Stew

IN a heavy skillet in 3 tablespoons olive oil brown 1 1/2 pounds veal cut into 2-inch cubes. Drain the cubes and put them into a braising kettle. In the fat remaining in the skillet brown lightly 1 onion, chopped, and 1 garlic clove, crushed. Stir in 1 tablespoon flour and add 2 cups chicken or veal stock, 3 large ripe tomatoes, peeled, seeded, and coarsely chopped, the juice of 1/2 lemon, a pinch of orégano, and salt and pepper to taste. Cook and stir this sauce for a moment and pour it over the veal. Cover the kettle and simmer the mixture slowly for 1 hour.

In a saucepan sauté in butter 12 whole mushrooms for 3 or 4 minutes and add them to the kettle. Cook the stew for 30 minutes longer, until the meat is tender. Turn it into a serving dish, sprinkle it with chopped parsley and garnish it with triangular croutons sautéed in butter. Serve with fluffy rice or baked potatoes and a mixed green salad.

Rollini di Vitello con Polenta
VEAL BIRDS WITH POLENTA

POUND 1 1/2 pounds of thinly sliced veal until it is paper thin and cut it into pieces about 5 by 3 inches. Combine 3/4 cup finely chopped *prosciutto*, 1 garlic clove, minced, 2 tablespoons chopped parsley, and salt and pepper to taste. Put 1 teaspoon of the filling in the center of each piece of veal, roll the meat, and secure with wooden picks.

Dredge the rolls in flour and brown them in a skillet in 3 tablespoons butter. Add 1 cup dry white wine and cook until the wine is reduced by half, turning the rolls occasionally. Add 2 cups chicken stock and simmer the rolls gently for 15 minutes. Add 1 carrot, 1 onion, and 1 stalk of celery, all finely chopped, and 1/2 teaspoon rosemary and cook the rolls for about 20 minutes longer. While the veal is cooking prepare *polenta*, or cornmeal mush.

Polenta

Bring 6 cups water to a boil. Add 1 teaspoon salt, stir in very gradually 2 cups cornmeal, and cook for about 5 minutes, stirring constantly, until the mixture is smooth and thick. Cook over boiling water for 30 minutes,

Veal Birds with Polenta

stirring occasionally. Beat in 2 tablespoons butter. Arrange the *rollini* on a warmed platter around a mound of *polenta* and strain the gravy over all.

Paupiettes de Veau en Casserole
VEAL ROLLS

HAVE the butcher cut 2 pounds veal for cutlets into thin slices. Pound the slices very thin with a mallet or cleaver and cut them into 3-inch squares. Combine 1/4 pound each of veal trimmings and lean ham, both finely chopped, with 1/2 cup grated Parmesan cheese, 2 eggs, 1/3 cup minced parsley, and salt and pepper to taste. Spread the veal slices with this stuffing, roll them carefully and tie each with string. In a large casserole heat 2 table-spoons each of olive oil and butter with 1 crushed garlic clove. Brown the veal rolls lightly in this fat and add 1 cup tomato sauce and 1/2 cup white wine. Cover the casserole and braise the meat in a moderately slow oven (325° F.) until is tender.

Veal Chops in Cream

BROWN 6 thick loin veal chops quickly in 6 tablespoons butter, pour 3 tablespoons heated brandy over them, and ignite the spirit. When the flame dies, transfer the chops to a flameproof serving dish and keep them warm. In the butter remaining in the pan, cook for 2 or 3 minutes 3/4 cup mushrooms, sliced. Sprinkle the mushrooms with 1/4 cup flour and stir in 1 1/2 cups light stock and 1 teaspoon *glace de viande* or a very little meat extract. Cook the sauce, stirring constantly, until it comes to a boil. Stir in 1 1/2 cups heavy cream and pour the sauce over the chops in the casserole. Add salt and pepper to taste, 1 bay leaf, and a pinch of dried thyme. Cover the dish and simmer the chops for about 45 minutes, until they are very tender. Just before serving, sprinkle the chops with grated Parmesan, dot them with butter, and glaze them briefly under the broiler. Serve in the baking dish.

Côtes de Veau à l'Estragon
VEAL CHOPS WITH TARRAGON

SEASON 6 thick veal chops with salt and pepper and rub them with flour. Sauté the chops slowly in 1/4 cup butter for about 12 to 15 minutes on each side and arrange them on a serving platter.

Parboil 3 dozen of the choicest leaves from 6 sprigs of tarragon in a little boiling salted water for 1 minute, drain them, and plunge them into cold water. Chop the remaining tarragon sprigs; add them to the pan in which the chops have been cooked with 1/3 cup white wine and cook for a few minutes, stirring in all the brown crustiness from the sides of the pan. Add 3/4 cup veal gravy or stock and 1 to 2 teaspoons beef extract and bring the sauce to a boil. Decorate the veal chops with the parboiled tarragon leaves and strain the gravy over them.

SEASON 6 inch-thick veal chops with a little salt and white pepper. Melt 2 tablespoons butter in a shallow casserole and sprinkle over the butter 2 tablespoons finely chopped onion. Set the chops side by side in the casserole. Mix together 2 cups fresh bread crumbs and 1 cup grated Parmesan cheese. Cover the chops with this mixture, pressing the crumbs and cheese together firmly to make a compact rounded topping, and sprinkle with melted butter. Add a generous 1/2 cup of white wine. Cover the casserole and braise the chops in a hot oven (400° F.) for 1 to 1 1/2 hours, or until the meat easily separates from the bone. During the cooking add water, a little at a time, as the liquid is reduced and baste the chops to give them a golden brown color. If the topping cracks, press it together firmly but carefully.

Côtes de Veau Braisées à la Chartres
BRAISED VEAL CHOPS

Transfer the chops to a serving dish. Pour the gravy from the casserole into a saucepan, bring it to a boil, and thicken with 1 tablespoon arrowroot or cornstarch mixed with a little cold water or stock. Correct the seasoning and strain the sauce through a fine sieve or muslin cloth. Serve with purée of spinach or with peas, carrots, or other vegetables.

MELT 2 tablespoons butter in a large skillet and add 3 tablespoons olive oil. Heat the mixture thoroughly and add half a 2-ounce can of flat anchovies cut into small pieces and 1/2 teaspoon dried rosemary or 1 teaspoon fresh rosemary, finely chopped. Cook the mixture over low heat for 5 minutes.

Veal Chops with Wine, Rosemary, and Anchovies

Season 6 veal loin chops to taste with salt and coarse, freshly ground pepper, put them in the skillet on top of the anchovy mixture, lower the heat, and brown the chops first on one side and then on the other. Sprinkle the second side with 1 tablespoon flour and add 1/4 cup dry white wine and a few drops of Worcestershire sauce. Tilt the pan back and forth to combine the mixture, and simmer the chops, covered, for 5 minutes.

Add the juice of half a lemon. Again tilt the pan and baste the chops with the sauce. Cover the skillet and simmer the chops for 10 minutes longer, or until they are done.

Arrange the chops on a heated serving platter, pour the sauce over them, and garnish with lemon wedges and freshly chopped parsley. Serve immediately.

This recipe may be used with lean loin or shoulder lamb chops or lean pork chops.

Veal Chops in Paper Cases

SEASON 6 veal chops, 1/2 inch thick, with salt and pepper. Sauté them gently in 3 tablespoons butter in a skillet for 20 to 25 minutes, or until they are golden brown on both sides.

Prepare a duxelles sauce as follows: Cook 1/2 pound mushrooms, minced, in a saucepan with 2 tablespoons butter, 1 teaspoon chopped shallot or onion, 1/2 teaspoon salt, and 1 teaspoon chopped parsley until all the moisture is cooked away. Add 1 cup thick cream sauce and mix thoroughly.

Cut into heart shapes 6 rectangles of white paper 8 1/2 by 11 inches. Butter the papers. Put thin slices of cooked ham about the size of the chops on one side of the heart shape and put a spoonful of duxelles sauce on the ham slices. Lay a cooked chop on this, pour the remaining sauce on the chops, and top with thin slices of cooked ham. Fold over the other side of the paper heart and roll and pinch the edges together securely. Put the packages on a large baking sheet and bake them in a hot oven (400° F.) for 5 to 6 minutes, or until the cases start to brown. Cut around the sides of each *papillote* with a small sharp-pointed knife and roll up the flap to uncover the contents. The chops, served on individual plates, are eaten from the paper cases.

Côtes de Veau en Papillotes
VEAL CHOPS
IN PAPER CASES

SCALLOPS are tender pieces of veal, usually cut from the leg in slices 1/8 inch thick. Cut 2 pounds veal sliced in this way into serving portions, cover each portion with wax paper, and pound the slices with the flat side of a cleaver or with a wooden mallet until they are very thin. Season the meat with salt and pepper and flour it lightly. Then cook as indicated.

Veal Scallops
also called
ESCALOPES DE
VEAU, SCALOPPINE
DI VITELLO
AND SCHNITZEL

IN a large skillet melt 1/4 cup butter and sauté the prepared veal scallops over high heat for 6 or 7 minutes, until they are golden brown on both sides. Arrange the scallops on a warm serving platter. Add 1/2 cup stock or water to the butter in the pan and cook for a few minutes, stirring in all the brown crustiness. Pour the sauce over the meat and sprinkle with finely chopped parsley.

Escalopes de Veau Sautées

BROWN 2 pounds prepared veal scallops on both sides in 1/4 cup each of butter and olive oil. Add 3 cups mushrooms, thinly sliced, and cook for 10 minutes. Add the juice of 1 lemon and 3/4 cup Marsala or Sherry, and simmer the *scaloppine* for 5 minutes more.

Veal Scaloppine al Marsala

*Escalopes
de Veau aux
Fines Herbes*

SAUTÉ 2 pounds prepared veal scallops and arrange the meat on a heated platter. To the butter remaining in the pan add 2/3 cup dry white wine and cook over high heat until the wine is reduced by half. Add 1 teaspoon each of chopped chives, tarragon, and parsley. Swirl in 2 tablespoons butter until it is just melted and pour the sauce over the meat.

*Escalopes
de Veau
à la Crème*

SAUTÉ 2 pounds prepared veal scallops and arrange the meat on a flame-proof platter. Pour over it 1/4 cup warmed Cognac and ignite the spirit. When the flame dies, add to the skillet in which the scallops were cooked 1 cup heavy cream and simmer, stirring in the brown crustiness in the pan, for 2 minutes. Pour the sauce over the veal.

Saltimbocca
VEAL SCALLOPS
ROMAN STYLE

SPRINKLE 2 pounds veal scallops with salt and pepper and a little powdered sage. Place a thinly shaved slice of *prosciutto* over each scallop and fasten it in place by threading with wooden picks. Sauté the meat in 3 tablespoons hot butter over high heat for about 2 minutes on each side and place it on a warm serving dish with the *prosciutto* side up.

To the juices in the pan add 1/4 cup light stock and stir, scraping the bottom and sides of the pan well. Swirl in 3 tablespoons butter and pour the sauce over the meat.

*Scaloppine
Modenese*

BEAT 1 egg and season it with salt and pepper. Dip 6 very thin veal scallops in the egg and then in fine bread crumbs. Sauté the scallops slowly in 1/4 cup of butter until they are golden brown on both sides. Arrange the scallops in a shallow baking dish, and place on each a thin slice of *prosciutto* and a thin slice of Mozzarella cheese. Garnish the dish with truffle slices and bake the *scaloppine* in a moderately hot oven (375° F.) until the cheese is melted.

*Paprika-
schnitzel*

SAUTÉ 2 pounds veal scallops in 6 tablespoons butter and transfer the meat to a heated serving platter. To the butter in the pan add 2 shallots, finely chopped, and sauté the shallots until they are golden brown. Stir in 1 table-spoon flour mixed with 1/2 tablespoon paprika and add gradually 1 cup hot light stock and 1/4 cup dry white wine, stirring constantly. Continue to cook, stirring constantly, until the sauce is thickened, lower the heat, and simmer the sauce for about 10 minutes. Stir in 1/2 cup sour cream and heat the sauce again but do not let it boil. Stir in a dash of lemon juice and pour the sauce over the veal.

SPRINKLE 2 pounds veal scallops with salt and pepper and dip them in flour. Dip them into lightly beaten egg and coat them with fine dry bread crumbs. Sauté the meat in 6 tablespoons hot butter over high heat for about 3 minutes on each side, or until the crumbs are golden, and arrange on a warmed serving platter. Top each schnitzel with a fried egg and garnish the platter with anchovy filets, thin slices of pickled beets, and dill pickles.

*Schnitzel
Holstein*

IN a skillet sauté 6 prepared veal cutlets cut 1/4 inch thick from the top sirloin over high heat until they are golden, turning them several times.

Kalvfilet Oscar
VEAL OSCAR

Arrange the meat on a warm serving dish and place on each piece 5 cooked asparagus tips. On top of the asparagus place 5 or 6 crabs' legs, cooked in butter.

To the juices remaining in the skillet add 3 tablespoons water, reduce this a little, and pour it over the meat. Put the platter in the oven to keep warm and, when ready to serve, pour béarnaise sauce over the meat, asparagus, and crabs' legs.

MAKE a *panade* as follows: Bring to a boil 2/3 cup water, a pinch of salt, and 1 tablespoon butter. Add 1/4 cup flour and stir with a wooden spoon over the heat until the mixture is smooth and does not cling to the sides of the pan. Remove from the heat, stir in 1 egg, and set aside.

Panade

Grind 1/4 pound veal with the sinews removed and 1/3 pound beef kidney suet, free of membranes, through the finest blade of food chopper. Add 1 teaspoon salt, a little pepper, and a grating of nutmeg. Add the *panade*, mix well, and spread on a flat plate. Cover with wax paper and chill for 3 to 4 hours.

Godiveaux
VEAL FORCEMEAT
SAUSAGES

Divide the farce into small pieces and roll the pieces into fingers about the size and shape of tiny sausages. Bake them on a flat baking dish in a slow oven (300° F.) for 10 to 15 minutes, or until they are firm but not crusty or brown.

CUT 1 to 1 1/2 pounds leftover veal into large dice. In a saucepan melt 2 tablespoons butter, add 3 tablespoons chopped onions, and cook until the onions begin to turn golden. Add 1 garlic clove, crushed, and 1 tablespoon flour and mix well. Add 1 cup each of red wine and stock, bring to a boil,

*Sauté de Veau
au Vin Rouge*
MATELOTE
OF VEAL

stirring constantly, and add 1/2 teaspoon salt, half a small bay leaf, crushed to powder, and a pinch of thyme. Cook for 20 to 25 minutes, stirring occasionally.

Sauté 12 to 15 small mushrooms in a little oil and cook 12 small white onions in butter with a little sugar until glazed and golden. Add the mushrooms, onions, and meat to the sauce and bring to a boil. Correct the seasoning with salt and add a little freshly ground pepper and 1 teaspoon chopped parsley. If the sauce is not quite thick enough, swirl in *beurre manié* made by creaming 1 tablespoon butter with 1 teaspoon flour. Serve with boiled potatoes or noodles.

Veal Cakes   CHOP finely 1 pound leftover cooked veal. Bake 3 large potatoes until they are tender and whip the pulp with a wooden spoon. Sauté 1/2 cup finely chopped onion in 2 tablespoons butter until it is golden. Add the meat and the potato pulp, 1 egg, beaten, 1 tablespoon chopped parsley, and a little salt and pepper, and mix thoroughly. Divide the mixture into portions the size of an egg, roll each one in flour, and flatten it into a patty about 3/4 inch thick. Brown the cakes on both sides in 3 tablespoons hot beef fat. Serve very hot.

Veal Salad   MARINATE 2 cups cooked veal, cut in thin slices, for 2 hours in 3 tablespoons oil, 2 teaspoons wine vinegar, 1/2 teaspoon salt, and 1/8 teaspoon black pepper. Arrange the slices of marinated meat on a platter and garnish them with slices of hard-cooked egg and sweet gherkins. Serve with a sauceboat of dressing made with 3 tablespoons oil, 2 teaspoons wine vinegar, 1 teaspoon sharp mustard, 3 anchovy filets, washed and chopped, and 6 washed and dried capers.

One stricture applies to all pork cookery—pork must always be very well done.

Roast Loin of Pork with Orange Sauce   SPRINKLE a loin of pork with salt and freshly ground black pepper and put it in a roasting pan, fat side up. Add 1 small onion, sliced, half an orange, peeled and divided into segments, 1/4 cup chopped celery, a little orégano, 1 cup orange juice, and 2 tablespoons wine vinegar. Roast in a moderate oven

Veal Salad

(350° F.) for 25 to 30 minutes per pound, basting frequently with the pan juices, until the meat is well done.

Arrange the loin on a heated serving platter. Remove the excess fat from the pan and strain the pan juices into a sauceboat. If desired, the sauce may be thickened with a little cornstarch or arrowroot mixed with cold water.

Hung Sao Tee Tzu
BRAISED FRESH HAM

COVER a 6- to 7-pound fresh ham in a large kettle with cold water and bring the water slowly to a boil. Cook for 5 minutes, remove the ham, and rinse it well in cold water. Put the meat in a Dutch oven with 1 cup each of stock or water and soy sauce, 1/3 cup dry Sherry, a slice of fresh ginger, and 2 scallions, trimmed. Bring to a boil, cover the Dutch oven, and simmer over low heat for 1 1/2 hours. Turn the ham over, add 1/3 cup brown sugar, and simmer for another 1 1/2 hours, basting occasionally.

Chinese Barbecued Pork

CUT a 2-pound strip of fresh pork loin in half lengthwise. Blend 1 tablespoon Sherry, 2 tablespoons each of soy sauce and sugar, 1 1/2 teaspoons salt, and 1/2 teaspoon ground cinnamon. Rub the pork strips with this mixture and let the meat absorb the seasonings for 2 hours. Cook the meat slowly under the broiler for about 1 hour, turning the strips frequently to insure even cooking, or roast the pork on a rack in a moderate oven (350° F.). Pork must be very well done. Cut the meat into very thin diagonal slices and serve it with hot Chinese mustard, dry mustard blended to a rather thin paste with water or stale beer. A pinch of turmeric will give additional color.

Mandarin Spareribs

MARINATE 4 to 5 pounds meaty spareribs for 12 hours in a mixture of 1 cup each of soy sauce and orange marmalade, 3 finely chopped garlic cloves, 1 teaspoon dried ginger, and a pinch of ground black pepper. Turn the ribs occasionally so that the marinade penetrates the meat evenly. Arrange the ribs on a rack in a roasting pan and roast them in a moderate oven (350° F.) for 1 1/2 hours, basting frequently with the marinade, until the ribs are glazed and golden brown and the meat is very tender. Cut the ribs into finger-size pieces with a sharp knife and serve hot.

Cassoeula
PORK STEW

MELT 2 tablespoons butter in a large heavy pan and in it brown lightly 2 slices of bacon, diced, 1 onion, sliced, 3 or 4 carrots, sliced, and 1 stalk of celery cut in 1/2-inch pieces. Add 1 1/2 pounds lean pork cut in thick slices, 1/2 pound Italian pork sausage, cut in chunks, and a small piece of bacon rind. Season with salt and pepper and 1 bay leaf, and sprinkle with 1 tablespoon flour. Blend in the flour and add 1 cup dry white wine. Cover the pot and cook the stew very slowly, adding stock or water if necessary, for about 1 to 1 1/2 hours.

Clean a medium-sized cabbage and boil it whole in salted water for 10 minutes. Drain the cabbage, cut it into quarters and add it to the meat. Cook the stew for about 30 minutes longer.

SEASON 6 thick pork chops and brown them very slowly on both sides in a little butter. Peel 6 tart apples and cut them into eighths. Put the half-cooked chops in a shallow casserole and arrange mounds of apples around them. Sprinkle chops and apples with a little melted butter and bake in a moderate oven (350° F.) for about 30 minutes, or until the pork is thoroughly cooked. Decorate the chops with paper frills and serve from the casserole.

Côtes de Porc à la Flamande
PORK CHOPS FLAMANDE

BROWN 6 thick loin pork chops well on both sides in butter. Transfer them to a baking dish and pour over them 3/4 cup each of cider and water. Sprinkle the chops with a generous pinch each of basil and marjoram, and with paprika, salt, and pepper to taste. Add to the casserole 3 medium onions, finely chopped. Cover the dish and bake the chops in a moderate oven (350° F.) for 45 minutes to 1 hour, or until they are tender. Serve the chops from the casserole.

Pork Chops in Cider

IN a skillet brown 1 garlic clove in 2 tablespoons olive oil. Discard the garlic and brown 6 pork chops on both sides. Sprinkle the meat with salt and pepper and add 3 tablespoons tomato purée mixed with 3 tablespoons white wine, 2 green peppers, finely cut, and 1 pound fresh mushrooms, sliced. Cover the skillet and cook for 20 minutes.

Pork Chops Neapolitan

There are all sorts and conditions of hams: smoked, ready to eat, "tenderized," and so on, most of which come from the packer with appropriate cooking instructions. The recipes that follow either elaborate on such instructions or take up where they leave off.

COOK a tenderized ham according to the packer's directions. Glazes are usually applied about an hour before the ham is ready to come from the oven. Remove the skin and some of the fat, brush the fat with beaten egg,

Champagne Glazed Ham

Ham Steak Virginia

score it in an attractive pattern, and stud it with a pattern of whole cloves. Pat brown sugar thickly over the surface and bake the ham in a moderate oven (350° F.) for 1 hour, basting it frequently with a mixture of 3/4 cup each of Champagne and pineapple juice, until the crust is richly browned. Remove the ham from the oven and continue to baste it with the pan juices for a few minutes. The ham will slice readily if it is allowed to stand for about 15 minutes before cutting. Put the ham on a heated platter and garnish with glazed small apples.

PUT a precooked ham in a roasting pan, pour over it 1 cup beer, and bake in a moderate oven (350° F.) for 45 minutes, basting occasionally with the beer in the pan.

Ham Glazed with Beer

Combine 1 cup brown sugar and 1 teaspoon dry mustard with 2 table-spoons vinegar and enough beer to make a smooth paste. Take the ham from the oven and score the fat diagonally in two directions to form diamonds. Spread the glaze over the ham, stud with whole cloves, and bake for 30 minutes longer, or until the ham is well glazed, basting it with drippings.

SOAK an aged country ham for 24 hours, scrub it well, and cut off the skin, leaving a generous layer of fat. (Or use an ordinary smoked ham that does not require soaking.) Stud the fat generously with whole cloves. Put the ham on a rack in a roaster and pour over it the following mixture: Combine 1 cup each of molasses, vinegar, and cider, 6 cups hot water, 2 bay leaves, and 1 tablespoon Worcestershire sauce. Cover the roaster and bake the ham in a slow oven (300° F.), basting it frequently with the cider sauce. Country hams require 5 to 6 hours cooking, an ordinary smoked ham about 20 minutes baking per pound; follow the packer's directions.

Baked Ham with Cider

IN a skillet melt 1/4 cup butter and in it sauté a slice of cooked smoked ham, 1 1/2 inches thick, until it is nicely browned on both sides. Transfer the ham to a heated serving platter to keep warm. To the pan in which the ham was cooked add 1/4 cup brown sugar and 1 cup Sherry and stir the mixture over low heat until the sugar melts. Add 2 teaspoons flour mixed to a paste with 1/4 cup water and cook the sauce, stirring constantly, until it is thick and smooth. Return the ham to the pan and simmer it in the sauce for 10 minutes, turning it to cook both sides evenly. Arrange the ham on the serving platter again and pour the sauce over it. Serve with creamed spinach.

Ham Steak Virginia

Tranches de Jambon Montmorency

HAM STEAKS WITH CHERRIES

IN a saucepan combine 1/2 cup water, 2 tablespoons sugar, 1 tablespoon finely chopped crystallized ginger, and a pinch of salt. Bring the mixture to a boil and add 3 cups pitted black cherries. Simmer gently for 5 minutes and add 1 tablespoon cornstarch mixed to a paste with 2 tablespoons water. Cook, stirring constantly, for a few minutes longer, or until the sauce is clear.

Arrange 2 cooked ham steaks, cut 3/4 inch thick, in a lightly buttered baking dish. Pour the sauce over the ham and bake the ham in a moderate oven (350° F.) for about 25 minutes, basting it frequently with the sauce. Transfer ham and sauce to a warm serving platter and serve with spiced sweet potatoes.

Stuffed Ham Slices

IN a saucepan melt 2 tablespoons butter and in it sauté 1/4 pound mushrooms and 1 large onion, both finely chopped, until they are soft but have not taken on any color. Add 1 teaspoon Dijon mustard, 3/4 cup bread crumbs, and enough chicken stock to moisten. Spread the mixture on thin slices of cold baked or boiled ham and fold the slices in half. Wrap each slice in aluminum foil and bake them in a moderate oven (350° F.) for 25 to 30 minutes.

Ham à la King

MELT 6 tablespoons butter in a saucepan, add 5 tablespoons flour, and cook the *roux* over very low heat for 5 minutes, stirring constantly and removing the pan from the heat from time to time to prevent the flour from browning. Add gradually 2 cups hot milk and 1 cup hot cream and cook, stirring, until the sauce is smooth and thick. Remove the pan from the heat and stir in 2 cups diced ham and 1/3 cup pimientos, cut into strips. Add a little of the sauce to 3 lightly beaten egg yolks and stir them into the sauce.

Sauté 3/4 cup green peppers, cut into slivers, and 1/2 pound sliced mushrooms in 2 tablespoons butter until tender but not brown. Combine the two mixtures, correct the seasoning with salt, and finish with 1/4 cup dry Sherry. The mixture may be reheated if necessary, but it should not be allowed to boil. Serve on freshly made toast or in heated patty shells.

Mousse de Jambon Florentine

HAM MOUSSE WITH SPINACH

PUT 1 pound cooked ham through the finest blade of a food chopper. Season it with white pepper and salt, if necessary, and pound it to a paste in a mortar. With a wooden spoon work in 2 egg whites. Force the mixture through a fine sieve into a bowl set in a bowl of ice. Very gradually work in 2 cups heavy cream. Fill a buttered ring mold with the mousse. Set the mold in a baking pan in an inch or two of hot, but not boiling, water and bake it in a moderate oven (350° F.) for about 45 minutes, or until the mousse is firm. Remove the mold from the hot-water bath and let it stand for a few minutes. Unmold the mousse on a serving platter and surround it with triangular croutons. Fill the center with a conical mound of cooked and seasoned spinach. Serve with a sauceboat of velouté sauce mixed with mushrooms.

Hot Ham
Home Style

PUT 1 tablespoon chopped shallot or onion in a saucepan with 3 or 4 leaves of tarragon and 1/2 cup dry white wine. Bring to a boil and cook until reduced to about one fourth the original quantity. Add 1/2 cup brown sauce or gravy or 1 to 2 teaspoons meat extract and 1/2 cup tomato purée. Cook very slowly for about 15 to 20 minutes. Add to this sauce an equal quantity of heavy sweet cream and cook slowly for about 10 minutes longer. Strain through a fine sieve, add 1 tablespoon butter, and correct the seasoning with salt.

Cut enough cooked ham for 4 servings in thin slices, arrange the slices in a chafing dish over hot water, and pour some of the sauce over the meat. Serve the remaining sauce separately. Serves 4.

Quiche
Bourbonnaise

LINE an 8-inch pie plate with rich pastry dough. On the bottom arrange 4 thin slices of cooked ham and sprinkle the ham with 1/4 cup grated dry Swiss cheese. Beat together 3 eggs and 1 yolk and stir in 1 cup heavy cream and 1/2 teaspoon salt. Pour the mixture into the pie shell and bake in a moderately hot oven (375° F.) for 30 to 35 minutes, or until the custard is set and the top is brown. Serve warm.

Ham Rolls

SAUTÉ 1/2 pound mushrooms, finely chopped, in 2 tablespoons butter. Add 1/2 teaspoon tarragon, 1/4 teaspoon dry mustard, and 1 tablespoon flour, and cook, stirring, until the mixture is well blended. Add 1 cup sour cream and salt to taste. Cool.

Spread 12 thin slices of cooked ham with the filling, lay 3 stalks of freshly cooked and cooled asparagus on each slice, and roll the ham. The asparagus tips should show at one end. Serve cold.

Pork sausages are part of the culinary folklore of many countries. They come in numerous shapes and sizes, but thin or fat, sweet or hot, all must be well cooked.

*Sausages
in Ale*

PRICK 1 1/2 pounds link sausages with the tines of a fork and brown the sausages quickly in 2 tablespoons hot butter. Pour off the excess fat, add 1 cup ale, and bring the liquid to a boil. Cover the pan and simmer the sausages in the ale for 30 minutes.

*Garbanzo
Casserole*

SOAK 2 cups chick-peas, or *garbanzos*, overnight in water to cover. Next day, drain the beans, cover them with fresh water and simmer for about 30 minutes, or until they are tender.

Cut 5 Italian or Mexican sausages in 1-inch lengths and brown them on all sides. In a flameproof casserole sauté 3 garlic cloves, chopped, and 1 cup each of chopped onions and green pepper in 1/4 cup olive oil for 2 to 3 minutes, or until the onion is transparent. Add the chick-peas, the sausages, 2/3 cup chopped celery, 1/2 cup chopped carrots, 2 tablespoons chili powder, 1/2 cup tomato paste, 3 cups stewed tomatoes, and 2 tablespoons parsley. Bring to a boil, cover the casserole, and simmer for 2 hours. Season to taste with salt.

*Toad-in-
the-Hole*

ROLL 1 1/2 pounds country sausage meat into small balls and brown the balls on all sides. Put the sausage balls in a casserole with 3 tablespoons of the sausage drippings and pour over them a batter made by combining 3 eggs, 1 1/2 cups each of flour and milk, a pinch each of thyme and cayenne, and 1/4 teaspoon salt. Bake the casserole in a very hot oven (450° F.) for 15 minutes, reduce the oven temperature to 350° F. and continue to bake until the pudding is puffy and brown.

*Country
Casserole*

FORM 1 1/2 pounds country sausage meat into 6 flat cakes, brown the cakes thoroughly on both sides, and arrange them in an ovenproof casserole. Put a slice of onion on each cake and cover with Spanish sauce. Cover sauce and sausage with an inch-thick layer of mashed potatoes, dot with butter, and sprinkle with grated Parmesan cheese. Bake the casserole in a moderate oven (350° F.) for 30 minutes, or until the topping is golden brown.

*Preparation of
Sweetbreads*

Sweetbreads are parboiled as a first step in any recipe for their preparation. Soak them in cold water for several hours, drain them, and cover them with cold salted water. Bring the water slowly to a boil, simmer the sweetbreads for 2 to 5 minutes, depending on their size, and drain them. Plunge them at once into fresh cold water. Cut away and discard the connecting tubes and tough sinews, spread the sweetbreads on a platter, and weight them down with a plate to flatten them as they cool.

SPREAD in a casserole 1 onion and 1 carrot, both sliced, and 1 tablespoon butter, and cook the vegetables until they are soft but not brown. Add a bay leaf, a few sprigs of parsley, and a little thyme. Lay the parboiled sweetbreads on this *mirepoix* and add 1/2 cup dry white wine and 1 cup white stock.

Bring the liquid to a boil, cover the casserole, and cook the sweetbreads in a moderately hot oven (375° F.) for 45 to 60 minutes, basting frequently, until the edges seem to crack slightly or begin to break at the touch of a fork. To braise sweetbreads *à brun*, remove the cover so that they brown as they cook; if the casserole is covered, the sweetbreads remain white, and are braised *à blanc*.

BRAISE 2 parboiled sweetbreads *à blanc*. Cut them in large dice. Melt 2 tablespoons butter in a saucepan, stir in 2 tablespoons flour and cook the *roux* for a few minutes, but do not let it brown. Add 1 3/4 cups hot milk and cook, stirring constantly, until the sauce thickens. Lower the heat and cook gently for 30 minutes longer, stirring often to prevent scorching. Add 1/4 cup cream mixed with 1 egg yolk. Add the sweetbreads and 1 cup diced cooked chicken, 1/2 cup sliced cooked mushrooms, and 2 tablespoons dry Sherry or Madeira. Mix carefully with a fork, taking care not to break the fragile sweetbreads. Serve in a *vol-au-vent* or in patty shells, on freshly made toast or with rice.

DICE 3 pairs parboiled sweetbreads and heat them in 1 1/2 cups cream sauce. Heat 3 cups cooked, drained spinach in a little butter. Put a narrow border of duchess potatoes around baking shells, or *coquilles*, and brown in a very hot oven (450° F.) or under the broiler. Put 1/2 cup spinach in the center of each shell and cover with the hot creamed sweetbreads. Sprinkle with finely chopped cooked ham and serve immediately.

SLICE 3 pairs parboiled sweetbreads diagonally and lard each slice with 1 or 2 small bits of bacon or salt pork. Heat 3 tablespoons butter in a pan and sauté the sweetbreads carefully to a light golden brown, turning them once. Sprinkle with 1 chopped garlic clove, 1 generous teaspoon each of chopped parsley and chopped chives, 1/2 teaspoon dried tarragon, a pinch of ground cloves and 1 1/2 cups chicken stock, and simmer these together for 3 or 4 minutes. Strain the sauce into another pan and thicken it by blending in 1 tablespoon butter, creamed thoroughly with 1 tablespoon flour. Cook for a moment and add 1 egg yolk and a few drops of lemon juice. Pour the sauce over the sweetbreads and serve very hot, on toast or in patty shells.

Mushroom and Sweetbread Casserole

IN 1/4 cup butter in a casserole sauté 3 pairs parboiled sweetbreads until they are golden on both sides. Add 1 cup Port, cover the casserole, and simmer until the wine is reduced by half. Stir in 2 cups heavy cream, 1/4 cup meat stock or gravy, a pinch of cayenne, salt to taste, and 1 pound small mushroom caps, browned briefly in butter. A truffle or two, thinly sliced, may also be added. Bake the casserole in a slow oven (300° F.) for 20 minutes.

Sweetbreads on Skewers

CUT 2 pairs prepared sweetbreads into slices. Trim 1/2 pound mushrooms and cut them into slices. Cut 6 slices of bacon, 1/8 inch thick, into squares.

Alternate the sweetbreads, mushroom slices, and bacon on 6 small skewers and sprinkle with salt and freshly ground pepper. Melt 6 tablespoons butter, spread soft breadcrumbs on a large plate, and brush each skewer generously with melted butter and roll it in the bread crumbs. Broil the skewers for about 15 minutes, turning them frequently.

Sweetbreads with Prosciutto

MELT 3 tablespoons butter in a large skillet. Season 3 pairs parboiled sweetbreads with salt and freshly ground pepper, put them in the skillet, and brown them lightly on both sides. Sprinkle over the sweetbreads 4 tablespoons finely chopped parsley, 3 tablespoons dry Marsala wine, and 4 slices of *prosciutto*, finely minced. Cover the pan and simmer the sweetbreads for 10 minutes. Serve immediately, with freshly made toast.

Fresh, smoked, and pickled tongues may be prepared by the same recipes, to achieve different ends. Taste the water in which a smoked tongue has boiled for 5 minutes; if it seems very salty, pour it off and add fresh water. Calf's tongue is very tender; if allowance is made for this, the same recipes apply.

Langue de Boeuf
BEEF TONGUE

WASH a small fresh beef tongue weighing about 4 pounds in warm water. Put it in a deep kettle with 1 onion stuck with 3 cloves, 1 carrot, sliced, 1 stalk of celery with the leaves, a small bunch of parsley, 1 bay leaf, and 6 peppercorns. Cover the tongue with boiling water and bring it slowly back to a boil. After the water has boiled for about 5 minutes, remove any scum and add 2 teaspoons salt. Reduce the heat and simmer for about 50 minutes to the pound, or until the tongue is tender.

Cool the tongue in the stock until it can be handled, remove it, and skin it with a sharp knife. Trim the tongue, removing the fat and tough portions near the throat end.

Tongue should be sliced thinly against the grain. Serve it hot or cold with a piquant sauce or bake it in a moderately hot oven (375° F.) for about 25 minutes, basting it frequently with 1 cup tomato or brown sauce.

When boiled tongue is basted with tomato sauce and garnished with saffron-flavored rice croquettes and stuffed tomatoes, it is called *langue de boeuf Sarde*. When it is finished with brown sauce and garnished with noodles, it is called *langue de boeuf suisse*. Garnished with cooked cauliflower rolled in melted butter and bread crumbs, it is known as *langue de boeuf polonaise.* A garnish of cooked artichokes and spaghetti with tomato sauce makes it *langue de boeuf italienne.*

Langue de Boeuf Sarde
Langue de Boeuf Suisse
Langue de Boeuf Polonaise
Langue de Boeuf Italienne

CUT the skin from the thick throat end of a 4-pound fresh beef tongue. Plunge it into boiling water for a few minutes and skin it with a sharp knife. Lard the tongue with strips of larding pork rolled in salt mixed with a little ground cloves, pepper, finely chopped parsley, and 1/4 teaspoon freshly grated garlic.

Heat 2 tablespoons beef drippings in a heavy braising kettle and in it brown the tongue, along with 3 onions and 2 carrots, both sliced. Drain the excess fat from the kettle and moisten the tongue with 2 cups white wine. Bring the wine to a boil and simmer until it is reduced to half its original quantity. Add enough thin brown sauce just to cover the tongue, salt and pepper to taste, and a *bouquet garni* of parsley, thyme, celery leaves, and a bay leaf. Cover the braising kettle tightly and cook gently for about 3 hours, or until the tongue is tender.

Place the tongue on a warm platter and surround it with buttered vegetables. Skim the fat and strain the sauce through a fine sieve into a heated sauceboat.

Langue de Boeuf Braisée
BRAISED BEEF TONGUE

SIMMER a smoked tongue, weighing about 4 pounds, in water to cover with a *bouquet garni* of 1 stalk of celery, 3 sprays of parsley, a sprig of thyme, and 1 bay leaf, for about 3 1/2 hours, or until the tongue is tender. Remove the skin and fat from the tongue and cut it into 1/2-inch slices.

In a saucepan melt 1 tablespoon butter, add 1 teaspoon sugar and cook until the sugar is caramelized. Add 2 cups of the liquid in which the tongue

Smoked Tongue in Beer Sauce

was cooked and bring the liquid to a boil. Add the grated rind of 1 lemon, 1 bay leaf, and 1 cup beer. Bring the sauce again to a boil, correct the seasoning, and add the sliced tongue. When the slices are heated through, arrange them on a warmed serving platter and serve the sauce separately.

Smoked Beef Tongue with Fruit Sauce

MELT 1 tablespoon butter, stir in 1 teaspoon flour, and add gradually 1/2 cup tarragon vinegar and 1/4 cup red wine, stirring constantly until the sauce is smooth and thickened. Add 1/2 cup sugar, stir until the sugar is dissolved, and add 1/4 teaspoon each of ground cloves and cinnamon. Add 1 cup soaked pitted prunes, 1/2 cup seedless raisins, and 1/4 cup blanched almonds.

Put a smoked beef tongue, cooked, skinned, and trimmed as for smoked tongue in beer sauce, in a heavy kettle and pour the sauce over it. Simmer the tongue in the sauce very gently for 30 minutes, turning it occasionally and basting it frequently. Slice the tongue thinly on a hot platter, surround it with the fruit and nuts, and pour some of the sauce over it. Serve the rest of the sauce separately.

Grilled Deviled Beef Tongue

SPLIT a beef tongue, cooked, skinned, and trimmed, in half lengthwise. Spread the surface of both halves with prepared mustard and coat them with buttered fine bread crumbs. Place them about 4 inches from the broiler and grill them slowly until the crumbs are golden brown. Serve with *sauce diable*.

Langue de Boeuf au Gratin

BEEF TONGUE
CASSEROLE

SLICE a cold cooked beef tongue as thinly as possible. Combine 6 small gherkins, chopped, 3 scallions, chopped, 1 tablespoon chopped parsley, 1/4 cup each of dry bread crumbs and white wine, and salt and pepper to taste. Spread a buttered casserole with half of the crumb mixture, add the slices of tongue, and cover with the remaining crumbs. Bake in a slow oven (300° F.) for about 30 minutes until the meat is heated through and the topping is browned.

Braised Tongue

PUT a 4- to 5-pound fresh tongue in boiling water and simmer it for 2 hours. Remove it from the water, skin it, and remove the fat and tough portions. Put the tongue in a deep pan with 1/3 cup each of carrots, celery, and onion, all diced, and a sprig of parsley. Heat 1/4 cup butter, add 1/4 cup flour, and cook the *roux* until it is golden. Add 4 cups water in which the tongue was cooked, salt, pepper, and a few drops of Worcestershire sauce, and pour the liquid over the tongue. Bake it for 2 hours in a slow oven (300° F.), turning it after 1 hour.

Although calf's liver brings the highest price at the meat market, it has a worthy rival in the far less expensive pork liver, which is equally tender and delicate in flavor. Beef liver has its adherents; the preferred variety comes from a young steer. The recipes for all three are interchangeable.

HAVE the butcher lard a whole calf's liver with strips of fat salt pork. In a deep pan just large enough to hold the liver put 1 tablespoon butter. Add 2 medium onions, sliced, 2 carrots, sliced, 1 garlic clove, and a faggot made by tying together 1 stalk of celery, 4 sprigs of parsley, 1 small bay leaf and 1 sprig of thyme. In another pan heat 2 tablespoons butter or suet, and in it brown the liver on all sides. Put the liver on the vegetables and cook them together over low heat until the onions and carrots start to brown.

Foie de Veau Braisé au Bordeaux

BRAISED
CALF'S LIVER
IN BORDEAUX

Add 2 tablespoons flour to the fat in the pan in which the liver was browned and cook the *roux* for a few minutes, stirring it constantly. Add 2 cups red wine and 1 cup water or stock, and cook, stirring, until the sauce is smooth. Strain the sauce over the liver. If necessary, add water to cover the liver well. Cover the pan and braise the liver in a moderately hot oven (375° F.) for 2 to 2 1/2 hours, turning it occasionally. Remove the liver to a serving dish. If the liquid has not already cooked down to about half the original quantity, reduce it further. Strain the sauce, skim off the fat, correct the seasoning, and serve the sauce with the liver.

DIP 6 thick slices of calf's liver in flour and sauté them gently in 6 tablespoons hot butter for about 3 minutes on each side. Remove the liver to a warmed platter, add 1/2 cup white wine to the pan, and stir in all the brown crustiness from the bottom and sides of the pan. Add 1 tablespoon finely chopped sweet basil and 2 tablespoons butter. Swirl the pan over the heat until the butter is melted and pour the sauce over the liver.

Calf's Liver and Sweet Basil

CUT 1 1/2 pounds calf's liver into finger-length strips, discarding the skin and tubes. Toss the liver strips in flour seasoned with salt, pepper, and paprika.

Calf's Liver Fines Herbes

Heat 1/4 cup butter in the blazer of a chafing dish placed directly over the heat and when it foams add the liver and sauté the strips for several minutes until they are brown, stirring frequently. Add 1/2 cup dry white wine and 1/2 teaspoon each of chopped parsley, chervil, tarragon, and chives and continue to cook for 2 minutes longer, stirring. Sprinkle the liver with 1 teaspoon lemon juice and serve from the blazer.

Calf's Liver in Sour Cream

BROWN 6 slices of calf's liver in 2 tablespoons hot butter and transfer them to a heatproof serving dish. In the same pan, melt 1/4 cup butter. Add 1/4 cup flour, stir well and add 1 teaspoon concentrated tomato paste, 1 teaspoon meat extract or *glace de viande* and 1 small garlic clove, crushed. Add slowly 1 1/2 cups light stock or water and 1/4 cup Sherry, and stir the sauce over moderate heat until it comes to a boil. Add slowly 1 cup sour cream, and heat the sauce well without permitting it to a boil again. Stir in 3 tablespoons Parmesan cheese and season the sauce with salt and freshly ground pepper to taste. Pour the sauce over the liver in the serving dish, dot it with butter, and sprinkle it with 2 tablespoons grated Parmesan. Set the dish in a moderate oven (350° F.) for about 10 minutes or until the cheese melts and browns.

Calf's Liver Mousse

MAKE 1 cup rich cream sauce. Let it cool slightly and stir in the beaten yolks of 2 eggs. Combine the sauce with 2 cups ground sautéed calf's liver, 1 small onion, finely chopped, 1 garlic clove, minced, 1/2 teaspoon each of salt and pepper, 1 tablespoon chopped parsley, and 2 tablespoons Madeira or brandy. Fold in the stiffly beaten whites of 2 eggs, pour the mixture into a buttered casserole, and dot the top with butter. Cover the casserole with wax paper, set it in a pan containing about 1 inch of hot water, and bake it in a moderately slow oven (325° F.) for 1 hour. Serve the mousse with mushroom Madeira sauce.

Foie de Porc aux Oignons
PORK LIVER WITH ONIONS

COOK 2 onions, sliced, in 2 tablespoons butter until they are golden brown. Season them with a little salt and pepper. Season 6 slices of pork liver with salt and pepper and rub them with a little flour. In another pan heat 3 tablespoons pork fat and in it brown the pork liver quickly on both sides. Remove the liver to a serving dish and keep it warm. Discard the fat from the pan but do not wash the pan. Add to the pan 2 tablespoons vinegar and the onions, and bring the mixture just to a boil. Cover the liver with the onions and sprinkle with chopped parsley.

Preparation of Calves' Brains

Remove the membranes and blood from the calves' brains and wash them well in cold water. Soak them in a large amount of cold water for several hours, changing the water frequently. Drain them, put them in a saucepan with water to cover and add 2 tablespoons vinegar, 1 teaspoon salt, 5 peppercorns, 1/2 onion, sliced, 1 small carrot, sliced, and a bouquet garni made by tying together 4 sprigs of parsley with a bay leaf and a little thyme. Bring the water to a boil, cover the saucepan, and simmer the brains for 25 to 30 minutes. Remove from the heat and leave the brains in their cooking liquor until ready to prepare. They should always be covered with the water.

CLEAN and cook 3 calves' brains. Drain them, and cut each one into 6 slices, 3 from each side. Dip the slices in flour and sauté them in hot oil or butter until they are brown on both sides. To serve, melt 6 tablespoons butter and cook it to a hazelnut-brown color. Pour the butter over the brains, sprinkle with parsley, and serve with a slice of lemon. The brains may be sprinkled with a few capers.

Calves' Brains Sauté

CLEAN and cook 3 calves' brains. Drain them, and cut them into thick slices. Dip the slices in flour and brown them on both sides in butter. Lightly brown about 10 slices of Canadian bacon on both sides in a little butter.

Cut into rather large julienne 1/8 pound each of lean cooked ham, smoked tongue, and cooked mushrooms, and 2 or 3 truffles. Make 1 1/2 cups *demi-glace* sauce flavored with Madeira and color it with tomato purée. Add to the sauce 1 teaspoon tarragon and combine it with the julienne.

Arrange the slices of brains and bacon alternately in an overlapping circle on a serving platter and surround them with a ring of the combined sauce and julienne. Sprinkle the garnish with chopped parsley.

Cervelles de Veau Zingara
CALVES' BRAINS ZINGARA

MELT 2 tablespoons butter and stir in 2 tablespoons flour. Add slowly 2 cups chicken stock and cook, stirring, until the sauce is smooth. Add 10 tiny peeled white onions and 1/4 pound mushrooms, stemmed. Simmer the vegetables until the onions are tender, about 30 minutes. Add 3 pairs cooked calves' brains, sliced, and simmer them for 15 minutes. Transfer the brains to a heated platter. Beat 2 egg yolks, stir in a little of the hot sauce, and return the eggs to the pan. Heat the sauce, but do not let it boil again.

Finish the sauce with 1 tablespoon lemon juice and pour it over the brains.

Cervelles de Veau à la Poulette
CALVES' BRAINS POULETTE

Veal kidneys are the first choice; their flavor is milder than that of lamb, and they are more tender and more delicate than the beef kidneys.

Rognons de Veau Sautés Badoise
VEAL KIDNEYS BADEN

REMOVE the membranes and tubes and trim the surplus fat from 4 veal kidneys, cut the kidneys in thin slices and season them with salt and pepper. Melt enough of the kidney fat to cover the bottom of a shallow pan. Cook the sliced kidneys in the hot fat over high heat for 5 to 6 minutes. Remove the kidneys from the heat and drain them in a colander. Discard the fat from the pan, but do not wash the pan. To the pan add 2 tablespoons butter and 1/2 pound sliced mushrooms, and cook the mushrooms until they are tender. Add 1 tablespoon chopped shallot and cook for 2 minutes longer. Add 1/3 cup dry white wine and 1 cup brown sauce.

Bring the mixture to a boil and add 1 teaspoon each of chopped parsley, tarragon and chervil, and 1/2 teaspoon chopped chives. Add 1 tablespoon butter and with a circular motion of the pan swirl the butter until it melts. Return the kidneys to the sauce and reheat them, but do not let the sauce boil. Serves 4.

Rognons de Veau au Chablis
VEAL KIDNEYS IN CHABLIS

REMOVE the skin from 4 veal kidneys and split the kidneys lengthwise. Remove the center core and slice each kidney crosswise into 3 pieces. Melt 2 tablespoons butter in a heavy casserole and add the slices of kidney and salt and pepper to taste. Cook the slices over very high heat for 5 minutes. Remove them to a warm platter and to the casserole add 5 large mushrooms, quartered. Cook them for 5 minutes and remove them to the warm platter. To the casserole add 1/2 teaspoon chopped shallots and cook them for 2 minutes, add 1/2 cup Chablis and cook until the liquid is reduced by half. Add 1/2 cup veal stock and cook the sauce for 2 minutes longer. Return the kidneys and mushrooms to the sauce in the casserole and add 1 tablespoon butter to thicken the sauce. Serves 4.

Preparation of Hearts

Veal hearts weigh about 1 pound each (it takes 2 or 3 to serve 6 persons) and are best for choice. Beef hearts, which weigh 3 1/2 to 4 pounds, are liable to be tougher. Pork hearts and lamb hearts, which are both slightly smaller than veal hearts, (allow 3 to serve 6 persons) also require tenderizing. An overnight soaking in buttermilk or sour milk or in water acidulated with a little vinegar will soften all. Split the heart and cut away the veins and hard parts within. Then follow any of the recipes.

WASH 3 veal hearts in several changes of cold water and cut out the veins and arteries and make a pocket for the stuffing. Cover the hearts with buttermilk and let them marinate in this tenderizing liquid for 1 hour or more.

Brown 3/4 pound sausage meat and remove the meat from the fat. In the fat brown lightly 3/4 cup each of chopped onion and chopped mushrooms. Toss the vegetables, meat, and fat with 1 1/2 cups soft bread crumbs. Add pepper and salt, if necessary, and 1 generous tablespoon chopped parsley.

Dry the hearts well, divide the stuffing evenly among them, and tie them securely with kitchen twine. Dredge the hearts lightly with flour and brown them quickly on all sides in butter in a casserole. Add 1 1/2 cups each of red wine and water, cover the casserole, and simmer the hearts until they are tender, about 2 hours, turning them occasionally.

Remove the strings, slice the hearts crosswise, and arrange the slices on a heated serving platter. Pour the sauce over them. If the sauce in the casserole seems too thin, thicken it slightly with a little *beurre manié*.

Braised Veal Hearts

SAUTÉ 1 pound mushroom caps in 1 tablespoon olive oil until lightly browned. Sprinkle them with salt and pepper and pour over them 2 tablespoons tomato paste mixed with 3/4 cup warm water. Cover the pan and simmer the mushrooms for 15 minutes over moderate heat.

Heat 2 tablespoons olive oil in a skillet and in it brown 3 veal hearts, thinly sliced, on both sides. Sprinkle the slices with salt and pepper and cook them over high heat for 5 minutes. Pour over them the mushrooms and sauce and cook them for 1 minute longer.

Veal Hearts and Mushrooms

SLICE a medium beef heart very thinly into a bowl with 3 tablespoons olive oil, 1/2 teaspoon salt, and 1/4 teaspoon pepper. Marinate the slices in the olive oil for 30 minutes, turning them frequently.

Sauté 1 garlic clove in 2 tablespoons olive oil. When it is brown, remove it and add the slices of heart. Brown them well on both sides over high heat and cook them for 8 minutes, turning them frequently. Add 3 anchovy filets, chopped, and cook them for 1 minute longer.

Arrange the heart slices and chopped anchovies on a heated serving dish and sprinkle them with salt, pepper, 2 teaspoons lemon juice, and 1 teaspoon chopped parsley. Serve immediately.

Pan Fried Heart Slices

Lamb Hearts en Casserole WASH 3 to 6 lamb hearts in warm water, dry them, and trim them. Roll them in flour and brown them on all sides in bacon drippings. Put the hearts in a casserole with 1 onion, chopped, 1 garlic clove, halved, 1 cup chopped tomatoes, and 1 bay leaf. Sprinkle with salt and pepper and pour in 1 cup tomato juice. Cover the casserole and bake in a moderate oven (325° F.) for 2 hours, turning the hearts several times during the cooking and adding a little more tomato juice as it may be needed.

To serve, arrange the hearts on a warmed serving platter and strain the gravy over them.

Tripe requires long slow cooking to transform it from a tough and rubbery bit of meat to a delightfully chewy, succulent morsel.

Tripes à la Saintongeaise CHOP 2 pounds calf's feet and cut 2 pounds tripe into large julienne. Combine 2 leeks, thoroughly washed and chopped, 2 cups diced carrots, 1 cup each of diced turnips and button mushrooms, 1 heart of celery, chopped, 20 small white onions, and 1 garlic clove, minced.

Put a layer of the chopped calf's feet and tripe in a large kettle and cover it with a layer of the mixed vegetables. Continue to add layers of meat and vegetables and season each layer with a little salt, pepper, nutmeg, parsley, and mustard. Pour in about 6 cups bouillon and 2 cups white wine, using just enough to cover the meat and vegetables. Bring the liquid to a boil, cover the kettle tightly, and cook the mixture over very low heat for 16 to 18 hours. Remove the fat from the surface before serving in a heated casserole.

Tripe Bordelaise PARBOIL 2 pounds tripe in salted water for 1 1/2 to 2 hours, drain it, and cut it into large julienne. Sauté 3 onions, chopped, in 2 tablespoons butter until golden. Add 1 garlic clove, chopped, 4 tomatoes, peeled, seeded, and chopped, 1 cup canned tomatoes or 1/2 cup tomato sauce, the tripe, 1 cup chicken stock, 1/2 teaspoon salt, a little pepper, and a *bouquet garni* of 3 sprigs of parsley, 2 stalks of celery, 1 bay leaf, and a sprig of thyme. Bring the liquid to a boil, cover, and cook over very low heat or in a moderate oven (350° F.) for about 3 hours, or until the tripe is tender. Add a little additional stock from time to time if necessary.

When ready to serve, discard the *bouquet garni*, skim the fat from the surface, correct the seasoning, and sprinkle with finely chopped parsley.

The extremities of meat animals are as delicious—and as neglected— as their innards.

CUT 2 oxtails, each weighing about 3 pounds, into serving pieces, put the pieces in a heavy kettle with 2 tablespoons lard, 3 slices of bacon, chopped, 2 onions and 1 carrot, both chopped, and 1 tablespoon chopped parsley, and brown the meat and vegetables well. Add 1/2 teaspoon each of salt and pepper and 1 1/2 cups dry red wine and simmer over low heat until the wine is almost evaporated. Add 1/4 cup tomato paste and water to just cover the meat, cover the kettle, and simmer for 4 hours. Add 6 stalks of celery, cut into pieces, and cook for 20 minutes.

Oxtail Roman Style

HEAT 2 tablespoons salad oil in a Dutch oven or a heavy kettle with a tight-fitting cover. Add 2 large oxtails, cut into sections about 1 1/2 to 2 inches in length, and brown the pieces well on all sides. Blend together 2 teaspoons each of chili powder, dry mustard, cornstarch or arrowroot, and salt. Stir in 1 1/2 cups orange juice, 2 tablespoons lemon juice, and a generous dash of Worcestershire sauce to make a smooth paste.

Add the paste and 1/2 cup seedless raisins to the browned oxtails and bring the mixture to the boiling point. Lower the heat, cover the kettle tightly, and simmer the meat for 2 to 2 1/2 hours, or until it is quite tender when tested with a fork. Stir in 1 cup ripe olives, coarsely chopped, 3 slices of pimiento, drained and cut in thin strips, and 3 stalks of celery, cut into thin diagonal slices. Continue simmering the meat and vegetables for 20 to 25 minutes longer. Serve with hot fluffy rice.

Oxtails with Olives

THE pigs' feet are cut very long to include most of the hock. Wrap them in cheesecloth to prevent the skin from breaking and poach them in salted, seasoned water until they are tender. Remove the cheesecloth and dry the feet. Then roll them in crumbs, grill, and serve with the following sauce: Add 3 shallots, chopped, and 8 peppercorns, crushed, to 1/3 cup dry white wine or vinegar and cook until reduced to a thick paste. Add 1 cup brown sauce, 1 teaspoon Worcestershire sauce, and 1/2 teaspoon minced parsley.

Pieds de Porc à l'Escargot

WRAP pigs' feet in cheesecloth to prevent the skin from breaking and poach them in salted, seasoned water until they are tender. Remove the cheesecloth and serve the hot *pieds* with the following sauce. In a saucepan heat 1/2 cup white wine and 1 tablespoon vinegar and let the liquid reduce

Pigs' Feet Sainte-Menehould

a little. Then add 1 tablespoon butter, 2 tablespoons finely chopped onion, 1/4 teaspoon salt, a pinch of thyme, 1 bay leaf, crumbled, and 1 cup *demi-glace* sauce. Cook the sauce for a few minutes and then add 1 teaspoon dry mustard, 1 tablespoon each of chopped sour pickle and finely chopped parsley and chervil, and a pinch of cayenne. Pour the sauce over the pigs' feet.

Deviled Pigs' Feet WASH and split in half 6 pigs' feet and put them in a kettle with 2 onions, 1 garlic clove, split, 2 bay leaves, 6 peppercorns, crushed, 1 lemon, sliced, 1 teaspoon salt, and 8 cloves. Cover the pigs' feet with water, bring the water to a boil, and simmer for about 2 1/2 hours, or until the feet are tender. Drain and cool.

Arrange the pigs' feet in a shallow pan, spread them with a mixture of 6 tablespoons each of English mustard and olive oil, and sprinkle them with 6 tablespoons fine bread crumbs. Broil the pigs' feet until they are golden and serve with mustard sauce, sauerkraut, and mashed potatoes.

Pigs' Knuckles and Sauerkraut PUT 2 pounds pigs' knuckles into a large saucepan with water to cover, add 1 stalk of celery, 1 parsnip, 2 carrots, and 1 leek, all cleaned and sliced, and salt and pepper to taste, and bring the water to a boil. Simmer the pigs' knuckles for 3 hours. Remove the knuckles from the broth and keep them hot, strain the broth through a fine sieve, and bring the broth again to a boil.

While the pigs' knuckles are cooking simmer 2 pounds sauerkraut with 2 apples and 1 onion, both peeled and chopped, for at least 2 hours. Serve the knuckles with the sauerkraut, potatoes cooked in their jackets, and the broth.

The need to make a little meat go a long way—a need encountered by most people at some time—has its happy results; among them, stuffed vegetables.

Stuffed Peppers WASH 12 peppers, cut a slice from the top of each, and remove the seeds and membranes. Cut out the stems carefully, reserving the tops for covers.

Sauté 1 1/2 pounds ground round steak in 2 tablespoons hot oil for 5 minutes. Add 6 tablespoons butter and 3 onions, finely chopped, and sauté for another 5 minutes. Add 1 cup uncooked rice and continue to sauté for 10 minutes, stirring constantly. Add 2 1/2 cups cooked, canned tomatoes, 1 teaspoon cinnamon, and salt and pepper and cook for 2 minutes.

Stuff the peppers with this mixture, replace the tops to keep the stuffing in place, and arrange them in a buttered baking pan. Add 1 1/2 cups hot beef stock or water and bake the peppers in a moderate oven (375° F.) for 1 hour, basting occasionally with the pan juices.

COMBINE 1/2 pound each of ground veal and pork, 1 tablespoon grated onion, and 1/4 cup bread crumbs. Season the mixture with salt and pepper and stir in gradually 1/2 cup each of cream and water.

Wash 2 pounds endives, split them, and remove the center cores, being careful not to break the outer leaves. Reserve the cores for salad and fill the outer leaves with the seasoned ground meat. Put two endive halves together and tie them securely with thread. Arrange the stuffed endives in a saucepan and sprinkle lightly with salt and pepper. Add 1/4 cup butter, cover the saucepan tightly, and braise the endives over low heat for 1 hour. Remove the threads before serving.

Endives Farcies
STUFFED ENDIVES

WASH 6 small summer squash or zucchini of uniform size and shape. Remove the tops and carefully scoop out some of the pulp with a thin-bladed knife, taking care not to break the skin.

Grind 1/2 pound lamb with 1 onion and brown the mixture lightly in butter. Add 1/4 cup shelled pine nuts and stir the mixture over the heat for a few minutes longer, until the nuts are brown. Stuff the squash with the mixture and replace the tops.

Put 2 or 3 lamb bones and the squash pulp in the bottom of a saucepan. Arrange the squash in rows over the bones and add 4 tomatoes, quartered, 1 teaspoon salt, and 1 cup water. Invert a plate on top of the squash, cover the saucepan, and bring the mixture to a boil. Simmer gently for about 1 hour and serve very hot. The stuffed squash must be removed to a platter without breaking the delicate skin.

Koosa Mahshie
STUFFED SQUASH

BREAK off the large outside leaves of a head of cabbage, pour boiling water over them, and let them stand for 10 minutes, or until the leaves are soft and pliable. Reserve the rest of the head for another use.

To make the stuffing, combine 1 pound ground beef, 1 beaten egg, 2 onions, finely chopped, 1 cup rice, 1/4 cup soft butter, 1/2 teaspoon cinnamon, and salt and pepper to taste. Moisten the stuffing with enough

Lahano-dolmades
GREEK STUFFED
CABBAGE LEAVES

hot water to make a soft paste and put about 1 tablespoon of it in the center of each cabbage leaf. Fold over the edges of the leaves and roll securely. Arrange the filled leaves side by side in a saucepan, dot them with 1/4 cup butter, and add 1 cup water. Weight the *dolmades* with a plate to prevent them from breaking, cover the saucepan, and cook the rolls for 35 minutes, or until the rice is tender.

Put the *dolmades* on a warmed serving platter. Beat 1 egg with the juice of 1/2 lemon, add the pan gravy, beating constantly, and pour the sauce over the cabbage rolls.

Laulaus with Curry Sauce

IN a saucepan melt 2 tablespoons butter and in it sauté 2 1/2 pounds finely diced lamb, well dusted with flour, until browned. Wash large spinach leaves. Arrange them in pairs, edges overlapping, to make larger leaves. Place a tablespoon of the browned lamb on each pair and sprinkle the lamb with finely chopped onion, salt, and freshly ground black pepper. Roll the leaves up, place each roll on 2 crossed cornhusks, and tie the corners of the husks together to form a package. Tie each package with string and steam the packages in a covered kettle for 2 hours. Remove the string and cornhusks and serve the *laulaus* with this Hawaiian curry sauce: In a saucepan melt 1 1/2 tablespoons butter and in it sauté 1 onion and 1 green gingerroot, both finely chopped, and 1 garlic clove, minced, until the onion is lightly browned. Add 1 tablespoon curry powder and 1/2 teaspoon brown sugar and mix well. Stir in 2 tablespoons flour and gradually add 4 cups coconut milk, stirring constantly. Cook, stirring, for about 10 minutes, or until the sauce is slightly thickened. Correct the seasoning with salt.

Onions with Almonds

PEEL medium onions, scrape the roots, and cut off the tops about 1/4 inch down. Boil the onions until they are almost tender, drain, and scoop out the insides, leaving 2 outer layers of onion. Chop the insides, and for each cupful add 1/4 cup each of melted butter, bread crumbs, and ground ham and 1/2 cup toasted chopped almonds. Season with salt and pepper. Stuff the onions and arrange them in a baking dish. Sprinkle a few bread crumbs on each and top with a split blanched almond and a little melted butter. Pour a little light cream into the dish and bake the onions in a moderately hot oven (375° F.) until they are tender.

Game

Today almost any game bird may be purchased through the kind offices of your butcher. Such birds are usually ready to cook and eat. But the hunter who shoots his own must know how to handle his birds. He should cool them in the open, so that the air can circulate freely around them, and delay plucking and drawing no longer than it takes him to reach camp or home. The birds should be plucked dry so that the skin will remain intact, and then hung again in a cool, airy place for the indicated length of time. It is generally safer to assume that a bird of unknown age and habitat is old and therefore tough, although rounded spurs and a flexible breastbone usually point to a younger bird.

Larding and Barding

MOST game birds are dry and lean of flesh, and require generous applications of fat in the cooking. Birds of any size may be barded by wrapping them in thin sheets of "larding pork," fat salt pork. Or large birds may be larded thus: Put a short larding needle part way into the flesh, thread it with a strip of pork, and push the needle out about an inch from the place where it was inserted. Pull the strip through so that the ends hang out. Usually 10 to 12 strips are required for the breast of a large bird. Pork fat is fragile and breaks easily; the experienced hand with the larding needle works very slowly and carefully, and avoids jerky movements that might tear the strips.

Wild duck, cooked à point—*there is some discussion as to the degree of rareness permissible, but no argument in favor of well done, and therefore dry, tough, and thus badly done duck—is an epicure's delight. All wild duck, mallard, canvasback, teal, and the rest should hang for at least 24 hours, and preferably for 48 hours, before cooking. The hanging serves a double purpose: it makes the flesh tender and it enhances the bird's exquisite flavor.*

Canards Sauvages Braisés à l'Ecu de France
BRAISED MALLARDS

CLEAN 3 mallard ducks and hang them for 48 hours. Singe the birds, wipe them inside and out with a damp cloth, and brush them several times inside and out with armagnac or Cognac.

To make the stuffing, cook the livers in a little chicken broth until tender, drain, and rub them through a coarse sieve. Cut 1/2 pound lean salt pork into small pieces, blanch them for 10 minutes in boiling water, and put them through the coarse blade of a food chopper. Add the sieved duck livers, 1 cup coarsely chopped onion, 1 garlic clove, chopped, 3 tablespoons each of parsley, green celery leaves, chives, and shallots, all finely chopped, 1 tablespoon chervil, 1/2 cup each of chopped pitted green olives and chopped mushrooms, 1 truffle, chopped, salt and pepper to taste, and a generous dash of nutmeg and thyme. Bind the stuffing with 3 egg yolks beaten with 1/3 cup brandy and stuff the cavities of the birds loosely.

Heat 1/3 cup equal parts of butter and olive oil in a braising kettle large enough to accommodate the 3 ducks. Add 1/4 cup each of chopped carrots, onions, celery, and green pepper, 1 large white leek, thinly sliced, 1/2 cup chopped raw lean veal, 2 cloves, a little salt, 8 bruised peppercorns, and a *bouquet garni* consisting of 1 bay leaf, 8 sprigs of parsley, and 1 sprig of thyme. Cook the *mirepoix* over high heat, stirring constantly, until it is well browned. Stir in 1/2 cup each of chicken stock and dry white wine and simmer the mixture for 15 minutes.

Brown the ducks on all sides in a mixture of equal parts of olive oil and butter and put them in the braising kettle. Cover the kettle tightly and braise the birds in a moderately hot oven (375° F.) for about 1 hour, or until they are tender. Turn them from time to time but do not prick the skin.

Arrange the birds on a heated platter and garnish with mushroom caps and artichoke bottoms, sautéed until tender in butter, and pitted green olives cooked in a little olive oil and well drained.

Braised Mallards

*Roast
Wild Duck
Provencale*

STONE 1 dozen ripe olives and soak them for 1 hour in a little olive oil flavored with a sliver of garlic. In a skillet sauté 1 onion and 3 tender stalks of celery, all finely chopped, in 1/4 cup butter until they are soft. Remove the skillet from the heat and add 3/4 cup toasted bread crumbs, the olives, 2 teaspoons Cognac, and salt and pepper to taste.

Divide this stuffing between 2 large wild ducks. Truss the ducks, butter the breasts generously, and sprinkle with salt and pepper. Place the ducks on a rack in a roasting pan, pour over them 1/2 cup red wine and 1/4 cup water, and roast them in a very hot oven (450° F.) for about 30 minutes, depending on the size of the ducks. Baste them frequently with the pan juices. Remove the ducks to a heated platter, skim off most of the fat from the pan juices, and stir in 1/2 tablespoon cornstarch mixed to a paste with a little cold water. Stir the gravy until it is smooth and slightly thickened. Correct the seasoning and swirl in 2 tablespoons butter. Pour a little of the gravy over the ducks and serve the rest in a heated sauceboat.

*Suprêmes
de Canards
Sauvages
à la Fine
Champagne*

BREASTS OF
WILD DUCK
IN BRANDY SAUCE

CLEAN 2 or 3 wild ducks and truss the legs and wings close to the body. Put the roasting pan in the oven and bring the temperature to very hot (450° F.). Put the ducks in the hot pan and cook them for 12 to 15 minutes, depending upon the weight of the birds. (Wild ducks are never served well done.) Let the ducks stand for about 10 minutes, then remove the breasts, and put them where they will keep warm but not cook. Save the blood. Chop the remaining carcasses and press in a duck press or, lacking a press, break up the carcasses and put them through a food chopper using the coarsest blade and strain the juice through a fine sieve.

Prepare the following sauce: Sauté 1 or 2 chicken or duck livers, chopped, in hot fat or butter for 2 to 3 minutes, turning them as they cook. They should be rare. Sprinkle them with salt and pepper. In another pan put 1 tablespoon chopped shallot, 1 small bay leaf, a little thyme, 5 peppercorns, and 6 tablespoons red wine, and cook slowly until the wine is reduced by one-third. Stir in 2 tablespoons brown sauce and bring again to a boil. Add the cooked livers, mix well, and pass through a fine sieve. Return the sauce to the pan and add very gradually the blood saved when the breasts were carved and the juice from the carcasses, having first skimmed off all the fat. Stir vigorously while reheating but do not boil or the sauce will curdle. Add 2 tablespoons Cognac. Slice the breasts, arrange the slices on a serving dish, and pour the sauce over them. Garnish with crescents of bread sautéed in butter.

WIPE 3 canvasback or other wild ducks inside and out with a damp cloth, then with a cloth dipped in gin. Stuff the birds with 1 crab apple, pared and cored, 1 tablespoon butter, 1 small onion stuck with 2 cloves, a small piece of celery stalk, 2 sprigs of parsley, and 1 small shallot. Sew up the opening, rub the birds with butter, and sprinkle them with a little freshly ground black pepper. Roast the ducks rapidly on a rotary spit for 15 to 20 minutes, basting them with melted butter and red wine. The flesh should be rare and bloody.

Spit Roasted Wild Duck

Remove the ducks from the spit, pour 1/2 cup warmed Cognac over them, ignite the spirit, and let the flame die. Carve the birds into serving portions. Combine the juices from the carving, the pan juices, and 1/4 cup red wine. Stir in a *beurre manié* composed of 1 tablespoon butter blended with 1 tablespoon flour, cook the sauce for a few minutes, and correct the seasoning with salt.

If your bag should include a goose of patriarchal stature, only braising —long, slow cooking in the moist heat of a covered kettle in the oven or on top of the stove—will make it tender. A tough old bird may be marinated as venison is marinated, and then braised in the marinade. If the bird is young, it may be prepared like wild duck.

DRAW a wild goose and hang it for about 5 days in a cool room; then pluck and singe it. Wipe the bird inside and out with a damp cloth and stuff it with raw apple quarters. Truss the goose, tying the legs and wings close to the body. Sprinkle with salt and pepper.

Roast Young Wild Goose

Roast the goose on a rack in a very hot oven (500° F.) for 30 minutes. Reduce the temperature to slow (300° F.), cover the pan, and roast the goose for 2 to 3 hours, or until the tines of a fork slip easily into the breast. Baste frequently with hot chicken stock and pour off the excess goose fat as it accumulates. Save this fat for other uses. Uncover the pan for the last 30 minutes of roasting.

RICE 10 boiled potatoes, reserving the water in which they were cooked. Sauté 1 cup chopped onions and 1/2 cup chopped celery in 1 tablespoon butter or fat until they are partially cooked but not brown. Stir the onions and celery into the potatoes with 1/4 pound ground salt pork, 4 slices of bread, crumbled, 2 beaten eggs, and salt, pepper, and poultry seasoning.

Roast Young Wild Goose with Potato Stuffing

Stuff a young wild goose with this forcemeat and truss it. Roast the goose as above, basting it from time to time with the potato water.

Wild Goose Stew

CUT a wild goose into serving pieces. Wipe the pieces dry with a cloth and place them in an earthenware crock with salt and black pepper, 1 bay leaf, 3 sprigs of parsley, 2 onions, sliced, and a pinch of thyme. Add 2 cups claret and 1/2 cup brandy and let the pieces marinate for several hours or overnight.

Put 1/4 pound bacon or salt pork, diced and parboiled, in a large casserole and heat the casserole for 10 minutes in a hot oven (425° F.). Dry the goose and add it to the casserole. Bake for 20 minutes, turning the pieces frequently to brown all sides. Then add the marinade, 1 garlic clove, crushed, and 2 cups coarsely chopped mushrooms. Add hot water to cover, cover the casserole tightly, reduce the oven temperature to very slow (325° F.), and simmer the goose for 1 hour, or until it is tender. Add a little more water to the casserole during the cooking, if necessary. Serve directly from the casserole with wild rice.

The grouse, in all its many species, is the most honored of American game birds. The gourmet particularly appreciates its characteristic wild flavor. The flesh of the grouse is rich in flavor, but its leanness demands the application of fat. Grouse can be eaten within twenty-four hours of killing, or it can be hung for a brief period.

Spit Roasted Grouse

CLEAN 6 plump grouse, season them with salt and pepper, and wrap them in thin slices of fat salt pork. Arrange them on a spit and roast them for 15 to 20 minutes. Remove the salt pork during the last few minutes of cooking so that the birds will brown. Take the birds from the spit and keep them warm. Skim the fat from the dripping pan and to the remaining pan juices add 1 teaspoon butter and 1/4 cup beef stock for each bird. Reduce this sauce quickly over high heat, stirring and scraping in the brown bits that cling to the pan.

Serve each bird on a piece of toast spread with *rouennaise* and accompanied by bread sauce and red currant jelly in separate dishes.

Broiled Grouse

SPLIT each cleaned grouse—1 to a person—down the back and wipe it well. Press the bird flat, brush it with olive oil, and sprinkle it with salt. Broil it, skin side down, for about 10 minutes. Turn the bird and broil it for 5 to 10 minutes more.

PLUCK, singe, and clean 2 large plump grouse, cut them into serving pieces, and dredge with flour. Melt 1/4 cup butter in a large skillet and in it sauté the pieces of grouse over moderate heat until they are golden on all sides. Sprinkle them with salt and pepper, lower the heat, and cook the grouse until it is tender. Keep the grouse warm.

Grouse in Sour Cream

To the juices in the pan add 2 teaspoons flour and, gradually, 2 cups warm but not boiled sour cream. Cook, stirring to blend all the rich brown bits with the cream, until the sauce is very hot and slightly thickened. Pour the sauce over the grouse. Serve with wild rice and mushrooms.

CLEAN 6 young wood grouse and wipe them with a damp cloth. Rub them inside and out with a cut lemon, sprinkle with salt, and put half a small carrot in each bird. Tie slices of bacon around the breasts and truss the birds. In a heavy kettle melt 1/2 cup butter and in it brown the birds on all sides. Cover the grouse with 1 cup stock and 1 1/2 cups milk, add the livers, and cover the kettle, leaving an opening for the steam to escape. Simmer the birds for 1 1/2 to 2 hours, or until they are tender, basting them frequently during the cooking and turning them every half hour so that they will cook evenly. When the grouse are tender arrange them on a warm serving platter and keep them hot.

Braised Grouse

Add 1 cup heavy cream to the liquid in the kettle and bring to a boil. Mix 1/4 cup flour and 1/2 cup heavy cream to a smooth batter and gradually stir the batter into the liquid. Cook, stirring, until the sauce is thickened. Remove the livers, mash them, and stir them into the sauce. Continue to cook the sauce for 5 minutes. Correct the seasoning.

Carve the birds on the platter and pour the sauce over them. Serve with a side dish of lingonberries or black currant jelly.

Hang partridge for at least four days before cooking it; then proceed in any of the following ways, or as for grouse, quail, or pheasant.

CLEAN 6 plump partridge that have hung for 4 days and rub them inside and out with mixed brandy and lemon juice lightly seasoned with salt and powdered thyme. Rub the birds with butter, wrap a thin sheet of larding pork around each and secure the larding with string. Arrange the partridge on a spit and roast them 20 to 30 minutes, depending on their size. Remove

Roast Partridge

the larding pork during the last few moments of cooking so that the birds will brown. Arrange the birds on a serving platter garnished with parsley or watercress, crisp croutons of bread sautéed in butter, and mushrooms simmered in water with a little lemon juice and sautéed. Serve the birds with the pan juices and accompany them with wild rice and red currant jelly.

Perdreaux Rôtis sur Canapés

ROAST YOUNG PARTRIDGE ON TOAST

CLEAN 6 small or 3 large partridge and truss the legs close to the bodies. Cover the breasts with sliced fat salt pork or bacon and tie the slices in place. Season with salt. Place the birds on their sides in a roasting pan and spread them with good fat. Roast the partridge in a very hot oven (450° F.) for 30 to 35 minutes depending upon their size, basting often. Turn the birds on their backs and cook them for about 5 minutes longer, or until they are done.

Remove the partridge from the oven and discard the trussing strings and the fat pork. Put the birds in a warm place. Pour all of the fat from the pan, add 1 tablespoon butter and, when it melts, add 1 cup water or stock. Cook, stirring in all the brown crustiness around the pan, and strain the gravy into a gravy boat. Serve a whole or half bird, according to size, on toast spread with *rouennaise*.

Salmi of Partridge

ROAST 3 large partridge as indicated for *perdreaux rôtis*, remove the breasts and set the legs and the carcasses aside. Put the breasts on a warm plate and spread them with butter or with fat from the roasting pan to prevent drying. Make a salmi sauce as follows: In 2 tablespoons salad or vegetable oil, sauté 1 onion, chopped, until it is golden brown. Add 1 tablespoon chopped shallot, 1 garlic clove, crushed, and 1 1/2 tablespoons flour and cook 2 minutes longer. Add 3/4 cup red or white dry wine and cook the mixture, stirring constantly, until it thickens. Add 1 cup stock or strained tomatoes, 1/2 teaspoon salt, 4 peppercorns, crushed, a pinch of thyme and a *bouquet garni* made by tying together 2 stalks of celery, 3 sprigs of parsley and 1 small bay leaf. Add the whole legs and the carcass, finely chopped, and simmer the mixture slowly for 1 hour. Strain the sauce and keep it hot.

Slice the leg meat from the bones and arrange it with the sliced breast meat on a serving dish. Simmer 12 mushroom caps in 1/2 cup water with 1 teaspoon butter and the juice of 1 lemon. Drain the mushrooms and use them to garnish the meat. Pour the sauce over the mushrooms and meat. Garnish the platter with triangles of bread sautéed in butter and spread with *rouennaise*.

Other game birds may be cooked in the same way.

ROAST 6 small partridge as for *perdreaux rôtis*, basting them frequently for 30 minutes. Turn the birds on their backs, remove and discard the trussing strings and the fat pork, and cover the breasts with 2 or 3 grape leaves. Continue to roast the birds until they test done. Remove the birds and pour off the fat in the pan. Add 1/4 cup Cognac, 1/3 cup white Burgundy, and 6 to 8 dozen red or white grapes, peeled. Cook the sauce for a few minutes, stirring in all the brown crusty bits in the pan. Add 1/2 cup white stock and 1 tablespoon butter. Arrange the birds on toast spread with *rouennaise* and serve the sauce separately.

Perdreaux aux Raisins
PARTRIDGE WITH GRAPES

SPRINKLE 3 plump, young partridge with salt and pepper to taste and rub them well with butter. Wrap a thin sheet of larding pork around each one and tie it with string. Roast the birds in a moderate oven (350° F.) for about 15 minutes, or until they are done to taste. Remove them from the pan, discard the fat pork, and halve the birds and arrange the halves on a heated serving platter. Skim the fat from the pan juices. Add 1 1/2 cups cream to the roasting pan and cook the liquid until it is reduced to one-third its original volume. Add 1/2 cup velouté sauce and bring the mixture to a boil. Correct the seasoning with salt and add the juice of 1/2 lemon. Serve the sauce separately.

Partridge with Cream Sauce Swedish Style

FOLLOW the directions for partridge with cream sauce Swedish style, substituting 1 tablespoon currant jelly for the lemon juice. Before serving, add to the sauce 2 tablespoons cooked ham cut in thin julienne strips or diced.

Partridge with Cream Sauce Danish Style

CLEAN 3 plump partridge. Cook the partridge livers with 1/2 pound chicken livers in 6 tablespoons melted butter or bacon drippings with 3 shallots, chopped, salt, pepper, 1 bay leaf, a pinch of thyme, and 2 tablespoons chopped parsley for 3 to 4 minutes over very high heat. Discard the bay leaf, force the mixture through a sieve, and bind it with 2 tablespoons brown sauce. Fill the cavities of the partridge with the liver forcemeat, truss them, and tie a strip of bacon over the breasts. Place the partridge side by side in a casserole. Add 1 cup game stock, cover the casserole, and cook the birds in a moderately hot oven (375° F.) for 30 to 40 minutes, or until they are tender. Halve the partridge and arrange the pieces on a warm serving platter. Reduce

Perdreaux à la Polonaise
PARTRIDGE POLISH STYLE

the pan juices to about 1/2 cup and pour it over the birds. Sprinkle the birds with the juice of 1 lemon.

Brown lightly 2 tablespoons fine dry bread crumbs in 6 tablespoons butter. Pour crumbs and butter over the partridge and garnish the platter with lemon slices dipped in chopped parsley.

Partridge Pie

CUT 3 partridge into serving pieces. Melt 5 tablespoons butter in a skillet and sauté the pieces gently until they are brown but not cooked through. Cut 1/2 pound each of veal and smoked ham into thin slices and line a deep, buttered pie dish with the meat slices. Add the partridge, 3 hard cooked eggs, sliced, 9 mushroom caps and salt and pepper to taste. Pour over the mixture 1 cup chicken stock and add another layer of thinly sliced veal and smoked ham. Cover the dish with a pie crust. Press the edges to the rim of the dish and make several slits in the top. Bake the pie in a moderate oven (350° F.) for 40 to 50 minutes. Serve hot or cold.

Chartreuse of Partridge

THIS is a good way to cook older, less tender birds. Clean the bird, truss it, and roast it in a very hot oven (450°F.) for about 20 minutes, turning it from side to side and on its back. Parboil 1 large cabbage, quartered, for 5 minutes. Drain the cabbage, rinse it and drain it again. Put 4 slices of salt pork or bacon in a deep saucepan and add a layer of a third of the cabbage leaves. Lay the bird on the cabbage leaves and add 1 carrot, 1 onion studded with a clove, and a faggot composed of 2 stalks of celery, 3 sprigs of parsley, 1/2 bay leaf, and a pinch of thyme. Add the second third of the cabbage leaves and 1 large piece of uncooked garlic sausage or Italian sausage.

In a separate pan, parboil 1/2 pound fat salt pork for 5 minutes. Drain it and add it to the saucepan.

Cover the pork with the remaining cabbage and add 1 quart stock. Cover the pan with a round of buttered paper with a tiny hole in the center to vent the steam. Adjust the lid of the pan and braise the bird in a moderately hot oven (375° F.) for 35 to 40 minutes, or until the sausage and fat pork are done. Remove and reserve the sausage and fat pork and continue to cook the *chartreuse* until the legs of the partridge fall away from its body, or for about 45 minutes longer. Remove the partridge and the carrot and discard the faggot.

Line a buttered, round-bottomed timbale mold with the sausage, sliced, slices of carrots, and small rectangles of the cooked salt pork in a neat pattern. Fill the timbale with thick layers of the cabbage and partridge meat. Finish with a final layer of cabbage leaves. Press with a fork, tilting the timbale so that any liquid will drain away. To serve, unmold the timbale on a heated platter.

If desired, the timbale need not be used and the partridge meat may simply be served on a bed of the cooked cabbage, garnished with the sausage, carrot, and salt pork.

The flavor of pheasant is only faintly gamy; the gamy quality may be increased by hanging, although it seems a pity to emulate certain hunters who hang a pheasant until its flesh almost literally decomposes and falls from the bones. Four days to a week is long enough to bring the pheasant to its peak of perfection for most of us. Recipes for grouse, partridge, and the like apply equally well to pheasant, which the former closely resemble.

CLEAN a large pheasant and make a stuffing as follows: Cut about 1/2 pound *pâté de foie gras* into large pieces or sauté 1/2 pound fresh goose liver in butter and combine it with 3 or 4 pieces of truffle, a little salt and pepper, a sprinkling of Cognac and 2 tablespoons *glace de viande* or 1 tablespoon beef extract. Stuff the bird and sew the opening neatly. Truss the legs and wings close to the body. Place the pheasant in a buttered roasting pan with 2 tablespoons butter and cover the breasts with slices of fresh larding pork. Cook the pheasant for about 35 to 40 minutes in a hot oven (400° F.). Discard the larding pork and the trussing strings and put the bird in an oval casserole just large enough to hold it. Add to the casserole 10 to 12 pieces of truffle tossed in hot butter. Discard the fat from the roasting pan and add to the remaining juices 1/4 cup Sherry or Madeira, 1/2 cup Madeira sauce, a few spoonfuls of truffle juice, and 2 tablespoons Cognac. Stir the sauce over low heat until it nearly reaches the boiling point and strain it over the pheasant in the casserole. Cover the casserole with a lid that has a small hole in the top to let the steam escape, seal the edges with a stiff paste made with flour and water, and bake the pheasant in a hot oven (400° F.) for 18 to 20 minutes. Serve in the casserole.

Pheasant Suvorov

CLEAN a pheasant and put 2 or 3 stalks of celery into the cavity. Put the bird in a kettle with chicken stock to cover, add 2 stalks of celery, and simmer the bird for about 45 minutes, or until it is tender. Serve with braised celery hearts or purée of celery, wild rice, and *sauce smitane*. Serves 2.

Faisan Poché au Céleri
PHEASANT WITH CELERY

Faisans Rôtis
au Madère

ROAST PHEASANT
WITH MADEIRA

CLEAN and dress 3 small pheasant, rub them with softened sweet butter, and place them on a rack in an open roasting pan. Roast them in a moderately hot oven (375° F.) for 15 minutes. Add 6 tablespoons Madeira and continue to roast for 30 minutes, basting the birds every 10 minutes with the juices in the pan. Fifteen minutes before serving the pheasant place 6 rounds of bread in the pan to brown and to absorb the juices.

Halve the pheasant and set the halves on a bed of watercress, surround them with the croutons, and garnish with slices of lemon.

Pheasant
Braised
in White Wine

SINGE and clean 2 pheasant and wipe them inside and out with a damp cloth. Put 3 shallots, minced, a few thin slices of tart apple, and the pheasant liver into the cavity of each bird. Lace the openings tightly and sauté the pheasant in 6 tablespoons hot butter in a deep skillet for 15 minutes, or until they are brown on all sides. Pour over them 1/4 cup warmed brandy and ignite the spirit. When the flame dies, transfer the birds to an earthenware casserole and keep them hot.

To the skillet in which the pheasant were browned, add 1/2 cup chicken stock and 1 cup dry white wine, stir in the brown bits, simmer for 2 minutes, and pour the sauce over the pheasant. Cover the casserole tightly and bake it in a hot oven (400° F.) for 30 to 40 minutes. Just before serving, add 1 cup hot heavy cream to the juices in the casserole. Correct the seasoning, arrange the pheasant on a hot serving platter, and pour the sauce over the breasts. Garnish with watercress and serve the birds with currant jelly and chestnut purée. Serves 4.

Faisan
à la Choucroute

PHEASANT WITH
SAUERKRAUT

COVER the bottom of a heavy kettle or casserole with 1 pound spareribs and distribute over them 2 pounds sauerkraut. On the sauerkraut put 1 pound smoked breast of pork, 1 dozen juniper berries, 1/2 pound large sausages, 1 onion stuck with 2 cloves, a *bouquet garni* of 4 sprays of parsley, 1 small stalk of celery with the leaves, 1 sprig each of marjoram and thyme, and 1 bay leaf. Top with another 2 pounds sauerkraut and pour over all 4 cups veal stock and 1 bottle dry white wine. Close the kettle with a tight-fitting cover and bake in a slow oven (250° F.), or cook over low heat, for 8 to 10 hours.

Put the sauerkraut on a long serving platter and put in the center of this bed 1 or 2 roasted pheasant, carved in serving pieces. Skim the fat from the pan and spoon the pan juices over the pheasant. Surround it with the sliced pork, grilled small sausages, and a few slices of broiled or baked ham.

SAUTÉ 3 plump pheasant in butter until they are brown. Peel, core, and dice 4 tart green apples, cook them briefly in a little butter, and put them in the bottom of a casserole. Put the browned birds in the casserole and over their breasts pour the butter in which they were browned. Cover the casserole and cook the birds very slowly for about 30 minutes. Add 1/3 cup each of Calvados and cream, and season to taste with salt and a little white pepper. Cover the casserole again and return it to the oven for 15 to 20 minutes longer, until the sauce is thick and the birds are tender.

Pheasant Normandy

The rich, dark meat of doves and pigeons lends itself to the preparation suggested for the tame varieties of the pigeon family (squab). Take the precaution of hanging the doves for 3 or 4 days before cooking them, and exercise some discretion in the selection of a recipe to suit the age and size of the bird: a young bird has darker flesh, less fat, and more flexible bones than its seniors.

Pigeons and Doves

The delicate, white-fleshed quail need not be hung at all; it never tastes better than it does when it is quickly dry-plucked and cleaned, wrapped in bacon slices, and broiled over a camp fire. For other methods of cookery, remember only that the quail is naturally dry, and this lack must be compensated for by larding or similar methods of adding fat.

Quail

SPLIT 6 quail down the back, clean and wipe them, and sauté them in butter until they are tender. Or rub the quail with butter and broil them. Or rub them with butter and roast them 15 to 20 minutes in a very hot oven (450° F.).

Quail: Sautéed, Broiled, or Roasted

PLUCK and clean 6 plump quail and rub them with a little salt and freshly crushed black pepper. Brown them lightly in melted butter and place them in a buttered casserole. To the skillet in which the birds were browned add 1 carrot, diced, 1 small onion, chopped, 2 tablespoons chopped green pepper, 1/2 cup chopped mushrooms, and 3 small slices of blanched orange peel. Cook the vegetables slowly for 5 minutes, stir in 1 tablespoon flour, and add

Quail in Wine

355

Quail Richelieu

gradually, stirring constantly, 1 cup chicken stock. Continue to stir until the sauce is thickened, correct the seasoning with salt and pepper, and simmer slowly for 10 minutes longer.

While the sauce is cooking, pour 1/2 cup white wine over the quail and bake the casserole in a moderate oven (350° F.) for 10 minutes. Pour the sauce over the birds, cover the casserole, and cook the birds for 20 minutes, or until they are tender.

CLEAN 6 tender, young quail and truss the legs close to the body. Wrap the birds in grape leaves, then in large thin slices of fat pork and tie the larding securely with string. Preheat a roasting pan in a very hot oven (450° F.). Lay the birds on their sides in the pan and roast them, basting frequently, for 5 minutes, then turn the birds and roast them for 5 minutes on the other side, and, finally, roast them for 5 minutes on their backs. Discard the larding pork and string.

Quail Richelieu

Remove the birds to a heatproof casserole and add a little water to the juices in the roasting pan, cooking and stirring in the brown crustiness. Parboil 3/4 cup each of carrots, celery, and onion, cut in very fine uniform pieces, for 2 or 3 minutes. Drain the vegetables and cook them until tender in 1 1/2 cups veal or chicken stock. Stir in a *beurre mainé* composed of 2 teaspoons butter kneaded with 1 teaspoon flour. Combine this with the quail juices and heat it well. Pour the sauce over the birds and simmer all together for 4 or 5 minutes longer.

CLEAN 6 tender, young quail and roast them as for quail Richelieu. Or the birds may be stuffed with chopped, sautéed chicken livers, trussed, poached in stock for 10 minutes, and browned under the broiler for 3 or 4 minutes. Cool the birds thoroughly, discard the salt pork and trussing strings, and prepare a vegetable julienne as for quail Richelieu. Parboil the vegetables, drain them and cook them until tender in 1 1/2 cups veal or chicken stock. To 1 cup of this mixture add 2 tablespoons Madeira or Sherry and 1 tablespoon gelatin softened in 1/4 cup cold water. Arrange the cold quail on a cold serving dish and when the gelatin mixture thickens, carefully spoon it over the birds. Chill the birds in the refrigerator until the gelatin sets. Finish with a final coating of aspic.

Quail Richelieu en Gelée

PLUCK, singe, and draw 6 fat young quail. Remove the heads, wing tips, and feet and reserve them. Stuff each quail with 2 tablespoons *foie gras* and 1 truffle and place the quail in a glass or crockery bowl. Sprinkle the quail

Quail with Muscat Grapes

generously with freshly ground black pepper, pour over them 1 cup Cognac, and marinate for 1 hour.

Put the heads, wing tips, and feet in a saucepan with 1 1/2 cups chicken stock and a *bouquet garni* of 4 sprigs of parsley, 1 small stalk of celery heart and the leaves, 1 sprig of thyme, and half a bay leaf. Bring the stock to a boil and simmer for 1 hour. Strain the broth, add the marinade from the quail, and continue to cook until the liquid is reduced by one-third. Correct the seasoning with salt and pepper. Reserve this broth for later use.

Wrap the quail in grape leaves, cover the breasts with thin slices of salt pork, and tie in place with string. In a roasting pan melt 6 tablespoons butter. Arrange the quail in the pan and roast them in a very hot oven (450° F.) for 15 to 20 minutes. Discard the barding.

Arrange 6 thick rounds of bread, sautéed in butter until crisp and golden, on an ovenproof platter. Place a quail on each crouton and add 1/2 pound muscat grapes, seeded. Heat birds and grapes together in a moderate oven (350° F.). To the juices in the roasting pan add 1/2 cup muscatel, bring it to a boil, and cook over high heat over until it is reduced by half. Add the reduced broth and bring to a boil. Stir in 1 teaspoon flour mixed to a paste with 1 tablespoon butter and cook, stirring, until the sauce is slightly thickened. Correct the seasoning, stir in 1 tablespoon lemon juice, and pour the sauce over the quail.

Wild turkey differs from its barnyard cousin in only one important particular; the wild turkey finds its food where it can and its lean flesh may taste pleasantly of nuts and acorns, or, less pleasantly, of berries not usually considered edible. If your wild turkey seems proud with years, eschew the roasting pan for the braising kettle; otherwise all the methods used for domestic turkey apply. Or cook it like wild goose.

Roast Wild Turkey

PLUCK and clean thoroughly a wild turkey. Rub it inside and out with salt and freshly crushed black pepper, sew up the openings, and truss the bird. Rub the skin with a creamed mixture of 1/3 cup butter and 1/4 cup flour. Lay the bird on a dripping rack in a roasting pan, cover the breast with thin slices of salt pork, and roast in a very hot oven (500° F.) for 30 minutes. When the bird is well browned, pour over it a mixture of 1/2 cup oil, the juice of a lemon, 1 teaspoon freshly ground black pepper, and 1 teaspoon salt. Reduce the temperature to slow (300° F.) and roast the turkey for 2 to

3 hours, depending upon its size. Baste it every 15 minutes with the pan drippings.

Simmer the liver, heart, and gizzard in a little water until they are very tender, drain, and chop finely. Thicken the pan drippings with a little browned flour and add the chopped giblets. Serve the sauce separately.

Among the shore birds likely to fall to the Nimrod's gun, woodcock and snipe are most familiar. These birds may be prepared like duck, but there are some forms of preparation that belong traditionally to them alone.

CLEAN and draw the birds, reserving the livers, and truss the legs close to the body. Tie a thin slice of fresh fat pork around each bird. Season the woodcock with salt and pepper and roast them in a very hot oven (450° F.) for 12 minutes, or until the fat pork is golden brown. Discard the fat pork. Remove the breasts from the birds and set them aside. Chop the carcasses and put them in a small pan. Pour over them 2 tablespoons warmed Cognac and ignite it. Chop the raw livers and add them, with the chopped carcasses, to the juices in the roasting pan in which the birds were cooked. Heat the mixture thoroughly without allowing it to boil and rub it through a fine sieve. Add 1/4 cup Cognac. Sauté slices of bread in butter, spread them with *rouennaise*, and arrange the breasts on them. Pour the sauce over the meat.

Woodcock au Fumet

HAVE a butcher clean and bone the woodcock, which should hang 3 days, reserving the intestines. One bird is a serving, generally. Make a forcemeat of *foie gras* mixed with diced truffles. Season it with salt, pepper, and poultry seasoning to taste and moisten with a few tablespoons of Cognac. Press the intestines of the woodcock through a fine sieve and mix the purée with the forcemeat. Stuff the birds, lard the breasts, and truss them. Sprinkle with salt and pepper.

Roast the woodcock in a well-buttered casserole in a very hot oven (450° F.) for 5 minutes. Reduce the oven temperature to 325° F. and roast the birds for another 15 to 25 minutes, depending on their size, basting them frequently with melted butter.

When the woodcock are almost cooked, put in the casserole 1 truffle, thickly sliced, for each bird and complete the cooking over low heat. Sprinkle the woodcock with warmed *fine Champagne* and ignite the spirit. When the

Bécasses Lucullus
WOODCOCK LUCULLUS

flame dies, stir 1/2 cup game stock into the pan juices and serve in the casserole, garnished with watercress.

The most popular furred game, at least among gourmets who must do their hunting at the butcher's, is venison, the meat of any antlered animal. The butcher will hang deer or elk meat for a period of two to four weeks before he offers it for sale; like beef, it must be well aged. Almost all cuts of venison, with the possible exception of the chops and steaks of a young animal, also need marinating to make them acceptably tender. And since venison, like other wild meat, is very lean, it should be larded through with strips of fat pork and cooked in a generous amount of fat.

Selle de Chevreuil Rôtie

ROAST SADDLE OF VENISON

REMOVE the furred skin from a saddle of venison, the second skin under it, and all the sinews. Cover the saddle in a deep bowl with cooked marinade for game and let it marinate in the refrigerator for 1 to 2 days, turning it frequently so that the marinade will penetrate the meat evenly.

Take the meat from the marinade and drain and dry it well. Lard the top with strips of fat salt pork and cover with slices of fat salt pork. Season the meat with salt, put it in a roasting pan with a generous amount of fat or oil, and roast it in a very hot oven (450° F.), basting it frequently. Venison should be rare and the time required to cook a saddle depends on its size. A 5- to 6-pound saddle takes about 45 minutes to 1 hour. About 15 minutes before the meat is done, add turned mushrooms that have been simmered for 5 minutes in a little water.

Remove the slices of fat pork, place the meat on a warm serving platter, and spread it lightly with *glace de viande*, if you wish. Garnish the saddle with the mushrooms, and garnish the platter with radish roses and watercress. Serve with a sauceboat of *sauce Grand Veneur*.

Roast Leg of Venison Cévennes

SKIN a 3- to 4-pound leg of venison, lard it with thin strips of salt pork, and marinate the meat for 48 hours in 2 cups dry white wine with a good pinch of thyme, 2 sprigs of parsley, 2 bay leaves, 10 peppercorns, 2 cloves, a pinch of savory, and 2 carrots and 2 onions, both sliced. Drain and dry the meat, season it with salt, and put it in a roasting pan on a bed of the vegetables and herbs, which have been drained from the marinade and well dried

Roast Saddle of Venison

between sheets of absorbent paper. Roast the venison in a slow oven (300° F.) for 1 hour, raise the heat to very hot (450° F.), and cook it for 15 minutes more.

Remove the fat from the pan juices, pour 3 to 4 tablespoons warmed Cognac over the meat, and ignite the spirit. When the flame dies, remove the meat, and keep it hot. Strain the marinade into the pan juices and reduce the liquid by one-fourth over high heat. Stir in 1/2 cup heavy cream, correct the seasoning, and serve the sauce with the meat.

Garnish the platter with whole cooked chestnuts and with large prunes, soaked, pitted, and cooked in white wine and stuffed with mousse of *foie gras* made by whipping *foie gras* with a little heavy cream.

Civet de Chevreuil

VENISON STEW

REMOVE and discard skin, bones, and sinews from about 3 pounds venison shoulder or neck. Cut the meat into cubes, put it in a bowl, and cover it with an uncooked marinade. Store the meat in the refrigerator to marinate for a day or two, stirring and turning it from time to time so that the marinade will penetrate it evenly. Drain and dry the meat thoroughly and reserve the marinade. Parboil 1 cup fat salt pork, cut in small dice, in water to cover, then drain it. Heat 1/2 cup salad oil in a heavy skillet and in it brown the salt pork dice. Skim off the cracklings and set them aside. In the hot fat in the pan brown lightly 12 to 15 small white onions. Add 1/2 cup carrots, cut in pieces and lightly sugared, and cook for about 5 minutes, until both onions and carrots are golden brown. Remove the vegetables from the fat with a skimmer and set them aside with the pork dice.

Sauté 1/2 pound cleaned mushrooms in the skillet until they are soft and the moisture is cooked out of them. If the mushrooms are very large, cut them in half. Skim off the mushrooms and put them with the pork and vegetables. Heat the fat well and in it brown the drained and dried venison, a few pieces at a time. Put the browned meat in a saucepan, sprinkle it with 2 tablespoons flour and cook it in the oven or on top of the stove until the flour is browned. Add 1 garlic clove, crushed, 1 tablespoon finely chopped shallot or onion, 3/4 cup red wine, the strained marinade and a faggot made by tying together 2 stalks of celery, 4 sprigs of parsley, 1/2 bay leaf and a pinch of thyme. Add water, if necessary, barely to cover the meat. Bring the liquid to a boil and simmer the meat for 1 1/2 hours. Add the brown pork dice and vegetables and continue to cook for 40 minutes longer, or until the meat is tender. Discard the faggot and correct the seasoning. Turn the stew into a serving dish and sprinkle it with finely chopped parsley.

BAKE 30 chestnuts in a hot oven (400° F.) for about 15 minutes and peel off shell and skin while the nuts are still hot. Follow the recipe for *civet de chevreuil*, and add the chestnuts to the stew along with the vegetables.

Venison Stew
with Chestnuts

TRIM sinew and bone from 2 pounds venison and cut the meat into cubes. Roll them in flour and brown them in 2 tablespoons melted fat in a deep kettle. Add 1 1/2 cups dry red wine, 1 teaspoon mixed dried herbs (marjoram, thyme, rosemary and parsley), 1 large onion, peeled and sliced, and salt and pepper to taste. Simmer for 2 hours, then add 3 medium carrots and 3 medium potatoes, peeled and quartered, and simmer for another hour.

Hunter's
Venison Stew

HAVE the loin of venison cut away from the bone and sliced into steaks 1 1/2 inches thick. Cover the meat with uncooked marinade and store it in the refrigerator for 24 to 48 hours, turning the pieces occasionally so that the marinade will penetrate them evenly. Drain and dry the slices well and brown them for about 3 minutes on each side in a generous amount of salad oil. Serve with *sauce poivrade* and puréed chestnuts.

Grenadins
of Venison
Saint Hubert

HAVE the loin of venison cut away from the bone and sliced into steaks approximately 1 1/2 inches thick. Put the steaks in a deep bowl and cover them with 1 onion, sliced, 2 carrots, sliced, 4 shallots, chopped, 4 sprigs of parsley, 1/2 teaspoon dried thyme, 1 teaspoon salt, 6 crushed peppercorns, 6 juniper berries, 1/2 cup red-wine vinegar, 1/4 cup olive oil or other vegetable oil, and enough red wine to cover the steaks.

Venison
Steaks
Polonaise

Put the bowl in the refrigerator for 24 hours, turning the pieces of meat occasionally so that the marinade will touch all areas of the venison. This marinating time is important since it develops the full flavor of the meat and acts as a tenderizer.

Drain the steaks and reserve 1/2 cup of the marinade. Wipe the meat dry.

In a large skillet heat 1/4 cup butter and cook the steaks on both sides until they are done to taste. Remove the steaks to a heated platter and keep them warm.

Add the reserved marinade to the skillet and bring it to a boil. Stir in 1 cup sour cream and heat the sauce thoroughly, but do not let it come to a boil. Season it to taste and serve separately in a heated sauceboat. Serve with wild rice.

The marinade in this recipe may be used for pheasant, rabbit, or other game.

Hunter's Venision Steaks

Cut a leg or loin of venison into steaks 3/4 inch thick and season the steaks with salt. Place them in a bowl and sprinkle them with 4 crushed peppercorns, 1 onion and 1 carrot, both sliced, 4 sprigs of parsley, and 1/2 teaspoon thyme. Add 1 bay leaf, 1/2 cup white wine, and 5 tablespoons olive oil and marinate the steaks for 24 hours, turning them occasionally in the marinade.

Remove the venison steaks from the marinade and pat them dry. In a frying pan heat 3 tablespoons olive oil and in it sauté the venison over high heat for about 3 minutes on each side. Remove the meat and keep it hot.

Drain the excess fat from the frying pan and to the juices remaining add 2 tablespoons butter and 2 shallots, minced. Stir in 1 tablespoon flour and cook, stirring, until the *roux* is lightly browned. Add 1/4 cup white wine, black pepper to taste, and 1 cup sour cream. Cook, stirring constantly, until the sauce is smooth and thickened. Correct the seasoning with salt and lemon juice and pour the sauce over the meat on a serving dish.

Wipe 5 pounds of meat from a haunch of venison with vinegar and cut it into 2-inch cubes. Melt 1/3 cup bacon drippings in a heavy kettle with 1 garlic clove and in it sauté the meat until it is browned on all sides. Add 1 1/2 cups each of carrots and celery, both diced, 1 cup minced onions, 2 cups red wine, 3 cups water, 2 bay leaves tied with 6 sprigs each of parsley and celery tops, and a sprig of thyme, 12 peppercorns, bruised, and 2 teaspoons salt. Cover the kettle and braise the meat in a slow oven (325° F.) for about 1 hour, or until it is tender.

Melt 1/4 cup butter in a saucepan and stir in 1/4 cup flour to make a *roux*. Strain the liquid in which the venison was cooked and add it gradually to the *roux*, stirring constantly over very low heat until the sauce is thickened. Continue to cook, stirring, for 3 minutes. Stir in 1 1/2 cups hot sour cream and 2 teaspoons paprika.

Transfer the venison and the vegetables to a serving dish and pour the sauce over them. Serve with buttered noodles and beach-plum or currant jelly. Garnish the dish with watercress.

After bear meat is hung and marinated, it may be cooked like beef. Bear fanciers claim that the ursine diet of vegetables, berries, and honey gives the meat an unsurpassable flavor. The neck and hindquarters of the bear are very tough, and suitable for nothing except perhaps hamburger.

Bear Steak
Fortier

MARINATE steaks cut from the bear's rump in an uncooked marinade for 2 days, turning the meat from time to time. Wipe the steaks dry and broil them quickly on both sides. Arrange the steaks on a heated platter. Strain the marinade, reduce it by two-thirds, and add to it 1 cup heated sour cream. Garnish the platter with French fried potatoes and watercress, and serve the sauce separately.

Larded Filet
of Bear

REMOVE the nerves from a whole filet of bear and trim it neatly. Lard it with long, narrow strips of larding fat and with strips of green pepper. Marinate the filet in a cooked marinade for several days.

Wipe the meat dry and roast it in a very hot oven (450° F.) for 15 minutes, turning it once to brown it well. Reduce the temperature to moderate (350° F.) and continue to roast, allowing from this point 12 minutes per pound. Baste frequently with melted butter. The meat should be very rare.

Place the roast filet on a heated platter covered with a thin layer of *sauce poivrade*. Garnish with cubes of wine jelly, thin slices of lemon, and watercress. Top with a few pitted black olives heated in butter for 3 minutes. Serve the remaining *sauce poivrade* separately.

Braised
Bear Liver

PARBOIL for 5 minutes a piece of bear liver weighing 2 1/2 to 3 pounds. Remove the tubes and the skin and lard the liver with narrow strips of larding pork. Cover the liver with 3 cups white wine and marinate it for 3 hours or longer, turning the meat occasionally. Wipe the liver dry and sear it well on all sides in 1/4 cup hot bacon drippings or lard.

Blend together 2 tablespoons each of onion and shallot, 4 sprigs of parsley, and 1/2 cup mushrooms, all finely minced, and 1/2 cup sausage meat. Season with a pinch each of thyme, sage, and tarragon, 1 teaspoon paprika, and salt, pepper, and cayenne to taste. Put this mixture through a food chopper, add the white of 1 raw egg, and put it through the food chopper again. Spread it on thin sheet of larding pork and wrap the pork around the liver.

Lay the liver in a buttered casserole and add the wine in which it was marinated, 8 crushed peppercorns, 2 bruised cloves, 8 sprigs of parsley tied with 1/2 bay leaf, and 2 slices of lemon. Cover the casserole tightly and braise the liver in a moderately slow oven (325° F.) for 1 1/2 hours, or until it is tender, turning it halfway through the cooking. Transfer the liver to a heated platter. Spoon off the excess fat from the liquid in the casserole. Strain the sauce and add 1 cup heated sour cream, salt, pepper, and 1 tablespoon paprika. Bring the sauce to the boiling point and pour part of it over the liver. Serve the rest of the sauce in a sauceboat. Garnish the platter with large mushroom caps sautéed in butter.

The wild pig, or peccary, is still hunted in some remote parts of this continent, as the boar, of which it is an American species, is still hunted in Europe. All wild pigs have in the middle of their backs a musk gland that must be removed as soon as the animal is killed. Young wild pigs may be cooked like domestic pork; older animals should be marinated.

CLEAN 1 pound fresh mushrooms and put them through a food chopper. Add 1 truffle, minced and cooked in 3 tablespoons Madeira for 5 minutes, 1/4 cup each of chopped blanched almonds, chopped parsley, and minced chives, 1 cup ground cooked ham, 1/2 cup each of ground lean veal and pork, and 2 cups fine dry bread crumbs soaked in 1 cup cream, squeezed dry, and shaken lightly to loosen. Season the dressing with 1/4 teaspoon each of sage, thyme, and marjoram, 1/8 teaspoon each of mace and allspice, and salt and coarsely ground black pepper to taste. Mix thoroughly and stir in 2 egg yolks, beaten until thick and pale in color, and 1 egg white, stiffly beaten.

Marcassin Rôti
ROAST BABY
WILD BOAR

Clean and wash a fat wild boar shoat or suckling and rub it well inside with salt, pepper, and lemon juice. Stuff the cavity with the dressing, sew up the opening, and truss the boar. Prop the mouth open with a 2-inch block of wood. Rub the outside with 1/4 cup olive oil and sprinkle with salt and pepper. Cut 4 parallel gashes in the skin on each side of the backbone and put the boar on a rack in a roasting pan, cavity side down. Pour 2 cups stock into the pan and cover the boar with a large piece of buttered paper.

Roast the boar in a very hot oven (450° F.) for 20 minutes, reduce the temperature to moderately slow (325° F.), and continue to roast, allowing 30 minutes for each pound of meat (drawn, unstuffed weight) and basting every 10 minutes with the liquid in the pan. Half an hour before the boar is ready to be served, discard the paper, brush the roast with sour cream, and return it to the oven to brown well.

To serve, place the boar on a platter with a cranberry in each eye cavity, a shiny red apple in the mouth, and a garland of watercress around its neck. Garnish the platter with baked apples stuffed with stewed cranberries and large cooked prunes. Serve with *sauce chasseur.*

REMOVE the rind from the hind leg of a plump young wild boar or peccary. Put the meat in an earthenware or enameled vessel and pour over it 2 cups vinegar and 1 bottle red wine. Add 10 sprigs of parsley, a spray of thyme, a spray of marjoram, 6 small stalks of celery with the leaves, and 1 bay leaf, all tied together. Also add 1 large onion, sliced, 3 garlic cloves, mashed,

Haunch of Wild Boar Prince de Chimay

1 carrot, sliced, 1 teaspoon bruised peppercorns, and salt' to taste. Let the meat marinate in this mixture in a cool place for 4 days, turning it at least twice a day.

Wipe the meat dry, place it in a braising kettle, and sear it well on all sides over high heat in 1/4 cup hot lard. If there is a good coating of fat on the ham, no lard is necessary. When the meat is well browned, set it aside and keep it hot.

Cook 1/4 cup flour in the fat in the braising kettle, stirring constantly, until it is well browned. Stir in gradually 4 cups of the marinade. Put the meat back into the kettle, cover tightly, and braise in a moderate oven (350° F.) for 3 hours, turning the meat twice during the cooking period.

Half an hour before serving, stir 1/4 cup brandy into the sauce and correct the seasoning. Place the meat on a hot serving platter, remove any excess fat from the sauce, and pour a little of it over the meat. Garnish the platter with fried apple rings and serve the remaining sauce in a sauceboat.

Grilled Filet of Wild Pig CUT thin slices from the leg portions of a wild pig. Pound them between sheets of wax paper with the back of a meat cleaver, lifting the paper a few times to sprinkle the meat with coarsely ground black pepper. The slices should be wafer thin. Season them to taste, dip them in melted butter, and broil them on both sides until they are delicately browned.

Arrange the slices on a heated serving platter and arrange around them small cottage cheese pancakes that have been spread with a little cottage cheese and rolled. Serve a side dish of Moscovite sauce and a side dish of unsweetened stewed apples, seasoned to taste with nutmeg and cloves.

A joint of fresh pork, marinated for 4 days in the marinade for game, may be prepared in the same manner as the meat of the wild boar or pig in the above recipes.

Buffalo—bison Americanus—is, thanks to the efforts of the conservationists, in fairly good supply on the market. Buffalo meat is lean and should be generously larded; otherwise it may be prepared like beef.

Potted Bison MIX together in a saucepan 2 cups dry white wine, 3/4 cup tarragon vinegar, 1/2 teaspoon dry mustard stirred with a little of the vinegar, 1/4 cup chopped onion, 2 tablespoons finely chopped green celery tops, a garlic clove, mashed,

2 cloves, 12 peppercorns, crushed, 3/4 teaspoon salt, and a dash of cayenne. Bring this mixture slowly to a boil and cook it for 5 minutes.

Cut a 2-pound piece of lean meat from a bison that has hung for 3 days. Put the meat in a bowl and pour the boiling marinade over it. Cover the bowl with a towel and marinate the meat for 3 days, turning it once every day. The meat should be completely covered with the marinade.

Wipe the meat dry and put it in a small casserole equipped with a tightly fitting cover. Cover the casserole with a buttered paper and adjust the lid. Braise the meat in a very moderate oven (325° F.) for 2 1/2 hours. When the meat is very tender, put it 3 times through the finest blade of a food chopper. Rub the ground meat through a fine sieve, moistening it with a little of the cooking marinade to make a smooth, but not liquid, mixture. Add salt and pepper to taste and cool. Pack the meat into small earthenware pots. Cover with a layer of clarified butter or melted lard and store the pots in a cool, dry, dark place.

Broiled Buffalo Steaks

WIPE 6 individual buffalo steaks, cut 1 inch thick, with a damp cloth, place them on a buttered broiler rack, and sear them well on both sides under high heat. Reduce the heat and broil the meat as desired, until it is medium-rare or rare, basting several times with melted butter during the broiling. Arrange the steaks on a hot serving platter and sprinkle with salt and pepper. Pour over them a little melted butter and dust generously with coarsely chopped parsley.

The meat of the domestic rabbit resembles chicken in flavor and texture; the wild rabbit and hare have the additional charm of a pleasant gamy tang.

Roast Hare

SKIN, draw, remove the heads, and lard 2 young hares. Reserve the livers. Wipe the hares with a damp cloth and put them in a china or earthenware dish. Pour over them 2 tablespoons olive oil and 1/2 cup each of brandy and water. Add 1 onion, 1 carrot, and 1 garlic clove, all sliced, 2 bay leaves, 4 sprays of parsley, 1 teaspoon salt, and 1/2 teaspoon thyme and marinate the hares in the refrigerator for 2 days, turning them frequently.

Roast the hares in a moderate oven (350° F.) for about 1 1/2 hours, or until they are tender, basting frequently with the marinade. Arrange the hares on a hot serving dish and to the juices in the roasting pan add 1/2 cup each of seeded white and black grapes, the mashed livers, and 1/4 cup heavy cream. Bring the sauce just to a boil and pour it around the hares.

Râble de Lièvre
à la Crème
Aigre

SADDLE OF HARE
WITH TART
CREAM SAUCE

SKIN, draw, and clean a hare and place the saddle or loin in a deep dish. Cover the meat with uncooked marinade and store it in the refrigerator for about 24 hours, turning the meat occasionally so that the marinade will penetrate it evenly. Drain and dry the meat thoroughly, lard it with strips of fat salt pork, and wrap it in thin slices of fat salt pork. Season with salt and pepper. Put enough salad oil in a roasting pan to cover the bottom of the pan generously and put the pan in a hot oven. When the oil is smoking hot lay the meat in it and roast it in a very hot oven (450° to 475° F.) for about 18 minutes. The meat should be medium rare. Remove the slices of salt pork and transfer the roasted meat to a hot serving platter.

Pour off the fat from the roasting pan. To the pan add 1 teaspoon chopped shallot or onion and 2 tablespoons vinegar and cook until it is reduced to almost nothing. Add 3 tablespoons *sauce poivrade* and reduce it to about 2 tablespoons. Add 1/2 cup heated heavy cream. If desired, the meat may be sliced and arranged on the platter, and the sauce poured over it. Or the sauce may be passed separately. Instead of the *sauce poivrade* you may add a few drops of lemon juice and one teaspoon beef extract or 1 tablespoon good gravy after adding the cream. Serve with château potatoes, small carrots, and red cabbage with wine garnished with fluted mushrooms.

Fricassee
of Hare

CLEAN and skin 2 young hares or rabbits. Rub them with a damp cloth and cut them into serving portions. Put the pieces in an earthenware bowl and cover with equal parts of vinegar and water. Add 2 or 3 slices of onion, 12 whole cloves, 2 large bay leaves, and salt and black pepper, coarsely ground, to taste. Marinate the rabbit for 2 days, turning the pieces frequently and being sure they are constantly covered with the liquid.

Drain the pieces of meat and sear them in an iron skillet in 3 tablespoons lard, turning the meat so that it is browned on all sides. Drain off the fat and pour in just enough of the marinade to cover the meat. Cover and simmer for 30 minutes, or until the meat is tender. When ready to serve, stir in 1 generous cup sour cream.

Hare Stew

CUT a hare into serving pieces, place the pieces in a bowl, and sprinkle them with salt and freshly ground black pepper. Pour over the hare 1/2 cup Cognac and 3 tablespoons olive oil, add 1 bay leaf, crumbled, 1/4 teaspoon thyme, and 1 onion, finely chopped, and marinate for 3 hours, turning the pieces occasionally. Chop the hare's liver and soak it in 1 cup dry red wine.

In a heavy kettle sauté 1 onion, finely chopped, in 1/4 cup butter until the onion is golden. Add 1 cup diced raw ham and stir in 2 tablespoons flour. Add the hare and the marinade, mix well, and stir in about 3 cups dry red wine, or enough almost to cover the meat. Add 1 garlic clove and a bouquet of parsley, cover the pot, and cook the meat over low heat for 1 hour.

Turn the contents of the kettle into an ovenproof casserole and add the liver and the wine in which it soaked and 12 mushrooms, sliced. Cover the casserole and bake in a slow oven (325° F.) for about 1 hour. Just before serving, the sauce may be thickened by stirring in 1 teaspoon flour mixed to a paste with 1 tablespoon butter. Sprinkle with chopped parsley and serve in the casserole.

Rabbit Curry

CUT 2 dressed rabbits into serving pieces. Sprinkle the meat lightly with flour and sauté it in 3 tablespoons hot butter until the pieces are browned on all sides.

In a saucepan melt 1/2 cup butter and in it sauté 1 crushed garlic clove for 3 minutes. Discard the garlic and add 1/2 cup minced onion, 1 cup chopped tart apple, and 1 tablespoon curry powder, or to taste. Cook, stirring occasionally, until the onion is soft. Stir in 3 tablespoons flour and 1 teaspoon salt and continue to cook for 3 minutes. Add 1 tablespoon lemon juice and stir in gradually 3 cups chicken stock. Add the pieces of rabbit to the sauce, cover, and simmer for about 30 minutes, or until the rabbit is tender, adding a little more stock from time to time if needed. Serve with rice.

Rabbit Terrapin Style

SKIN and clean a young 3-pound rabbit, wash it thoroughly in warm water, and sponge it dry. Rub it thoroughly inside and out with equal parts of ground cinnamon, allspice, cloves, salt, and black pepper. Let the rabbit stand for at least 1 hour, to allow the spices to penetrate the flesh, then cut it into regular serving portions. Put the rabbit meat in a heavy kettle, cover with equal parts of water and white wine, and add a large *bouquet garni* composed of 4 sprigs of green celery leaves, 8 sprigs of parsley, 1 bay leaf, and 6 green onion tops, all tied together, 8 peppercorns, crushed, and a tiny pinch of salt. Bring to the boil, lower the heat, and simmer the meat for 45 minutes, or until it is tender. Drain the broth into a saucepan, reduce it to 1 1/2 cups over high heat, and strain it through a fine sieve.

Remove the meat from the rabbit bones and cut it into small pieces. Mash 4 hard-cooked egg yolks with 3 tablespoons each of prepared mustard and flour and 3/4 cup heavy cream. Blend well and add the whites of 4 hard-cooked eggs, coarsely chopped, salt, pepper, and a pinch each of cayenne and nutmeg. Add this to the reduced broth. Boil for 2 minutes, stirring constantly, then add the rabbit meat. Mix well and simmer gently for 10 to 15 minutes. Stir in 1/4 cup Sherry and serve on a heated platter, in individual patty shells or on toast, sprinkling each serving with a little paprika.

Rabbit with Lentils

SOAK 1 pound lentils in cold water to cover for an hour or two.

Cut 2 dressed rabbits into serving pieces. Rub the pieces with a cut garlic clove, roll them in flour, and sauté them in hot butter or olive oil until they are browned on all sides.

Drain the lentils, cover them with fresh water, and add 1 teaspoon salt. Bring the water to a boil and simmer the lentils for about 20 minutes, or until they are tender but not mushy. Drain and stir in 3 onions, diced, and 1/4 cup soft butter. Season to taste with salt and cayenne.

Rub a casserole with garlic and line the bottom with strips of bacon. Put a layer of the lentils in the bottom, arrange the rabbit pieces on the lentils, and cover the meat with more lentils. Sprinkle with 1 cup sliced mushrooms, cover the casserole, and bake the rabbit in a moderate oven (350° F.) for 1 1/2 hours.

Lapereau à la Normande

WILD RABBIT NORMANDY STYLE

CUT a 4-pound dressed rabbit into about twelve uniform pieces and marinate the pieces overnight in an uncooked marinade. Melt 3 tablespoons butter in a large skillet. Drain and dry the rabbit pieces and sauté them without permitting them to take on color. Season the meat with salt and a little pepper, sprinkle it with 1 teaspoon flour, and remove it from the skillet. Then add to the skillet 2 green apples, peeled, cored and sliced, and 3 medium onions, sliced. Lay the rabbit on top of this mixture and add 1 1/2 to 2 cups cream, barely to cover the meat. Cover the pan and cook the rabbit slowly for 1 to 1 1/2 hours, or until it is tender. Transfer the meat to a serving dish and keep it hot. Force the sauce through a fine sieve, or purée it in a blender, reheat it, correct the seasoning with salt and pepper and finish with the juice of 1/2 lemon. Pour the hot sauce over the meat and serve.

In a large skillet try out 2 ounces salt pork for a few minutes. Add 1/4 cup olive oil and 1 garlic clove, crushed, and cook for a few minutes. Cut a rabbit into serving pieces and brown the meat on all sides. Reduce the heat and cook the rabbit for 25 minutes, turning the pieces once during the cooking period.

Sweet and Sour Rabbit

Add to the skillet 1/2 cup each of chicken broth and dry white wine, 6 peppercorns, crushed, a little salt, the juice of 1 lemon, 1 tablespoon brown sugar, and 1/4 cup tomato purée. Cover the skillet and let the rabbit simmer in the sauce for 10 minutes. Add 1/4 cup seedless raisins and 1/4 cup shelled pine nuts and simmer the mixture for 10 minutes longer. Correct the seasoning with salt, remove the pieces of rabbit to a serving dish, and add to the sauce in the pan another 1/2 cup wine. Heat the sauce and pour it over the meat. Sprinkle all with 2 tablespoons chopped parsley. If the sauce seems too thin, it may be thickened with a little cornstarch mixed to a paste with water or wine.

Squirrel has been an American favorite since colonial days, when these lively little animals provided sport and meat for the early pioneers. The flavor of squirrel is not to everyone's taste; the meat is distinctively gamy, and if the glands in the small of the back and under the forelegs are not carefully removed, the meat is easily tainted. But if you live in squirrel country, you can discover for yourself why the earliest American ordinaries, or inns, featured squirrel on their menus.

Skin, clean, and disjoint 3 young squirrels. Sprinkle each piece with salt and pepper, dip it in milk, and roll it in flour. Heat enough fat in a heavy skillet to cover the bottom 1 inch deep. When the fat is smoking hot, fry the squirrel to a rich brown. Drain it on absorbent paper and keep it warm on a heated platter.

Fried Squirrels

Pour off the frying fat and add to the skillet 2 tablespoons butter. Stir in 2 tablespoons flour and add gradually, stirring and scraping the pan, 1 1/2 cups hot milk. Simmer the sauce for 5 minutes, stirring continually to prevent sticking. Stir in 1/2 cup cream, season with salt and pepper, and bring just to the boiling point. Serve this gravy in a heated sauceboat.

Squirrel Stew   SKIN, clean, and disjoint 3 squirrels. Melt 3 tablespoons good fat in a heavy kettle and stir in 2 tablespoons flour. Add 12 crushed allspice, 3 sprigs of sweet marjoram, 2 sprigs of thyme, 1 bay leaf, 1 garlic clove, crushed, 1 large onion, sliced, 6 fresh tomatoes, peeled, seeded, and chopped, 1/2 cup dry red wine, and 4 cups water. Bring the liquid to a boil, add salt to taste and a pinch of cayenne, and simmer for 5 minutes. Add the squirrels and the juice of 1 lemon and simmer the meat for about 45 minutes, or until it is tender. Serve with rice.

Squirrels   SKIN, clean, and disjoint 3 plump squirrels. Soak the pieces in cold salted
in Cider   water for 20 minutes, wipe them dry, and dust them with flour seasoned with salt and pepper. In a heavy skillet brown 1/4 cup diced fat ham. Add the squirrel and brown the pieces well on all sides in the ham fat. Add enough hard cider barely to cover the squirrel, cover the skillet, and simmer the liquid until most of it has evaporated and the meat is tender. Add 2 tablespoons butter, increase the heat, and quickly brown the pieces of meat once more. Remove the squirrel to a warm serving platter and to the juices remaining in the skillet add 1 cup hot cream and stir in all the brown bits from the bottom and sides of the pan. Stir in, bit by bit, 1/2 tablespoon flour mixed to a paste with 1 tablespoon butter, correct the seasoning with salt and pepper, and strain the sauce into a gravy boat.

Casserole of   SKIN, clean, and disjoint 3 squirrels. Wash the pieces in cold salted water
Squirrels   and wipe them dry. Roll the pieces in flour seasoned with salt and pepper
and Wild Rice   and brown them lightly on all sides in butter. Arrange them in a buttered casserole with 3/4 cup washed and soaked wild rice, 2 green peppers, seeded and chopped, 1 cup diced celery, and 1 cup sliced tart apples. Add boiling water to cover, cover the casserole, and bake it in a slow oven (300° F.) for 1 1/2 hours, or until the rice is cooked and the meat is tender.

With the exception of rabbit, small game is seldom available at the market; we include the recipes that follow for the benefit of the hunter.

Roast Stuffed   DRESS an opossum as you would a piglet by removing the entrails, head,
Opossum   and tail. Be certain to remove the small kernels or glands in the small of

the back and the larger ones found under the forelegs. Hang the opossum outdoors for several cold nights.

Wash thoroughly inside and out with salted hot water. Cover the opossum with cold water, add 1 cup salt, and let it stand overnight. In the morning, drain off the water and rinse the opossum well in several changes of boiling water. To prepare the stuffing, cook 1 large onion, finely chopped, in 1 tablespoon butter until it begins to color. Chop the opossum liver fine and add to the onion. Cook over low heat, stirring constantly, until the liver is tender and well done. Stir in 1 cup bread crumbs, 1 finely chopped hard-cooked egg, 1/4 green pepper, finely chopped, and 1 tablespoon each of chopped parsley and chives. Season with salt and a dash of Worcestershire sauce and sufficient beef bouillon to moisten.

Stuff the opossum with this mixture and fasten the openings with skewers or thread. Put the meat in a roasting pan. Add 1/4 cup each of chopped carrots, white turnips, and the green part of leeks, 1 onion, quartered, two of the quarters stuck with a whole clove, and a *bouquet garni* composed of 1 large bay leaf, 8 sprigs of fresh parsley, 1 sprig of thyme, 1 sprig of marjoram, and 2 sprigs of green celery tops, all tied with kitchen thread. Add 1 1/2 cups cold water. Roast in a hot oven (425° F.) for 20 minutes, turning the meat frequently until it is well seared on all sides. Reduce the temperature to moderate and continue to roast for 1 1/2 to 1 3/4 hours, depending on the size of the animal. Baste frequently with the liquid in the roasting pan. Discard the *bouquet garni*. Serve with pan gravy and baked sweet potatoes.

Roast Opossum and Sweet Taters

PREPARE opossum as for roasted stuffed opossum and put it in a deep pan with 4 cups water. Lay 4 slices of bacon across the breast and bake in a moderate oven (350° F.) for 1 hour, basting frequently with the water in the roasting pan.

Make a stuffing with 3 cups dry bread crumbs, 1 onion, minced and sautéed in 1/4 cup butter until golden brown, and salt and pepper. Moisten the dressing with a little of the juice from the roasting pan. Parboil 6 sweet potatoes or yams in their jackets until they are almost tender.

Remove the opossum from the oven, drain off all but 2 cups of the roasting liquor, and stuff the opossum with the dressing. Put the stuffed opossum back in the roasting pan. Peel the sweet potatoes, cut them in half lengthwise, and arrange them around the meat. Sprinkle the potatoes with a little cinnamon and brown sugar and bake the meat for about 1 hour longer, or until it is brown and crisp, basting frequently with the pan gravy.

Serve with a dish of turnip greens, cooked with a pig's jowl, and with corn bread.

Roast Raccoon   SKIN and carefully clean a young raccoon, removing the kernels from the small of the back. Hang it for several cold nights in the open air. Parboil the raccoon for 1 hour in salted water with 1 onion stuck with 2 cloves, 1 bay leaf, 2 pods chili pepper, with the seeds and veins removed, and 1 carrot, sliced.

Toss 3 cups dry bread crumbs with 1 onion, minced and sautéed in 1/4 cup butter until golden brown. Season this stuffing with salt and pepper and moisten it with a little of the liquid used to boil the meat.

Stuff the raccoon and close the openings with skewers or thread. Put the meat in a roasting pan. Add 1/4 cup each of chopped carrots and white turnips, 1 onion, quartered, two of the quarters stuck with a whole clove, and a *bouquet garni*, as for roast stuffed opossum. Add 1 1/2 cups cold water. Roast the meat in a hot oven (425° F.) for 20 minutes, turning it frequently until it is well seared on all sides. Reduce the temperature to moderate (350° F.) and continue to roast for 1 1/2 to 1 3/4 hours, depending upon the size of the animal. Baste the meat frequently with the liquid in the pan. Discard the *bouquet garni*. Serve with pan gravy and sweet potatoes.

Potted Muskrat   SKIN and clean 2 plump muskrat, removing the musk glands with the skin. Care should be taken to avoid cutting into these glands, and a little meat around them should be trimmed away. Clean the muskrat thoroughly, removing the feet and head. Wash them in lukewarm water and soak them overnight in cold water mixed with 1/2 cup vinegar and 1/2 cup baking soda.

Drain the muskrat, wipe them dry, and cut them into serving pieces. Season the pieces with salt, pepper, and crushed marjoram leaves and sauté them in 1/2 cup each of butter and oil over high heat until lightly browned. Put the meat in a casserole. Add to the fat in the frying pan 2 tablespoons chopped shallots, 1/2 cup each of carrots, leeks, and celery, all finely chopped. Cook the vegetables for 5 minutes and add the juice of 2 lemons, 6 tomatoes, peeled and chopped, 1 garlic clove, chopped, and 1 tablespoon chopped chives. Add 2 cups water, mix thoroughly, and pour over the meat in the casserole. Bake the meat in a slow oven (325° F.) for about 1 1/2 hours, or until it is tender. Sprinkle with chopped parsley and serve in the casserole.

Woodchuck or   SKIN and clean a young woodchuck or muskrat and remove the kernels
Muskrat Pie   under the front legs and in the small of the back. Soak overnight in water seasoned with a handful of salt. In the morning, wash, rinse, and wipe

the animal dry. Put the meat in a large pan, cover with fresh water, and add a large *bouquet garni* composed of 6 sprigs of green celery leaves, 1 large bay leaf, and 2 sprigs of fresh thyme, all tied together, an onion stuck with a clove, 10 peppercorns, and salt to taste. Cook for about 2 hours, or until the meat is tender, skimming the broth from time to time. Remove the meat, discard the *bouquet garni,* and reduce the cooking liquid over high heat to about 1 quart. In the reduced liquid cook until tender 2 onions, sliced, and 1 1/2 cups each of raw potato cubes, chopped celery, and chopped carrots.

Remove the meat from the bones and cut it into small pieces. Put the meat in a deep baking dish and add the cooked vegetables. Strain the stock and reduce it to 1 generous cup. Add 3 tablespoons Sherry and stir in 1/2 tablespoon flour mixed to a paste with 1 tablespoon butter. Pour the sauce over the meat. Top with 1 cup mushroom caps, cooked in butter and drained. Cover the baking dish with flaky pie pastry, moisten the edge, and press it carefully around the rim of the dish. Cut several gashes in the pastry to allow for the escape of steam. Brush with melted butter and bake in a hot oven (425° F.) for 10 minutes. Reduce the temperature to 400° F. and bake the pie for another 20 minutes, or until the crust is brown.

SKIN a young woodchuck and clean the carcass, being careful to remove the little red kernels or glands in the small of the back and in each foreleg near the body. Cut the woodchuck into serving pieces and soak them for 1 hour in cold water mixed with 1/2 cup vinegar and 1 teaspoon baking soda. Drain and dry the pieces, sprinkle them with salt and pepper, and roll them in flour. Heat 3 tablespoons fat in a heavy pot with 1 garlic clove. Brown the pieces of meat on all sides, add 1 cup water, and a *bouquet garni* containing 3 sprigs of parsley, 1 spray of celery leaves, 1/2 bay leaf, and 1 sprig of fresh thyme, all tied together, and cover the pot tightly. Let the meat simmer for about 2 hours, or until it is tender, adding a little water as needed. Just before serving, stir in 2 tablespoons butter and 1 teaspoon Worcestershire sauce.

Woodchuck Pot Roast

SKIN a young woodchuck and clean the carcass, being careful to remove the little red kernels or glands in the small of the back and in each foreleg near the body. Put the woodchuck in cold salted water for 30 minutes,

Roast Woodchuck

377

drain it, and wipe it dry. Sprinkle with salt, pepper, and curry powder. Fill the woodchuck with this prune stuffing: Sauté 1 small onion, finely chopped, in 2 tablespoons butter until lightly browned. Combine with 1 1/2 cups bread crumbs, 1 cup each of chopped celery, diced cooked prunes, and chopped tart apples, and 1/4 teaspoon salt. Blend thoroughly. Sew the filled woodchuck carefully into shape and truss it by cutting the sinews under both front and hind paws, bending the forepaws backward and the hindpaws forward, and pinning each securely into position by means of skewers. Tie a string around the neck, catch it on the first set of skewers, pass it around the body, and fasten it securely on the second set.

Bring to a boil enough water to cover the woodchuck and add to it 1 slice of onion, 1 bay leaf, a 2-inch stick of cinnamon, 1 tablespoon vinegar, and 1 teaspoon salt. Wrap the woodchuck in cheesecloth, put it in the boiling water, and simmer it for 1 hour. Remove the cheesecloth and put the wood-chuck in a baking pan. Sprinkle with 1/4 cup flour, letting some fall on the bottom of the pan. Insert a strip of bacon along the back. Roast the woodchuck in a moderately hot oven (375° F.) until the flour browns. Add to the pan 3 cups hot water mixed with 1/2 cup butter and 1/2 teaspoon pickling spice and baste the woodchuck every 10 minutes for 1 hour. Roast it without basting for 1 hour longer.

Remove the skewers and string, arrange the woodchuck on watercress, and garnish with strips of bacon and lemon slices. Serve with gravy from the pan seasoned with minced cooked onion and sliced cooked carrots.

Hunter's Skilligalee

THIS recipe is necessarily inexact, since it is based on the contents of the hunter's bag, whatever they may be. Skilligalee is always impromptu.

Disjoint the rabbit or squirrel. Cut the small birds into halves. Cut the duck or pheasant into quarters, and the venison into large cubes.

Heat a Dutch oven and in it brown some bacon or salt pork. Then add a few onions, sliced, and let them become golden in the fat. Add the miscellaneous game and sear it lightly on all sides, being careful not to let the onions burn. When the meat is seared, add 1 to 2 cans of tomato paste, a small bouquet of herbs, and salt and pepper and cover all the ingredients generously with hot water. Cover the pot and simmer for 2 to 3 hours.

About 30 minutes before serving time, add vegetables such as quartered potatoes, coarsely chopped celery, sliced carrots, green beans, small white onions, and slices of sweet pepper. If the broth cooks down too rapidly, add more boiling water. Remove any bones from which the meat has fallen, correct the seasoning, and serve the skilligalee in large soup bowls sprinkled with finely chopped parsley.

All furred game should be marinated for at least two or three days; some cuts will benefit from marinating for a week. The marinade tenderizes and flavors the meat. Uncooked and cooked marinades may be used interchangeably, but the uncooked marinade is usually specified when the marinade is to become part of the sauce, as it does for less tender cuts that require long slow cooking. Always use an enamel or earthenware vessel for marinating. It is important that the meat is well drained and dried afterward.

Marinades for Game

IN a bowl combine 1 carrot and 1 onion, both sliced, 4 sprigs of parsley, 1 bay leaf, 1 small pinch of thyme, 1 teaspoon salt, 6 to 8 peppercorns, 1 tablespoon salad oil, and 3/4 cup white wine.

Uncooked Marinade

IN a saucepan combine 4 cups water, 1 1/2 cups vinegar, 2 onions, chopped, 1 carrot, sliced, 1 garlic clove, 1 teaspoon thyme, 2 bay leaves, 4 sprigs of parsley, 12 peppercorns, and 1 tablespoon salt. Bring the mixture to a boil and simmer it for 1 hour. Cool the marinade thoroughly before pouring it over the meat.

Cooked Marinade

These are classic sauces for game.

PUT 6 tablespoons salad oil in a saucepan. Add 1 carrot and 1 onion, both diced, and cook until they are golden brown. Stir in 1/2 cup flour and cook until the flour turns golden brown. Add 3 cups brown stock or double-strength beef consommé and 1 cup tomato purée, mix well with a whip, and cook, stirring, until the mixture is well blended. Add 3 or 4 sprigs of parsley, 1 bay leaf, and a little thyme. If any bones of the game are available, brown them well in the oven and add them. Cook for 1 1/2 hours, stirring occasionally and skimming as needed.

    Put 1/2 cup each of vinegar and liquid from the marinade and 6 peppercorns, crushed, in another pan and cook until the liquid is reduced by about two-thirds. Strain the sauce into the reduced vinegar mixture and cook all together for about 30 minutes longer, skimming carefully as the fat rises. Add 1/2 cup red wine. Use for game.

Sauce Poivrade

BRING to a boil 2 cups *sauce poivrade* and add 2 tablespoons truffles cut in julienne. Thicken the sauce with the blood of a rabbit or hare, swirling it in slowly off the heat. Serve at once. Use for furred game.

Sauce Grand Veneur

Sauce Diane   FOLD into 1 1/4 cups hot *sauce poivrade* 1 cup heavy cream, whipped, 1 tablespoon chopped truffles, and 1 tablespoon chopped hard-cooked egg.

Sauce Moscovite   SIMMER 1 teaspoon juniper berries in 1/4 cup water for 15 minutes. Strain the infusion and add it to 1 1/2 cups hot *sauce poivrade.* Add 1/2 cup Malaga grapes and 2 tablespoons each of shredded, toasted almonds and seedless raisins, plumped in meat stock. Blend well and add salt and pepper to taste. Use for game.

Sauce Chasseur
HUNTER'S SAUCE   COOK 2 tablespoons thinly sliced mushrooms and 1 scant teaspoon minced shallots in a little butter until tender. Moisten with 1/2 cup dry white wine and reduce the liquid over high heat by half. Stir in 1 tablespoon tomato purée and 1 cup brown sauce. Boil the sauce up twice, remove it from the heat, and beat into it 1 tablespoon sweet butter and 1/2 teaspoon each of minced parsley and tarragon. For game.

Sauce Rouennaise   PUT 1 cup red wine, 10 peppercorns, 1 bay leaf, 1 teaspoon thyme, and 4 shallots, chopped, in a saucepan. Bring the mixture to a boil and cook until it is reduced by two-thirds. Add 1/4 cup brown sauce or 1 tablespoon butter creamed with 1 teaspoon flour. Bring again to the boiling point, remove from the heat and keep the sauce hot without boiling. Add 5 to 6 finely chopped raw duck or chicken livers, mix all together well, and rub through a fine sieve. If there is any blood from the duck available, stir this slowly into the sauce. Finish with 1/4 cup Cognac. Use this sauce with wild or domestic duck.

Rouennaise
POULTRY
LIVER PASTE   HEAT well 2 tablespoons rendered salt pork fat. Add 1 cup chicken or duck livers, a pinch of thyme, 1 bay leaf, 1 teaspoon salt and a little pepper. Cook for 3 or 4 minutes over high heat. Add 3 tablespoons Cognac or Sherry. Crush the livers and rub them through a sieve. This paste is spread on toast or croutons used to garnish game and poultry dishes.

Bread Sauce   BRING to a boil 2 cups milk, 1 onion studded with 2 cloves, 1/2 teaspoon salt, and a little cayenne pepper. Cook this mixture for 5 minutes, strain it, and add 1 cup fresh bread crumbs. Correct the seasoning with salt and, if desired, add a little butter or heavy cream. Use bread sauce for roast wild birds, especially grouse.

Bread Sauce

Barbecue and Spit Roasting

When backyard cookery was exclusively a male province, as it is no longer, it was likely to begin and end with steaks. It took the ladies to realize that outdoor cookery can comprise, within the bounds set by time, equipment, taste, and common sense, anything that is normally cooked on a range or in a broiler under a roof. Somehow, everything tastes better with the roof off.

Charcoal Broiled Steak

HAVE the steak, sirloin, porterhouse, or tenderloin, cut 1 1/2 to 2 inches thick, allowing from 3/4 to 1 pound of meat per person. Let the steak stand at room temperature for 2 hours before cooking it.

Place the steak on a grill 3 to 4 inches above a deep bed of glowing coals and broil it for 5 to 10 minutes. The exact cooking time cannot be given; the type of grill, and the kind and thickness of the steak, the distance of the steak from the fire, and the intensity of the coals determine this. Turn the steak, sprinkle the cooked side with salt and pepper, and continue to broil until it is done to taste.

Place the steak on a warm serving platter, sprinkle the second side with salt and pepper, and put several pats of sweet butter on the steak to melt and mingle with the juice as the steak is carved. Cut the meat in diagonal slices with a sharp carving knife.

BLEND 1/4 pound Roquefort cheese with 1/4 cup olive oil and a garlic clove crushed in 1 tablespoon brandy. Broil a thick steak, spread it with this mixture, and put it back on the grill again, just long enough to melt the cheese.

Steak Roquefort

SPRINKLE a 2-inch-thick porterhouse steak with salt and pepper, brush it with olive oil and let it stand at room temperature for 2 hours, turning it occasionally. Then grill the steak over charcoal for about 8 minutes on each side, or until it is done to taste. Put the steak on a heated platter, sprinkle with 1 teaspoon lemon juice, and garnish with half a lemon, cut into wedges.

Beefsteak Firenze

MARINATE a flank steak for 1 hour or more in a highly seasoned French dressing. Broil it quickly close to the coals to sear both sides and leave the center very rare. Slice very thinly on the diagonal.

Flank Steak

COMBINE 2 pounds chopped fresh lean beef with 1/2 cup finely chopped beef marrow and 1/3 cup cold water. The liquid makes the meat more juicy. Season with salt and pepper, and, if desired, add 1/4 cup finely chopped onion cooked until soft in 2 tablespoons butter. Shape the mixture into flat rounds, brush with butter, and broil the hamburgers over charcoal for about 4 to 5 minutes on each side for medium or a little longer for well-done.

Hamburgers

For variety, season the meat with 2 tablespoons minced onion and moisten it with 1/4 cup heavy cream. Or flavor it with garlic, puréed in a press, or with thyme and/or sage, or with a generous quantity of chopped parsley or chives, or with chili powder and chopped green pepper and onion. The cooked hamburger may be sandwiched on toasted rolls or buns or on English muffins, with cheese, raw or cooked onions, or tomato slices. Any desired bottled condiment or barbecue sauce or any of the various relishes and chutneys are possible additions.

IN a saucepan melt 3 tablespoons butter and in it sauté 3 onions, sliced, and 2 garlic cloves, minced, until lightly browned. Stir in 1 tablespoon curry powder, 1/2 teaspoon salt, and 3 tablespoons hot water, and simmer for 15

Kebab Curry

Steak Saté

minutes. Add 3 large tomatoes, quartered, and 1/2 cup hot beef stock and simmer for 45 minutes. Cool this marinade before using it.

Cut 2 1/2 pounds tender steak into 1 1/2-inch cubes. Pour the sauce over the meat and let the meat marinate in the sauce for 2 hours. Remove the meat from the sauce and skewer it, alternating the cubes with slices of onion, and sliced fresh ginger. Brown the meat on all sides over a hot charcoal fire, basting it frequently with melted butter. Serve with cooked rice and the marinade, reheated to the boiling point.

CUT 2 pounds sirloin steak into thin strips 1 inch wide and moisten the strips in a marinade made of 1/2 cup each of soy sauce and sesame oil, 1/3 cup minced onions, and 1 garlic clove, crushed. Roll the strips in toasted and crushed sesame seeds and return them to the marinade for 1 hour. Thread the meat on skewers and broil it very quickly over a hot charcoal fire to char the surface while the center of the meat remains rare. Serve with saffron rice.

Steak Saté

Skewer cookery originated in the Near East, where the most popular meat is lamb. The seasonings for skewered lamb inevitably display an Oriental flair.

POUND together 2 teaspoons ground coriander seeds, 1/2 teaspoon dried ground chili pepper, 1 teaspoon cuminseeds, 1/2 teaspoon saffron, 1 teaspoon powdered ginger, 2 garlic cloves, minced, and 2 teaspoons salt. Cut 3 pounds lamb into 1-inch cubes. Roll the cubes in the seasoning mixture and marinate them in 1 cup vinegar for 1 hour. Drain and dry the meat and arrange it on skewers. Brush the meat with melted butter or peanut oil and broil it over a hot charcoal fire.

Saté Kambing
SKEWERED LAMB

MARINATE 2 pounds lamb, cut in 1 1/2-inch cubes, for 4 hours in a marinade composed of 1 cup olive oil, 1/3 cup lemon juice, 1 garlic clove, crushed, salt and pepper to taste, and 1 bay leaf. Arrange the lamb on skewers alternately with uniform slices of parboiled sweetbreads and tomato quarters. Broil the meat quickly over a hot charcoal fire, turning the skewers to brown it on all sides.

Near East Kebabs

TOSS 2 pounds lamb cut in 1 1/2-inch cubes in a mixing bowl with 1 large onion, finely chopped, 2 tablespoons ground cuminseed, 1 tablespoon paprika, 1/2 cup finely chopped parsley, 2 garlic cloves, crushed, 2 bay leaves, salt

Moorish Kebabs

and pepper to taste, and 6 tablespoons olive oil. Cover the bowl and set it in a cool place for 3 to 4 hours. Arrange the meat on skewers and broil it over a hot charcoal fire.

Oriental Kebabs

CUT 2 pounds tender lamb in 1 1/2-inch cubes and marinate the meat for 2 hours in a mixture of 1 cup pineapple juice, 1 garlic clove, crushed, and 3 tablespoons soy sauce. Arrange the meat on skewers alternately with cubes of pineapple. Brush the *kebabs* with melted butter and broil them over a hot charcoal fire.

Arni Souvlakia
GREEK
SKEWERED LAMB

CUT 2 pounds loin of lamb into 1-inch squares. Dip the squares into 1/2 cup lemon juice seasoned with 1/2 teaspoon orégano and salt and pepper to taste. Thread the square of meat on 6 skewers, with a tomato half at each end. Cook over charcoal, turning to brown all sides. Serve with rice pilaff.

Charcoal Broiled Lamb Chops

SEASON lamb chops with salt and brush them with butter. Broil them over a hot charcoal fire for 3 to 5 minutes on each side for rare, depending on the thickness of the chops, or a little longer for medium or well-done.

Charcoal Broiled Mutton Chops

MUTTON chops are usually served rare or medium-rare. They are cut thicker than lamb chops and have more fat on them. Broil thick mutton chops over charcoal for about 15 minutes. Brush them with melted butter from time to time. If the chops include the kidney, cook for about 5 minutes longer.

California Skewered Lamb

HAVE a 5- to 6-pound leg of lamb boned and cut the flesh into large regular chunks. Put the meat in a bowl and sprinkle it with 1 teaspoon each of salt and coarsely ground pepper, 3 tablespoons finely chopped parsley, and 1/2 teaspoon each of thyme and orégano. Add 1 bay leaf and 2 garlic cloves, split, and pour over the meat 3/4 cup olive oil and red wine to cover. Let the meat marinate at room temperature for 4 to 5 hours or in the refrigerator overnight.

Arrange the lamb on skewers, alternating the pieces with a slice each of onion and green pepper, a tomato quarter, and a mushroom cap. Grill the skewers over hot coals, turning them frequently and brushing them with the marinade. Serves 10.

CUT 1 1/2-inch-thick steaks from a leg of lamb, sprinkle with salt and pepper, and marinate them for 1 hour in 1/2 cup olive oil with 1 garlic clove, crushed, 1 tablespoon each of chopped parsley and celery leaves, and 2 sprigs of rosemary. Grill the lamb steaks over hot coals for about 10 minutes on each side, brushing them often with the seasoned oil.

Barbecued
Lamb Steaks

SECTION 2 racks of lamb breast. Sprinkle with salt and pepper and brush with this barbecue sauce: Pour 1 large can of tomatoes into a saucepan, breaking up the chunks with a fork. Add 1 medium onion, chopped, 1 garlic clove, chopped, 1 tablespoon each of brown sugar and butter, 1/2 cup each of ketchup, Worcestershire sauce, and vinegar, 1 teaspoon salt, 1/4 teaspoon each of pepper and dry mustard, and a dash of cayenne. Bring to a boil, lower the heat, and simmer the sauce for 45 minutes. Roast the lamb in a hot oven (400° F.) for 1 hour, occasionally turning and basting.

Barbecued
Lamb Riblets

Pork must be thoroughly cooked—broil it at length and slowly, at some distance from the glowing coals, until the meat is very tender and no tinge of pink remains.

CUT 2 pounds pork tenderloin into large dice and cut 6 slices of bacon into 6 pieces each. Sauté 12 mushroom caps in 3 tablespoons butter until they are lightly browned. Arrange the meat and mushrooms on 6 individual skewers, starting and ending each skewer with a mushroom. Roll the skewers in melted butter, then in fine bread crumbs.

Broil the pork rather slowly over a charcoal fire for about 20 minutes, until it is very well done, turning the skewers so that the meat and mushrooms will brown on all sides. The pork may also be broiled in the oven.

Brochette
of Pork
Tenderloin

TRIM the fat from 2 pounds boneless pork and cut the meat into 1-inch cubes.

Mix together 1 1/2 cups orange juice, the juice of 1 lemon, 3 garlic cloves, finely chopped, 3/4 teaspoon sugar, 1 1/2 tablespoons *ketjap* (or soy sauce) and salt to taste. Marinate the pork in this mixture for 2 to 4 hours. Thread the meat on skewers and broil it slowly over a charcoal fire for 15 to 20 minutes, or until the pork is cooked through and very tender. Serve with the following sauce: In a saucepan combine 1 teaspoon butter, 2 tablespoons

Saté with
Peanut Sauce

peanut butter, 1 tablespoon *ketjab* (or soy sauce), 1 teaspoon lemon juice and 1 teaspoon *sambal oelik* (or finely crushed dried red pepper). Simmer this mixture over low heat for about 15 minutes, blend in 1/4 cup cream, and reheat. Use this sauce as a dip for the *saté*.

Pork Saté   CUT 2 pounds lean pork into 1 1/4-inch cubes. Mix together in a bowl 6 grated Brazil nuts, 2 tablespoons coriander seeds, finely ground, 2 garlic cloves, finely minced, 1 tablespoon salt, and 1 hot red pepper, seeded and finely minced. Less red pepper may be used, to taste, as it is very hot. Or the pepper may be replaced by 1 tablespoon chili powder. Pound the mixture to a smooth paste and blend it with 8 small red onions, grated, 3 tablespoons lemon juice, 2 tablespoons brown sugar, 1/4 cup soy sauce, and 1 teaspoon freshly ground black pepper. Rub the spice mixture over the meat cubes until they are thoroughly saturated. Thread the meat on skewers and broil it slowly over a charcoal fire to brown it on all sides, basting often with olive oil or melted butter.

Teriyaki   CUT 2 pounds boneless pork into cubes 1 1/2 by 2 inches and marinate the meat for 3 or 4 hours in a mixture of 1 cup soy sauce, 1/4 cup Sherry, 1 garlic clove, crushed, and 1 teaspoon sugar. Arrange the meat on skewers and broil it slowly over charcoal, basting it frequently with the marinade, until the pork is cooked through and very tender.

Costillas   CUT 5 pounds lean spareribs into small serving pieces, season with salt, black
con Salsa   pepper, and paprika and arrange them in a glass or enamel vessel with a cover.
Barbacoa   Crush 2 garlic cloves and combine with 1/2 cup Sherry or Madeira and
              the juice of 1 lemon. Pour this marinade over the ribs evenly, cover, and
BARBECUED   marinate in the refrigerator for several hours or overnight. Turn the spareribs
SPARERIBS   once or twice.
                   Sauté 2 large onions, minced, and 1/2 cup finely diced celery in bacon
or other fat. Add 1/2 cup cooked tomatoes, 1/2 cup tomato paste, 1 tablespoon prepared mustard, 1 teaspoon each of crushed dried thyme and crushed cuminseed, 2 tablespoons each of Worcestershire sauce, sugar, and chili powder, 2 finely chopped chili peppers or 1/4 teaspoon Tabasco sauce, and 1 cup vinegar. Mix well and boil for 2 minutes. Brush the drained ribs with

Teriyaki

some of this sauce. Broil the ribs slowly over charcoal until they are well browned, turning and basting with the sauce every 15 minutes.

Jambon
Forestière

IN a saucepan melt 2 tablespoons butter and in it sauté 1/4 pound finely chopped mushrooms until they are lightly browned. Add 1 garlic clove, finely chopped, and stir in 2 tablespoons tomato paste. Season the mixture to taste with salt and pepper and stir in enough dry bread crumbs to thicken the liquid. Spread thin slices of baked or boiled ham with this stuffing and fold the slices in half. Wrap each slice in buttered aluminum foil and bury the packages in hot ashes to cook for 20 to 30 minutes.

Smoked Ham
Steaks

A moderately thick slice of smoked ham serves two. Brown the ham steaks slowly on both sides over a bed of glowing charcoal, brushing them frequently with a mixture of melted butter and white wine.

Glazed Ham
Steaks

IN a bowl combine 1 cup honey with 1 tablespoon each of dry mustard and prepared mustard. Stir in 1 teaspoon lemon juice and beat thoroughly. Grill the ham steaks slowly over a bed of glowing charcoal, brushing them frequently with the honey sauce until they are brown and glazed on both sides.

Long, slow cooking will insure tender, well-done veal and at the same time help to retain juiciness.

Barbecued
Veal Chops

HAVE the butcher cut veal chops, including the kidney, about 1 1/2 inches thick. Dip the chops in seasoned oil and coat both sides with crushed rosemary. Grill very slowly, at some distance from the heat, until the chops are cooked through.

Skewered Veal

CUT 2 pounds veal round steak into cubes 3/4-inch square and marinate the cubes for 2 hours in a mixture of 1/4 cup each of salad oil, lemon juice, and soy sauce. Thread the meat on skewers and broil it or put it over a hot charcoal fire. Turn the skewers frequently until the meat is brown on all sides.

TRIM all but a thin layer of fat from 4 veal kidneys, split them, season with salt and pepper and put them on skewers to keep them flat. Brush the kidneys with melted butter and broil them rather slowly over hot coals, about 8 minutes on each side. Serve the kidneys with broiled bacon or ham and broiled mushrooms or tomatoes, and with maître d'hôtel butter.

Rognons de Veau Grillés

The skin of barbecued chicken should be browned, not charred, and the bird should be cooked only until the juices that follow the fork are clear.

SEASON 3 small broilers with salt and brush them with butter. Put them in a pan in a hot oven (400° to 425° F.) and cook for 10 to 15 minutes, or just long enough to make the flesh firm and to give the skin a slight golden color. Make a *diable* mixture: Cream 1/2 cup butter with 1 tablespoon English mustard and a few drops of Worcestershire sauce and mix it with 3 cups fine fresh bread crumbs. Remove the chicken from the oven and take out any of the bones that can be easily withdrawn.

Spread the chicken with a layer of the *diable* mixture. The chicken may then be set aside until 30 minutes before serving time. Finish the cooking over a charcoal fire out-of-doors. Grill the broilers slowly for 20 to 25 minutes, until they are just cooked, but not charred and dry. Serve hot or cool, but not chilled.

Deviled Chicken

IN a small saucepan combine 3 tablespoons butter, 1 teaspoon each of thyme and freshly grated lemon rind, 1/2 teaspoon each of dry mustard and salt, 1/4 teaspoon freshly ground black pepper, and a dash of lemon juice and stir over low heat until the butter is melted. Adjust the seasoning to taste.

Split 3 broilers and sprinkle them generously with salt, pepper, and thyme. Put the halves in a hinged double broiler and broil them, skin side up, about 2 inches from the coals, for 10 minutes. Stick a hollowed-out lemon half on the end of a long fork and using it as a dipper, baste the chickens frequently with the prepared sauce. Turn the chickens and broil them for about 10 minutes longer, until the skin is evenly browned and the meat thoroughly cooked. Serve the chickens on heated plates, and pour over them the remaining basting sauce. Garnish the plates with watercress.

Barbecued Herb Chicken

SELECT 3 plump broilers. Remove the backbones and neck with a sharp knife so that the halves will lie flat on the grill. Place the chicken halves in a shallow

Barbecued Broilers

Chicken Mixed Grill

pan and sprinkle them with salt. Make a marinade of 1 cup olive oil, 1/2 cup white wine, 1 cut garlic clove, and 6 crushed peppercorns. Marinate the chickens for 30 minutes.

Place the chickens on the grill, skin side down at first, 5 inches from the glowing coals and broil them for 25 to 30 minutes. Turn the halves frequently to cook them evenly and baste often with the marinade.

Melt 1/2 cup butter in a saucepan, add 6 shallots, finely chopped, 1 tablespoon each of chopped chives and chervil or parsley, and 1 teaspoon chopped sweet basil. Bring the butter almost to a boil and pour it, foaming, over the chicken.

SPLIT 3 broilers, dip each piece in melted butter, sprinkle with salt and pepper, and arrange them skin side down on a buttered broiler rack. Broil the birds about 2 inches from the heat for 10 to 12 minutes on each side, basting occasionally with melted butter.

Chicken Mixed Grill

Cut the stem ends from 6 small tomatoes. Sprinkle the tomatoes with salt and bread crumbs, dot with butter, and bake them in a moderate oven (350° F.) while the chickens are broiling.

Sauté 12 slices of lean bacon until crisp. Drain the bacon on absorbent paper and, in the fat remaining in the pan, pan-broil 6 sausages until they are brown all over and well cooked. Sauté 12 mushroom caps in butter until they are golden and sprinkle them with lemon juice and finely chopped parsley. Use all these to garnish the chicken.

BEGIN each skewer arrangement with a mushroom cap lightly sautéed in butter and fill the skewers with alternating halves of chicken livers and squares of bacon and lastly a cooked mushroom cap. Roll the skewers in flour, then in oil, and broil them lightly over charcoal, turning each brochette once or twice to brown both sides. Do not overcook.

Foies de Volaille en Brochette
SKEWERED CHICKEN LIVERS

QUARTER 2 ducklings and rub them with a mixture of 2 egg yolks, 1/3 cup soy sauce, and 1/4 cup honey. Broil the quarters over a low fire, cut side down first, for 45 to 60 minutes. Turn the pieces occasionally toward the end of the cooking time and bring them closer to the fire to crisp the skin.

Broiled Duckling

SPLIT in half a small turkey, weighing from 6 to 8 pounds, and remove the backbone. Place the halves in a shallow pan, sprinkle them with salt, and add 1 cup each of white wine and olive oil and 1/4 cup minced tarragon leaves.

Barbecued Baby Turkey Tarragon

Let the turkey soak in this marinade overnight. Broil the turkey in a hinged rack over hot coals, turning the bird frequently and basting with the marinade from time to time, for about 1 1/2 hours, until the juices that run when the bird is pierced show no pink.

A hinged broiler, which encloses fragile fish, or other suitable food, between twin racks, permits the fish to be turned, broiler and all, without danger of breaking.

Grilled Salmon

SPLIT a whole salmon, weighing from 8 to 12 pounds, rub it on both sides with salt and olive oil and put it in a well-oiled hinged broiler. Broil the salmon, flesh side down, until it is lightly browned. Turn, cover the flesh with a mixture of 1/2 cup butter, the juice of 1 lemon, and 1/4 cup minced parsley, and broil it slowly, skin side down, for about 35 minutes, or until the flesh flakes easily. Do not overcook it.

Almost any fish may be split and cooked in this way.

Grilled Bass

CLEAN and split a 4- to 5-pound bass. Sprinkle it lightly with salt and pepper and put it in an oiled hinged broiler. Broil the fish, skin side up, over hot coals for about 20 minutes, basting frequently with 1/2 cup butter melted with 2 tablespoons chopped fresh mint. Turn the fish and continue to broil, basting often, until the flesh flakes easily.

Broiled Bluefish

CLEAN and scale a bluefish, leaving it whole. Brush the fish with olive oil and sprinkle it with seasoned flour. Arrange the fish in a hinged double broiler and brown it on both sides over the coals, brushing it frequently with oil. The fish is done when it flakes easily with a fork. Serve with melted butter and lemon wedges.

This method applies equally well to other whole fish.

Barbecued Salmon Steaks

DIP salmon steaks, cut 1 inch thick, in melted butter and arrange them on a hinged broiler. Broil the steaks quickly over hot charcoal, turning to brown both sides. During the broiling brush the steaks frequently with melted butter mixed with a little white wine or lemon juice.

Barbecued Fish

Other fish steaks adaptable to this recipe are swordfish, tuna, and halibut.

CUT salmon steaks into large chunks and string the chunks on skewers, alternating the fish chunks with mushroom caps, halved tomatoes, sliced onions, and strips of green or red pepper. Put the skewers in a shallow pan and pour over them 1 cup olive oil and 1/2 cup white wine. Sprinkle the fish and vegetables with salt and freshly ground pepper, and marinate them for 3 hours. A little finely chopped fresh dill may be added to the marinade if desired.

Charcoal Broiled Skewered Salmon

Broil the salmon over charcoal until it is lightly browned, turning the skewers and basting occasionally with the marinade. Serve with potatoes baked in the ashes.

DIP freshly shucked clams in melted butter, sprinkle them with lemon juice and a little freshly ground pepper, and wrap them in small squares of aluminum foil. Roast the clams in the hot coals for 3 to 4 minutes and serve hot in the aluminum package as an hors-d'oeuvre.

Coal Roasted Clams

RINSE soft-shelled crabs in salt water. Cut off the heads about one-fourth inch behind the eyes and discard the green bubble. Lift the soft shell where it comes to a point at each side and cut off the white gills. Peel back the apron and cut it off. Arrange the crabs on an oiled, hinged broiler and grill them over glowing coals for about 5 minutes on each side, basting them frequently with a mixture of 1/2 cup each of fresh tomato juice, white wine, and melted butter, 1 garlic clove, minced, and salt and pepper to taste. Serve the crabs with the remaining sauce poured over them.

Barbecued Crabs

MIX together 1 pound fresh crab meat, 1 teaspoon each of salt, dry mustard, and chopped chives, 3 tablepoons Sherry, and 1 cup white bread crumbs to make a firm paste. Form the mixture into small balls the size of a walnut. Wrap a strip of bacon around each ball and secure it with a toothpick. Broil the balls over hot coals for 15 to 20 minutes, or until the bacon is nicely browned on all sides. Serve with a dip of hollandaise sauce sprinkled with finely chopped chives.

Crab Meat Brochette

TURN live lobsters on their backs and split them lengthwise with a heavy knife or cleaver. Crack the large claws and discard the intestinal vein and the small sac behind the head. Brush the flesh with melted butter and broil the lobsters, flesh side down, for 3 to 4 minutes, or just long enough to brown. Turn the lobsters and continue to broil, shell side down, for about 15 minutes,

Charcoal Broiled Lobsters

basting frequently with melted butter. Serve with melted butter and lemon wedges.

Japanese Broiled Lobster WASH 3 large lobsters, split them in half lengthwise, discard the intestinal vein and the sac behind the head, and marinate them in a mixture of 5 tablespoons soy sauce and 3 tablespoons Japanese sweet wine *(mirin)* or white wine with 1/2 teaspoon sugar. Broil rather quickly over hot coals, basting two or three times with the sauce. Serve with plain boiled rice.

Oysters en Brochette DRAIN freshly shucked oysters, reserving the juice, and wrap each in a piece of bacon. Arrange from 3 to 6 wrapped oysters on a skewer and place the skewers in a hinged broiler. Spread the oysters with a little butter and broil them quickly over hot coals until the bacon is cooked. Serve on toast with the oyster liquor heated with a little butter.

Skewered Scallops DIP washed and dried scallops in melted butter and then in cracker meal seasoned to taste with salt and mixed herbs. Arrange 4 or 5 scallops on each skewer with a whole slice of bacon, weaving the bacon slice back and forth between the scallops. Brown lightly over hot coals, turning the skewers frequently for even cooking. Serve with melted butter seasoned with lemon juice and parsley.

Chinese Skewered Shrimps SHELL and devein large shrimps and soak them for 30 minutes in a mixture of equal parts of dry Sherry, soy sauce, and olive oil. Finely chopped ginger, garlic, or fresh herbs may be added. Thread the shrimps on metal skewers with sliced water chestnuts and squares of bacon. Broil them over hot coals, turning several times and basting with the marinade. Serve hot from the grill on a bed of rice garnished with fresh tomatoes.

Grilled Shrimps SHELL and devein 2 pounds jumbo shrimps. Put the shrimps in a bowl or jar and add 3 garlic cloves and 1 onion, both finely chopped, 1/4 cup chopped parsley, 1 teaspoon each of chopped basil, dry mustard, and salt, 1/2 cup olive oil, and the juice of 1 lemon. Let the shrimps marinate in the jar for several hours. Grill them over hot coals for about 5 minutes, or until they are bright pink.

Broiled Shrimps

ARRANGE 1 1/2 pounds shrimps, shelled and cleaned, side by side in a shallow baking dish. Pour over them 1/2 cup each of dry white wine and olive oil and sprinkle them with 4 or 5 shallots, finely sliced, 2 tablespoons finely chopped parsley, 1 spray of fresh dill, tarragon, or thyme, finely chopped, and 1/2 teaspoon each of freshly ground black pepper and salt. Let the shrimps marinate for 2 hours, spooning the marinade over them from time to time.

Broil the shrimps on a hinged broiler over hot coals for 5 minutes. Turn the broiler and broil the shrimps for 5 minutes longer, or until they are cooked, basting them several times with the marinade.

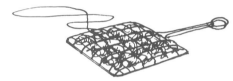

Barbecue marinades are combined tenderizing and flavoring agents.

Marinade for Game or Beef

With a fork combine 1 cup olive oil and 1/2 cup red wine. Add 2 garlic cloves and 4 shallots, both finely chopped, 12 crushed peppercorns, 1 bay leaf, 1/2 teaspoon each of chopped orégano and sweet basil, and salt to taste and mix thoroughly to blend the ingredients.

Marinade for Lamb

With a fork combine 1 cup each of olive oil and red wine. Add 6 cloves, 12 crushed peppercorns, 1 tablespoon each of finely chopped mint leaves and parsley, a pinch of rosemary, and salt to taste and combine the mixture thoroughly.

Marinade for Shrimp or Soft Shelled Crabs

With a fork combine 1 cup white wine and 3/4 cup olive oil. Add 1/2 tablespoon crushed peppercorns, 6 shallots, finely chopped, 1 garlic clove, split, 1 bay leaf, 3 tablespoons finely chopped parsley or chervil, and salt to taste. Mix well.

Marinade for Poultry

With a fork combine 1 cup olive oil, 1/2 cup dry white wine, and 1 tablespoon vinegar. Add 1 garlic clove, minced, 10 peppercorns, 1/2 teaspoon chopped sweet basil or tarragon, and salt to taste and mix well.

Marinade for Fish

With a fork combine 1/2 cup each of olive oil and dry white wine. Add 2 garlic cloves, finely chopped, 1 tablespoon crushed peppercorns, and 1 teaspoon each of salt, Worcestershire sauce, and paprika.

Barbecue sauces give individuality and distinction to simply grilled meats, fish, and poultry.

Uncooked Barbecue Sauce

MIX together 1 1/2 cups ketchup, 1 dry chili pepper, soaked in water until soft and finely chopped, 1/4 cup lemon juice, 1 teaspoon each of prepared mustard and freshly ground black pepper, and 1 tablespoon Worcestershire sauce. Add 1 garlic clove, split, 1 onion, halved, and 1 bay leaf. For meat or poultry.

Cooked Barbecue Sauce

IN a saucepan sauté 5 garlic cloves, chopped, in 1/3 cup olive oil until the garlic is golden. Add 1/2 cup red wine, bring the wine to a boil, and simmer for 2 minutes. Add 1/4 cup A.1. sauce, 2 tablespoons brown sugar, 1 teaspoon each of salt, pepper, mustard, and orégano, 1 cup brown stock, and 1/2 cup tomato paste and simmer over low heat for 15 minutes. Correct the seasoning to taste with a dash of Tabasco and lemon juice. For meat, game, or poultry.

Sweet and Sour Barbecue Sauce

IN a saucepan mix 1 cup each of red-wine vinegar, water, and brown sugar. Add 3 tablespoons ketchup, 1 tablespoon soy sauce, 1 teaspoon dry mustard, 1 cup pineapple chunks, fresh or frozen, 1 green pepper, seeded and cut into strips, and 2 tomatoes, peeled and cut into wedges. Bring the sauce to a boil and simmer it gently for 10 minutes. Stir in 1 1/2 tablespoons cornstarch, mixed to a smooth paste with 1/4 cup cold water and cook the sauce, stirring, until it is clear and thickened. For shrimps, roast pork, or spareribs.

California Barbecue Sauce

COMBINE 1 1/2 cups olive oil, 1 cup red wine, 1/4 cup vinegar, 1 teaspoon chopped parsley, 1 tablespoon salt, 2 garlic cloves, crushed, and 1/4 teaspoon freshly ground black pepper. For basting grilled meats and poultry.

Creole Barbecue Sauce

IN a saucepan melt 1/2 cup butter and in it sauté until lightly browned 1 onion, 2 garlic cloves, 1 green pepper, seeded, and 1 stalk of celery, all coarsely chopped. Add 2 cups tomatoes, freshly stewed or canned, 1/2 cup each of tomato purée, water, and brown sugar, 2 tablespoons vinegar, 1 teaspoon each of salt and pepper, and a dash of Tabasco. Bring the sauce to a boil and simmer it gently for 30 minutes. Correct the seasoning and keep the sauce hot. Use with meat or fish.

MIX together 1 cup soy sauce, 2 garlic cloves, crushed, 1 tablespoon grated fresh ginger, and 1/2 cup each of Sherry and tomato ketchup. Use as a marinade for spareribs and other pork cuts and for basting the meat.

Chinese Ginger Barbecue Sauce

SAUTÉ 1/2 cup onions, finely chopped, in 1/4 cup olive oil until the onions are golden but not brown. Add 1 cup tomato paste, 2 tablespoons Worcestershire sauce, 1/2 cup strained honey, and 1 teaspoon each of basil and salt. Simmer the sauce for 5 minutes, stirring constantly, and add 1/2 cup red wine. Strain the sauce through a fine sieve and use it for basting grilled fish.

Fish Barbecue Sauce

IN a saucepan combine 1 cup butter with 1/4 cup each of lemon juice and Sherry, 1 teaspoon Worcestershire sauce, 1 garlic clove, 1 teaspoon chopped parsley, and 1/2 teaspoon salt. Bring the mixture to the boiling point but do not cook it. Use for basting grilled meats and poultry.

Lemon Butter Barbecue Sauce

IN a saucepan combine 1 cup tomato ketchup, 1/2 cup butter, 1 tablespoon Worcestershire sauce, 1 teaspoon salt, the juice of 1 lemon, and 4 thin slices of lemon. Simmer the mixture for 10 minutes. Use for basting grilled meats, poultry, or fish.

Maryland Barbecue Sauce

COMBINE 1 cup olive oil, 1/2 cup vinegar, 3 tablespoons each of finely minced shallot and green pepper, 1 cup tomato juice, 1 teaspoon orégano, 1 tablespoon chili powder, 4 garlic cloves, crushed, and 1 tablespoon salt. Simmer the mixture gently for 10 minutes and strain it. Use for basting meats and fish.

Mexican Barbecue Sauce

IN 1 cup olive oil, sauté 4 garlic cloves, crushed, and 3/4 cup chopped onions until they are golden but not brown. Add 1 cup each of ripe olives and tomatoes, both finely chopped, 1 cup red wine, 2 tablespoons Worcestershire sauce, 1/2 cup each of orange juice and brown sugar, the juice of 1 lemon, the grated rind of 1 orange, 1 teaspoon rosemary, 3 tablespoons chopped green pepper, and 1/4 cup chopped parsley. Bring the mixture to a boil and simmer it gently for 20 minutes. Strain and use for basting grilled meats and poultry.

Orange Barbecue Sauce

There are portable and makeshift ovens capable of turning out an acceptable biscuit over a charcoal fire; for the most part the outdoor cook will prefer to bring his bread to the party, and heat or toast it over the coals at the last minute.

Butter Bread   SPLIT a long French or Italian bread lengthwise, or cut it into rather thick slices, but not through the bottom crust. Combine 1/2 cup butter with 2 or more garlic cloves forced through a press. With a pastry brush, spread the cut surfaces of the bread with garlic butter. Reshape the loaf, wrap it in foil, and heat it on the back of the grill for about 20 minutes. The butter may be mixed with a generous amount of chopped chives, parsley, and or chervil, instead of the garlic, or the herbs may be omitted entirely.

Griddle Scones   POUR 1 1/2 cups buttermilk into a large bowl and stir in 1/3 cup chopped chives, 1/2 cup cream, 1 1/2 tablespoons sugar, 1 teaspoon soda, 1/2 teaspoon each of baking powder and salt, and enough sifted flour to make a soft dough. Drop the dough from a tablespoon onto a greased heated griddle and bake the scones until small bubbles appear on top. Carefully turn the scones and brown the other side. Split the scones, butter them, and serve them hot.

Any vegetable preparation that can be cooked quickly in saucepan or skillet can be cooked outdoors as well. Generally the simpler, more robustly flavored of these preparations earn a heartier welcome from cook and consumer. As for charcoal-broiled and grilled vegetables and fruits, their unique flavor cannot readily be duplicated by other cookery methods.

Roast Corn   OPEN the husk at the top of each ear of corn and pull out the silk. Dip the ears in water and grill them over medium coals for 10 to 15 minutes, or until the kernels are cooked, turning the ears frequently. Serve with sweet butter, salt, and freshly ground pepper.

Corn in Cream   CUT enough fresh corn from the cobs to fill a buttered earthenware casserole. Sprinkle the corn with salt and freshly ground pepper and add heavy cream almost to cover. Cover the casserole and simmer the corn on top of the grill for 5 minutes.

Griddle Scones

Skewered Cucumbers and Mushrooms

PEEL large firm cucumbers and cut them in 1-inch slices. Arrange the slices on skewers alternately with large mushroom caps. Dip in melted butter and cook over hot coals for 8 to 10 minutes. Brush the vegetables with more melted butter and sprinkle them with freshly ground pepper.

Grilled Eggplant

PEEL a large eggplant and cut it into 1/2-inch slices. Dip the slices in melted butter and in seasoned flour. Broil the slices over the hot coals until the underside is brown, turn them, dot them with butter, and brown the other side. If desired, the half-cooked eggplant may be generoulsly sprinkled with grated Parmesan cheese; the cheese will melt as the underside of the eggplant browns.

Skewered Eggplant

PEEL and cut a large eggplant into 1 1/2-inch cubes. Marinate the eggplant for an hour or more in highly seasoned French dressing. Thread the cubes on individual skewers and broil slowly over the coals, basting from time to time with the marinade.

Grilled Mushrooms

CHOOSE very large mushrooms and cut away the stems, which should be reserved for other purposes. Dip the caps in melted butter and arrange them on a narrow-screen grill close to the hot coals, round side down. Add more butter as the mushrooms cook, until they are tender.

Grilled Onions

PEEL large sweet onions and slice them crosswise into thick discs. Dip them in melted butter and arrange them in a hinged broiler. Broil them quickly on both sides—the onions should still be crisp—and sprinkle them with salt and freshly ground black pepper.

Coal Roasted Onions

WASH large sweet onions, but do not peel them. Wrap each onion in aluminum foil and bury the packages in the hot coals to roast for 45 to 60 minutes.

Grilled Sweet Pepper

QUARTER green peppers, discard seeds and pith, and parboil the quarters for 2 minutes in boiling salted water. Dip in melted butter and grill rather slowly until they are brown on both sides. Serve with grilled mushrooms or onions, as an accompaniment to meat or poultry.

BOIL sweet potatoes in their jackets until they are barely tender. Peel, cut into large uniform pieces, and arrange on individual skewers alternately with chunks of canned pineapple. Dip the skewers in melted butter and grill them on all sides until they are delicately browned.

Skewered Sweet Potatoes

BAKE potatoes in the usual way, split them, and scoop out the pulp. Mash and season the pulp with salt, pepper, butter, and a little grated onion, and add enough milk to make a smooth mixture. Pack the shells with the seasoned mixture and put the halves together. Wrap each potato separately in aluminum foil. Heat the stuffed potatoes on the back of the grate while the meat is cooking, for 20 to 30 minutes.

Barbecued Stuffed Potatoes

SCRUB 1 large baking potato for each serving. Bury the potatoes in the hot coals for 40 minutes, or until they test done when pierced with a fork. Serve with butter, salt, and freshly ground pepper. The potatoes may be wrapped in aluminum foil for faster cooking.

Ash Roasted Potatoes

FILL an iron cauldron or kettle 3/4 full with common rosin. Melt the rosin over a wood fire out in the open. Put the potatoes in their jackets into the hot rosin. The potatoes are cooked when they come to the surface. Remove the potatoes from the rosin with a wrought-iron spoon, taking care not to puncture the skins. Roll each potato in 2 or 3 thicknesses of newspaper and twist the ends of the paper tightly. The rosin cools at once and sticks to the paper. Cut the wrapped potato across the middle and break it open. The skin will pull away with the paper. Season with butter, salt, and freshly ground black pepper.

Rosin Potatoes

CUT large, firm tomatoes in half, brush with melted butter, and place them cut side down on the side of the grill away from the intense heat. Cook the tomatoes from 1 to 3 minutes, depending on the fire, but be careful not to overcook them or they will be difficult to turn. Turn the tomatoes and prick the flesh with a fork. Sprinkle the cut surface with a little finely chopped dill and pour a little melted butter on each. Continue to cook the tomatoes until the skin blisters.

Tomatoes with Dill

Barbecued Apples

SPLIT zucchini lengthwise, brush the halves with melted butter, and grill them over the coals for 2 to 3 minutes on each side, or until they are tender. Sprinkle with salt and pepper and serve hot from the grill.

Grilled Zucchini

WASH and cut into 1-inch slices 1 medium zucchini for each guest. Marinate the slices in 1/2 cup olive oil with 1 medium onion and 1 teaspoon marjoram, both finely chopped, for an hour or more. Arrange the slices of zucchini on skewers alternately with thin slices of green tomato and cook over hot coals, turning frequently to brown evenly.

Skewered Zucchini

MAKE a stuffing of equal parts of soft bread crumbs and chopped parsley and twice as much chopped cooked ham or tongue. Add salt and pepper to taste, some chopped chives, and enough soft butter to bind the mixture. Split zucchini and scoop out a little of the center. Fill the halves with the stuffing, mounding it high, and lay the zucchini on the grill, some distance from the coals. Broil the zucchini until it is tender and the filling is warmed through.

Stuffed Zucchini

CORE but do not peel large tart apples. Cut the fruit into thick rings and dip the rings in melted butter. Grill the slices over the coals, turning them often, until they are brown on both sides. Sprinkle lightly with sugar and let the sugar melt.

Barbecued Apples

CHOOSE slightly green bananas. Lay the fruit on the grate over the coals and cook them for about 15 minutes, turning them carefully with two spoons or a pair of tongs. Serve in the shell. To eat, each guest strips off a section of the peel and scoops out the soft pulp with a teaspoon. Sprinkle with a little rum and sugar, if desired.

Grilled Bananas

CUT grapefruit and remove the seeds, but do not free the sections. Brush the cut surface with melted butter and sprinkle it with sugar, white or brown, and a little cinnamon or nutmeg. Grill the fruit, shell side down, until it is heated through. Glaze the fruit by passing over it a hot coal,

Grilled Grapefruit

405

held in tongs. Maple syrup or honey may be used as sweetener instead of sugar, and a spoonful of cordial or brandy may be added as a final flourish. Serve as a first course or as dessert.

Broiled Orange Slices

DIP thick unpeeled slices of seedless oranges into melted butter and arrange them in a hinged double broiler. Brown the fruit quickly on both sides and serve it with duck or other poultry.

Grenadine Peaches

CUT firm, ripe freestone peaches in half and remove the seeds. Or, if desired, the peaches may be dipped into boiling water, and the peel slipped off. Brush the cut surface well with grenadine and put the fruit on the grill, cut surface up. When the fruit is tender, turn it for a few minutes to gild the other side.

Spiced Peaches

MAKE a paste of brown sugar and Madeira or Sherry, and with it coat liberally the cut side of preserved peaches. Sprinkle the fruit with ground cloves and grill it, round side down, until it is heated through. Caramelize the sugar with a hot coal held in tongs.

Grilled Pineapple

SPLIT a large fresh pineapple lengthwise into segments. Brush the flesh with olive oil and grill the segments at some distance from the coals until they are lightly browned.

Glazed Pineapple

DIP slices of canned pineapple in melted butter and dredge them with brown sugar. Grill on both sides for a few minutes and sprinkle with a little warmed brandy.

Curried Apples

SELECT 4 large cooking apples of uniform size and peel them. Cut the apples into wedges about 1/2 inch thick and remove the cores. Arrange the slices on baking pans and sprinkle them with 3 tablespoons melted butter, 1/2 teaspoon curry powder, and 1 tablespoon sugar. Bake the slices in a moderate oven (350° F.) for about 15 minutes, or until they are tender but not soft enough to break when tested with a fork.

Remove the slices from the oven and sprinkle them with 1 tablespoon sugar or to taste, or a little brown sugar. Serve as an accompaniment to lamb, pork, or ham.

Spit-roasted meats bear little resemblance to oven-roasted, or more accurately, baked, meats, since spit roasting is true roasting, in the open, with no steam to confuse the objectives. The proud owner of an electric rotisserie will also be the proud owner of the manufacturer's book of instructions for the use of same; experience with this invaluable piece of equipment will bring the courage to adapt to its use recipes that call for "roasting" in the oven. To insure efficient operation of the rotisserie, the meat must be arranged on the spit in such a way that it is perfectly balanced and will not slip as the spit turns. The recipes that follow are intended to serve as guide-posts for spit-cookery in general; the motor driven spit of the charcoal barbecue presents no additional problems. If you cannot judge doneness by nose and feel, use a meat thermometer.

When game and game birds have been prepared for cooking by aging, larding, and marinating, as prescribed, the procedure for spit roasting them differs in no way from that for domestic meats.

SECURE a short fork on the spit with the prongs pointed toward the end of the spit. Weave a 5-pound slab of marinated ribs in the spit, running it through the flesh after every fifth rib. Fasten the meat in place with the second meat fork and fit the spit in the roaster so that one entire surface of the slab faces the heat. Brush the top of the meat generously with some of the marinade, turn on the heat, and cook the meat until one side is well browned. Switch on the motor to rotate the spit and expose the underside to the heat. Brush again with the marinade and continue to roast until the second side is brown, about 1 1/2 hours.

MARINATE a leg of lamb for 24 hours, turning it several times, in the marinade for lamb, omitting the mint leaves.

Fasten a short meat fork on the spit with the prongs pointed toward the end of the spit. Drive the spit lengthwise through the thick flesh on the leg and fasten it securely with the second meat fork. The lamb must be well balanced and centered on the spit. Grasp an end of the spit in each hand and, if the lamb rotates the spit in the hands, the spit should be relocated in the leg, to insure a proper balance. Insert a meat thermometer in the lamb and place the spit in the roaster. Turn on both the motor and the heat and roast the meat for about 22 minutes to the pound, or until the thermometer registers medium-rare.

Strain the marinade into a saucepan and add 1 tomato, peeled, seeded,

Rotisserie Cooking

Spit Roasted Spareribs

Roast Marinated Leg of Lamb

and chopped, 4 mushrooms, sliced, and 3 gherkins, chopped. Simmer the sauce for 15 minutes and serve with the meat.

Roast Filet
of Beef

WRAP a filet of beef in thin slices of larding pork and tie the slices securely in several places. Fasten a short fork on the spit with the prongs pointed toward the end of the spit. Drive the spit lengthwise through the filet and fasten it on the spit with the other short fork. Sprinkle the filet with salt and pepper, rub it with 1/2 teaspoon rosemary, and insert a meat thermometer. Place the spit in the roaster, turn on the heat and the motor, and roast the filet for about 12 minutes per pound, or until the meat thermometer registers rare.

Spit Roasted
Baby Turkey

RUB the inside of a 5- to 6-pound turkey with salt and pepper and put in the cavity 4 or 5 shallots, sliced, several sprays of parsley, and a sprig of thyme. Fold the wing tips under the wings and truss the legs and wings close to the body.

Rub the skin of the bird generously with butter and sprinkle with salt and pepper. Fasten a short meat fork on the spit with the prongs pointed toward the end of the spit. Press the turkey on the spit, running the spit diagonally from the crotch of the breast bone through the tail. Secure the bird on the spit with the second meat fork and place the spit in the roaster. Turn on both the motor and heat and roast the bird for about 1 1/2 hours.

Poularde
Gennoise
à la Broche

ROAST a chicken on a spit—charcoal gives it excellent flavor—and put it on a serving platter.

Garnish the platter with mushrooms prepared as follows: Put the yolks of 6 hard-cooked eggs through a fine sieve, add tiny julienne strips of truffle, salt and pepper to taste, and a sprinkling of finely chopped garlic. Add enough soft butter to bind the mixture. Use this mixture to stuff 6 large perfect mushrooms that have been soaked briefly in water acidulated with lemon juice. Arrange the mushroom caps, stuffing up, in an earthenware baking dish, dot them with butter and add 1 cup sparkling white wine. Cover the dish and bake the mushrooms in a slow oven (300° F.) for 20 minutes.

Brown lightly in butter rounds of bread cut the same size as the mushrooms. Cover each crouton with a round slice of *foie gras* cut to fit and top each with a stuffed mushroom. Carve the chicken and re-form it. Garnish the platter with the mushroom canapés and watercress.

Aspics and Pâtés

Aspic has four uses: it is used to bind other ingredients, or to line a mold into which other ingredients are to be packed; it is cut into shapes or chopped or rubbed through a coarse sieve and used for garnishing, and, of course, it is used to coat cooked meats, poultry, or fish.

In handling aspics, have all ingredients and utensils very cold. To line a mold, bank it with crushed ice. When the cold aspic is swirled around the inside of the mold, it will congeal almost immediately. To make a thicker coating, add another layer of aspic. Decorations should be affixed between layers of aspic. It is important to allow enough time for each coating of aspic to set completely before the next coat is added; return the food to the refrigerator between steps.

A piece of meat, fish, or poultry that is to be coated with aspic should be so thoroughly chilled that the aspic begins to set as soon as it touches the surface. The aspic should be liquid, but on the verge of congealing.

As a final precaution, keep the finished aspic in the refrigerator until the last possible moment before serving. If the party is a large one, use two small serving dishes, rather than one large one, for each aspic preparation, so that the second serving can be kept cold in the refrigerator.

Meat Aspic PUT in a large kettle 3 pounds each of beef bones and veal shin bones, 6 prepared calves' feet, 3 carrots, 3 onions, and 3 leeks, all sliced, 1 stalk of celery, 2 tablespoons salt and 2 gallons water. Bring the liquid to a boil, skim it and boil it gently for about 5 hours, skimming as needed. Strain the stock, cool it and remove the fat from the surface. Clarify as follows: Beat slightly 4 egg whites, mix them with 1 pound lean chopped beef and add the mixture to the cold broth. Add 12 peppercorns, 1 tablespoon salt, 4 sprigs each of tarragon and chervil, 6 sprigs of parsley and 1 bay leaf. Heat slowly, stirring constantly just until the boiling point is reached, and simmer the stock very gently for 30 minutes. Strain the stock through

Sherry or Madeira Aspic fine muslin and add 1/2 cup Sherry or Madeira. If calves' feet were not available, add to the hot strained broth 2 tablespoons gelatin softened in 1/2 cup cold water.

It is a sensible precaution to test aspic to make sure that it will have the proper stiffness. Chill a little of the stock; if it does not stiffen, it may be reduced further or it may be stiffened with gelatin. Use 1 envelope gelatin, softened in 1/4 cup cold water, to jell 1 quart stock that has congealed lightly, but is not stiff enough.

Calf's Feet Prepared for Aspic Have the butcher split the feet. Wash them well, put them in a kettle, add salted water to cover and bring the water to a boil. Cook the bones for about 5 minutes, until the scum stops coming to the top. Rinse the bones well and add them to the soup kettle with the other ingredients for aspic.

Chicken Aspic To the recipe for meat aspic, add a fowl and some chicken feet.

Chicken Feet Prepared for Aspic Chop off the nails and discard them. Wash the feet and put them in a kettle with salted water to cover. Bring the water to a boil. When the skin loosens, plunge the feet into cold water, remove the skins and discard them. Add the cleaned feet to the soup kettle with the other ingredients for aspic.

Fish Aspic PUT 2 pounds trimmings and bones of flounder, whiting, or other inexpensive fish in a saucepan with 2 onions, sliced, 4 sprays each of tarragon and parsley, and 1 bay leaf. Add 1 cup white wine and the juice of 1 lemon, and bring the liquid to a boil, shaking the pan frequently to prevent scorching. Reduce the liquid over high heat by half. Add 2 quarts water and a little salt and pepper, bring the water to the boil, and skim carefully. Simmer the stock for 20 minutes, strain it into a large deep pan, cool it, and skim it again.

Add 6 tablespoons gelatin softened in 3/4 cup cold water, a pinch of saffron, and the stiffly beaten whites and crushed shells of 2 eggs. Bring the stock slowly to a boil, stirring constantly, and boil it up a few times. Let the stock stand in a warm place for 30 minutes and strain it through a sieve lined with a flannel cloth wrung out of cold water. Cool the aspic to lukewarm and flavor it with 1/2 cup Champagne or white Burgundy.

Game Aspic

To the ingredients for meat aspic, add 2 or 3 carcasses of such game birds as partridge or pheasant. To clarify a game aspic, use ground meat of the game that is to give the aspic its flavor in place of the ground beef. Cool the aspic to lukewarm and flavor it with a little brandy.

Chicken Tomato Aspic

IN a saucepan combine 3 cups chicken stock, 1 cup tomato juice, 2 tablespoons dry white wine, 1 tablespoon tarragon vinegar, 4 tablespoons gelatin softened in 1/2 cup cold water, salt and pepper to taste, and the crushed shells and stiffly beaten whites of 2 eggs. Heat the mixture slowly, stirring, until it boils. Remove from the heat, let it stand for 10 minutes, and strain it through a sieve lined with a flannel cloth wrung out of cold water.

Tomato Aspic

PUT into a saucepan 1 cup light stock, 1 cup tomato juice, 1/2 teaspoon sugar, 1 crushed egg shell, 1 egg white, lightly beaten, 2 tablespoons gelatin softened in 1/4 cup cold water, and salt and pepper to taste. Bring the mixture slowly to a boil, stirring constantly, and strain it through a sieve lined with wet flannel.

Port Wine Aspic

PUT into a saucepan 3 cups chicken consommé, 1 cup Port, 2 tablespoons dry white wine, 1 tablespoon tarragon vinegar, 4 tablespoons gelatin softened in 1/2 cup cold water, salt and pepper to taste, and the crushed shells and stiffly beaten whites of 2 eggs. Heat the mixture slowly, stirring constantly, until it boils up in the pan. Remove from the heat, let it stand for 10 minutes, and strain it through a sieve lined with a flannel cloth wrung out of cold water.

Mayonnaise Collée

SOFTEN 2 tablespoons gelatin in 1/2 cup cold water and stir it over hot water until it is completely dissolved. Fold the gelatin into 2 cups mayonnaise and blend well. Use at once, before the gelatin sets. It may be reheated and used again, if required.

Chaud-Froid Blanc

JELLIED WHITE SAUCE

MELT 1/4 cup butter in a saucepan, stir in 1/4 cup flour, and stir in gradually 2 cups hot chicken broth. Add salt to taste and continue to stir until the sauce is smooth and thickened. Cook the sauce over low heat for about 30 minutes. Strain it, add 2 tablespoons gelatin softened in 1/3 cup cold water and 1 cup heavy cream, and stir well.

Chaud-Froid Brun

JELLIED BROWN SAUCE

SOFTEN 2 tablespoons gelatin in 1/2 cup cold water. Combine 2 cups brown sauce with 1 cup stock or consommé, bring the sauce to a boil and skim it well. Dissolve the gelatin in the sauce. Add a scant 1/2 cup Madeira or Sherry and strain the sauce through a fine sieve.

Aspic of Filets of Sole

FOLD 12 small filets of sole in half and poach them in butter and lemon juice for about 4 minutes on each side, or until the flesh flakes easily but is not at all brown. Put them on a platter to cool.

Set a decorative quart mold into a bed of cracked ice. Pour a few tablespoons of cool but still liquid fish aspic into it and rock and turn the mold to coat the bottom and sides with the aspic. As soon as the jelly begins to set, decorate it artistically with small crescents, diamonds, or circles of truffle and hard-cooked egg white. Leaves of tarragon or thin slices of tiny radishes may also be used.

Sprinkle a few drops of liquid aspic over each decoration to prevent it from shifting and as soon as this aspic sets, add cold liquid aspic to cover the decorations with an inch-thick layer. Place the mold in the refrigerator for about 15 minutes, or until the jelly is firm.

Arrange 6 of the sole filets on the jelly with tails overlapping and cover them with a little jelly. Continue to add thin layers of aspic, chilling each layer for about 15 minutes, or until it is set, until the layer of jelly covering the filets measures about 1/2 inch.

Arrange the remaining 6 filets in reverse order and fill the mold with cold liquid aspic. Chill the mold for at least 1 hour, or until set.

To Unmold Aspic

To serve, run a knife blade around the edge of the mold and dip the mold in and out of hot water three times. Each dip should last about 1 second. The water should be very hot, but not hot enough to scald the hand. Turn the aspic out onto a chilled serving platter and garnish the dish attractively with romaine, watercress, green olives, radishes, sliced tomatoes, or thin slices of cucumber.

Aspic of Filets of Sole

Filets de Sole en Gelée à la Parisienne
JELLIED FILETS OF SOLE À LA PARISIENNE

POACH 6 filets of sole in court bouillon for about 15 minutes, or until the fish is cooked. Lay the filets on a rack to drain and cool, and coat them with *mayonnaise collée.* Chill the filets until the *collée* is set and repeat to make a thicker coating. Use 1 to 1 1/2 cups *collée* in all. Decorate the fish with tarragon leaves or truffles cut into shapes, or make daisies with the whites of hard-cooked eggs for petals and sieved hard-cooked egg yolks for centers, fixing the decorations in the sauce. Chill and coat with clear aspic. Combine cooked vegetables cut in fine dice with *mayonnaise collée* and arrange this salad on a serving dish. Lay the fish filets on the vegetables. Garnish with little cucumber baskets made by cutting cucumbers into 1 1/2 inch lengths and scooping the slices out about two-thirds from the top. Fill the basket with tiny cherry tomatoes dressed with vinaigrette sauce. Or hollow out small tomatoes and fill them with cucumber salad. Or arrange slices of hard-cooked egg on tomato slices and place a ripe olive in the center of each egg yolk.

Truite Saumonée Glacée à la Norvégienne
JELLIED SALMON TROUT NORWEGIAN

CLEAN a salmon trout weighing from 3 to 4 pounds. Wipe it with a damp cloth and tie it securely in cheesecloth. Place it on its stomach on the rack of a fish kettle, securing it with string through the holes in the rack. Steam the fish for about 15 minutes per pound, or until the flesh flakes easily. Remove the trout and cool it in the same position.

Prepare a boat-shaped rice socle. The hollow in the top will hold the fish securely. When the fish is cold, unwrap it and carefully remove all the skin except a little near the head and the tail. Place the trout in the hollow of the rice socle and brush it several times with clear liquid aspic, chilling it between the applications of the layers.

Decorate both sides of the fish with cutouts of truffle. Place a row of poached shrimps along the spine of the fish, then coat fish and garnishings with several more layers of aspic very lightly tinted with red food coloring. Surround the rice socle with chopped aspic and garnish the platter with peeled small tomatoes, lemon wedges, and thick slices of cucumbers hollowed out and filled with chopped shrimps bound with mayonnaise. Harpoon the trout's head with an *attelet* or decorated skewer bearing a tiny heart of lettuce. Serve with a sauceboat of mayonnaise.

Saumon Glacé
GLAZED POACHED SALMON

CLEAN a salmon weighing about 10 pounds, leaving head and tail intact. Place it on a thin wooden board that will fit on the rack of the *saumonière*, or fish kettle, wrap the fish and board in a piece of cheesecloth, and tie it in place with string. Put this in the kettle with enough court bouillon for shellfish to cover generously. Bring the court bouillon to a boil and simmer the salmon for 1 to 1 1/2 hours, or about 10 minutes per pound. Turn off the heat and leave the salmon in the water until it is cold.

Lift out the fish, drain it well, and remove the string and cheesecloth. Take off the skin and the dark flesh from one side of the fish. Carefully turn it onto a serving platter so that the skinned side is underneath. Remove skin and dark flesh from the side now uppermost.

Coat the fish with a thin layer of cool but still liquid aspic and decorate it with fanciful shapes—flowers, crescents, and circles—made of carrot, hard-cooked egg, watercress, tarragon leaves, lemon peel, and pimiento. Coat the fish with several layers of aspic and chill it until ready to serve. Garnish the platter with congealed aspic stirred into fragments with a fork, with serrated slices of lemon, and with parsley. Put a cherry tomato in the salmon's mouth. Serve the aspic with a sauceboat of green mayonnaise.

Darnes de Saumon en Gelée
SALMON STEAKS IN ASPIC

IN a saucepan poach 6 salmon steaks, about an inch thick, in white-wine court bouillon for about 10 minutes, or until the flesh flakes readily. Put each steak in a shallow individual serving dish and garnish it with thin slices of cucumber and hard-cooked egg, and leaves of fresh tarragon.

Brush the decorated fish steaks with cool but still liquid fish aspic and chill them. When the glaze is firm, fill the dishes with aspic and return them to the refrigerator. Serve the jellied fish with a sauceboat of green mayonnaise.

Mousse de Saumon en Gelée

PLACE a fish mold on a bed of cracked ice and coat the bottom and sides with a thin layer of cool but still liquid fish aspic. Outline the fins, tail, and mouth with thin strips of pimiento and the scales down the back with tiny thin crescents of hard-cooked egg white. A round of truffle for the eye completes the garniture. Sprinkle some liquid aspic over each piece to set the decorations and, when it is firm, pour in aspic 1/2 inch deep.

Mash 1 1/2 cups well-packed poached salmon flakes. Force the salmon through a fine sieve and mix thoroughly with 1 tablespoon gelatin softened in 1/2 cup cold water and dissolved over hot water, 3 tablespoons mayonnaise, and 3 heaping tablespoons whipped cream. Flavor the mousse with lemon juice, salt, and cayenne to taste. Pile the mousse in the mold, using a pastry bag fitted with a large round tube, but keep the mousse away from the sides of the mold. Chill the mousse until it is set. Fill the mold with

Clam Aspic in Half Shells

fish aspic, chill until firm, and unmold on a large glass or silver platter. Surround the fish with chopped aspic and garnish with a large bouquet of watercress.

SKIN and clean an eel weighing about 2 1/2 pounds. Remove the bones and cut the meat into 2-inch lengths. Bring to a boil 1 1/2 quarts water with 1 cup vinegar, 10 peppercorns, 1 tablespoon salt, 2 bay leaves, 1 onion, sliced, 3 cloves, and a few sprigs of parsley. Add the eel and simmer gently for 20 minutes. Remove the eel, simmer the broth until it is reduced to 1 quart, and use it to make fish aspic.

Anguille en Gelée
EEL IN ASPIC

Place a ring or timbale mold on a bed of cracked ice and coat the bottom and sides of it with a layer of fish aspic. Line the bottom of the mold attractively with slices of hard-cooked egg, pour over the egg slices a little of the aspic, and chill the jelly until it is firm.

Put the pieces of eel in the mold, cover them with aspic and chill again until set. Unmold the aspic on a serving platter and garnish with lemon wedges, romaine, and watercress.

POACH 6 slices of halibut, about 3/4 to 1 inch thick, in court bouillon for 5 minutes. Remove them from the stock, cool them, and chill them. Strain the court bouillon and reserve it to use in making the fish aspic. Coat each slice of halibut with fish aspic and chill again until the aspic is set. Place the halibut slices on a bed of curly chicory or romaine and encircle them with some diced aspic. Serve with green mayonnaise and pickled mushrooms.

Halibut in Aspic

SELECT 1 dozen large chowder clams. Scrub and rinse them well. Put the clams in a saucepan with just enough water to cover the bottom of the pan, cover the pan tightly and cook the clams over high heat until the shells open. Remove the clams from their shells and reserve 12 perfect half shells for later use.

Clam Aspic in Half Shells

Heat 1 cup of the strained clam broth, add 1 cup dry white wine and 1/3 cup finely minced heart of celery, and season the mixture with a little Tabasco and salt. Soften 1 tablespoon gelatin in a little cold broth or wine and add it to the liquor. Put the clams through the finest blade of a food chopper and add them to the broth. Pour the mixture into a shallow pan to set. Just before the aspic becomes firm, stir it with a fork and spoon it onto the reserved half shells. Chill the filled shells well. Serve 2 to a person and garnish each shell with a spoonful of caviar or with a dab of sour cream and with capers or chopped parsley.

Crab Meat Mold

SOAK 1 teaspoon gelatin in 1/4 cup cold water for 5 minutes, dissolve the gelatin over hot water, and let it cool. Stir the gelatin into 1/2 cup mayonnaise.

Combine 2 cups crab meat, 1 cup finely chopped celery, 1 tablespoon each of chopped parsley and chopped chives, and 1/2 teaspoon chopped tarragon. Bind this mixture with the mayonnaise, put it in a quart mold for several hours, and unmold it on a bed of shredded lettuce. Garnish the serving dish with quartered hard-cooked eggs, black olives, and cold cooked shrimps dipped in Russian dressing. Serves 4.

Homard en Belle Vue à la Parisienne

LOBSTER IN ASPIC PARISIAN

COOK a large lobster in boiling salted water for about 20 minutes. Cool it and remove all the meat, keeping the tail meat in one piece and being careful not to damage the main shell. Place the empty shell on a bed of lettuce and elevate the thorax with a small round head of lettuce.

Cut the tail meat of the lobster into cutlets and coat the surface of each cutlet with aspic. Decorate each with cutouts of truffle, pieces of the lobster coral, and leaves of chervil, and chill thoroughly. Glaze the cutlets with several layers of aspic, chilling them between each procedure. Place them down the back of the entire shell, each piece slightly overlapping the other.

Garnish the platter with tomatoes, peeled, seeded, and filled with mixed cooked vegetables bound with *mayonnaise collée* and halved hard-cooked eggs, all decorated with truffles and coated with aspic. Complete the decoration by inserting an *attelet* in the head of the lobster.

Homard Froid Figaro

COLD LOBSTER FIGARO

BOIL 3 lobsters weighing 1 1/2 pounds each for 6 to 8 minutes in court bouillon. Cool the lobsters and split them in half lengthwise. Remove the tail meat in one piece and trim it neatly. Chop the claw meat finely, add the tail trimmings, the tomally, 2 cups fresh crab meat, 1 teaspoon chopped chives, and 1 teaspoon each of chopped parsley, tarragon, and chervil. Mix 3 tablespoons chili sauce with 2/3 cup mayonnaise, correct the seasoning and combine the mayonnaise with the seafood mixture. Fill the empty half shells with this mixture, top with the tail meat and decorate with thin strips of pimiento, anchovy filets, and capers. Coat the whole with fish aspic and chill. Serve with mayonnaise.

Aspic de Homard

LOBSTER IN ASPIC

LINE the bottom and sides of a decorative mold placed on ice with a thin layer of fish aspic. Garnish the bottom of the mold symmetrically with cutouts of sliced truffle and hard-cooked egg white, lobster coral, and leaves of tarragon. Fix the decorations with a few drops of aspic, let them set, and cover the bottom with an inch-thick layer of aspic.

When the jelly is firm, arrange on it, alternately and slightly overlapping, thin slices of lobster meat and slices of truffles. Cover the lobster and truffles with another inch of aspic and continue to fill the mold with layers of sliced lobster meat and jelly until the mold is full, chilling each layer until it is set.

Chill the aspic until it is firm. Unmold it on a cold serving platter garnished to taste with watercress, olives, radishes, or tomatoes.

PLUNGE 3 pounds live lobsters into boiling salted water to cover, with 1 onion and 1 carrot, sliced, and a *bouquet garni* of chervil, parsley, thyme, and 1 bay leaf, and simmer for 6 to 8 minutes. Cool the lobsters in the liquid in which they were cooked, split them, and remove the flesh. Reserve the tips of the claws for garnishing and pound the rest of the meat and the coral to a smooth paste in a mortar.

Soufflé de Homard Froid

COLD LOBSTER SOUFFLÉ

Soften 1 tablespoon gelatin in 1/4 cup cold water and dissolve it in 1 cup hot fish *fumet*. Add the lobster and 1 cup fish *velouté* and stir the mixture over a bowl of cracked ice until it is cool and beginning to set. Fold in 1 1/2 cups cream, whipped until stiff, and correct the seasoning with salt.

Butter a soufflé dish and tie a standing collar of wax paper around it. Turn the mixture into the dish and chill it until it is set. Remove the paper collar, decorate the top with the tips of the lobster claws, brush lightly with cool but still liquid fish aspic, and return the dish to the refrigerator until the aspic sets.

COAT a ring mold with aspic. When the aspic begins to set, arrange slices of hard-cooked egg all around the sides of the mold, and garnish the bottom with capers and sliced ripe olives. Chill. Add 1 teaspoon prepared mustard, 1/4 teaspoon Worcestershire sauce, 1 tablespoon chopped parsley, and 1/2 teaspoon mixed chopped tarragon, chervil, and chives to 2 cups *mayonnaise collée*. Combine this sauce with 1/3 cup shrimps cut in pieces, 1/3 cup diced lobster, and 1 cup lump crab meat. Fill the mold with the seafood salad and cover the salad with a layer of cool liquid aspic. Chill until thoroughly set. Spread a thin layer of cold aspic on a serving dish and chill it until it is

Turban de Crustacés en Gelée

RING OF SHELLFISH IN ASPIC

set. Unmold the salad on the dish and garnish it with tomatoes stuffed with cucumber salad.

Buisson de Crevettes à la Pompadour

JELLIED
VEGETABLE SALAD
WITH SHRIMPS

CUT 1 cup each of artichoke bottoms and celery knob in 1/4 inch cubes. Slice string beans and asparagus stalks diagonally in 1/2-inch pieces to make 1 cup of each. Prepare 1 cup shelled green peas. Cook each of the vegetables separately in boiling salted water, cool them and combine them. Season the vegetables to taste with salt, pepper, olive oil and vinegar, and mix them well with 2 cups *mayonnaise collée*. Pour the vegetable mixture into an oiled, cone-shaped mold and chill it until it is set. Unmold the salad on a serving dish and pile cooked shrimps up around the cone. Around the base of the mold pipe a ribbon of mayonnaise tinted green and another tinted pink. Arrange slices of hard-cooked egg around the ribbons and finish with two more ribbons of mayonnaise, a green and a pink, around the egg slices.

Boeuf à la Mode en Gelée

JELLIED
BRAISED BEEF

LARD a 4-pound piece of beef cut from the rump with 12 strips of larding pork soaked in brandy, sprinkle the meat with salt, pepper, and nutmeg, and soak it for 24 hours in a marinade for game, using red wine.

Dry the meat well and sear it in 3 tablespoons lard in a skillet. Transfer the meat to a Dutch oven and discard the fat. Add 1/2 cup water and cook, stirring in all the brown bits. Pour this over the meat in the Dutch oven and add the strained marinade, 1 cup cooked tomatoes, 2 calf's feet prepared for aspic, some veal bones, 2 cups red wine, 3 tablespoons brandy, 1 garlic clove, and a bay leaf tied with a few green celery tops and sprigs of parsley. Cover the Dutch oven and braise the meat in a moderate oven (350° F.) for 3 hours, turning it twice.

Transfer the meat to another kettle, remove the calf's feet, skim all the fat from the surface of the liquid, and strain the liquid over the meat. Add 12 small young carrots and 12 small white onions. Remove the meat from the calf's feet, cut the meat into small cubes and add it to the kettle with the beef. Cover the kettle tightly, return it to the oven and continue cooking for 1 hour or until the vegetables are tender. Remove the meat from the kettle and cool it in the liquid. When the meat is cold, place it on a serving dish and chill it. Remove the onions and the carrots and chill them. Strain the sauce, add 1/2 cup Madeira, and cool it. Arrange the vegetables around the meat and spread the sauce over all. Chill until the sauce is congealed, then coat the whole with meat aspic. Or slice some of the meat, arrange the slices in front of the rump, and coat meat and vegetables as indicated above.

HAVE the butcher remove the bone from a 3- to 4-pound piece of veal cut from the center part of the leg and lard the top of the meat with small strips of fat salt pork. Have the bone sawed into pieces. In the bottom of a casserole, spread the bones, 1 onion, 1 carrot, sliced, and a faggot made by tying together 1 piece of celery stalk, 4 sprigs of parsley, 1 small bay leaf, and a sprig of thyme. Season the veal with 1/2 teaspoon salt and lay it on top of the vegetables. Spread 1 tablespoon butter or veal or beef fat over the meat. Braise the meat in a hot oven (425° F.) for 20 minutes, until the meat is golden brown and the vegetables begin to cook. Add 1 cup chicken stock, cover the casserole and continue to cook the meat about 2 hours, basting it often, until the liquid is reduced by half. Add 1/2 cup more stock and continue to cook until the meat is tender, basting often. Add a little more stock if necessary. Uncover the casserole and cook the meat for 15 to 20 minutes longer, basting the meat frequently to glaze it. If there is not enough liquid, add a little bouillon.

Remove the meat to a serving dish and let it cool. Discard the faggot and strain the sauce through cheesecloth. There should be less than a cup of syrupy liquid. Cool this sauce, and if it does not jell, reheat it and add 1/2 tablespoon gelatin softened in 1/4 cup cold water. Slice enough meat for one serving for each guest and arrange the slices and the unsliced meat on a serving platter. Garnish the platter with cooked carrots or carrot balls and small cooked white onions, glazed with melted butter and a sprinkling of sugar. Coat the meat and the vegetables with the cooled sauce and chill the platter until the coating is firm. Then coat meat, vegetables, and garniture with clear, cold, but still liquid aspic.

Fricandeau de Veau Braisée en Gelée
JELLIED BRAISED VEAL

TRIM veal chops to uniform size and shape them. Braise them in the usual way until they are well done. Let the chops cool, and chill them. Cut cooked vegetables and hard-cooked egg white into fancy shapes with small French cutters, and decorate the chops attractively, sticking each cutout on with a little cool aspic. Use an individual mold for each chop or a shallow pan in which the chops can be arranged side by side.

Pour a thin layer of aspic into the molds or pan and let it set. Lay

Côtes de Veau en Gelée
JELLIED VEAL CHOPS

the cold garnished chops on the aspic, decorated side down, and cover with more meat aspic. Chill. When ready to serve dip the molds or the pan in hot water and invert the jellied chops onto a cold platter. Garnish the platter with chopped aspic and watercress.

Chinese Jellied Lamb

HAVE the butcher cut 2 1/2 pounds shoulder of lamb into 2 1/2-inch cubes. Parboil the meat for 3 minutes, rinse it in cold water, and put it in a heavy kettle. Add 2 scallions, trimmed, 2 garlic cloves, 6 or 8 tablespoons soy sauce, 3 tablespoons dry Sherry, 1 tablespoon brown sugar, and water barely to cover. Bring to a boil and simmer gently for about 2 hours, or until the meat is tender and the flavors well blended. Cool the stew, discard the scallions and garlic, and remove the meat. With two forks, shred the lamb and free it from any bones.

Soak 3 tablespoons gelatin in 3/4 cup cold water for 5 minutes and add 1 cup hot water, stirring until the gelatin is dissolved. Reheat the lamb stock, add the gelatin, and bring to a boil, stirring constantly. Add the meat and heat for 5 minutes. Pour the meat and gravy into shallow loaf pans, and chill until set. Serve sliced, with shredded scallions.

Côtelettes d'Agneau à la Gelée

LAMB CHOPS
WITH ASPIC

SEASON with salt and pepper 6 large lamb chops cut 1 1/2 inches thick. In a skillet brown the chops on both sides in a little fat. Remove them to a heavy saucepan. Discard the fat in the skillet and add 1 tablespoon butter and 2 carrots, 2 onions, and 2 stalks of celery, all cut into small dice. Cook the vegetables until they are soft and spread them over the chops in the saucepan. Add sufficient white stock to cover the meat, cover the pan, and braise the chops over low heat for about 45 minutes, or until they are very tender when tested with a fork.

Strain the braising liquid, skim off the fat, and pour the liquid over the chops. Weight them down to keep them flat and cool them in the liquid. Drain them, dry them, and trim them neatly.

Make meat aspic, using the strained braising liquid as part of the stock. Fill a ring mold with some of the aspic. Coat the chops with cool but still liquid aspic and sprinkle them heavily with sieved hard-cooked egg yolks mixed with a little minced truffle. Spoon more aspic carefully over the egg and decorate the center with small truffle circles. Cover the decorations with more aspic. Chill the chops well between coatings.

Cover the bone ends with paper frills, and stand the chops, frills up, in a circle within the unmolded aspic ring. Garnish the platter with chopped aspic and with quarters of hearts of lettuce and of hard-cooked egg. Serve *sauce tartare* or mayonnaise separately.

COOK 2 fresh tongues, each about 4 pounds, and cool them in the stock. Remove the skins and the tough root portions and chill the tongues. Place the larger and better-shaped tongue in a narrow pan with sides 2 to 3 inches high. Let the tip of the tongue curl over the side so it will retain its tongue-shape as it cools.

Langue de Boeuf à la Rochefort

BEEF TONGUE ROCHEFORT

Rice Socle

A socle, or pedestal, of rice supports the tongue. It may be eaten, but its primary purpose is support. Wash 2 cups rice in cold water and cover it well with cold water in a saucepan. Bring to a boil and simmer the rice for 2 minutes. Drain it in a sieve and rinse it with cold water. Return the rice to the pan and cook it with 5 cups water and 1 teaspoon salt for about 20 minutes, or until the rice is tender and all the water is evaporated. Soften 2 tablespoons gelatin in 1/4 cup cold chicken consommé for 5 minutes. Add 1 cup hot chicken consommé and stir until the gelatin is thoroughly dissolved. Combine the gelatin with the rice and pack the mixture firmly into an oval mold about 2 1/2 inches deep lined with wax paper. Chill until firm and unmold onto a chilled platter.

Arrange the shaped tongue on the rice socle with the tip hanging over the edge of the rice wall. Coat both tongue and rice with 4 layers of *chaud-froid blanc*, chilling between layers.

Decorate the tongue with thin slices of truffle cut into circles, petals, and crescent shapes, dipping each piece into a little liquid aspic to make it adhere. Garnish the rice pedestal all around with overlapping slices of the second tongue and coat the whole piece—*chaud-froid*, truffle decorations, rice, and tongue—with 2 coatings of liquid aspic, chilling each layer until it is set. Around the tongue on top of the rice put a circle of whipped aspic and around the platter arrange more chilled aspic that has been coarsely chopped into cubes. Insert in the thick end of the tongue two or three *attelets*, each threaded with a truffle, a rectangle of tongue, and another truffle.

COOL a cooked smoked tongue slightly, remove the outside skin, cut off the root, and trim. Chill the tongue well and slice it as thinly and regularly as possible. Also slice the meat from a smoked turkey breast and trim the slices to match the tongue slices.

Smoked Tongue Aspic Gastronome

Soften 2 tablespoons gelatin in 1/2 cup dry white wine. Add 2 cups hot, clear chicken consommé and stir until the gelatin is thoroughly dissolved. Bring the liquid to a boil, skim carefully, and strain it through a sieve lined with a wet flannel cloth. Let the aspic set almost to the congealing point. Dip the slices of tongue and turkey into the jelly, let the coating set, and dip again. Using alternate slices of tongue and turkey, reshape the tongue in its original form. Arrange the meat on a chilled serving platter and brush it with the aspic. Let the first coat set and brush again with aspic. Repeat until 3 coats have been applied.

Decorate the platter with tarragon leaves, thin slices of stuffed olive, some sprigs of parsley, and hard-cooked eggs and cooked vegetables cut into fancy shapes. Apply 3 more coats of aspic to the tongue, letting each coat set before another is applied.

Aspic Cutouts   Heat the remaining gelatin mixture without boiling. Stir in 1/4 cup Sherry. Pour the mixture into a wet shallow pan to set. When the aspic is firm, cut it into fancy shapes and use it to decorate the serving platter. Garnish the platter with bunches of crisp watercress sprinkled with paprika.

Langue de   BOIL a tongue until it is tender. Cool it, remove the skin, and trim away the
Boeuf en   butt end and the bones. Put the tongue on a rack and coat it with cool liquid
Gelée au Porto   aspic flavored with a little Port and colored with a few drops of red food
TONGUE   coloring. Chill the tongue well. Coat a serving dish with aspic, place the tongue
WITH PORT   on it and decorate the platter with truffles, hard-cooked eggs, and more aspic,
WINE JELLY   chilled in a shallow pan and cut into decorative shapes.

Aspic   REMOVE the skin from a cooked tongue weighing about 5 pounds, cut off the
de Langue   root, and trim the tongue. Bend it into ring form while it is still hot and
à la Parisienne   skewer it through the tip and the fleshy part to keep it in shape. Cool and
TONGUE IN ASPIC   then chill it thoroughly before removing the skewer. Slice the tongue and
PARISIAN   reshape it.

Put a round mold in a pan containing cracked ice and cover the bottom with a thin layer of aspic. When it is firm, decorate it with slices of cooked carrots, hard-cooked egg white, truffles, olives, pimientos, gherkins, or sliced cooked beets cut in fancy shapes. Cover with more aspic, adding it by careful spoonfuls to avoid disarranging the garnishings.

When the aspic is firm, lay the tongue in the mold. Gradually fill the mold with layers of aspic, decorating the sides of the mold and letting each layer of aspic set before another is added. Chill for at least 4 hours before unmolding on a cold platter. Garnish the platter around the base of the jellied tongue with watercress.

Ham Mousse   PUT 4 cups ground cooked ham 4 or 5 times through the finest blade of a food chopper with 2 tablespoons tomato purée. Stir in 2 tablespoons Sherry, 2 teaspoons prepared mustard, and a little cayenne. Soak 2 tablespoons gelatin

Tongue in Aspic Parisian

in 1/3 cup cold water for 5 minutes, add 1 cup boiling meat stock or chicken stock, and stir until the gelatin is dissolved. Add the gelatin to the ham, mix well, and rub the mixture through a fine sieve. Cool, stirring occasionally, and fold in 1 cup heavy cream, whipped.

Oil a 1 1/2-quart mold, fill it with this ham mousse, and chill it for several hours, or until it is firm. To serve, unmold the mousse in the center of a large chilled serving platter and surround it with coronets made of thin scalloped circles of cooked ham filled with ham mousse, pressed through a large fluted nozzle, and garnished with tiny rounds of truffle.

The mold may be coated with a thin layer of aspic and the aspic decorated with truffle slices and crescents of hard-cooked egg before the mousse is added. The mold must be chilled until the aspic sets and each decoration must be stuck in place with a little cold, but still liquid aspic.

Mousse de Jambon Hongroise

HUNGARIAN HAM MOUSSE

COMBINE 2 cups ground cooked lean ham, 1/2 cup each of butter and heavy cream, 2 tablespoons tomato purée, and 1 cup cold thick *béchamel sauce*. Season well with Hungarian paprika and add a very little red food coloring. Force the mousse through a fine sieve.

Line a charlotte mold with Port-flavored aspic and decorate it with cutouts of truffle and hard-cooked egg white. Fill the mold with the mousse, using a pastry bag with a large, round tube, but keep the mousse away from the sides. Chill the mousse until it is firm.

Fill the mold with aspic and chill for at least 1 hour. Unmold on a round serving platter and garnish with cutouts of firm aspic and sprigs of crisp watercress.

Jambon à la Gatti

HAM IN ASPIC GATTI

CHILL a ham in the liquor in which it was cooked and remove all the skin except a portion around the bone. Cut the edges of this remaining skin into sharp points. Coat all the ham, except the skin, with several layers of *chaud-froid blanc* or *mayonnaise collée*, chilling each layer for about 25 minutes before adding another.

Decorate the sides of the ham with sprays of leaves, making the stems of thin strips of truffle and the leaves of pistachio nuts. Make a symmetrical design on top of the ham of cutouts of truffle slices and mask the decoration, the *chaud-froid*, and the exposed skin with several layers of clear, cold, but still liquid aspic, chilling between layers.

Arrange the ham on a rice socle on a large silver platter. The surface of the socle may be spread with mayonnaise. Surround the ham with finely chopped or whipped aspic and decorate the platter with large cubes of jelly and hard-cooked eggs cut in half and heaped with chopped aspic. Cover the bone with a paper frill and insert an *attelet* stuck with a large truffle on one side, parallel to the bone.

SOAK a country ham overnight and scrub it thoroughly under running water. Cover it with cold water, bring the water to a boil, and simmer the ham for 18 to 20 minutes per pound. Let it cool and cut the skin away. Or use a ready-to-eat or tenderized ham and follow the packer's directions. Carve from the top of the ham several thin slices and cut small uniform circles from these. Cut matching rounds of *pâté de foie gras* and sandwich them with rounds of ham. Coat these medallions with Madeira aspic and decorate each with a small circle of truffle.

Jambon Glacé à la Monselet
GLAZED HAM MONSELET

Arrange a small dome of cold cooked vegetables—carrot balls, peas, and potato balls—glazed with aspic on top of the ham and arrange an overlapping ring of ham-and-goose-liver medallions around the vegetables. Edge the ring with chopped aspic mixed with chopped truffles. Coat the sides of the ham and the shank bone with aspic and decorate to taste with small cutouts of carrot and truffle. Cover the end of the shank bone with a paper frill.

Garnish the platter with small tart shells made with puff paste or with unsweetened tart pastry and filled with cooked peas, small cooked carrots, and potatoes cut in olive shapes, all chilled and glazed with aspic. Cut a slice from the top of small tomatoes, scoop out pulp and seeds, and fill the tomatoes with the same vegetables bound with aspic or *mayonnaise collée*. Use to complete the garnish.

HAVE the butcher remove all the bones from a large pig's head. Clean and scrape it thoroughly and wipe it dry. Combine 1 pound salt, 2 tablespoons brown sugar, 1 tablespoon saltpeter, and 1 teaspoon mixed nutmeg, cloves, and cinnamon. Rub the head inside and out with this mixture for 6 days, using a sixth part daily.

Jellied Pig's Head

Mix together thoroughly 1 pound each of lean pork and veal, both finely ground, 2 truffles, finely chopped, 1/2 pound mushrooms, sliced and sautéed in butter until they are lightly browned, and 1 cup dry bread crumbs. Season the forcemeat mixture with salt, pepper, and nutmeg and bind it with 2 beaten eggs. Remove the ears from the head and stuff the head with the forcemeat, pressing it into shape as it is stuffed. Place a flat plate at the back of the head and tie plate and head securely in a large cloth.

Place the stuffed head in a large kettle with 2 onions, each stuck with 2

427

Chaud-Froid of Chicken

cloves, a small bunch of parsley, 8 peppercorns, and 1 bay leaf and simmer the head slowly for 5 to 6 hours in stock or water to cover. Add more water as needed.

Remove the head from the liquid, press it again into shape, and chill it. Cook the ears for about 1 hour in a little of the pot liquor, cool them, and with wooden picks fasten them in place on the head, now unwrapped.

Coat the head 2 or 3 times with clear aspic, chilling it thoroughly between coatings. Place radishes, lady apples, or any other small, bright object in the eye sockets and stud the forehead and snout with whole cloves.

Place the head on a silver platter or a wooden plank and garnish it colorfully with lady apples, limes and lemons, apricots, parsley or watercress, or a bunch of grapes draping the brow. Any tart fruit or combination of fruits will give contrast to the rich meat. Cranberries, apples, citrus fruits, and the less sweet grapes are suitable.

Chaud-Froid de Poularde
CHAUD-FROID OF CHICKEN

PUT twice through the finest blade of a food chopper 3/4 pound raw chicken meat—leg, wing, and back meat—1/4 pound each of veal and lean pork, and 1 pound fat pork. Add 1 tablespoon salt and a dash of Parisian spice and pound the mixture to a paste in a mortar. Rub the forcemeat through a fine sieve. Slit the skin over the breastbone of a 4-pound capon and remove each breast in one piece. Cut out the breastbone. Stuff the cavity loosely with the forcemeat, replace the breasts, and reshape the capon. Sew up the skin and truss the bird. Put it in a deep pan just large enough to accommodate it, add white stock to cover, and poach it, covered, for about 1 hour, or until it is tender. Cool the capon in the stock, remove it, and chill it. Coat the entire bird with *chaud-froid blanc* made with the strained stock from which the fat has been skimmed and decorate it with slices of truffle cut in flower shapes, circles, and crescents. Chill well and finish with a coating of clear chicken aspic.

Poularde à la Néva
CHICKEN NEVA

POACH a plump capon and the giblets in white stock for about 2 hours, or until it is tender. Cool the bird in the stock and use the stock to make aspic. Remove the capon breasts and slice into cutlets. Place the cutlets on a baking sheet and mask them with several layers of *chaud-froid blanc*. Decorate each cutlet with a slice of truffle, then glaze with several coats of cold but still liquid aspic, chilling it between coatings.

Soften 2 tablespoons gelatin in 3/4 cup water for 5 minutes. Stir over hot water until the gelatin is dissolved, remove from the heat, and cool to room temperature.

Mash 1 pound *foie gras* and force it through a fine sieve. Add to it the dissolved gelatin and 2 truffles, chopped, and mix well. Fold in 6 table-spoons whipped cream.

Cut out the breast bone from the capon, fill the cavity with the *foie gras* mousse, reshaping the breast, and chill the capon until the mousse is set.

Coat the capon with several layers of *chaud-froid blanc* and place the cutlets over the breast on each side, each cutlet slightly overlapping the next. Arrange the bird on a serving platter and coat the bird with several layers of clear aspic. Chill the remaining aspic until it is set. When ready to serve, chop the aspic with a sharp knife on a wet board and surround the chicken with it.

Poularde Soufflée Rose de Mai

CHICKEN
ROSE OF MAY

IN a saucepan put 1 onion, 1 leek, 3 sprigs of parsley, 2 stalks of celery, 3 quarts of water, and either some chicken bones or chicken feet. If chicken feet are used, chop off the nails, scald the feet, and peel off the skin. Bring the water to a boil, skim well, and simmer for 1 hour. Strain the broth into a kettle large enough to hold a chicken. Into the broth put a 4-pound young capon or chicken, cleaned, singed, and trussed, bring the broth to a boil, and simmer the chicken until it is tender. Let the chicken cool in the stock, then with a sharp knife carefully detach the breast meat from the bones and cut away the bones that remain under the breasts, leaving the back and sides with the legs and second joints intact and an open cavity.

Tomato Mousse

Peel 8 large tomatoes. Cut them in half and press out the juice and seeds. Chop the tomato flesh and press it through a fine sieve to make a purée. Mix 1 cup of the purée with 1 cup tomato juice and season the mixture to taste with about 1 teaspoon salt. Soften 2 tablespoons gelatin in 1/3 cup cold water and stir it over hot water until the gelatin is dissolved. Stir the gelatin into the tomato mixture and again press through a fine sieve. Stir in 1 1/2 cups heavy cream.

Put the bird on a rack to steady it and stuff the cavity with the tomato mousse, rounding it up in the shape of the bird. Trim the skin from the breast, slice the meat neatly, and arrange the slices carefully on either side of the exposed rounded part of the mousse.

Coat the chicken with *chaud-froid blanc*, leaving the mousse and the legs uncovered. Stripe the *chaud-froid* with lines of tomato mousse and decorate the bird with fresh chervil leaves and with small slices of truffle cut in circles, crescents, and flower shapes. Spoon clear cold but still liquid aspic over the entire bird. Put it on a platter on a layer of congealed aspic and garnish the platter with chopped aspic.

Serve the chicken with small tomatoes stuffed with whipped cream mixed with horseradish and topped with rosettes of thinly sliced cucumber.

Cut a 4- to 5 pound fowl into serving pieces and put them in a large kettle with 1 onion stuck with 2 cloves, 1 carrot, 1 stalk of celery, and several sprigs of parsley. Add water to almost cover the chicken and bring to a boil. Cover, lower the heat, and simmer for 1 hour. Season with 2 teaspoons salt and several peppercorns and cook until the fowl is very tender when tested with a fork. Cool the chicken in the stock until it is cool enough to handle. Strip the meat from the bones, discard the skin and bones, and arrange large pieces of meat in a mold or in a loaf pan. Garnish with slices of hard-cooked eggs, cooked sliced vegetables, and olives or pimiento.

Chicken in Aspic

Strain the stock, reheat it, and stir in 1 tablespoon gelatin softened in 2 tablespoons dry white wine. Pour it over the chicken and chill the dish for several hours or until the mold is firm. Shortly before serving, unmold the chicken aspic on a cold platter and garnish it with sprigs of watercress. Serve well-seasoned mayonnaise with the chicken.

Poach 2 chickens, each weighing about 3 pounds, in white stock until they are tender.

Poularde Glacée Belle de Lauris
JELLIED CHICKEN WITH ASPARAGUS

Cool the chickens in the stock and use the stock to make aspic. Remove the chicken breasts and cut them into cutlets. Place them on a baking sheet and mask them with several layers of *chaud-froid blanc* or *mayonnaise collée*. Decorate the cutlets with a flower motif, using leaves of tarragon for the stem and leaves, round petals cut from pimiento, and a small circle of hard-cooked egg yolk for the center of each flower. Glaze the cutlets with several coats of clear, cold, but still liquid aspic, chilling between coatings.

Cut out the breast bone from one of the chickens and remove the legs from both. Grind the meat from the legs in a mortar or run it through the finest blade of a food chopper several times and then force it through a fine sieve. Measure the chicken purée and add an equal amount of purée of *foie gras* and 24 green tips of asparagus, cooked and put through a sieve. Work the mixture with a wooden spatula, adding to it gradually 1 tablespoon gelatin softened in 1/2 cup cold water and dissolved over hot water, 1/2 cup Port, and 1/2 cup heavy cream, lightly whipped. Put this mousse in the refrigerator to cool, stirring it gently from to time to keep it from setting in a solid mass.

Correct the seasoning of the mousse, which will be an emerald green color, and with it reshape the chicken with the breast bone removed, filling out the breast and reshaping the thighs. There should be some mousse left for garnishing. Place a piece of heavy paper, lightly oiled and cut into a long triangle, over the breast filling and mask the entire chicken with *chaud-froid blanc* or *mayonnaise collée*. When the *chaud-froid* is set, remove the paper triangle carefully to reveal the green mousse. Cover the mousse at regular intervals with small squares of sliced truffles and hard-cooked egg white to make a green, black, and white checkerboard effect. Coat the decoration and *chaud-froid* with several layers of cool liquid aspic, chilling it between layers.

To serve, place the chicken on an oval rice socle at one end of a long serving platter coated with a thick bed of jelly. In the center of the platter arrange a fan of cooked asparagus stalks, placing the cut ends of the stalks under the shoulders of the chicken. Around the asparagus arrange the decorated breast cutlets in a half-oval formation, the cutlets overlapping slightly. Form small balls of the remaining mousse and roll one-third of them in finely chopped pistachios, and one-third in finely chopped truffles. Coat the remaining balls of mousse with *chaud-froid* and arrange them so that the colors alternating around the base of the socle carry out the color scheme of the *poularde*. Complete the décor by inserting in the end of the chicken two or three *attelets*, each garnished with three of the different colored balls of mousse.

Suprêmes de Volaille Pompadour

BREASTS
OF CHICKEN
POMPADOUR

SIMMER a 3 1/2- to 4-pound chicken until it is tender, cool it and remove the breast meat. Cut each breast filet lengthwise to make three servings. Flatten the filets and trim them evenly. Spread each filet with 1 tablespoon *mousse de foie gras*, making a smooth rounded surface, and chill the filets thoroughly in the refrigerator.

Color and season 2 1/2 cups *chaud-froid blanc* with 2 or 3 tablespoons sweet paprika. Cool the sauce. Arrange the breasts on a rack and coat them well with the sauce, which should be on the point of congealing. Decorate the filets with truffles cut in decorative shapes and tarragon or chervil leaves. Arrange the decorated filets on a serving dish, chill well and cover with clear chicken aspic. Chill until the aspic is set.

Chicken Pie in Jelly

REMOVE the breasts from a tender 3- to 3 1/2-pound chicken and cut each breast in two pieces. Remove the skin and bones from the second joints and cut each joint in two pieces. Put the meat in a casserole and add 8 to 10 mushrooms, cleaned and sliced, 2 tablespoons finely chopped onion, 1 tablespoon chopped parsley, 1/2 teaspoon each of Worcestershire sauce and salt, a little pepper, 1/4 cup Sherry and 1 quart chicken aspic. Cover the casserole with pie dough, slash the dough in a decorative pattern, and bake the pie in a moderate oven (350° F.) for 50 minutes to 1 hour. Cool the pie and chill it in the refrigerator until the jelly sets. Carefully lift off the crust and garnish the filling with sliced cooked ham and sliced hard-cooked eggs. Replace the crust, cover it with a glaze of clear aspic jelly, and sprinkle it with chopped parsley.

CUT up enough freshly poached breast of chicken to make 2 cups and put the chicken through the finest blade of a food chopper with 1 cup velouté sauce made with chicken stock. Rub the mixture through a fine sieve and cool it. Gradually add to it 2 cups chicken aspic. If the aspic does not jell, reheat it and add 1 tablespoon gelatin softened in 1/4 cup cold water. Fold in 1 cup heavy cream, whipped until stiff, and season the mixture to taste. Coat the inside of a large mold (or individual molds) with clear aspic and decorate it with truffles cut in fancy shapes. Chill until the aspic is set, coat again with more aspic, and chill until the second coat is set. Fill the mold with the chicken mixture and chill thoroughly. To serve, unmold on a chilled serving dish.

HAVE the butcher bone a 7-pound capon.

Cut 1 pound veal cutlet into filets about 4 inches long and 1 inch thick and grind together 1 pound veal and 1 pound pork. Let the veal filets marinate in 1/4 cup brandy for about 1 hour and season the ground meat with salt and pepper.

To stuff the capon, place the filets of veal next to the flesh, lengthwise in the cavity, sprinkle the filets with finely chopped truffles, and fill the remaining space with the ground meat. Fasten the incision down the back with wooden picks or sew it firmly with kitchen needle and thread. Wrap the stuffed bird tightly in a cloth and tie the cloth at both ends.

Place 3 or 4 onions and 2 carrots, all sliced, in the bottom of a heavy kettle. On top of the vegetables place 4 slices of bacon and a calf's foot, cleaned and cut up. Add the cleaned capon giblets and a *bouquet garni* of 3 sprigs of parsley, 1 sprig of thyme, and 1 bay leaf, tied together. Place the kettle over moderate heat and when the onions begin to color, add the capon, 1 cup white wine, and enough chicken stock just to cover the capon. Bring the liquid to a boil, skim well, and correct the seasoning with salt and pepper. Reduce the heat to low, cover the kettle tightly, and cook slowly for 2 hours.

Let the capon cool before removing it from the cloth and then chill it thoroughly. Use the broth to make aspic.

When the capon is well chilled, place it on a rack and spoon over it some of the aspic. Chill the capon again until the glaze is set and serve it on a bed of watercress. Slice directly across and through the bird to serve.

*Caneton
à l'Orange
Froid*

COLD DUCK
À L'ORANGE

IN a saucepan combine 3 cups chicken stock, 1 cup orange juice, 1 table-spoon tarragon vinegar, 2 tablespoons dry Sherry, 4 tablespoons gelatin, salt and pepper to taste, and the crushed shells and stiffly beaten whites of 2 eggs. Heat the mixture slowly, stirring constantly, until it boils. Remove the aspic from the heat, let it stand for 10 minutes, and strain it through a sieve lined with a flannel cloth wrung out in cold water.

Pour 2 cups of the aspic into a round or oval mold. When the foundation aspic sets, arrange on it in an attractive pattern slices of cooked duck, sliced truffles, cooked carrots, cooked mushrooms, and the skinned sections of 2 blood oranges. Cover the arrangement carefully with the remaining aspic, which should be cold but still liquid. Chill the mold until the aspic is firm. To serve, unmold the aspic on a serving platter and garnish it with a ring of watercress.

*Caneton
Montmorency
en Gelée*

DUCKLING IN ASPIC
WITH CHERRIES

*Mousse de
Foie Gras
et Rouennaise*

GOOSE LIVER AND
ROUENNAISE
MOUSSE

CLEAN a duck weighing about 5 pounds and truss it to hold wings and legs close to the body. Roast the duck in a hot oven (425° F.) for 40 to 45 minutes, or until it is done. Let the duck cool. Remove the breasts and cut them in thin slices. Fill the carcass with the following goose liver and *rouennaise* mousse: Prepare a *rouennaise* using 1 cup chicken livers. Measure 3 times as much purée of *foie gras* as finished *rouennaise* and work the goose liver with a wooden spoon until it is very light. Combine the *rouennaise* with an equal amount of sweet butter that has been well creamed. Gradually work the *rouennaise*-butter mixture into the *foie gras*. Press the mousse through a very fine sieve into a bowl set on a bed of cracked ice and work in the same amount of whipped cream as butter.

Cover the outside where the breasts were removed with the same mix-ture, reconstructing the duck to give it its natural form. Then carefully lay the thin slices of breast meat over the mousse, overlapping them neatly to cover it. Cover with chicken aspic flavored with Port or Madeira and colored a light pink with a drop or two of food coloring. Arrange the duck on a flat oval platter, surround it with chopped aspic, and decorate it with pitted red cherries and slices of orange.

If preferred, the mousse can be arranged in a mound on an entrée dish and the slices of duck placed on it, then the whole coated with aspic and garnished with cherries.

*Galantine
de Caneton*

GALANTINE
OF DUCK

HAVE a butcher bone a duck, or follow the instructions for boning a chicken, reserving the carcass and liver. Detach the meat gently from the skin and cut the meat into thin strips, discarding the sinews.

Put into a large kettle 1/4 pound beef chuck and 1/2 pound veal shank, both diced, a calf's foot, chopped into several pieces, a strip of bacon rind, blanched, the heart, liver, and gizzard of a large chicken, and the carcass and any scraps of meat from the duck. Add 2 1/2 quarts water, bring to a boil, and remove the scum. Add 1 carrot, 1 onion stuck with 1 clove, salt, 8 peppercorns, and a *bouquet garni* of 3 sprays of parsley, 1 bay leaf, and 1 sprig each of thyme and marjoram. Simmer for 3 hours. Strain the stock into another large kettle, cool, and remove the fat.

Marinate 1/2 pound *foie gras*, 1/4 pound each of tongue and ham, 1/8 pound fresh pork fat, and about 12 truffles in 1/4 cup each of Sherry and Cognac for several hours. Reserve the marinade and cut the *foie gras*, tongue, ham, and lard into thin strips. Sprinkle with salt and pepper.

Make this forcemeat: Grind 1/2 pound fresh pork fat through the finest blade of a food chopper and melt it in a skillet over low heat. Add 4 mushrooms, chopped, 1 shallot, minced, 1 sprig of thyme, 1 small bay leaf, 1 chicken liver, the duck liver, and salt and pepper. Cook slowly, stirring, for 5 minutes, or until the mushrooms are tender, but not browned. Then grind this mixture in a mortar and press it through a fine sieve. Grind 1/2 pound veal in a mortar and add, little by little, the reserved marinade and 1 beaten egg. Force the veal through a sieve, combine it with the cooked farce, and correct the seasoning with salt, pepper, allspice, thyme, and bay leaf.

Spread the duck skin on a heavy cloth and spread over it a layer of the forcemeat. Over the forcemeat put the marinated strips of *foie gras*, tongue, ham, and lard, lengthwise, in alternating colors, and sprinkle with chopped pistachios. Arrange the strips of duck lengthwise in the middle and place between them a row of truffles. Cover the strips with the remaining forcemeat. Wrap the skin around the stuffing, pressing the galantine into a long, regular roll, and sew the overlapping skin with kitchen thread. Put thin strips of fat on top, wrap the cloth around, and tie it securely at both ends.

Lower the galantine gently into the stock, add 1 cup white wine and 1 teaspoon meat extract, and bring the stock to a boil. Lower the heat, poach the galantine for 1 1/2 hours, and then remove it to a flat platter to cool. Place a board on top and weight it down with a few dinner plates so that it will drain as it cools.

Cool the cooking liquor and remove the fat. Add 1/4 pound ground beef or game and 2 beaten egg whites and bring slowly to a boil, whipping gently and constantly. Cook over low heat for 15 minutes, stir in 1/4 cup Sherry, and strain through a sieve lined with a double thickness of cheesecloth wrung out of cold water.

When the galantine is cool, remove the cloth and thread and chill it thoroughly in the refrigerator. Put it on a wire cake rack, with the overlapping edges on the bottom and spoon 1 cup of cool but still liquid broth over it for a smooth glaze. Decorate it with truffles cut in circles, crescents, and flower shapes. Chill the galantine until serving time. Surround it with a ring of jellied aspic, beaten lightly with a fork, and garnish with aspic cutouts.

Terrine de Canard à l'Ancienne
TERRINE OF DUCK

REMOVE the skin of a 5-pound duck in one piece and reserve it. Cut the breast meat into long thin strips and put them in a bowl with 1 tablespoon chopped shallot or onion, a pinch of thyme, 2 bay leaves, 1/2 teaspoon salt, a little pepper and 1/3 cup white wine or Madeira. Remove the meat from the legs and the second joints and sauté it lightly in butter. Break up the rest of the duck carcass and put it into a saucepan with 1 carrot, 1 onion, a small leek, a little parsley, 1/2 teaspoon salt and 1 quart water. Cook slowly, skimming as necessary, to make 1 1/2 to 2 cups rich broth.

Season 2 pounds duck livers with salt and pepper and sauté them quickly in butter for about 3 or 4 minutes. The livers should be medium rare. Peel, core, and quarter 4 apples and put them in a pan with 1 teaspoon sugar, 1 tablespoon butter and the juice of 1/2 lemon. Cook slowly until the apples are soft. Put the apples, the sautéed livers, and the meat from the legs and second joints through a fine sieve. Add 1 large egg and correct the seasoning with salt. Line an earthenware casserole, or terrine, with thin slices of fat salt pork and spread the skin of the duck over this. Put in half the liver mixture and the marinated duck meat. If desired, the liver may be dotted with pieces of truffle wrapped in thin slices of fat pork. Cover with the remaining liver mixture and fold over the skin of the duck to enclose the filling. Lay thin slices of fat salt pork over the skin and top with 4 or 5 bay leaves. Cover the casserole, put it in a pan of hot water and cook it in a moderate oven (350° F.) for 1 1/2 hours.

When the pâté is done, the fat that cooks out on top will be very clear. Weight the casserole lightly with a board or plate and cool it thoroughly. Turn the pâté out of the casserole, scrape off all the fat from the outside and put the pâté back into the casserole, bottom side up. Decorate it with truffles. Soften 1 tablespoon gelatin in 1/4 cup cold water and dissolve it in 1 1/2 cups of the hot duck broth, strained through fine muslin. Cool the aspic, add 2 tablespoons Madeira or Sherry and pour the congealing aspic over the pâté. Chill until the aspic sets, and serve from the casserole.

Molded Goose

CUT away as much fat as possible from an 8- to 10-pound goose. Put the goose in a deep kettle with an onion stuck with 2 cloves, 2 or 3 carrots, a pinch each of thyme and orégano, 3 sprigs of parsley tied with a small bay

Terrine of Duck

leaf, and 2 cups white wine. Let the goose stand for about an hour, then add boiling water to cover and 2 teaspoons salt and simmer until the goose is tender.

Remove the goose from the broth and cool it. Skin the bird and remove the meat from the bones. Skim the fat from the broth, return the carcass to the kettle, and reduce the broth by two-thirds. Skim the broth again and strain it through several thicknesses of cheesecloth. To each 2 cups liquid, add 1 tablespoon gelatin dissolved in 1/4 cup cold water. Correct the seasoning and cool the aspic until it thickens slightly. Pour a thin layer of the aspic into the bottom of a mold and chill the mold. Arrange the goose meat, cut into serving pieces, in the mold. Cover the meat with the remaining liquid aspic and return the mold to the refrigerator to set. To serve, unmold on a chilled platter and serve with potato salad and with mayonnaise flavored with tarragon.

Terrine de Foie Gras Truffé au Porto

TRUFFLED
GOOSE LIVER IN
PORT WINE ASPIC

DIVIDE in half a firm goose liver weighing about 2 pounds and trim each half to make regular-shaped pieces. Save the trimmings. Make a hole in each half with a skewer and insert a piece of truffle. Season the liver with 1/2 teaspoon salt mixed with a pinch of poultry seasoning, place it in a bowl, and sprinkle with 3 tablespoons Cognac. Let the liver marinate for 2 hours, turning occasionally. Cut 3/4 pound lean fresh pork and 1 pound fat fresh pork in pieces, mix with the trimmings of the goose liver, and put the mixture through the finest blade of a food chopper. Add 1/4 to 1/2 cup truffles cut into small dice, season with 1/2 teaspoon salt mixed with a pinch of poultry seasoning and 1/2 cup Madeira or Sherry. Mix well.

Line the bottom and sides of a terrine with very thin slices of fresh larding pork, and cover the bottom with the ground seasoned pork mixture, using about one-third of it. Place one of the pieces of seasoned goose liver on this and cover with another layer of the pork mixture, the other piece of seasoned goose liver, and the remaining pork mixture. Cover with thin slices of larding pork, a small bay leaf, and a little thyme. Cover the terrine and seal the edges with a roll of firm dough made by mixing flour with water. Make a small slit in the center of the dough to allow the steam to escape.

Place the terrine in a shallow pan of boiling water and cook it in a moderately hot oven (375° F.) for 1 1/4 to 1 1/2 hours, or until steam comes out of the slit in the cover and the liquid that boils out is clear and colorless. Remove the dough, take off the cover, and place a stack of 4 or 5 plates on the mixture to compress it as it cools. Let it stand overnight. To unmold the pâté, dip the terrine quickly into hot water to melt the fat, then run a knife blade around the edge, and invert the pâté on a dish. Remove the slices of fat pork, clean the terrine, and return the pâté to it. Fill the terrine with Port wine aspic and chill the terrine until the aspic is set. Unmold the terrine on a chilled platter and slice to serve.

PLACE a whole cooked goose liver (these are available in cans) on a cold serving platter and mask the liver with several layers of cool but still liquid chicken aspic, chilling thoroughly between layers. On each side of the liver arrange 3 large slices of truffle and again mask the liver with several layers of aspic. Put the platter in the refrigerator until serving time, and serve the *foie gras* with hot Melba toast and watercress.

Foie Gras
Suvorov

COAT small decorative molds with a layer of Port wine aspic and put in the bottom of each a large slice of truffle. On top of the truffle put a cube of *foie gras* 2 to 3 inches in diameter, depending on the size of the molds, and fill the molds with cold liquid aspic. Chill thoroughly.

To serve, unmold the aspics in circle formation on a chilled platter. Surround them with chopped aspic and place a small pyramid of whole truffles in the center.

Petits Aspics
de Foie Gras
FOIE GRAS ASPICS

SET a deep round mold in a bed of cracked ice and coat it with chicken aspic. Decorate the bottom of the mold with crescents and flower shapes cut from thin slices of truffle and garnish the sides of the mold with circles of truffle slices and slices of hard-cooked egg white. Affix each piece of the decoration with a few drops of aspic and let the aspic set. Then cover the bottom of the mold with a layer of aspic 1/2 inch thick and chill the mold until the aspic is set.

Soften 1 1/2 tablespoons gelatin in 3/4 cup water for 5 minutes. Stir over hot water until the gelatin is dissolved, remove from the heat, and cool to room temperature. Mash 2 cups *purée de foie gras* and force it through a fine sieve. Stir in the dissolved gelatin and fold in 1/3 cup cream, whipped.

Fill the mold to within 1/2 inch of the top with the *mousse de foie gras* and chill until the mousse is set. Fill the mold with cool but still liquid aspic and chill again until the aspic is firm.

When ready to serve, unmold the mousse on a round serving platter,

Mousse de Foie
Gras en Aspic
FOIE GRAS MOUSSE
IN ASPIC

Mousse de
Foie Gras

fill the center with watercress, and decorate the platter with crescents of aspic and with aspic cutouts set with truffle shapes.

Turkey Mousse   SOAK 1 1/2 tablespoons gelatin in 3/4 cup cold chicken broth for 5 minutes. Beat 4 large or 5 small egg yolks, stir in 3/4 cup chicken broth, 1/4 teaspoon salt, and a pinch each of pepper and nutmeg, and cook the mixture over simmering water, stirring constantly, until it thickens. Add the softened gelatin and stir until the gelatin is thorough dissolved. Stir in 1 1/2 cups finely ground cooked white meat of turkey and stir over cracked ice until the mousse is cold and begins to set. Fold in 1 1/2 cups cream, whipped until stiff, and 1/2 cup mayonnaise. Reserve 1 cup of the mousse for garnish and turn the rest into a ring mold or tall decorative mold rinsed in cold water. Chill the mousse for about 2 hours, or until it is set.

Roll thin scalloped slices of cooked ham into cornucopias and fasten with wooden picks. Fill the cornets with the reserved mousse, pressing it through a rolled paper cone fitted with a large fluted tube. If the mousse is too thin, chill it before filling the cornets. Garnish each cornet with a small round of truffle or black olive slice.

Invert the mold on a chilled serving platter and garnish the platter with watercress and the cornets of ham.

Mousse de   PLUCK, singe, and clean 2 plump young partridge that have been hung for
Perdreaux   four days. Skin them and remove all the bones, reserving the meat and the
aux Truffes   partridge livers, and break the carcasses into small pieces.
MOUSSE OF   In a saucepan melt 1/4 cup butter and in it sauté over high heat 1/3 cup
PARTRIDGE   ground ham and the partridge carcasses, heads, feet, and skins for 5 minutes,
WITH TRUFFLES   shaking the pan constantly. Reduce the heat, add 1 carrot and 1 onion, both coarsely chopped, and cook gently, still shaking the pan, until the vegetables are golden. Add 1 sprig of thyme, 1 bay leaf, and 1 cup dry white wine, cover the pan, and simmer until the wine is reduced by half.

Strain the liquor from a 7-ounce can of truffles and reserve it. In a small deep saucepan melt 1 tablespoon butter, add 1 tablespoon each of finely chopped onion and carrot, 1 spray of parsley, and a pinch each of powdered thyme and bay leaf, and cook gently, stirring constantly, until the vegetables are tender but not browned. Add the truffles and their liquor and 2/3 cup Madeira, cover the pan, and simmer for 5 minutes. Remove the truffles from the liquid, wipe off any particles of vegetable adhering to them, and chill them. Continue to cook the vegetables until the liquid is reduced by half. Add this mixture, together with 3 cups beef stock, to the pan containing the partridge carcasses. Cover and simmer for 1 hour.

Strain the stock into a saucepan, add 2 egg whites, stiffly beaten, and 2 tablespoons gelatin, and bring the stock to a boil, stirring constantly. Strain the clarified stock into an eathenware bowl through a sieve lined with a double thickness of cheesecloth wrung out of cold water. Combine 2 beaten egg yolks with 1/4 cup of the hot stock and strain the egg mixture into the stock, stirring rapidly. Cool.

Heat 2 tablespoons butter in a skillet and in it brown the partridge meat and the livers over high heat. Transfer the meat and livers to a plate and cool them in the refrigerator. Put the chilled partridge meat and livers through the finest blade of a food chopper, add a few tablespoons of the aspic, and work the mixture into a smooth purée, using a mortar and pestle. Rub the purée through a fine sieve into an earthenware bowl, and blend it gradually and thoroughly into the cool but still liquid aspic. Reserving one whole truffle, stir in all the rest, chopped or cut into thin julienne strips, and fold in 2 cups heavy cream, whipped until thick but not stiff. If necessary, correct the seasoning with salt and freshly ground white pepper.

Coat a mold with aspic. Peel the reserved truffle, slice it thinly, and cut the slices into fancy shapes. Arrange these in the mold in an attractive design, fastening them in place with more aspic. Other fancy shapes, cut from thin slices of beef tongue, ham, hard-cooked egg whites, and colorful cooked vegetables, may also be used for decoration.

Fill the mold with the mousse and chill thoroughly. To serve, turn the mousse out on a cold platter and garnish it with a wreath of watercress.

CLEAN a large pheasant and remove the skin without tearing it. Cut off the breasts and leg meat. Save the rest of the bird to make aspic. Cut each breast into 6 slices. Cut 6 slices of lean fresh pork or veal, or both, the same size, put the meat in a bowl and cover it with the following marinade: Mix together 1/2 teaspoon salt mixed with a pinch of Parisian spice or poultry seasoning, 1/4 cup dry Sherry, Madeira, or white wine, 2 tablespoons Cognac, 1 small bay leaf, and a pinch of thyme. Place 3 sprigs of parsley, 1 small garlic clove, and 3 slices of onion on the meat and sprinkle it with 1 tablespoon olive oil. Cover the bowl and set it in the refrigerator overnight.

Prepare a farce as follows: Remove the sinews from the pheasant's leg meat and combine the meat with 3/4 pound lean fresh pork, or pork and veal, and 3/4 pound fresh fat pork. Put the meat through the finest blade of a food chopper. Add 2 or 3 tablespoons goose liver, 2 tablespoons finely

Terrine de Faisan Truffée au Madère

TERRINE OF PHEASANT

chopped truffles, and 1 egg, and mix all together well. Pour over the meat a mixture of 1/4 cup dry white wine, 2 tablespoons Cognac, 1 tablespoon olive oil, 1/2 teaspoon salt, and a pinch of Parisian spice. Cover the bowl and put it in the refrigerator for a few hours or overnight.

Remove the sliced pheasant breast and the pork from the marinade. Cut 6 large julienne strips of cooked ham or tongue 1/2 inch thick and 1/2 inch wide. Also make 6 large strips of goose liver and 12 of truffles. With the skin of the pheasant line a straight-sided casserole, or terrine, with a cover. Cover the skin on the bottom and sides of the casserole with thin slices of fat salt pork. Strain the marinade from the sliced meat into the bowl containing the farce and its marinade and mix all together well. Pack one-third of this mixture firmly in the bottom of the prepared terrine and on it lay half the slices of marinated pheasant breast alternately with half the slices of pork and half the julienne of ham, truffles, and goose liver. Cover this with another one-third of the farce and pack firmly. Add the remaining sliced pheasant breast, pork, and julienne of ham, truffles, and goose liver, alternating them as before. Add the rest of the farce and press it down. Cover the terrine with thin slices of fat salt pork, pull the edges of skin over all to cover it completely, and place a small bay leaf on top. Cover the casserole and seal the edges with a roll of stiff dough made of flour and water. Set the terrine in a pan of hot water and bake it in a hot oven (400° F.) for about 2 hours. Remove the dough seal and the cover. If the melted fat on top of the terrine is clear, the terrine is done. If it is cloudy, replace the cover and return the terrine to the oven.

Remove the cover and cool the pâté under the weight of several plates. Unmold the pâté and scrape off the fat. Wash the casserole and return the pâté to it, bottom side up. Fill the terrine with game aspic made with one-third the amounts indicated in the recipe and flavored with 2 tablespoons Madeira instead of brandy. Chill the terrine until the aspic is set. Slice the pâté and serve it directly from the terrine.

Chaud-Froid de Pigeonneaux
BONED SQUAB
IN ASPIC

HAVE the butcher bone 6 plump squabs. Rub them inside and out with salt and pepper.

Pound 1/2 pound each of ground lean veal and fresh fat pork to a smooth paste in a mortar. Add the yolks of 3 eggs, mix thoroughly, and rub the farce through a fine sieve. Season with a little salt and a pinch each of cayenne, nutmeg, and allspice. Add 2 ounces each of larding pork, ham, and tongue, all cut into 1/4-inch dice, 1 truffle, chopped, and 3 tablespoons chopped pistachios. Mix well and chill.

Divide the stuffing into 6 parts and wrap a boned squab around each, pressing the squab into shape and securing it with wooden picks or kitchen thread. Wrap each bird firmly in cheesecloth and place them in a deep kettle or casserole with 2 ounces larding pork, 1 carrot, 1 leek, and 1 onion, all sliced, 1 stalk of celery, chopped, 2 sprigs of parsley, 1 garlic clove, crushed, 10 peppercorns, 1 bay leaf, 2 cloves, and a pinch of thyme. Add chicken stock to cover and 2 pairs of cleaned chicken feet and season to taste with salt and pepper. Cover the casserole tightly, bring the liquid to a boil, and simmer gently for 45 to 60 minutes. Cool the squabs slightly, unwrap them, and cool them in the liquid.

Place the squabs on cake racks. Coat them evenly with *chaud-froid blanc* and decorate them with tiny cutouts of hard-cooked egg yolk, pimiento, and truffle or with leaves of tarragon, parsley, or chives. Press the decorations lightly into the soft *chaud-froid* and chill the squabs until the sauce is set. Glaze by spooning over them some of the cool but still liquid aspic and chill again until the aspic is set. Serve on a bed of watercress.

SLICE off the tops of 2 large or 3 medium green peppers and remove the pith and seeds. Mash the yolks of 4 or 5 hard-cooked eggs and add to them 1/2 cup chopped red pimientos and 1/2 cup *mayonnaise collée*. Pack this mixture into the peppers and chill them. Poach 6 or 8 eggs and trim and chill them. With a sharp knife, cut the stuffed peppers into 1/2-inch slices and arrange a poached egg on each slice. Finish with a coat of clear aspic.

Oeufs Pochés Louisiane
POACHED EGGS LOUISIANA

POACH 6 eggs, trim them evenly and put them on a rack to cool. Coat the cold eggs with *chaud-froid blanc*, chill them until the sauce is set and repeat twice more to give each egg a generous coating. Fill the hollows of 6 cooked and chilled artichoke bottoms with *mousse de foie gras* and set one of the coated eggs on each. Decorate the eggs with sliced truffles or with tarragon leaves and chervil. Chill thoroughly and finish with a final coating of aspic.

Oeufs Pochés Rachel
POACHED EGGS RACHEL

BRING 2 cups clear chicken stock to a boil and dissolve in it 1 tablespoon curry powder. Soften 1 1/2 tablespoons gelatin in 1/4 cup cold water for 5 minutes, and dissolve the gelatin in the stock. Chill the stock until it starts to thicken. Blend in 1 1/2 cups mayonnaise and fold in 3 hard-cooked eggs, sliced, and 6 stuffed olives, cut in rings. Season to taste with salt. Pour the

Egg Curry Ring

PÂTÉ EN CROÛTE · *Pâté Dough*

mixture into a ring mold dipped into cold water, and chill until the aspic is set. Unmold on a chilled platter.

Oeufs Pochés à l'Estragon
POACHED EGGS WITH TARRAGON IN ASPIC

Cover the bottom of small *cocottes* or small individual molds with Madeira aspic. When it is almost set, lay on it tarragon leaves that have been drawn through hot water and diamonds cut from truffle slices. Lay on these two crosspieces of thinly sliced cooked ham. Dribble aspic thinly over this decoration, let it set and cover it with more aspic. Let this set and put a trimmed poached egg in each mold. Cover the egg with aspic and let it set. Cover the aspic with a layer of mixed ham and truffles, both finely chopped, and finish with a thin layer of aspic. Chill the molds.

Dip the molds in hot water, unmold them onto a chilled serving platter and surround them with chopped aspic and with finely minced parsley. Decorate the edge of the platter with triangles of aspic.

Légumes en Gelée
VEGETABLES IN ASPIC

Combine cold cooked peas, tiny white turnips and carrots cut in small dice or *bâtonnets* (little sticks), green beans, sliced slantwise, and tiny Lima beans, and add enough *mayonnaise collée* to hold the mixture together. Line small cylindrical molds with cold but still liquid aspic and chill the molds. When the aspic has congealed, fill the molds with the vegetable mixture. Add a layer of clear aspic at the top. Chill until the aspic is set. Unmold the salad and use to garnish cold main dishes.

Pâté en Croûte

The exalted meat pie of la haute cuisine, *the* pâté en croûte, *may be baked in an ordinary loaf tin, but a pâté mold makes for maximum efficiency and ease in unmolding the pâté. The pâté mold has no bottom and must be placed on a baking sheet. The sides of the mold, whatever its shape, are hinged at one side and closed with a metal pin at the other. When the pâté is baked, the mold may be opened and the pâté removed from the baking sheet to a serving platter.*

The pâté en croûte *may be served hot or cold, as a main dish at luncheon, as an hors-d'oeuvre at dinner, or as part of an elegant buffet.*

Pâté Dough

Make a pâté dough by mixing together, in the order given, 4 cups flour, 1 teaspoon salt, 1 cup butter, 1 cup lard, 1 egg and about 1/2 cup cold water.

Handle the dough very lightly. Wrap the dough in wax paper and store it overnight in the refrigerator.

When the dough is ready to use, reserve one-quarter of it for the top crust of the pâté. Roll the remaining three-fourths into a large round or oval sheet, depending upon the shape of the mold, 1/8 inch thick and 1 inch larger around than necessary to cover the bottom and sides of the mold to allow for shrinkage. Put the buttered mold on a buttered sheet and fit the dough into it, carefully and firmly pressing the dough into all the indentations of the mold. Trim the edge evenly, leaving a 1/2-inch border. Moisten the top rim of the mold, fold the overlapping dough back under itself, and press it firmly against the moistened rim. Bake the dough in a very hot oven (450° F.) for 10 minutes to set it. Cool and fill the shell as specified.

Roll out the remaining dough into a sheet slightly thicker than the dough used for lining and 1 inch wider than the top of the mold. Adjust this cover on top of the filling. Moisten the edge of the partially baked lining, fold over the overlapping edge of the covering dough, and press firmly together with the tines of a fork.

Decorate the top of the *pâte en croûte* with leaves or flowers cut from the leftover dough. Prick the top in several places with a fork and make a small hole in the center of the covering to allow steam to escape. Insert a pastry tube or wax-paper funnel in the hole to keep it from closing during the baking. Brush the surface of the pâté with an egg beaten lightly with 1 tablespoon water. Bake as directed.

LINE a springform loaf pan with pâté dough and bake it for 10 minutes.

Grind together 1/2 pound each of veal, lean pork, and fat pork. Add 2 eggs, mix well, and pound the forcemeat to a smooth paste in a mortar. Add salt and pepper to taste. Ignite 2 tablespoons warmed Cognac and stir it in. Press the forcemeat through a sieve or purée it in a blender.

Cut 3/4 pound each of lean ham and tongue into uniform sticks or batons about 1 inch thick and as long as possible. Cut the contents of a can of truffles into similar, smaller sticks. Cover the bottom of the prepared loaf pan with a layer of forcemeat. Arrange parallel rows of truffles and ham and tongue sticks down the length of the pan. Cover these with a layer of forcemeat and proceed in this fashion until the mold is full, arranging pink and black batons to make an attractive cross-section pattern when the pâté is sliced. Wrap one row of ham or tongue sticks in larding pork, if desired. Fill the mold to the top with forcemeat and cover it with a thin layer of larding pork and with the remaining dough. Decorate the crust and insert the tube, as indicated in the directions for lining a pâté mold.

Bake the pâté in a moderate oven (350° F.) for about 1 1/2 hours, brushing it once or twice with *dorure* and covering it with buttered heavy paper if it browns too quickly. Cool in the pan. Pour cool but still liquid aspic through the hole in the crust to fill spaces created by shrinking during the cooking.

Chill the pâté well and remove it to a serving platter. Garnish with aspic cutouts and with ribbons of finely minced parsley and aspic stirred to fragments with a fork. If desired, a few slices may be cut from the loaf before the pâté is brought to the buffet.

Pâté de Lièvre en Croûte

WILD RABBIT OR HARE PÂTÉ

SKIN, clean and draw a 3- to 4-pound hare and remove the sinews. Cut the loin and the tender part of the legs away from the bones and cut the meat into narrow slices. Weigh this meat and add to it an equal amount of similarly sliced loin of fresh pork and of veal. Put the meat in a deep bowl and cover it with an uncooked marinade made with a generous 1/4 cup white wine, 2 tablespoons olive oil, 1 tablespoon Cognac, 1 onion and 1 carrot, sliced, 1 small bay leaf, a pinch of thyme, 4 sprigs of parsley, 1 garlic clove and 1 teaspoon salt mixed with a little poultry spice. Cover the bowl and marinate the meat overnight in the refrigerator.

Cut the rest of the meat from the bones, discard the sinews and put the meat, the heart, and the liver, free of the bitter gall, through the finest blade of a food chopper, along with 3/4 pound lean fresh pork and 1 pound fat fresh pork. Add a generous 1/2 cup dry white wine, 2 tablespoons olive oil, 1 tablespoon Cognac and 1 teaspoon salt mixed with poultry spice. Blend this forcemeat well and put it in a bowl. Lay a few slices of onion and a few sprigs of parsley on the farce, cover the bowl, and store it overnight in the refrigerator.

Remove and discard the onion and parsley from the forcemeat. Add to the forcemeat the marinade in which the meat slices have stood overnight. Mix marinade and forcemeat together well. Wrap each slice of meat in a thin sheet of fresh fat pork.

Line a pâté mold with dough and fill it with alternate layers of forcemeat and meat slices interspersed with bits of truffle, beginning and ending with forcemeat. Cover the pâté in the usual fashion.

Bake the pâté in a moderately hot oven (375° to 400° F.) for about 45 minutes for each pound. When it is done, the juice which boils up in the wax paper tube will be perfectly clear. Cool the pâté thoroughly and pour into it, through the hole in the crust, as much Madeira-flavored aspic jelly as it will hold. Return it to the refrigerator until the aspic sets. Unmold the pâté and serve it sliced.

SOAK 4 pairs sweetbreads in cold water for 2 hours. Drain them and put them in a saucepan with fresh cold water to cover. Add 1 small carrot, cut into strips, 1 small onion stuck with 1 clove, 1/2 bay leaf, 1 pinch of thyme, 1 stalk of celery with leaves, 2 sprigs of parsley, 1 small strip of lemon peel, salt, and 6 peppercorns. Simmer the sweetbreads in this court bouillon for 15 minutes and then plunge them into cold water, reserving the liquid in which they were cooked. When the sweetbreads are cool, remove the membranes and tubes and cut each kernel into quarters.

In a skillet sauté 1 pound mushrooms, sliced, in 3 tablespoons butter until they are tender and delicately browned. Set them aside. In a saucepan melt 3 tablespoons butter, blend in 3 tablespoons flour, and add gradually 1 1/2 cups of the court bouillon in which the sweetbreads were cooked and 1/2 cup Sherry or Madeira, stirring constantly over low heat until the sauce is smooth and thickened. Season to taste with salt and pepper and finish with 1/4 cup heavy cream. Combine the sweetbreads, mushrooms, and sauce and allow the mixture to cool while making a veal forcemeat.

Mix together well 1 1/2 pounds ground veal, 2 tablespoons finely chopped shallots, 1 tablespoon chopped parsley, and 2 eggs. Season the mixture with salt and pepper and add gradually 1/4 cup heavy cream.

Line a partially baked pâté shell with a thin layer of this forcemeat, reserving enough to make a border around the top. Fill the shell with the sweetbreads and encircle the filling with a border of forcemeat packed closely to the inside edge of the mold. Cover the pâté in the usual fashion. Bake it in a very hot oven (450° F.) for 10 minutes. Reduce the temperature to moderate (350° F.) and bake the pâté for 50 minutes longer. Brush the top crust with the egg-and-water mixture once or twice more during the baking period. When the pie is browned, remove it from the oven. Lift the mold carefully from the cookie sheet to a serving platter. Remove the sides of the mold and serve surrounded by sprigs of parsley or watercress and radish roses.

LINE a loaf pan with pâté dough and bake it in a hot oven (400° F.) for 10 minutes.

Grind coarsely 2 pounds each of pork liver and lean fresh pork. Add salt and freshly ground black pepper to taste, 2 garlic cloves, minced, 1 tablespoon chopped parsley, and 1 egg, lightly beaten. Mix thoroughly. Line the bottom and sides of the prepared shell with tiny slices of fresh larding pork. Divide the liver pâté into 4 parts and fill the mold with alternate layers of the pâté and thin slices of fresh larding pork, finishing with a layer of the larding pork and 1 bay leaf. Cover the pâté with the remaining dough and bake it in a very hot oven (450° F.) for 10 minutes. Reduce

Ris de Veau en Croûte
SWEETBREADS IN CRUST

Veal Forcemeat

Pâté de Foie de Porc en Croûte
PORK LIVER PÂTÉ IN CRUST

Quail Pâtés

the temperature to slow (300° F.) and bake the pâté for 1 hour and 20 minutes longer. Just before the end of the baking time, pour through the pastry-tube funnel 1/2 cup hot consommé and 1 tablespoon brandy. May be served hot or cold.

Pheasant Pâté en Croûte

FOLLOW the directions for terrine of pheasant, but line the casserole with pâté dough instead of with the skin of the bird. Cover the top of the pâté with more pastry and pinch the edges together to seal the crust. Make a small hole in the top crust and put in it a tube of wax paper, to form a steam vent. Bake the pâté in a hot oven (425° F.) for 1 3/4 to 2 hours, reducing the temperature to moderately hot (375° F.) if the dough browns too rapidly. When the juice that rises in the wax paper is clear, the pâté is done. Cool the pâté and pour cooled, but still liquid, Madeira aspic through the hole in the top crust.

Petits Pâtés de Caille
QUAIL PÂTÉS

PLUCK and bone 3 quail and sauté the birds in 6 tablespoons hot butter until they are lightly browned on all sides. Cut the birds in half through the center of the breast and cut each half of the breast into 2 scallops. Keep the thigh and leg meat intact.

Grind 1/4 pound each of fresh pork meat and chicken livers and mix with 1/4 cup Cognac, 1 truffle, finely chopped, 1 egg yolk, and a little salt and pepper.

Spread 6 slices of cold cooked ham on the table. Place a breast scallop on each slice of ham. Place a tablespoon of the chopped liver-pork mixture on the scallop, place one of the leg and thigh meat pieces on the liver-pork mixture and top this with another scallop of breast. Fold the ham slice around the filling.

Roll out puff paste 1/3 inch thick on a lightly floured board and cut 6 rectangles about 1/2 inch larger on all sides than the ham rolls. Cut 6 more rectangles 1 inch larger on all sides than the ham rolls. Place each ham roll on one of the smaller rectangles of puff paste and cover it with one of the larger rectangles of puff paste. Moisten the edges of the paste and pinch them together securely. When all the ham rolls have been enclosed in paste, cut a small vent in the top of each, and brush the pâté with a beaten egg. Bake the rolls on a baking sheet in a very hot oven (450° F.) for 15 minutes. Reduce the temperature to moderate (350° F.) and continue to bake for 25 minutes longer, or until the paste is puffed and golden brown. Serve hot or cold.

Pâté de Poulet
CHICKEN IN CRUST

CLEAN and singe a 4- to 4 1/2-pound young capon or roasting chicken. Carefully pull the skin back over the breast without tearing it and remove the breast bone.

Cut 1/2 to 3/4 pound goose liver into large pieces, roll them in flour, and sauté them for a few minutes in butter or goose fat. Or use sliced *pâté de foie gras* but do not sauté it. Put the goose liver in a bowl with 4 or 5 large pieces of truffle, sprinkle with 2 tablespoons Cognac, and blend with 1 cup *mousseline* of chicken. Stuff the capon with this forcemeat, sew the opening neatly, and truss the bird. Rub the outside with a little salt. Melt 2 or 3 tablespoons butter in a pan large enough to hold the capon or chicken, and cook the bird either in the oven or on top of the stove until it is well browned.

Make a *mirepoix* as follows: Melt 2 tablespoons butter in a small saucepan and add 1 carrot, 1 onion, and 1 stalk of celery, all finely chopped, a pinch of thyme, half a bay leaf, finely crushed, and a little salt and pepper and cook the vegetables slowly until they are soft but not brown.

Make a pie dough from 4 cups flour, 1 teaspoon salt, 1 cup lard or other shortening, 1/2 cup butter, and about 6 tablespoons water. Roll out a generous third of the pastry into an oval about 1/4 inch thick and about 2 inches larger than the bird. Lay the bird on this and spread the *mirepoix* over the breast and legs. Arrange a few thin slices of raw ham on top and cover with thin slices of fresh larding pork. Roll out the remaining pastry and cover the bird. Moisten the edge of the lower pastry, press top and bottom together, and pinch or flute the edge attractively. Cut a small hole in the top to allow the steam to escape. Brush with an egg beaten with a little milk. Bake the pie in a hot oven (425° F.) until the crust starts to color, then lower the temperature to moderate (350° F.), and bake for 1 1/2 to 1 3/4 hours.

To serve, cut a slice from the top of the pastry to permit carving and give each guest a piece of pastry, a piece of chicken, a piece of ham, and some of the stuffing. Serve *sauce périgourdine* separately.

For an alternate method to make this dish place the browned capon, the *mirepoix*, ham slices, and larding pork in an oval casserole just large enough to hold the bird. Add a little gravy, cover with a lid that has a small hole in it for the steam to escape, and seal the edge with a stiff paste made of flour and water. Bake 1 1/2 to 1 3/4 hours.

Beefsteak and Kidney Pie

MIX together in a deep casserole 1 pound beefsteak and 4 veal kidneys, cut in very small dice, 8 mushrooms, sliced, 1 large onion, and 1 teaspoon parsley, finely chopped, 1/2 teaspoon Worcestershire sauce, 1/2 cup Madeira, and 1 1/2 cups brown sauce. Cover the filling with any pie dough and cut slits in the crust to allow the steam to escape. Bake the pie in a moderate oven (350° F.) for 50 to 60 minutes, or until the pie is well browned and the meats are tender. Serves 4.

Tourte de Veau

VEAL PIE

CHOP very finely enough leftover cooked veal to make about 3 cups. Soak 3/4 cup fresh bread crumbs in milk to cover for a few minutes, drain well, and combine them with the veal. Add 2 tablespoons finely chopped onion sautéed until golden in 1 tablespoon butter, 1 tablespoon chopped parsley, 1/2 teaspoon salt, a little pepper, 1 egg, beaten, and 1/3 cup veal gravy and mix thoroughly. The consistency should be about that of hash. A few finely sliced cooked mushrooms may be added.

Line a deep pie plate or shallow casserole with pie dough, put in the veal filling, and cover with a thin layer of dough. Brush the top with a little milk, prick the dough with a two-tined fork, and bake the pie in a moderately hot oven (375° F.) for 35 to 40 minutes, or until the crust is well browned.

Tart Pastry for Timbales

MIX 1/2 cup butter, 1 tablespoon sugar, 1 teaspoon salt, and 1 egg. Cut this mixture into 2 cups sifted flour and add just enough cold water, about 4 or 5 tablespoons, to hold the mixture together. Work this dough as little as possible, because too much handling toughens it.

To shape the timbale, roll out a circle about 1/8 to 1/4 inch thick and large enough to cover the bottom and sides of the mold. Sprinkle the sheet of dough lightly with flour and fold it in half, but do not crease the fold. With the open edges facing forward, pull the two ends around to the front to form what looks like a skull cap and stretch the dough gently to get a bowl-shaped piece when the halves are opened. Fit this into the well-buttered mold, working it into the edges so that the finished timbale will have the exact mold shape.

If the mold has a decoration on the sides, it will, of course, show on the finished timbale. Let about 1/2 inch lap over the edge of the mold like a flange and decorate with a pastry wheel or pastry leaves or pinch it neatly. Line the mold with wax paper and fill it with dried beans to weight down the pastry and keep it from puffing up and out of shape as it bakes. Bake in a hot oven (400° F.) until the shell is golden brown. Discard the beans, remove the wax paper, and carefully unmold the timbale. Let it dry in a warm place until ready to fill and serve.

If a pastry cover is to be added, roll out a piece of the dough and cut it the size of the top of the timbale to fit nicely on the 1/2-inch flange at the top of the timbale. Decorate the edge of the cover like the flange. Leaves are usually cut from the pastry and arranged in a kind of wreath on this cover. Finally, three small circles of dough, graduated in size, are placed in the center, one on top of the other, for a knob. Bake the cover on a flat pan or cookie sheet.

Timbale molds vary in height from 2 1/2 inches to 7 or 8 inches. Any straight-sided mold can be used, a charlotte mold, a deep pie dish, or a porcelain or earthenware casserole. Usually covers are made only for the very high timbales, and when the timbale is covered, the contents of the timbale are not elaborately garnished. When the timbale is not high, the filling is garnished with "turned" mushrooms, truffles, or other decorations, and the mixture is piled up a little higher than the edge of the timbale. The pastry cover is then omitted. A dome-shaped, high silver cover is always placed over the open timbale when it is served.

Timbale de Filets de Sole Grimaldi

TIMBALE OF FILETS OF SOLE GRIMALDI

MELT 2 tablespoons butter in a shallow pan and add 1 teaspoon chopped shallots or onions and 12 mushrooms, stemmed.

Spread 6 filets of sole with fish mousse, roll them up, and fasten the rolls with toothpicks. Put the rolls, or *paupiettes*, in the pan and add 1/2 cup dry white wine or 1 cup water or fish stock acidulated with 1/2 teaspoon lemon juice. If the bones of the fish are on hand, lay them on top and remove them when the fish is cooked.

Cut a round of paper, wax or buttered, the size of the pan and make a small hole in the center. Place this over the fish and cover the pan. Bring the liquid to a simmer and poach the fish for 10 to 12 minutes, or until it is done. Discard the bones and transfer the *paupiettes* and the mushrooms to a plate to keep warm.

Cook the liquid in the pan until it is reduced by half and add 1 cup cream sauce or *velouté*, 1/4 cup heavy cream, and 1 tablespoon butter. Correct the seasoning with salt and a little freshly ground white pepper and strain.

Cook in boiling salted water enough spaghetti, broken into 2-inch pieces, to make 2 cups. Drain the spaghetti thoroughly and sauté it in a little butter.

Place a baked timbale about 3 to 3 1/2 inches deep on a serving platter and spread some sauce over the bottom. Arrange the spaghetti on the sauce and the fish *paupiettes* and mushrooms on the spaghetti. Pour the remaining sauce over the fish and arrange slices of truffle on each *paupiette*. Serve very hot.

BRAISE 3 pairs prepared sweetbreads *à blanc*.

Make a good *sauce suprême* by adding to 1/2 cup chicken broth the stems and peelings of the 12 mushrooms to be used for garnishing, the liquid in which they were cooked, and a little truffle juice. Boil this rapidly until it is reduced by half. Add 1 cup *sauce velouté*, combine well, and add 1 cup heavy cream. Correct the seasoning with salt and thicken the sauce with 2 egg yolks mixed with a little cream. Heat the sauce until it almost comes to a boil and strain it through a fine sieve.

In another saucepan heat together 12 turned and cooked mushrooms, 12 cooked cockscombs, and 12 to 15 *mousselines* of chicken decorated with truffles cut in half-moon shapes. Heat them with 1/2 cup of the sauce and 1/4 cup dry Sherry or Madeira.

Place a baked timbale 3 inches deep on a serving platter and spread some of the sauce in the bottom. Arrange the sweetbreads over it with the mushrooms, cockscombs, and *mousselines* of chicken over and around them. Add more sauce and serve immediately.

Timbale de Ris de Veau à la Régence
TIMBALE OF SWEETBREADS

BRAISE 2 pairs of sweetbreads *a blanc* and dice them. In a saucepan cook 1 1/2 tablespoons shallots in 3 tablespoons butter for a moment. Add 1 cup mushrooms, sliced, and cook for 3 minutes. Stir in the sweetbreads and 1/3 cup dry white wine or dry white vermouth and cook over brisk heat until the liquid has almost evaporated. Season the mixture with salt, freshly ground pepper, and 1 tablespoon fresh tarragon or chervil.

In a separate saucepan melt 2 tablespoons butter, add 2 1/2 tablespoons flour and cook, stirring constantly, until the *roux* is smooth but not colored. Stir in 1 cup heated light cream, salt and pepper to taste, and cook, stirring constantly, until the sauce is smooth and thick. In a bowl, beat 1 egg yolk with 1/4 cup cream and very gradually beat in the thickened sauce. Return it to the saucepan and cook over low heat for 1 minute, stirring. Remove the sauce from the heat and combine it with the sweetbreads mixture.

Put a baked timbale 3 inches deep on a serving platter and spoon in the sweetbreads mixture. Serve immediately.

Ris de Veau à la Crème
SWEETBREADS IN CREAM

Timbale of Game and Sweetbreads à la Soyer

BRAISE 2 pairs prepared sweetbreads *à blanc*, without browning them, and slice each in half to make 2 *escalopes*. Remove the breasts from a broiled pheasant, partridge, or grouse and cut each one in thin slices to make 6 *escalopes*. Prepare, as for *timbale de ris de veau à la Regénce*, a garnish of 12 turned mushrooms, 12 cockscombs, and 12 small *mousselines* made with the meat of game birds.

In a buttered saucepan cook 1 onion, sliced, 2 tablespoons ground ham, 1/2 cup ground veal, 1/4 cup ground game trimmings, and 1/2 cup veal stock until the stock has almost evaporated. Add 2 1/2 cups veal stock, 1 tablespoon each of chopped parsley and celery, 1/2 bay leaf, a pinch of thyme, 4 peppercorns, 1 clove, 1 tablespoon truffle juice, and the stems and peelings of the mushrooms to be used for garnish. Simmer the liquid slowly until it is reduced to half its original quantity and the vegetables are tender. Strain the liquid through a fine sieve and add 1 cup brown sauce, 1 tablespoon *glace de viande*, 2 truffles, sliced, and salt to taste.

In another saucepan put half of each of the garnishings and 1/2 cup of the hot sauce. Spread some of the sauce on the bottom of a baked timbale 3 to 3 1/2 inches deep, edged with small leaf cutouts of pastry. Arrange the game and sweetbread *escalopes* in the timbale alternately with the sauced garnishings. Add more sauce, if necessary, and heap in the center the remaining turned mushrooms, cockscombs, and *mousselines*, and 12 small rounds of truffle heated in 1/4 cup Sherry or Madeira.

Vol-au-Vent de Ris de Veau

SWEETBREADS
IN PUFF
PASTE SHELL

BRAISE 3 pairs prepared sweetbreads *à blanc*. If they are very large, cut them diagonally into 2 or 3 thick slices before braising. Place in a saucepan 12 quenelles of chicken, 12 mushrooms caps, cooked until tender in water barely to cover, and 1/2 cup dry Sherry. Heat gently and keep the mixture hot, being careful not to let it scorch.

For the sauce, reduce to 1/2 cup the liquid in which the mushrooms were cooked, adding the chopped stems of the mushrooms and a little juice of truffles, if obtainable. Add 4 cups *velouté* or béchamel sauce, and cook the mixture until it is well combined and slightly reduced. Add 2 1/2 cups heavy cream little by little. The sauce should be thick enough to coat the back of a silver spoon. Correct the seasoning with salt and strain the sauce through a fine sieve.

Combine half the sauce with the quenelles and mushrooms. Arrange the sweetbreads in a ring in a *vol-au-vent* shell, fill the center with the other mixture, and cover all with sauce. Serve the remaining sauce in a heated sauceboat. Garnish the *vol-au-vent* with turned mushrooms and quenelles of chicken. Leave the cover of the *vol-au-vent* off or half off to display the garnish.

Garden Vegetables

The gourmet finds it to his gastronomic advantage to treat vegetables with the respect due them, not because they are "good for one"—oh, kiss of death—but simply because they are good to eat. Our Anglo-Saxon custom of relegating vegetables to a subordinate position on the meat plate can logically be blamed for the disrepute into which the vegetable tribe has fallen; it is understandably difficult to wax enthusiastic about a spoonful of watery mashed potatoes or an anonymous stew of peas. In France, vegetables frequently are served as a separate course, and so get the undivided, appreciative attention they merit.

Included in the following pages, along with some very important vegetables, are the lesser preparations that nevertheless make a valuable contribution to the menu, and the savory vegetable mixtures *en casserole* that can be expected to make converts of the most prejudiced meat eaters.

REMOVE the tough or discolored outer leaves from well-rinsed artichokes and cut off about 1 inch of the top leaves with a knife or scissors. Trim the base and stem of each with a sharp knife and put lemon slices on the bases to keep them white. Tie the artichokes with kitchen thread to secure the leaves and lemon during cooking and cook them in a large quantity of well-salted boiling water for 45 minutes to 1 hour, or until they are tender. When a leaf pulls out easily, the artichokes are done.

Remove the strings and lay the artichokes upside down to drain. Lift

Whole Artichokes

out and discard the fine prickly leaves in the center and the fine hairy section, or choke, that covers the heart. Serve the artichokes hot with seasoned melted butter or hollandaise, or cold with vinaigrette sauce.

Artichokes alla Romana

REMOVE the hard outer leaves of 12 very small artichokes, trim the points of the others, and remove the chokes, putting minced garlic, parsley, mint, salt and pepper in their place. Make a bouquet of the artichokes in a terra-cotta casserole, moisten them with 1/4 cup oil, and cook them over moderate heat for 10 minutes. Add 2 cups dry white wine and 1/2 cup stock. Cover the casserole and let the artichokes cook until they are tender and the sauce is well reduced.

Artichauts à la Mireille

CLEAN and trim 6 artichokes. Put them in a casserole with 1 cup chicken bouillon, 1/2 cup olive oil, and 12 small onions, peeled. Add 4 tomatoes, peeled and quartered, and sprinkle with salt and pepper. Cover the casserole and bake it in a hot oven (425° F.) for about 30 minutes, or until the artichokes and onions are tender. Serve from the casserole.

Artichokes Majorca

TRIM and cook 6 artichokes. Remove the outer leaves and arrange the hearts in a baking dish. Sprinkle them with 1 garlic clove, finely chopped, and the juice of 1 lemon.

Prepare a mushroom sauce as follows: Remove and chop the stems of 12 raw mushrooms and dry them in a hot oven (400° F.). With a mortar and pestle grind the dry stems to a coarse powder. Slice the mushroom caps and sauté them lightly in butter. Add 1 tablespoon flour, mix well and add 2 tablespoons sour cream, stirring constantly. Season the creamed mushrooms with salt and pepper and spoon them into the artichoke hearts. Sprinkle the stuffed artichokes with the dried mushroom powder and bake them in a moderately hot oven (375° F.) for 5 minutes.

Fonds d'Artichauts Sautés

REMOVE the stems from large artichokes, trim the bottoms and rub them with lemon juice to keep the flesh from darkening. With a sharp knife cut off the leaves about 1/2 inch from the base. Cut each artichoke into 6 to 8 pieces, depending upon the size, and remove the chokes.

In a saucepan, mix 1 tablespoon flour with a little water and add 1 teaspoon salt and 1 tablespoon vinegar or 1 teaspoon lemon juice. Add 1 quart water, bring the liquid to a boil, and add the artichoke pieces. Cook the artichokes over moderate heat for about 30 minutes, or until they are

Artichauts à la Mireille

tender. Drain them well. In a shallow pan heat 2 tablespoons butter until it turns a hazelnut brown, add the artichoke pieces, and sauté them for a few minutes on each side.

*Braised
Artichokes*

CUT the top third from 6 artichokes and trim the base. Put them in boiling salted water and cook them for 15 to 20 minutes. Cool them in cold water, drain, and remove the prickly chokes. Prepare a stuffing as follows:

Melt 1/4 cup butter in a saucepan, add 2 teaspoons finely chopped shallots or 2 tablespoons finely chopped onions, and cook until these are soft but not brown. Add 1/2 cup mushrooms, finely chopped, and cook them for a few minutes, or until the moisture is cooked away. Add 2 tablespoons chopped cooked ham, 2 teaspoons chopped parsley, 1/2 teaspoon salt, a little pepper, and 1/4 cup tomato sauce or tomato purée. Fill the artichokes with this mixture, wrap a piece of fat salt pork around each, and tie the artichokes with a string to hold them in shape.

Place in a casserole 1 carrot and 1 onion, both sliced, 2 sprigs of parsley, 1 small bay leaf, and a little thyme and add 1/2 cup each of white wine and meat stock or water, 2 tablespoons tomato purée and a little lemon juice. Add the artichokes. Bring the liquid to a boil over direct heat, cover the casserole, and braise the artichokes in a moderate oven (350° F.) for about 1 hour. Remove them to a serving dish and discard pork and string. Strain the liquid in the casserole, skim the fat, and cook the sauce until it is reduced by about half. Spoon some of it into each artichoke, dot with chopped parsley, and pour the rest of the sauce around the vegetables.

*Fonds
d'Artichauts
Sarah
Bernhardt*

ARTICHOKE
BOTTOMS
SARAH BERNHARDT

TRIM 6 artichokes as for sautéed artichoke bottoms, but do not cut them into pieces. In a saucepan combine 3 pints water, 1 tablespoon flour, 2 teaspoons salt, and the juice of 1 large lemon or 3 tablespoons vinegar. Bring the water to a boil, add the artichokes, and cook them for 45 to 50 minutes. Separate the leaves and remove the chokes.

Prepare the following garnish: Trim the stems from 1/2 pound small mushrooms and season the caps with salt and pepper. Melt 2 tablespoons butter in a shallow pan and in it sauté the mushrooms until they are golden brown, shaking the pan to brown them evenly. Add 1/2 cup cream, cover the pan, and cook the mushrooms very gently for about 10 minutes. Arrange 2 or 3 mushrooms in the center of each artichoke. Continue to cook the sauce until it thickens a little, and combine it with 1 egg yolk beaten with a little of the hot sauce. Correct the seasoning with salt, add 2 or 3 drops of lemon juice, and fold in 1 tablespoon whipped cream. Cover the mushrooms with the sauce and brown them under the broiler.

Place the artichokes on a serving dish and around each arrange 3 to 4 cooked asparagus tips and a few small carrot balls, cooked and glazed with a little butter and sugar until they are golden brown.

ARRANGE 6 cooked artichoke bottoms in a baking pan and sprinkle them with 1/4 cup finely chopped mushrooms. In the center of each heart put 1 teaspoon *pâté de foie gras*. Add 1/4 cup each of Madeira and beef stock or consommé. Dot each heart with butter and sprinkle with salt and pepper. Bake the hearts in a hot oven (400° F.) for 15 minutes.

Artichoke Hearts Parisienne

FILL cooked artichoke bottoms with buttered cooked spinach, piling it up in the center. Cover the artichokes with Mornay sauce, sprinkle with grated cheese, and glaze them under the broiler.

Other vegetables, cooked and tossed in a little butter, may be used in place of spinach, such as green beans, mushrooms, asparagus tips, or a macédoine of mushrooms and peas.

Fonds d'Artichauts à la Florentine

CUT 6 artichoke hearts, trimmed as for sautéed artichoke bottoms, in quarters and cooked them for 10 minutes in salted water to which has been added the juice of 1 lemon and 1 tablespoon flour mixed to a paste with a little cold water. Drain the hearts and put them in the center of a casserole. Pour over them 1/2 cup each of dry white wine and veal gravy.

Place around the artichoke hearts handfuls of fresh vegetables—small new carrots, turnips cut in quarters, small white onions, peas, tiny new potatoes, and tomatoes, quartered. Sprinkle with salt, pepper, and finely chopped chervil and dot with butter. Cover the casserole and bake it in a moderate oven (350° F.) for 35 to 40 minutes. Serve from the casserole.

Fonds d'Artichauts à la Printaniére

IN a saucepan melt 1/4 cup butter, stir in 6 tablespoons flour, 1 teaspoon salt, and 1/4 teaspoon pepper, and add gradually 1 cup milk, stirring constantly. Bring the sauce to a boil, remove it from the heat and set it aside

Artichoke Ring

459

to cool. Force 12 cooked artichoke bottoms through a food mill or purée them in a blender. Lightly butter a 9-inch ring mold and set it in a pan in 1/2 inch of water. Combine the puréed artichokes and the cooled sauce. Add 2 teaspoons scraped onion, 3 tablespoons grated Parmesan and 4 eggs, well beaten. Blend the mixture thoroughly and pour it into the prepared mold. Bake the ring in a moderate oven (350° F.) for 1 hour. Unmold it on a warm serving platter and serve it with hollandaise sauce.

Artichoke
Fritters

CUT off the stalks and tips of 12 very small artichokes and discard the tough outer leaves. Cut the artichokes in half lengthwise and remove the chokes. Cut each half into thirds, lengthwise. Place the slices in a large bowl and cover them with water. Add the juice of 1 lemon and allow the artichokes to soak for a few minutes. Drain them on absorbent paper. Dip them in fritter batter for meat and vegetables and fry them in hot deep fat (370° F.) until they are golden. Serve hot.

Jerusalem artichokes are really tubers.

Purée of
Jerusalem
Artichokes

PEEL 2 pounds Jerusalem artichokes and cook them in boiling salted water for 20 to 30 minutes, or until they are tender. Drain the tubers and put them through a ricer. Whip them with butter and cream until the purée is smooth. Season it to taste with salt and pepper and pile it into a serving dish. Serve hot.

Jerusalem
Artichokes
à la Crème

PEEL 18 to 20 Jerusalem artichokes and cut them into large olive shapes, dropping them into cold water as they are peeled so that they will not blacken. Bring the water to a boil and cook the artichokes for 15 minutes. Drain the tubers and turn them into a buttered casserole. Dot with butter, sprinkle with salt and pepper, and cover with heavy cream. Bake the casserole in a hot oven (425° F.) for 20 minutes.

Hot Asparagus
Vinaigrette

WASH 3 pounds asparagus, snap off the tough ends, and peel the stalks a few inches below the tips to remove the scales. Stand the asparagus tips up, in the bottom of a double boiler half full of boiling water. Cover the pan with the inverted top part of the double boiler and cook the stalks for 12 to 20 minutes, or until they are just tender. The stalks cook in the boiling water and the tips in the steam. Place the asparagus on a serving dish. Pour French dressing over them and sprinkle with chopped parsley.

Cook 3 pounds prepared asparagus until it is tender and drain it on absorbent paper. Arrange a layer of the asparagus in a shallow buttered baking dish, dot it with butter and sprinkle it with 1/4 teaspoon lemon juice and 1 tablespoon each of grated Parmesan and grated Swiss cheese. Alternate layers of asparagus and butter, lemon juice and grated cheese to within 1/4 inch from the top of the dish, finishing with butter, lemon juice, and cheese. Bake the asparagus in a hot oven (375° to 400° F.) for 10 minutes and serve it immediately on hot plates.

Asperges au Four
BAKED ASPARAGUS

Arrange 3 pounds cooked asparagus in a baking dish and over it pour 1/3 cup melted butter and 1/2 cup dry white wine. Sprinkle the asparagus lightly with salt and pepper and generously with grated Parmesan cheese. Place the dish in a hot oven (425° F.) for about 10 minutes, or until the cheese browns lightly.

Asperges au Vin Blanc

Cook 3 pounds asparagus and drain it thoroughly. Wrap bunches of 3 stalks in thin slices of *prosciutto* or ham. Put the bundles in a buttered baking dish, dot them with 1/4 cup butter, and sprinkle them generously with grated Parmesan cheese. Place the dish in a hot oven (400° F.) for 5 minutes. Sprinkle with another 1/4 cup melted butter.

Asparagus Tips with Prosciutto

In a saucepan melt 1/4 cup butter. Add 1 cup very coarse cracker crumbs, 1/2 teaspoon grated onion, 1 tablespoon chopped parsley, 1/2 teaspoon salt, and 1/4 teaspoon freshly ground black pepper. Sauté the mixture briefly. In a mixing bowl beat 2 eggs lightly and add gradually 2 cups hot milk, stirring constantly. Add the sautéed crumbs and 4 cups cooked asparagus cut into 1-inch lengths. Blend the mixture well, pour it in a buttered bread pan or timbale, and bake it in a moderate oven (350° F.) for 30 to 40 minutes, or until the loaf is firm. Serve with curry sauce.

Asparagus Timbale

In a saucepan melt 1/3 cup butter, add 1/3 cup flour and cook it for a few minutes. Add 3 cups white stock—chicken or veal—1/2 teaspoon salt and a little white pepper, and cook the mixture, stirring, until it thickens. Add 2 tablespoons grated Parmesan cheese and continue cooking the sauce, stirring occasionally, until it reduces to about 2 1/2 cups and is very thick but light

Chicken Asparagus Divan

and creamy. Remove the sauce from the heat, add 2 tablespoons Madeira, blending well, and set it aside.

Arrange 2 pounds cooked asparagus in a baking dish and pour over it 1 cup of the sauce. Cover this with a layer of thinly sliced cooked white meat of chicken or turkey and add the remaining sauce. Sprinkle generously with grated Parmesan and bake the dish in a moderately slow oven (325° F.) until the sauce begins to bubble. Brown the top under the broiler.

Bamboo Shoots
Bordelaise

DRAIN 1 large can of bamboo shoots. Cut them into 1-inch pieces and sauté them in 3 tablespoons butter over low heat. The pan should be gently shaken back and forth and the pieces of bamboo turned once, very carefully, with two forks.

Sauce Bordelaise
Maigre

When the pieces of bamboo are heated through, but not brown, place the bamboo shoots in a heated serving dish and pour over them the following sauce: Chop 6 medium-sized shallots very finely and sauté them in 1 tablespoon butter over low heat until they are transparent. Add 1/2 cup red wine and boil it gently until it is reduced by half. Just before serving, add 1 generous tablespoon finely chopped chervil or parsley. Serves 4.

Sautéed
Bamboo
Shoot Tips
CHAO TUNG SUN

CUT the contents of a can of bamboo shoot tips into 2-inch lengths and slice them lengthwise 1/8 inch thick. Heat 1/2 cup lard in a skillet and in it sauté the slices of bamboo shoots for 3 minutes. Add 1/4 teaspoon salt, 1/2 teaspoon sugar, and 3/4 cup chicken stock and cook for 2 minutes. Stir in 1 teaspoon cornstarch mixed with 2 tablespoons cold water and continue to stir until the gravy is smooth. Serves 4.

Green beans and wax beans may be used interchangeably in these recipes. The important thing is that the beans cook quickly and briefly; overcooking destroys color and texture.

Haricots Verts
aux Amandes
GREEN BEANS
WITH ALMONDS

WASH and remove the ends of 1 1/2 pounds young green beans and cut them into 1-inch lengths. Or slice each bean down the center lengthwise and then in half, to make 4 pieces. Or slice the beans slantwise into thin diagonal strips. If the beans are very small and young, they may be left whole. Cook the beans in boiling salted water to cover for 20 minutes or less, until they are barely tender. Drain them well and toss them with butter, salt and pepper to taste, and 1/4 cup slivered toasted almonds.

Toss 1 1/2 pounds cooked whole green beans in 3 tablespoons hot butter with 1 tablespoon chopped parsley. Sauté lightly and add salt and pepper to taste. *Haricots Verts à la Française*

Cook 1 1/2 pounds sliced green beans until they are just tender. Drain them well and stir in 1 cup sour cream mixed with 1 teaspoon flour, 1 teaspoon each of finely chopped parsley, chives, fennel, and dill, 3 tablespoons butter, and salt and pepper to taste. Heat the mixture over hot water for about 15 minutes and serve hot. *Green Beans Smitane*

Cook 1 1/2 pounds young green beans until they are barely tender and drain them. While the beans are cooking, cook 2 cups celery, cut in thin slices, in 1/4 cup butter for about 10 minutes with a garlic clove. The celery should not become limp. Discard the garlic and combine celery and beans. Season with salt and a pinch each of basil and paprika and serve hot. *Green Beans and Celery*

Wash, trim, and cut into diagonal strips 1 1/2 pounds tender green beans. In a flameproof casserole melt 1/4 cup butter and in it sauté 1 cup tiny white onions, peeled, and 2 green peppers, seeded and chopped, until the onions are golden, stirring frequently. Add the beans and 1/4 cup chopped parsley, sprinkle with salt and pepper, and mix thoroughly. *Green Bean Casserole*

Cover the casserole tightly and bake it in a moderate oven (350° F.) for about 1 hour, or until the beans are tender.

Wash 1 1/2 pounds tender young green beans and snap off the ends. Cook the beans in boiling salted water until they are tender but still crisp. Add 1 1/2 teaspoons dry mustard and 1 1/2 tablespoons butter to 3 egg yolks and with a wire whisk beat the mixture until it is light and frothy. Scald 3/4 cup milk and add it to the egg yolk mixture. Cook the mixture in a double boiler until it is thick, stirring constantly. Add 3 teaspoons vinegar, *Green Beans with Mustard Dressing* salt to taste and the green beans. Cook the dressed beans for 4 minutes longer.

Beets Biarritz   REMOVE the tender greens from 12 medium-sized beets and wash the greens thoroughly. Place them in a kettle with just enough water to cover and sprinkle lightly with salt. Bring the water to a boil and cook the greens for 15 minutes. Drain them, chop them finely, and season them with freshly ground pepper, a generous lump of butter, the juice of 1 lemon, and salt to taste.

Cook the beets in boiling salted water for about 45 minutes, or until they are tender. Drain them, peel them, and hollow out the centers to form shells. Fill the beet shells with the chopped greens and dot the greens with a lump of butter. Place the beets in a baking dish, cover, and bake it in a moderate oven (350° F.) for about 15 minutes. Garnish with sieved yolks of hard-cooked eggs mixed with chopped parsley.

Russian Beets   GRATE enough raw beets to make 4 cups. In a saucepan heat 2 tablespoons butter and add the beets, the juice of 1 lemon, 1 1/2 teaspoons salt, and a little pepper. Cover the pan and cook the beets over very low heat for 25 minutes, stirring occasionally. Sift 1 tablespoon flour over the beets, cover, and continue to cook for 15 minutes longer. Stir in 1/2 cup boiling water and keep the beets hot over boiling water.

Beets Baked   WASH 1 dozen medium beets, place them in a casserole, and bake them
with   in a moderate oven (350° F.) for about 1 hour, or until they are tender.
Sour Cream   Remove the skins and slice the beets thinly into a buttered casserole. Sprinkle them with salt and pepper, pour over them 1 cup sour cream, and return the casserole to the oven until the cream bubbles.

Orange Beets   COOK, peel, and slice 18 small beets. In a saucepan blend 3 tablespoons butter, 2 tablespoons cornstarch, 1/4 cup each of lemon juice and sugar, and 2 cups orange juice. Cook this sauce until it is slightly thickened, season it with salt and pepper to taste, and pour it over the sliced hot beets.

Broccoli   WASH 1 large bunch of broccoli in cold water. Discard the coarse leaves and the tough lower parts of the stalks and split the stalks lengthwise. Soak the broccoli for 30 minutes in salted water and drain it. Cook it standing with the flowerets out of the water, in a deep covered saucepan half-filled with boiling water for about 10 minutes, or until it is barely tender. Drain the broccoli.

Broccoli may be served with hollandaise sauce, or with a spoonful of sour cream, or with butter and grated cheese, or it may be sprinkled while still hot with 1/4 cup olive oil and salt and pepper to taste.

WASH and trim a large bunch of broccoli and cut the stalks and the flowerets lengthwise into thin slices. Pour 1 tablespoon olive oil into a skillet and add a layer of thinly sliced onions, a scattering of pitted, sliced black olives, and an anchovy filet cut in pieces. Add a layer of broccoli and sprinkle it generously with grated Provolone cheese, olive oil, and seasonings to taste. Repeat the process and pour over the 4 layers 1 cup dry red wine. Cover the pan and cook the broccoli over low heat for about 30 minutes, or until it is just tender.

Broccoli alla Siciliana

COOK 1 large bunch of broccoli until it is just tender and cool it. Combine 1/4 cup olive oil and 2 tablespoons lemon juice with 1 garlic clove, crushed, salt and pepper to taste, and 2 tablespoons minced chervil. Pour the dressing over the broccoli and chill before serving.

Broccoli with Chervil

COOK 1 large bunch of broccoli in salted water until it is just tender and drain it. Steep 1 garlic clove, crushed, in 1/2 cup hot butter for 2 minutes, discard the garlic, and stir in 1/2 cup minced ripe olives, salt and pepper to taste, and 1 teaspoon lemon juice. Pour this over the broccoli.

Broccoli with Ripe Olive Sauce

PICK over 1 1/2 pounds Brussels sprouts, remove any yellowed leaves, and trim the stems. Wash the sprouts and make an incision in the bottom of each. Cook them in 2 quarts boiling water with 2 teaspoons salt for about 10 to 15 minutes, or until they are just tender, and drain well. Finish them as in the recipes that follow.

Brussels Sprouts

TRIM and cook 1 1/2 pounds Brussels sprouts and sauté them for a few minutes in butter. Use the buttered sprouts to fill a ring made of equal

Brussel Sprouts in Ring

465

parts of mashed sweet potato and purée of lentils, seasoned with butter and salt, and browned on a heatproof platter.

*Brussels
Sprouts
Ménagère*

SAUTÉ 2 or 3 slices of bacon cut in dice in 2 tablespoons butter until the bacon is crisp and golden brown. Add 1 1/2 pounds cooked Brussels sprouts and toss well together. Season with salt and pepper and sprinkle with parsley.

*Brussels
Sprouts with
Chestnuts*

COOK 1 1/2 pounds Brussels sprouts until they are tender and turn them into a colander to drain.

Blanch and shell 1 pound chestnuts, simmer them, covered, in boiling salted water for 30 minutes, or until they are just tender, and drain them. Combine the chestnuts and sprouts and toss them with 1/4 cup melted butter.

*Brussels
Sprouts
Soubise*

Purée Soubise
ONION PURÉE

COMBINE 1 pound cooked Brussels sprouts with 1 1/2 cups purée Soubise. Sprinkle with 1/3 cup grated cheese and brown well under the broiler.

To make purée Soubise, or onion purée: Mince 4 large onions and place them in a pan with 3 tablespoon hot butter. Cover the pan and cook the onions gently until they are soft. Add 1/2 teaspoon salt, 1/4 cup rice, and 1/2 cup boiling water. Mix well, cover tightly and simmer gently for about 40 minutes, or until the water has virtually disappeared. Rub through a fine sieve and combine with 1/2 cup thick béchamel sauce.

*Brussels
Sprouts
Louisiana*

MAKE a ring of overlapping rounds of sliced cooked sweet potatoes, alternating them with small pieces of pineapple. Sprinkle potatoes and fruit with maple syrup and glaze them in the oven, basting frequently with syrup. Fill the center of the ring with 1 pound Brussels sprouts cooked, sautéed in butter, and mixed with 1 cup cooked chestnuts sautéed in butter.

*Red Cabbage
with Wine*

CLEAN 1 large or 2 small heads of red cabbage, cut in quarters, and remove the hard core. Cut the cabbage in fine julienne and parboil it in boiling water for 10 minutes. Cool it in cold water and drain well. Season with 1 teaspoon salt, a little pepper, and a few grains of nutmeg. Melt 2 tablespoons butter or fresh goose fat in a saucepan, add 1 onion, finely chopped, and cook until it is soft. Add 1 tablespoon vinegar, 2 cups white or red wine, and 2 cups water. Add the drained cabbage and cook it gently for 30 minutes. Add 2 or 3 green apples, peeled, cored, and chopped, and cook for 25 to 30 minutes longer, adding more water if necessary to keep the cabbage from scorching.

REMOVE the wilted outer leaves and the hard core from a head of cabbage and cut the cabbage into thick slices. Cook it gently for 5 minutes in 3 tablespoons melted butter in a covered skillet. Add 1/2 teaspoon salt, a little freshly ground pepper, and 1 1/2 cups flat ale or beer and continue to cook, covered, for 5 to 7 minutes longer, or until the cabbage is just tender.

Alsatian Cabbage

CUT 1 head of Chinese cabbage into strips about 1/4 inch wide. Heat 3 tablespoons olive oil in a large skillet, add the cabbage, and stir for 3 minutes. Add 1 1/2 teaspoons salt and 1/2 cup water and stir for 3 minutes longer. Mix together 1 cup water, 3 tablespoons each of vinegar and sugar, and 1 tablespoon cornstarch. Add this sweet-sour mixture to the cabbage and cook and stir until the sauce is clear.

Chinese Cabbage Sweet and Sour

BRING about 1 inch of water to a boil in a large saucepan and add 1 teaspoon salt and 1 small onion, finely chopped. Simmer until the onion is transparent.

Add 2 small heads of Chinese cabbage, washed and coarsely shredded. Cover the pan and cook rapidly for about 6 minutes, or until the cabbage is barely tender. Turn it into a serving dish with all or part of the water, pour some melted butter over the cabbage, and sprinkle liberally with chopped parsley.

Chinese Cabbage

SCRAPE 36 tender young carrots. Melt 1 cup butter in a baking dish and add the carrots, a little salt, and about 1 teaspoon sugar. Sprinkle with 1/3 cup Cognac. Cover the baking dish and bake the carrots in a moderate oven (350° F.) for 45 minutes to 1 hour, or until they are tender. Serve from the baking dish.

Carottes au Cognac
CARROTS
IN COGNAC

COOK 10 medium-sized carrots in salted water until they are tender and drain and mash them. Sauté 2 tablespoons grated onion and 1/2 green pepper, finely chopped, in 2 tablespoons butter until the onion is golden in color. Stir in 1

Carrot Pudding

Cauliflower with Cheese Sauce

tablespoon each of flour and sugar, and salt and pepper to taste and then add gradually, while stirring, 1 cup hot milk, Continue to stir until the sauce is slightly thickened and then combine this mixture with the carrot purée. Turn the mixture into a buttered casserole, cover the top with bread crumbs, dot with butter, and bake the casserole in a moderate oven (350° F.) for 30 minutes.

PUT in a saucepan 1 cup carrots, scraped and diced or cut into small balls. Add 1 tablespoon each of butter and sugar and enough water to half cover the carrots. Bring the water to a boil, cover the pan and simmer the carrots until they are tender and the water has entirely cooked away. Cook 2 cups shelled peas separately in salted water, drain them, and add them to the carrots. Add 1 cup *sauce crème*—1 cup béchamel reduced to 3/4 cup and mixed with 1/4 cup heavy cream. Toss well.

Carottes et Pois à la Crème
CREAMED CARROTS AND PEAS

Sauce Crème

WASH and scrape 2 bunches of carrots and slice them 1/4 inch thick. Place them in a saucepan with just enough water to cover and let them cook for about 10 minutes, or until they are tender enough to pierce with a toothpick. Add to the water in the pan 1/2 teaspoon salt, 3/4 cup honey, and 1 tablespoon lemon juice, and simmer the carrots gently for about 20 minutes. Brown 3 tablespoons flour in 3 tablespoons butter and add the mixture to the carrots, shaking the pan to distribute it evenly. Let the carrots cook for another 5 minutes, turn them into a shallow buttered casserole, and lightly brown the top under the broiler.

Honey Glazed Carrots

TRIM a whole cauliflower and cook it in salted water until it is barely tender and still crisp. Drain it well, inverting it on a towel for several minutes to assure dryness. Arrange the cauliflower on a round serving dish, cover it with hot Mornay sauce, and sprinkle it with 1/2 cup slivered toasted almonds. Serve immediately.

Chou-Fleur Mornay aux Amandes
CAULIFLOWER WITH CHEESE SAUCE

STEAM a large head of cauliflower until it is tender, but do not overcook it.
Blend 3/4 tablespoon flour with 1 generous tablespoon butter, in the top of a double boiler. Add salt, pepper, and a good grating of nutmeg. Pour in gradually 1/3 cup cider and 2/3 cup heavy cream, stirring well. Simmer for just a minute, stirring constantly until the sauce becomes slightly thickened. Put the pan over boiling water and cook the sauce for 10 minutes. Finish with a little lemon juice and pour the hot sauce over the cauliflower.

Chou-Fleur Normande

Céleri Braisé
BRAISED CELERY

SPLIT 6 hearts of celery in half or leave them whole, depending on the size, and trim off the leafy tops. Parboil them for 5 or 6 minutes and drain them. Place a few slices of onion and carrot in the bottom of a casserole. Add the celery and just enough stock or water to cover it. Add a small piece of fresh beef suet and season with salt. Bring the liquid to a boil, cover the casserole, and braise the celery in a moderately hot oven (375° F.) for about 1 to 1 1/2 hours, or until it is very tender.

Remove the celery to a serving dish, cover it with chicken or veal gravy, and glaze it quickly under the broiler. The liquid in which the celery was cooked, reduced to about 1/2 cup and thickened with *beurre manié* made by creaming together 1 tablespoon butter and 1 teaspoon flour, may be used instead of gravy. Serve braised celery with braised or roasted meat.

Purée of Celery

DRAIN braised celery well and force it through a sieve or purée it in a blender. The celery purée may be mixed with an equal amount of mashed potatoes to give it a firmer consistency.

Creamed Celery

FOLLOW the recipe for braised celery, using about 1 quart of the outside stalks, cleaned and scraped to remove the stringy fibers and cut in 2-inch lengths. While the celery is braising, melt 2 tablespoons butter in a saucepan, add 1 tablespoon flour, and cook the *roux* until it just starts to turn golden. Drain the cooked celery thoroughly, reserving the liquid, and arrange it in a serving dish. Skim off the fat, strain the cooking liquid into the *roux*, and cook the sauce, stirring, until it is reduced to about 1/2 cup. Add 1/4 cup cream, bring the sauce to a boil, and pour it over the celery.

Stewed Celery

CUT 6 trimmed celery hearts in half, soak them in cold water for 30 minutes, and drain them. Put them in a saucepan with chicken stock barely to cover, cover the saucepan tightly, and simmer for about 30 minutes, or until the hearts are just tender. Serve with grated Parmesan cheese.

Celery Sauté

DISCARD the tough outer stalks and leaves from 3 bunches of celery. Clean the inside stalks thoroughly and dry them on absorbent paper. Cut each stalk on a sharp diagonal into strips 1/8 to 1/4 inch thick. Heat 6 tablespoons salad oil to the smoking point in a large skillet. Add the celery and sauté it for 3 minutes, stirring constantly. Stir in 1/4 cup soy sauce and 1 teaspoon sugar and cook the celery for 2 minutes longer, stirring to blend.

PEEL 3 or 4 celery knobs and slice them 1/8 inch thick. Boil the slices for 40 to 50 minutes in salted water and drain them. Melt 2 tablespoons butter, add 1 tablespoon flour, and cook the *roux*, stirring, until it is golden. Add gradually 1 cup consommé, and cook the sauce, stirring, until it is smooth and thickened. Stir in 1/2 teaspoon *glace de viande*, 1 teaspoon brandy, salt and pepper to taste, and a few thinly sliced truffles. Put the celery in a casserole and pour the sauce over it. Sprinkle the sauce with bread crumbs and grated Swiss cheese, dot with butter, and brown the top in a moderately hot oven (375° F.).

Céleri-Rave au Gratin

DISCARD the outer leaves from 2 1/2 pounds Chinese chard. Wash the chard thoroughly, dry it, and cut it into 2-inch lengths. Heat 6 tablespoons chicken fat or lard in a skillet over high heat. When the fat is very hot, add the chard and cook it, stirring quickly, for 6 to 8 minutes. Add 1/2 teaspoon each of salt and sugar, and 1/2 cup chicken consommé and cook the mixture, stirring, for another 2 minutes.

Hearts of Chard
TSAI SING

SOAK 2 ounces dried black mushrooms in boiling water for 30 minutes, remove them, and discard the stems. Discard the outer leaves from 2 pounds Chinese chard, wash the chard twice in cold water, and cut it into 1 1/2-inch lengths. Heat 5 tablespoons salad oil in a skillet and sauté the chard for 4 or 5 minutes, stirring constantly. Season with salt and 1/2 teaspoon brown sugar and sauté the chard for 1 minute longer. Add 2 cups soup stock, 1 1/2 table-spoons soy sauce, the mushrooms, and 1/3 cup bamboo shoot tips, very thinly sliced. Cook the mixture over moderate heat for about 5 minutes.

Chard with Mushrooms
TUNG KOO
CHAO TSAI

WITH a sharp knife make a slit in the convex side of 1 pound chestnuts. Place them in a saucepan with water to cover and bring the water to a boil. Remove the pan from the heat without draining. Take the chestnuts from the pan, one by one, when they are cool enough to handle, and remove the shells and the inner skins.

Chestnuts
To Blanch and Shell

As a Vegetable Put the chestnuts in a saucepan with a few stalks of celery and cover them with white stock. Simmer the chestnuts, covered, for 30 minutes, or until they are tender.

Chestnut Purée To make the chestnut purée that is a usual accompaniment to game and game birds, force the cooked chestnuts through a ricer. Season with butter, salt and pepper, and, if necessary, add cream or a little of the cooking liquid to make a light, fluffy mixture.

Braised Chestnuts PEEL and skin chestnuts and put them in a buttered casserole. Sprinkle with a little salt, cover with strong veal stock, and add a bouquet of celery. Cover the casserole and bake the chestnuts in a moderate oven (350° F.) for about 45 minutes, or until they are tender. Serve as a garnish for meat, game, or poultry.

Sautéed Water Chestnuts SLICE thinly 1 pound canned water chestnuts and heat them in a saucepan with 2 tablespoons butter and a little of their own juice. Turn them into a warm serving dish and sprinkle them with salt, fresh lime juice, and finely chopped parsley.

Sweet Corn Purée COOK freshly picked ears of corn in boiling salted water for about 7 minutes. With a knife or sharp-tined fork, rip down the rows of kernels to split them open, and press out the pulp with the side of the fork. Add 2 cups of this pulp to 2 tablespoons butter melted in a saucepan, season with salt and pepper, and reheat it. A little cream may also be added, if desired.

Corn Turban Washington MELT 1 tablespoon butter in a saucepan, add 1 1/2 cups pulp from freshly cooked corn, and cook until the juice is reduced to almost nothing.

Melt 2 tablespoons butter in a saucepan, add 2 tablespoons flour, and cook the *roux* until it just starts to turn golden. Add 1 cup hot milk and cook, stirring constantly, until the sauce thickens. Continue cooking slowly for about 15 minutes, stirring with a whip to keep the sauce very smooth. Add 1 whole egg and 2 egg yolks beaten together. Add the corn pulp and reheat, being careful not to let it boil.

Correct the seasoning and pour the mixture into a well-buttered ring mold set in a pan of hot water. Bake in a moderately hot oven (375° F.) for 20 to 25 minutes, or until the pudding is firm. Remove from the oven but leave the pudding in the mold for a few minutes to set. Loosen the edges with a

Corn Turban Washington

small knife. Invert the pudding and unmold the ring on a heated serving dish. Fill the center with baby Lima beans or with mushrooms and Lima beans, heated in butter and sprinkled with chopped parsley.

Corn in Sour Cream   SAUTÉ 6 strips of bacon, diced, over low heat, stirring frequently until they are crisp and brown. Remove the bacon and sauté 3 tablespoons onion in the bacon fat. Add 1 teaspoon sugar, 2 cups corn pulp, freshly scraped, 1 tablespoon chopped pimiento, and salt and pepper to taste. Cook the mixture for 10 minutes. Add 1 1/2 cups sour cream, reheat the mixture, and add the diced bacon. Serve on toast points and garnish with curls of crisp bacon.

Beignets de Maïs
CORN PUFF FRITTERS   BRING 1 cup water or half milk and half water to a boil with 1/2 teaspoon each of salt and sugar, and 1/4 cup butter. Add 1 cup flour and cook, stirring rapidly, until the mixture is smooth and rolls away from the sides of the pan. Remove the pan from the heat, cool the batter a little, and add 4 large eggs, one at a time, beating each one in thoroughly before adding the next. Stir in 1 cup well-drained cooked corn. Drop the batter from a tablespoon into hot deep fat (375° F.) and fry the fritters until they are puffed and brown on all sides. Drain on absorbent paper and serve very hot.

Corn Soufflé   COMBINE 1 cup freshly cooked and scraped corn pulp with 1 cup cream sauce made with 2 tablespoons each of butter and flour and 1 cup hot milk. Add 4 egg yolks, well beaten, and heat without boiling. Add salt and pepper to taste and fold in 5 stiffly beaten egg whites. Pour the mixture into a baking dish or soufflé dish, buttered and floured, and bake it in a moderately hot oven (375° F.) for about 30 minutes, or until the soufflé is well puffed and nicely browned. The soufflé may be garnished before baking with a few whole kernels of corn cut from the cob.

Cucumbers in Butter   PEEL 3 cucumbers, quarter them lengthwise, and cut each quarter into 1-inch pieces. Simmer the pieces in boiling salted water for 3 minutes. Drain and put them in a casserole containing 1/4 cup melted butter. Sprinkle with salt and pepper, cover the casserole, and cook the cucumbers slowly for 20 minutes, or until they are tender. Serve in the casserole with chopped parsley and a dash of lemon juice.

Cucumbers in Cream   Cucumbers prepared in this way may be finished with 1/2 cup heavy cream. The casserole should then be returned to the oven for 5 minutes.

Or they may be mixed before baking with béchamel sauce, and baked *au gratin* with a sprinkling of buttered bread crumbs and grated Swiss cheese.

PEEL cucumbers and cut them in half lengthwise. Scoop out the seeds and cut the halves into 1-inch lengths. Parboil the cucumbers in boiling salted water for 10 minutes, drain and dry them, and sprinkle them lightly with salt. Sauté them in butter until they are golden.

DREDGE 2 cups peeled sliced cucumbers with flour and sauté them slowly in hot olive oil with 1 garlic clove until they are brown on both sides. Sprinkle the slices with salt and pepper and keep them in a warm serving dish. Melt 1/4 cup butter in the cooking pan and add 2 cups peeled and chopped tomatoes. Cook, stirring, for 3 minutes. Stir in 2 tablespoons finely chopped parsley and pour the tomatoes and sauce over the cucumber slices.

CUT 3 eggplant in half lengthwise and make a few deep incisions in the flesh with a sharp knife. Sprinkle them well with salt and let them stand for 30 minutes. Drain off the juices and dry the cut surfaces. Cook the eggplant in 6 tablespoons hot olive oil in a large frying pan, covered, for about 10 minutes on each side, or until they are tender, adding more oil if needed. Scoop out the flesh, being careful not to cut through the skins, and chop it coarsely in a wooden bowl.

Melt 3 tablespoons butter in a skillet, add 3 onions, sliced, and cook them slowly until they are soft but not brown. Add 6 tomatoes, peeled, seeded, and chopped, and the chopped eggplant, cover, and cook over low heat for 5 minutes. Fill the eggplant shells with the mixture and sprinkle with dry bread crumbs and grated Parmesan cheese. Cut 6 anchovy filets into thin strips and lay the strips over the bread crumbs and cheese. Sprinkle with butter and finely chopped herbs and brown under the broiler.

CUT 3 medium eggplant in half. Cut the flesh away from the skin, lift it out, and cut it into 1/2-inch slices. Sprinkle the slices with salt and pepper. Cover the bottom of a skillet generously with olive oil and in it sauté 3 onions, finely sliced, until the onions are transparent. Add the eggplant slices and sauté them quickly for 3 minutes on each side. Return the slices, with the onions, to the eggplant shells and cover with thin slices of *prosciutto*. Sprinkle generously with grated Parmesan cheese and bake in a moderate oven (350° F.) for about 10 minutes.

Eggplant Florentine

ARRANGE a bed of cooked buttered spinach in the bottom of a *cocotte* and on it arrange slices of eggplant sautéed in butter. Cover the eggplant with Mornay sauce and put the *cocotte* under the broiler for a few seconds to lightly brown the top.

Eggplant Provençale

PEEL a medium eggplant and cut it into large dice. Season the dice with salt and dredge with flour. Heat 2 tablespoons salad oil in a shallow pan until very hot and sauté the dice until they are golden brown, adding more oil if necessary. In another pan, heat 2 tablespoons salad oil and in it sauté 4 tomatoes, peeled, seeded, and chopped. Combine the two vegetables, add 2 garlic cloves, crushed, and cook for a few minutes longer. Serve sprinkled with parsley.

Eggplant Basquaise

ADD to eggplant Provençale 4 or 5 sweet green peppers, sliced and sautéed in oil. There should be equal amounts of eggplant, tomatoes, and green pepper in this dish. Omit the garlic, but cook the vegetables together for at few minutes to blend the flavors.

Deviled Eggplant

PEEL 2 large eggplant and 1 small onion and slice them. Boil them in a small amount of salted water until the eggplant slices are very tender. Drain the liquid from the pan and add 3 tablespoons butter, a dash of Worcestershire sauce, and salt and pepper to taste. Mix the eggplant and onion slices well with 1 cup ground ham. Place the mixture in a baking dish or in individual dishes, cover with cracker crumbs, and dot liberally with butter. Brown the top in a hot oven (400° F.) just before serving. This mixture will keep well and may be prepared for the oven ahead of time.

Eggplant Ankara

IN a saucepan sauté 1/2 onion, finely chopped, in 2 tablespoons olive oil until it is golden. Add 1/2 cup chopped parsley, 1 teaspoon salt, and 3 small eggplant, peeled and diced. Stir in 1 1/2 tablespoons flour and cook until the vegetables are simmering. Add 1/2 cup hot water, cover, and cook over very low heat until the eggplant is tender. Add 3 sprigs of fresh dill, chopped, and just before serving stir in from 1/2 to 1 cup sour cream.

SLICE 2 medium eggplants 1/4 inch thick and soak the slices in salted water for 20 minutes. Drain, cover with boiling water, and drain again. Dry the slices thoroughly.

Eggplant with Cheese

In a skillet melt 1/2 cup butter and in it sauté the eggplant for about 2 minutes on each side, or until they are browned. Arrange the slices in a baking dish, alternating the layers with layers of thinly sliced Swiss cheese and a sprinkling of freshly ground pepper. Bake the casserole in a moderate oven (350° F.) for 30 minutes, or until the cheese it melted and bubbling.

PEEL 2 medium eggplant and cut them into 1/2-inch slices. Dip the slices in flour and sauté them in a skillet in 1 cup hot olive oil for about 2 minutes on each side, or until they are almost tender. Drain the slices on absorbent paper.

Panini Gravidi Melanzana
EGGPLANT SANDWICH

Combine 2 egg yolks, 1/2 pound Mozzarella cheese, finely diced, and 2 tablespoons grated Parmesan cheese. Spread about 1 tablespoon of this mixture on half the eggplant slices, and cover the filling with the remaining eggplant slices, sandwich fashion. Dip the sandwiches in beaten egg, roll them in bread crumbs, and brown them on both sides in the oil remaining in the skillet.

SAUTÉ slices of eggplant in hot oil until they are soft and delicately browned. Place a layer of the eggplant slices in a large flat pie dish and season with salt, pepper, very finely minced parsley, and a little minced fresh thyme. Cover with a layer of sliced tomatoes. Season these with salt, pepper, parsley, finely chopped onion, and chopped green pepper. Cover the tomatoes with slices of Mozzarella cheese.

Torta di Melanzana
EGGPLANT PIE

Beat 3 egg yolks into 1 1/2 cups milk and pour the mixture over the pie. Bake in a moderately slow oven (325° F.) for 30 minutes, or until the custard is firm and the cheese slightly brown.

Cut the *torta* in wedges and serve with a bowl of grated Parmesan on the side.

WASH 2 pounds endives and arrange them in a single layer in a buttered earthenware casserole. Sprinkle the endives with salt and pepper, dot them with 1/4 cup butter, and cook them over very low heat for 30 minutes or

Endives à l'Americaine

until they are very brown. Turn the endives and cook them for 15 minutes, adding butter if necessary. Sprinkle them with 2 tablespoons grated onion and cover them with a layer of thinly sliced Swiss cheese, and continue to cook for 15 minutes longer, or until the cheese is melted. Serve in the casserole.

Endives
Mornay

WASH and drain 2 pounds endives and place them side by side in a deep saucepan. Add the juice of 1 lemon, 1 teaspoon salt, 3 tablespoons butter, and 1 cup water. Bring the liquid to a boil, cover the saucepan, and simmer the endives for 35 to 40 minutes, or until tender. Arrange them in a shallow baking dish and pour over them 2 cups Mornay sauce. Sprinkle with 1 tablespoon melted butter and brown under the broiler.

Each head of endive may be wrapped in a thin slice of ham before the sauce is added.

Endives
and Eggs
Béchamel

WASH 2 pounds endives and simmer them in water with the juice of 1 lemon for 20 minutes. Drain and arrange them in a buttered casserole and cover them with 6 hard-cooked eggs, thickly sliced. Sprinkle with salt and pepper and pour over the eggs 3 cups béchamel sauce. Sprinkle with 1/2 cup each of grated Swiss cheese and fine bread crumbs, dot with 2 tablespoons butter, and bake in a moderate oven (350° F.) for about 30 minutes, or until the endives are tender and the sauce is brown and bubbling.

Baked Kale
Gruyère

DISCARD the imperfect leaves and the tough midribs of 2 1/2 pounds kale. Wash the tender leaves several times in warm water, rinse them in cold, and drain them well. Place the kale in a large kettle and pour over it 1 quart boiling salted water. Cover tightly and boil steadily for 20 minutes, or until the kale is tender. Drain it and chop it finely.

Add 1/4 cup grated Gruyère cheese to 1 cup medium cream sauce and season it with pepper and a grating of nutmeg. Combine the sauce with the kale and transfer the mixture to a buttered baking dish. Sprinkle with 1/2 cup buttered fine bread crumbs mixed with 1/4 cup grated Gruyère. Bake in a hot oven (425° F.) until the topping is brown and bubbly.

Cooked kale may be used in any preparation for spinach.

Torta
di Pasqua
KALE PIE

TRIM the coarse center stalks from 1 pound kale. Chop the tender leaves, sprinkle them with salt, and soak them in water to cover for 2 hours. Drain the kale thoroughly and sauté it in 3 tablespoons olive oil with 2 onions, sliced, until the kale is wilted. Stir in 3 tablespoons grated Parmesan cheese.

Combine 1 3/4 cups ricotta cheese, 1 tablespoon flour, 1/4 cup sour cream, 5 tablespoons grated Parmesan, and 4 eggs, well beaten, and mix well.

Sift 5 cups flour onto a pastry board and make a well in the center. In the well put 2 eggs, lightly beaten, 1/2 teaspoon salt, and 3 tablespoons olive oil. Gradually work in the flour, adding enough warm water to make a soft dough. Work the dough vigorously, lifting it up and crashing it down on the table until it becomes elastic and cleans the board. Divide the dough into 12 parts and let them stand for 30 minutes covered with a damp cloth. Then, on a lightly floured board, roll each part out into a paper-thin rectangle the size of a large oblong baking dish.

Pour a little olive oil on the bottom of the baking dish and place the first layer of dough in the dish. Sprinkle the dough with olive oil or melted butter and place the second sheet of dough on top. Repeat this operation 6 times. Fold the edges of the dough over and flute them to make a standing rim.

In a large bowl combine the kale and ricotta mixture with 8 eggs, a little olive oil, salt and pepper to taste, and 1/4 cup butter, broken into bits.

Turn the filling into the dough-lined pan and cover it with the other thin layers of dough, sprinkling each layer with olive oil or melted butter. With a large needle puncture the dough in several places and bake the *torta* in a moderate oven (350° F.) for about 45 minutes. Serves 8.

Lima Beans in Cream

PUT 1 quart freshly shelled baby Lima beans into a saucepan containing an inch of boiling water. Add 1 tablespoon butter, cover the pan, and simmer the beans for 10 minutes. Add 1 teaspoon salt and continue to cook the beans, covered, for 10 to 15 minutes longer, or until they are tender. Stir in 1/4 cup each of butter and chopped parsley, turn the beans into a casserole, and sprinkle with freshly ground pepper. Pour over the beans 1/2 cup heavy cream, cover the casserole, and heat well.

Lima Bean Casserole

HEAT 3 tablespoons butter in a saucepan and in it sauté until golden 3 tablespoons chopped onion. Add 1 1/2 cups cooked tomatoes and salt and pepper to taste and simmer for 10 minutes. Add 2 cups fresh Lima beans cooked in boiling salted water to cover for 10 minutes and well drained. Pour the vegetables into a casserole and sprinkle generously with fine dry bread crumbs and grated Parmesan cheese. Bake in a moderately hot oven (375° F.) for 30 minutes, or until the topping is nicely browned.

Lima Beans and Mushrooms

CLEAN and slice 1/2 pound fresh mushrooms. Melt 2 tablespoons butter in a saucepan, add 1 tablespoon finely chopped shallots or onion, and cook until soft. Add the mushrooms and cook until the moisture is evaporated. Add 1 cup light cream and cook until the liquid is reduced to 1/2 cup. Thicken by adding *beurre manié*, made by creaming 1 tablespoon butter with 1 teaspoon flour. Add 2 cups cooked fresh young Lima beans, return to the boil, and season with salt and freshly ground pepper.

Lima Beans Bonne Femme

IN a saucepan sauté gently 12 tiny onions and 1/2 cup diced lean ham in 2 tablespoons butter for about 4 minutes, stirring constantly. Stir in 1 teaspoon flour and add 3 cups baby Lima beans, 3 or 4 lettuce leaves, shredded, 1 cup water, 1 teaspoon salt, and 1 tablespoon chopped parsley. Cover tightly, bring to a boil, lower the heat, and cook the beans for about 20 minutes, or until they are tender. Keep them hot and stir in 3 tablespoons butter just before serving.

Sautéed Mushrooms with Sherry

SAUTÉ 2 cups thinly sliced mushrooms in 3 tablespoons hot butter for 3 minutes, stirring frequently. Add 2 tablespoons Sherry and 1 tablespoon finely chopped dill and serve hot.

Sautéed Mushrooms with Marjoram

REMOVE the stems from 1 pound large mushrooms, reserving them for another use. In a skillet melt 1/4 cup butter and 1 tablespoon olive oil and in it sauté 1 garlic clove, crushed, until the garlic is lightly browned. Put the mushroom caps in the skillet cap side down, sprinkle them with salt and pepper and 1 teaspoon minced marjoram leaves, and sauté for about 5 minutes, or until they are golden. Turn the caps, sprinkle each with a drop or two of lemon juice, and sauté them for 5 minutes longer.

Broiled Mushrooms with Olive Sauce

TRIM 1 pound large mushrooms and remove the stems. Make a slit in the top of each mushroom and put them in a bowl with a garlic clove. Pour 1/2 cup olive oil and 1 teaspoon lemon juice over the mushrooms and let them marinate for 30 minutes. Arrange the mushrooms on a broiler pan and sprinkle them with salt and pepper. Broil them two inches from the heat for several minutes on each side.

Discard the garlic from the oil in which the mushrooms marinated, add to the oil 1/4 cup each of parsley, green onions, and ripe olives, all minced, and heat the sauce well. Serve the broiled mushrooms on toast with the sauce over them.

Mushrooms in Sour Cream

SAUTÉ 1/2 cup minced scallions and 1 pound whole button mushrooms in 1/4 cup butter until they are lightly browned. Stir in 1 tablespoon flour and add gradually 1/2 cup stock. Cook, stirring, until the sauce is thickened, add salt and pepper to taste and 1 teaspoon chopped dill, and simmer for 10 minutes. Stir in 1 cup sour cream and reheat to the boiling point.

Mushrooms Provençale

WASH 1 pound mushrooms and remove the stems and chop them finely. In a skillet or the blazer of a chafing dish sauté the caps in 3 tablespoons olive oil. Remove the caps and keep them warm.

To the juices in the skillet or blazer add 1 tablespoon olive oil, the mushroom stems, and 1 garlic clove and 3 shallots, both minced, and sauté for 3 minutes. Stir in 1 tablespoon flour, add gradually 1 cup dry white wine, stirring constantly, and cook, stirring, until the sauce is thickened. Add 1 tablespoon each of chopped parsley and tomato paste, 1/2 teaspoon thyme, and salt and pepper to taste and cook, stirring occasionally, for 10 minutes. Reheat the mushroom caps in this sauce and serve as a garnish for meat or on buttered toast.

Champignons sous Cloche
MUSHROOMS IN CREAM UNDER GLASS

SAUTÉ mushroom caps in butter for about 3 minutes, or until they are golden. Moisten them with heavy cream and season with a little salt and pepper. Cover the pan and simmer the mushrooms over low heat until the cream is reduced by half.

Put each slice of toast in a small baking dish, arrange the mushrooms on the toast in pyramid form, and pour over the mushrooms a few tablespoons of the sauce. Cover each serving with a glass bell and bake the mushrooms in a slow oven (250° F.) for 20 minutes. The glass bells are removed at the table.

Stuffed Mushrooms Tarragon

TRIM 1 pound large mushrooms and remove the stems. Chop the stems and sauté them in 2 tablespoons butter with 2 tablespoons chopped shallots for 5 minutes. Add 1 tablespoon each of finely chopped tarragon and parsley, 1 egg, beaten, 2 tablespoons brandy, 1/2 cup dry bread crumbs, and salt and pepper to taste.

Sauté the mushroom caps in 3 tablespoons butter until they are golden, place them cap side down on a baking sheet, and stuff them with the bread mixture. Dot each mushroom with butter and broil them under medium heat for several minutes, or until they are brown. Serve the mushrooms surrounded by watercress and garnished with lemon wedges.

Baked Stuffed Mushrooms with Crab Meat

SAUTÉ gently in butter 1/4 cup finely chopped shallots until they are transparent. Add 1 tablespoon dry English mustard and simmer for 1/2 minute. Add 1 pound picked-over crab meat, heat the meat, pour in 1/4 cup warmed Sherry and ignite the spirit. When the flame dies, add 2 cups thick cream sauce, 2 hard-cooked eggs, finely chopped, and 2 tablespoons chopped chives. Simmer for 10 minutes and stir in a pinch of cayenne, salt, and strained lemon juice to taste.

Stem 12 large mushrooms and sauté the caps in butter for about 5 minutes, or until they are half-cooked. Cool and fill them with the deviled crab meat. Bake them for 5 minutes on a buttered baking sheet in a very hot oven (450° F.). Serve the mushrooms on a bed of cooked and well-seasoned wild rice and pour some browned butter over all. Serves 4 as a luncheon entrée.

Mushrooms Stuffed with Ham

COOK large mushrooms, allowing at least 2 for each person, in boiling salted water for about 20 minutes, or until they are just tender. Drain them, remove the stems, and chop them finely. For each cup of stems add 1 cup finely ground cooked ham, pork, or tongue, 1 tablespoon each of finely chopped celery, pine nuts, and chives, and 2 tablespoons sliced ripe olives. Season with salt and pepper and cook gently in 3 tablespoons melted butter for 10 minutes. Stir in 1 egg, beaten with 2 tablespoons heavy cream and 1 tablespoon Cognac, and let the mixture cool. Place the mushroom caps on a buttered baking sheet and fill them with the stuffing, heaping it up in the center. Sprinkle with bread crumbs, place a dab of butter on each mound, and brown the tops under the broiler. Serve each mushroom on a small circle of bread sautéed in butter until it is golden brown.

Mushroom Pie

TRIM 2 pounds fresh mushrooms. In a large skillet heat 1/4 cup butter, add the mushrooms, and sprinkle them with salt, pepper, and the juice of half a lemon. Cover the skillet and cook the mushrooms for 10 minutes, shaking the pan frequently. Arrange the mushrooms in a buttered quart baking dish and to the juices remaining in the pan add 2 more tablespoons

Baked Stuffed Mushrooms with Crab Meat

butter and stir in 3 tablespoons flour. Gradually stir in 1/2 cup each of Madeira and hot heavy cream and season the sauce with salt and freshly ground pepper. Pour the sauce over the mushrooms and cover with a layer of flaky pie dough. Brush the dough with beaten egg, make a few slits in the top, and bake in a very hot oven (450° F.) for 15 minutes. Reduce the heat to moderate and bake for 10 to 15 minutes longer.

Soufflé aux Champignons

TRIM 1/2 pound fresh mushrooms and chop them very finely—they should be almost a purée. Put them in a saucepan with 1 cup milk, bring the milk to a boil, and cook the mixture slowly for 10 to 15 minutes. In another saucepan, melt 2 tablespoons butter, add 3 tablespoons flour, and cook the *roux* until it starts to turn golden. Stir in the hot milk-and-mushroom mixture. Return the pan to the heat and cook the sauce, stirring constantly, for about 5 minutes. Season the sauce with 1/2 teaspoon salt, a little pepper, and a little grated nutmeg. Beat 5 egg yolks until they are light and add them to the mushroom mixture. Heat the mixture to the boiling point, but do not let it boil. Remove the pan from the heat and stir the sauce for a few minutes as it cools. Beat 5 egg whites until they are stiff but not dry. Fold into the mixture thoroughly and carefully one-fourth of the beaten egg whites and add the remaining egg whites, cutting them in lightly and completely by raising and folding the mixture over and over. Pour the batter into a buttered and floured mold and bake the soufflé in a moderate oven (350° F.) for 25 to 30 minutes, or until it is well puffed and golden brown.

Mushroom Purée

WASH 1 pound mushrooms, chop them, and purée them in a blender. Cook the purée, stirring over high heat until the moisture evaporates. Add 1 cup béchamel sauce and salt, pepper, and nutmeg to taste, and heat well.

The floppy orange cèpes *of Europe are available in this country only in cans.* Morilles, *on the other hand, are never in the market, but can be found by earnest hunters in the deep dark woods of several of our states. Recognize them by their conical shape and honeycombed surface.*

Cèpes à la Bordelaise

DRAIN a 1-pound can of *cèpes*. Cover the *cèpes* with hot water, drain, and dry them on a towel. Leave the small ones whole; cut the larger ones in pieces. Cover the bottom of a shallow pan with salad oil, heat the oil until it is very hot, and add the *cèpes*. Cook them until they are golden brown and drain off the oil. Heat 3 tablespoons butter in the pan and season the *cèpes* with salt and pepper. Add 1 garlic clove, crushed, and 1 tablespoon each of chopped shallots, parsley, and fresh bread crumbs. Cook the mixture until the crumbs are golden brown, shaking the pan constantly to combine the ingredients. Serve very hot.

Trim and discard the bulbous stem ends from 1 pound morels, wash the morels well, and dry them thoroughly. Leave them whole or cut them into halves or quarters, according to size. Heat 3 tablespoons butter in a saucepan, add the morels, and sauté them for 8 to 10 minutes, or until they are light golden brown. Add 1 tablespoon flour and mix well. Add 1 cup hot light cream, mix well, cover the pan, and cook the mixture slowly for 10 to 15 minutes. Season with salt and a little pepper and serve with hot toast.

Morilles à la Crème
CREAMED MORELS

Trim and clean 1 pound morels well and dry them thoroughly. Melt 2 tablespoons butter in a saucepan and in it cook 1 tablespoon finely chopped onion until it is soft. Add the morels and cook them for 8 to 10 minutes. Add 2 teaspoons curry powder, stir well, and finish with 1/2 cup thin cream sauce.

Morilles à l'Indienne
CURRIED MORELS

Follow the recipe for *morilles à l'indienne*, substituting paprika for the curry powder.

Morilles à la Hongroise

Heat 1/4 cup salad oil in a saucepan and add 1 1/2 cups diced cooked ham. When the ham is golden brown, spoon it out and drain it. Add 1 pound cleaned and trimmed morels to the hot oil in the pan. Add 1/4 cup finely chopped onion and cook it until it is golden brown.

Morilles Sevilla
MORELS WITH HAM

Drain as much of the oil as possible from the pan. Add the ham to the morels and onion, along with 1/2 cup Sherry. Cook until the wine is reduced to about 1/4 cup. Add 1/2 cup veal or chicken gravy or 1/2 cup Madeira sauce to thicken the mixture, 1 to 2 red pimientos, cut in julienne, and a little salt and freshly ground white pepper to taste. Cook slowly for 20 to 25 minutes and serve in a large *croustade*.

Make the *croustade* by removing the crusts from a loaf of bread and hollowing out the center to form a cavity for the filling. Brush the shell on all sides with butter and brown in the oven.

Croustade

485

Honey Glazed Onions

HEAT 1 tablespoon butter and 2 tablespoons salad oil in a saucepan, add 1 pound trimmed and cleaned morels—whole or cut in halves or quarters —and sauté them over high heat for 8 to 10 minutes. In another pan heat 1 tablespoon salad oil and add 1/4 cup diced fat pork, fresh or salt. Sauté the pork dice until they are golden brown, lift them out, and add them to the morels. Add 2 tablespoons chopped shallots and salt and a little freshly ground white pepper to taste. Cook the mixture for 15 minutes. Add 2 teaspoons chopped parsley and serve immediately.

Morilles Sautées Bonne Femme

IN a skillet render 5 slices of bacon, cut in 1-inch strips, until the strips begin to crisp. Add 3 cups okra cut in thin slices and cook until the okra is browned. Add 3 cups tomatoes, peeled, seeded and cut in wedges, and 1 small bay leaf. Simmer very slowly for 3 hours. Season to taste with salt and pepper. If the mixture becomes too thick, add a little tomato juice.

Okra Casserole

COOK small white onions in boiling salted water for 20 minutes, or until they are tender. Drain them well. Melt 1/4 cup butter in a saucepan. Add 1/4 cup honey and stir until the mixture is blended. Add the onions and cook slowly, turning them occasionally, until they are glazed.

Honey Glazed Onions

Carrots, sweet potato balls, or tiny beets may be glazed in the same way.

Honey Glazed Vegetables

PEEL and slice 6 large onions into rings and separate the rings. Heat 1/4 cup beef fat, bacon drippings, or butter in a skillet and cook the onions in the fat, covered, over very low heat until they are transparent and tender, but not mushy. Season with salt, pepper, and a little paprika, to taste.

Smothered Onion Rings

PEEL and parboil 3 dozen small white onions. Drain them and place them in a skillet with 1/4 cup butter. Sprinkle the onions with 1 teaspoon sugar and brown them slowly, turning them frequently. Remove the onions to a flat baking dish and stick a whole clove in a each. To the butter-sugar mixture remaining in the skillet add 1/4 cup cold water and cook, stirring, until the liquid is brown and syrupy. Pour the syrup over the onions and add 1 cup thin cream sauce. Bake in a moderate oven (350° F.) for 20 to 25 minutes.

Creamed Onions

If desired, the onions may be turned into a baking dish, sprinkled with salted peanuts and bread crumbs, and browned lightly in the oven.

Onions and Peanuts

487

*Parsnips with
Parmesan*

PEEL 6 parsnips and cook them in boiling salted water for about 30 minutes, or until they are tender. Slice the parsnips in half lengthwise. In a skillet melt 1/4 cup butter and in it sauté the parsnips until they are lightly browned on both sides. Sprinkle with salt, pepper, and grated Parmesan cheese, turn the parsnips, and cook until the cheese blends with the butter. Place the parsnips in a warm serving dish, pour the butter-cheese sauce over them, and sprinkle lightly with paprika.

*Creamed
Parsnips*

PEEL parsnips and cut them into small sticks, as for French fried potatoes. Cook them in boiling salted water until they are tender, about 15 minutes, and drain. For 2 cups parsnips, melt 1 tablespoon butter in a saucepan, add 1 tablespoon flour, and cook the *roux* until it just starts to turn golden. Add 3/4 cup hot milk and cook, stirring constantly, until it cooks down to about 1/2 cup. Season with salt, add the parsnips, and cook for a few minutes longer, shaking the parsnips in the sauce until all the pieces are coated. For a richer sauce, add 2 tablespoons cream.

Parsnip Balls

PEEL 6 parsnips, drop them into boiling salted water, and cook them for about 30 minutes, or until they are tender. Press the parsnips through a fine sieve. Stir in 1 tablespoon flour, 2 eggs, beaten, and salt and pepper to taste. Form the parsnip mixture into small balls and press the meat of 1 whole walnut into each. Sauté the parsnip balls to a golden brown in hot butter and serve on a hot platter garnished with parsley.

*Spring Peas
and Thyme*

SHELL 2 pounds peas and put them into a saucepan with 2 tablespoons melted butter. Sprinkle with salt and shake the pan until the peas are coated with the butter. Add 2 tablespoons hot water, cover tightly, and cook for about 10 minutes, or until tender. Add 1 teaspoon finely minced thyme just before serving.

*Spring Peas
and Herbs*

Mint, basil, orégano, and other herbs, may be used to flavor green peas as desired.

*Baked
Green Peas*

PLACE 4 cups freshly shelled peas on a large lettuce leaf in a quart casserole or baking dish. Add 2 tablespoons water, cover tightly, and bake the peas in a moderate oven (350° F.) for 10 minutes. Add 3 tablespoons sweet butter and salt and freshly ground pepper, cover again, and continue to bake for about 25 minutes longer, or until the peas are tender.

COOK 4 cups freshly shelled peas in a tightly covered saucepan with 1/4 cup boiling water, salt and pepper to taste, 1 clove, and a *bouquet garni* of 6 sprigs of parsley, 1 bay leaf, and 1 large mint leaf for 12 to 15 minutes, or until the peas are tender and the water is evaporated. Add 3 tablespoons butter and 3/4 cup heavy cream and heat the cream to the boiling point.

Discard the *bouquet garni*, turn the peas and sauce into a warm serving dish, and sprinkle with a little finely chopped mint.

Green Peas Bayou

PARBOIL 1/2 cup fat salt pork, diced, for 5 minutes. Drain off the water. Melt 1 tablespoon butter in a saucepan, add the pork dice, 1/2 cup carrots, scraped and diced, and 10 tiny white onions. Cook the vegetables, shaking the pan occasionally, until they are all a light golden brown. Remove the vegetables from the pan with a skimmer.

In the fat in the pan, brown lightly 1 teaspoon flour. Add 3/4 cup chicken stock, bring the liquid to a boil and add the browned carrots, onions and pork dice, 2 cups freshly shelled peas, 4 shredded leaves of lettuce, and 4 sprigs each of parsley and chervil tied in a faggot. Add 1 tablespoon sugar, bring the liquid to a boil, cover the pan and simmer the vegetables for 30 minutes, or until they are tender. Discard the faggot. Reduce the liquid, if necessary, to 1/2 cup. Correct the seasoning with salt.

Petits Pois Paysanne
PEAS COUNTRY STYLE

COOK 1/2 pound cleaned shrimps in hot peanut oil until they turn pink. Soak 8 dried mushrooms in water to cover. Heat 2 tablespoons peanut oil in a heavy pan and in it cook over high heat for 2 minutes, stirring, 1/4 pound trimmed snow pea pods, 1/2 cup sliced Chinese cabbage, 1/4 pound each of bamboo shoots and water chestnuts, sliced, and the drained mushrooms. Add the mushroom liquid, 1 tablespoon each of soy sauce and Sherry, a dash of sesame oil, and the prepared shrimps. Heat quickly and serve at once.

Snow Peas

PARBOIL small potato shapes—balls, ovals, dice, or slices—for 5 minutes in salted water and drain them well. Or cut raw potatoes into similar shapes. Sauté them to a rich golden brown in a generous quantity of beef fat, rendered chicken or goose fat, or clarified butter—butter poured off the

Pommes au Beurre

Clarified Butter

sediment that settles at the bottom of the melting pan. Season the potatoes to taste with salt and pepper and, if desired, sprinkle them with chopped parsley.

Pommes Château   *Pommes château* are cut in oval shapes and browned as above.

Pommes Rissolées   *Pommes rissolées* are cut in balls and browned on a shallow baking pan in butter in the oven.

Pommes de Terres Pont-Neuf   PEEL and trim potatoes into squares and cut them into rectangles 1/2 inch thick and of uniform length. Wash the potatoes in cold water, dry them well, and fry them in hot deep fat (375 F.) until they are crisp and golden.

French Fried Potatoes   Potatoes for deep fat frying may be cut into any size or shape. They should be of uniform size, and should be kept in cold water until frying time to prevent them from discoloring. Dry them well before plunging them into hot deep fat; the larger shapes should be cooked in fat at a temperature of 375° F., the smaller and thinner at 390° F.

Potatoes Clemenceau   PEEL and cut 1 pound potatoes into small uniform dice and French fry them in hot deep fat (395° F.) until they are golden brown. Combine the potatoes with a scant 1/2 pound mushrooms, sliced and sautéed in butter until tender, and 1/2 pound green peas, cooked until tender in a little water and drained. Add salt and pepper to taste.

Pommes Soufflées Chatouillard
PUFFED POTATO RIBBONS   PEEL Idaho potatoes and cut them into long spiral ribbons 1/8 inch thick, using a special cutter, a potato peeler, or a very sharp knife.

Fill 2 deep saucepans, each equipped with a handle and a deep-fat thermometer, half-full with melted fat. Any type of fat or vegetable shortening may be used. Heat the fat in one saucepan until the thermometer registers 350° F. Heat the fat in the other saucepan to 400° F. and maintain this temperature.

Drop a handful of potato ribbons, one at a time, into the fat at 350° F. Remove the saucepan from the heat and shake it constantly to keep the ribbons moving. The potatoes will come to the surface. When the temperature of the fat goes down to 250° F., put the saucepan back on the heat and continue shaking the pan until the ribbons just begin to puff. This will take from 6 to 10 minutes, and the temperature of the fat should not be allowed to rise above 300° F.

Remove the potatoes from the fat with a large skimmer and plunge them into the fat at 400° F. in the other pan. They will puff immediately and bob around on the surface of the fat. Turn the puffs constantly until they are well browned on both sides. Remove them from the fat to drain on absorbent paper. Sprinkle them with salt and keep in a warm place until ready to serve.

If the *pommes Chatouillard* are not to be served immediately, they may be removed from the hot fat when they are well puffed and lightly golden to cool. Drain them on absorbent paper, well separated, and place them between two towels for several hours or even overnight. They will deflate but will puff again when dropped into hot fat (400° F.). Turn the ribbons constantly until they are well browned on both sides, drain, sprinkle with salt, and serve hot.

SLICE hot, freshly boiled potatoes and brown them quickly in bacon drippings or beef suet. Season with salt and pepper and serve at once.

Cottage Fried Potatoes

BROWN cooked potatoes, cut in any desired shape, in hot oil. At the last moment, add minced garlic to taste and a generous quantity of finely chopped parsley.

Pommes de Terre Provençale

SCRUB the skin from tiny new potatoes, cook them in boiling salted water to cover for 2 or 3 minutes and drain them well. For each cup of potatoes, heat well 2 tablespoons good beef, chicken, or goose fat. Cook the potatoes in the fat until they are tender and golden brown all over. Drain them and pour off the fat from the pan. Return the potatoes to the pan, add 1 tablespoon butter for each cup of potatoes and roll the potatoes in the butter as it melts. Season with a little salt and sprinkle with finely chopped parsley.

New Potatoes

PEEL 2 pounds potatoes, cut them into even pieces, and cook them in boiling salted water to cover until they are soft but not mushy. Drain and dry them by shaking the pan over the heat until the moisture has evaporated. Rub the potatoes through a sieve or put them through a ricer. Add 2 tablespoons butter, 1 teaspoon salt, pepper to taste, and 2 eggs slightly beaten with 2 egg yolks and beat the mixture with a spoon until it is fluffy.

Pommes de Terre Duchesse
DUCHESS POTATOES

Duchess potatoes are commonly used to garnish serving dishes; the mixture is piped through a pastry tube in an attractive design and browned in the oven or under the broiler.

Potato Croquettes

PREPARE *pommes duchesse* and shape the mixture into croquettes of any desired shape. Coat the croquettes with flour and dip them into a mixture of 1 egg beaten with 1/4 cup milk, 1 tablespoon oil, and 1/2 teaspoon salt and in fine, dry bread crumbs. Fry them in hot deep fat (370° F.) to a rich, golden brown. Drain on absorbent paper.

Potato Croquette Variations

A few trimmings of truffle, finely minced, may be added to the *pommes duchesse* mixture to make *croquettes à la périgourdine*, or the mixture may be flavored with grated Parmesan cheese, or with sautéed onion, or with chives or chervil or parsley, to taste.

Pommes de Terre Dauphine

ADD to *pommes duchesse* a third as much *pâte à chou*. Let the paste cool well, shape it into balls or other shapes, and roll the balls in flour. Fry them in hot deep fat (390° F.) until the fritters are puffed and brown. Drain on paper toweling and serve hot.

Pommes de Terre Crécy

PEEL and slice potatoes into thin rounds. Butter a round mold or small baking dish generously and line the mold with a thick layer of overlapping potato slices. Sprinkle with salt and spread with 1 tablespoon butter. Add a layer of sliced carrots, cooked until they are barely tender in a little salted water and seasoned with butter, and proceed in this fashion, using 2 cups carrots in all and spreading each layer of potatoes with 1 tablespoon butter, until the mold is full. Finish with a final tablespoon of butter and bake the casserole in a hot oven (400° F.) for about 40 to 50 minutes, until the potatoes are cooked. To serve, invert the mold on a hot platter and garnish with parsley.

Pommes Anna

When the carrots are omitted, this dish is called *pommes Anna*.

Panier de Pommes de Terre

POTATO BASKET

PEEL 2 pounds potatoes and drop them into cold water. Cut one potato at a time into uniform slivers the size of matchsticks and drop the strips into a small bowl of cold milk. Potatoes discolor quickly out of liquid.

Line the bottom and sides of a generously buttered, shallow, round glass, earthenware, or copper pan with the potatoes in a basket-weave pattern. Pack the remaining potatoes into the lined pan, and sprinkle with salt and pepper.

Melt 1 cup butter and pour it over the potatoes. Cover the pan with a lid and bake the potatoes in a moderate oven (350° F.) for 30 minutes. Uncover the potatoes and add 1/4 cup melted butter. Raise the temperature to hot (400° F.) and continue to bake, uncovered, for 15 minutes longer or until the potatoes are golden brown on top and bottom.

Turn the potatoes out of the mold and sprinkle them with salt, pepper, and finely chopped parsley.

BAKE 3 very large Idaho baking potatoes until they are tender. Cut the potatoes in half lengthwise and scoop out the pulp, leaving the shells intact. Mash the pulp with 2 egg yolks and season it with cream, butter, and salt and pepper to taste. Whip the mixture until it is smooth and fold in 2 egg whites, beaten until stiff. Pile the mixture in the potato shells, using a pastry tube, if desired, to make an attractive pattern. Sprinkle lightly with buttered bread crumbs and bake the potatoes in a moderate oven (350° F.) until the filling is hot and the topping browned. The pulp may be seasoned to taste with minced onion, chives, grated cheese, or minced green pepper, or with chopped onion lightly sautéed in rendered chicken fat. In this case, omit the butter and cream.

To stuff whole potatoes, use 1 medium potato for each serving. Bake the potatoes and make a circular opening on one flat side of each. Scoop out some or all of the pulp and fill the potato with any well-flavored creamy preparation such as might be served in a patty shell or in a crêpe. Or mash and season the pulp and return it to the shell. These potato boats are an excellent way to serve simple preparations of buttered or creamed peas, carrots or baby onions.

Pommes de Terre Fourées
BAKED STUFFED POTATOES

BOIL 6 large potatoes in their skins for 15 minutes, drain them, and with a teaspoon scoop out a deep hole in the center of each.

Mash and brown 1 pound sweet Italian sausage. Add 3 slices of bread soaked in water and squeezed dry, 2 tablespoons each of butter, chicken stock, and chopped parsley, and 1 egg yolk and mix well. Stuff the potatoes

Sausage Potatoes

493

with this forcemeat and place them in a buttered baking dish. Dot them with butter, sprinkle with salt and pepper, and bake the potatoes in a hot oven (400° F.) for about 30 minutes, or until they are tender.

Pommes de Terre à la Hongroise

BUTTER a baking dish generously and cover the bottom with a 1/2-inch-thick layer of chopped onions. Season well with salt and paprika and add 1 large tomato, peeled, seeded, and coarsely chopped. Peel and slice thinly 5 or 6 potatoes and add them to the casserole. Add beef bouillon barely to cover the potatoes and bake the mixture in a moderately hot oven (375° F.) for about 1 hour, until the potatoes are soft. Sprinkle with chopped parsley and serve hot.

Latkes

POTATO PANCAKES

PEEL 6 medium potatoes and grate them; or cut them into small pieces and put them in a blender with 1/4 cup water until they are reduced to a thick purée. Drain off as much as possible of the potato liquid and beat in 2 large eggs and salt and pepper to taste. Add fine cracker crumbs or matzo meal to make a batter that will barely hold its shape. Fry the batter by tablespoons in a generous amount of hot fat, turning the cakes to brown and crisp both sides. A little grated onion or minced parsley may be added to the batter, if desired. Serve with applesauce.

Papas Rellenas

STUFFED POTATOES

SCRUB 6 large potatoes and cook them in boiling water until they are just tender and still firm. Drain them thoroughly. In a skillet sauté 6 leeks, finely chopped, in 2 tablespoons butter with 1 red chili pepper, seeded and crushed, and a pinch of garlic salt until the leeks are golden. (Make the garlic salt by rubbing a cut garlic clove into salt in a wooden bowl until it is granular.) Peel the potatoes thinly. Make a hole in one side of each and scoop out the pulp, leaving a shell 1/2 inch thick. Be careful not to break the potato. Mash about half the potato pulp, reserving the other half for another use, with 2 tablespoons butter, and add the pulp to the leek mixture. Add 1 1/2 cups minced cooked chicken, 1/2 cup sliced mushrooms, sautéed in butter, 1 1/2 tablespoons chopped pimiento, and 3 pinches of tarragon. Add a little more garlic salt and Tabasco to taste and blend the mixture thoroughly. Let the mixture stand, covered, for 5 minutes. Stuff the potato shells with the mixture, pressing it in firmly. Dip the potatoes lightly in beaten egg and put them in a frying basket, stuffed side up. Fry the potatoes in hot deep fat (370° F.) until they are crisp and brown. Drain the potatoes and sprinkle them with paprika before serving. Any leftover cooked meat may be substituted for the chicken.

PEEL and grate 6 to 8 large potatoes and combine the gratings thoroughly with 1/4 onion, grated, 3 eggs, well beaten, 1 cup hot milk, 6 tablespoons melted butter, and 1 1/2 teaspoons salt.

Pour the mixture into a well-buttered shallow baking pan and bake the pudding in a moderate oven (350° F.) for 1 hour and 15 minutes.

Potato Râpure

SEASON 4 cups mashed potatoes highly with salt and black pepper and beat in 1/4 cup rendered chicken or goose fat. Add 4 eggs, one at a time, beating well after each addition, and pile the mixture lightly into a baking dish that has been coated with the same fat used in the pudding. Bake the pudding in a moderately hot oven (375° F.) for 35 minutes, or until the pudding is crusted and richly browned.

Potato Pudding

Yams and sweet potatoes may be used interchangeably in these recipes.

COOK unpeeled sweet potatoes in boiling water for about 20 minutes or until they are tender. Drain, cool, and peel them. Cut the potatoes in 1/4-inch slices and brown them in hot deep fat (390° F.). Drain the potatoes on absorbent paper and sprinkle them with a little salt.

Fried Sweet Potatoes

PARE raw sweet potatoes and cut them in thin slices, then in thin strips the size of a matchstick. Drop the julienne strips immediately into very cold water to which a few tablespoons of lemon juice have been added. Drain the sweet potatoes and dry them in a towel. Fry the strips in hot deep fat (395° F.) until they are golden brown and crisp. Drain the sweet potatoes on absorbent paper, sprinkle with salt, and serve.

Julienne Sweet Potatoes

BOIL 3 pounds sweet potatoes until they are soft. Peel and mash them. Stir in 1/2 cup sugar, 3 tablespoons butter, 1/2 teaspoon each of cinnamon and nutmeg, 1/4 teaspoon salt, and about 1 cup milk. Turn the mixture into a casserole, sprinkle it with sugar, and bake it in a hot oven (400° F.) for about 15 minutes.

The potatoes may be further flavored with grated orange rind and

Spiced Sweet Potatoes

Sweet Potato Rum Casserole

brandy, and sprinkled with chopped roasted peanuts or almonds before baking.

MEASURE 4 cups boiled, riced sweet potatoes into a mixing bowl. Beat in thoroughly 1/4 cup each of butter and cream, 1/4 teaspoon nutmeg and, gradually, 1/4 cup rum. Season to taste with salt and pepper. Heap the sweet potatoes in a casserole and sprinkle the surface with melted butter and 1 tablespoon grated orange rind.

Sweet Potato Rum Casserole

Bake the casserole in a hot oven (400° F.) until the top is lightly browned.

WASH 6 medium sweet potatoes and cook them in slightly salted boiling water to cover until they are tender, but not mushy. Peel and cut them crosswise into 1/4-inch slices. Butter a casserole generously and in it place the sweet potato slices. Pour over them 1 cup honey, sprinkle with cinnamon or nutmeg, and dot with 1/4 cup butter. Bake the potatoes in a moderate oven (350° F.) for 35 minutes, basting them occasionally with the spiced honey, until they are nicely glazed.

Honeyed Sweet Potatoes

COOK 3 pounds uniform sweet potatoes in their skins until they are tender. Drain and peel them and cut them into slices. Drain the syrup from a can of apricot halves and reserve it. In a generously buttered casserole, arrange alternate layers of apricot halves and sweet potato slices. Place apricot halves on the top and pour the reserved apricot syrup over all. Dot the casserole with 2 tablespoons butter and bake it for 45 minutes in a moderate oven (350° F.). Cover the top with buttered paper if it browns too quickly.

Apricot Sweet Potato Casserole

WASH sweet potatoes of medium size and uniform shape. Cook them in slightly salted boiling water to cover until they are tender, but not mushy. Remove the skins and cut them crosswise into 1-inch slices. On small skewers arrange alternately the potato slices, quartered slices of canned pineapple, and pieces of bacon. Place the skewers on a generously buttered baking pan, pour the pineapple syrup over them, and dot with butter. Bake the skewers in a hot oven (400° F.) for about 15 minutes, basting occasionally.

Skewered Sweet Potatoes

BOIL 6 sweet potatoes until they are just tender. Peel and cut them lengthwise in 1/2-inch slices and arrange the slices in a shallow, buttered baking

Candied Sweet Potatoes

497

dish. Season them with salt and paprika and sprinkle them with 3/4 cup brown sugar, 1/2 teaspoonful grated lemon rind, and 1 1/2 tablespoons lemon juice. Dot the sweet potatoes with 2 tablespoons butter. Bake them uncovered in a moderately hot oven (375° F.) for 20 minutes, basting often until the potatoes are well glazed.

Sautéed Yams   Boil small yams in salted water until they are tender. Remove the skins and cut each yam in half lengthwise. Heat a generous amount of butter in a large skillet and in it sauté the potatoes gently without letting them brown, turning them often so that both sides become saturated with the butter, until the yams are heated through. Sprinkle one end of each half with finely chopped parsley and use as a garnish.

Pumpkin Purée   Wash and cut into quarters a ripe pumpkin, discarding the seeds and fibers. Arrange the quarters on a baking pan in 1/2 inch hot water and bake them in a moderate oven (350° F.) for 1 1/2 to 2 hours, or until they are tender. Scrape the pulp from the rind and rub it through a sieve or put it through a food mill or a blender.

Stir the purée over moderate heat until most of the moisture evaporates. Season it with butter, salt, pepper, and a little sugar. A pinch of ginger may also be added, to taste.

Baked Pumpkin   Cut 2 pounds pumpkin into serving pieces. Peel the wedges and discard the seeds and fibers. In a small saucepan melt 1/2 cup butter and add 1/4 cup each of brown sugar and chopped, preserved ginger. Score the pumpkin wedges with a sharp knife, spread them with the butter-sugar mixture, and sprinkle them lightly with salt. Bake the pumpkin in a moderate oven (350° F.) in 1/2 inch water on a shallow baking pan for 1 1/2 to 2 hours, or until it is tender, basting the wedges frequently with melted butter.

Bundewa
RUMANIAN
PUMPKIN
   In a saucepan lightly brown 1 onion, finely chopped, in 2 tablespoons melted butter. Add 1 tablespoon flour, blend well, and stir in 1 cup hot water. Add 1/2 teaspoon salt and 1 tablespoon finely chopped dill and cook, stirring, until the mixture is smooth and slightly thick. Add 2 pounds pumpkin, peeled and cut in thin julienne strips about 2 inches long. Cover

the pan and cook the pumpkin over low heat for 1 hour, or until it is tender. Add 2 teaspoons lemon juice and 1/2 cup cream and heat well.

DRAIN 2 pounds sauerkraut well and put it in a casserole with a generous sprinkling of freshly ground black pepper, 6 juniper berries, and 1/2 cup goose or bacon fat. Add half white wine and half chicken or veal stock to barely cover the sauerkraut and bring the liquid to a boil. Cover the casserole and bake the sauerkraut in a slow oven (325° F.) for 1 1/2 hours, or until most of the liquid has been absorbed.

Sauerkraut Casserole

SAUTÉ 8 strips of bacon, diced, until they are crisp. Add 2 large onions, chopped, and continue to sauté until the onions are golden. Transfer the onions and bacon to a heavy kettle, and add 2 pounds sauerkraut and enough chicken or veal stock to half cover the kraut. Bring the stock to a boil, cover the kettle, and simmer for 10 minutes. Add 8 tart apples, peeled, quartered, and cored, and continue to cook for about 15 minutes, or until the apples are very soft. Sprinkle 2 teaspoons flour over the apples, stir it in thoroughly, and cook the mixture rapidly, uncovered, for 10 minutes, stirring occasionally.

Apfelkraut
SAUERKRAUT AND APPLES

WASH thoroughly 5 pounds sorrel and cook it over high heat for 10 to 15 minutes in the water that clings to the leaves, or until it is very soft. This is called "melted" sorrel. Drain the sorrel, pressing out as much water as possible. Rub it through a sieve. In a casserole melt 3 tablespoons butter, add 2 tablespoons flour and cook the mixture until it begins to color. Add the sorrel purée, 1/2 teaspoon salt, 1 tablespoon sugar, and 1/2 cup stock. Stir the mixture well and bring it to the boiling point. Cover the pan with a piece of buttered paper, adjust the lid, and braise the sorrel in a moderate oven (350° F.) for about 1 hour. Remove the casserole from the oven and beat in 2 beaten eggs. Bring the mixture back to the boiling point over direct heat, but do not allow it to boil. Correct the seasoning with salt and and add 2 tablespoons cream.

Oseille Braisée
BRAISED SORREL

WASH thoroughly 3 pounds sorrel and blanch in boiling water for 10 minutes. Drain off all the liquid and rub the sorrel through a sieve or purée it in a blender. Melt 1 tablespoon butter in a heavy saucepan, stir in 1 tablespoon flour and cook for several minutes. Lay the sorrel on this without mixing, cover, and let stand in a warm place for 30 minutes to soften the

Sorrel à la Crème

499

flavor. Add 1 cup béchamel, 1/2 cup heavy cream, and 1 egg, well beaten. Season to taste with salt, pepper, and nutmeg and beat thoroughly. Reheat the sorrel over low heat, stirring well.

The best way to cleanse spinach of the sand that lurks in the crevices of the leaves is to wash it in several changes of water, first lukewarm, and then cold, lifting the spinach out of the water so that the sand falls to the bottom of the bowl. The practice of cooking freshly washed spinach without additional water is modern, American, and our preference.

Spinach Near East

Cook 3 pounds well-washed spinach in the water left on the leaves, covered, for about 5 minutes and drain it. Melt 1/4 cup butter in a saucepan, add the spinach, and cook for 5 minutes longer, stirring occasionally. Sprinkle the spinach with salt and pepper to taste and stir in 3 tablespoons shelled pine nuts and 1 tablespoon raisins.

Epinards à l'Italienne
SPINACH IN OLIVE OIL

Wash well 3 pounds fresh spinach, cook it for about 5 minutes in the water that clings to the leaves, drain it well, and press out as much water as possible. Heat 1/4 cup olive oil in a pan with a split garlic clove. Toss the spinach well with the oil, add salt and nutmeg to taste, and stir it over the heat until the spinach has reduced in volume and the water has entirely evaporated.

Epinards à la Crème
CREAMED SPINACH

Clean and cook 3 pounds spinach. Drain, pressing out as much water as possible. Chop the spinach very finely, purée it in a blender, or force it through a coarse sieve. Melt 2 tablespoons butter in a saucepan, add 2 teaspoons flour, and cook the *roux* until it begins to turn golden. Stir in the spinach and cook it for a few minutes until it is quite dry. Season with 1/2 teaspoon salt and, if desired, a grating of nutmeg. Stir in 1/2 cup milk or cream, bring the mixture to a boil and cook it for a few minutes longer. Garnish with small triangles of bread browned in butter, or with quarters of hard-cooked egg.

Spinach and Radishes with Chicken Sauce
CHI CHIH LO CHIU

Wash thoroughly 1 pound spinach, chop it coarsely, and put it in water to cover. Bring the water just to the boiling point, remove and drain the spinach, and put it through a sieve.

Clean and peel 2 bunches of radishes, boil them in water for 5 minutes, and drain. Put them in a saucepan, pour over them chicken stock to cover, and add a pinch of salt. Simmer the radishes for 20 minutes, drain them, and arrange them on one half of a heated platter.

Heat 2 tablespoons rendered chicken fat in a skillet, sauté the puréed spinach in it for 2 minutes, and arrange it on the other half of the platter.

Heat 2 tablespoons chicken fat in a saucepan and blend in 2 cups chicken stock, 1/2 teaspoon sugar, a pinch of salt, and 1 1/2 teaspoons cornstarch dissolved in 2 tablespoons cold water. Cook, stirring constantly, until the sauce is smooth and thickened and blend in 3 tablespoons light cream. Pour the sauce over the vegetables and sprinkle with a spoonful of minced ham. Serves 4.

Soufflé d'Épinards au Jambon

WASH and cook 2 pounds spinach, drain it well, and rub it through a coarse sieve. Melt 1 tablespoon butter in a saucepan, add the spinach and cook it over high heat, stirring constantly until all the water has cooked away. Add 1 1/2 tablespoons flour, a little salt and pepper, and a grating of nutmeg. Stir well, add 1/2 cup boiling chicken stock or hot milk and mix thoroughly. Bring the liquid to a boil, cover the pan and cook the spinach for 10 minutes.

Remove the pan from the heat and add 1/4 cup grated Parmesan cheese, 1/2 cup lean Virginia ham cut in very small dice, 1 tablespoon butter and 3 beaten egg yolks. Beat the mixture thoroughly and fold in 4 stiffly beaten egg whites. Turn the mixture into a buttered soufflé mold or baking dish, round the surface into a dome shape and sprinkle it with grated Parmesan and a little melted butter. Bake the soufflé in a moderate oven (350° to 375° F.) for 25 to 30 minutes, or until it is well puffed and lightly browned.

Soufflé d'Épinards aux Oeufs Pochés

WASH and cook 3 pounds spinach and rub it through a sieve. There should be about 1 cup thick spinach purée. Melt 1 1/2 tablespoons butter in a saucepan and add the spinach purée. Season with 1/2 teaspoon salt, a little pepper, and a little grated nutmeg. Cook the purée over low heat, stirring it constantly, until all the moisture cooks away. In another pan, melt 2 1/2 tablespoons butter, add 3 tablespoons flour, and cook the *roux* until it starts to turn golden. Stir in 1 1/4 cups hot milk, return the pan to the heat, and cook the sauce for 8 to 10 minutes, until it is very thick, stirring it constantly with a whip. Beat 6 egg yolks, combine them with the milk mixture, and heat all together just to the boiling point. Do not allow the mixture to boil. Add the spinach purée. Beat 6 egg whites until they are stiff but not dry. Fold into the mixture thoroughly and carefully one-fourth of the beaten egg whites and add the remaining egg whites, cutting them in lightly and completely by raising and folding the mixture over and over. Spread about one-third of the batter in the bottom of a buttered and floured ovenproof casserole or square dish and arrange 6 well-drained, lightly poached eggs on it. Cover the eggs with the remaining soufflé mixture. Bake the soufflé in a moderate oven (350° F.) for 25 to 30 minutes, or until it puffs and browns. To serve, cut down through the soufflé with a spoon so that one egg is included in each serving.

The hard-fleshed winter squashes, whatever their shape or the name they bear, may be used as pumpkin is, even for pies and puddings.

Baked Butternut Squash

WASH 3 butternut squashes, split them in half, and remove the seeds. Coat the meat thickly with butter and sprinkle it with sugar, salt and pepper to taste and a little ginger. Arrange the squashes, cut side up, in a shallow baking dish in 1 inch of water. Bake them in a moderate oven (350° F.) for about 1 hour, or until they are brown and very tender when tested with a fork. Serve in the shell.

Baked Acorn Squash

CUT 3 small acorn squashes in half lengthwise and remove the seeds. Place 2 tablespoons slivered Brazil nuts in each lightly salted half, sprinkle on each 1 tablespoon brown sugar and dot with 1/2 tablespoon butter. Place the squashes in a baking pan in 1 inch of water. Bake them in a moderate oven (350° F.) for about 1 hour, or until the flesh is tender.

Hubbard Squash in Cream

PEEL and slice thinly enough Hubbard squash to measure 1 quart and put it in a well-buttered baking dish. Sprinkle it with salt and pepper and 1/4 cup sugar. Add 1 cup heavy cream, sprinkle with 1 teaspoon cinnamon, and bake in a slow oven (300° F.) for about 50 minutes, or until the squash is tender. Serve from the baking dish.

Baked Hubbard Squash

CUT Hubbard squash into serving sections. Arrange the pieces on a baking sheet, cut side up, and spread the surface with softened butter. Season the squash with salt and pepper, brush the sections with honey, and sprinkle with bacon cut into small pieces. Bake in a moderate oven (350° F.) for 45 minutes, or until tender when tested with a fork.

Zucchini is a summer squash that has only recently come into its own in our country. It looks something like a cucumber, but its taste and texture are uniquely delicious. Peel the zucchini or simply scrub it for the pot.

SAUTÉ 1 cup red Italian onion rings and 1 cup green pepper strips in 1/4 cup butter. When the vegetables begin to take on color add 2 cups zucchini, cut in 1-inch slices, and sauté for 5 minutes longer. Add 4 tomatoes, peeled and cut in wedges, and cook until the tomatoes are soft, or about 5 minutes. Season with freshly ground black pepper and salt. Turn the vegetables into a casserole and sprinkle them with grated Parmesan cheese. Just before serving time, bake the casserole in a moderately hot oven (375° F.) until the topping browns and the vegetables are hot.

Zucchini Casserole

REMOVE and reserve for another use the stems from 1 pound uniformly sized mushrooms. Sauté the caps with 1 garlic clove and 1 pound zucchini, cut into 1-inch slices, in 1/4 cup butter for 5 minutes. Discard the garlic, add 2 tablespoons flour to the vegetables, and cook for 2 minutes. Add 1 cup sour cream and 1 teaspoon finely chopped dill and mix well. Reheat before serving.

Zucchini and Mushrooms

SCRUB uniform zucchini but do not peel them. Cut them into 1/4-inch-thick slices. Sauté the zucchini in a generous amount of melted butter until it is transparent, but do not let the slices brown. Sprinkle them lightly with salt and pepper to taste and lavishly with crumbled orégano. Serve hot.

Zucchini Orégano

CUT small firm tomatoes in half and put them, cut side down, in a little melted butter in the blazer of a chafing dish placed directly over the heat. Cook the tomatoes for about 3 minutes, turn them carefully with a spatula and sprinkle with salt and pepper. Continue to cook the tomatoes for another 3 minutes, or until they are just tender, basting several times with the juices in the pan. Sprinkle with chives.

Pan Broiled Tomatoes

HALVE 6 ripe tomatoes and sprinkle each half lightly with salt, pepper, and a few grains of cayenne. Top the tomatoes with fine dry bread crumbs or with crumbs mixed with chopped tarragon and dot them with bits of butter.

Broiled Tarragon Tomatoes

Broil the tomatoes 3 inches from the heat for about 6 minutes, or until the crumbs are brown and the tomatoes hot. Arrange them on a heated platter and sprinkle with finely chopped tarragon.

Pennsylvania Dutch Tomatoes

CUT 6 large, firm tomatoes, either red or green, into thick slices. Dip the slices in flour and sprinkle them with salt and pepper. Arrange the slices in a large skillet in 1/4 cup hot butter, sprinkle them with brown sugar, and cook them over moderate heat until they are brown underneath. Turn the slices and sprinkle again with brown sugar. Cook slowly, so that the sugar and butter blend but do not burn, until the slices are tender. Add 1 cup heavy cream and continue to cook until the cream begins to bubble. Arrange the tomatoes on a warm serving platter and pour the sauce over them.

Soufflé de Tomates

CHOP coarsely 5 or 6 large ripe tomatoes. Melt 1 tablespoon butter in a saucepan, add the tomatoes, and cook them until all the liquid has cooked away and the mixture is quite thick. Strain the mixture and discard skin and seeds. Add 3 tablespoons canned tomato paste, 1 tablespoon sugar, and 1/2 teaspoon salt, and bring the mixture to a boil.

Make a thick white sauce as follows: Melt 2 tablespoons butter, add 3 tablespoons flour, and cook, stirring, until the *roux* starts to turn golden. Stir in 1 cup hot milk and cook the sauce for about 5 minutes, or until it is very thick, stirring it constantly with a whip. Combine this with the tomato mixture and 2 tablespoons Parmesan or dry Swiss cheese. Beat 5 egg yolks, add them to the tomato mixture, and heat all together just to the boiling point, stirring briskly. Do not allow the mixture to boil. Remove the pan from the heat and continue to stir for a few minutes longer. Beat 5 egg whites until they are stiff but not dry. Fold into the mixture thoroughly and carefully one-fourth of the beaten egg whites and add the remaining egg whites, cutting them in lightly and completely by raising and folding the mixture over and over. Pour the batter into a buttered and floured 8-inch soufflé dish and run your forefinger to the depth of 1/2 inch around the inside of the mold to separate the batter from the dish. Bake the soufflé in a moderate oven (350° F.) for 25 to 30 minutes.

Tomatoes Stuffed with Rice

WASH 6 large, ripe tomatoes, cut off the stem ends and scoop out the seeds, forming large tomato cups. Place the cups upside down to drain. Wash 1 cup long-grained rice in several changes of cold water. Cover the rice with 3 cups cold water, bring the water to a lively boil, boil the rice for 10 minutes and drain.

Arrange the tomatoes cup side up close together in a baking dish. Sprinkle them with salt and coarsely ground black pepper and fill the cups with the rice. Sprinkle with 2 garlic cloves, minced, and pour over the tomatoes 3 cups chicken stock, moistening the rice thoroughly. Season again with salt and pepper and sprinkle with 4 strips of bacon, shredded. Cover the baking dish and bake the tomatoes in a very hot oven (450° F.) for about 25 minutes, or until the rice is tender, basting occasionally with the pan juices. Uncover and continue to bake until most of the pan juices have been absorbed and the bacon is brown and crisp. Sprinkle with 3 tablespoons chopped parsley.

Tomatoes Stuffed with Tuna

CUT the tops from 6 ripe tomatoes and scoop out the pulp. Force the pulp through a fine sieve and add to the tomato purée 1 cup flaked cooked tuna fish, 6 anchovy filets, chopped, 2 tablespoons chopped parsley, 1 teaspoon chopped basil, 1/2 garlic clove, minced, 1/4 teaspoon chopped orégano, 2 slices of bread soaked in water and squeezed dry, 2 tablespoons soft butter, and salt and pepper to taste. Stuff the tomatoes with the filling, arrange them in an oiled baking dish, and bake them in a moderately hot oven (375° F.) for 20 minutes.

Pomodori alla Veneziana
VENETIAN TOMATOES

PEEL 6 medium-sized firm tomatoes, cut a slice from the stem end of each, and scoop out the seeds.

In a saucepan brown 1 small onion, chopped, in 2 tablespoons olive oil and 1 teaspoon butter. Add 1 garlic clove, mashed, 1 tablespoon parsley, 2 mushrooms, 4 anchovies, chopped, and salt and pepper. Simmer the sauce for 5 minutes and add 6 oysters and 3 tablespoons concentrated stock. Bring the sauce to a boil. Arrange the prepared tomatoes in a buttered baking dish and stuff them with the mixture, topping each with an oyster. Sprinkle with a few drops of lemon juice and some bread crumbs. Brown the topping in a hot oven (400° F.).

Tomato Flan

LINE a flan ring with pie dough and bake it in a very hot oven (450° F.) for 7 to 8 minutes.

In a skillet heat 3 teaspoons olive oil and in it sauté 2 large onions and 1 garlic clove, both chopped, until browned. Add 6 large tomatoes, peeled and sliced, 1 small zucchini, sliced, 3 tablespoons chopped parsley, a pinch of sage, and salt and pepper to taste. Simmer until the vegetables are tender, pour the mixture into the partially baked pie shell, and cover the top with

505

2 eggs, well beaten. Sprinkle with grated cheese and bake the flan in a hot oven (400° F.) for about 15 minutes, or until the pastry is golden.

Tomato and Cheese Casserole

IN a saucepan cook 1 tablespoon onion gently in 1/2 cup melted butter, stir in 1/2 cup flour, and add gradually 2 1/2 cups hot milk, stirring constantly until the sauce is thick and smooth. Cook, stirring frequently, for 10 to 20 minutes. Season the sauce with 1/2 teaspoon salt and a little pepper and paprika.

Beat 2 egg yolks with 1/4 cup cream and gradually stir in the hot thick sauce. Stir over low heat until the sauce almost reaches a boil and add 3/4 to 1 cup grated Swiss or Parmesan cheese.

Cut the tops from 6 firm tomatoes. Squeeze them very gently to remove seeds and excess liquid. Arrange them in a shallow baking dish and pour the sauce over them. Bake the casserole in a hot oven (425° F.) for about 15 minutes, or until the topping is richly browned.

Truffes au Champagne

STRAIN the liquid from 6 large canned truffles and reserve it.

Cook 3 cups white stock until it is reduced to 3/4 cup. Stir in 2 teaspoons arrowroot, blended with 2 tablespoons cold veal stock, and cook, stirring, until the sauce it thickened. Strain the sauce through a fine sieve and keep it warm over hot water.

In a small deep saucepan heat 1 tablespoon butter and in it cook gently, stirring, 1 tablespoon finely chopped carrot, 2 teaspoons chopped onion, and 1 teaspoon minced celery until the vegetables are tender but not browned. Add the truffles and their strained liquor, season with salt and freshly ground white pepper, and add 1 1/2 cups dry Champagne. Cover the saucepan with 3 or 4 layers of cheesecloth, place the lid on the saucepan, and simmer the truffles gently for 6 minutes.

Remove the truffles and wipe off any particles of vegetable adhering to them. Place the truffles in a small covered silver casserole or singly in 6 covered silver or porcelain ramekins and keep them warm.

Strain the sauce in which the truffles were cooked through a fine sieve and cook the liquid until it is reduced to 2 tablespoons. Stir in the veal sauce and heat almost to the boil. Pour the sauce over the truffles, heat the casserole or ramekins containing them on an asbestos mat over low heat for about 10 minutes without letting the sauce boil, and serve immediately.

Truffes sous Feuilletée

PUT 6 large canned truffles and their liquor in a small saucepan. Add 1 cup white stock, 1/4 cup Maderia, 1 tablespoon brandy, 1 sprig of thyme, 1 bay leaf, salt, and freshly ground white pepper. Cover the pan tightly and simmer the truffles for 6 minutes. Place the pan, still covered, in the refrigerator and chill the truffles in the sauce.

Roll out puff paste 1/8 inch thick and cut 6 circles about 3 1/3 inches in diameter. On one side of each puff paste circle place a slightly smaller half circle of thinly sliced goose liver or *pâté de foie gras* and sprinkle with salt and pepper. Dry the truffles on absorbent paper, reserve the sauce, and place one truffle on each slice of goose liver. Moisten the edges of the dough circles, fold them in half, and seal the edges with the tines of a fork. Brush the dough with beaten egg yolk, pierce the top of each turnover once, and bake them in a very hot oven (450° F.) for about 20 minutes or until the pastry is puffed and golden.

Strain the sauce through a fine sieve and cook it until it is reduced to 1/2 cup. Stir in 2 teaspoons Maderia and serve the sauce separately.

PEEL 6 medium white turnips and cook them in salted water with a few caraway seeds until they are very tender. *Turnip Purée*

Shred and sauté 3 onions over low heat in a generous amount of butter, with 2 tablespoons chopped parsley and a few drops of lemon juice until they are transparent.

Drain and mash the turnips with 2 tablespoons butter and turn them into a hot serving dish. Put the sautéed onions in the center and serve hot.

WASH, peel, and dice 1 pound turnips and cook the dice in boiling salted water to cover for about 10 minutes, or until they are tender. Drain the turnips, mash them, and combine them with an equal amount of freshly cooked and mashed potatoes. Add 2 tablespoons cream and 1 well-beaten egg, and season the mixture to taste with salt and pepper and 1/2 teaspoon dry mustard. Pile the purée in a buttered casserole and bake it in a hot oven (400° F.) for 20 minutes. *Mashed Turnips*

COOK 4 rutabagas for about 30 minutes, until they are tender, in a small quantity of salted water in a covered saucepan. Drain the rutabagas and mash them. Simmer 2 peeled and quartered apples in a little water for about 10 minutes, or until tender. Put the apples through a sieve. Combine the apple purée and the mashed rutabagas, add 2 tablespoons butter, and beat well. Season with salt and pepper to taste. *Rutabagas and Apples*

A casserole of dried beans can serve a double purpose; it will take the place of meat, or a place alongside meat, and is especially welcome on informal occasions.

Kidney Bean Casserole

PICK over and wash 2 cups kidney beans and soak them overnight. Drain the beans and put them in a heavy saucepan with 2 quarts cold water and 1 onion, sliced. Bring the water to a boil, cover the saucepan, and simmer the beans gently for about 1 1/2 hours, or until they are tender but not soft.

Sauté in 1/4 cup olive oil until they are tender 1 onion, 2 garlic cloves, and 1 green pepper, all finely chopped. Add 5 tomatoes, peeled, seeded, and chopped, 1 teaspoon salt, 1/2 teaspoon pepper, 1 bay leaf, and 1/2 teaspoon thyme. Cover the skillet and simmer for 30 minutes.

In a casserole combine the sauce and beans with 2 tablespoons chopped chives and 1/4 cup chopped parsley. Bake in a moderate oven (350° F.) for about 40 minutes. Sprinkle with grated Parmesan cheese and bake another 5 minutes or until the cheese is lightly browned.

Fagioli all'Uccelletto

DRIED BEANS
UCCELLETTO

SOAK 3/4 pound white beans overnight, drain them and put them in a large saucepan with 2 tablespoons olive oil, 1/2 teaspoon powdered sage, 2 garlic cloves, 4 cups water, and 1 large tomato, peeled and chopped. Cover the saucepan and cook the beans over low heat for about 3 hours, or until they are tender. Add salt and pepper to taste and 2 tablespoons olive oil.

Fava Bean Casserole

PICK over 1 pound dried *fava* beans and soak them overnight in water to cover. Drain them and cover with fresh water. Add 2 small onions, each stuck with 1 clove, 1 garlic clove, 3 peppercorns, 1/2 teaspoon salt, and a *bouquet garni* consisting of 2 sprigs of celery, 4 sprigs of parsley, 3 peppercorns, and 1 bay leaf. Bring this to a boil, lower the heat, and simmer the beans gently for about 1 hour, or until they are tender. Drain them, reserve the liquid, and discard the *bouquet garni*.

Melt 3 tablespoons butter in a saucepan and stir in 2 tablespoons flour. Add gradually 1 1/2 cups of the liquid in which the beans were cooked, stirring until the sauce is smooth and thickened. Stir in 1/2 cup heavy cream. Turn the beans into a buttered baking dish and pour the sauce over them. Arrange strips of bacon across the top and bake in a moderate oven (350° F.) for 30 minutes, or until the bacon is crisp.

SOAK 2 pounds black beans overnight in water to cover. In the morning cook the beans in the water in which they were soaked with 2 onions, sliced, salt and pepper, and a *bouquet garni* of 6 sprigs of parsley, 2 bay leaves, and 2 stalks of celery with the leaves until the beans are tender, adding boiling water from the kettle as the liquid cooks away.

Transfer the beans to a large casserole and thicken the liquid slightly with a little flour rubbed to a paste with an equal amount of butter. Stir in 1/4 cup dark rum and strain the sauce over the beans. Cover the casserole tightly and bake the beans in a moderate oven (350° F.) for 30 minutes. Serve hot with cold sour cream. Serves 12.

Casserole of Black Beans with Sour Cream

LIGHTLY sauté 3 tablespoons chopped onion and 2 tablespoons chopped salt pork in 1 tablespoon olive oil or bacon drippings. Stir in 3 cups cooked rice and 1 cup cooked lentils and heat the mixture thoroughly.

Arroz con Lentejas

SOAK 2 cups dried Lima beans in water to cover for several hours or overnight. Add 1 cup water, 1/2 teaspoon salt, a stalk of celery tied with 3 sprigs of parsley and 1/2 bay leaf, and 1 small onion stuck with 1 whole clove. Bring to a boil, cover, and simmer the beans 3 hours.

Drain and reserve the liquid. Discard the seasoning vegetables and rub the beans through a sieve. Add a little cream and cooking liquid. Add salt and white pepper to taste. Finish with 2 tablespoons butter.

Purée of Lima Beans

The mixed-vegetable casseroles that follow are universally pleasing and are therefore a particularly happy choice for the informal buffet.

SLICE crosswise 6 to 10 green onions, depending on their size, and include some of the green top as well as the bulb. Dice coarsely 3 stalks of celery. Cook onions and celery briefly in 1/4 cup melted butter, but do not allow them to brown. Add 1 1/2 cups light cream and continue to cook the mixture until it is reduced by half, stirring often to prevent scorching. Add 2 cups fresh green peas, cooked until they are barely tender in a little water, and simmer all together for a few minutes. Adjust the seasoning and serve the vegetables very hot.

Légumes à la Crème
VEGETABLES IN CREAM

COMBINE 3 large tomatoes, peeled, seeded, and chopped with 1 cup sliced okra, 1 teaspoon salt, a dash of freshly ground pepper and 2 tablespoons minced celery. Cover the pan and simmer the vegetables for 5 minutes. Add

Southern Succotash

1 cup fresh Lima beans and simmer the mixture for 15 minutes more, adding a little chicken stock if necessary. Add 1 cup freshly scraped corn pulp and simmer the succotash for 8 minutes, or until the vegetables are tender. Add 2 tablespoons butter, correct the seasoning, and serve hot.

Vegetable Curry

IN a large saucepan melt 1 cup butter with 1/2 tablespoon curry powder and a pinch of salt. Add the following vegetables: 1 cup each of peas, fresh Lima beans, and green beans, 3 tomatoes, peeled and cut in wedges, 8 finely chopped leeks, and 1 small cauliflower broken into flowerets. Toss lightly together and add 1 cup hot water. Cover the pan and simmer very slowly until all the vegetables are tender, shaking the pan from time to time to prevent the vegetables from burning.

Vegetable Ghivetch

ARRANGE the following vegetables in a large earthenware casserole: 6 baby carrots, sliced, 2 potatoes, diced, 1/2 eggplant, unpeeled but cut in dice, 1/2 cup each of green peas, fresh Lima beans, and seedless grapes, 1/2 cup green beans, sliced lengthwise, 1/2 green pepper, sliced into strips, 1/2 small head each of cabbage and cauliflower, cut up, 1/2 summer squash, diced, 1/2 celery root, diced, 5 tomatoes, quartered, and 2 garlic cloves. Sauté 2 onions, sliced, in 1/4 cup butter or olive oil until they are golden, add 1 cup stock and bring to a boil. Pour over the vegetables in the casserole 1/2 cup boiling olive oil and add 1 teaspoon salt, freshly ground pepper to taste, and the onion mixture. Cover the casserole and bake the vegetables in a moderate oven (350° F.) for 25 minutes or until the vegetables are tender and the liquid has been absorbed. Serve hot or cold.

Salads

Cooked, chilled vegetables in almost any assortment may be dressed with French dressing or mayonnaise and served as a salad; some of these are described among the vegetable hors-d'oeuvre.

Raw vegetables, too, make interesting salads; they should be young and tender, and shredded or cut thin and small for easy mastication. So far as we know the only raw young vegetable that is not eligible for salad-making is the potato, and there are those who include even this in their raw-vegetable mixtures. All leafy greens are candidates for the salad bowl; and this includes, in addition to the usual lettuces, cress, endive, escarole, and other such acknowledged salad greens, the young leaves of chard and spinach, beet tops, and dandelion.

Elegant Aftermaths

In the epicurean kitchen yesterday's provender comes to an elegant end in croquettes, turnovers, crêpes, fritters, and soufflés. These recipes take well and naturally to substitutions and changes.

Almost any leftover food finds a happy home in the croquette. Prepare the croquette mixture as indicated in the individual recipe. Spread the mixture on a platter and chill thoroughly. Shape into small pear shapes, cones, balls, or cylinders and coat the shapes à l'anglaise, *that is, first with flour, then with a mixture of 1 egg beaten with 1/4 cup milk, 1 tablespoon oil, and 1/2 teaspoon salt, and finally with fine dry bread crumbs. Fry croquettes in hot deep fat (385° F.) a few at a time to a rich, crisp brown. Drain them on absorbent paper and garnish with parsley. Serve with a suitable sauce.*

Croquettes

Coating à l'Anglaise

MELT 1/4 cup butter in a saucepan, stir in 6 tablespoons flour, and cook, stirring, until the *roux* turns golden. Stir in gradually 1 1/2 cups hot milk and cook, stirring constantly, for 10 to 15 minutes, or until the sauce is smooth and very thick. Add 1/2 teaspoon salt and a little white pepper and stir in 2 egg yolks and 1 whole egg beaten with a little sauce. Makes 2 cups sauce.

Béchamel Sauce for Croquettes

511

Lobster Croquettes COMBINE 2 cups finely diced cooked lobster, 6 cooked mushrooms, finely diced, 1 tablespoon chopped truffles, and 2 cups hot béchamel sauce for croquettes. Cook, stirring, until the mixture rolls away from the sides of the pan without sticking. Correct the seasoning with salt and spread the mixture on a flat buttered dish to cool. Shape as desired, coat *à l'anglaise*, and fry in hot deep fat (385° F.) until golden brown. Serve on béchamel sauce for fish with a little tomato sauce streaked through it.

Fish Croquettes FOLLOW the recipe for lobster croquettes, substituting cooked fish, such as haddock, sole, or cod, without the skin or bones, for the lobster.

Tuna Croquettes TO 1 cup béchamel sauce for croquettes add 2 cups minced cooked tuna, 1 tablespoon each of chopped parsley and onion, and salt and cayenne to taste. Cook over low heat for 10 minutes, stirring occasionally. Beat 1 egg lightly with 2 tablespoons heavy cream and stir it into the croquette mixture. Cook, stirring, for 1 minute, remove the pan from the heat, and add 1 teaspoon lemon juice.

Cool the mixture in a buttered shallow dish and shape it into croquettes. Roll them in fine bread crumbs, in 1 egg lightly beaten with 2 tablespoons water, and again in bread crumbs. Fry the croquettes in hot deep fat (385° F.), and serve them with any fish sauce.

Puerto Rican Chicken Croquettes MIX 1 cup each of finely chopped cooked chicken and veal with 1/3 cup chopped coconut, and season the mixture with salt, pepper, and a generous pinch each of curry powder and mace. Add 1 cup béchamel sauce for croquettes, blend the paste thoroughly, and spread it on a cold platter to chill.

Shape cylindrical croquettes, dip them in egg beaten with a little Cognac, roll them in soft bread crumbs mixed with an equal amount of chopped blanched almonds, and plunge them into hot deep fat (385° F.) for a minute or two, until they are well browned. Fry only a few at a time. Drain the croquettes and serve them around a mound of fluffy rice, with a sauceboat of curry sauce.

Chicken Croquettes COMBINE 2 cups finely diced cooked chicken, 6 cooked mushrooms, finely diced, and 2 cups hot béchamel sauce for croquettes. Cook, stirring, until the mixture rolls away from the sides of the pan without sticking. Correct the seasoning with salt and spread the mixture on a flat buttered dish to cool. Shape the croquettes, coat *à l'anglaise*, and fry them in hot deep fat (385° F.)

Lobster Croquettes

until golden brown. Cooked sweetbreads may be substituted for half the chicken, or a few tablespoons of finely chopped truffles or cooked ham may be added.

Turkey and Chestnut Croquettes

MELT 2 tablespoons butter in a saucepan, stir in 2 tablespoons flour, and add gradually, while stirring, 1/2 cup hot chicken stock. Continue to stir until the sauce is thickened and smooth. Add 1/2 cup heavy cream, 2 cups ground cooked turkey meat, 1 cup cooked and riced chestnuts, 1 teaspoon lemon juice, 1 tablespoon finely chopped parsley, and salt and pepper to taste. Mix well, remove the sauce from the heat to cool slightly, and stir in the lightly beaten yolks of 3 eggs. Chill the mixture, shape the croquettes, coat them *à l'anglaise*, and fry them in hot deep fat (385° F.). Serve with *sauce suprême* or turkey gravy.

Sweetbread Croquettes

COMBINE 3 pairs cooked sweetbreads, cut into small cubes, with 2 cups béchamel sauce for croquettes. Add 2 tablespoons finely chopped shallots, 1 tablespoon finely chopped parsley, and salt, pepper, and cayenne to taste. Chill the mixture, shape it, coat the shapes *à l'anglaise*, and fry them in hot deep fat (385° F.). Serve with butter caper sauce.

Beef Croquettes

TO 2 cups ground cooked beef add 1 tablespoon chopped parsley and salt and pepper to taste. Melt 3 tablespoons butter in a saucepan. Stir in 3 tablespoons flour, and add gradually 3/4 cup stock. Cook the mixture, stirring until it is smooth and thickened, and add the beef mixture and 1/2 cup chopped mushrooms. Cook slowly for about 20 minutes until it is very thick. Correct the seasoning, cool a little, and stir in the lightly beaten yolks of 2 eggs. Spread the mixture in a shallow pan and chill. Shape the croquettes, coat them *à l'anglaise*, and fry them in hot deep fat (385° F.). Arrange them on a hot serving dish, garnish with mushroom caps sautéed in butter, and serve with *sauce smitane*.

Game Croquettes

DICE finely enough cooked game to make 2 cups. Add 6 cooked mushrooms, finely chopped, and 2 to 3 tablespoons chopped truffles. Reduce 1 1/2 cups Madeira sauce until it is very thick and mix with the other ingredients. Cool, shape the mixture into croquettes, coat the croquettes *à l'anglaise*, and fry. Serve with Madeira sauce.

MELT 1/4 cup butter in a saucepan, stir in 5 tablespoons flour, and add gradually 1 1/2 cups hot milk. Continue to stir until the sauce is smooth and thick. Stir in 1/4 cup heavy cream and 1/2 pound Swiss cheese, diced. Stir the mixture until the cheese is melted, remove from the heat, let it cool a little, correct the seasoning, and stir in 3 well-beaten egg yolks. Pour the mixture into a buttered shallow pan and chill it.

Swiss Cheese Croquettes

Shape the croquettes, coat them *à l'anglaise*, and fry them in hot deep fat (385° F.). Serve with tomato sauce.

COMBINE 12 hard-cooked eggs, finely chopped, with 1 cup béchamel sauce for croquettes, the beaten yolks of 2 eggs, 2 tablespoons finely chopped parsley, 1 teaspoon salt, and a little pepper. Chill the mixture, shape the croquettes, coat them *à l'anglaise*, and fry them in hot deep fat (385° F.). Garnish with parsley fried in the same fat and serve with Hungarian sauce.

Egg Croquettes

COMBINE 2 cups finely chopped assorted cooked vegetables with 1 cup béchamel sauce for croquettes. Cool the mixture, shape the croquettes, coat them *à l'anglaise*, and fry them in hot deep fat (385° F.) until they are golden brown.

Croquettes Printanière

Call them turnovers, call them piroshki, *call them patties or pasties or* empanadas; *— these pretty packages supplement soup or salad at a simple meal. In* petit *versions, they appear on the hot hors-d'oeuvre tray; in king size, they make an ample all-in-one-entrée.*

The pastry for these fancies may be pie dough, or puff paste—scraps and trimmings will do—or biscuit dough. Roll any of these thin for the happiest result.

COMBINE 1 1/2 cups ground cooked chicken, 1 tablespoon each of finely chopped parsley and chives, 6 slices of crisp crumbled bacon, and just enough sour cream to bind. Taste for seasoning and add salt and pepper to taste. Put a tablespoon of this filling on each 4-inch round of pie dough. Fold the dough in half over the filling and seal the edges securely. Prick well with the tines of a fork and bake the turnovers in a hot oven (400° F.) for about 15 minutes, or until nicely browned.

Chicken Turnovers

Veal and Ham Patties   ROLL out puff paste 1/8 inch thick and cut it into twelve 4-inch rounds. Combine 1 cup each of finely diced cooked ham and veal, 1 onion, chopped, the grated rind of 1 lemon, a good pinch of mace, and salt and pepper to taste. Stir in 1 cup béchamel sauce. Place 2 to 3 tablespoons of the filling in the center of half the rounds. Moisten the edges of the dough, place another round on top of the filling, and seal the edges securely. Bake the patties in a hot oven (400° F.) for about 15 minutes, or until the paste is puffed and golden.

Turkey Turnovers Rouennaise   COMBINE 1 1/2 cups chopped cooked turkey meat and 1 tablespoon each of finely chopped parsley, chives, onion, and green pepper. Stir in 1/2 cup turkey gravy and 2 tablespoons Sherry. Roll out pie dough 1/8 inch thick and cut it into 4-inch squares. Put a tablespoon of the filling on each square, fold the dough over the filling into triangles, and seal the edges securely. Brush the dough with 1 egg yolk lightly beaten with 2 tablespoons cream and bake the turnovers in a hot oven (400° F.) for about 15 minutes, or until the pastry is golden.

Minced Ham Turnovers   COMBINE 2 cups ground cooked ham, 1 small onion, ground, and freshly ground pepper to taste. Stir in 1 cup rich cream sauce. Roll out flaky pie dough 1/8 inch thick on a lightly floured board and cut it into circles or squares. Place 1 tablespoon of the filling in the center of each triangle, fold the dough in half over the filling, and seal the edges. Brush the turnovers with beaten egg and bake them in a hot oven (400° F.) for 15 minutes, or until the pastry is golden.

Lamb Turnovers   COMBINE 2 cups finely chopped leftover lamb, 1 onion, chopped, 1 tablespoon each of finely chopped green pepper and parsley, a pinch of celery salt, and salt and pepper to taste. Add just enough chili sauce to bind the filling and stir in a dash of Worcestershire. Roll out pie dough 1/8 inch thick and cut it into 4-inch rounds. Place a heaping tablespoon of the filling on each round. Fold the dough in half over the filling, seal the edges securely, and bake the turnovers in a hot oven (400° F.) for about 15 minutes, or until the pastry is golden.

Cornish Pasties   COMBINE 1 pound chopped round steak, 1 cup raw finely diced potatoes, 1 1/4 cups chopped onions, and salt and pepper to taste.
     Roll out flaky pie dough 1/8 inch thick and cut it into 5-inch rounds.

Place 2 or 3 tablespoons of the filling on each round, sprinkle each filling with 1 tablespoon finely chopped parsley, and dot with butter. Moisten the edges of the dough, fold the dough in half over the filling, and crimp the edges securely. Prick the tops of the turnovers with the tines of a fork, brush with beaten egg, and bake them in a hot oven (400° F.) for 10 minutes, lower the temperature to moderately slow (325° F.), and bake the pasties for 50 minutes longer. About 15 minutes before the pasties are done, make a small incision in the tops and pour 2 tablespoons heavy cream through a small funnel into each pasty.

Beef Pasty

MIX well 2 pounds ground lean raw beef and 3 strips of bacon, ground, with 1/4 cup tomato ketchup, 2 tablespoons each of grated onion and finely chopped parsley, 1 small garlic clove, finely chopped, 2 tablespoons Worcestershire sauce, a pinch each of powdered mace, clove, thyme, and bay leaf, and salt and pepper to taste. Form the meat into 12 small cylindrical loaves. Cut a sheet of flaky pie dough rolled out 1/4 inch thick into twelve 4-inch squares. Brush each square lightly with prepared mustard and wrap the dough around the meat. Moisten the edges of the dough with a little cold water and press them together. Brush the dough with egg yolk beaten with a little milk, and bake the pasties on a lightly oiled baking sheet in a very hot oven (450° F.) for 5 minutes. Lower the temperature to moderate (350° F.) and bake for 25 to 35 minutes, or to taste, until the crust is delicately browned.

William IV's Ruffs

MASH enough freshly boiled potatoes to measure 1 cup. Stir in 1 cup flour and 2 well-beaten eggs and enough cream to make a soft dough. Cut 1 pound sirloin steak into thin slices and sprinkle the slices generously with salt and pepper. On a lightly floured board roll out the potato dough 1/4 inch thick and cut it into 3-inch rounds. Place a piece of steak on each round and sprinkle it with a little grated onion and freshly ground black pepper. Brush the edges of the dough with water, fold in half, and crimp the edges deeply. Fry the ruffs in hot deep fat (370° F.) until golden and drain on absorbent paper.

Empanadas

GRIND coarsely 1 cup each of lean beef and pork and 1/2 cup ham, a small pimiento, and 2 tablespoons shelled almonds. Mix the meat with 3 tablespoons each of seedless raisins and sliced olives and 1 tablespoon capers. Sprinkle it with salt and pepper and lightly with Worcestershire sauce, and add a few drops of Tabasco. Stir in just enough melted butter to make a spreadable mixture. Roll out pie dough and cut out 8-inch squares. On one half of each, spread a liberal scoop of the meat mixture, fold the other half over, and seal the edges. Bake the *empanadas* in a moderate oven (350° F.) for 25 to 35 minutes, or until they are golden brown.

Empanadas de Orno SAUTÉ 3 onions and 1 green pepper, both chopped, in 3 tablespoons butter until the onion is golden. Add 1 pound ground beef and continue to sauté for 10 minutes. Add 1 cup cooked corn, 1/2 cup each of pitted ripe olives and raisins, and salt and pepper to taste.

Roll out pie dough 1/8 inch thick and cut it into rounds 3 inches in diameter. Place 1 tablespoon of the filling on each round and lay a slice of hard-cooked egg on the filling. Fold the rounds in half and pinch the edges together securely. Sprinkle the top of the *empanadas* with brown sugar and bake them in a hot oven (400° F.) for about 20 minutes, or until the pastry is lightly browned.

Calzoni DISSOLVE 1 package granular yeast or 1 cake compressed yeast in 1 cup water at temperature given on page 573. Sift 4 1/2 cups flour onto a pastry board, add the yeast and 2 tablespoons oil, 1 teaspoon salt, and a little pepper. Knead the dough thoroughly, cover it with a cloth and let it rise in a warm place for 2 hours, or until it doubles in bulk.

Separate the dough into 6 parts and roll it out lightly, or stretch it by hand into circles 1/4 inch thick. Brush each circle with oil, using about 1/4 cup in all. Slice thinly 1/2 pound Mozzarella cheese, and mix it with 1/4 pound *prosciutto* and 1/8 pound salami, both cut in slivers, 1/8 teaspoon salt, and 1/4 teaspoon pepper. Spread the dough with this mixture, moisten the edges, fold into half circles, and seal the edges with the floured tines of a fork. Brush the *calzoni* with oil and bake in a hot oven (400° F.) for about 20 minutes or until they are golden brown. Serve hot with tomato sauce and grated Romano cheese.

Ground Steak Pirog DISSOLVE 1 package granular yeast or 1 cake compressed yeast in 1 cup milk at temperature given on page 573. Stir in 1 cup flour and let the sponge stand in a warm place for about 1 hour, or until it is foamy. Add 1 teaspoon salt, 2 teaspoons sugar, 3 eggs, lightly beaten, and 1/2 cup butter, melted and cooled, and stir in about 4 cups flour, or enough to make a dough that does not stick to the hands. Turn the dough out on a lightly floured board and knead until it is smooth and elastic. Put the dough in a bowl, brush it with melted butter, and let rise in a warm place, lightly covered, for about 3 hours, or until double in bulk.

Sauté 1 onion, finely chopped, in 1/4 cup butter until the onion is transparent. Add 3 tablespoons butter and 1 pound of ground round steak and continue to sauté, stirring, until the meat is brown. Sprinkle the meat with salt and pepper, stir in 1/4 cup each of meat gravy and finely chopped parsley, and cool. Stir in 2 hard-cooked eggs, chopped.

Punch down the dough and roll it out on a well-floured heavy cloth into a rectangle about 24 by 15 inches. Spread the filling in the center of the dough, leaving a 4-inch border on all sides. Moisten the edges of the dough, bring the long sides of the dough to the center of the *pirog*, and pinch the edges together firmly over the filling. Then bring the two short sides to the center and seal securely. Put a buttered and floured baking sheet alongside the *pirog* and roll the *pirog* onto the baking sheet by raising the cloth so that the folded edges of the *pirog* will be underneath. Cut 3 or 4 slits in the dough for the steam to escape and let the *pirog* rise in a warm place for 30 minutes. Brush the *pirog* with egg yolk beaten with a little cold water and bake in a hot oven (400° F.) for 15 minutes. Reduce the temperature to moderate (350° F.) and bake the *pirog* for 20 to 30 minutes longer, or until it is well browned.

REMOVE the stems from 2 pounds mushrooms and reserve them for another use. Slice the caps thinly and put them in a saucepan with 1/4 cup butter, 1 teaspoon lemon juice, and 2 tablespoons chopped parsley. Simmer the mushrooms, covered, for 10 minutes. Add 6 scallions, finely chopped, 3/4 cup sour cream, and salt and pepper and simmer for 10 minutes longer. Mix 1 tablespoon each of flour and butter to a smooth paste, stir it into the mushroom mixture, and cook, stirring constantly, until the sauce is smooth and thick. Cool.

*Mushroom
Pirog*

Sift 2 cups flour into a bowl with 1 teaspoon salt and 2 teaspoons baking powder. With the fingertips or a pastry blender quickly work in 1/2 cup butter, or 1/4 cup each of vegetable shortening and butter. Beat 1 egg lightly and combine it with enough water to measure 1/2 cup. Stir the liquid into the flour mixture, adding a little more water if necessary to make a soft dough. Turn the dough out on a lightly floured board.

Roll out half the dough into a circle 1/4 inch thick and line a 9-inch pie plate. Spread half the mushroom filling over the dough, cover the filling with 4 hard-cooked eggs, chopped, and cover the eggs with the remaining filling. Roll out the rest of the dough into a circle 1/4 inch thick and cover the filling. Trim and pinch the edges of the dough securely together. Cut a slit in the top for the steam to escape, decorate with leaves cut from the scraps of dough, and chill. Brush the *pirog* with an egg yolk beaten with a little water and bake in a hot oven (425° F.) for 10 to 15 minutes, reduce the temperature to moderate, and bake for 10 to 15 minutes longer, or until the crust is golden.

Calf's Liver Pirog SAUTÉ 1 pound sliced calf's liver with 1 onion, chopped, in 2 tablespoons butter until the liver is golden brown on both sides. Cut the cooked liver into chunks and put it through the finest blade of a food chopper. Slice 1/2 pound mushroom caps and sauté them in 2 tablespoons butter until lightly brown and tender. Mix the liver and mushrooms with salt and pepper to taste, 2 hard-cooked eggs, chopped, and 2 tablespoons chopped parsley. Blend the filling gently and moisten it with 1/2 cup chicken stock or Madeira.

Roll out biscuit dough on a lightly floured board into a rectangle about 24 by 15 inches and spread the filling in the center of the dough, leaving a 4-inch border on all sides. Moisten the edges of the dough and bring the long sides of the dough to the center of the *pirog* and pinch them together firmly. Then bring the short sides to the center and pinch them together in a neat ridge. Pinch together the edges of the dough from the center to each corner. Lift the *pirog* gingerly with two spatulas and transfer it to a buttered and floured baking sheet. Cut two slits in the top and brush the *pirog* with egg yolk beaten with a little water. Bake in a hot oven (400° F.) for 15 minutes, reduce the temperature to moderate (350° F.), and bake for 10 to 15 minutes longer, or until the crust is golden.

Carrot Piroshki CHOP finely 12 cooked carrots and sauté them in 1/4 cup butter for about 4 minutes. Add 1/4 cup sour cream and cool. Stir in salt and pepper to taste, 2 tablespoons finely chopped parsley, and 3 hard-cooked eggs, chopped.

Roll out biscuit dough or rich pie dough 1/4 inch thick and cut it into rounds about 4 inches in diameter. Place 1 1/2 tablespoons of the carrot filling in the center of each round, moisten the edges of the rounds, and pinch the dough together in a neat ridge along the center of the *piroshki.*

Transfer the *piroshki* to a buttered and floured baking sheet and bake them in a hot oven (400° F.) for about 15 minutes, or until the crust is golden.

MIX 5 cups shredded cabbage with 2 tablespoons salt and let it stand for 15 minutes. Put it in a colander, pour boiling water over it, and drain thoroughly.

Sauté 2 onions, finely chopped, in 1/4 cup butter. Add the cabbage, cover tightly, and braise for 20 minutes. Stir in 2 tablespoons minced parsley and 2 hard-cooked eggs, chopped, and cool the mixture.

Use this filling as in the recipe for carrot *piroshki*.

SIMMER 1 pound fish filets in salted water for about 8 minutes, or until the flesh flakes easily, cool it, and flake it. Sauté 1 onion, finely chopped, in 2 tablespoons butter until the onion is transparent, but not brown. Stir the onion into the flaked fish with salt and pepper to taste. Add 1 hard-cooked egg, chopped, and mix lightly but well. Use this mixture as a filling for *piroshki*.

For the ingenious cook, pancakes are a never failing resource; they appear at any meal and at any course. The filled crêpes which follow make a most acceptable luncheon or supper dish—and, incidentally, offer delightful accomodation for leftovers—and in suitably diminished portions, serve admirably as hors-d'oeuvre at luncheon or at dinner.

The crêpes for dessert will be found in another chapter, along with some less ethereal, if no less delicious, pancakes.

SIFT together 1 cup flour, 1/2 teaspoon salt, and 1 teaspoon sugar and add gradually 2 beaten eggs and 1 3/4 cups milk. Stir the mixture to make a smooth batter the consistency of heavy cream and strain it through a fine sieve. Let the batter stand for 2 hours before cooking the crêpes.

Brush a 5- to 6-inch seasoned hot skillet with melted butter. Pour a generous tablespoon of batter into the pan and tip the pan to coat it with a thin layer of batter. When the crêpe is brown on the bottom, turn it and brown the other side. Or the crêpes may be cooked on one side only and rolled around the filling, cooked side in, and the outside browned in butter just before serving.

Crêpes
de Fruits de Mer

Melt 1/4 cup butter in a flat pan and remove the pan from the heat. To the butter add 2 shallots, finely chopped, 1 teaspoon each of parsley and chervil, finely chopped, a pinch of tarragon, 12 mushrooms, sliced, and salt and pepper. Lay on the vegetables 1 pound assorted fish filets (salmon, snapper, striped bass, whitefish, halibut, sole) cut into small pieces. Pour over the fish 3/4 cup Champagne and 1/4 cup fish stock. Add a pinch of cayenne pepper and cover the pan with a buttered paper. Bake the fish in a moderately hot oven (375° F.) for about 15 minutes, and just before it is cooked, add 1/4 cup cooked lobster meat cut in small pieces. Return the pan to the oven and continue cooking until the fish flakes readily with a fork. Remove the fish from the pan to a heated dish.

Reduce the broth over high heat by two-thirds and add 3 tablespoons heavy cream. Let the sauce boil for 2 minutes, remove it from the heat, stir in 1/4 cup hollandaise, and correct the seasoning. Reserve 1/2 cup of the sauce and mix the rest with the fish.

Spread half the reserved sauce on the bottom of an ovenproof serving dish. Fill 12 prepared crêpes with the fish mixture, roll them up and arrange them on the dish. Garnish each crêpe with 1 sautéed mushroom cap and 1 cooked shrimp. Cover the crêpes with the rest of the sauce and a little hollandaise, and glaze them quickly under the broiler.

Crêpes Louise

Sauté 6 shallots, finely chopped, in 3 tablespoons butter and add 1/2 pound picked-over crab meat. Add 2 beaten egg yolks and 1 tablespoon Madeira to 1 cup béchamel sauce. Reserve 1/4 cup of the sauce and add the crab meat and shallot mixture to the remaining sauce along with 1 tablespoon finely chopped chives.

Spread 12 prepared crêpes, made with a dash each of nutmeg and pepper, with the crab meat filling, roll them and arrange them on a buttered earthenware platter. Fold 3 tablespoons whipped cream into the reserved sauce and mask the pancakes with it. Glaze them under the broiler for about 2 minutes and serve very hot.

Crêpes Niçoise

Combine 1 cup each of ground lean veal and ground pork, 1/4 cup finely chopped shallots, 1 tablespoon minced parsley, a dash of cayenne, and salt and pepper to taste. Sauté this in 2 tablespoons butter over moderate heat for about 20 minutes, or until it begins to take on color, stirring constantly from the bottom of the pan. Stir in 3/4 cup heavy cream. Knead together 1 tablespoon each of butter and flour and add to the mixture, bit by bit.

Crêpes de Fruits de Mer

Continue to cook over low heat until the mixture is well blended and thick, stirring constantly.

Make 12 crêpes for luncheon in the usual way. Place 1 heaping table-spoon of the meat stuffing in the center of each pancake, roll the crêpes, and arrange them side by side in a shallow baking dish.

Poach 1 cup thinly sliced mushrooms for 10 minutes in the juice of 1 lemon and just enough water to cover. Add the drained mushrooms to 2 cups béchamel sauce and pour the mushroom sauce over the filled crêpes. Sprinkle generously with grated Parmesan or Swiss cheese and brown under the broiler.

Crêpes de Volaille Versaillaise   Melt 5 tablespoons butter in a saucepan. Stir in 5 tablespoons flour and cook the *roux* until it is lightly browned. Stir in gradually 1 cup each of hot milk and hot chicken broth and continue to stir until the sauce is smooth and thickened. Cook it over low heat for about 25 minutes, stirring occasionally.

Sauté 1/4 cup chopped mushrooms in 1 tablespoon butter until they are lightly browned. Add 3 shallots, chopped, and cook for another minute. Combine this mixture with 2 cups diced cooked chicken meat, 3 tablespoons Sherry, and three-fourths of the sauce. To the remaining sauce, add 1 egg yolk beaten with 1/4 cup warmed heavy cream, stir over low heat for 2 minutes without boiling, and set aside.

Make 12 crêpes—adding a dash of nutmeg and pepper to the batter—browned on both sides. Spread them with the chicken filling, roll them, and arrange on a buttered earthenware platter. Fold 2 tablespoons whipped cream into the reserved sauce and mask the pancakes with it. Glaze them under the broiler for about 2 minutes and serve very hot, garnished with buttered green beans or asparagus tips.

Crêpes Polonais   Work into a smooth paste 2/3 cup each of grated Emmenthaler, or Swiss cheese, and soft butter. Season the mixture to taste with salt, pepper, and nutmeg and stir in 1 egg, lightly beaten. Divide the mixture into portions about the size of marbles and enclose each portion in a very thin pancake, or crêpe. Roll the crêpes in beaten egg and in fine bread crumbs, and fry them, a few at a time, in hot deep fat (375° F.). Drain on absorbent paper, sprinkle lightly with salt, and garnish with fried parsley.

Rissoles   Mix 2 cups cooked veal or pork, ground or minced, with 1/2 cup minced mushrooms, sautéed until lightly browned in 2 tablespoons butter.

Brown to a light golden color 1/2 cup flour in a heavy frying pan or skillet. Stir in 1/4 cup melted butter and add gradually 2 cups hot beef stock, stirring constantly. Season the sauce lightly with salt to taste, 1/4 teaspoon freshly ground black pepper, 1/2 teaspoon nutmeg, and 1 teaspoon onion juice and continue to stir until the sauce is smooth and thickened. Add the meat and mushroom mixture and blend the sauce thoroughly.

Prepare a pancake batter as follows: Melt 1 1/2 teaspoons butter, cool it, and stir it into 3 well-beaten egg yolks. Sift together 6 tablespoons flour, 1/4 teaspoon salt, and 1 teaspoon sugar and beat them into the egg mixture. Add gradually 3/4 cup milk and, lastly, fold in 3 stiffly beaten egg whites.

Bake 12 very thin pancakes about 7 inches in diameter. Fill them with the meat mixture and roll them up, tucking in the ends. Dip the *rissoles* in 2 beaten eggs, roll in fine, dry bread crumbs, and arrange them side by side in a buttered baking dish. Bake them in a hot oven (400° F.) for about 15 minutes, or until they are brown and crisp, basting frequently with a mixture of 2 tablespoons water and 1 tablespoon melted butter.

Fritter batters are used in two ways: leftover meat, fish, or vegetables may be minced and folded into the batter, or larger slices of food may be coated with the batter one by one. The basic procedure for fritters is our concern here, and two batters for entrée fritters are given below, with examples of their use to serve as a pattern. Fritters should fry in hot deep fat at 390° F., the temperature at which a bread cube will brown in forty seconds.

SIFT into a bowl 1 cup flour and a pinch of salt. Add gradually 1 egg yolk beaten with 3/4 cup lukewarm water and 1 tablespoon oil. Mix quickly and lightly and put the batter in a warm place for 3 to 4 hours. Fold in the white of 1 egg, beaten until stiff, just before using.

Fritter Batter for Meat and Vegetables

SIFT 1/2 cup flour, a pinch of salt, and 1 tablespoon sugar into a bowl and stir in enough white wine to make a batter the consistency of heavy cream. Stir in 1 tablespoon melted butter and let the batter rest for 1 hour. When ready to use, fold in 2 egg whites, stiffly beaten.

Wine Batter for Fritters

IN a bowl combine 1/2 cup sifted flour, 1 egg, and 1 egg yolk. Stir in 3 tablespoons milk, 1 tablespoon melted butter, and 1/4 teaspoon salt. Beat the mixture with a rotary beater until it is smooth. Add 3 tablespoons milk

Parsley Fritters

Ham Fritters

and 1 teaspoon baking powder and mix thoroughly. Fold in 1 egg white, stiffly beaten, and chill the batter for 30 minutes. Beat the batter before using.

Wash and dry thoroughly 24 sprigs of curly parsley with long stems. Hold each sprig by the stem, dredge it with flour, then dip it in the batter. Shake off any excess batter, as the sprigs should be thinly coated. Dip the sprigs, one or two at a time, in hot deep fat (370° F.). Drain the fritters on absorbent paper and sprinkle them with salt.

Sprigs of watercress may be used in place of parsley.

To the basic fritter batter add 1 cup ground ham, 1 tablespoon each of chopped green pepper and pimiento, and freshly ground black pepper to taste. Drop the mixture by tablespoons into hot deep fat (390° F.) and brown the fritters on both sides. Drain well on absorbent paper and serve with any desired sauce. *Ham Fritters*

Cut leftover cooked veal into squares and marinate it for about 1 hour in a mixture of 2 tablespoons olive oil, a few drops of vinegar, 1 tablespoon chopped parsley, and a little salt and pepper. Turn the pieces occasionally. Drain the squares and dip them in fritter batter. Brown the fritters in hot deep fat (390° F.), drain them on absorbent paper, and serve with fried parsley, lemon wedges, and tomato sauce. *Veal Fritters*

The soufflé, for all its aura of glamor and luxury, often is, in actuality, yet another thrifty means of using up the remains of yesterday's meals.

To the basic recipe given below, add 1 cup finely chopped, puréed cooked food and the appropriate seasonings; the enterprising cook can thus achieve an endless variety of soufflés.

Melt 3 tablespoons butter and stir in 3 tablespoons flour. Add slowly 1 cup milk or light cream and cook the sauce, stirring constantly, until it is thick and smooth. Do not let it boil. Fold in 1 cup puréed cooked vegetables, grated cheese, or finely chopped cooked meat, fish or fowl, and seasonings to taste. Stir in 4 well-beaten egg yolks. Beat 5 egg whites until they are stiff. Fold into the batter thoroughly and completely one-fourth of the egg whites. Fold in the remaining egg whites, cutting them in lightly and carefully by raising and folding the batter over and over. Pour the batter into a buttered and floured straight-sided soufflé dish. Bake the soufflé in a moderate oven (350° F.) for 25 to 30 minutes, until it is well puffed and lightly browned. Serve at once. *Entrée Soufflé*

Cheese and Eggs

There is no dessert so dear to the heart of the sophisticated gourmet as cheese. Meltingly ripe Camembert with a sweetly succulent pear; a crumbling morsel of Roquefort with a tart-fleshed apple; a few grapes and a biscuit spread with fresh, sweet cream cheese—any of these is a fitting finale to a splendid meal, and has the further grace of justifying yet another glass of wine! A famous dessert is the heart made of fresh cottage cheese and cream, the *coeur à la crème*. And there are, of course, the numerous cheesecakes and the desserts that follow herewith.

Ricotta Condita IN a bowl combine 1 pound ricotta cheese and 1/2 cup milk and beat until the mixture is smooth and creamy. Gradually beat in 2 1/2 tablespoons fine granulated sugar and 3 tablespoons rum, turn the mixture into a serving bowl or individual custard cups, and chill. Just before serving, sprinkle the dessert lightly with grated semisweet chocolate.

Ricotta Croquettes CRUSH 1/2 pound macaroons and press the crumbs through a fine sieve. Add to the crumbs 1 pound ricotta cheese, 2 eggs, lightly beaten, and a dash of cinnamon, and mix well. Shape the mixture into small balls, dip into beaten egg, and roll in bread crumbs. Sauté in butter until golden on all sides.

BEAT 1/4 cup flour, 2 scant tablespoons sugar, and 2 beaten eggs into 1/2 pound ricotta. Stir in the grated rind of 1/2 lemon, 2 tablespoons brandy, and a pinch of salt. Let the mixture stand for 1 hour or longer before frying. This will make the batter thicker so it will hold its shape when dropped into the hot oil.

Put a fritter the size and shape of a walnut in the bowl of a long-handled spoon and hold the spoon in the hot oil for 10 seconds, or until a crust forms on the fritter. Withdraw the spoon gently and put in another *frittella*. Sprinkle the *fritelle* with confectioners' sugar and serve piping hot.

Frittelle di Ricotta

ITALIAN CHEESE FRITTERS

PUT 1/2 pound ricotta cheese through a sieve and mix it thoroughly with 1/2 cup sugar. Blend into the cheese and sugar 2 egg yolks, and add 3 whole eggs, one at a time, beating constantly. Into this mixture stir 1/4 teaspoon each of salt, cinnamon, and nutmeg, and the grated rind of a small lemon. Pour the pudding into a 1-quart buttered mold, lightly sprinkled with bread crumbs, place the mold in a pan of water, and bake the pudding in a moderately slow oven (325° F.) for 1 hour.

Roman Cheese Pudding

SOFTEN 6 ounces cream cheese, add 3/4 cup sour cream, and beat until smooth. Stir in 2 tablespoons honey, a pinch of salt, and the beaten yolks of 3 eggs. Fold in 4 egg whites, stiffly beaten, and turn the mixture into a buttered baking dish. Bake in a moderate oven (350° F.) for 35 minutes and serve immediately with heavy cream and strawberries or raspberries, sweetened to taste.

Cream Cheese Soufflé

SOAK a whole Camembert overnight in enough dry white wine just to cover. Next day scrape off any discolored portion of the crust and mash the cheese with 1/2 cup soft sweet butter until the mixture is smooth. Chill and re-form the cheese into its original shape. Cover the top and sides with finely chopped toasted almonds and chill again. Remove the Camembert from the refrigerator about 30 minutes before serving and serve as a dessert with hot toasted crackers.

Soused Camembert

PRESS 1/2 pound Roquefort cheese through a fine sieve. Add gradually 1/2 cup light cream and mix thoroughly. Stir the cheese and cream mixture in the top of a double boiler over hot water until it becomes smooth. Remove from the heat, chill, and beat in 1 cup heavy sweet cream. Turn the mousse into a shallow mold or refrigerator tray and freeze it for about 4 hours, or

Roquefort Cheese Mousse

until the mousse is firm. Unmold the mousse on a chilled serving dish and surround it with rounds of toast.

Cheese, bread, and beer or wine make the classic impromptu meal, but the sturdy native virtues of cheese are equally valuable in cookery.

Swiss Fondue   RUB the inside of an earthenware casserole with a garlic clove. Place the pot in the bottom pan of the chafing dish, adding just enough water to the pan to protect the bottom.

Heat 1/2 bottle dry white wine in the casserole and add 1 pound Swiss cheese, grated or cubed. Heat the mixture, stirring constantly until the cheese is melted and well blended with the wine. Care should be taken to keep the bottom of the chafing dish pan covered with water during the entire process. Stir into the cheese 3 tablespoons flour mixed to a paste with a little cold water. Season with a pinch of nutmeg and salt and pepper to taste. Add 1/4 cup kirsch.

The fondue is eaten directly from the earthenware casserole, which should be kept warm over low heat. Should the fondue thicken too much, stir in a little more kirsch. The guests spear pieces of bread with their forks and dip them into the fondue.

Fondue   IN an earthenware casserole protected from direct contact with the heat
Chez Soi   by an asbestos pad, melt 2 tablespoons butter and add 2 cups cottage cheese. Cook the cheese very slowly in the butter, stirring constantly, until the fondue is creamy. Serve with cubes of bread to be dipped into the fondue.

Fondue   REMOVE the crusts from 8 slices of white bread and spread the slices with
en Casserole   butter, using about 3 tablespoons butter for all the slices. Arrange the bread in a buttered casserole alternately with 8 thin slices of sharp Cheddar cheese. Beat 3 eggs, add 1 teaspoon Worcestershire sauce, 1/2 teaspoon dry mustard, a little freshly ground pepper, and 1 1/2 cups beer. Pour the egg mixture over the bread and cheese in the casserole and bake in a moderate oven (350° F.) for 40 minutes. Sprinkle on top 1/4 pound bacon, diced and sautéed until golden and crisp.

IN a saucepan or the pan of a chafing dish placed over simmering water melt 1 tablespoon butter. Add 1 pound grated Swiss or Cheddar cheese and gradually, as the cheese melts, stir in with a wooden spoon 3/4 cup stale beer. Combine 1 tablespoon beer with a dash of cayenne, 1 tablespoon dry mustard, 1/4 teaspoon salt, and 1 teaspoon Worcestershire sauce and when the cheese is melted and smooth, stir in this mixture. Add 1 egg and stir rapidly until the egg is well combined with the cheese. Serve at once on hot buttered toast triangles.

Welsh Rabbit

MELT 3 tablespoons butter in the top pan of a chafing dish over low heat. Add 1 small onion, finely chopped, and 1/2 green pepper, chopped, and sauté until the onions are transparent. Place the blazer over hot water. Add 2 tablespoons flour and blend well. Gradually add 1 cup milk, stirring constantly until thick and smooth. Stir in 2 cups grated American cheese and, when it is melted, add 1 1/2 cups stewed or canned tomatoes, 1/2 teaspoon salt, and red pepper to taste. Continue to cook the mixture for about 10 minutes, stirring frequently. Stir in 2 well-beaten egg yolks and continue to stir for about 2 or 3 minutes. Serve the rabbit hot on freshly made toast in individual heated dishes.

Mexican Rabbit

SOAK 1 cup bread crumbs in 1 cup milk for 15 minutes. Place the top pan of the chafing dish over hot water, melt 2 tablespoons butter, and add 2 cups Cheddar cheese cut in small pieces. When it is melted, add the soaked bread crumbs, 1 well-beaten egg, and salt and pepper to taste. Stir the mixture constantly for 2 or 3 minutes and keep it hot over the hot-water pan. Serve hot on toasted crackers or English muffins.

English Monkey

IN the bottom of 6 individual buttered ramekins place a slice of toast, trimmed and cut into two triangles. Beat 4 egg yolks with 1 1/2 cups cream until well blended. Stir in 1 1/2 cups grated Swiss cheese, 1/8 teaspoon nutmeg, and a pinch of salt and fold in 4 egg whites, stiffly beaten. Pour the mixture into the prepared ramekins and bake in a moderately hot oven (375° F.) for about 30 minutes, or until the cheese is melted and the tops are golden brown.

Cheese Ramekins

SAUTÉ 2 garlic cloves in 1/4 cup olive oil for 1 minute and turn garlic and oil into a baking dish. Coat the bottom and sides of the dish well with the oil and cover the bottom with slices of sharp Cheddar. Beat 3

Cheddar Custard

531

eggs with 1 tablespoon rice or potato flour and stir in 1 1/2 cups milk and 1/2 cup heavy cream. Pour the mixture over the cheese and bake in a moderately hot oven (375° F.) for 15 minutes. Sprinkle with grated Parmesan and continue to bake for about 5 minutes longer, or until the custard is set. Serves 4.

Petites Tartes Danoises WITH a pastry blender, cut 3 ounces cream cheese, 5 tablespoons crumbled Danish blue cheese, and 1 tablespoon butter into 1 cup flour and press the crumbs together to make a dough. Chill the dough thoroughly, roll it out as thinly as possible, and cut it into fluted rounds. Line tiny tartlet pans with the rounds, prick the dough with a fork, and fill with dried beans or rice. Bake the tart shells on a baking sheet in a moderate oven (350° F.) for about 10 minutes, or until the dough is set but not browned. Discard the beans and cool the shells.

Sauté 3 or 4 minced scallions in 2 tablespoons butter and put a little in each shell. Crumble a little Danish blue cheese in each. Beat 3 eggs lightly, stir in 1 1/2 cups cream and a pinch each of salt and pepper, and fill the shells with this mixture. Bake the *petites tartes* in a moderately hot oven (375° F.) for about 10 minutes, or until the custard is set and the shells are browned. Serve the tarts hot.

Gruyère Tarts LINE tart pans with flaky pie dough. Dredge 1/2 pound grated imported Gruyère or Swiss cheese with 1 tablespoon flour and half fill each of the tart shells with the mixture. Beat 3 eggs well with 1 cup each of light cream and milk and season the mixture to taste with salt, pepper, and grated nutmeg. Pour the custard over the cheese and bake the tarts in a hot oven (400° F.) for 10 to 15 minutes. When they puff and brown slightly, reduce the temperature to moderate (350° F.) and bake them for about 10 minutes longer, or until the filling is set.

Cheddar Pie LINE a 9-inch pie pan with rich tart dough. Flute the edge and brush the bottom with beaten egg. Bake the shell in a very hot oven (450° F.) for about 10 minutes, or until the dough is set but is not browned. Sauté 12 slices of bacon slowly until crisp, drain on absorbent paper, and crumble the bacon into the pastry shell. Cover the bacon with 1 cup sliced ripe olives and top the olives with 1 cup grated Cheddar cheese. Scald 1 cup heavy cream, stir in 2 eggs, lightly beaten, 1/2 teaspoon salt, and a little freshly ground pepper, and pour the mixture into the pie crust. Bake in a moderate oven (350° F.) for about 30 minutes, or until the custard is set and the crust browned. Serve hot or cold.

BEAT 2 cups creamy cottage cheese until it is smooth and press it through a fine sieve. Add 1/4 cup sour cream, 2 1/2 cups hot mashed potatoes, and 1/2 teaspoon salt, and mix well. Line the bottom and sides of a 10-inch pie plate with pie dough and fill the plate with the cheese and potato mixture. Brush the top with a little milk and dot with small pieces of soft butter. Bake the pie in a moderate oven (350° F.) for about 45 minutes, or until the shell and filling are golden brown, and serve warm.

Cottage Cheese Potato Pie

IN a saucepan melt 3 tablespoons butter, remove the pan from the heat, and stir in 3 tablespoons flour. Cook, stirring, for 2 minutes, then stir in gradually 1 cup hot milk. Cook over low heat for 5 minutes, stirring constantly, until the sauce is smooth and thickened. Add 1/2 wheel, or about 1 cup, Camembert, finely diced, and cook, stirring, until the Camembert is almost melted. Remove the sauce from the heat and stir in 4 egg yolks, lightly beaten with a pinch each of salt and cayenne. Cool. Carefully fold in 6 egg whites, stiffly beaten, and turn the mixture into a buttered soufflé dish. Bake in a moderate oven (350° F.) for 35 to 40 minutes. Wrap a folded napkin around the soufflé dish, sprinkle the top of the soufflé with paprika, and serve immediately. Serves 3 or 4.

Camembert Soufflé

MELT 1/4 cup sweet butter in a saucepan, stir in 1/2 cup flour, and cook the *roux* until it starts to turn golden. Add 2 cups hot milk, stirring well with a whip, return the sauce to the heat, and cook it, stirring constantly, for about 5 minutes, or until it is very thick. Add 1/2 teaspoon salt, a little pepper, and a little nutmeg, and remove the pan from the heat. Beat 5 egg yolks until light, combine them with the sauce, and heat the mixture just to the boiling point, stirring briskly. Do not allow it to boil. Remove the pan from the heat and stir in 1 cup grated Parmesan cheese. Beat 5 or 6 egg whites until they are stiff but not dry. Fold into the mixture thoroughly and carefully one-fourth of the beaten egg whites and add the remaining egg whites, cutting them in lightly and completely by raising and folding the mixture over and over. Pour the batter into 2 small soufflé dishes, buttered and floured, and bake the soufflés in a moderate oven

Parmesan Soufflé

(350° F.) for 25 to 30 minutes, or until they are puffed and lightly browned. If desired, very thin diamond-shaped slices of Swiss cheese can be arranged in a circle on the soufflé. As the soufflé bakes, they will melt and form a decorative design in the crusty surface.

Cheese and Olive Roll　CREAM together 1/2 pound each of blue cheese and cream cheese and 1/4 cup butter. Stir in 1 tablespoon each of minced chives and brandy and 1/2 cup minced ripe olives. Form the mixture into a roll, cover with chopped toasted almonds, and chill. Slice and serve with toasted crackers on a plate garnished with watercress.

Salade de Fromage　CHOP 6 hard-cooked eggs very finely and combine them with 1/2 pound finely diced Swiss cheese. Stir in 1/2 cup sour cream, 1 1/2 teaspoons dry mustard, 1 teaspoon grated horseradish, a pinch of ground cuminseed, and 1/2 teaspoon each of salt and freshly ground black pepper. Arrange individual servings on beds of crisp romaine or watercress garnished with cherry tomatoes.

Délices d'Emmenthal　MELT 1/4 cup butter over low heat, add 6 tablespoons flour, and stir until the *roux* is golden. Stir in 1 1/2 cups hot milk and cook, stirring constantly, until the sauce is smooth and very thick. Cook the sauce for about 10 minutes and season it with salt and pepper. Add 1/2 pound grated Swiss cheese and stir until the cheese is melted. Stir in 3 egg yolks, well beaten, and continue to cook, stirring, for 3 minutes, being careful not to let the mixture boil. Spread the mixture in a well-buttered shallow dish about 6 by 9 inches and cool. Cover with wax paper and chill the mixture for 2 hours, or until needed.

Cut the cream into 18 equal portions and form each portion into a croquette. Roll the croquettes in flour and then into 2 eggs, beaten with 2 tablespoons milk and 1 tablespoon olive oil. Drain the croquettes on paper and roll them in fine bread crumbs. Fry the croquettes in hot deep fat (380° F.) for 1 to 1 1/2 minutes, or until golden. Drain the *délices d'Emmenthal* on absorbent paper and serve them with tomato sauce or stewed tomatoes.

SCRAPE the rind from a whole Camembert and press the cheese through a fine sieve. Add soft butter in the amount of one-third the weight of the cheese, 2 tablespoons flour, and 1 tablespoon potato or rice flour and mix well. Stir in 1/2 cup milk, season with a little cayenne pepper, and stir the mixture over very low heat until it has the consistency of very thick cream. Turn the cream onto a plate to cool.

Délices Printanières

Form the cream into small cork shapes and roll them in flour. Dip in beaten egg, roll in fine, dry bread crumbs, and fry in hot deep fat (380° F.) until golden brown.

To 3/4 pound grated or finely chopped Mozzarella cheese add 1 1/2 tablespoons flour, 2 small eggs, lightly beaten, and 1/2 teaspoon salt and mix until well blended. Shape the mixture into small croquettes, roll them in flour or fine dry bread crumbs, and fry a few at a time in hot deep fat (370° F.) until golden brown. Drain the *nocette* on absorbent paper and serve hot.

Nocette di Mozzarella
MOZZARELLA CROQUETTES

CUT 3/4 pound Mozzarella into 3-inch squares, 1 inch thick. Roll the squares in flour, dip them in beaten egg, in bread crumbs, again into egg, and once more in bread crumbs. Fry the squares in hot deep fat (375° F.) for about 2 minutes, or until the crumbs turn golden. Drain on absorbent paper and serve hot with tomato sauce.

Fried Mozzarella

CUT slices of bread into rounds with a large cookie cutter and cover each round with a slice of Mozzarella cut the same size as the bread. Roll bread and cheese in flour, dip into beaten egg, and brown on both sides in hot oil to cover until golden. Serve very hot.

Mozzarella in Carrozza

CUT the crusts from thin slices of bread and spread each slice with grated Swiss cheese mixed to a paste with heavy cream. Put a thin slice of ham between each two slices of bread, dip the sandwiches in beaten egg, and fry them in hot butter until golden brown on both sides. Serve with a cream sauce flavored with grated Swiss cheese.

Croque Monsieur

BUTTER a slice of white bread and cover it with lean baked ham and chicken. Butter a second slice on both sides, place it on the meat, and cover it with thinly sliced Swiss cheese. Butter a third slice and place it, butter down, over the cheese. Trim the crusts and cut the sandwich in two. Secure the sandwich

Monte Cristo Sandwich

Mozzarella Loaf

with picks, dip it in beaten egg, and fry in butter on all sides until golden brown. Remove the wooden picks and serve with currant jelly, strawberry jam, or cranberry sauce.

SLICE a small loaf of unsliced Italian or French bread almost but not quite through at half-inch intervals. Place thin slices of Mozzarella cheese between the slices and brush the loaf generously with soft butter. Put the loaf on a baking sheet, arrange thin strips of anchovy filets on top, and sprinkle with orégano. Bake in a very hot oven (450° F.) for about 10 minutes, or until the cheese melts and bubbles and the bread is golden.

Mozzarella Loaf

REMOVE all but the bottom crust from a loaf of unsliced bread. Cut the loaf lengthwise through the center to within 1/2 inch of the bottom, then slice crosswise at 1/2 inch intervals down to, but not through, the bottom crust. Spread all surfaces generously with soft butter and sprinkle with grated Parmesan cheese. Bake on a cookie sheet in a moderate oven (350° F.) for about 10 minutes, or until the loaf is browned.

Toasted Cheese Bread

Eggs are probably the most versatile of all our foods. They fit into every menu, into every hour of the day, into almost every known cookbook category. We have arbitrarily abstracted from this chapter those recipes that are primarily for hors-d'oeuvre or for desserts. The egg dishes that follow are suitable for breakfast, luncheon, and supper; this does not mean to say many of them, in discreetly smaller portions, will not be equally welcome as a first course at dinner.

SIMMER eggs in water at the simmering point for 10 to 12 minutes, turning them four or five times to set the yolk at center—an important refinement when the eggs are to be stuffed. Cool them by plunging them at once into cold water. This prevents the formation of a greenish ring around the yolks.

Hard-Cooked Eggs

MELT 1/2 cup butter in a saucepan and in it sauté 1 large onion, minced, until it is golden, stirring occasionally. Stir in 1 tablespoon curry mixed with 2 tablespoons flour and add slowly 1 1/2 cups hot chicken stock, stirring constantly. Continue to stir until the sauce is smooth and thickened. Correct

Curried Eggs

537

the seasoning, stir in 1/2 cup heavy cream, and add 12 hard-cooked eggs, cut in half. Heat together over boiling water, basting the eggs occasionally with the sauce. Serve with fluffy rice and chutney.

Stuffed Curried Eggs   SIMMER 12 eggs for 10 minutes, cool them under cold running water, and peel immediately. Slice the eggs in half lengthwise and mash the yolks with 1/2 cup mayonnaise and 1 tablespoon each of curry powder, soy sauce, minced onion, and parsley. Season with salt, freshly ground black pepper, and cayenne. Stuff the eggs with the yolk mixture, put the halves together again, and let them stand for several hours in the refrigerator.

Arrange the stuffed eggs in a shallow, well-buttered casserole and cover them with 4 cups hot rich cream sauce. Bake the eggs in a moderate oven (350° F.) for 15 to 20 minutes, or until the sauce is bubbling.

Stuffed Eggs in Tomato Cream Sauce   CUT in half lengthwise 12 hard-cooked eggs. Mash the yolks with 3 table-spoons butter, 6 tablespoons concentrated tomato purée, 1 teaspoon salt, and a dash of pepper. Stuff the egg whites, arrange them in a shallow buttered casserole, and put the casserole in a moderate oven (350° F.) until the eggs are heated through but not browned. Combine 1 cup concentrated tomato purée with 2 cups hot béchamel sauce and coat the eggs with this mixture. Sprinkle with 1 hard-cooked egg, chopped, and with parsley and chervil.

Eggs Venice   SAUTÉ 2 onions, chopped, in 3 tablespoons butter until they are soft and golden. Stir in 1 1/2 tablespoons flour and add gradually, stirring constantly, 1 1/2 cups hot milk. Continue to stir until the sauce is smooth and slightly thickened. Add 6 hard-cooked eggs, chopped, 1 tablespoon minced parsley, a drop or so of Tabasco, to taste, 1/2 teaspoon paprika, 1 tablespoon lemon juice, and salt and pepper to taste. Cook the mixture over boiling water for 15 minutes. Just before serving, stir in 2 egg yolks lightly beaten with a little of the hot sauce.

Cut 12 slices of fresh tomato about 3/4 inch thick. Roll them in flour and brown them quickly in 3 tablespoons hot butter. They should be quite firm. Brown 12 rounds of bread, cut the same size as the tomato slices, in another 3 tablespoons butter.

Place 2 of these croutons on each individual serving dish, lay a slice of fried tomato on each, and top generously with the egg mixture. Serve with a tossed green salad.

CUT in half lengthwise 12 hard-cooked eggs. Mash the yolks with 2 teaspoons prepared mustard, 1/2 cup béchamel sauce, and salt to taste. Stuff the egg whites and press the halves together. Put two stuffed eggs into each of 6 individual buttered casseroles and cover them with Mornay sauce, using 3 cups in all. Sprinkle with grated Parmesan cheese and brown under the broiler. Sprinkle with paprika and serve very hot.

Hot Deviled Eggs

ADD 1 tablespoon vinegar and 1 teaspoon salt to 1 quart boiling water in a shallow pan. Break one egg at a time and slip it gently onto the surface of the water. Simmer the eggs over low heat for 3 minutes, or until the whites are barely firm. Remove the eggs from the water with a perforated spoon and trim the whites evenly.

Poached Eggs

MASH 12 washed anchovy filets and combine them with 1/4 cup butter and a few drops of lemon juice. Use this anchovy paste to butter 12 toasted croutons. Place a poached egg on each crouton and make a cross on each egg with 2 anchovy filets. Serve 2 eggs for each portion.

Poached Eggs on Anchovy Toast

SAUTÉ very large mushroom caps in butter until they are tender. Put each cap, top down, on a round crouton slightly larger than the mushroom and in each mushroom place a freshly poached egg. Sprinkle with finely chopped parsley and serve with the following Chateaubriand sauce: Simmer 1/2 cup dry white wine with 1 shallot, finely chopped, until the wine is slightly reduced. Add 2 tablespoons *glace de viande*, 1 tablespoon butter, 1 teaspoon finely chopped tarragon, a pinch of cayenne, and a dash of lemon juice.

Poached Eggs with Mushroom Caps
Chateaubriand Sauce

CUT a slice from the top of 6 fresh tomatoes and hollow them slightly. Arrange the tomatoes on a baking sheet, dot them with butter, sprinkle with a little salt, and put them in the oven for about 8 minutes. The tomatoes should be cooked through but not mushy. Transfer the tomatoes to a warm serving plate and sprinkle them with crumbled crisp bacon. Cover each tomato with a poached egg and a little tomato sauce.

Poached Eggs à la Bayard

POUND 1 cup cooked diced chicken meat with a pestle to a smooth paste. Gradually beat in 1/4 cup cream, or enough to make a soft filling. Season the filling with salt and cayenne to taste and rub it through a fine sieve. Line 6 baked unsweetened tart shells with a little of the chicken purée.

Oeufs Royale
EGGS ROYALE

Lightly poach 6 eggs. Trim the eggs neatly, slip one into each tartlet, and cover the egg with more of the purée, shaping it into a dome in the center. Sprinkle with fresh bread crumbs mixed with a little grated cheese, place a star cut from a slice of truffle in the center, and dot with butter. Bake the tartlets in a moderate oven (350° F.) for 5 minutes, until the topping browns lightly.

Oeufs Pochés
Béatrice
POACHED EGGS
BEATRICE

PLACE poached eggs on rounds of toast, cover them with Mornay sauce to which sliced cooked mushrooms have been added, sprinkle with grated Parmesan cheese, and brown under the broiler. Garnish alternate rounds of toast with asparagus tips and with tomato sauce.

Oeufs Pochés
Encore
POACHED EGGS
ENCORE

IN a patty shell put 1 tablespoon picked-over crab meat heated in cream. Cover the crab meat with a lightly poached egg and spread the egg with a little Mornay sauce. Sprinkle with grated Parmesan and brown quickly under the broiler. Garnish with a thin slice of truffle.

Oeufs
Beaugency
EGGS BEAUGENCY

ARRANGE poached eggs on large cooked artichoke hearts, mask them with *sauce béarnaise*, and top each with a slice of beef marrow that has been poached for 3 minutes in salted water.

Poached Eggs
Grand Duke

ARRANGE poached eggs on round croutons of sautéed bread in a circle on a serving dish. Cover the eggs with Mornay sauce and grate a little Parmesan cheese over the yolks. Put the dish under the broiler for a minute to melt the cheese. Garnish the dish with little bouquets of cooked asparagus tips dipped in melted butter. In the center of the ring, pile sautéed mushrooms and truffles, cut in julienne strips and bound with a little *demi-glace*.

Poached Eggs
Parmentier

CUT large baked Idaho potatoes in half lengthwise. Scoop out of each half a well just large enough to hold a poached egg, reserving the scooped out pulp. Pour a little melted butter into each well and sprinkle with grated cheese and with diced crisp bacon. Put a well-drained poached egg into each potato case. Sprinkle with salt and pepper and with fine bread crumbs and dot with butter. Mash the reserved potato pulp, season to taste, and whip it until light and fluffy with a small quantity of hot cream. Use a pastry tube to pipe a border of this whipped potato around the egg. Put the potatoes under the broiler for a few moments to brown and serve at once.

In an individual *plat* or casserole melt 1 teaspoon butter. Break in 2 eggs, sprinkle with a little salt but no pepper, and cook over low heat for 1 minute. Drip 1 teaspoon melted butter over each yolk and cook in a moderate oven (350° F.) until the whites are set. Do not overcook. The whites must be creamy and soft and the yolks liquid with just a transparant white film, *au miroir*, over them.

Oeufs au Miroir or *Sur le Plat*
SHIRRED EGGS

In an individual *plat* or casserole melt 1 teaspoon butter. Break in 2 eggs, sprinkle with a little salt, and cook over low heat for 1 minute. Pour 1/4 cup hot heavy cream over the eggs and finish cooking in a moderate oven (350° F.).

Oeufs à la Crème
EGGS SHIRRED
IN CREAM

When eggs shirred in cream are garnished with cooked asparagus tips heated in butter, the name of the dish becomes *oeufs Argenteuil*.

Oeufs Argenteuil

Sauté 2 slices of bacon and drain the crisp strips on absorbent paper. Pour 1 tablespoon of the bacon fat into an individual *plat* or casserole. Break in 2 eggs, sprinkle with a little salt, and cook over low heat for 1 minute. Tip the dish and spoon the hot bacon fat over the egg yolks. Finish cooking in a moderate oven (350° F.) and garnish the plate with the bacon strips and tomato slices sautéed in butter.

Oeufs à l'Anglaise
SHIRRED EGGS
ENGLISH STYLE

In an individual *plat* or casserole melt 1 teaspoon butter. Break in 2 eggs, and cook over low heat for 1 minute. Cover each egg with a thin slice of Gruyère, pour over this 1/4 cup hot heavy cream, and bake in a moderate oven (350° F.) until the eggs are set and the cheese is melted.

Oeufs Gruyère
GRUYÈRE EGGS

Garnish shirred eggs with cooked lobster meat and truffles, cut in dice, and surround with a ring of Newburg sauce.

Shirred Eggs Victoria

Cook eggs *sur le plat*. Garnish the plate with tiny grilled sausages and surround the eggs with tomato sauce.

Eggs Bercy

Eggs
à l'Andalouse

COOK eggs in olive oil instead of butter in a *plat* rubbed with a cut garlic clove. Garnish with a mixture of chopped tomatoes and diced sweet peppers cooked in olive oil until tender.

Eggs
à la Chaville

COOK eggs in a *plat* or casserole lined with chopped mushrooms sautéed in butter. Surround the cooked eggs with stewed tomatoes and sprinkle with chopped tarragon.

Oeufs
Archiduc
EGGS ARCHDUKE

COOK eggs in a *plat* or casserole lined with chopped onion cooked until tender in butter and seasoned with paprika. Garnish with sliced truffle warmed in butter and surround the eggs with *sauce suprême* flavored to taste with paprika.

Oeufs
à la Florentine
SHIRRED EGGS
FLORENTINE

LINE an individual *plat* or casserole with chopped spinach cooked until tender in butter. Break 2 eggs on the spinach and mask them with Mornay sauce. Sprinkle with grated Parmesan and melted butter and bake in a moderate oven (350° F.) until the eggs are set and the sauce is lightly browned.

Shirred Eggs
Grand Duke

MASK 2 eggs in a buttered *plat* or casserole with Mornay sauce. Sprinkle with grated cheese and melted butter and bake in a moderate oven (350° F.) until the eggs are set. Garnish the plate with diced truffle and asparagus tips heated in a little melted butter.

Oeufs Bibesco
SHIRRED EGGS
BIBESCO

ARRANGE 3 thin slices of tongue in a buttered ramekin. Break 2 eggs into the ramekin and bake in a moderate oven (350° F.) for 10 to 12 minutes, or until the whites are set. Garnish each egg with a ring of *Périgueux* sauce.

Oeufs Opéra
EGGS OPERA

GARNISH one side of a ramekin containing shirred eggs with sautéed chicken livers in Madeira sauce, the other side with cooked asparagus tips.

BREAK 2 eggs into a buttered ramekin and bake in a moderate oven (350° F.). Take the eggs from the oven just before the whites are set and pour over them 1 tablespoon butter which has been seasoned with a dash of vinegar and cooked until dark brown. The hot butter will finish cooking the eggs. Garnish with 1/2 teaspoon capers.

Oeufs au Beurre Noir
SHIRRED EGGS IN BLACK BUTTER

GARNISH shirred eggs with a broiled sausage link, a sautéed chicken liver, a strip of broiled bacon, and a broiled tomato half.

Shirred Eggs Américaine

GARNISH 2 shirred eggs with 3 shrimps, diced and sautéed in butter. Finish with a ring of Nantua sauce and a slice of truffle for each yolk.

Shirred Eggs Nantua

IN a saucepan heat 3 tablespoons olive oil and add 1 large onion, sliced, 1 large green pepper, sliced, and 1 garlic clove, crushed. Cook the vegetables gently for 3 minutes. Blend in 1 tablespoon flour and add 3 1/2 cups peeled, diced, and sautéed tomatoes. Cook, stirring, for a few minutes, and season the sauce with salt, pepper, and chili powder, and add cuminseed orégano to taste. Cook the mixture for 5 minutes longer, discard the garlic, and pour the sauce into a shallow baking dish.

Break 6 eggs into the dish and with a teaspoon make a depression under each egg so that it will slip down into the sauce. Dot the sauce between the eggs with cubes of sharp Cheddar cheese and pitted black olives. Bake the mixture in a moderate oven (350° F.) for about 12 minutes, or until the eggs are set.

Huevos Rancheros
RANCH STYLE EGGS MEXICAN

MIX 2/3 cup ground raw beef with 2 tablespoons butter and spread the mixture over the bottom of a baking dish. Sprinkle with 2 tablespoons finely chopped onion, and season with salt and pepper. Break 6 eggs over the mixture, sprinkle them with 1/4 cup sour cream, and bake them in a moderately hot oven (375° F.) until they are set. Sprinkle with 2 tablespoons finely chopped parsley and serve immediately.

Oeufs Tartare

MIX 1/4 pound cooked ham, chopped, with 3/4 cup grated Parmesan cheese. Butter 6 custard cups, break 1 egg into each, season to taste, and cover with the ham and cheese mixture. Set the cups in boiling water and bake the eggs in a moderately hot oven (375° F.) for 10 minutes. Turn them out on heated plates and serve immediately with warm hollandaise sauce.

Baked Eggs with Hollandaise

543

Baked Ham and Eggs COMBINE 6 tablespoons ground ham with 2 tablespoons minced parsley and a little pepper. Butter generously 6 muffin tins and pat onto the sides and the bottom of each tin some of the ham-parsley mixture, reserving about a third for topping. Break an egg into each prepared tin, sprinkle with the reserved ham-parsley mixture, and dot with butter. Bake in a moderate oven (350° F.) for about 12 minutes, or until the eggs are set.

Spanish Eggs SAUTÉ 3 large onions and 3 green peppers, chopped, in 1/2 cup olive oil. Add 3 large tomatoes, peeled and chopped, and cook gently until the tomato is soft. Season the sauce with salt, pepper, and a little chili powder. Put a little of this sauce into each of 6 individual baking dishes, and on it arrange 6 shelled shrimps, cooked for 5 minutes in salted water, and 1 *chorizo*, or Spanish garlic sausage, parboiled for 5 minutes. Break 2 eggs into each dish. Bake the eggs in a moderate oven (350° F.) for about 12 minutes, until the whites are just set. Serve with hot garlic bread and a green salad.

Eggs en Croûte REMOVE the crust from a large loaf of unsliced sandwich bread and cut in into 6 thick slices. Scoop out the inside of each slice with a sharp knife, leaving a 1/2-inch shell. Spread the shells inside and out with soft butter and place them on a buttered cookie sheet. Fill with creamed chicken and break an egg on top of each. Dot the eggs with butter and bake in a moderate oven (350° F.) for about 12 minutes, or until the whites are set. Dust with paprika.

Baked Eggs Provençale FOR each person cut off the top of 1 large, ripe tomato. Scoop out the pulp and place the shells in a well-buttered baking dish. Sprinkle with salt and pepper and put in the center of each 1 teaspoon finely chopped parsley and 1/2 garlic clove. Bake the tomatoes in a moderate oven (350° F.) for 6 minutes. Discard the pieces of garlic and break an egg into each shell. Dot with butter and return to the oven to bake for another 10 minutes, or until the eggs are set. Remove the dish from the oven, sprinkle the eggs with grated Parmesan, and brown quickly under the broiler.

Swiss Eggs CUT 6 thin slices of bread into large circles and brown them in butter on one side only. Arrange the croutons, browned side up, in a buttered baking dish. Sprinkle them with salt and pepper and place on each a thin round of Swiss cheese. Break an egg on the cheese and sprinkle the eggs

Spanish Eggs

with 2 tablespoons grated Swiss cheese. Pour 1/2 cup heavy cream around the eggs and bake them in a moderate oven (350° F.) for about 12 minutes or until the cheese is melted and the eggs are set.

Fromage Vaudois
EGGS AND GRUYÈRE

CUT 1 1/2 pounds Gruyère into slices 1/2 inch thick and dip the slices into fritter batter. In a large skillet melt 1/4 cup butter and in the butter sauté the cheese slices to a golden brown on both sides, turning them only once with a spatula. Arrange the slices in a long baking dish and pour over them 8 eggs lightly beaten with a little salt and pepper. Bake the eggs in a moderately hot oven (375° F.) for about 12 minutes, or until they are cooked and puffed. Sprinkle the top with finely chopped parsley and serve immediately.

Oeufs Brouillés
SCRAMBLED EGGS

BREAK 6 eggs into a bowl and beat them until the whites and yolks are well mixed, but not too foamy. Melt and heat well 1 1/2 tablespoons butter in a skillet or in the top of a double boiler and add the eggs. Cook, stirring constantly, over low heat or over hot water and, as the eggs begin to set, add 1 tablespoon butter and 2 tablespoons cream. Correct the seasoning with salt and white pepper. Serves 3.

Scrambled Eggs à la Reine

FILL a heated patty shell with a layer of scrambled eggs, a layer of creamed chicken, and a final layer of scrambled eggs. Garnish with a slice of truffle.

Scrambled Eggs Princesse

GARNISH scrambled eggs with asparagus tips and slices of truffle.

Scrambled Eggs Magda

GARNISH scrambled eggs with tomato sauce and sprinkle them with finely chopped parsley and grated Parmesan cheese.

Chafing Dish Eggs with Artichokes

CUBE 3 cooked artichoke bottoms and toss them in the top pan of a chafing dish with 1/4 cup butter and 1 garlic clove, split. When the butter melts, discard the garlic and add 6 eggs, lightly beaten and seasoned with salt and pepper. Cook, stirring constantly, until the eggs just begin to set, add

2 tablespoons cream and 1 tablespoon butter and cook for a moment longer. Serve on hot buttered toast spread with anchovy paste. Serves 3.

MELT 3 tablespoons butter in a skillet and in it sauté lightly 2 cups cooked ham cut into small dice.

Beat 12 eggs lightly with a fork, season with pepper and a little salt, and pour them over the ham cubes. Lower the heat and cook, stirring constantly, until the eggs are barely set and are still soft and creamy. Stir in 2 teaspons chopped parsley and serve at once, with a sprinkling of paprika for color.

Ham Scramble

MELT 1/4 cup butter in a heavy skillet. Add 1 cup light cream, 1/2 teaspoon salt, and a little freshly ground pepper. Add 1 cup flaked crab meat and heat it through. Beat 12 eggs until well blended but not frothy. Pour the eggs into the skillet and stir gently until they thicken. Do not overcook. The mixture should be soft, moist, and creamy. Sprinkle with 2 tablespoons finely chopped parsley.

Scrambled Eggs with Crab Meat

BREAK 8 eggs into a bowl and add the juice from a small can of truffles. Beat the eggs lightly and season to taste with salt and white pepper.

Place the top pan of a chafing dish over boiling water and in it melt 3 tablespoons butter. Add the truffles, diced, season them with salt and white pepper, and cook gently for about 2 minutes, or until the truffles begin to release their aroma. Add the beaten eggs and stir them constantly until they are just firm enough to be taken up on a fork but are still soft and creamy. Stir in 2 tablespoons heavy cream and serve immediately on hot buttered toast. Serves 4.

Oeufs Brouillés aux Truffes
SCRAMBLED EGGS WITH TRUFFLES

IN the blazer of a chafing dish melt 2 tablespoons butter and add 1/2 cup heavy cream. When the cream is hot place the blazer over the dish containing hot water and add 1/2 pound Gruyère cheese, grated. Stir until the cheese is almost melted, then stir in 6 eggs, lightly beaten with 1/2 teaspoon salt. Cook, stirring constantly, until the eggs are softly scrambled. Stir in 2 tablespoons butter and 3 tablespoons dry Sherry and serve

Sherried Eggs with Gruyère

547

Scotch Woodcock

on toast covered with a slice or two of grilled Canadian back bacon. Serves 4.

MELT 6 tablespoons butter in the top pan or blazer of a chafing dish placed over boiling water. Add 8 egg yolks lightly beaten with 1 cup heavy cream and stir until the yolks and cream become a thick sauce. Spoon the sauce over triangles of hot toast buttered and spread with mashed anchovy filets. Sprinkle with freshly ground pepper and parsley. Serves 4.

SCRAMBLE 7 eggs and add to them 4 more eggs, lightly beaten. Add salt and cayenne to taste. Butter 6 individual molds and garnish them with a decorative pattern of mushroom slices. Fill the molds with the egg mixture and put them in a baking pan, with hot water reaching halfway up the sides of the molds. Bake in a moderate oven (350° F.) for about 15 minutes, until the eggs are set. Let the molds stand for a few minutes before turning them out on rounds of buttered toast. Cover them with purée of mushrooms and garnish with strips of pimiento. To make the mushroom purée, put 1/3 pound mushrooms through the finest blade of a food chopper, add 1 cup béchamel sauce, and stir the sauce over moderate heat for 15 minutes. Add 1/4 cup hot cream and salt, pepper, and nutmeg to taste. Stir in 2 tablespoons butter.

The basic omelet may be varied by the addition of almost anything that comes to hand: cooked vegetables, seafood, or smoked meats may be added to the beaten egg; creamed mixtures may be folded into the omelet before serving it. Various combinations of potatoes, ham and bacon, green pepper, onions, and tomatoes make a popular country-style omelet with universal appetite appeal. The omelet is a logical last hiding place for culinary odds and ends of many sorts. In a word, the omelet is very much in the service of an imaginative cook. See the omelets for dessert in the dessert chapter.

FOR each serving, mix 2 eggs lightly with a fork and add 1/2 teaspoon salt. Heat a 7- to 8-inch omelet pan over high heat and in it melt 1 teaspoon butter. The pan should be so hot that the butter sizzles at once, but not so hot that the butter browns. Immediately pour in the eggs and stir them briskly with a fork, shaking the pan constantly. When the fork makes a visible track through the eggs, the omelet is set. The omelet will set in a minute or less. Remove the pan from the heat.

If the omelet is to be served with a filling, put the filling in the center of the omelet at this point.

Gently raise the handle of the pan and let the omelet slide toward the opposite edge of the pan. Fold the edge nearest the handle over the center (or over the filling) with the aid of the fork. Hold the pan over a heated oval platter and turn it upside down to deposit the omelet on the dish. The omelet will be an oval with three folds. The whole procedure should take less time than it takes to describe. As each omelet is cooked, keep it warm in a very slow oven (200° F.) until the others are finished.

Omelette aux Champignons
MUSHROOM OMELET

SAUTÉ 1/2 cup chopped mushrooms in 1/4 cup butter for 2 minutes, stirring constantly. Stir the mushrooms and their juices into 4 beaten eggs and add 2 tablespoons milk. Make the omelet in the usual fashion.

Or, sprinkle 1/4 pound sliced mushrooms with 1 tablespoon brandy and let them marinate for 30 minutes. Add 1 tablespoon butter and stir over the heat for 5 minutes, until all the liquid has evaporated. Add 2 tablespoons cream and salt and pepper to taste, and heat well. Spread this mixture on the omelet before folding it.

Omelette aux Fines Herbes

To the beaten eggs add salt, pepper, and 1 tablespoon mixed herbs, finely chopped. Parsley, chervil, chives, and tarragon, in any combination, are suitable. Make the omelet in the usual way and pour over it just before serving 1 tablespoon melted butter mixed with 1 tablespoon mixed chopped herbs.

Omelette à la Reine

FILL an omelet with 3 tablespoons creamed chicken and fold it. Surround the omelet with a ribbon of béchamel sauce and garnish it with parsley or watercress.

Omelette aux Tomates
TOMATO OMELET

PEEL 3 ripe tomatoes, squeeze out the seeds, and chop the pulp rather coarsely. Cook the pulp in 3 tablespoons oil with 2 slices of onion, finely chopped, until the mixture thickens slightly. Add salt and pepper to taste and 1 tablespoon finely chopped parsley. Spread this mixture on a cooked omelet just before folding it.

FILL a cooked omelet with 3 tablespoons freshly cooked, well-drained spin-ach and fold it. Or fill it with 3 tablespoons creamed spinach purée.

Omelet Florentine

FILL a cooked omelet with asparagus tips, cooked until tender and dipped in melted butter.

Asparagus Omelet

FOR each serving broil or sauté a thin slice of ham and top the ham with an omelet made in the usual way, but not rolled. Slip it like a pancake onto the ham and sprinkle liberally with grated Cheddar cheese. Put the omelet under the broiler until the cheese is melted.

Omelette Savoyarde

MINCE finely 3 tablespoons richly flavored ham and stir it into the beaten eggs. Make the omelet in the usual fashion, but reduce the amount of salt to taste.

Or, heat the ground ham in a little butter, sprinkle it with a little flour, and stir in 1/4 cup cream. Cook, stirring, until the mixture thickens slightly, and spread the creamed ham in the center of the omelet just before folding it.

Ham Omelet

HEAT 1/3 cup lard or shortening in a skillet and in it sauté for 1/2 min-ute 1 scallion, trimmed and chopped, and 1 teaspoon minced fresh ginger. Add 1/2 pound crab meat and stir in 1 tablespoon dry Sherry and 2 well-beaten eggs. Sprinkle with salt and white pepper to taste and cook the omelet in the usual fashion. Serves 2.

Chinese Crab Meat Omelet

FOR each serving have ready 2 slices of bacon, fried until cooked but not crisp, and 3 oysters, heated in their own juices. Lay the bacon in the oiled top pan of a chafing dish, over direct low heat. Set the oysters on the bacon, and pour over all 2 eggs, slightly beaten and seasoned to taste. Cook without stirring until the eggs set. Turn the eggs out upside down onto a warm plate.

Hangtown Fry

PARBOIL 1/3 cup diced salt pork, bacon or ham, for a few minutes and drain it. Melt 1 tablespoon butter in an omelet pan, add the pork and

Omelette Paysanne

sauté it until it is brown. Remove the meat and reserve it. Sauté 3/4 cup potatoes, finely diced, in the same pan until they are cooked and golden brown. Return the meat to the pan. Add 6 lightly beaten eggs combined with 1 cup cooked sorrel, drained, 1 teaspoon each of finely chopped parsley and chervil, and 1/2 teaspoon salt.

Cook, stirring the eggs with a fork and moving the pan about with a circular motion. When the omelet begins to set around the edges, lift it and add 1 tablespoon butter to the pan. When the first faint odor of browning is evident, turn the omelet and brown it lightly on the other side. Slide it onto a heated platter and serve.

Finnan Haddie Omelet

SOAK 1/2 pound finnan haddie in 1/2 cup each of water and milk for about 2 hours. Simmer the fish gently in the same liquid until it flakes easily when tested with a fork. Drain it thoroughly and separate the fish into small flakes. Cook the smoked haddock in a small saucepan with 2 tablespoons each of cream and butter for several minutes. Remove it from the heat and let it cool.

Separate the yolks from the whites of 4 eggs. Beat the yolks with 1 tablespoon cream, a little salt, and pepper. Beat the egg whites until they hold a soft shape and fold them into the yolks along with the fish and 1 tablespoon grated Parmesan cheese.

Cook the omelet in the usual fashion and serve it unfolded on a heated platter. Garnish with watercress.

Shrimp Omelet Mirepoix

IN a saucepan in 1 1/2 tablespoons butter put 1/2 carrot, grated, 1 small onion, finely chopped, 1/2 small stalk of celery and the leaves, finely chopped, 1/2 teaspoon chopped parsley, 1 bay leaf, a pinch each of marjoram, thyme, salt, and pepper. Simmer the mixture for about 8 minutes.

Stir in 3 tablespoons tomato paste, 1/2 cup each of white wine and light stock or water, and 1 teaspoon brandy. Cover, and simmer the mixture for 15 to 20 minutes, or until it has reduced by one-third. Add 1 cup diced shrimps, cooked, shelled, and deveined.

Spread part of this sauce on the cooked omelet just before folding it. Serve the remaining sauce on top of the omelet.

Rice and Pasta

For much of the world, rice and pasta are basic foods, staple articles of diet that are literally the staff of life. It is our good fortune, in this land of plenty, that we enjoy rice and pasta freely, embellishing their honest simplicity with lavish saucing and spicing and additional ingredients *ad lib.*

Neither rice nor pasta should be overcooked. Pasta should be *al dente*, resistant to the teeth, and rice tender and dry.

Rijsttafel Rice

WASH 3 cups rice 6 to 8 times in cold and warm water alternately. Soak the rice for 15 minutes in cold water, then drain it. Add the rice to 4 1/2 cups cold water and bring it to a boil. Stir the rice once, cover the kettle tightly and turn the heat down as low as possible. Cook the rice for 20 minutes without removing the cover. Lift the cover and test the rice for firmness but do not stir it. If the rice is not sufficiently cooked, sprinkle a little hot water over it, replace the cover, and steam the rice for 3 to 5 minutes longer. Turn off the heat and let the kettle stand for 5 minutes. Serve the rice without stirring. It should be soft, but grainy and fluffy and entirely dry. The rice that adheres to the pot should be discarded. This rice is served with Indian and Javanese curries.

Rice Pilaff

MELT 1 tablespoon butter in a casserole and in it brown lightly 1 small onion, finely chopped. Add 1 cup uncooked rice and stir for a minute or two, until the grains of rice are coated with butter. Add 2 cups boiling chicken stock and 1 teaspoon salt and cover the casserole tightly. Bake the rice in a moderate oven (350° F.) about 30 minutes, or until the grains are tender, stirring it occasionally and adding a little chicken stock if necessary. Or cook the rice over direct heat, in a tightly covered pan, for about 25 minutes. Remove the rice to a serving dish, add 1 tablespoon butter, and toss with a fork to separate the grains.

*Pakistani
Pilaff*

MELT 1/2 pound butter in a deep pan fitted with a lid. Sauté 1 large onion and 2 garlic cloves, both finely chopped, until they are golden. Add these spices, tied in a cheesecloth bag: 12 black peppercorns, 12 cloves, 12 whole cardamoms, 2 sticks of cinnamon, each about 2 inches long, and 1/2 teaspoon whole allspice. Sauté the onions with the spices for 5 minutes, then remove the spice bag, add 1 pound well-washed long-grain white rice to the pan, and sauté the rice until it is golden. Add salt to taste and sufficient boiling water to cover the rice by about 2 inches. Add the spice bag and steam the rice until the water has evaporated and the rice is fluffy. Watch the rice carefully and occasionally toss it with a spatula to ensure each grain being cooked. When the rice is nearly done, discard the spice bag, add 1 cup sultanas (white raisins), and 1/2 cup blanched almonds that have been lightly sautéed in butter and salted. Heap the pilau on a hot platter and garnish it with toasted almonds, a few cloves, and finely chopped green onions.

*Brown
Rice Pilaff*

WASH 2 cups brown rice well and put it in a heavy pot with 4 cups consommé and salt to taste. Add a piece of fresh gingerroot the size of a walnut, bring the consommé to a boil, stir the rice once, and cover the pot tightly. Simmer the rice over very low heat for about 45 minutes, until it is just tender and the liquid is absorbed. Turn the rice into a heated serving dish and sprinkle it with 2 tablespoons minced scallions.

Risi e Bisi

PEAS AND RICE

HEAT 1/4 cup oil and 2 tablespoons butter in a heavy saucepan and in it sauté 3/4 cup chopped onions until they are very lightly browned. Mix in 1 1/2 cups well-washed long-grain rice and sauté it until it is translucent. Add 3 tablespoons dry Sherry and cook the mixture over low heat for 1 minute. Add 3 cups shelled fresh peas, 2 cups hot chicken broth, and salt and pepper. Cover the pan, bring the liquid to a boil, and cook the mixture over low heat for 10 minutes. Add 1 more cup hot chicken broth and cook the mixture, covered, for 10 minutes longer, or until the rice is dry and tender. Season to taste and mix in 1/4 cup grated Parmesan cheese and 2 tablespoons butter.

Soak 2 cups dried lentils for several hours and drain them. Brown a large onion on all sides in olive oil. Cook lentils, onion, and 1/2 cup rice in 6 cups salted water until the lentils are tender. Discard the onion, turn the rice and lentils into a serving dish, and top them with a little chopped onion sautéed until tender in oil.

Mujaddarah
ESAU'S POTTAGE

In a heavy skillet heat 3 tablespoons oil or fat. Add 3/4 cup finely diced roast pork, salt and pepper to taste, and 2 cups cold cooked rice. Cook the mixture over moderate heat, stirring constantly, for 5 minutes. Add 1 green pepper, seeded and finely chopped, and cook, stirring constantly, for 5 minutes. Sprinkle with 2 tablespoons soy sauce. Add 2 eggs, lightly beaten, and cook, stirring, for 5 minutes longer. Add 2 tablespoons finely chopped scallions and 2 medium tomatoes, peeled, seeded and chopped, and cook, stirring, for 1 minute more. Serves 2.

Sub Gum Chow Fon
CHINESE FRIED RICE

In a skillet heat a little peanut oil. Sauté 2 cups cold cooked rice in the fat until the rice is hot, stirring constantly with a fork to separate the grains. Add 2 scallions, coarsely chopped, salt, pepper, and 1/2 cup lobster meat, cut in small dice. Make a hole in the center of the rice and break in 3 eggs. Stir the eggs until they begin to set, then toss eggs and rice together. Stir in 2 tablespoons chopped parsley and 1 tablespoon soy sauce.

The rice may be quickly packed into a cup and unmolded for serving. Serves 2.

Lobster Fried Rice

Beat 2 whole eggs and 2 egg yolks lightly with 2/3 teaspoon salt and a dash of white pepper. Add 2 scallions, finely chopped, and continue beating until well combined.

Heat 3 tablespoons lard in a skillet. Add the egg mixture, cook, stirring, for just 2 minutes, and turn into a bowl.

In the same pan heat 1 tablespoon lard and in it sauté 4 cups cooked rice for 6 minutes. Add the scrambled eggs and mix well. Add 1 cup cooked diced pheasant or chicken meat, 1/4 cup seedless raisins soaked in boiling water for 20 minutes and drained, and 2 tablespoons each of diced ham and butter. Sauté the mixture over moderate heat for 3 minutes and serve at once. Serves 4.

Royal Pheasant and Rice
SAN CHI CHAO FAN

In a saucepan heat 2 tablespoons olive oil and in it sauté 1 garlic clove, minced, 1/3 cup chopped onions, and 2 tablespoons chopped green pepper until the onion is transparent and golden. Add 3 ripe tomatoes, peeled, seeded, and

Shrimp and Olive Jambalaya

chopped, 2 cups chicken stock, 3/4 cup washed rice, half a bay leaf, 1/2 teaspoon chili powder, 1/8 teaspoon each of cloves and thyme, 1 teaspoon salt, and a dash of cayenne. Cover closely and simmer for 20 minutes. Add 1 cup cleaned shrimps, 1/2 cup diced cooked ham, and 1 cup coarsely chopped ripe olives, cover, and cook for 10 minutes longer, or until the rice is tender and most of the liquid has been absorbed.

Nasi Goreng

FRIED RICE
WITH CHICKEN

CLEAN and wipe a plump 5-pound chicken. Rub the bird inside and out with lemon juice, truss it, and put it in a kettle with cold water to cover, 1 medium onion, 4 peppercorns, 2 leeks, 1 bay leaf, 2 sprigs of parsley and 2 teaspoons salt. Bring the liquid to a boil and cook the chicken over medium heat for 1 1/2 hours, or until tender. Remove the chicken from the kettle and strain and reserve the stock. Remove the meat from the chicken bones and slice it into strips. Wash 2 1/3 cups rice in several changes of water. Put 3 1/2 cups chicken stock in a deep saucepan with the rice and 1 teaspoon salt. Cover the saucepan and cook the rice over low heat for 20 minutes or until the rice is tender. Heat 1/3 cup peanut oil in a large skillet. Add 4 chopped onions and 2 garlic cloves, minced, and sauté the vegetables for 10 minutes, stirring frequently. Add the rice and cook it until it is brown, stirring frequently. Add the chicken slices, 1 1/2 cups cooked shrimps, 1 cup cooked crab meat, 1 cup cubed ham, 2 teaspoons ground coriander seeds, 1 teaspoon ground cumin-seeds, 1/4 teaspoon mace, 1/2 teaspoon ground dried hot red peppers and 1/4 cup peanut butter. Cook the mixture over low heat for 10 minutes, stirring gently.

Crayfish Risotto

IN a kettle combine 2 cups each of dry white wine and water, 1 carrot, 2 shallots, finely chopped, 1 large onion, 10 white peppercorns, 2 teaspoons salt, and *a bouquet garni* consisting of 3 sprays of parsley, 1 spray each of thyme and tarragon and 1 bay leaf, tied together with kitchen thread. Bring the court bouillon to a boil and simmer it for 15 minutes. Wash 2 dozen crayfish well and remove their intestinal tracts. Cook them for 5 minutes in the simmering court bouillon and transfer them to a heated dish to keep warm. Strain the court bouillon and reserve it.

In the top of a double boiler over direct heat sauté 3 tablespoons finely chopped onion in 2 tablespoons butter until the onion begins to brown. Add 1 cup long-grain rice and cook, stirring constantly, for 2 minutes. Add 3 cups of the reserved court bouillon and cook over hot water, without stirring, for about 20 minutes, or until the rice is tender but not at all mushy.

Remove the crayfish meat from the shells and sauté it gently in 2 tablespoons butter for a few minutes. Sprinkle the crayfish with 1 tablespoon flour and sauté for a few minutes longer, stirring frequently. Add gradually 1 cup heavy cream and heat thoroughly, stirring constantly, without allowing the sauce to boil. Remove the pan from the heat and add the beaten yolk of 1 egg, mixed with a little of the hot sauce.

Shape the *risotto* into a ring on a round serving platter and fill the ring with the crayfish. Garnish with sprays of parsley.

IN a large earthenware casserole melt 1/2 cup butter and in it brown 1 small onion, sliced, 5 thin slices of *prosciutto*, cut in slivers, 1/4 pound sweetbreads, parboiled and cut in dice, and 2 tablespoons dried mushrooms, previously soaked in water for 30 minutes and squeezed dry. Add 1/2 cup each of dry white wine and Sherry, 1 cup shelled peas, 1 thinly sliced truffle, and 3/4 cup rice and cook the mixture over low heat, stirring, until all the wine has been absorbed. Combine 1 cup each of water and stock, 1 tablespoon *glace de viande*, and salt and pepper to taste and cook slowly for 20 minutes, or until the rice is tender. Toss gently with 1/4 cup butter and sprinkle with freshly grated Parmesan.

Risotto alla Fregoli

MELT 1/4 cup butter and in it brown 6 trimmed lamb kidneys, cut in half. Remove the kidneys and reserve them. In the same butter brown lightly 1 sliced onion. Add 6 sliced mushrooms and sauté them for 2 minutes. Add 1 tablespoon tomato paste and 2 cups rice and cover the rice with boiling beef stock. Cook the rice slowly until it has absorbed the liquid and is nearly tender. Add more stock from time to time if necessary. Slice the reserved lamb kidneys and add them to the rice along with 6 tomatoes, peeled, seeded and sliced. Turn the *risotto* into an earthenware casserole, sprinkle it with grated Parmesan and dot it generously with butter. Cover the casserole and bake it in a moderate oven (350° F.) for 10 minutes. Sprinkle with more grated cheese and serve at once.

Risotto of Lamb Kidneys

MELT 1/4 cup butter in an earthenware casserole, add 1/4 cup beef marrow and 1 onion, finely chopped, and cook until the onion starts to brown. Add 2 cups rice and stir constantly over the heat until the rice takes on color. Add 3 cups boiling chicken or beef stock, 1/4 cup white wine, a pinch of powdered saffron, and salt and pepper to taste. Mix all together well and cook for 20

Risotto alla Milanese

to 25 minutes, stirring occasionally, until the liquid is absorbed and the rice is tender. Sprinkle the *risotto* generously with freshly grated Parmesan and with 1/4 cup melted butter.

Risotto con Funghi
RISOTTO WITH MUSHROOMS

MELT 1/4 cup butter in an earthenware casserole, add 1/4 cup beef marrow and 1 onion, finely chopped, and cook until the onion colors. Add 1 1/2 cups sliced mushrooms and cook for 5 minutes longer. Add 2 cups rice and cook, stirring constantly, until the rice begins to take on color. Pour in 3 cups beef stock and salt and pepper to taste, mix all together well and simmer the rice, stirring from time to time, for 20 to 25 minutes until the liquid is absorbed and the rice is tender. Just before serving sprinkle the *risotto* generously with freshly grated Parmesan and 1/4 cup melted butter.

Chicken Liver Risotto

MELT 1/2 cup butter in an earthenware casserole. Add 1 onion, finely chopped, and brown it lightly. Add 1 cup chicken livers, cook them for a minute or so and add 1/2 cup chopped mushrooms, 1/2 red pepper, chopped, salt and pepper to taste and 2 cups rice. Cook, stirring constantly, until the rice takes on color. Add 1/2 cup Marsala and 4 cups boiling chicken stock. Cover the casserole and cook the rice over very low heat until it is tender and all the liquid is absorbed, adding more stock if necessary. Sprinkle the *risotto* generously with grated Parmesan and serve very hot.

Risotto Marinara

HEAT 2 tablespoons olive oil in an earthenware casserole and in it brown 1 large onion, finely chopped. Add 10 anchovy filets, finely minced, and sauté the mixture for 5 minutes. Add 1/2 cup water and 2 tablespoons tomato paste, bring the mixture to a boil and simmer it for 20 minutes. Add 2 cups rice, 3/4 cup dry white wine, 3 teaspoons finely chopped parsley, a pinch of sage, and salt and pepper to taste. Cook the mixture slowly until the wine is almost absorbed. Add 1 1/2 cups water and cook for 10 minutes longer. Sprinkle generously with grated Parmesan or Romano cheese and serve hot.

Shrimp Risotto

SHELL and devein 1 pound fresh shrimps. Reserve the shells. In a saucepan in 2 tablespoons hot olive oil sauté 2 tablespoons each of finely chopped onion and carrot, 1 tablespoon minced celery, and 1 garlic clove. When the garlic is golden discard it. Add to the vegetables 1 cup dry white wine and the reserved shells from the shrimps, bring the liquid to a boil and simmer it for 10 minutes. Add 5 cups hot water and 1 teaspoon salt, cover the saucepan and cook the stock for 30 minutes more.

In another pan brown lightly 2 tablespoons finely chopped onion in 6 tablespoons butter, add the prepared shrimps and sauté all together for 5 minutes. Add 2 cups rice and cook, stirring, for 3 to 4 minutes. Strain the stock and skim the fat from the surface. Add 2 cups of this broth to the shrimp and rice mixture. Cook the mixture for about 20 minutes, until the rice is tender, adding more broth as necessary. Correct the seasoning. Sprinkle the *risotto* with 1/3 cup freshly grated Parmesan and dot it with 3 tablespoons butter. Serve hot.

WILD rice, which is technically not a rice but a berry, may be served in any of the ways suggested for white rice, but its own flavor is so distinctive and so delicious that it needs little ornamentation. Simply toss the cooked rice with butter and seasonings, or with sautéed mushrooms or toasted slivered almonds, and use it to accompany ordinary meats and poultry as well as game and game birds.

Wild Rice

Soak 1 cup wild rice in cold water for 30 minutes and wash it in several changes of cold water. Bring 3 cups water to a boil with 1 teaspoon salt, add the rice, and cook without stirring for about 30 minutes, until the rice is barely tender. Drain if necessary and keep hot over low heat or in a slow oven.

PUT 1/2 cup water, 1/4 cup butter, and a little salt in a saucepan and bring to a boil. Remove from the heat and add, all at once, 1/2 cup flour. Return to the heat and cook, stirring briskly, until the mixture rolls away from the sides of the pan without sticking. Remove the pan from the heat and add 2 eggs, one at a time, mixing well after each one is added. To this mixture add 3/4 cup cooked wild rice mixed with a little butter. Drop by spoonfuls into hot deep fat and increase the temperature of the fat as the *beignets* cook. They will turn by themselves when cooked on the underside.

Beignets of Wild Rice

Other grains find favor with gourmets as well as with country folk; buckwheat, cornmeal, parched crushed wheat, and barley head the list.

HEAT 1 tablespoon butter or rendered chicken fat in a heavy skillet. Add 1 1/2 cups *kasha*, or coarse-grained groats, and cook for 10 minutes over moderate heat, stirring constantly. Add 1/3 cup finely chopped onion, salt and pepper to taste, 3 tablespoons butter, and 4 cups chicken consommé.

Kasha and Mushroom Casserole

Cover tightly and cook over very low heat for 25 minutes, stirring occasionally. If the *kasha* becomes too dry, add a little boiling water. Stir in 1 cup sliced mushrooms, browned in 2 tablespoons butter or rendered chicken fat, and turn the *kasha* into an ovenproof casserole. Cover the casserole and bake in a moderate oven (350° F.) for 30 minutes. The *kasha* should be tender but moist.

Buckwheat Groats with Noodles

To the baked *kasha* and mushroom casserole add 1/2 pound cooked noodle shells. Toss well, add a little more butter or chicken fat, and serve as a supper main dish.

Scrapple

COMBINE 6 cups water with 2 large onions and 1/2 pound fresh pork, half fat and half lean, both put through the finest blade of a food chopper. Add 1/2 teaspoon each of thyme, sage, and black pepper, and 1 1/2 teaspoons salt. Bring the liquid slowly to a boil and simmer it for 15 minutes, stirring it with a fork to prevent the meat from forming lumps. Add very slowly, in a thin trickle, 1/2 pound water-ground yellow cornmeal, stirring constantly. Continue to cook and stir until the mixture is thick and smooth, about 10 minutes. Taste for seasoning and add more salt and pepper as needed. Pour the scrapple into a square loaf pan to cool and set. To serve, unmold the loaf and cut it into 1/2-inch-thick slices. Brown the sliced scrapple on both sides on an ungreased griddle and serve it with scrambled eggs, tart applesauce, and toasted muffins.

Gnocchi Bourbonnaise
GNOCCHI WITH MUSHROOMS

BRING to a boil 1 cup milk with 2 tablespoons butter, 1 teaspoon salt, and a pinch of nutmeg. Add gradually 1 cup flour, mixing thoroughly with a wooden spoon. Remove from the heat and add 4 eggs, one at a time, mixing well after each addition. Add 2 tablespoons grated Parmesan cheese.

Bring a kettle of water to a boil. Put the dough in a pastry bag fitted with a tube with a 1/4- to 3/8-inch opening and force the dough through, cutting it into 1/2-inch pieces to drop into the boiling water. Boil the *gnocchi* slowly for 5 to 8 minutes, or until firm. Remove with a skimmer and dry on absorbent paper.

Slice 12 to 15 mushroom caps. Put them in a pan with 1 tablespoon butter, a little salt, and a few drops of lemon juice. Cook until the juice from the mushrooms cooks away. Prepare 2 cups Mornay sauce.

Put some sauce in the bottom of a timbale or deep baking dish and spread over it a layer of *gnocchi*, then a layer of cooked mushrooms, more sauce, *gnocchi*, and the remaining mushrooms. Cover generously with sauce, because the *gnocchi* puff up during cooking. Sprinkle with grated dry Swiss or Parmesan cheese and a little melted butter and bake in a moderatly hot oven (375° to 400° F.) for 20 to 25 minutes, or until well browned. Serve immediately because the puffed-up *gnocchi* will collapse if allowed to stand.

POUR 1 pound coarse cornmeal very slowly into 2 quarts rapidly boiling water with 2 teaspoons salt, stirring constantly with a wooden spoon. Cook the mixture gently over low heat for about 35 minutes, or until it is very firm. The *mamaliga* may be served from the pan, with pot cheese and melted butter, or it may be cooled in a mold.

    The molded *mamaliga* is cut with a taut string into slices which are sautéed in butter or fat until brown. Serve them plain with grated cheese or with gravy, meat, or fish sauce. Or rub the slices with garlic, roll them in melted butter, and wrap each in a slice of bacon. Place them side by side in a baking dish and bake them in a hot oven (400° F.) until golden brown.

Mamaliga Romanian
CORNMEAL MUSH

ADD 1 cup hominy grits slowly to 4 cups boiling water seasoned with 1 teaspoon salt and 2 tablespoons butter. Cook, stirring constantly, until the mixture begins to thicken. Lower the heat and cook the grits for about an hour, stirring frequently. Season with paprika and white pepper to taste and serve with butter or with gravy, as an accompaniment to meat.

Hominy Grits

IN a mixing bowl combine 2 cups cooked hominy, 2 eggs, beaten, 1/2 cup cream, 3 tablespoons butter, and salt and pepper to taste. Beat the mixture well, pour it into a buttered baking dish, and bake in a moderate oven (350° F.) for about 1 1/2 hours, or until the hominy is set.

Baked Hominy

COMBINE 2 cups cooked hominy grits with 1 cup light cream and stir the mixture over low heat until it is heated through and free of lumps. Add 1/2 teaspoon salt, 1/4 cup butter, and the beaten yolks of 2 eggs. Mix

Hominy Spoon Bread

thoroughly and let it cool. Then fold in the stiffly beaten whites of 3 eggs. Pour the batter into a buttered baking dish and bake in a moderate oven (350° F.) for 30 to 40 minutes, or until the top is lightly browned.

Baked Barley Casserole   SOAK 1/2 cup navy beans overnight in cold water. Drain the beans and cook them in 1 quart boiling water until they are tender. Add 1/2 cup barley and 2 teaspoons salt, and cook slowly until the barley is tender, about 30 minutes, adding chicken stock as necessary. Add salt and white pepper to taste and 2 tablespoons butter or rendered chicken fat. Turn the mixture into a casserole and bake it in a moderate oven (350° F) for about 30 minutes, without letting it brown.

Bulgur   SAUTÉ 3 onions, chopped, in 1/3 cup fat until they are golden. Add 3 cups bulgur, parched crushed wheat, and stir and cook until the fat is absorbed. Add 5 cups boiling water or chicken stock and salt and pepper to taste, cover the pan, and cook the bulgur slowly until the grains are tender. Serve with tomato sauce or meat gravy.

The dumplings that go into the soup plate will be found elsewhere; these dumplings are served with a sauce and for their own sake.

Won Ton
MEAT DUMPLINGS   TO 2 cups sifted flour add about 1/2 cup cold water, to make a very light dough. Cover the dough with a damp cloth and let it rest. Prepare this filling:

Put 1 pound lean pork through the finest blade of a food chopper with 6 spring onions, white and green together. Add 1/2 teaspoon finely chopped gingerroot and 1 tablespoon soy sauce. Chop very finely 1 pound Chinese cabbage and the white parts of 6 leeks, and add them to the mixture with salt to taste and 2 tablespoons olive oil. Combine the ingredients thoroughly.

Divide the dough into four parts and knead each part well on a lightly floured board. Roll the dough into long strips about 1 inch wide. Cut the strips into 1-inch lengths and with a rolling pin roll each small piece into a very thin circle. The circles should be about 3 inches in diameter. Put a heaping teaspoon of the filling on each, fold over the dough, and seal the edges by pinching them together.

Cook the *won ton* in boiling salted water for 8 minutes. Remove them with a perforated spoon and serve at once, with a bowl of soy sauce as condiment. The *won ton* may be served in soup, or they may be fried in hot deep fat, and served as an hors-d'oeuvre.

SIFT 1 1/2 cups flour and 1/2 teaspoon salt onto a pastry board and make a well in the center. Break 2 eggs into the well and gradually work the flour into the eggs. Knead the paste until it is smooth and elastic, adding a little more flour, if necessary, to make a firm dough. Roll the dough out 1/8-inch thick and cut it into 4-inch rounds.

Mix 3 cups cooked *kasha* with 3 egg yolks, 1 onion, diced and sautéed until tender in rendered chicken fat, and salt and black pepper to taste. Put a spoonful of this filling in the center of each round, fold the rounds in half, and pinch the edges securely to seal in the filling. Let the dumplings dry on the board for 10 minutes. Drop them into boiling salted water and cook them for 12 to 15 minutes, until the dough is cooked through. Put a thin layer of rendered chicken fat in the bottom of a baking dish, coat the *varenikes* with the fat, and brown them lightly in a moderate oven (350° F.) for about 15 minutes.

Kasha Varenikes
BUCKWHEAT GROAT DUMPLINGS

BRING to a boil 4 cups milk, 1/4 cup butter, and 1/2 teaspoon salt. Stir in 1/4 pound farina and cook the mixture over low heat, stirring frequently, for 20 minutes, or until it is smooth and thick. Remove the mixture from the heat and beat in 3 eggs and 1 cup each of grated Emmenthal or Swiss cheese and chopped cooked spinach, well drained. Cut the gnocchi with a spoon into oval shapes and lay them in a well-buttered shallow baking pan. Sprinkle them with 1/2 cup flour beaten with 4 eggs, 1 2/3 cups milk, and salt, pepper, and nutmeg to taste. Bake the gnocchi in a moderate oven (350° F.) for 20 minutes, or until they are lightly browned.

Cheese Gnocchi with Spinach

PEEL 4 large potatoes and boil them in salted water until they are tender when tested with a fork. Drain the potatoes and work them through a ricer. When cool, beat in about 1 1/2 cups flour, 1/2 teaspoon salt, and 1 egg, beaten. With the hands, work the mixture into a dough, adding more flour if the dough is too moist. Shape it into dumplings the size of golf balls, drop them into a large kettle of boiling salted water, and boil them for 15 minutes. Lift the dumplings from the water with a slotted spoon and drain them well. To serve, split the dumplings in half with two forks and arrange them on a hot platter. Pour over them 1/4 cup hot browned butter and sprinkle them with 1/2 cup fine bread crumbs browned in butter.

Erdäpfelknödel
POTATO DUMPLINGS

Cuscinetti di Ricotta
RICOTTA PILLOWS

WORK 2 1/4 cups flour with 2 generous tablespoons butter and 1/2 teaspoon salt and add gradually enough lukewarm water to make a dough that is soft but does not stick to the hands in the kneading. Shape the dough into a smooth ball, cover, and let stand for 1 hour.

Roll the dough out thinly on a lightly floured board and cut it with a floured cookie cutter into circles 2 1/2 inches in diameter. Combine 1 1/4 pounds ricotta cheese, 2 eggs, and 3 tablespoons Parmesan. Place 1 generous teaspoon of the filling on each round, fold the dough over, and pinch the edges together firmly so that none of the filling will escape. Fry the *cuscinetti*, a few a time, in hot deep fat (370° F.) until golden brown. Serve with spaghetti sauce and grated Parmesan, or simply with the cheese.

Conchiglie Ripieno
STUFFED SHELLS

COOK 1 pound large *conchiglie* in boiling salted water for about 15 minutes, or until the shells are tender. Drain the shells, cool, and stuff them with the ricotta filling used for *cuscinetti di ricotta*.

Arrange the stuffed shells in a buttered baking dish, pour over them 2 cups tomato sauce for pasta or 1/2 cup melted butter, and sprinkle generously with grated Parmesan. Bake the *conchiglie* in a moderate oven (350° F.) for 20 minutes. Other large hollow pasta shapes may be used in the same way.

Ravioli alla Genovese
Ravioli Dough

To make ravioli dough, sift 3 cups flour into a bowl with a dash of salt. Stir in 2 eggs, lightly beaten, and enough lukewarm water to make a stiff dough. Knead the dough until it is smooth, cover it with a warm bowl, and let it rest for 30 minutes. Roll out the dough on a lightly floured board into two thin, identical sheets. Drop the prepared filling by teaspoons 2 inches apart on one sheet, cover with the second sheet, and press firmly around each mound to form small filled squares. With a pastry cutter, cut the dough between the mounds. Boil the ravioli in boiling salted water for about 8 minutes, until the dough is cooked through but not mushy.

For the Genovese filling, sauté half a chicken breast, 1 sheep's brain, a pair of sweetbreads, and 1 chicken liver lightly in 2 tablespoons butter. Cover the skillet and simmer the meats for 15 minutes. Put the cooked meat twice through the finest blade of a food chopper and add 2 tablespoons slivered ham, 1 cup cooked sieved spinach, 1/4 cup chicken stock, salt, pepper, and nutmeg to taste, and the yolks of 2 eggs. Use this mixture to fill the ravioli.

Pesto
Serve the cooked ravioli with *pesto*: In a mortar mix 3 garlic cloves, chopped, 2 tablespoons minced sweet basil leaves, 2 tablespoons grated cheese, 1 tablespoon chopped walnuts and 1/4 teaspoon salt. Pound the mixture with a pestle to a smooth paste. Still pounding, add gradually about 3 tablespoons olive oil and work the mixture thoroughly to make a smooth sauce.

Stuffed Shells

Agnolotti   COMBINE 1 cup each of minced cooked lamb or pork and chopped cooked spinach, 1 tablespoon grated Parmesan cheese, 1 egg yolk, 2 slices each of *prosciutto* and Italian salami, finely chopped, and salt, pepper, and nutmeg to taste. Use this lamb filling for ravioli. Serve the cooked *agnolotti* with melted butter and grated Romano or Parmesan cheese.

Cappelletti alla Romana   SAUTÉ 1 chicken breast gently in 3 tablespoons butter until it is lightly browned on both sides. Season the meat with salt and pepper and cook until it is tender. Chop the chicken breast very finely and mix it thoroughly with 1/2 pound ricotta cheese, 2 tablespoons grated Parmesan cheese, 1 egg and 1 egg yolk, a pinch of nutmeg, a grating of lemon rind, and salt to taste.

Roll out ravioli dough on a lightly floured board into thin sheets and cut the sheets into circles 2 1/2 inches in diameter. Place 1 teaspoon of the filling in the center of each circle and fold in half, pressing the edges firmly together. Join the two extreme ends of each half circle to form a "little hat," or *cappelletto*.

Cook the *cappelletti* in rapidly boiling salted water for about 10 minutes, or until the dough is tender, drain, and serve with a spaghetti sauce and grated Parmesan.

Manicotti   SIFT 4 cups flour and 1/2 teaspoon salt onto a pastry board and make a well in the center. In the well put 1 tablespoon soft butter and 3 beaten eggs and gradually work the flour into the center ingredients, adding enough warm water to make a medium soft dough. Knead the dough for about 3 minutes, or until it is smooth. Roll the dough out thinly on a lightly floured board and cut it into rectangles 4 by 6 inches. Spread 1 1/2 tablespoons ricotta cheese on each rectangle and roll it up like a jelly roll. Moisten the edges of the dough and seal the rolls securely along the seam and ends to prevent the filling from seeping out.

Cook the *manicotti* in a large quantity of boiling salted water for about 10 minutes, or until the dough is tender. Remove the "little muffs" carefully with a skimmer and arrange several side by side on individual baking dishes. Cover the *manicotti* with a spaghetti sauce, sprinkle with a little finely chopped sweet basil, and bake in a hot oven (400° F.) for 10 minutes. Serve with grated Romano cheese.

Lasagne Parmigiana   IN a skillet sauté 1 onion and 1 garlic clove, both chopped, in 1/4 cup olive oil until they are golden. Add 1 stalk of celery, finely chopped, 4 cups Italian tomatoes, 1/2 cup tomato paste mixed with 1/2 cup hot water, and

1/2 teaspoon sugar, cover the skillet, and simmer gently for about 1 hour, stirring frequently. Add salt and pepper to taste.

Cook 1 pound lasagne noodles in 5 quarts rapidly boiling salted water for about 15 minutes, or until just tender, stirring frequently to prevent the noodles from sticking together. Drain the noodles and arrange them in layers in a baking dish. Cover each layer of noodles with some of the tomato sauce. Cover the sauce with thin slices of Mozzarella cheese and sprinkle the Mozzarella with grated Parmesan cheese. Bake the lasagne in a moderate oven (350° F.) for 20 minutes. Cut into serving portions and serve on individual heated plates, each portion topped with more sauce and grated Parmesan.

IN a skillet sauté 1 pound pork shoulder in 1 tablespoon olive oil until the meat is brown on all sides. Add 1 small onion and 1 garlic clove, both chopped, and cook until the onion is golden. Add 1 tablespoon minced parsley, a little salt and pepper, and 1 1/2 cans Italian-style tomato paste mixed with 2 cups hot water. Cover the skillet and simmer for 2 hours, adding a little water from time to time, if needed. Remove the pork from the sauce and serve it as a separate course or reserve it for another meal.

Lasagne di Carnevale alla Napolitana
LASAGNE WITH MEAT SAUCE

Cook 1 pound lasagne noodles in 5 quarts rapidly boiling salted water for about 15 minutes, or until just tender, stirring frequently to prevent the noodles from sticking together, and drain.

Mix 1 pound ricotta cheese with about 1 tablespoon warm water to make a soft paste.

Arrange the noodles in layers in a baking dish. Cover each layer of noodles with some of the sauce, cover the sauce with a layer of the ricotta paste, and sprinkle the ricotta with grated Parmesan cheese. Bake the *lasagne* in a moderate oven (350° F.) for 20 minutes. Serve the remaining sauce separately.

BEAT 3 eggs lightly and add about 2 cups flour, or enough to make a stiff dough. Work the dough until it is elastic, adding more flour if necessary. Let the dough rest for 10 minutes. Divide it into three parts and roll out each part as thinly as possible on a lightly floured board. Cut the sheets into strips and let them dry for 20 minutes.

Noodle Dough

Drop the noodles into boiling salted water and cook them for about 8

Noodles

Fettuccine Verdi

minutes, or until just tender. Drain the noodles and toss well with 1/2 cup soft butter.

SIFT 4 cups flour with 1 teaspoon salt to form a mound on a pastry board. Make a well in the center of the mound and pour into the hollow 2 well-beaten eggs and 3/4 cup spinach purée. Combine the dry and the wet ingredients to make a rather stiff dough. If necessary, add a little water. Turn the dough out on a floured board and roll it into a very thin rectangle. Roll the sheet up tightly and slice it in very narrow strips. Scatter the strips on the board and let them dry thoroughly before using them. They should be quite brittle.

Cook the *fettuccine* in rapidly boiling salted water for about 8 minutes, or until it is just tender. Drain it well and toss it over low heat or in the top pan of a chafing dish over hot water with 1 cup each of sweet butter and grated Parmesan cheese. Sprinkle each serving with Parmesan and serve more butter and cheese separately.

COOK 3/4 pound homemade noodles in boiling salted water until they are tender. Drain the noodles thoroughly and toss them well with 1/4 cup butter, 2/3 cup slivered and toasted almonds, and 1 tablespoon toasted caraway seeds.

COOK 1 1/2 pounds homemade noodles in rapidly boiling salted water for about 8 minutes. Drain them well and keep them warm.

Mash 1 cup creamy cottage cheese with 6 ounces cream cheese and 1 cup sour cream. Mix this with the noodles and season with 1/4 teaspoon each of salt and pepper. Mix in lightly 1/3 cup chopped scallions or chives and turn the mixture into a generously buttered 2-quart baking dish. Sprinkle with 1/2 cup grated Parmesan cheese, dot with butter, and bake in a moderate oven (350° F.) for 30 minutes.

BOIL 1 pound spaghetti in salted water until it is cooked through but not too soft. Drain. Bring 2 cups tomato sauce to a boil and add 1/2 cup each of cooked ham and cooked tongue, 8 cooked mushrooms, and 2 truffles, all cut in julienne. Mix the cooked spaghetti with the sauce and add 1/2 cup grated Parmesan cheese. Spread a layer of this mixture on the bottom of a deep, well-buttered ring mold.

Cook 3 lamb's or calf's brains in court bouillon, drain, and sauté them in butter. Fill the timbale and top with the remaining spaghetti mixture. Serve very hot.

About one-third of the cooked spaghetti mixed with just enough of the sauce to hold it together may be baked in a ring mold in a moderate oven (350° F.) for about 15 to 20 minutes. Let the mold set for 5 minutes after removing it from the oven and then unmold on a serving dish. Fill the center with a layer of the sauced spaghetti, the brains, and the remaining spaghetti.

Pasta and Beans alla Veneta

SOAK 3/4 pound dried beans overnight. Drain the beans and cook them slowly in 2 quarts unsalted water. Before the beans are tender add salt to taste.

Heat 1/4 cup oil in a deep saucepan and add a sprig of rosemary. Cook slowly about 3 minutes and discard the rosemary. Add 3 chopped garlic cloves and 1 tablespoon chopped parsley to the oil and brown lightly without allowing the herbs to burn. Stir in 1 tablespoon flour and cook for several minutes, stirring until the *roux* is smooth. Add a generous tablespoon of tomato paste and cook until the mixture has the consistency of a thick sauce. Add the cooked beans and about 3/4 cup of the liquid in which the beans were cooked and bring to a boil. Add a little less than 1/2 pound of the pasta known as *ditalini*, or any other small pasta. Cook the pasta until it is barely tender, cover the pan, and set in a warm place for 10 minutes before serving.

Connoisseurs insist that every one of the scores of pasta shapes has its own distinctive taste. For most of us, the shapes are interesting, but the sauce makes the difference.

Garlic Sauce

COOK 2 garlic cloves, finely chopped, in 2/3 cup olive oil, without burning them. Pour the sauce over 1 pound of cooked pasta, sprinkle with chopped sweet basil and parsley, freshly ground pepper, and grated Parmesan cheese, and toss gently.

Salsa Marinara

BROWN 2 garlic cloves, chopped, in 1/3 cup olive oil. Add 4 cups tomatoes, peeled, seeded, and chopped, 2 tablespoons finely chopped parsley, 1 teaspoon each of chopped sweet basil and salt, and 1/4 teaspoon freshly ground black pepper and cook over low heat for 30 minutes. Add 3 tablespoons grated cheese and 1/8 teaspoon orégano and cook for 15 minutes, or until the sauce is very thick, stirring to prevent burning.

PEEL, quarter, and seed 6 large ripe tomatoes. Put them in a saucepan with 1/2 teaspoon salt, a small onion stuck with 2 cloves, 1/2 cup chicken stock, and a few leaves of sweet basil. Cover and simmer for 35 to 40 minutes, or until the tomatoes are very soft. Strain them through a fine sieve and stir in 1 tablespoon butter.

Tomato Sauce for Pasta

SAUTÉ 2 garlic cloves, chopped, in 1/4 cup olive oil until the garlic begins to color. Add 1 pound mushrooms, sliced, and simmer for 10 minutes. Add 2 1/2 cups tomatoes, 2 leaves of sweet basil, a pinch of cayenne, and salt to taste. Cover and simmer for 1 hour over low heat, stirring occasionally.

Mushroom Tomato Sauce

SAUTÉ 1 onion and 1 garlic clove, both chopped, in 2 tablespoons olive oil, until the onion is golden. Add 1 can tomato paste, stir, and cook for 3 minutes. Add salt and pepper to taste, 2 1/2 cups warm water, 1/2 pound of chopped lean beef or pork, and 1 bay leaf. Cover and simmer for 1 1/2 hours.

Meat Sauce

SAUTÉ 1/2 pound of chopped beef, 1 cup sliced mushrooms, and 1 garlic clove, chopped, in 1/4 cup olive oil for 5 minutes, stirring constantly. Add 1/8 teaspoon red pepper and 2 1/2 cups cooked tomatoes and simmer over low heat for 45 minutes, stirring occasionally. Stir in 1/2 can tomato paste and salt to taste. Cover and simmer for 30 minutes longer, stirring occasionally.

Mushroom Meat Sauce

IN a small skillet melt 1 tablespoon butter and in it sauté 1/4 pound lean bacon, diced, until it is crisp. Add 1 teaspoon coarsely ground pepper and pour the sauce over cooked spaghetti. Sprinkle with grated Romano cheese.

Bacon and Pepper Sauce

IN a saucepan heat 1/4 cup each of olive oil and butter and in it sauté 2 garlic cloves, minced, and 2 tablespoons finely chopped shallots until

White Clam Sauce

571

the shallots are golden. Add 1 cup clam juice and simmer for 5 minutes. Stir in 1 cup minced clams and 1/4 cup finely chopped parsley and bring the mixture to a boil. Pour the sauce over cooked spaghetti.

Spaghetti aux Fruits de Mer

In a large saucepan heat 1/4 cup olive oil and in it sauté 3 small onions and 6 shallots, both finely chopped, until they are soft but not brown. Add 1 1/2 pounds of tomatoes, peeled, seeded, and chopped, 1 tablespoon fresh tarragon leaves, a pinch of saffron, and salt and pepper to taste and simmer for 1 1/4 hours. Add 1 pound shrimps, shelled and deveined, and 1 pound of lobster meat and continue to simmer for 10 minutes longer. Pour the sauce over 1 pound of cooked spaghetti.

Ragout Bolognese

This meat "ragout," which is more than a sauce, may be served with pasta.

Brown together slowly in a saucepan 3/4 pound of chopped beef, 1/4 pound each of chopped pork, veal, and salt pork, 1 onion and 1 carrot, both sliced, and 1 stalk of celery, chopped. Add 1 /4 cups stock and simmer until the liquid is almost entirely evaporated. Add 1 teaspoon tomato paste, salt and pepper, 1 clove, and just enough water to cover. Cover the pan and simmer over low heat for about 45 minutes to 1 hour. Add 1/4 pound sliced mushrooms and 2 chickens livers, diced, and cook 10 minutes longer. Finish with 1 sliced truffle and 1/2 cup cream.

Spaghetti alla Siciliana

In a skillet heat 1/2 cup olive oil and add 2 garlic cloves cut into quarters. Allow them to brown and then remove them from the oil. Add half a medium-sized eggplant, peeled and cut into small cubes, and 6 large ripe tomatoes, peeled and cut into pieces. Simmer the mixture over low heat for about 30 minutes.

Partially cook 2 large green peppers on all sides under the broiler, peel off the loosened skin, and cut out the ribs and seeds. Cut the peppers into slices and add them to the eggplant mixture along with 1 tablespoon fresh basil, chopped, 1 tablespoon drained capers, 4 anchovy filets cut into small bits, 12 small black olives, pitted and sliced in half, and salt and pepper to taste. Cover the pan and simmer the sauce for about 10 minutes. Pour the sauce over 1 pound cooked and drained spaghetti.

Breads and Crêpes

No home baker can hope to produce a loaf of daily bread to match the perfect product of the experienced professional baker, who works with scientifically designed equipment under scientifically controlled conditions. He can expect to achieve a pleasantly palatable loaf, but his real reward must come from the basic pleasure inherent in mixing and baking bread at home. The sweet breads, however, are another story. Homemade breads enriched with eggs and butter can rival the commercial product, and even best it.

Compressed yeast in cake form will dissolve best in water that feels comfortably warm to the wrist, 80–86° F., and dry yeast in granular form in slightly warmer water, 110–115° F.

All yeast doughs should be allowed to rise in a warm place, 80–85° F., free from drafts.

Brioche à Tête

DISSOLVE 1 package granular yeast or 1 cake compressed yeast in 1/4 cup water at temperature given on page 573. With the fingertips mix in 1/2 cup flour, adding, if necessary, a little more lukewarm water to make a soft dough. Roll the dough into a ball, cut a cross on top, and put it in a bowl of lukewarm water to rise while you make the brioche paste.

Sift 1 1/2 cups flour onto a pastry board and make a well in the center. Break 2 eggs into the well and begin to knead the paste, adding, little by little, a third egg, to make a soft dough. A good brioche dough is very elastic. Scoop the paste up in the hand, and crash is violently against the table or pastry board. Repeat this crashing technique about 100 times, or until the dough becomes very elastic and detaches itself cleanly from the fingers and the board.

Knead into the beaten dough 1/2 teaspoon salt and 1 tablespoon sugar. Knead 3/4 cup butter until soft and mix it in gently but thoroughly, being careful that the dough does not lose its elasticity.

By this time the yeast dough will have doubled its bulk and will be floating. Remove it carefully from the water to a towel and sponge off the excess moisture. Mix the two doughs together well. Shape the dough into a ball and put it in a floured bowl. Cover the bowl and let the dough rise in a warm place for about 3 hours, or until double in bulk. Turn the dough onto a lightly floured board and punch it down to its normal size. Return the dough to the bowl, cover it, and chill it for 6 hours or overnight.

During the chilling it will rise a little. In the morning punch it down, and it will be ready to shape and bake.

Cut off 1/4 of the dough for the "head," roll the rest into a large ball, and put it in a buttered fluted brioche mold. Roll the remaining dough into the shape of a pear and push the pointed end well into the center of the large ball. Cover and let it rise for about 30 minutes, or until double in bulk. Cut around the base of the head with a sharp pointed knife to keep it separate from the body of the brioche during the baking and brush the brioche with 1 egg yolk beaten with a little water. Bake the brioche in a hot oven (425° F.) for 30 to 45 minutes, or until it tests done.

Les Petites Brioches

INDIVIDUAL brioches are fashioned in the same way as the larger *brioches à tête*. Use small fluted molds or large muffin pans. The bases of the brioches should just half fill the pans. Bake them in a very hot oven (450° F.) for 10 to 15 minutes.

Brioche Couronne

BRIOCHE CROWN

ROLL brioche dough into a ball on a lightly floured pastry board and make a hole through the center with the forefinger. Rotate the finger, enlarging the hole with each rotation, until a large crown is formed. Let it rise on a buttered baking sheet for about 30 minutes, or until double in bulk. Brush it with egg yolk beaten with a little water.

With kitchen scissors make a series of small triangular snips around the top. With the thumb bend the tip of each triangle toward the outer edge of the crown. Bake the brioche in a hot oven (425° F.) for about 35 minutes.

SIFT 1 cup flour into a bowl and make a hole in the center. In the hole *Gannat* put 1 package granular yeast or 1 cake compressed yeast dissolved in 1/4 cup water at temperature given on page 573, and mix together into a firm dough, adding a little more lukewarm water if necessary. Put the dough in a deep pan filled with lukewarm water to rise.

Sift 3 cups flour into another bowl, make a hole in the center, and add 1 cup butter, 4 to 5 tablespoons Cognac, 6 eggs and 6 egg yolks beaten together, and 1/2 teaspoon salt. Mix to a soft dough and work in 1 cup diced Swiss cheese.

When the ball of yeast dough rises to the surface of the water, remove and knead it gently into the egg dough. Put the dough in a large bowl, cover it with a towel, and set it in a warm place to rise until it doubles in bulk. Punch down the dough, put it in a buttered round baking pan with sides from 1 1/2 to 2 inches high, and let it rise again until it doubles in bulk. Brush the dough with beaten egg and milk, and bake in a hot oven (425° F.) for 40 to 50 minutes, or until golden brown.

DISSOLVE 2 packages granular yeast or 2 cakes compressed yeast in 1/4 cup *Basic Sweet* water at temperature given on page 573. Scald 1 cup milk, add 1/2 cup *Yeast Dough* sugar, 1 teaspoon salt, and 1/2 cup butter and cool the mixture to lukewarm (80° to 85° F.). Stir in 3 cups flour to make a thick batter, add the softened yeast and 2 lightly beaten eggs, and beat the batter thoroughly. Then add about 2 cups flour to make a dough that is soft but does not stick to the hands.

Turn the dough out on a lightly floured board and knead it for about 5 minutes until it is smooth and satiny. Place the dough in a buttered bowl, cover it lightly with a towel to prevent a crust from forming, and let it rise in a warm place for 1 1/2 hours, or until it doubles in bulk. Punch down the dough and let it rest for 10 minutes before shaping it into rolls. This recipe makes three dozen rolls or three coffeecakes.

SHAPE yeast dough into rolls and arrange the rolls on a buttered pan. Let *Rolls* them rise in a warm place, covered with a towel, for 3/4 hour, or until they double in bulk.

Glaze the rolls with milk, plain or slightly sweetened, with unbeaten egg white mixed with 1 tablespoon cold water, or with an egg yolk stirred with a little cream. Brush the rolls with the glaze before baking them and again a few minutes before taking them from the oven. After the second glazing, the rolls may be sprinkled with coarse salt, poppy seeds, or caraway seeds. Rolls should be baked quickly, in a hot oven (425° F.), for 12 to 18 minutes, until they are golden brown.

Parker House Rolls Roll yeast dough out 1/4 inch thick and spread it with very soft butter. Cut it into rounds with a 3-inch cookie cutter and, with the back of a knife, make a deep impression across each round slightly off center. Fold each round so that the smaller half overlaps the larger. Press the crease tightly and put the rolls close together on a buttered baking sheet.

Cloverleaf Rolls Shape yeast dough into balls the size of large marbles and put three balls into each cup of a buttered muffin pan.

Crescents Roll yeast dough into a circle about 10 inches in diameter and 1/4 inch thick and cut it into 8 wedges. Roll each triangle loosely, from the base toward the point, and shape the dough into a crescent. Place the crescents on a buttered baking sheet 1 inch apart.

Butterflies Roll yeast dough into a rectangle 1/4 inch thick and 6 inches wide. Brush the dough with melted butter and roll it up like a jelly roll. Cut the roll into 2-inch pieces and place the pieces—on their sides, not on the cut ends—on a buttered baking sheet, 2 inches apart. Press across the center of each piece with the back of a knife to make a deep impression.

Emperors Break off pieces of dough about the size of plums and form them into smooth round balls. Put the balls in the cups of a buttered muffin pan and cut each ball in half, then in quarters, with kitchen shears, cutting almost but not quite through.

Figure 8's Fasten the two ends of a strip of dough, cut as for snails, twist it in the middle, and stretch it into a figure 8. Place the rolls on a buttered baking sheet 1 inch apart.

Rosettes Tie a strip of dough, cut as for snails, into a knot. Bring one end up through the center of the knot and tuck the other end over the side. Place the rosettes on a buttered baking sheet 1 inch apart.

Snails Roll out yeast dough into a long rectangle 12 inches wide and 1/4 inch thick. Spread the sheet with melted butter and fold it in half lengthwise. Trim the edges and cut the dough into strips 1/2 inch wide.

Hold one end of each strip down on a buttered baking sheet and wind the dough around and around, snail-fashion. Tuck the end firmly underneath. Place the snails 1 inch apart on the baking sheet.

The traditional breads from foreign lands baked for the Christmas and Easter seasons take little more time than other breads, and add the finishing touch to the festive board.

COMBINE 1 1/3 cups boiling water, 1/2 cup butter, 2 teaspoons salt, and 1/2 cup sugar, and cool to lukewarm. Add 2 packages granular yeast or 2 cakes compressed yeast dissolved in 1/4 cup water at temperature given on page 573, 1/2 teaspoon nutmeg, and 1 teaspoon each of allspice and caraway seeds. Stir in about 6 cups flour, or enough to make a soft dough. Knead until the dough is smooth and satiny and work in 1 cup currants, 3/4 cup sultana raisins, and 1/2 cup chopped citron. Let the dough rise in a warm place until it doubles in bulk, punch down, and knead again for several minutes. Put the dough into 2 buttered loaf pans and let the loaves rise again until they double in bulk. Bake the loaves in a hot oven (400° F.) for 10 minutes, reduce the temperature to moderate (350° F.), and bake the loaves for 50 minutes longer.

English Christmas Bread

DISSOLVE 1 package granular yeast or 1 cake compressed yeast in 1/4 cup water at temperature given on page 573. Stir in 1/2 cup flour and let the sponge stand in a warm place until bubbly. Cream together 3/4 cup butter and 1/2 cup sugar. Beat in 3 eggs and 2 egg yolks and stir in the yeast. Add 1 teaspoon vanilla, 1/2 teaspoon salt, and about 4 cups flour, or enough to make a dough that is soft but not sticky. Add 1/4 cup lukewarm milk if needed. Divide the dough and to half of it knead in 1/3 cup seedless raisins and 1/2 cup each of mixed shredded candied peel, citron, and chopped blanched almonds. Let both portions of the dough rise in a warm spot to double in bulk, punch them down, and knead them again for 3 minutes. Butter a tube pan well, sprinkle it with sugar, and stud it with whole blanched almonds. Roll out the plain dough into a long triangle. Roll out the fruit dough the same size and lay it on top of the plain. Roll up the dough, beginning at the base of the triangle, fit the roll into the prepared pan, and let it rise in a warm place until it is double in bulk. Bake the *panettone* in a hot oven (400° F.) for 10 minutes, reduce the oven temperature to moderate (350° F.), and continue to bake for about 50 minutes, until the cake tests done.

Panettone di Natale
ITALIAN CHRISTMAS FRUIT BREAD

Kulich

RUSSIAN EASTER
BREAD

IN a large mixing bowl combine 2 cups milk, scalded and cooled to lukewarm, 1 teaspoon salt, 1 cup sugar, 1 cup sifted flour, and 1 package granular yeast or 1 cake compressed yeast dissolved in 1/4 cup water at temperature given on page 573. Set the batter in a warm place to rise for 1 hour, until it is very light.

Beat 6 egg yolks with a generous 1/2 cup sugar and incorporate the eggs into the risen batter. Add, little by little, 1 1/2 cups sweet butter, melted, and 7 cups sifted flour, alternately.

Combine 1/4 pound each of candied fruits, ground blanched toasted almonds, and raisins. Soak 1/2 teaspoon saffron in 2 tablespoons brandy. Scrape the seeds from a vanilla bean and pound 12 cardamom seeds to a powder. Add the fruits, spices, and strained saffron infusion to the dough and knead it until it is smooth and elastic. This may take as long as an hour. Beat 3 egg whites until they are stiff and work them into the mixture.

Line a tall, cylindrical baking pan with buttered paper and turn the dough into it to fill halfway. Let the dough rise to the top of the pan. Bake the *kulich* in a moderate oven (350° F.) for about 1 hour. Ice with pink or white confectioners' sugar frosting and decorate with a small paper rose.

To serve the *kulich*, cut horizontal slices from the top; the crusted and iced first slice is always saved to use as a lid for the cake.

Christöllen

SCALD 2 cups milk and add 1 cup sugar, 2 teaspoons salt, and 1 1/3 cups butter. Stir until the butter is melted and let cool to lukewarm. Add 2 packages yeast or 2 cakes compressed yeast dissolved in a little water at temperature given on page 573, and stir in 2 cups flour. Let the batter rest in a warm place until it is bubbly. Then stir in 4 eggs, beaten, and about 6 cups flour, or enough to make a light but not sticky dough. Knead in 1 1/2 cups each of chopped blanched almonds and raisins, softened in a little hot water and thoroughly drained, 1/2 cup each of chopped citron and currants, 1/4 cup each of candied cherries and chopped candied pineapple, 1 tablespoon candied orange peel, the grated rind of 1 lemon, and 2 teaspoons vanilla. Continue to knead the dough until it is smooth and elastic. Cover the dough lightly and let it rise in a warm place until double in bulk. Punch down the dough, divide it into three parts, and let the parts rest for 10 minutes. Flatten each part into an oval about 3/4 inch thick, brush with melted butter, and sprinkle with sugar and cinnamon. Fold the ovals not quite in half (like large Parker House rolls), pinch the ends firmly together, and place the loaves on oiled baking sheets. Brush the loaves with melted butter again and let them rise for about 1 hour, or until double in bulk. Bake in a hot oven (425° F.) for 10 minutes, reduce the temperature to moderate (350° F.) and bake the loaves for 40 minutes longer. Cool, glaze with confectioners' sugar icing, and decorate with large pieces of fruit and nuts.

COMBINE 1/2 cup each of sliced dried pears, raisins, chopped blanched almonds, and mixed chopped green and red candied cherries. Add 1/4 cup chopped citron, 1 teaspoon grated lemon rind, 1/2 teaspoon each of cloves, cinnamon, and nutmeg, and 2 tablespoons brandy. Let the fruit and nuts soak in the brandy overnight.

Swiss Christmas Bread

Scald 1 cup milk, add 1/4 cup each of butter and sugar and 1 teaspoon salt, and cool to lukewarm. Stir in 1 package granular yeast or 1 cake compressed yeast dissolved in 1/4 cup water at temperature given on page 573, 1 egg, beaten, and about 4 cups flour, or enough to make a dough that is soft but not sticky. Let the dough rise until it is double in bulk, punch it down, and knead for about 3 minutes. Work in the spiced fruit mixture, mold into 2 loaves, and put the dough into oiled bread pans. Let the loaves rise until double in bulk and brush with melted butter. Bake in a hot oven (400° F.) for 10 minutes, reduce the temperature to moderate (350° F.), and bake the loaves for 50 minutes longer. Turn the bread out onto a rack, cool, and frost the loaves with confectioners' sugar icing flavored with almond extract.

SCALD 1/2 cup each of milk and cream, add 1/2 cup butter, and cool to lukewarm. Dry 1 tablespoon saffron in a slow oven (250° F.) until it is crisp, pound it to a powder in a mortar, and add it to the milk. Stir in 1 egg, beaten, 1/4 cup sugar, and 1 package granular yeast or 1 cake compressed yeast dissolved in 1/4 cup water at temperature given on page 573. Stir in about 4 cups flour, or enough to make a thin dough, add 1 teaspoon salt and 1 cup raisins, and continue to stir vigorously until the dough is thick and glossy. Cover the dough and let it rise in a warm place until double in bulk. Add more flour, or enough to make a firm dough, turn out the dough onto a floured board, and knead until it no longer sticks to the board.

Saffron Bread

The dough may be shaped into buns, crescents, or a Christmas wreath. To make the wreath form the dough into a long roll and fashion a large ring on an oiled baking sheet. With scissors cut the ring almost but not quite through at 1/2-inch intervals and turn the slices alternately to the right and to the left.

Brush the buns or wreath with lightly beaten egg, sprinkle with sugar and slivered blanched almonds, and let rise in a warm place for about 1 hour, or until double in bulk. Bake in a moderately hot oven (375° F.) for about 20 minutes for buns, about 45 minutes for the wreath.

Cornish
Saffron Bread

KNEAD into the saffron bread 1/3 cup each of chopped, candied lemon peel, citron and walnut meats, and 1 cup each of currants and raisins.

Mákos és
Diós Kalács
HUNGARIAN
CHRISTMAS BREAD

SOFTEN 1/2 package granular yeast or 1/2 cake compressed yeast in 2/3 cup milk at temperature given on page 573. Stir in 1 teaspoon sugar. Let the yeast stand in a warm place until the mixture bubbles. In a bowl combine 1 cup soft butter, 1/4 cup sugar, 1/2 teaspoon salt and the grated rind of 1 lemon. Add alternately 2 1/2 cups flour and the yeast mixture. Knead the dough well on a floured board, adding a little more flour if necessary to make a dough that is soft but not at all sticky. Turn the dough into a buttered bowl, cover it with a cloth, and let it rise in a warm place for about 1 hour, until it doubles in bulk.

Combine 1 cup each of ground poppy seeds and sugar, 1/2 cup each of raisins and milk, and the grated rind of 1 lemon. Cook over boiling water, stirring constantly, until the mixture is of spreading consistency.

Divide the dough in half, punch it down, and roll out each half into a rectangle 1/4 inch thick. Spread the rectangles with the poppy seed filling and roll like a jelly roll. Place the rolls on an oiled baking sheet and brush with beaten egg. Let them rise for 30 minutes, brush them again with beaten egg, and bake in a moderately slow oven (325° F.) for about 45 minutes, or until they are lightly browned.

Tea breads are distinguished from other breads because they are quick: that is, they are leavened with baking powder or with soda, rather than with yeast. They are also sweetened, and are likely to contain fruits, nuts, and other ameliorations.

Date and
Nut Bread

POUR 1 cup boiling water over 2 cups cut-up dates and 1 cup coarsely chopped walnuts and cool to lukewarm.

Cream together 1/4 cup butter and 3/4 cup brown sugar until the mixture is light and smooth. Add 1 egg, beaten, and beat thoroughly. Sift together 2 cups sifted cake flour, 1/2 teaspoon salt, and 1 teaspoon soda. Add the dry ingredients and the fruit-nut mixture alternately to the butter-sugar mixture, beating after each addition until the ingredients are blended. Stir in 5 tablespoons cold water and turn the batter into a buttered loaf pan. Bake in a moderate oven (350° F.) for 45 minutes, or until a cake

Hungarian Christmas Bread

tester inserted in the center comes out clean. Remove the bread from the pan to a rack to cool.

Apricot Bread COVER 1 cup dried apricots with cold water, bring the water to a boil, and simmer the apricots, covered, until they are soft. Uncover and cook over low heat until nearly all the water is cooked away. Press the apricots through a fine sieve, add 1/2 cup sugar to the purée, and beat until the sugar is dissolved. Cool the purée.

Sift into a mixing bowl 2 cups sifted flour, 2 teaspoons baking powder, and 1/2 teaspoon salt. Cut in 1/4 cup butter and stir in 1 cup milk combined with 2 beaten eggs. Pour half the batter into a buttered loaf pan, cover the batter with the apricot purée, and add the remaining batter. Sprinkle the batter with 2 tablespoons each of melted butter and brown sugar and bake in a moderately hot oven (375° F.) for 30 to 40 minutes, or until the loaf tests done.

Whole Wheat Honey Bread PEEL 3 medium oranges in narrow strips and simmer the peel slowly in 2 cups water for 25 to 30 minutes, or until it is tender. There should be just 1/4 cup liquid left. Add 1 cup honey, bring to a boil, and cook until the syrup is thick.

Sift together into a mixing bowl 2 3/4 cups whole wheat flour, 4 teaspoons baking powder, and 3/4 teaspoon salt. Add 1 cup cold milk and the warm orange strips and syrup gradually to the sifted dry ingredients and beat well. Stir in 1/2 cup chopped nuts, dredged in a little flour. Turn the dough into 1 large or 2 small buttered loaf pans and bake in a moderate oven (325° F.) for about 1 hour, or until the bread tests done. Cool before slicing.

Walnut Bread SIFT 3 cups sifted flour with 4 teaspoons baking powder, 1 teaspoon salt, and 3/4 cup sugar. Add 1 cup chopped walnuts and mix lightly. Beat 1 egg with 1 1/2 cups milk and add this to the dry ingredients, stirring only until the flour is moistened. Stir in 2 tablespoons melted butter. Turn the batter into a buttered loaf pan and bake it in a moderate oven (350° F.) for 1 hour. Turn the loaf out on a rack to cool. Serve thinly sliced with cream cheese and preserves.

Banana Tea Bread SIFT together 1 3/4 cups sifted flour, 2 teaspoons baking powder, 1/4 teaspoon soda, and 1/2 teaspoon salt. Cream 1/3 cup butter, add gradually

2/3 cup sugar, and beat until light and fluffy. Add 2 eggs, well beaten, and beat thoroughly. Add the sifted dry ingredients alternately with 1 cup mashed ripe bananas, beating after each addition until the batter is smooth. Turn the batter into a buttered bread pan and bake in a moderate oven (350° F.) for about 1 hour and 10 minutes.

SIFT together 1 3/4 cups sifted flour, 2/3 cup sugar, 1 1/2 teaspoons baking powder and 1/2 teaspoon each of soda and salt. Stir in 1 beaten egg. In a measuring cup place the juice and grated rind of 1 orange and 2 tablespoons butter. Add boiling water to make 3/4 cup and stir the liquid into the dry ingredients, mixing well. Combine 1 cup washed and dried blueberries or huckleberries, 1 cup chopped pecans, and 1/4 cup sifted flour. Add the fruit to the batter, blending gently but thoroughly. Pour the batter into a large buttered loaf pan and bake in a moderate oven (350° F.) for 1 hour, or until the bread tests done. *Huckleberry Pecan Bread*

Stone-ground white or yellow cornmeal has a superior flavor to either white or yellow roller-milled cornmeal, but there is little difference in their baking properties.

STIR 1/2 cup yellow cornmeal very slowly into 2 cups boiling water. Add 2 tablespoons shortening, 1/2 cup molasses, and 1 teaspoon salt and cool the mixture. Dissolve 1 package granular yeast or 1 cake compressed yeast in 1/4 cup water at temperature given on page 573, add to the meal, and sift in 5 cups flour, or more if needed to make a stiff dough. Turn the dough onto a lightly floured board and knead well. Put the dough in a warm place and let it rise to more than double its bulk. Shape it into loaves and let them rise until light. Bake the bread in 2 loaf pans in a moderately hot oven (400° F.) for 1 hour. *Anadama Bread*

SPREAD an 8-inch pie pan with bacon drippings and put it in a very hot oven (450° F.) to heat. Sift together 2 cups white cornmeal, 1 teaspoon salt, 1/2 teaspoon soda, and 1 teaspoon baking powder. Add 1 1/4 cups buttermilk and 2 tablespoons bacon drippings. Mix the batter and pour it into the heated pie pan. Bake the bread for 20 minutes or more, until it is well browned. *Buttermilk Corn Bread*

Corn Sticks

BEAT 2 eggs with 1/2 teaspoon salt until they are thick and pale in color. Add to them 2 tablespoons sugar and continue beating until the sugar is dissolved. Stir into the egg-sugar mixture 2 tablespoons melted butter. Sift together 1 cup stone-ground cornmeal, 1 cup sifted flour, and 2 teaspoons baking powder. Add these dry ingredients alternately with 1 cup milk, stirring after each addition until all the ingredients are well blended. Pour the batter into a buttered 8-inch-square cake pan and bake in a hot oven (425° F.) for 20 minutes.

Johnnycake

HEAT 1 cup milk to the scalding point and remove it from the heat. Add 2 tablespoons butter and 1 tablespoon sugar and stir until the butter is melted. Stir in 1 beaten egg, 2 cups yellow cornmeal mixed with 2 teaspoons baking powder and 1/2 teaspoon salt. Bake in hot buttered cornstick pans in a very hot oven (450° F.) for 12 to 15 minutes. Serve hot.

Corn Sticks

COMBINE 1 1/2 cups yellow cornmeal, 1/2 cup sifted flour, 1 teaspoon each of salt and sugar, and 3 tablespoons baking powder. Add 3 eggs lightly beaten with 1 cup milk and beat until the batter is thoroughly blended. Stir in 1/4 cup heavy cream and 1/3 cup melted butter.

Spread the batter about 1/2 inch thick in a shallow buttered baking pan, 16 inches by 12 inches, and bake the bread in a hot oven (400° F.) for 20 minutes or more, until it is well browned.

Rich Corn Bread

TO 1 cup stone-ground white cornmeal add enough boiling water to make a mush the consistency of oatmeal. Season with salt to taste and stir in 1/4 cup melted bacon drippings. Brush hot cookie sheets with drippings and spread the mush over them very thinly. Bake in a hot oven (425° F.) for about 6 minutes, or until the bread is lightly browned. Cut into squares and serve hot.

Cornmeal Wafers

STIR 2 cups stone-ground cornmeal gradually into 2 cups rapidly boiling water. Continue to stir over a low heat until the mixture is smooth. Add 1/4 cup melted butter and 1 teaspoon salt and stir in slowly 1 1/2 cups milk. Remove the pan from the heat and stir in the beaten yolks of 3 eggs. Let the mixture cool a little and then fold in the stiffly beaten whites of 4 eggs. Pour the batter into a buttered 1-quart baking dish and bake it in a moderate oven (350° F.) for 30 minutes, until it is well puffed and brown. Serve with a spoon.

Virginia Spoon Bread

Crackling Bread   SIFT together 2 cups stone-ground cornmeal, 1 teaspoon salt, and 3 teaspoons baking powder. Stir gradually into the dry ingredients 1/2 cup each of milk and water and beat the mixture until it is smooth. Add 1 egg and beat again. Stir in 1 cup cracklings, which have been broken into small pieces. Bake in a moderately hot oven (400° F.) for 30 minutes.

Biscuits and muffins are, technically, quick rolls. We list some of the variations on the basic theme; the possibilities are endless.

Basic Biscuits   SIFT 2 cups flour into a bowl with 1 teaspoon salt and 2 teaspoons baking powder. With two knives or a pastry blender, quickly cut into the dry ingredients 4 to 6 tablespoons butter. Stir in about 3/4 cup milk to make a soft but not sticky dough. Knead the dough on a lightly floured board with floured fingertips for just 30 seconds and roll it out into a sheet from 1/2 to 1 inch thick, depending on whether thin crusty biscuits or thick soft biscuits are desired. Cut the dough with a floured biscuit cutter or a knife into rounds and bake them on a baking sheet in a very hot oven (450° F.) for 12 to 15 minutes, or until the biscuits are golden brown.

Apple Biscuits   Make basic biscuits, but add 1/2 teaspoon cinnamon or nutmeg and 1/2 cup shredded apple to the flour and butter mixture before adding the milk. Brush the biscuits with beaten egg, place a thin slice of apple on each, and sprinkle lightly with sugar. Bake as usual.

Bacon Biscuits   Roll out basic biscuit dough into a rectangle 1/4 inch thick and spread it lightly with soft butter. Sprinkle it with 1/2 cup bacon, diced and sautéed until crisp and golden. Roll the dough like a jelly roll and cut it into slices 1/2 inch thick. Bake as usual.

Lemon Biscuits   Cut basic biscuit dough into small rounds. Press half a lump of sugar, dipped in lemon juice, into each biscuit, sprinkle them with grated lemon rind, and bake.

Herbed Biscuits   Add to the flour for basic biscuits 1/2 cup finely chopped parsley. Roll out the dough 1/2 inch thick on a lightly floured board and cut it into small rounds. Brush the rounds with melted butter and bake as usual.

     Fresh basil, chives, or tarragon, or any favored herb may be substituted for the parsley.

Maple Biscuits   Roll out basic biscuit dough 1/4 inch thick on a lightly floured board and cut it into rounds. Place the rounds in a buttered baking pan, brush them with melted butter, and sprinkle generously with 1/2 cup shaved maple sugar. Bake as usual.

Honey Biscuits

Roll out basic biscuit dough 1/2 inch thick on a lightly floured board and spread it with softened butter. Sprinkle over the butter 2 tablespoons sugar and 1/2 cup each of seeded raisins and chopped pecans and roll the dough like a jelly roll. Slice the roll 1/2 inch thick. Butter a baking pan generously and pour into it a half inch of honey. Lay the biscuits in the pan and bake them in a hot oven (400° F.) for 15 minutes, or until they are delicately browned. Remove them at once from the pan after baking and pour over them any honey in the pan.

Cream Biscuits

SIFT 2 cups sifted flour with 1/2 teaspoon salt and 2 teaspoons baking powder. Cut in 1/4 cup butter and add about 3/4 cup heavy cream to make a soft, but not sticky, dough. Roll out the dough 1/4 inch thick on a lightly floured board and cut it into rounds. Bake as usual.

Shortcake Biscuits

To make shortcake biscuits, brush the rounds with butter and bake them in pairs, sandwich style. Split them, butter them again, fill with sweetened fruit and top with whipped cream.

Sweet Potato Biscuits

SIFT 1 cup flour into a bowl with 1/2 teaspoon salt and 2 teaspoons baking powder. With the fingertips or a pastry blender, quickly work in 6 tablespoons shortening. Stir in 6 tablespoons milk and 1 cup cooked, mashed sweet potatoes. Knead the dough on a lightly floured board for a half a minute. Roll out the dough to the desired thickness and cut it with a floured biscuit cutter. Thin biscuits are crisp and crusty, thick biscuits are tender and flaky. Bake the biscuits on a buttered baking sheet in a very hot oven (450° F.) for 12 to 15 minutes, or until they are well browned.

Basic Muffins

SIFT together into a mixing bowl 2 cups flour, 2 tablespoons sugar, 2 teaspoons baking powder, and 1/2 teaspoon salt. Add 1 cup milk combined with 1 well-beaten egg and 1/4 cup melted butter and mix just enough to moisten the dry ingredients; do not beat. Pour the batter into well-buttered muffin pans, filling them two-thirds full, and bake in a hot oven (400° F.) for 20 to 25 minutes.

For sweeter muffins double or triple the amount of sugar.

Apple Muffins   Make basic muffins and sift 1 teaspoon cinnamon and an additional 1/4 cup sugar with the dry ingredients. Fold into the batter 1 cup shredded raw apple.

Blueberry Muffins   Increase the sugar in the basic recipe to 1/2 cup. Fold into the batter 1 cup blueberries sprinkled with 1 tablespoon flour.

Cranberry Muffins   Combine 1 cup raw, chopped cranberries with 1/2 cup sugar and fold into the basic muffin batter.

Date Muffins   Add to basic muffin batter 1 cup pitted dates, cut in small pieces.

Berry Muffins   Increase the sugar in the basic muffin recipe to 1/3 cup and fold into the batter 1 cup blackberries, raspberries, or loganberries, sprinkled with 1 tablespoon flour.

Honey Bran Muffins   SIFT together into a mixing bowl 1 cup sifted flour, 1 teaspoon baking powder, and 1/2 teaspoon each of soda and salt. Add 1 cup bran and 1/2 cup chopped walnuts, and mix thoroughly. Add 1 egg, beaten, 3 tablespoons strained honey, and 3/4 cup sour milk or buttermilk, and stir just enough to combine the ingredients. Stir in 3 tablespoons melted butter. Fill buttered muffin tins two-thirds full and bake in a hot oven (425° F.) for 15 to 18 minutes.

Cheese Popovers   PUT an iron popover pan in a very hot oven (450° F.). Sift 1 cup flour with 1/2 teaspoon salt and 1/4 teaspoon paprika. Add 1 cup milk and 2 large eggs, well beaten, and stir in 1/4 cup grated Cheddar cheese. Beat the batter well; it should be as thick as cream, and if the eggs are small it may be necessary to add another one. Butter the hot pan well and fill it half full with the cheese batter. Bake the popovers in a hot oven (450° F.) for 30 minutes. Reduce the temperature to moderate (350° F.) and bake them for about 10 minutes longer, or until they are browned and crisp, inside and out. Slit each popover with a sharp knife and serve hot, with butter.

Popovers may be used as cases for various creamed mixtures or for salad mixtures. The cheese may be omitted.

SIFT 2 cups flour with 2 tablespoons sugar, 1/2 teaspoon salt, and 2 teaspoons baking powder. Rub in 3 tablespoons butter and add 2/3 cup cream, to make a soft dough. Pat the dough into rounds 1/2 inch thick and of any desired diameter. Cut the rounds into quarters and bake the triangles on a buttered baking sheet in a very hot oven (450° F.) for about 12 to 15 minutes, until they are browned. Serve hot, with generous amounts of butter.

Cream Scones

SIFT together 2 cups pastry flour, 2 teaspoons baking powder, 1 teaspoon soda, and 1/2 teaspoon salt. Beat 3 egg yolks until they are light and stir in 1 1/2 cups buttermilk. Add the liquid to the dry ingredients to make a smooth batter. Stir in 1/2 cup butter, melted, and fold in 3 egg whites, stiffly beaten. Bake on a waffle iron. Serve with hot maple syrup and butter.

Buttermilk Waffles

Waffles may be varied by such additions to the batter as cheese, crumbled crisp bacon or ham, raisins, nuts, or fruits. The last three are then served with whipped cream or ice cream, for dessert.

The classic dessert crêpe is gossamer light, leaf thin, and faintly redolent of brandy or rum.

COMBINE 1 cup flour, 1 tablespoon sugar, and a pinch of salt. Beat 2 eggs with 2 egg yolks and stir in 1 3/4 cups milk. Beat the liquid gradually into the dry ingredients, to make a smooth batter. Add 2 tablespoons melted butter and 1 teaspoon Cognac or rum. The batter should be the consistency of heavy cream. Let the batter stand for 2 hours before using it. Brush a small, hot skillet with melted butter. Pour a generous tablespoon of batter into the pan and tip the pan to coat it with a thin layer of batter. When the crêpe is brown on the bottom, turn it and brown the other side. Or the crêpes may be cooked on one side only, rolled around the filling, cooked side in, and browned in butter just before serving.

Crêpes for Dessert

Bake crêpes for dessert and put 2 tablespoons sliced and sugared strawberries on each. Roll the crêpe to enclose the filling and arrange the rolls side by side in a shallow, buttered baking dish. Sprinkle them with blanched, shredded, and lightly toasted almonds and put the dish under the broiler until the crêpes blister. Serve hot, with whipped cream sweetened and flavored to taste.

Crêpes Elizabeth

Sliced and sweetened nectarines, peaches, plums, or any berry may be substituted for the strawberries in this recipe.

Crêpes Frangipane Bake crêpes for dessert, spread them with *crème frangipane* and roll them or fold them in quarters. Arrange the crêpes side by side on the buttered blazer of a chafing dish over direct heat. Sprinkle them lightly with sugar and cook them until the butter sizzles and the crêpes are warmed through. Pour over them 1/4 cup warmed Cognac and ignite the spirit. When the flame dies sprinkle the crêpes with finely chopped pistachio nuts and serve at once.

Crêpes à la Bourbonnaise Bake crêpes for dessert. Put a generous tablespoon *crème pâtissière* on each, roll the crêpes, and arrange them side by side in a chafing dish. Pour over the crêpes hot, thin apricot purée and sprinkle them with warmed rum. Ignite the spirit and serve the crêpes flaming.

Fruit Blintzes Make dessert crêpes and bake them on one side only. For the filling, mash 1/2 pound cottage cheese, pot cheese, or farmer cheese and flavor to taste with grated lemon rind, sugar, and cinnamon. Add 1 egg, well beaten, and, if the filling seems too dry, a little sour cream. Fold in 1 cup drained blueberries, cherries, or pineapple, cut in small, even pieces. Put a tablespoon of the filling in the center of the cooked side of each crêpe and roll it up, folding in the ends. Brown in hot butter, turning to cook both sides, and serve with sour cream and with a spoonful of the fruit used for the filling or with a compatible jelly.

Crêpes Flambées Bake crêpes for dessert and fold them in quarters. Arrange them in a buttered chafing dish blazer. Heat the crêpes for a few minutes and pour over them 1/4 cup Cognac and 2 tablespoons each of kirsch and anisette. Sprinkle generously with confectioners' sugar and ignite the spirits. Spoon the flaming sauce over the crêpes until they are thoroughly saturated, and serve two or three crêpes to a portion, with a little of the sauce.

Crêpes Soufflées with Berries Beat together to a smooth paste 5 tablespoons flour, 2 tablespoons sugar, 1 whole egg, 3 egg yolks, and 1/8 teaspoon vanilla. Add gradually enough cold milk to make batter the consistency of heavy cream. Fold in 2 stiffly beaten egg whites and a few grains of salt.

Have ready fresh or frozen raspberries or strawberries, soaked for a few minutes in brandy or liqueur, drained, and rolled in confectioners' sugar.

Heat several individual skillets to sizzling, brush them generously with melted butter, and pour into each 1 tablespoon of the batter. Tilt the pans to spread the batter evenly over the bottom. As soon as the batter begins to set, put 5 or 6 berries on each pancake and pour over the berries another tablespoon of batter. Quickly put the pans in a very hot oven (450° F.)

or under the broiler until the pancakes are firm and delicately brown on top. Sprinkle each with a little sugar and serve as soon as the sugar caramelizes.

Other fruits may be used to make *crêpes soufflées*.

Crêpes Soufflées Alsacienne

Melt 1 1/2 tablespoons butter, stir in 1/2 tablespoon flour, and stir the *roux* over low heat until it begins to turn golden. Add 1/4 cup milk and cook, stirring briskly, for a minute or two. Remove the pan from the heat and stir in 3 egg yolks beaten until light with 1 tablespoon sugar. Fold in 3 egg whites, stiffly beaten with 1 tablespoon sugar, and a few drops of vanilla extract.

Prepare crêpes for dessert and in the center of each put a tablespoon of the soufflé mixture. Fold the crêpes in four and arrange them in buttered individual shallow baking dishes, three to a dish, with the filling exposed so that it can rise. Bake the crêpes in a hot oven (425° F.) for about 5 minutes, or until the filling rises and browns lightly. Serve them in the baking dishes, with a separate dish of apricot sauce flavored with kirsch.

Shrove Tuesday Pancakes

SIFT 2 cups flour and a pinch of salt into a bowl. Add 2 eggs, lightly beaten, and about 2 cups milk, or enough to make a thin batter, and beat until the batter is smooth.

Pour the batter on a well-buttered hot griddle to make very thin cakes about 5 inches in diameter. Bake until the cakes are delicately brown on the under side, turn, and brown the other side. Spread each pancake with jam or sprinkle with confectioners' sugar and roll up. Serve hot, with a slice of lemon if sugar is used.

Lefser
NORWEGIAN SKILLET CAKES

STIR 1 cup sugar into 1 cup sour cream. Add 1 teaspoon soda and 1 tablespoon melted butter. Add about 3 1/2 cups flour, or enough to make a soft dough. Knead the dough until it is smooth. Roll it out 1/8 inch thick on a lightly floured board, using a *Lefse* rolling pin, and cut it into rounds. Bake the rounds in a heavy greased skillet over low heat until the cakes are well browned on both sides.

Plättar
SWEDISH PANCAKES

SIFT 1 cup flour with 2 tablespoons sugar and a pinch of salt. Beat 3 eggs with 3 cups milk and add the liquid to the flour. Stir to make a smooth, light batter and let it stand in a cool place for 2 hours. It will be the consistency of heavy cream. Bake in a buttered *plättar* pan—a griddle divided into small rounds—over moderate heat; turn the pancakes once to brown both sides. Or form small cakes on an ordinary griddle. Serve them hot, with lingonberry sauce or preserves. ·The lingonberry resembles our native cranberry.

Cottage Cheese Pancakes

RUB 1 cup cottage cheese through a fine sieve, stir in 6 well-beaten eggs, and mix thoroughly. Add 6 tablespoons each of sifted flour and melted butter and a pinch of salt and beat until well blended. Drop the batter by spoonfuls onto a buttered hot griddle and brown both sides, turning the cakes only once. Serve with tart currant jelly or with jam.

Omelet Puffs

BEAT the yolks of 4 eggs until they are thick and light. Beat in 1/4 cup each of water and sifted flour to make a smooth batter. Fold in 4 egg whites beaten until stiff. Drop the batter by tablespoons onto a buttered hot griddle and bake the puffs to a delicate brown on both sides, turning them only once. Serve with tart fruit preserves.

Blackberry Pancakes

BEAT 2 eggs until they are light and fluffy and beat in 2 cups buttermilk and 1 teaspoon soda. Sift together 2 cups sifted flour, 1 teaspoon salt, 1 tablespoon sugar, and 2 teaspoons baking powder. Gradually add the flour to the liquid, beating after each addition to make a smooth, rather thin batter. Stir in 1/4 cup melted butter and fold in 1 cup blackberries. Fry the cakes until brown on a hot buttered griddle. Turn the cakes only once and serve immediately.

Berry Pancakes

Other berries may be used the same way.

German Apple Pancakes

SIFT 1 cup flour, add 1/2 teaspoon salt and 2 teaspoons sugar, and sift together into a bowl. Gradually stir in 1 1/2 cups milk to make a smooth paste. Add 4 eggs, one at a time, beating briskly after each addition.

Peel and core 3 large apples, grate them or cut them into fine julienne strips, and marinate them in 1/2 cup lemon juice .

Fold the apples and juice into the batter and pour the batter into buttered hot individual skillets. Brown the underside and flip the pancakes; or sprinkle with cinnamon and sugar and glaze the top under the broiler. Serve hot, with more cinnamon and sugar, or with honey or preserves.

Cottage Cheese Pancakes

Grimslich   SOAK 1/2 loaf of white bread in water until it is quite soft, wrap the bread in a towel and press out as much of the water as possible. Add 2 egg yolks, 1/2 cup sugar, 1/4 cup each of raisins and finely pounded blanched almonds, and 1 teaspoon cinnamon. Beat well and fold in 2 egg whites, beaten until stiff. Drop the batter by tablespoons into a generous amount of melted butter and brown the cakes well on both sides, turning them only once. Serve the *grimslich* with a compote of cooked fruits.

Buckwheat   DISSOLVE 1 package granular yeast or 1 cake compressed yeast in 1/4 cup
Blini   water at temperature given on page 573 and combine it in a mixing bowl with 1 cup milk, scalded and cooled to lukewarm. Sift 2 cups buckwheat flour with 1 tablespoon salt and stir enough flour into the yeast and milk to make a thick sponge. Cover the bowl and let the sponge rise in a warm place for about 3 hours. Beat 3 egg yolks well with 1 cup lukewarm milk, 1 tablespoon melted butter and 1 teaspoon sugar. Add the liquid to the sponge alternately with the remaining buckwheat flour. The batter should be fairly thin; if necessary, add a little more milk. Beat the batter well and let it stand, covered, for 30 minutes. Fold in the 3 egg whites, beaten until stiff, and bake the *blini* in 3-inch cakes on a hot buttered griddle.

   Blini are part of the traditional Russian *zakuski* and are usually served with red and black caviar, smoked salmon, pickled herring, melted butter, and sour cream.

Adirondack   SEPARATE 4 eggs. Mix the yolks with 2 tablespoons sugar and 1/2 tea-
Flapjacks   spoon salt. Sift 2 cups flour with 2 teaspoons baking powder and stir the dry ingredients into the egg yolks alternately with 2 cups milk. Stir in 6 tablespoons melted butter, and fold in the egg whites, stiffly beaten. Bake the cakes on a hot griddle and serve with shaved maple sugar.

Hominy   IN a sieve drain thoroughly 2 cups cooked hominy. Put the hominy through
Tortillas   a food chopper and season it with salt to taste. Add 2 or 3 tablespoons fine white cornmeal. Blend in a little cold water, a few drops at a time, to make a smooth dough that can be kneaded.

   Form the smoothly kneaded dough into balls the size of eggs and flatten the balls between the hands, patting first with one hand on top, then the other, until the dough is as thin as pie pastry. Moisten the hands occasionally with cold water. Bake the *tortillas* on both sides on a hot un-buttered griddle until they are slightly brown and blistered.

Corn Cakes

To 3 cups cornmeal add 1 teaspoon salt, 2 tablespoons molasses, 1/4 cup melted butter and 2 eggs, lightly beaten. Add gradually about 3 cups milk, to make a batter the consistency of heavy cream. Bake on a very hot lightly buttered griddle in cakes about 3 inches in diameter. If the batter should thicken with standing, add a little more milk.

Scotch Oatcakes

Put 4 cups fine, steel-cut oats or oatmeal into a bowl and stir in 1 tea-spoon soda and 2 teaspoons salt. Stir in 6 tablespoons melted shortening and about 1 cup hot water, or enough to make a firm dough. Roll the dough out very thinly on a board sprinkled generously with oatmeal and cut it into 9-inch circles. Cut the circles into pie-shaped quarters (farles) and bake them on a hot griddle until the edges curl. Turn and bake the oatcakes briefly on the other side.

Irish Griddle Scones

Sift 4 cups flour with 1 teaspoon each of sugar, soda, and salt. Add grad-ually about 2 cups milk, to make a rather soft dough. Turn the dough out onto a floured board and knead it lightly for 5 minutes. Pat the dough into rounds 1 inch thick and of any desired diameter. Cut each round into quarters. Bake the triangles on a hot, floured griddle until they are brown on the underside; turn them to brown the other side. To serve, split, toast, and butter generously.

Flannel Cakes

Sift together 1 cup sifted flour, 2 tablespoons sugar, 1 tablespoon baking powder, and 1/2 teaspoon salt. In a separate bowl beat 2 eggs until they are light and stir in 1 cup milk and 2 tablespoons melted butter. Blend the flour and egg mixture together as lightly as possible. Drop the batter by table-spoons onto a greased hot griddle and brown the cakes lightly on both sides. Serve them with butter and warmed maple syrup or honey.

Noodle Cakes

Cook enough very fine noodles in boiling salted water to make 3 cups cooked noodles and drain them thoroughly. Beat 3 eggs until they are light and com-bine them with the noodles. Season to taste with salt, pepper, and nutmeg. Melt 6 tablespoons butter in a large skillet and drop heaping tablespoons of the noodles into the pan. Brown the cakes lightly on both sides.

Vanilla Pots de Crème

$\mathcal{D}$esserts

According to the scientists, there are only four flavors: sweet, sour, bitter, and salt. According to the gourmet, the greatest of these is, indisputably, sweet. We are inclined to sympathize with those who consider a meal merely the straightest line to dessert, and see great logic in the suggestion that one avoid the dreadful dilemma of being too full to enjoy dessert by having dessert first, and proceeding backward to soup or hors-d'oeuvre!

Out of deference to the old-fashioned housewife who customarily climaxed every meal with dessert *and* cake or cookies, we have listed these different kinds of sweets separately. In the pages that follow, you will find our choice of an endless variety of sweets, all as beautiful as they are good.

The flavored mixtures of eggs and milk known broadly as custards form the basis of bland nursery desserts and of the most elaborate entremets *a professional chef can devise. Our collection of custards runs the gamut.*

SCALD 2 cups cream with a 1-inch piece of vanilla bean and 1/2 cup sugar and cool it slightly. Beat 6 egg yolks until they are light and lemon colored and add the cream, stirring constantly. Strain the mixture through a fine sieve into small earthenware pots or custard cups. Set the pots in a pan of water, cover the pan, and bake them in a moderately slow oven (325° F.) for about 15 minutes, or until a knife inserted near the center comes out clean. Serve chilled.

Pots de Crème à la Vanille
VANILLA
POTS DE CRÈME

597

Pots de Crème Variations	Flavor the basic mixture for *pots de crème à la vanille* with 1 tablespoon coffee extract, 4 ounces sweet chocolate, melted, for half the sugar, or 2 tablespoons any desired liqueur, rum, or brandy, or with any combination of these, such as chocolate and coffee or chocolate and rum.

Soft Custard BEAT 4 egg yolks lightly and stir in 1/4 cup sugar and a dash of salt. Add gradually 2 cups milk, scalded with a 1-inch piece of vanilla bean. Cook the mixture over hot water, stirring constantly, until it coats the spoon. Be careful not to overcook. Cool the custard, stirring it occasionally, and store it in the refrigerator until wanted. Instead of the vanilla bean, 1/2 teaspoon vanilla extract may be added to the cooled custard.

Oeufs à la Neige aux Fruits
SNOW EGGS

BEAT the whites of 4 eggs until they are stiff, adding gradually 3/4 cup sugar. Using a wet spoon, form the meringue into egg-shapes and slip them off the spoon into boiling water. Poach them for about 2 minutes, turn them, and poach them for 2 minutes longer. Remove the snow eggs from the water with a skimmer and drain them on absorbent paper. Put sliced fresh fruit or berries in the bottom of a deep dish and arrange the eggs on the fruit. Pour cold vanilla sauce or soft custard around them and sprinkle with toasted slivered almonds or grated chocolate.

Zabaglione Orientale IN the top of a double boiler beat with a rotary beater 6 egg yolks and 1/2 cup sugar until the mixture is thick and pale in color. Gradually beat in 2/3 cup Oriental mixture: 2 tablespoons vodka, 1/4 cup Cointreau, and enough water to make 2/3 cup in all. Place the pan over boiling water and continue to beat until the mixture foams and begins to thicken. Be careful not to overcook it. Strain into sherbet glasses lined with ladyfingers or pound cake and serve hot.

Sabayon Meringué BUTTER a large baking dish and cover the bottom with 18 crushed dry macaroons. Beat 6 egg yolks well with 2 tablespoons confectioners' sugar and 1/3 cup Madeira. Cook this mixture over hot water, beating it constantly with a rotary beater, until it is hot and foamy. Do not let it boil. Pour the hot custard over the macaroon crumbs in the baking dish. Beat 6 egg whites with a pinch of salt until they stand in soft peaks, then beat in 1 scant cup confectioners' sugar and 1/2 teaspoon vanilla. Continue to beat the meringue mixture until it is very stiff. Spread the meringue evenly over the custard in the baking dish, being sure that it touches the edge of the dish all around.

Decorate the meringue with blanched almonds. Bake the pudding in a moderate oven (350° F.) until the meringue and nuts are lightly browned. Serve at once.

Strawberry Custard

BEAT the yolks of 4 eggs until they are light and very pale in color, and combine them with 1 cup hot milk and 1 tablespoon sugar. Stir over very low heat until the custard coats a spoon. Remove the pan from the heat, stir in 1 teaspoon brandy and cool thoroughly.

Whip 2 cups heavy cream and fold in the stiffly beaten whites of 4 eggs. Fold in the cooled custard and 2 cups washed, hulled, sliced, and chilled strawberries. Serve the custard immediately.

Pineapple Custard

PEEL and grate a fresh pineapple and strain the juice from the pulp. Combine 1 cup pineapple juice and 1/2 cup sugar, bring to a boil, and boil vigorously for 10 minutes. Remove the pan from the heat and pour the syrup gradually over 3 beaten egg yolks, beating constantly. Return the mixture to the heat and cook over low heat, stirring, until the custard coats the spoon. Do not let it boil. Cool. Put the grated pineapple in a serving dish. Fold 3 stiffly beaten egg whites into the cooled custard and pour the custard over the pineapple. Chill and serve with a topping of whipped cream sweetened to taste.

Zuppa Inglese al Crèma de Cacao

ITALIAN TRIFLE WITH CRÈME DE CACAO

COMBINE 1/3 cup flour, 1/2 cup sugar, and 1/4 teaspoon salt. Gradually stir in 2 cups hot milk and beat until smooth. Stir this gradually into 4 slightly beaten egg yolks and cook the mixture over boiling water, stirring constantly, until the custard is thick, taking care not to let it curdle. Strain the custard through a fine sieve. Cool, flavor with 1/2 teaspoon vanilla, and set aside.

Make a meringue as follows: Beat 4 egg whites until they are frothy, add a pinch of salt, and beat the whites until they are stiff but not dry. Beat in gradually 1/4 cup sugar.

Line the bottom of an ovenproof dish with a layer of spongecake sprinkled with 3 tablespoons dark rum. Cover the cake with the custard and sprinkle the custard with 1 tablespoon finely shredded candied fruit. Place over the custard another layer of spongecake and sprinkle it with 1/4 cup crème de cacao. Spread the meringue over the entire surface right up to the rim of

599

the dish. Sprinkle the meringue with a little sugar and set the dish in a moderate oven (350° F.) until the meringue is lightly browned.

Trifle   LINE the bottom of a cut-glass bowl with an inch-thick layer of day-old spongecake. Moisten the cake with Madeira and spread it thinly with tart currant jelly. Cover the cake with chilled soft custard and top it with 1 cup sweetened whipped cream. With a pastry tube, pipe whipped-cream rosettes around the trifle and decorate the center with flowers made of angelica and crystallized cherries.

English Bilberry Trifle   SANDWICH 2 dozen ladyfingers in pairs with bilberry (blueberry) jam. Arrange half of these in rows in a glass serving dish and sprinkle them with 3 tablespoons Port or Sherry. Add the remaining ladyfingers, with the rows running in the opposite direction, and sprinkle them with 3 more tablespoons of the wine.

Pour over all cooled soft custard and chill the trifle until serving time. Sprinkle the entire surface with 6 crumbled almond macaroons. Whip 1 cup heavy cream with 1 tablespoon sugar. Spread the cream over the trifle and garnish it with 3 tablespoons slivered and toasted almonds stuck upright.

Sherry Trifle   COOK in the top of a double boiler 4 egg yolks, 3/4 cup Sherry, 1/2 cup sugar, and a pinch of salt. Add 1 tablespoon flour and cook for about 2 minutes longer. Cool and fold in 4 stiffly beaten egg whites. Pour the Sherry custard over 12 macaroons soaked in Sherry, spread with whipped cream, and garnish with almonds.

Chestnuts with Coffee Sauce   SLIT the shells of 1 pound large chestnuts and simmer the chestnuts in water to cover for 5 minutes. Working very quickly, when the nuts are cool enough to handle, remove and discard the shells and the skins. Put the chestnuts in fresh boiling water with 3 tablespoons sugar, and cook them gently until they are tender, for 20 to 30 minutes. Drain the nuts well, chill them, and pile them in sherbet glasses.

Beat 4 egg yolks with 3 tablespoons sugar and add 1/2 cup each of double-strength coffee and heavy cream. Cook the mixture over hot water, stirring constantly, until it is thick enough to coat a spoon, but do not let it boil. Chill the sauce well, stirring it from time to time, and serve the sauce over the chestnuts in the sherbet glasses.

To 1 quart milk add 2 tablespoons water and bring almost to a boil. Mix 5 tablespoons cornstarch, 1/4 cup sugar, and a dash of salt with enough cold water to make a smooth paste. Add the paste slowly to the milk, stirring constantly, and simmer for about 15 minutes, or until the mixture begins to thicken to nearly the consistency of whipped cream. Remove from the heat and stir in 2 tablespoons rose water. Pour the pudding into sherbet glasses, decorate with halved blanched almonds placed in a rosebud design, and sprinkle with coarsely chopped pistachio nuts.

Muhailabien
MILK PUDDING

Baked custards may be turned out of their molds to serve or, for less formal occasions, spooned out of the dish and masked with sauce.

SCALD 3 cups milk with a 1-pinch piece of vanilla bean and cool it slightly. Beat 4 whole eggs, 4 egg yolks, and 1/2 cup sugar until the mixture is light and lemon colored and add the milk, stirring constantly. Strain the mixture through a fine sieve into a buttered baking dish or individual custard cups. Set the dish or cups in a pan of hot water, cover, and bake in a moderately slow oven (325° F.) for 30 minutes to 1 hour, or until the custard is set and a knife inserted near the center comes out clean.

To serve the custard, let it cool, loosen it from the sides of the baking dish with a knife, and invert the mold on a serving dish.

Crème Renversée à la Française
BAKED CUSTARD

COMBINE 1/2 cup strong coffee with 2 cups scalded milk and follow directions for *crème renversée à la française.*

Coffee Custard

COOK 1/2 cup water and 1/4 pound grated sweet chocolate over low heat, stirring constantly, until the mixture is smooth. Combine with 2 1/2 cups scalded milk and follow directions for *crème renversée à la française.*

Chocolate Custard

SCALD 1 cup each of cream and milk with a piece of vanilla bean. Beat together thoroughly 3 whole eggs, 2 egg yolks, and 1/2 cup sugar. Discard the vanilla bean from the hot milk and gradually pour the milk into the egg mixture, stirring vigorously.

Heat 1 cup sugar in a heavy skillet until it is melted. Gradually stir in

Caramel Custard with Peaches

1/2 cup water and cook the syrup until it becomes caramel in color. Pour the caramel syrup into a ring mold and turn the mold around and around until the entire inside is well coated. Let the caramel set and pour in the custard. Set the mold in a pan of hot water and bake it in a moderate oven (350° F.) for about 45 minutes, or until a knife inserted near the center comes out clean. Cool the custard and, when ready to serve, unmold it onto a serving dish. Fill the center of the mold with 12 peach halves, poached in vanilla syrup until tender, and cover the peaches with whipped cream, sweetened and flavored to taste, piling it high in the middle. Decorate the cream with candied cherries and pistachio nuts.

Crème Sainte-Cécile aux Fruits
CUSTARD RING WITH FRUIT

SCALD 3 cups milk with a piece of vanilla bean and let the mixture steep for 15 minutes. Mix together 4 whole eggs and 4 egg yolks, add 1/2 cup sugar, and work all together well. Remove the vanilla bean from the milk and add 3 tablespoons finely crushed almond praline. Stir the milk slowly into the egg mixture and pour the custard into a well-buttered ring mold. Set the mold in a shallow pan of hot but not boiling water and bake it in a moderately slow oven (325° F.) for about 45 minutes, or until the custard is set. Add a little cold water occasionally to keep the water below the boiling point. The custard is done when a knife inserted near the center comes out clean. Let the custard stand until it is lukewarm.

Prepare a macédoine of mixed cooked fruit cut in dice or slices, using any desired combination—pears, pineapple, peaches, cherries, oranges, and so on. Drain the juice from the fruit. To each cup of juice, add 1 teaspoon cornstarch or arrowroot mixed with 2 tablespoons cold juice, and cook the juice until it thickens slightly. For each cup of fruit add 1 tablespoon kirsch, Cointreau, or Grand Marnier and 2 tablespoons puréed stewed dried apricots and a little of the thickened fruit juice. Keep the fruit warm. Invert the custard ring on the serving dish and unmold it. Fill the center of the ring with fruit and pour the remaining juice around the ring. Pour a little heated kirsch, rum, or Cognac over the fruit and ignite the spirit. Serve flaming.

Crème Santa Clara
CUSTARD RING SANTA CLARA

PREPARE a custard ring for *crème Sainte-Cécile aux fruits*. The praline may be omitted.

Fill the center of the ring with prunes prepared as follows: Soak 1/2 pound prunes for several hours in cold water and drain them. Simmer them with 1 cup each of red wine and water and 2 slices of lemon until they are soft and the liquid is reduced to 1 cup. Add 3 tablespoons purée of cooked dried apricots. Pile the prunes in the center of the mold and pour around the ring the sauce in which the fruit was cooked. Serve warm.

COMBINE 1/2 cup sugar, 2 tablespoons flour, and 1/2 teaspoon freshly grated nutmeg. Stir in 1 1/2 cups heavy cream and 1/2 cup thinly sliced citron peel. Stir in the beaten yolks of 6 eggs and turn the mixture into a buttered shallow pudding dish. Bake the custard in a moderate oven (350° F.) for about 30 minutes, or until a knife inserted near the center comes out clean and the top is browned.

Citron Custard

MIX together 1 cup cooked, puréed pumpkin, 2 lightly beaten eggs, and 1/2 cup brown sugar mixed with 1/2 teaspoon each of salt and cinnamon and 1/4 teaspoon ginger. Stir in 1 cup cream and the grated rind of half an orange. Pour the mixture into buttered custard cups and set the cups in a pan of hot water. Bake the custard in a moderately slow oven (325° F.) for 40 minutes, or until a knife inserted near the center comes out clean.

Pumpkin Custard

CREAM together 1 cup sugar, white or brown, and 2/3 cup butter. Add 2 beaten eggs and 2 cups grated raw sweet potato and beat well. Add the grated rinds of 1 orange and 1/2 lemon, 1/2 teaspoon each of ginger and mace, and a dash of cinnamon. Beat the custard again well and bake it in a well-buttered baking dish in a moderate oven (350° F.) for 1 hour.

Sweet Potato Custard

    Like custards, rice desserts can be very simple or very elegant; they lend themselves to infinite variation.

WASH 1 cup rice in cold water, put it in a saucepan, and add cold water to cover generously. Bring to a boil, turn off the heat, and let the rice stand for 5 minutes. Drain it in a sieve and rinse it well in running cold water. Return the rice to the pan or put it in the top of a double boiler with 2 1/2 cups scalded milk, 6 tablespoons sugar, 1/2 teaspoon salt, and a piece of vanilla bean. Bring the milk to a boil and add 1 tablespoon butter. Cover the pan and simmer the rice very gently for about 30 minutes or cook it in the top of a double boiler for about 45 minutes, or until it is tender. Toss the rice with a fork to separate the grains and add 3 egg yolks mixed with 2 tablespoons cream, tossing all together carefully with a fork. Spread the mixture on a platter to cool This rice for *entremets*, or desserts, is used for many of the elaborate desserts that follow.

Rice for Entremets

**Croquettes
de Riz à la
Confiture**

RICE CROQUETTES
WITH JAM

SHAPE cold rice for *entremets* into small balls and put 1/2 teaspoon apricot jam in the center of each. Roll the balls in flour, dip them in beaten egg, and roll in fine fresh bread crumbs. Fry them in hot deep fat (380° F.) until they are golden brown and drain on absorbent paper. Serve on hot plates with sabayon or fruit sauce.

**Croquettes
de Riz
Fructidor**

RICE CROQUETTES
WITH
CANDIED FRUITS

PREPARE half the recipe for rice for *entremets*, but use 3 eggs. Return the mixture to the heat and cook it, stirring, until it thickens and leaves the sides of the pan. Stir in 1/2 cup mixed candied fruits, finely chopped and moistened with 2 tablespoons kirsch. Spread the cream in a shallow pan and chill it. At serving time, mold the mixture into pear-shaped croquettes, roll the croquettes in flour, in an egg beaten with 1/4 cup milk and 1 tablespoon oil, and in finely chopped blanched almonds. Fry the croquettes in hot deep fat (385° F.) until they are browned. Drain them on absorbent paper and insert in the top of each, to resemble the stem of a pear, a small stick of angelica softened in lukewarm water. Serve with sabayon sauce or a fruit sauce.

**Apricot
Rice Pudding**

PREPARE rice for *entremets* and spread it 1 1/2 inches thick in a buttered baking dish. Drain cooked apricot halves and arrange them on the rice, rounded side up. Cover with a meringue made by beating 1/2 cup sugar gradually into 2 stiffly beaten egg whites, making attractive swirls or designs. Sprinkle with confectioners' sugar and brown for 15 minutes in a moderate oven (350° F.). Decorate between the meringue swirls with melted red currant jelly, alternately with thick apricot purée forced through a pastry tube.

**Fruit
Bourgeoise**

SPREAD a thick layer of freshly cooked rice for *entremets* in a heatproof serving dish. Arrange cooked fruit—apricots, pears, apples, or pineapple—on the rice and cover all with *crème pâtissière*. Sprinkle with chopped almonds or macaroon crumbs and then with a little sugar. Place in a hot oven (450° F.) or under the broiler to brown.

**Apples
Dauphin**

PEEL and core baking apples of uniform size and put them in a baking dish. Put a little sugar and a little butter in the center of each and sprinkle with sugar. Pour just enough water into the pan to prevent scorching. Bake in a moderate oven (350° to 375° F.) until the apples are soft and golden brown.

Apricot Rice Pudding

Spread in the serving dish a layer of freshly cooked, still-warm rice for *entremets*. Arrange the hot baked apples on the rice and decorate each with a daisy made of almonds. Pour apricot sauce over them.

Riz à la Condé
RICE CONDÉ

TURN rice for *entremets* into a flan ring on a serving platter and chill the rice well. Remove the ring and cover the rice with a layer of poached fruit such as apricots, apples, or pears, all cut in half, rounded side up. Decorate the rice with candied cherries and bits of angelica, and moisten it with a little of the syrup in which the fruit was poached. The syrup may be flavored with any liqueur.

Rice for Impératrice Variations

WASH 1/2 cup rice in cold water and cover it well with cold water in a saucepan. Bring the water to a boil and simmer the rice for 2 minutes. Drain it in a sieve and rinse it by letting cold water run through it. Return the rice to the pan and cook it with 1 1/4 cups milk until it is very tender. Do not stir the rice while it is cooking.

Combine 4 egg yolks with 1/2 cup sugar in the top of a double boiler. Stir in 3/4 cup hot milk, add a 1-inch piece of vanilla bean, and cook over boiling water, stirring, until the sauce is smooth and thick. Stir in 1 tablespoon gelatin softened in 2 tablespoons cold water and strain the custard through a fine sieve. Add the rice, blend thoroughly, and chill until the mixture just begins to set.

Poires à l'Impératrice
PEARS IMPÉRATRICE

PREPARE rice for *impératrice* variations and turn it into a buttered ring mold. Chill the mold for about 4 hours, or until it is well set. Turn it out onto a serving dish.

Follow the recipe for *pâte à genoise* and bake part of the batter in a small round mold of a size that will fit within the rice ring. Bake the rest of the batter in a thin sheet. Set the cake in the ring.

Poach about 12 pear halves in a light syrup of 2 cups water and 1 cup sugar until they are tender and let them cool. Set them close together, wide ends down, upright on the rice in a circle around the cake. Cut 2 of the halves into thirds and lay these pieces in a star-shape on the top of the cake. Brush pears and cake generously with apricot glaze.

Press between the pears, into the rice ring, and onto the top of the cake halves of candied cherries and jewel-shaped cutouts of angelica. Put half a cherry in the center of the pear star. Chill the *pièce montée* thoroughly.

At serving time, garnish the plate with small triangles cut from the thin *génoise*. Sprinkle alternate triangles with confectioners' sugar.

PREPARE rice for *impératrice* variations, but omit the gelatin. Stir in 3/4 cup chopped mixed candied fruit marinated in a little kirsch and fold in 1 cup heavy cream, whipped. Turn the rice into a large glass dish and chill it well. To serve, cover the rice decoratively with whipped cream forced through the fluted nozzle of a pastry bag, piling it high in the center. Around the edge of the dish form a circle of large, perfect strawberries. Glaze the berries by brushing them with currant jelly heated to spreading consistency. Return the dish to the refrigerator for a few minutes to allow the jelly to set.

*Fraises
à l'Impératrice*
STRAWBERRIES
IMPÉRATRICE

REMOVE a thin layer of the peel from 3 mandarin oranges or tangerines and cut it into very fine julienne. Cover it with boiling water, simmer for 2 minutes, and drain.

*Riz à la
Mandarin*
MANDARINS
IMPÉRATRICE

Make rice for *impératrice* variations and add the blanched peel and 1 cup heavy cream, whipped. Add a small amount of orange food coloring and chill the rice in a decorative mold for at least 4 hours.

When ready to serve, unmold the rice onto a chilled platter and arrange around the base a circle of peeled mandarin sections which have been marinated for 30 minutes with a little sugar, apricot marmalade, and Curaçao. Sprinkle with a little blanched julienne of peel.

IN the top of a double boiler bring 4 cups milk to a boil. Add 1 cup rice, 3/4 cup sugar, and 1/2 teaspoon salt and cook the rice over boiling water for about 45 minutes. Add 2 teaspoons unsalted butter and cook the rice for 45 minutes longer. Add 1 teaspoon vanilla and 1/2 teaspoon lemon juice to the rice and set it aside to cool.

*Rice and
Oranges
à la Russe*

Soften 2 tablespoons gelatin in 1/4 cup water and dissolve it in 1/2 cup boiling water. Stir the gelatin into the rice. In a mixing bowl whip 2 cups heavy cream until it is stiff and fold it into the rice. Turn the rice mixture into a serving bowl and chill it for at least 4 hours.

Peel 5 seedless oranges and cut them into thin slices. In a saucepan make a syrup by boiling together for 5 minutes 1 cup each of sugar and water, 1/4 cup orange juice, and 1 tablespoon grated orange rind. Add the orange slices to the hot syrup. Chill the fruit and serve it with the rice.

WASH 1 cup rice and cook it in 1 quart water for about 25 minutes, or until it is very tender. Do not stir. Drain and set it aside to cool.

*Rice Pudding
Amandine*

Whip 3 cups heavy cream until it is stiff. Stir in 3 tablespoons brandy,

3 tablespoons sugar or more to taste, about 20 almonds, blanched and grated, and the rice. Mix thoroughly.

Put one-third of the rice cream in a large glass serving bowl. On this arrange 12 macaroons soaked in brandy. Put another third of the rice cream on the macaroons and cover it with more brandied macaroons. Finish with the rice cream and chill the dessert for several hours. Decorate with whipped cream forced through a fluted nozzle and serve with strawberry sauce.

Riz aux
Fraises
STRAWBERRY RICE

IN a heavy saucepan cook 1/4 cup rice and 2 cups milk over low heat, stirring constantly, until the mixture comes to a boil. Cook slowly, stirring occasionally, until the rice is very soft and creamy. Soften 2 teaspoons gelatin in the juice of 1 lemon, dissolve it over hot water, and stir it into the hot rice. Remove the pan from the heat, pour a little of the hot mixture into the lightly beaten yolks of 2 eggs and add the eggs to the rice. Put the pan in a bowl of crushed ice and stir the cream until it is cold. Carefully fold in the stiffly beaten white of 1 egg, 1 cup whipped cream flavored with 1 teaspoon *eau-de-vie de framboise*, and 2 cups sliced strawberries. Turn the cream into a serving bowl and chill.

Hot Rice
Pudding
à l'Anglaise

COOK 2 cups milk, 1/2 cup rice, and a small piece of vanilla bean in the top pan of a double boiler for about 45 minutes, stirring from time to time. Mix together 2 egg yolks and 1/4 cup each of sugar and cream and stir the mixture gently into the rice and milk. Bring to the boiling point, remove the vanilla bean, and turn the rice into a baking dish. Brown the top quickly in a very hot oven (450° F.) or under the broiler. Serve hot, with cream.

Reismeringue
RICE WITH
MERINGUE

IN the top of a double boiler over hot water cook 1 cup rice with 2 cups hot water and 1 teaspoon salt for 30 minutes without removing the cover.

In a saucepan mix 3/4 cup sugar with 2 tablespoons softened butter. Heat it slowly, stirring constantly until it is lightly browned. Add the juice of 1 lemon and 1 orange and 1/4 cup light rum. Cook, stirring, until the mixture is well blended and syrupy. Carefully fold in the cooked rice, mixing lightly with a fork until the grains are coated. Cover the bottom of a buttered baking dish with 1 1/2-inch layer of the rice mixture and top with 1/4-inch layer of apricot jam, making alternate layers, ending with rice. Whip 3 egg whites until they are stiff and fold in 3 tablespoons sugar, 1/2 teaspoon vanilla extract, and 1/4 teaspoon salt. Swirl the meringue over the rice in peaks, and bake it in a moderate oven (350° F.) until it is lightly browned.

When gelatin is used to thicken and stiffen a cream, the result is light, fluffy, insubstantial, and entirely delightful. Gelatin creams may be cooked or uncooked; both sorts are included here.

SOFTEN 1 tablespoon gelatin in 2 tablespoons cold water. In a saucepan combine 4 egg yolks and 1/2 cup sugar and beat the mixture with a wooden spoon until it is smooth and creamy. Gradually add 1 cup hot milk, stirring rapidly. Add a 1-inch stick of vanilla bean and cook the mixture over simmering water, stirring constantly, until the cream is thickened and smooth. Discard the vanilla bean and add the softened gelatin, stirring until it is thoroughly dissolved. Cool the cream, stirring occasionally to prevent a skin from forming on the surface.

Crème à l'Anglaise Collée
JELLIED ENGLISH CUSTARD

WHILE the *crème à l'anglaise collée* is cool but not firm fold in 1 cup heavy cream, whipped until stiff. The cream may be flavored with coffee, chocolate, or any liqueur, to taste.

Bavarois Variés
BAVARIAN CREAMS

IN a saucepan beat 5 egg yolks and 1/4 cup sugar until the mixture is thick and pale in color. Add 1 tablespoon gelatin softened in 1/4 cup cold water and 1 1/2 cups hot milk and stir constantly over low heat until the mixture is hot and thick. Do not allow it to boil. Stir the cream over cracked ice until it cools and begins to set. Fold in the stiffly beaten whites of 3 eggs and 1/2 cup cream, whipped until it stands in well-defined peaks, and flavor with 1 tablespoon kirsch. Pour into a 1-quart mold dipped in cold water and chill for 2 hours. Unmold on a chilled platter and garnish with fresh strawberries.

Bavarois au Kirsch
KIRSCH BAVARIAN CREAM

CRUSH 1 quart fresh raspberries and strain them through a fine sieve. Add 1 tablespoon lemon juice and 3/4 cup sugar and stir until the sugar is completely dissolved. Soften 2 tablespoons gelatin in 1/4 cup cold water, dissolve it over hot water, and stir it into the raspberry purée. Stir the mixture over cracked ice until it cools and begins to thicken and fold in 2 cups heavy cream, whipped until it stands in peaks.
Rinse a 2-quart mold in cold water, pour the raspberry cream into it, and

Bavarois aux Framboises
RASPBERRY BAVARIAN CREAM

609

chill it for at least 2 hours. To serve, unmold on a large chilled serving platter and garnish with whole raspberries.

Other berries may be used in the same way.

Bavarois
aux Oranges

ORANGE
BAVARIAN CREAM

GRATE the rind of 2 small oranges and 1/2 lemon and soak it in 1/2 cup boiling water for 30 minutes. Beat 4 egg yolks with 1 cup sugar until the mixture is very light and creamy, add to it the strained juice of 4 oranges and 2 lemons and blend well. Add the grated rind and the water in which it was soaked, and mix thoroughly. Put the mixture into the top of a double boiler and cook it over hot but not boiling water, stirring constantly, until the custard is thick. Set it aside to cool.

Soften 1 tablespoon gelatin in 1/4 cup cold water for 5 minutes and dissolve it over hot water. Add the gelatin to the custard, blend well, and strain the mixture into a mixing bowl. Whip 2 cups heavy cream until it is very stiff and fold it gently into the orange mixture. Turn the cream into a ring mold that has been dipped in cold water and chill it for at least 3 hours, until it is thoroughly set.

Whip 1 cup heavy cream until it is stiff with 1/4 cup sugar and a little vanilla to taste. To serve, unmold the pudding on a serving dish, fill the center of the ring with whipped cream and sprinkle the cream with finely chopped candied orange peel.

Peach Cream

BEAT 1 cup sugar and 4 egg yolks until the mixture is light and lemon colored. Add 1 cup fresh peach pulp forced through a sieve, 1/2 cup white wine, 2 tablespoons lemon juice, and 1 tablespoon peach brandy. Cook the mixture in the top of a double boiler, stirring constantly, until is smooth and thick. Soften 2 tablespoons gelatin in 1/2 cup water and stir it over boiling water until the gelatin is dissolved. Add the gelatin to the fruit, turn the mixture into a bowl, and stir it from time to time until it cools. Fold in 1 cup cream, whipped, and 4 egg whites, beaten until stiff. Pour the pudding into a glass serving bowl and chill it for an hour or more.

Ginger Cream

BEAT together 2 egg yolks, 1/4 cup sugar, and a pinch of salt until well blended. Over the egg mixture pour gradually 1 cup milk, scalded, and cook, stirring constantly, until the custard thickens. Remove the pan from the heat. Soak 1 tablespoon gelatin in 1/4 cup cold water for 5 minutes, dissolve it over boiling water, and stir it into the hot custard. Add 3 tablespoons Chinese ginger syrup, 1 teaspoon vanilla, and 1/4 cup of the preserved ginger, cut into tiny pieces. Stir the mixture over cracked ice until it begins to set and fold in 2 cups heavy cream, whipped. Pour the cream into a cold, wet mold and chill it until ready to serve. Unmold and decorate with 1 cup whipped cream sweetened with 1/4 cup sugar and 1 teaspoon vanilla.

BEAT 3 egg yolks and 1/3 cup sugar with a whip until the mixture is smooth and creamy. Scald 1 cup milk with a piece of split vanilla bean and add the milk gradually to the egg yolks, mixing thoroughly. Cook the mixture slowly, stirring constantly until it almost reaches the boiling point, but be careful that it does not boil. Remove the vanilla bean and stir in 1/2 tablespoon gelatin softened in 2 tablespoons cold water. Cool, stirring from time to time to prevent a crust from forming on the surface. Fold in 3/4 cup heavy cream, whipped, and pour the mixture into a ring mold rinsed out in cold water. Chill until set.

Turban de Fraises Printanier
SPRING STRAWBERRY RING

To serve, loosen the edges and invert the cream on a serving dish.

Wash and drain 2 cups strawberries and put them in a bowl with the juice of 1 lemon and 2 tablespoons sugar. Prepare 1 cup apricot sauce and add 2 tablespoons kirsch. Put a few strawberries around the outside of the unmolded cream, fill the center with the remaining berries, and spread apricot sauce over them. Decorate around the ring with whipped cream and crystallized violets.

IN the top of a double boiler scald 2 cups light cream with 2 ounces bitter-sweet chocolate. Stir in 1/4 cup cocoa and 1/2 cup sugar. Soften 1 1/2 tablespoons gelatin in 1/4 cup cold water and dissolve the gelatin over hot water. Stir it into the chocolate-cream mixture. Pour the pudding into a mixing bowl and cool it, stirring occasionally. Stir in 1 teaspoon or more vanilla and fold in 6 egg whites, beaten until stiff. Pour the mixture into a glass bowl and chill it. Just before serving, garnish the pudding with whipped cream and sprinkle it with grated chocolate.

Chocolate Cream

SOAK 1 tablespoon gelatin in 1/4 cup cold water for 5 minutes and dissolve it in 1 cup boiling water. Stir in 1 cup sugar and continue to stir the mixture over cracked ice until it cools and begins to thicken. Beat the mix-

Almond Pudding

ture with a rotary beater until it is frothy. Fold in 5 egg whites, beaten until stiff, and 1/2 teaspoon almond extract. Pour a layer of this into a mold that has been dipped in cold water, and cover it with a layer of blanched chopped toasted almonds. Continue in this fashion until the mold is filled, using 1 cup almonds in all. Chill the pudding until it is thoroughly set, unmold it, and serve it with the following sauce: Scald 2 cups milk in the top of a double boiler. Beat 5 egg yolks with 1/4 cup sugar and a dash of salt until they are very light. Slowly add the eggs to the milk and cook, stirring constantly, until the mixture is thick enough to coat the spoon. Cool the custard, add 1/2 teaspoon vanilla, and fold in 1 cup whipped cream.

Charlotte Russe aux Amandes

LINE a cylindrical charlotte mold with split ladyfingers. Begin at the bottom of the mold by placing a small round piece of the sponge in the center. Cover the bottom with ladyfingers cut into triangles, placing them close together around the center piece and radiating from it like the petals of a flower. Place split ladyfingers upright and close together all around the inside wall.

Fill the mold with almond Bavarian cream and put it in the refrigerator to set for at least 2 hours. Unmold the charlotte on a round serving plate. Serve with apricot sauce and whipped cream.

Bavarois aux Amandes
ALMOND BAVARIAN CREAM

In a saucepan combined 2 cups milk and 1/2 cup almond paste. Cook over low heat, stirring constantly, until the cream is smooth. Stir the mixture slowly into 4 beaten egg yolks and cook over hot water, stirring, until the custard is hot and slightly thickened. Add 1 tablespoon gelatin softened in 1/2 cup cold water and continue to cook and stir until the gelatin is dissolved. Stir the cream over cracked ice until it cools and begins to set. Stir in 1 teaspoon vanilla and fold in 2 cups heavy cream, whipped until it stands in soft peaks.

Almond Milk

POUND 1 cup blanched sweet almonds and 2 bitter almonds to a paste in a mortar. Add 2 cups water, a little at a time, and continue to pound until the liquid becomes milky. Strain the mixture through a sieve lined with muslin to extract as much of the almond milk as possible.

Coffee Blancmange

Soften 1 1/2 tablespoons gelatin in 1/2 cup cold water for 5 minutes and combine it with the almond milk, 1 cup cream, and 1/2 cup sugar. Bring the mixture slowly to the boiling point, stirring to dissolve the sugar and the gelatin. Cool, and stir in 2 tablespoons coffee extract. Pour the mixture into an oiled ring mold and set it in the refrigerator until the blancmange is firm. At serving time, dip the mold quickly into hot water, loosen the blancmange carefully with a knife blade, and turn it out onto a chilled platter. Decorate the mold to taste with sweetened and flavored whipped cream forced through a pastry tube.

BEAT 5 whole eggs and 5 egg yolks until they are very light and fluffy. *Lemon Cream* Add 1 cup sugar and continue to beat until the mixture is thick and pale in color. Add the grated rind of 3 lemons. Soften 1 tablespoon gelatin in the juice of 3 lemons and stir over hot water until the gelatin is dissolved. Stir the mixture into the eggs and fold in 4 cups heavy cream, whipped. Chill the *fromage* and serve it with whipped cream.

CHOP enough peeled nectarines to make 1 cup. Add 1/2 cup confectioners' *Nectarine* sugar and 1 tablespoon brandy. Soak 1 tablespoon gelatin in 1/4 cup cold *Cream* water for 5 minutes, dissolve it over hot water, and stir it into the nectarine mixture. Cool and fold in 1 cup cream, whipped until it stands in peaks. Turn the mixture into a ring mold dipped in cold water and chill the mold for at least 3 hours. Unmold onto a chilled serving platter, fill the center with brandied kumquats, and top with whipped cream. Peaches may be used in this recipe.

SOFTEN 2 tablespoons gelatin in 1/2 cup cold water and add it to 2 cups *Hawaiian* very hot milk. Add 1/2 cup sugar and stir until the sugar and gelatin are *Pineapple* dissolved. Remove from the heat and stir in 1 teaspoon vanilla. Pour the *Pudding* flavored milk slowly into 5 beaten egg yolks, stirring vigorously, and beat until the mixture is cool. Stir in 1 cup shredded pineapple and 1/2 cup each of ground macaroons, chopped blanched almonds, and raisins. Beat 5 egg whites until they are stiff and fold them into the custard. Turn the pudding into a mold and chill it for 5 hours. When ready to serve, turn the pudding out on a chilled platter and garnish with triangular pieces of pineapple and whole strawberries.

SOFTEN 2 tablespoons gelatin in 1/2 cup cold water and dissolve it in *Coffee* 2 cups hot double-strength coffee. Add 1/2 cup sugar and a pinch of salt. *Cream Jelly* Cool the mixture to the syrupy stage and fold in 1 cup dry macaroon crumbs and 1 1/2 cups cream, whipped until stiff. Chill the jelly well and serve it piled high in sherbet glasses, garnished to taste with sweetened and flavored whipped cream.

The cold soufflé is a trompe-l'oeil *dessert, actually a cold but not frozen mousse. It stands above the rim of the dish in proud imitation of the soufflé.*

Cold Chocolate Soufflé

IN a bowl beat 4 whole eggs, 3 egg yolks, and 1/4 cup sugar with an electric beater until the mixture is very thick and pale in color, or place the bowl over hot water and beat vigorously with a rotary beater. Melt 3 ounces of sweet chocolate over boiling water with 2 tablespoons strong coffee and cool. Add the chocolate to the eggs with 2 tablespoons gelatin, softened in 1/2 cup cold water and dissolved over hot water, and mix well. Fold in 1/2 cup heavy cream, stiffly beaten.

Butter a soufflé dish and tie a standing collar of wax paper around the edge. Turn the cream into the dish and chill it until set. Remove the paper collar and decorate the top of the soufflé with whipped cream pressed through a pastry bag fitted with a fluted tube.

Cold Orange Soufflé

IN a bowl beat 4 whole eggs, 3 egg yolks, and 6 tablespoons sugar until the mixture is very thick and pale in color. Add the grated rind of 1 large orange. Soften 1 1/2 tablespoons gelatin in 5 tablespoons orange juice, stir over hot water until the gelatin is completely dissolved, and combine it thoroughly with the egg mixture. Fold in 1 cup heavy cream, whipped, and proceed as for cold chocolate soufflé.

Garnish the mousse with skinned orange sections and pour over the orange 2 tablespoons red currant jelly dissolved in 2 tablespoons hot water. Return the mousse to the refrigerator until serving time.

Byculla Soufflé

BEAT 5 egg yolks with 1/2 cup sugar until the mixture is thick and pale in color. Stir in 3/4 cup brandy, 1/2 cup Sherry, the juice of 1 lime, 2 liqueur glasses of Bénédictine, and 2 tablespoons gelatin softened for 5 minutes in 1/2 cup water and dissolved over hot water. Fold in the stiffly beaten whites of 5 eggs and 1 cup heavy cream, whipped. Proceed as for cold chocolate soufflé.

Cold Apricot Soufflé

BEAT 1/2 cup sugar, 4 whole eggs, and 3 egg yolks until the mixture is thick and pale in color. Stir in 1 cup purée of stewed dried apricots and 1 tablespoon Cognac. Add 2 tablespoons gelatin softened in 2 tablespoons lemon juice and dissolved over hot water, and fold in 1/2 cup heavy cream, whipped. Proceed as for cold chocolate soufflé.

COMBINE 1 cup sugar, 1/2 cup water, and 1/4 teaspoon cream of tartar, stir over moderate heat until the sugar is dissolved, and cook without stirring until the syrup spins a long thread or registers 240° F. on a candy thermometer. Pour the syrup very gradually, in a thin stream, into 5 well-beaten egg whites, beating continually with a rotary beater until the meringue stands in firm peaks. Set the bowl in a bowl of cracked ice to chill.

Cold Strawberry Soufflé

Make 1 1/2 cups strawberry purée by forcing fresh strawberries through a fine sieve. In the top of a double boiler cook the purée with 1 1/2 cups sugar and 6 egg yolks, stirring constantly until the custard thickens. Cool the custard.

Whip 3 cups heavy cream until stiff. Stir the strawberry custard into the cream along with an additional 3/4 cup strawberry purée. Fold in the meringue. Proceed as for cold chocolate soufflé. Decorate with whole strawberries, if desired. Serves 18.

BEAT 3 whole eggs, 2 egg yolks, and 3 tablespoons sugar until the mixture is very thick and pale in color. Soften 1 1/2 tablespoons gelatin in 1/2 cup Sherry for 5 minutes, stir the mixture over hot water until the gelatin is completely dissolved, and combine it with the egg mixture. Stir in 1/2 cup praline powder and fold in 1/2 cup heavy cream, whipped until stiff, and proceed as for cold chocolate soufflé.

Cold Praline Soufflé

Garnish the soufflé with a design of almonds, blanched and toasted, and decorate it with whipped cream pressed through a pastry bag fitted with a fluted tube.

There are those who believe that fresh fruit is its own excuse for being, and that to tamper with it is to gild the lily. Here are several dozen cool, restrained arguments to the contrary. We deal elsewhere with more complicated preparations in which fruit plays a secondary role.

CRUSH 2 cups juicy fruit or fresh berries and force them through a fine sieve. Or purée them in a blender and strain out the seeds. Sweeten the purée to taste and chill it thoroughly.

Fresh Fruit Purée

Apples Frangipane

SOFTEN 1 tablespoon gelatin in 1/4 cup cold water and dissolve it over hot water. Combine the gelatin with 2 cups fruit purée, 1 cup sugar, and 2 cups heavy cream, whipped until stiff. Flavor to taste with almond extract, lemon juice, fruit brandy, or a fruit liqueur. Pour the cream into a 1 1/2-quart mold and chill it until firm. Unmold the cream on a chilled platter and garnish it with slices of the fruit that made the purée, or with whole berries, and with sprigs of mint.

Fruit Purée Cream

COMBINE 1/2 cup each of strawberry purée and raspberry purée, and add 2 tablespoons brandy. Chill the purée well and fold in 1 cup cream, whipped until stiff and sweetened to taste. Serve the mousseline as a sauce with fresh fruit, chilled and sweetened, using sliced peaches, nectarines, apricots, bananas, pears, apples, and pineapple, or whole berries.

Fruit Mousseline

BRING to a boil 1 cup sugar, 1/2 cup water, 1 small stick of cinnamon, and the rind of 1 lemon. Cook the syrup for 5 minutes and discard the lemon rind and cinnamon stick. Put 2 pounds washed and drained blackberries, strawberries, raspberries, or any desired berry in the syrup, bring the syrup to a boil, and simmer the fruit gently for 2 to 3 minutes. Chill the compote well and serve it with soft custard, whipped cream, or ice cream.

Berry Compote

PLUNGE fresh peaches into boiling water for 1 minute, then into cold water, and slip off the skins. Leave the peaches whole, or cut them in half and discard the pits.

Poached Peaches

Dissolve 3/4 cup sugar in 2 cups water, add a 2-inch piece of vanilla bean, and bring to a boil. Cook for 5 minutes. Add the peaches to the syrup, cover the saucepan, and simmer very gently until the fruit is tender. Serve warm or chilled with plain or half-frozen heavy cream.

Other fruits may be poached in syrup in the same way.

Poached Fruit

COOK to a syrup 1/2 cup water, 1/4 cup apricot jam or purée of stewed dried apricots, 3 tablespoons sugar, and a little grated orange rind. Peel, core, and cut in half 4 large tart apples, and poach them in the syrup until they are just tender.

Apples Frangipane

Chill the poached apple halves and fill them with *frangipane* pastry cream, using a pastry bag fitted with a rose tube. Pour over the filled apples the syrup in which they were poached and garnish them with slivered toasted almonds.

617

Baked Apples   CORE 6 large baking apples without cutting through the blossom end, and pare them one third of the way down. Arrange them side by side in a baking dish and add enough water or wine to the pan to keep the fruit from sticking. Put a little butter in each cavity, and any of the following: chopped raw cranberries or pineapple, sweetened and spiced; chopped nuts and raisins with brown sugar, maple sugar, or honey; chopped dates and figs with candied ginger; quince, apricot, or greenage jam; prune or apricot purée, sweetened with brown sugar and flavored with a little rum. Or put only butter into the cavities and baste the apples with maple syrup. Bake, uncovered, in a moderately hot oven (375° F.) for 30 to 45 minutes, until the fruit is tender, but not mushy.

Baked Apple Compote   SLICE 2 pounds tart cooking apples, peeled and cored, into a generously buttered baking dish. Sprinkle the slices with a little lemon juice and 1 cup brown sugar and dot with 1/4 cup butter. Bake them, uncovered, in a moderately hot oven (375° F.) for 30 minutes, or until they are tender. Serve with heavy cream.

Applesauce   STEW unpeeled tart apples (red-skinned fruit makes the most attractive sauce) in a little water until the fruit is just tender. Force the sauce through a sieve or a food mill and discard the skins. Add sugar, cinnamon, nutmeg, or mace to taste. Or omit the spices and add slivers of candied ginger or raisins plumped in a little Calvados, Cognac, or rum.

Baked Applesauce   PUT a layer of seasoned applesauce in a buttered baking dish, sprinkle it with ground blanched almonds and with macaroon crumbs, dot with butter, and bake in a hot oven (400° F.) for 15 minutes. Serve hot, with whipped cream.

Apricots and Cream   SOAK 1 pound dried apricots overnight in water barely to cover. Cook the fruit in the same water until it is very tender. Force the apricots through a sieve or purée them in a blender. Chill the purée well, add sugar to taste, and pour it into a crystal serving bowl. Spread with whipped cream, sweetened and flavored with Cognac to taste.

CHILL 3 avocados. Cut them in half lengthwise, discard the seeds, and remove the flesh. Mash the pulp with a silver spoon, press it through a sieve, and beat the purée until it is smooth with 3 teaspoons confectioners' sugar. Stir in 3 tablespoons fresh lime juice and fold in 1/2 cup heavy cream, whipped. Pile the purée into sherbet glasses and serve at once.

Avocado Cream Whip

PEEL 6 bananas, cut them in half lengthwise, and sprinkle with sugar. Dip the pieces in flour, in beaten egg, and again in flour. Sauté them in 3 tablespoons butter until lightly browned on both sides. The bananas should be soft but not mushy. Arrange them side by side on a warm serving platter and sprinkle them with sugar. Pour over them 3 ounces warmed kirsch, ignite the spirit, and serve flaming.

Bananes Flambées
BANANAS ABLAZE

LAY six large bananas, yellow but not flecked with brown, on a rack in a baking pan in their skins. Slit them horizontally almost to the bottom skin, and fill the opening with a paste of butter creamed with sugar in equal amounts. Bake the bananas in a moderate oven (350° F.) for about 25 minutes.

Baked Bananas

SLIT the skins of 6 bananas with a sharp knife and remove the fruit without breaking the skins. Slice the bananas in 1-inch slices without cutting all the way through. Marinate the fruit for 30 minutes in 1/2 cup each of Madeira and brandy with 1/3 cup sugar.

Return the bananas to their skins and arrange them in a baking dish. Open the skins and pour melted butter, a little sugar, and 1 teaspoon of the marinade on each banana. Bake the bananas in a moderate oven (350° F.) for 20 to 30 minutes, or until they are cooked. Serve the bananas in the skins, using the remaining marinade as a sauce.

Baked Bananas Congo

WASH 2 cups each of dried black and white figs and soak them overnight in 2 quarts water. In the morning simmer the figs gently in the water in which they have been soaking for about 20 minutes, or until the fruit is tender and the liquid is syrupy. Serve hot or cold with heavy cream.

Stewed Figs with Cream

PUT 12 fresh figs in the top pan, or blazer, of a chafing dish with 1/2 cup each of sugar and water, boiled together for 5 minutes. Put the pan over the heat until the figs and syrup are heated through. Sprinkle the figs with

Fresh Figs Flambé

about 3 tablespoons fine granulated sugar and pour over them 1/2 cup warmed brandy. Ignite the spirit and let the flame die. Serve the figs topped with whipped cream.

Figs in Port   WASH 12 fresh ripe figs and prick them in several places with the tines of a fork. Sprinkle the figs with cinnamon, cover them with Port, and marinate them in the refrigerator for at least 8 hours or overnight. Sprinkle the figs with chopped cooked chestnuts and serve with whipped cream, sweetened and flavored to taste.

Baked Figs   PRICK 12 fresh ripe figs in several places with the tines of a fork and arrange the figs in a buttered baking dish. Sprinkle them generously with sugar and add 1/2 cup water. Bake the figs in a slow oven (300° F.) for about 30 minutes, or until they are tender, basting them frequently with the syrup.

Remove the baking dish from the oven and sprinkle the figs with powdered cloves. Pour over them 1/4 cup warmed liqueur such as Grand Marnier, Cointreau, Curaçao, or Bénédictine, and ignite the spirit. Serve with whipped cream sweetened to taste and flavored with the liqueur.

Cantaloupe à la Gelée

CANTALOUPE WITH WINE JELLY

SOFTEN 4 tablespoons gelatin in 2 cups cold water for 5 minutes. Put it over hot water and stir until the gelatin is thoroughly dissolved. Add 1/4 cup each of sugar and raspberry, lime, or lemon juice, and 2 cups dry white wine and stir until thoroughly mixed. Let the wine-gelatin cool until it has the consistency of a very thick syrup. Reserve 1 cup and divide the rest among 6 small cantaloupe halves, pouring it into the cavities from which the seeds have been removed.

Chill the cantaloupes along with the reserved jelly until the jelly is set. To serve, garnish each cantaloupe half with the remaining jelly whipped with 2 tablespoons *eau-de-vie de framboise* until it is spongy.

Melon Rafraîchi en Surprise

CHILLED MELON SURPRISE

CUT a circular piece from the stem end of a large cantaloupe, honeydew, or cassaba. Reserve the cover and discard the seeds and filaments. Scoop out the pulp and sprinkle the interior of the melon shell generously with confectioner's sugar. Fill it with a macédoine of fresh fruits and berries in season such as black pitted cherries, strawberries, raspberries, blueberries, diced pineapple, peach slices, or apricots, mixed with the melon balls or dice. Pour over the mixed fruits 1 cup strawberry purée flavored to taste

Cantaloupe with Wine Jelly

with sugar and kirsch. Replace the plug, sealing the cut with butter to make it airtight, and chill the melon for at least 2 hours.

Melone d'Oro
MELON WITH WINE

CUT a circular piece from the stem end of a large melon and remove the seeds and filaments with a silver spoon. Sugar the interior lightly and pour into it 1 1/2 cups Port, Madeira, Champagne, Sherry, or a white dessert wine such as Sauternes. Replace the plug and set the melon on a bed of chopped ice in the refrigerator to mellow for 2 hours. To serve, spoon the fruit onto individual chilled serving plates and ladle over them the wine.

Watermelon Bowl

SPLIT a watermelon lengthwise and remove the flesh with a French ball scoop, discarding the seeds. Combine watermelon balls with balls of honeydew, cantaloupe, or cassaba melon, papaya, sliced peaches, pitted ripe cherries, blueberries, and raspberries and heap the mixture in the melon shells set on beds of crushed ice. Sprinkle the fruit with fine granulated sugar and keep in the refrigerator.

To serve, pour about 2 cups chilled Champagne into each shell and garnish with sprays of mint.

Nectarines with Raspberry Syrup

WASH 6 fresh nectarines and poach them in 2 cups boiling water for 3 to 4 minutes. Remove the fruit from the water and slip off the skins. Place the nectarines in a glass bowl. Return the skins to the poaching water along with 1 cup sugar and 1 pint fresh raspberries. Cook all together rapidly for 10 minutes and strain the syrup through cheesecloth. Return the syrup to the heat and cook it for 5 minutes longer, or until it has thickened and reduced slightly. Cool the syrup to lukewarm, add 2 tablespoons kirsch, and pour it over the nectarines. Do not chill.

Nectarines in Sour Cream

PEEL and slice as many chilled nectarines as are required into a glass bowl. Sprinkle them with maple sugar and cover with sour cream. Serve at once.

Fruit in Sour Cream

Other fruits to taste may be substituted for the nectarines. Pineapple, peaches, bananas, strawberries, and blueberries are particularly delicious served in this way. The sugar may be omitted, or it may be replaced by fine granulated sugar.

POACH 6 peaches in the usual way. Prepare *sauce sabayon.*

Arrange portions of pistachio ice cream on dessert plates. Top each scoop with a peach, pour a spoonful of the *sauce sabayon* over the fruit and sprinkle the whole with chopped pistachio nuts.

DISSOLVE 1 cup sugar in 1 1/2 cups water, bring the syrup to a boil and cook it for 10 minutes. Add 6 peeled peaches and simmer them for about 5 minutes, or until the fruit is just tender. Remove the peaches and syrup to the blazer of a chafing dish over direct heat. Bring the syrup again to a boil, pour over the fruit 1/4 cup warmed Cointreau and ignite the spirit.

CAREFULLY remove the rind from 6 large oranges and cut it in thin julienne strips. Put the strips in a bowl and cover them with Irish whiskey. Strip off and discard the white pith from the oranges and arrange the fruit in a baking dish with 1 teaspoon each of butter and sugar on each orange. Bake the oranges in a moderate oven (350° F.) for 10 minutes. If the sugar has not caramelized sufficiently, brown the fruit for a few minutes under the broiler.

In a saucepan make a syrup of the juice of 2 oranges and 2 tablespoons sugar, add the julienne rind and whiskey and cook the syrup until it thickens and reduces slightly.

Place the baked oranges in the blazer of a chafing dish. Pour 1 tablespoon warmed Irish whiskey over each orange and ignite the spirit. As the flame dies, add the hot orange syrup and cook it for 2 minutes. Finish the sauce with 1 tablespoon heavy cream.

IN a saucepan dissolve 3/4 cup sugar in 1 cup each of water and claret. Bring the mixture to a boil and add a cheesecloth bag containing 2 whole cloves, 1 stick of cinnamon, and 2 slices each of unpeeled tangerine and unpeeled lemon. Cook the mixture for 5 minutes and discard the spice bag.

Remove the skin of 6 large oranges and peel the membranes from each segment. Pile the orange sections in a serving bowl and pour the hot wine syrup over them. Marinate the fruit in the refrigerator for several hours and serve it very cold.

WITH a sharp knife cut a 1/2-inch slice from the tops of 6 oranges and remove the flesh, leaving the shells clean. Dice the orange flesh and combine it with 12 dates, stoned and shredded, and 6 teaspoons each of chopped

Pears in Red Wine

walnuts, seeded raisins, and grated fresh coconut. Sweeten the mixture to taste and pile it into the orange shells. Arrange the filled oranges in a flat baking dish containing 1/2 inch hot water and bake them in a very slow oven (250° F.) for 40 minutes. Take them from the oven and cover the toppings generously with a meringue made by beating 1/4 cup honey gradually into the stiffly beaten whites of 2 eggs. Sprinkle the meringue with a little sugar and then with shredded coconut. Increase the oven temperature to very hot (500° F.) and return the shells to the oven for a few minutes to brown the meringue.

COMBINE in a serving dish 3 cups orange segments and 2 cups grapefruit sections, free from pith and membranes. Sprinkle the fruit with 1/4 cup sugar. Add 1/2 cup Grand Marnier and chill the bowl thoroughly before serving. Garnish with sprays of fresh mint and serve a little confectioners' sugar separately.

Citrus Bowl

PEEL, core, and mince 5 or 6 apples. Cook the pulp until it is soft in 1 tablespoon butter with 1/4 cup sugar and a piece of cinnamon stick. Discard the cinnamon and add 3 tablespoons chopped walnuts. Bring to a boil 1/2 cup red wine, 1 cup sugar, a small piece of cinnamon stick, and a piece of lemon rind. Peel 6 pears and poach them in the wine syrup until they are tender. Put the apple mixture in a serving bowl and arrange the pears on top. Cook the syrup until it is reduced by about half and pour it over the pears. Just before serving, pour over the fruit 1/4 cup warmed rum or Cognac and ignite the spirit at the table.

Poires des Vignerons
PEARS IN RED WINE

PEEL, quarter, and core 6 firm, ripe pears and put them at once into cold water acidulated with a few drops of lemon juice. In a saucepan boil 2 cups water and 3/4 cup sugar for 5 minutes. Cook the pears in the syrup until they are tender and transparent, but not mushy. Turn pears and syrup into a serving bowl and let them cool for a few minutes. Add 1 cup Cointreau and finish the cooling, spooning the syrup over the fruit from time to time. Serve chilled.

Pears in Cointreau

PEEL 12 ripe pears and slice them thinly into a serving bowl. Sprinkle the pears with 2 tablespoons sugar, pour over them 2 cups freshly squeezed orange juice, the juice of 1/2 lemon, and 1/2 cup Curaçao, and marinate the pears in the refrigerator for an hour before serving.

Sliced Pears in Curaçao

Persimmon Cup PEEL a persimmon and put it point down in a sherbet glass. Scoop out some of the pulp from the center and fill the fruit to overflowing with pieces of orange and grapefruit, and with brandied grapes or other fruits.

Pineapple in Port PEEL, slice, and core a large ripe pineapple. In a saucepan combine the grated rind of 1 orange and 1/2 lemon, 1 cup pineapple juice, a generous 1/2 cup sugar, and 1/2 cup Port. Bring the mixture to a boil and simmer it for 10 minutes. Add the fruit and remove the syrup from the heat to cool. Chill before serving.

Pineapple Snow PEEL and grate a ripe pineapple. Beat 4 egg whites until they are stiff, beat in 1/2 cup fine granulated sugar, 1 tablespoon at a time, and continue to beat until the meringue is thick and glossy. Whip 2 cups heavy cream and fold it into the meringue. Fold in 1 tablespoon Sherry and as much grated pineapple and juice as the meringue cream will hold without becoming too soft. Pile the dessert in sherbet glasses and serve very cold with ladyfingers.

Pineapple au Liqueur PEEL a ripe pineapple and cut it into thin slices or wedges. Put the pineapple into a serving bowl, sprinkle it with fine granulated sugar and 1/4 cup of any fruit-flavored liqueur, or with crème de menthe, and chill it for several hours, or overnight.

Ananas Sautés
SAUTÉED
PINEAPPLE
PEEL half a ripe pineapple and cut it into finger-size pieces. In the blazer of a chafing dish melt 1/4 cup butter and sauté the pineapple until it is lightly browned on both sides. Sprinkle it with 2 generous tablespoons sugar, slowly add 6 tablespoons kirsch, and cook it until the kirsch is almost absorbed. Pour 3/4 cup heavy cream over the pineapple but do not stir. As soon as the cream is thoroughly heated, serve the dessert from the chafing dish. Serve ladyfingers separately.

Ananas à la Crème
CREAM-FILLED
PINEAPPLE
REMOVE the top of a fresh pineapple and cut out the pulp, leaving a shell about 1/2 inch thick. Cut the pulp in thin slices and cook it in a light sugar syrup for about 10 minutes. Fill the pineapple with alternating layers of *crème pâtissière* and the cooked pineapple, starting and finishing with the *crème*. Reserve some slices of pineapple for garnishing. Sprinkle with macaroon

crumbs and a little melted butter. Bake the pineapple in a hot oven (425° F.) until golden brown. Arrange it on a heated serving dish, garnish it with the remaining pineapple slices, and brush the slices with apricot sauce.

CUT a ripe pineapple in half lengthwise, keeping the leaves intact. Cut each half pineapple lengthwise in half again. With a flexible knife, cut away the core from the rind, score each wedge deeply in several places, and return it to the rind.

Pineapple with Coconut

Rearrange the split halves of the pineapple, end to end, in a large serving dish and sprinkle the scored flesh with crème de menthe and with 1 cup freshly grated coconut. Chill well before serving.

MAKE a syrup of 2/3 cup sugar and 1 cup each of Sauternes and water. Add 4 cloves and a 2-inch stick of cinnamon, and boil the syrup for 5 minutes. Add 2 pounds greengage or red plums, washed but not peeled or stoned, and simmer them for about 5 minutes, until the fruit is tender but not mushy. Serve chilled, plain or with whipped cream or soft custard.

Plum Compote

SKIN, stone, and mash 3 dozen ripe blue plums. Stir in 1 cup chopped blanched almonds. Put the mixture in a glass dish and pour over it 1 1/2 cups thin caramel syrup. Chill the plums thoroughly and serve them with whipped cream.

Plum Caramel

SIMMER 1 pound prunes, covered, in the water in which they were soaked with a stick of cinnamon for about 20 minutes, or until almost tender. Add 6 thin slices of lemon and simmer the prunes for 5 minutes longer. Drain the prunes and add 1 cup Port to the sauce. Replace the prune pits with walnut halves and chill the prunes in the sauce.

Prune Compote with Port

SOAK 1 pound very large prunes overnight in a mixture of red wine and water to cover. Add 1/2 cup sugar, cover the pan tightly, and simmer the prunes gently for about 20 minutes, until they are plump and just tender.

Stuffed Prunes

Drain the prunes, slit them carefully, and discard the pits. Reserve the syrup.

Shape fondant, flavored with rum or brandy to taste, into large ovals and reshape the prunes around this filling. Press half a pecan or blanched almond into the fondant.

Reduce the cooking liquid quickly to a thick syrup, dip the prunes in the syrup, and put them on an oiled baking sheet to dry. The prunes may be served at room temperature, with a little of the reduced syrup poured over them, and with a pitcher of lightly whipped cream.

Stewed Rhubarb

WASH 1 pound rhubarb and cut it into 1/2 inch pieces. Put the pieces in the top of a double boiler with a pinch of salt, the peeled sections of 1/2 orange and the juice of 1/2 orange, and from 1/2 to 3/4 cup sugar to taste. Cook the rhubarb over boiling water until it is just tender.

Baked Rhubarb

WASH 2 pounds rhubarb and cut the stalks into 1/2-inch pieces. Put layers of the rhubarb in a buttered baking dish alternately with 2 cups sugar. Sprinkle the rhubarb with 1/2 teaspoon nutmeg and the grated rind of 1 lemon, dot with butter, and bake in a slow oven (300° F.) for about 30 minutes, or until the rhubarb is tender.

Rhubarb Ring with Strawberries

CUT about 1 1/2 pounds rhubarb into 1-inch pieces. Put it in a saucepan with 2 cups sugar and 1 cup boiling water, bring to a boil, and simmer the rhubarb for about 5 minutes, or until tender. Add 2 tablespoons gelatin softened in 1/2 cup cold water for 5 minutes and stir until it is thoroughly dissolved. Pour the rhubarb into a ring mold, cool it, and chill it.

To serve, unmold the rhubarb ring onto a cold serving platter and fill the center with 2 cups washed and hulled strawberries. Sprinkle the berries with 1/4 cup confectioners' sugar and top with 1 cup heavy cream, whipped.

Strawberries with Champagne

SPRINKLE washed and hulled whole strawberries with sugar and chill them well. Serve them in glass dishes with Champagne poured over them.

Strawberries Fédora

CUT a very large pineapple in half lengthwise. Discard the core and cut the flesh into small slices or dice. Mix the pineapple pieces with an equal quantity of strawberries. Add sugar to taste and flavor with kirsch. Let the fruit marinate in the refrigerator for a few hours.

Put a layer of orange ice in the bottom of a pineapple shell, then add a layer of fruit, a layer of orange ice, one of fruit, and so on until the pineapple is filled.

IN a saucepan combine 1 cup sugar and 1/4 cup water, bring the syrup to a boil, and boil it for 5 minutes or until it is thick. Flavor the syrup to taste with a little Grand Marnier. Pour the syrup over 2 quarts washed and hulled strawberries in another saucepan, and let the mixture cool completely. Bring the berries quickly to a boil, remove them at once from the heat, and cool them again. Serve very cold in a glass serving dish on a bed of crushed ice.

Strawberry Compote

WASH, hull, and cut strawberries in half. Stir them into whipped cream sweetened with confectioners' sugar and flavored with a few drops of vanilla extract. Chill for 2 hours before serving.

Fraises Chantilly

Fruit soups may be strange to American palates, but Europeans know and welcome them equally as first course and as dessert, accompanying them accordingly with salted crackers or with sweet cookies or plain cake.

PEEL and core 1 pound tart apples and cut them into small pieces. Place them in a saucepan with 4 1/2 cups water, 1/2 tablespoon grated lemon rind, a 1-inch stick of cinnamon, and a pinch of salt. Cover the saucepan tightly and cook the apples until they are very tender. Strain the apples and the juice through a fine sieve into another saucepan, add 1/2 cup sugar, and stir in gradually 2 1/2 tablespoons cornstarch mixed to a paste with 2 tablespoons cold water. Cook the mixture, stirring, until it is thickened. Add 1/4 cup white wine and 1 tablespoon lemon juice and bring it again to a boil. Serve warm or cold as a dessert with whipped cream and macaroons.

Apfel-Suppe

WASH in warm water 3/4 pound dried apricots. Wash, peel, quarter, and remove the stones from 3 ripe fresh peaches. Combine the fruits, cover with 5 cups water, add 1/2 cup sugar, and allow the mixture to stand overnight. Cook the fruit in the water in which it soaked until it is very soft and strain the fruit and the juice through a fine sieve. Heat the strained soup to the boiling point, stir in gradually 1/4 cup tapioca, and cook, stirring constantly,

Norwegian Apricot Søtsuppe

until the soup is thickened and clear. Remove from the heat, stir in a little lemon juice, and serve warm or cold.

Polish Blackberry Soup

WASH and pick over 1 pint ripe blackberries and put them in a saucepan with 2 small lemons, thinly sliced, 2 cups cold water, 1/2 cup sugar, a 1-inch stick of cinnamon, and 2 cloves. Bring the liquid to a boil, lower the heat, and simmer the fruit gently for 10 minutes, or until it is soft. Rub the soup through a fine sieve and chill it well. Just before serving, stir in 2 cups chilled sour cream.

Hungarian Sour Cherry Soup

IN a saucepan combine 1 pound sour cherries, pitted, 1 teaspoon salt, 2 table-spoons sugar, and 1 quart water. Bring the liquid to a boil and cook the cherries for 20 minutes. Strain the juice from the cooked cherries into another saucepan placed over low heat and thicken it by stirring in 1 tablespoon flour mixed to a paste with a little cold water. Rub the cherries through a fine sieve and stir the purée into the thickened juice. Allow the soup to cook for another 5 minutes, remove from the heat, and stir in 1 cup sour cream. Cool the soup and serve it well chilled.

Plum Soup

COOK 1 1/2 pounds halved and seeded plums with 1/2 cup sugar, a 1-inch stick of cinnamon, and 2 quarts water, until the fruit is soft. Force fruit and juice through a fine sieve. Return the soup to the heat and stir in 5 tablespoons cornstarch mixed to a paste with a little cold water. Bring the soup to a boil and cook it for 5 minutes longer. Add 1/2 cup dry white wine and chill the soup well. Serve it in chilled bouillon cups with a dab of whipped cream on each portion. Serve with cookies.

Raspberry White Wine Soup

COOK 1 quart ripe raspberries and 1 cup dry white wine slowly for 15 minutes, until the fruit is tender. Strain fruit and juice through a fine sieve. Return the strained soup to the heat and stir in 1/2 tablespoon cornstarch mixed to a paste with 1 tablespoon water. Bring the soup to a boil, lower the heat, and simmer it gently for 10 minutes, stirring frequently and skimming from time to time. Season with salt, white pepper, and sugar to taste, add 1/2 cup each of orange juice and white wine, and chill well. Serve as dessert with cookies or spongecake.

WASH 2 pounds young rhubarb, cut it into 1-inch pieces, and cook it in 1 quart water until soft. Strain the fruit and juice through a fine sieve and return the soup to the heat. Stir in 1 tablespoon cornstarch mixed with a little cold water and sweeten the soup with sugar to taste. The amount of sugar will depend on the tartness of the rhubarb. Let the soup simmer for 5 minutes, stirring constantly with a wooden spoon. Whip 1/2 cup heavy cream and combine it with the yolk of 1 egg. Stir the hot soup into the whipped cream and serve at once with cookies or cakes. Or chill the soup and add the cream at serving time.

Rhubarb Soup

WASH and hull 4 cups very ripe sweet strawberries and rub them through a fine sieve. Mix the purée with 1 cup each of sugar and sour cream. Add 4 cups cold water and 1 cup claret and heat the mixture very slowly over low heat, stirring constantly with a wooden spoon. Do not let the soup boil. This soup may be served either hot or cold with thin wafers. When it is served cold, garnish each portion with a few whole strawberries.

Russian Strawberry Soup

IN a saucepan combine the following fruits, all finely chopped: 1/2 cup each of stoned peaches, hulled strawberries, fresh rhubarb, oranges, peeled and seeded, and fresh pineapple, peeled. Add 3/4 cup sugar, 2 tablespoons unstrained lemon juice, 1/2 teaspoon salt, and 2 whole cloves. Add 2 quarts water and bring the liquid slowly to a boil. Lower the heat and simmer the soup gently for 15 minutes. Rub the soup through a fine sieve or purée the mixture in a blender. Chill the soup thoroughly and serve with toasted crackers.

Medley Fruit Soup

Fruit charlottes and the other fruit puddings in which bread plays a part were undoubtedly invented as an economy measure; in their case, it is gastronomically smart to be thrifty.

CUT stale brioche or coffeecake into slices about 1/4 inch thick. Place the slices in a baking pan, sprinkle with a little sugar, and brown them under the broiler or in a hot oven (400° F.). Put a piece of canned pineapple on each slice, spread with apricot sauce, and top with half a cherry, maraschino or glacéed. Arrange the pieces in a circle, overlapping them to make an attractive ring. Heat whole small apricots or halves of large apricots in a

Croûtes aux Abricots Flambés
FLAMING APRICOT RING

631

kirsch-flavored apricot sauce and fill the center with them. Sprinkle with warmed kirsch or rum and ignite the spirit. Serve flaming.

Brioche Parisienne   PUT enough brioche dough in a buttered deep round mold, like a charlotte mold, to half fill it and let the dough rise in a warm place until it almost fills the mold. Tie a piece of white paper around the top to make a collar 1 inch high above the mold. Brush the top of the brioche with *dorure* and bake it in a hot oven (425° F.) for about 25 minutes, until it tests done. If the brioche browns too quickly, cover it with a piece of white paper. Cool the brioche and turn it out of the mold. Slice off the top and scoop out most of the inside, leaving a shell about 3/4 to 1 inch thick. Spread the outside of the shell and the top slice with thick apricot jam and sprinkle it with chopped toasted almonds or decorate it with almond halves and angelica. Fill the shell with assorted cooked fruits mixed with apricot jam flavored with a little rum or kirsch. The fruit may be warm or cold as preferred. Put back the cover. Cut through the crust and serve the fruit and sauce with a piece of the crust.

Apricot Charlotte   CUT bread into slices 1/4 inch thick. Remove the crusts and dip each slice into melted butter. Cover the bottom and sides of a charlotte mold or any deep, round mold with the bread, overlapping the slices to make a firmer support for the filling. Peel, core, and slice 2 large or 3 small apples. Heat 2 tablespoons butter in a saucepan and add the apple slices and an equal amount of well-drained canned or stewed apricots. Cook the mixture until it is soft and most of the moisture is cooked away. Add the juice of 1/2 lemon. Fill the center of the mold with the mixture. Bake the mold on a baking sheet in a hot oven (425° F.) for 40 to 45 minutes, until it is golden brown. Invert on a serving dish and serve with apricot sauce while the charlotte is still warm.

Apple Pudding   PEEL and cut 1 1/2 pounds tart apples into thin sections. In a well-buttered baking dish arrange a layer of the apple sections, sprinkle the fruit with brown sugar, fine dry bread crumbs, and a little cinnamon, and add a few dabs of butter. Fill the dish with alternate layers of apples and crumbs, sugar, cinnamon, and butter, and finish with crumbs on top. Allow about 1 1/2 cups crumbs, 3/4 cup sugar, 5 tablespoons butter, and 1 teaspoon cinnamon in all. Pour over the pudding 1/2 cup cherry brandy and bake it in a moderate oven (350° F.) for about 35 minutes, or until the apples are tender. Cool and serve with whipped cream.

Brioche Parisienne

Rhubarb Brown Betty

COMBINE 1/4 cup sugar, the grated rind of 1 lemon, and 1/2 teaspoon nutmeg. Melt 1/2 cup butter, pour the butter over 2 cups bread crumbs, and mix well. Cover the bottom of a buttered pudding dish with one-third of the crumb mixture and spread over it 1 cup stewed rhubarb. Sprinkle with half the sugar mixture, then repeat the layers, covering finally with the remaining crumbs. Bake the pudding in a moderate oven (350° F.) for 40 minutes, covering the dish for the first 15 minutes. Serve hot, with heavy cream.

Cranberry Crisp

BRING to a boil 1 cup sugar, 1/2 cup orange juice, and 1/2 teaspoon cinnamon. Add 2 cups cranberries and cook for 2 minutes. Pour 1/2 cup melted butter over 3 cups soft bread crumbs. Arrange alternate layers of crumbs and cranberry mixture in a buttered baking dish, finishing with crumbs. Cover the dish and bake in a moderately hot oven (375° F.) for 20 minutes. Uncover and bake for 15 minutes longer, or until the top is brown and crisp.

Beat 1 egg yolk with 2 tablespoons sugar until the mixture is thick and pale in color. Fold in 1 cup cream, whipped, and 1 teaspoon orange-flower water. Serve the pudding hot with the cold sauce.

Banana Pudding

MASH 12 bananas with 1/4 cup rum. Stir in 2 eggs, beaten, 1/2 cup each of sugar and melted butter, and nutmeg and cinnamon to taste. Sift 1/2 cup flour with 2 teaspoons baking powder, and add the banana purée. Bake the pudding in a moderate oven (350° F.) for about 1 hour, or until a silver knife inserted in the middle comes out clean. Serve cool, with whipped cream flavored with rum and a dash of nutmeg.

Persimmon Pudding

MIX together 2 cups mashed and sieved persimmon pulp, 3 beaten eggs and 1 3/4 cups milk. Sift together 2 cups sifted flour, 1 1/2 cups sugar, 1 teaspoon each of salt and coriander, and 1/2 teaspoon soda. Pour the liquid mixture into the dry ingredients, add 3 tablespoons melted butter and stir the pudding briefly. Bake it in a buttered shallow pan in a moderately slow oven (325° F.) for about 1 hour. Cool the pudding, cut it into squares, and serve it with whipped cream.

Apricot Mold

SOAK 1/4 pound stale ladyfingers in 1 1/2 cups hot milk for about 10 minutes. Press the mixture through a sieve and add 1/4 cup sugar and 4 eggs, beaten. Pour the batter into a buttered and sugared mold and bake it in a pan of hot water in a moderate oven (350° F.) for 30 to 40 minutes, or until the pudding is set. Unmold the pudding onto a serving dish and arrange well-drained stewed apricot halves, rounded side down, around it. Fill the hollow of each apricot with a piece of glacéed marron or cherry and coat with apricot sauce.

Most of our hearty, hot puddings originated in cold countries where hot desserts provided central heating. They are nevertheless welcome in our steam-heated dining rooms.

MELT 1/2 cup butter and stir in 1/2 cup sifted flour. Add gradually 2 cups hot milk and cook the mixture over low heat for 5 minutes, until it is thick and smooth.

Princess Pudding

Cool the sauce and beat in 6 well-beaten egg yolks. Add a dash of salt, 2 teaspoons sugar and 1 teaspoon vanilla. Fold in the stiffly beaten whites of 6 eggs and turn the batter into a 2-quart melon mold thickly buttered and generously sprinkled with brown sugar and chopped nuts. Cover the mold tightly and steam the pudding for 2 hours. Turn the pudding out on a heated platter and serve it with whipped cream.

IN a large bowl, mix the following ingredients thoroughly: 1 1/2 cups fine dry bread crumbs, 1 cup finely chopped or ground suet, 3/4 cup flour, 2/3 cup sugar, 1/2 cup each of seeded raisins, currants, and sultanas, washed and steeped for 1 hour in a little *fine champagne* (a French liqueur brandy), 1/4 cup each of finely diced preserved orange rind, lemon rind, citron, finely chopped dried figs, and chopped blanched almonds, 1/2 cup chopped apple, 2 1/2 tablespoons chopped preserved ginger, 3/4 teaspoon cinnamon, 1/2 teaspoon each of nutmeg and salt, 1/4 teaspoon each of ground cloves and mace, and the juice and grated rind of 1 orange and 1/2 lemon. Sprinkle the ingredients with 1 cup *fine champagne* and blend well. Cover the bowl with a towel and put it in the refrigerator for 6 to 8 days, adding a few spoonfuls of *fine champagne* and tossing the mixture each day.

Plum Pudding à la Fine Champagne

The day the pudding is to be served, stir 6 beaten eggs into the batter and pack it firmly into a buttered mold, cover the mold closely, and steam for 5 hours.

To serve, unmold the pudding onto a serving platter and decorate the top with a spray of holly. Sprinkle the pudding with fine granulated sugar, pour over it 1/2 cup warmed *fine champagne*, ignite the spirit, and serve flaming.

Marmalade Pudding

IN a mixing bowl combine 2 cups cranberries, coarsely chopped, and 1 1/2 cups flour sifted with 2 teaspoons soda and 1/2 teaspoon salt. Combine 1/2 cup each of molasses and hot water and stir the mixture into the flour mixture. Turn the batter into a buttered pudding mold, cover, and steam for 3 hours. Serve hot with a sauce made by cooking together for a few minutes 1 cup each of sugar and heavy cream, 1/2 cup butter, and a pinch of salt. Stir in 1 teaspoon vanilla extract and serve hot.

Steamed Cranberry Pudding

CREAM 2 tablespoons butter with 1 cup sugar and stir in 3 egg yolks, lightly beaten, 1/4 cup flour, and a pinch of salt. Stir in the grated rind of 1 lemon, 5 tablespoons lemon juice, and 1 1/2 cups milk and fold in the stiffly beaten whites of 3 eggs.

Lemon Pudding

Turn the batter into a buttered and sugared 2-quart baking dish, set the dish in a shallow pan of hot water, and bake it in a moderate oven (350° F.) for 45 minutes, until it is golden brown. Serve hot.

SIFT together 1 cup sifted cake flour, 1 1/2 teaspoons baking powder, 1/2 teaspoon cinnamon, and 1/4 teaspoon salt.

Marmalade Pudding

Cream 1/4 cup butter, add 2/3 cup sugar, and cream these together until the mixture is light and fluffy. Add 2 eggs, beaten, and beat until well blended. Stir in the sifted dry ingredients alternately with 1/4 cup each of milk and hot water, beating the mixture after each addition until it is smooth. Stir in 1 teaspoon vanilla extract.

Heat 1 cup orange marmalade and turn it into a buttered baking dish. Pour the batter over the marmalade and bake the pudding in a hot oven (400° F.) for 25 to 30 minutes, or until it is well browned and tests done. Serve warm, with whipped cream.

COMBINE in a saucepan 1 quart milk, 1/2 cup sugar, 3 tablespoons butter, a piece of vanilla bean, and 1/2 teaspoon salt. Bring the mixture to a boil and sprinkle in slowly 1 cup farina, stirring constantly. Cook slowly for 20 to 25 minutes, stirring from time to time. Turn the mixture into a bowl and remove the vanilla bean. Add 2 tablespoons butter and 6 egg yolks, well beaten. Fold in 4 egg whites, stiffly beaten. Butter a cylindrical mold or a mold with a tube in the center and sprinkle the mold with a little farina. Fill it with the pudding, set it in a pan of boiling water, and bake the pudding in a moderate oven (350° F.) for 25 to 30 minutes. Let the pudding stand for 10 minutes before unmolding it onto a serving dish. Serve with fruit sauce or sabayon sauce.

Pouding à la Semoule

FARINA PUDDING

Baked Indian Pudding SCALD 3 cups milk, stir in 6 tablespoons cornmeal, and cook the mixture over boiling water for 15 minutes, stirring constantly. Stir in 1/2 cup dark molasses, 1/4 cup each of butter and sugar, and 1/2 teaspoon each of ground ginger, cinnamon, and salt. Turn the batter into a buttered baking dish, and pour over it 1 cup cold milk. Set the baking dish in a pan of hot water and bake in a slow oven (250° F.) for 3 hours. Serve the pudding hot with whipped cream or vanilla ice cream.

Bread and Fruit Pudding Stephanie SAUTÉ 2 cups bread cut into small dice in 3 tablespoons butter, tossing them in the butter until they are golden on all sides. Add 1 1/2 cups hot milk. Peel and core 2 tart apples, cut them in dice, and put them in a bowl with 1/4 cup finely chopped candied orange peel, 1/2 cup each of ground almonds, seedless raisins, and sugar, and the grated rind of 1 lemon. Add the milk and bread and mix all together. Add 3 beaten egg yolks and fold in 3 egg whites, beaten until they are stiff. Butter a 1-quart mold and fill it with the mixture. Set the mold in a pan of hot water and bake the pudding in a moderate oven (350° F.) for 45 minutes. Let it stand for about 15 minutes before unmolding it onto a serving dish. Serve with a red wine sauce made as

Red Wine Sauce follows: Boil 1 cup red wine with 2 tablespoons sugar for 2 to 3 minutes and add 3 tablespoons thick purée of cooked dried apricots or apricot jam. Serve the sauce warm.

Pouding au Pain à la Française
BREAD PUDDING FRENCH STYLE SCALD 1 quart milk and in it soak 5 to 6 cups soft bread crumbs and 1 cup sugar. Rub the mixture through a fine sieve. Beat together 4 eggs and 6 egg yolks and combine them thoroughly with the bread crumb mixture. Fold in 4 egg whites, beaten until stiff. Butter a tall 2-quart cylindrical mold, sprinkle it with fine dry bread crumbs, and fill it with the mixture. Set the mold in a deep pan of hot water and bake the pudding in a moderate oven (350° F.) for about 40 to 45 minutes, or until it is firm. Let it stand for about 15 minutes before unmolding it onto a serving dish. Serve hot or warm with vanilla or sabayon sauce, or any fruit sauce.

Cabinet Pudding SOAK 2 tablespoons raisins in a little warm water to make them plump. Drain them and mix them with 3 tablespoons diced candied fruit and 1 tablespoon kirsch or another liqueur. Scald 2 cups milk with a piece of vanilla bean. Beat together 3 eggs, 2 egg yolks, and 1/2 cup sugar. Add the milk slowly to the egg and sugar. Strain the custard. Spread half the mixed fruit in the bottom of a buttered charlotte mold and cover it with 3 ladyfingers or macaroons broken in small pieces. Pour half the strained custard over the fruit. Add a second layer of ladyfingers and the rest of the custard. Cover the mold, set it in a pan of hot water, and bake the pudding in a moderate oven (350° F.) for 40 to 50 minutes, or until the mixture is set. Let the pudding stand for 10 minutes before unmolding it on a warmed serving dish and serve it warm with vanilla or sabayon sauce.

Pouding au Chocolat

IN a warm bowl work 1/4 cup butter with a wooden spoon until it is creamy. Add 1/2 cup confectioners' sugar and 1/4 teaspoon vanilla extract or a few seeds scraped from a split vanilla bean and continue to cream the mixture until it is fluffy. Work in 6 egg yolks, one at a time. Melt 1/4 pound bitter chocolate over hot water and add it to the creamed mixture with 3 tablespoons flour and 2 tablespoons arrowroot or cornstarch. Fold in 5 egg whites, beaten until stiff. Butter and flour a 1 1/2-quart round or oblong mold and fill it with the pudding mixture. Set the mold in a pan of hot water and bake the pudding in a moderate oven (350° F.) for about 45 minutes. Let it stand for 10 to 15 minutes before unmolding it onto a serving dish. Serve warm with chocolate cream sauce.

Greek Honey Pudding

CUT some slices of stale bread into rounds with a fluted cutter, soak them in milk until they are quite soft, and drain them. Dip the soaked slices in lightly beaten egg and in fine bread crumbs and fry them in butter until they are golden brown on both sides. Sprinkle the rounds with chopped pistachio nuts and serve them warm with honey poured over them.

There are two schools of thought on the baking of a soufflé: one school, in the classic tradition, bakes a soufflé quickly and briefly; about 20 minutes in a hot oven produces a soufflé which is puffed and delicately browned, but so soft that it has a creamy liquid center. In a word, a soufflé baked in this manner makes its own sauce. The second school, and most Americans prefer to follow this line, insists that a soufflé be cooked through, and therefore bakes the soufflé for as long as 45 minutes in a moderate oven. Consult your own preferences as well as the baking time indicated in the soufflé recipes that follow.

639

Dessert Soufflé I

MELT 2 tablespoons butter, add 1 1/2 tablespoons flour and cook, stirring, until the *roux* just starts to turn golden. Add 1/2 cup scalded milk and a 1-inch piece of vanilla bean (or add 1/2 teaspoon vanilla extract after the mixture has cooked). Cook the sauce, stirring constantly until it thickens, and then continue cooking, stirring constantly for 5 minutes longer. Remove the vanilla bean or add the extract. Beat 5 egg yolks well with 3 tablespoons sugar and combine them with the batter. Beat 6 egg whites until they are stiff, adding 1 tablespoon sugar during the last minutes of beating. Fold thoroughly and carefully into the mixture one-fourth of the beaten egg whites and add the remaining egg whites, cutting them in lightly but completely by raising and folding the mixture over and over. Pour the batter into a buttered and lightly sugared soufflé dish and bake the soufflé in a hot oven (400° F.) for 20 minutes or in a moderate oven (350° F.) for 35 to 45 minutes. Serve at once.

Dessert Soufflé II

SCALD 1/2 cup milk with a 1-inch piece of vanilla bean. If vanilla extract is used, it must be added later. Mix 1 tablespoon flour and 1/4 cup sugar to a paste with 3 tablespoons cold milk. Add the paste to the hot milk and cook the mixture, stirring constantly, until it thickens. Remove the vanilla bean, or add 1/2 teaspoon vanilla extract, and add 1 tablespoon butter. Remove the pan from the heat. Beat 4 egg yolks until they are light and foamy and combine them with the batter. Beat 5 egg whites until they are stiff, adding 1 tablespoon confectioners' sugar during the last few minutes of beating. Fold thoroughly and carefully into the mixture one-fourth of the beaten egg whites and add the remaining egg whites, cutting them in lightly but completely by raising and folding the mixture over and over. Pour the batter into a buttered and lightly sugared soufflé dish and bake the soufflé in a hot oven (400° F.) for 20 minutes or in a moderate oven (350° F.) for 35 to 45 minutes. Serve at once.

Dessert Soufflé III

BEAT 4 egg yolks well with 1/2 tablespoon sugar and add 1/3 cup *crème pâtissière*. Add the pulp scraped from a 1-inch piece of vanilla bean, or add 1/2 teaspoon vanilla extract. Beat 5 egg whites until they are stiff, adding 1 tablespoon sugar during the last few minutes of beating. Fold into the mixture thoroughly and carefully one-fourth of the beaten egg whites and add the remaining beaten egg whites, cutting them in lightly and completely by raising and folding the mixture over and over. Pour the batter into a buttered and sugared soufflé dish and smooth off the top with a spatula. Bake the soufflé in a hot oven (400° F.) for 20 minutes or in a moderate oven (350° F.) for 35 to 45 minutes. Serve at once.

FOLLOW the recipe for dessert soufflé I or II. In the hot milk, melt 1 1/2 squares or ounces grated sweet chocolate and add 1 tablespoon sugar.

Chocolate Soufflé

FOLLOW any one of the recipes for dessert soufflé. Add to the thickened base 2 tablespoons double-strength coffee.

Coffee Soufflé

FOLLOW any of the recipes for dessert soufflé. Omit the vanilla and add to the mixture just before folding in the egg whites the finely grated rind of 1 lemon and juice of 1/2 lemon.

Lemon Soufflé

FOLLOW any one of the recipes for any dessert soufflé. Omit the vanilla and add to the mixture just before folding in the egg whites the finely grated rind of 1 small orange and 2 tablespoons orange juice or 1 tablespoon Cointreau.

Orange Soufflé

ADD to the batter for dessert soufflé II 1 cup nectarine pulp forced through a sieve and 1/2 cup macaroon crumbs soaked in a little brandy. Fold in the 5 egg whites, beaten until stiff. Butter a soufflé dish, sprinkle it with sugar and bake the soufflé in the usual way. Serve with whipped cream flavored with brandy. Peaches may be substituted for the nectarines.

Nectarine Soufflé

POUR two-thirds of the batter for dessert soufflé I into a buttered and sugared soufflé dish. Make a shallow depression in the batter. Carefully fold into the rest of the batter 2 tablespoons melted chocolate. Pour the chocolate batter into the center of the vanilla batter, leaving a rim of vanilla. Smooth the soufflé with a spatula and run a finger around the inside edge of the mold. Bake as usual and serve at once.

Soufflé Jeanette

To the batter for dessert soufflé I, add 3/4 cup ground walnuts, 1/2 teaspoon black walnut flavoring extract, and 1 tablespoon brandy and remove the pan from the stove. Stir in thoroughly 4 beaten egg yolks and let the mixture cool. Then fold in the stiffly beaten whites of 5 eggs and turn

Walnut Soufflé

the batter into a buttered soufflé dish. Bake the soufflé in a moderately hot oven (375° F.) for 35 to 45 minutes. Other nuts may be substituted for the walnuts. Serve at once.

Soufflé au Grand Marnier PUT half the mixture for dessert soufflé I into a buttered and sugared soufflé mold or a straight-sided baking dish, place 6 or 8 ladyfingers soaked in Grand Marnier on top, and cover with the rest of the soufflé mixture. Bake the soufflé in a hot oven (400° F.) for 20 minutes. If a glaze is desired, sprinkle the top with a little confectioners' sugar a few minutes before the soufflé is done. Serve immediately with a sauce made by adding 2 tablespoons each of whipped cream and Grand Marnier to 1/2 cup vanilla sauce.

Avocado Soufflé TO the batter for dessert soufflé II add 1 tablespoon lime juice and 1 cup mashed and sieved avocado pulp. Cool, and fold in the 5 stiffly beaten egg whites. Bake the soufflé in the usual way, and serve immediately with slightly sweetened whipped cream flavored with the grated rind of the lime.

Soufflé Valtesse PREPARE 2 separate batters for dessert soufflé I, using 3 egg yolks in each. Into one soufflé mixture stir 3 ounces melted unsweetened chocolate, 1 teaspoon praline powder, and 1/4 cup plus 1 tablespoon sugar. Into the second soufflé mixture stir 1/4 cup sugar, 1 teaspoon praline powder, and 2 teaspoons vanilla extract. Fold 5 egg whites, stiffly beaten, into each soufflé.

Turn half the vanilla soufflé into a large buttered and sugared soufflé dish and over it arrange 6 ladyfingers cut up and soaked in maraschino liqueur. Cover the ladyfingers with all the chocolate soufflé and add another layer of the soaked ladyfingers. Cover these with the rest of the vanilla soufflé mixture and sprinkle lightly with powdered macaroons and granulated sugar. Bake in the usual way and serve at once.

Orange and Vanilla Soufflé MAKE basic dessert soufflé I and divide the batter in half before folding in the egg whites. Flavor half with vanilla and half with 1 tablespoon orange juice and 1 tablespoon grated orange rind. Divide the stiffly beaten egg whites in half and fold them into the two batters. Put the orange batter in the bottom of a buttered and sugared soufflé dish. Soak ladyfingers in an orange-flavored liqueur and cover the orange soufflé with them. Cover the ladyfingers with the vanilla batter and bake the soufflé as usual.

COVER 1 pound dried apricots with cold water. Bring the apricots to a boil, cover, and cook over low heat for about 35 minutes or until the fruit is very tender when tested with a fork. Drain, reserving the juice for other uses, and force the apricots through a fine sieve or purée them in a blender. This makes about 1 cup apricot purée.

Apricot Soufflé

    Blend into the warm purée 1/2 cup sugar, 2 teaspoons lemon or lime juice, 1/2 teaspoon grated lemon or lime rind, and a pinch of salt. Beat 5 egg whites until they hold their shape when the beater is lifted, and fold in the apricot mixture very gently. Turn the mixture into a buttered and sugared soufflé dish and bake the soufflé in a moderate oven (350° F.) for about 35 minutes. Serve with sweetened whipped cream.

WASH and hull 1 pound fresh, ripe strawberries, put them through a fine sieve and add 1/2 cup sugar and 3 tablespoons kirsch. Beat 6 egg whites until they are very stiff, gradually adding 1/2 cup confectioners' sugar. Fold the egg whites gently into the strawberry mixture. Butter a soufflé dish, sprinkle it lightly with sugar, and pour into it the soufflé mixture. Bake the soufflé in a moderate oven (350° F.) for 20 to 35 minutes, or until it is well puffed and lightly browned. Serve at once.

Strawberry Soufflé

PUT 2 cups cranberries through the finest blade of a food chopper. Heat 1 cup sugar with 2 tablespoons lemon juice, stirring until the sugar is melted. Add the cranberry pulp and cook it for 2 minutes. Cool. Stir in the grated rind of 1 lemon and a pinch of salt.

Cranberry Soufflé

    Beat 4 egg yolks until they are light and fold in the cranberry mixture. Fold in 4 egg whites, stiffly beaten, and turn the batter into a buttered soufflé dish. Bake in a moderate oven (350° F.) for 25 to 40 minutes and serve at once with whipped cream.

COMBINE 1 cup sliced dates and 1/2 cup milk in a saucepan. Bring the milk to a boil and cook the dates until they are soft. Remove the pan from the heat and with a wooden spoon mash the dates to a paste. Beat in 2 tablespoons each of rum and cream, 1 teaspoon vanilla extract, and 4 egg yolks, beaten. Whip 4 egg whites until they are stiff, adding gradually

Date Soufflé

DESSERTS · Hot Soufflés

1/2 cup sugar, and fold them into the date mixture. Butter a soufflé dish and sprinkle it with sugar. Pour in the soufflé batter and sprinkle it lightly with finely ground almonds and sugar. Bake the soufflé in a moderate oven (350° F.) for 25 to 40 minutes, until it is well puffed and lightly browned. Serve at once with heavy cream.

Prune Nut Soufflé

WASH 1 pound prunes, cover them with hot water, and soak them for about 2 hours. Bring the prunes to a boil in the water in which they were soaked, cover, and simmer them gently for about 25 minutes, or until they are tender. Drain the prunes, reserving the juice for other uses, pit them, and force the pulp through a fine sieve. This makes about 1 cup purée.

Stir a pinch of salt, 1 tablespoon lemon juice, 1/2 teaspoon grated lemon rind, and 1/4 cup sugar into the warm prune purée and fold the purée and 1/2 cup chopped nut meats into the stiffly beaten whites of 5 eggs. Turn the mixture into a buttered and sugared soufflé dish and bake the soufflé in a moderate oven (350° F.) for about 35 minutes. Sprinkle generously with confectioners' sugar and serve with whipped cream.

Banana Soufflé

FORCE 6 peeled bananas through a fine sieve and flavor the purée with 1 tablespoon rum. Blend 1 1/2 tablespoons each of flour and sugar with 1/4 cup cold milk to make a smooth paste and stir in 1 1/4 cups hot milk. Bring the mixture to a boil and cook it, stirring constantly, until it thickens. Stir into the banana purée 3 egg yolks, beaten, and 2 tablespoons soft butter. Beat 4 egg whites until they are stiff and add them to the mixture, cutting them in lightly but completely by raising and folding the mixture over and over.

Fill individual casseroles or soufflé dishes with the mixture and bake the soufflés in a hot oven (425° F.) for about 10 minutes. Shortly before taking them from the oven, sprinkle them with a little sugar.

Pudding Soufflé

CREAM 3 tablespoons butter with 6 tablespoons flour until the mixture is light and fluffy. Scald 3/4 cup milk with a 1-inch piece of vanilla bean. If vanilla extract is used it must be added later. Add the butter and flour mixture to the milk, and cook the mixture, stirring constantly until it rolls away from the sides of the pan. Remove the pan from the heat. Remove the vanilla bean or add 1/2 teaspoon vanilla extract. Add 4 egg yolks, well beaten with 3 tablespoons sugar and a pinch of salt, and mix all together well. Beat 4 egg whites until they are stiff, adding 1/2 teaspoon sugar during the last few minutes of beating. Fold the egg whites lightly but com-

Prune Nut Soufflé

pletely into the first mixture, raising and folding the mixture over and over.

Pour the batter into a buttered and sugared mold with a tube in the center. The mold should be only three-quarters full. Set the mold in a pan of hot water and bake the soufflé in a moderate oven (350° F.) for 40 to 50 minutes. If the soufflé browns too quickly, cover it with a piece of buttered paper. Remove the mold from the oven and let the pudding settle for a minute. To serve, unmold the soufflé onto a serving dish and cover it with custard or sabayon sauce. If the pudding drops from standing too long, put the mold in a pan of hot water and reheat the pudding in the oven until it puffs again.

The famed French crêpes for dessert and a number of variations on the theme, plus some other dessert pancakes, will be found elsewhere in this volume. The near and neglected relative of the dessert pancake is the dessert omelet.

Dessert Omelet for Two

MEDIUM-SIZED omelets are as a rule better than larger ones because an omelet made of too many eggs is difficult to handle. Mix 4 eggs lightly with a fork and add 1/4 teaspoon salt. Be careful not to overbeat the eggs. Place 1 tablespoon butter in an omelet pan and let it become hazelnut brown. Put the eggs in the butter and stir briskly with a fork to prevent the eggs from sticking to the pan. They should congeal immediately upon contact with the butter. Remove the pan from the heat. If the omelet it to be served with a filling, put it in at this point. Gently raise the handle of the pan and let the omelet slide toward the opposite edge of the pan. Fold the edge nearest the handle over the center (or over the filling) with the aid of the fork. Hold the pan over a heated oval platter and turn it upside down to deposit the omelet on the dish.

The dessert omelet is often filled with fresh or stewed fruit, or served with a fruit sauce.

Jam Omelet Flambée

PREPARE a plain omelet and when it is half cooked, put 1 or 2 tablespoons fruit jam in the center. Roll the omelet, finish the cooking, and sprinkle the top with confectioners' sugar. Pour over it 2 tablespoons warmed rum or kirsch and ignite the spirit. Or score the top by drawing a piece of red-hot iron at intervals across the omelet, sprinkle with liqueur, and ignite the spirit. Serve flaming. Serves 2.

Omelette à la Marmelade

SPREAD a plain omelet with jam or marmalade and roll it. Warm 2 or 3 tablespoons rum in a pan. Turn the omelet onto a hot serving dish and sprinkle it with sugar. Pour the warmed rum over the omelet, ignite the spirit, and serve the omelet flaming. Serves 2.

Rum Omelet

BEAT the yolks and whites of 4 eggs separately until the yolks are creamy and the whites are stiff. To the yolks add 3 tablespoons heavy cream, the grated rind of lemon, 1 tablespoon sugar, 1/2 teaspoon rum, and a tiny pinch of salt. Fold in the whites gently but thoroughly. Melt 2 tablespoons butter in the omelet pan and pour in the eggs. Sprinkle with sugar and place under a very hot broiler just long enough to caramelize the sugar. Warm 2 tablespoons rum, pour it over the omelet, and ignite the spirit. Serve flaming.

Omelet Soufflé

ADD 5 tablespoons sugar and the pulp scraped from a 1-inch piece of vanilla bean to 4 egg yolks, and beat the mixture until it is very light. Beat 4 egg whites until they are stiff, adding 1/2 tablespoon sugar during the last few minutes of beating, and fold them lightly but completely into the first mixture. Heap the mixture into an oval-shaped mound about four inches high on a well-buttered flameproof serving platter. Smooth the mixture with a spatula, then draw the spatula lengthwise across the top to make a furrow about two inches deep. Bake the soufflé in a hot oven (400° F.) for 20 minutes, until the soufflé is well puffed and browned. A few minutes before taking the soufflé from the oven, glaze the top by sprinkling it with a little sugar. Serve at once.

Orange Omelet Soufflé

BEAT 6 egg yolks with 1 1/4 cups sugar until the mixture is light and thick, and add the grated rind of 1 orange. Beat 8 eggs whites until they are stiff and fold them gently into the egg mixture. Turn the mixture into a buttered and sugared soufflé dish, piling it higher in the center than at the edge, and bake it in a hot oven (400° F.) for about 20 minutes, or until it is well puffed. Sprinkle the omelet with confectioners' sugar, put it under the broiler for 1 minute to glaze, and serve immediately.

Fruit fritters, for which various fruits are dipped into special fritter batters and deep-fried to brown puffiness, are restricted to the dessert course in almost every country except our own; here apple fritters, for instance, are likely to garnish the turkey on its platter or to appear at breakfast along with sausage cakes and a pitcher of warm maple syrup.

Fritter Batter for Fruit

SIFT 3/4 cup flour and 1 tablespoon sugar into a bowl and stir in 1 tablespoon melted butter and about 1/4 cup warm water, or enough to make a smooth batter. Stir in 2 tablespoons Cognac, a pinch of salt, and 1 beaten egg yolk. The batter should be the consistency of thick cream. If it is too heavy, thin it with a little of the wine in which the fruit was marinated. Just before using the batter, fold in 1 egg white, stiffly beaten.

Beer Fritter Batter for Fruit

SIFT together 1/2 cup flour and 1/4 teaspoon salt. Beat 1 egg lightly with 1 tablespoon melted butter and stir it into flour. Add gradually 1/2 cup beer, stirring only until the batter is smooth. Let it stand in a warm place for 1 to 2 hours to become light and foamy. Before using, fold in 2 stiffly beaten egg whites.

Beignets de Fruit

FRUIT FRITTERS

MAKE a fritter batter. Dip pieces of fruit marinated in wine into the batter and fry the fritters in hot deep fat (370° F.) until they are golden brown. Drain the fritters on absorbent paper and serve them hot, sprinkled with sugar or with a sauceboat of fruit purée, sweetened and flavored with a compatible liqueur.

Pommes Frites Princesse

APPLE FRITTERS PRINCESS

PEEL and core 3 large apples, cut them into thin slices, and sprinkle the slices with sugar, cinnamon, and a few drops of rum or kirsch. Cover the fruit and let the slices stand for about 1 hour. Drain well, adding any juice to the fritter batter. Dip the slices into the batter and fry a few at a time in hot deep fat (370° F.) until they are golden brown. Drain the fritters on absorbent paper and arrange them in a shallow pan. Sprinkle with sugar and glaze the fritters in a hot oven (400° F.) for about 5 minutes. Serve sprinkled with chopped pistachio nuts.

PEEL and halve ripe peaches. Sprinkle the halves with sugar and with a little kirsch, rum, or Cognac and let them stand for 30 minutes. Drain the marinade from the peaches and reserve it for use in making the fritter batter. Dry the fruit halves, dip them in fritter batter, and fry them a few at a time in hot deep fat (370° F.) until they are delicately brown. Drain the fritters on absorbent paper and arrange them on a flameproof platter. Sprinkle with fine granulated sugar and glaze the fritters under the broiler.

Beignets de Pêches
PEACH FRITTERS

Arrange the fritters on a napkin in the form of a pyramid, *en buisson.* Serve *sauce sabayon* separately.

PEEL, halve, and stone 6 nectarines. Sprinkle the fruit with the grated rind of 1 lemon and 3 tablespoons sugar, and pour over it 1/2 cup Madeira. The fruit should marinate for about 3 hours. Drain the nectarines and dip them, one by one, into fritter batter. Fry a few at a time in hot deep fat (370° F.) until golden brown. Drain the fritters on absorbent paper, sift a little confectioners' sugar over them and serve hot.

Nectarine Fritters

Apricots or peaches may be used in this recipe.

PEEL and split 4 ripe bananas lengthwise. Cut the halves crosswise into two or three pieces and sprinkle with 2 tablespoons each of sugar, lemon juice, and rum. Cover the bananas and marinate them for 30 minutes, turning them several times.

Banana Fritters Flambé

Use the liquid from the bananas for a fritter batter for fruit, dip the pieces into the batter, and drop them one by one into hot deep fat (370° F.). Fry the fritters until they are brown and puffed. Drain them on absorbent paper. Arrange the fritters on a serving dish, sprinkle with sugar, and pour over them 6 tablespoons warmed rum. Ignite the spirit, and serve flaming.

MIX and sift together into a mixing bowl 1 cup sifted flour, 1 1/2 teaspoons baking powder, 1 teaspoon sugar, and a pinch of salt. Beat 1 egg with 1/4 cup milk, stir the liquid into the dry ingredients, and beat until the dough is smooth. Mash 2 large bananas and stir them into the dough.

Banana Fritters

The dough may be flavored with rum, brandy, grated lemon or orange rind, or finely chopped candied ginger. Drop the dough by teaspoons into hot deep fat (370° F.) and fry the fritters until they are golden brown. Drain on absorbent paper.

Schlosserbuben
PRUNE FRITTERS

SOAK 1 pound large sweet prunes overnight in water to cover. In the morning bring the liquid to a boil and simmer the prunes until they are tender. Cool. Remove the pits. Insert a blanched almond in each prune and chill. Make a batter by combining 1 cup each of flour and dry white wine and a pinch of salt. Beat the batter until smooth. Dip the prunes in the batter and fry them in hot deep fat (370° F.) for 3 to 4 minutes, or until they are browned. Remove the prunes from the fat with a slotted spoon and drain them on absorbent paper. Mix 1 cup semisweet grated chocolate with 1/2 cup sugar. Roll the prunes in this mixture while they are still hot. Serve immediately.

Berry Fritters

SIFT 1 cup sifted flour, 2 tablespoons sugar, 1 teaspoon baking powder, and 1/2 teaspoon salt into a bowl. Stir in gradually 2 egg yolks lightly beaten with 3 tablespoons water, mixing until the batter is smooth after each addition. Fold in 2 egg whites, stiffly beaten, and 3/4 cup blueberries or raspberries. Drop the batter by spoonfuls into hot deep fat (370° F.) and fry the fritters until they are lightly browned. Drain on absorbent paper and sprinkle generously with confectioners' sugar.

Cranberry Fritters

COOK 3/4 cup cranberries in 1/2 cup water with 1/4 cup sugar until the skins burst. Drain the berries and proceed as for berry fritters.

Crème Frite aux Raisins Flambée
FRIED CREAM WITH GRAPES

MIX together 1 cup flour, 1/4 cup sugar, and a pinch of salt. Add 1 egg and 2 egg yolks mixing thoroughly. Then add a second egg and 2 egg yolks, mixing thoroughly, and finally a third egg and 2 yolks. The mixture should be worked with a spoon until it is well combined and very smooth.

Scald 2 cups milk with a piece of vanilla bean. Remove the bean and pour the hot milk slowly into the egg mixture, stirring briskly with a wire whip. Add 2 tablespoons butter and cook for about 2 minutes, stirring vigorously all the time. Pour the cream into a buttered shallow pan in a layer 3/4 inch thick. Chill thoroughly.

Turn the pan upside down on a lightly floured board and turn out the thickened cream. Cut it in 1 1/2-inch squares or other decorative shapes. Sprinkle each piece with flour and dip it in beaten egg and then in fine fresh bread crumbs. Fry the squares in hot deep fat (370° F.) until they are golden brown.

To make the sauce, drain the liquid from 2 cans white grapes. Put the grapes in the top of a double boiler or a chafing dish over hot water. Cook the liquid in a saucepan until it is reduced by half. Add an equal amount of apricot sauce. If the sauce is thin, the mixture may be thickened with a little arrowroot or mixed with a very little cold water. When this is added, boil the sauce for a minute or two longer. Add 1/4 cup prunelle liqueur, pour the sauce over the grapes in the chafing dish, and keep them hot until ready to serve. Just before serving, heat 1/2 cup kirsch and pour it over the grapes. Ignite the spirit and serve the sauce flaming.

Beignets Suzette

HEAT 2 cups milk with a piece of vanilla bean and gradually add 1/2 cup farina, stirring briskly to prevent lumps. Cook the mixture, stirring occasionally, for about 10 to 15 minutes, or until it is very thick. Remove the vanilla bean. Add 1/2 cup sugar, 1 tablespoon sweet butter, and 2 slightly beaten egg yolks, and mix all together well. Return the pan to the heat and cook for 2 minutes longer, stirring constantly. Spread the batter about 3/4-inch thick on a buttered shallow pan or baking sheet, and chill it. Turn out the dough on a floured pastry board and cut it with a doughnut cutter. Dip the *beignets* in flour, in beaten egg, and in fine white bread crumbs, and sauté them in butter until they are golden on both sides. Arrange the fritters in a ring and put a candied cherry in the center of each. Sprinkle with powdered sugar and serve hot, with a fruit sauce.

Dumplings are probably the plainest of all desserts; they are also among the most welcome and most satisfying.

Steamed Fruit Dumpling

Suet Dough

MAKE a suet dough by sifting together into a mixing bowl 2 cups sifted flour, 2 teaspoons baking powder, and 1/2 teaspoon salt. Rub into the dry ingredients 3/4 cup finely chopped suet. Stir gradually into this mixture enough cold water to form a dough that is soft but not sticky. Turn the dough onto a lightly floured board and knead it for 20 seconds. Roll out the dough 1/4 inch thick and line a greased bowl with part of it.

Fill the bowl two-thirds full with apples, pears, or peaches, peeled and sliced, or with blueberries or other berries, fresh in season, or frozen and partially defrosted. Add sugar according to the fruit used and flavor with a little nutmeg or cinnamon. Cover the top of the bowl with the remaining suet dough, cover with greased paper, put it in a steamer, and steam the dumpling for 2 hours.

Pot Cheese Dumplings

CREAM together 2 tablespoons each of sugar and butter. Add 2 lightly beaten eggs, stirring vigorously, and 2 cups dry flaky pot cheese put through a sieve. Add 3 cups flour and, gradually, about 6 tablespoons milk, or enough to make a soft dough.

Roll out the dough into a thin sheet on a lightly floured board and cut it into 2-inch squares. In the center of each square place a small blue plum or apricot or a spoonful of diced apple. Pinch the corners together and roll the dumpling into a ball. Drop the dumplings into a large pot of boiling slightly salted water and simmer them for 8 to 10 minutes. Test one dumpling to be sure the dough is cooked. Serve hot with cinnamon and sugar and with melted butter.

Cherry Vareniki

BEAT 1 large egg until it is frothy. Sift in 2 cups flour sifted with 2 teaspoons salt and add enough warm water to make a soft dough. Knead the dough gently on a lightly floured board. Cover it with a cloth and let it rest for 10 minutes. Knead again until the dough is very smooth.

Roll out the dough on a floured board into a thin sheet and cut it into 1 1/2-inch squares. In the center of each of half the squares place 3 or 4 black cherries, stoned and sugared. Cover each square with another, sealing the edges securely with a little cold water. Drop the *vareniki* into briskly boiling water and cook them for about 8 minutes, or until they rise to the top. Remove them immediately and drain them in a sieve. Serve hot with sour cream and a sprinkling of sugar.

Cranberry Grunt

WASH 1 quart cranberries and put them in a 2-quart casserole with 2 cups each of sugar and water. Let them come to a boil, drop dumpling batter by the tablespoonful on top of the berries, cover closely, and simmer the mixture for 20 minutes without removing the cover. Serve in the casserole.

To make the dumpling batter, sift together into a mixing bowl 2 cups sifted flour, 2 tablespoons baking powder, 1/4 cup sugar and 1/2 teaspoon salt. Add 2 eggs beaten with 1 cup milk, stirring only enough to combine the ingredients.

PARE and core 6 fine apples and fill the cavities with brown sugar. Add 1 clove and 1 teaspoon butter. Roll out suet dough 1/4 inch thick and cut it into rounds that are large enough to wrap around the apples. Place an apple in the center of each round, lightly wet the edges, and press the dough firmly together at the top of each apple. Tie each dumpling in a well-floured pudding cloth, put it into boiling water, and boil gently for 40 to 50 minutes. Serve with cream and sugar.

Boiled Apple Dumplings

New electrically powered freezing churns have taken the arm-ache out of the process that produces velvety, smooth-as-cream ice creams. Your appliance may require special techniques, but in general, the process is the same as for hand-powered churns. Chill the cream mixture and fill the freezer only three-fourths full. Pack the can in a mixture of rock salt and ice; 3 or 4 parts of ice to 1 part rock salt is best, because more salt, while it shortens freezing time, makes for coarser texture. Churn until the paddles stop, then remove the paddles and pack down the cream in the can. Close the can, seal it, and insulate it with blankets or layers of newspaper. Most ice creams profit from a spell of mellowing, so allow two or three hours before serving.

Ice Cream, Freezer Method

The success of homemade ice creams depends largely upon the churning, so refrigerator ice creams lack the smoothness characteristic of a perfect ice cream. A hand or electric-powered ice cream freezer lacking, proceed in this way. Freeze the cream in the refrigerator as quickly as possible for an hour, or until it is mushy, but not solid. Then turn it into a chilled bowl and beat it rapidly with a rotary beater, also chilled, until it is smooth. Work quickly to minimize melting. Return the cream to the refrigerator, and when it is almost solid, beat it smooth again and finish the freezing. Cover the tray with plastic wrap, wax paper, or aluminum foil to help prevent ice crystals from forming on top of the cream.

Bearing in mind the limitations, you may freeze in a refrigerator tray any ice cream recipe that contains a thickening agent such as gelatin, egg yolk, flour, or cornstarch.

Ice Cream, Refrigerator Tray Method

BRING to a boil 2 2/3 cups cream and 1 1/3 cups milk with a piece of split vanilla bean. Beat 8 egg yolks and 1 cup sugar with a wire whip until the mixture is smooth and creamy. Pour the hot milk mixture over the egg yolks, stirring briskly, and cook the custard over very low heat until it almost reaches the boiling point. Be careful that it does not boil or it will curdle. Strain

Glace Vanille
VANILLA CUSTARD
ICE CREAM

it through a fine sieve, chill it quickly, and freeze it. If desired, 1 cup cream, whipped, may be folded into the ice cream just before it becomes firm.

This is a basic recipe that may be varied by the addition of various extracts and liqueurs, nuts, or chopped or puréed fruits.

Glace aux Fraises
STRAWBERRY
ICE CREAM

Follow the directions for vanilla ice cream, adding to the egg yolk mixture 1 cup mashed fresh strawberries.

Glace Moka
MOCHA ICE CREAM

Follow the directions for vanilla ice cream. Melt 6 ounces semisweet chocolate in 2 tablespoons double-strength coffee and add it to the egg mixture.

Glace Praliné
PRALINE ICE CREAM

Follow the directions for vanilla ice cream, omitting the vanilla. Stir in 3/4 cup pulverized praline before freezing.

Apple
Ice Cream

COMBINE 1 1/2 cups cream, whipped, with 1 1/2 cups grated raw apple, including the skin, 1/2 cup sugar, 1/3 cup lemon juice, and a pinch of salt, Freeze the ice cream.

Apricot
Ice Cream

BEAT 2 eggs with 1 cup sugar and 1/2 teaspoon salt. Stir in gradually 2 cups hot milk and cook the custard over boiling water until it coats the spoon, stirring constantly. Cool. Add 1/2 teaspoon almond extract, 2 cups apricot purée, and 1 cup heavy cream, mix well, and freeze the ice cream.

Avocado
Ice Cream

WITH a silver fork mash the pulp of 2 avocados and press it through a fine sieve. Stir in 1/4 cup lemon or lime juice, 3/4 cup sugar, and a pinch of salt and continue to stir until the sugar is dissolved. Stir in 2 cups cream and 1 teaspoon gelatin softened in 1 tablespoon cold water and dissolved over hot water. Mix thoroughly and freeze the ice cream.

Banana Peach
Ice Cream

CRUSH 3 bananas and 6 ripe peaches and press the pulp through a fine sieve. Mix the purée with 2 cups sour cream, 1 cup sugar, and 1/4 cup lemon or lime juice and freeze the ice cream.

Berry
Ice Cream

CRUSH 2 cups berries and force the pulp through a fine sieve to remove the seeds. Add 1 cup sugar to 2 cups heavy cream and stir until the sugar is dissolved. Stir in the berry purée and 2 tablespoons lemon juice, and freeze the ice cream.

Raspberries, strawberries or boysenberries may be used in this recipe.

MELT 2 squares bitter chocolate and combine it with 1 1/4 cups sugar, 1 tablespoon flour, and 1/4 teaspoon salt. Beat in 2 lightly beaten eggs and add gradually, stirring briskly, 2 cups scalded milk. Cook the mixture over hot water, stirring, until it is thickened. Cool and strain it through a fine sieve. Stir in 1 tablespoon vanilla and 2 cups heavy cream. Freeze the ice cream. *Old Fashioned Chocolate Ice Cream*

SCALD 2 cups milk in the top of a double boiler. Mix 1/2 cup confectioners' sugar and 1 1/2 tablespoons flour to a paste with a little of the milk, add the paste to the scalded milk, and cook the mixture, stirring constantly until it is thick and smooth. Beat 2 eggs well, mix them with a little of the hot sauce, and add the eggs to the sauce. Continue to cook, still stirring, until the custard is thick enough to coat the spoon. Remove the pan from the heat and stir in 1/2 teaspoon salt and 1 teaspoon gelatin softened in 1 tablespoon cold water. *Coffee Rum Ice Cream*

Cool the cream, stirring it from time to time. Add 2 tablespoons each of coffee extract and dark Jamaica rum, and fold in 2 cups heavy cream, whipped until stiff. Freeze the ice cream.

SCALD 1/2 cup milk and stir it slowly into 2 well-beaten egg yolks. Cook the mixture over boiling water, stirring constantly, until the custard coats the spoon. Cool and fold the custard into 1 1/2 cups heavy cream, whipped. Peel 1 quart ripe figs thinly and press them through a sieve. Sprinkle the fig purée with 1 tablespoon lemon juice, stir in 1/2 cup sugar and 1 teaspoon vanilla, and add it to the custard. Blend the ingredients thoroughly and freeze the ice cream. *Fig Ice Cream*

HEAT 1 cup maple syrup. Beat 3 egg yolks until they are light, gradually stir in the heated syrup, and cook the mixture over hot water, stirring constantly, until the custard coats the spoon. Stir in 1 teaspoon vanilla and cool. Fold in 3 egg whites, stiffly beaten, and 1 cup heavy cream, whipped. Freeze the ice cream until it is mushy, then stir in 1 cup chopped walnuts and finish the freezing. *Maple Walnut Ice Cream*

*Lime
Ice Cream*

BEAT 2 eggs well and gradually beat in 1/2 cup sugar. Stir in 1 1/2 cups milk, 1/2 cup white corn syrup, 1/4 cup lime juice, and 1 teaspoon grated lime rind. Freeze the ice cream. An hour before serving, fold in 1 cup heavy cream, whipped, and finish freezing. Let the ice cream soften slightly before serving.

*Peach
Ice Cream*

MASH thoroughly 2 cups fresh peaches, peeled and sliced, with 1 cup sugar and 1 tablespoon lemon juice. Let the mixture stand for 30 minutes, stir it into 1 quart heavy cream, and freeze the ice cream.

*Pineapple
Ice Cream*

Pineapple may be substituted for the peaches and the sugar increased to taste.

*Hokey Pokey
Ice Cream*

SOFTEN 4 tablespoons gelatin in 1 cup milk.

In a saucepan combine 2 quarts milk, 4 lightly beaten eggs, 1 1/2 cups sugar, the thinly peeled rind of 1 lemon, and a pinch of salt. Mix all together well and cook the mixture over high heat, stirring constantly, until the cream is thick. Add the gelatin and mix well.

Pour the cream into a bowl, set the bowl in a pan of cracked ice, and stir the mixture until it cools. Freeze the ice cream.

With a few exceptions, ices and sherbets, like ice creams, benefit appreciably from the steady beating of the churn freezer. If the same tiny crystals and smooth texture are to be attained in the refrigerator tray, the sherbet should be beaten well and often during the freezing process; first after an hour or so, when the mixture is set around the sides but still mushy in the center, and every 30 minutes thereafter until the ice is frozen solid. Ices are, strictly speaking, water *ices; they include neither eggs nor milk.*

Lemon Ice

COMBINE 4 cups water and 2 cups sugar, bring the syrup to a boil, and boil it for 5 minutes. Cool. Add 1 tablespoon grated lemon rind and 1 cup lemon juice. Freeze the ice in a churn freezer or in a refrigerator tray.

Apricot Ice

COMBINE 2 cups water and 1 cup sugar, bring the mixture to a boil, and cook it for 5 minutes. Cool the syrup and add 2 cups sieved apricot purée and the juice of 1/2 lemon. Freeze the ice in a churn freezer or in a refrigerator tray.

FOLLOW the recipe for apricot ice, substituting 2 cups crushed pineapple for the apricot purée, and flavor with 1 tablespoon rum.

Pineapple Ice

FOLLOW the recipe for apricot ice, substituting raspberry purée for the apricot purée, and flavor with 2 tablespoons *eau-de-vie de framboise*.

Raspberry Ice

COMBINE 1 1/2 cups water and 1 cup sugar in a saucepan, bring the mixture to a boil and cook it for 5 minutes. Cool the syrup and add 1 1/2 cups finely crushed pineapple and 1/2 cup white crème de menthe. Blend well and freeze the ice.

Pineapple Crème de Menthe Ice

WASH 1 quart raspberries and press them through a fine sieve to remove the seeds. Add 1/2 cup lemon juice and 1/4 cup orange juice. In a saucepan combine 2 1/2 cups each of sugar and water, bring the syrup to a boil, and simmer it for 5 minutes. Cool it and stir it gradually into the fruit mixture. Freeze the ice.

Italian Raspberry Ice

By natural progression we move from simple water ices to the slightly more complicated sherbets.

MANY sherbets owe their characteristic lightness to the whipped-egg froth of an Italian meringue, made with 1 egg white or more in the following proportions:

    Dissolve 1/2 cup sugar in 3 tablespoons water, add a pinch of cream of tartar and boil without stirring until the syrup reaches the soft ball stage, 240° F. on a candy thermometer. Pour the syrup very gradually in a thin stream into 1 stiffly beaten egg white, beating constantly with a rotary beater. Continue to beat with a rotary beater until the meringue is cool. Italian meringue may be flavored with various extracts or liqueurs and used as a cake frosting. It should be very thick.

Italian Meringue

Sorbet
aux Cerises
CHERRY SHERBET

BOIL 2 cups water and 1 cup sugar for 5 minutes. Add 1 cup strained cherry juice, a pinch of salt, and 3 tablespoons lemon juice and cool the mixture. Freeze the sherbet.

About 1 hour before serving, make an Italian meringue, using 1 egg white, and stir it into the frozen sherbet. Continue to freeze and, at the last moment, just before serving, stir in 1/4 cup chilled maraschino liqueur. Serve the sherbet in sherbet glasses and pour a little maraschino over each serving.

Orange
Sherbet

BOIL 2 cups water and 1 cup sugar for 5 minutes. Add the grated rind of 1 orange, 1 cup orange juice, and 2 tablespoons lemon juice. Cool the syrup and strain it through a sieve lined with cheesecloth. Freeze the sherbet.

About an hour before serving, make an Italian meringue with 1 egg white and stir it into the frozen sherbet. Continue to freeze and, at the last moment, just before serving, stir in 1/2 cup chilled Cointreau, Curaçao, or Grand Marnier and spoon the sherbet into chilled sherbet glasses.

Cranberry
Orange
Sherbet

DISSOLVE 1 cup sugar in 1 1/2 cups water, bring to a boil, and boil rapidly for 5 minutes. Cool the syrup and combine it with 2 cups cranberry juice, the juice of 1 lemon, and 1 cup orange juice. Freeze the sherbet.

About an hour before serving, fold into the sherbet an Italian meringue made with 1 egg white. Serve in small chilled sherbet cups with 1 tablespoon Cointreau poured over each portion.

Wine
Sherbet

BOIL 2 cups water and 1 cup sugar for 5 minutes. Add 1 cup orange juice and 1/4 cup lemon juice and cool and chill the syrup. Stir in 2 cups cold wine and freeze the sherbet. Just before serving stir in an Italian meringue made with the whites of 2 eggs. Pile the sherbet into sherbet glasses and top each serving with 1 tablespoon of the wine. Sauternes, Chablis, Rhine wine, Moselle, Madeira, Marsala, and Port are favorite wines for sherbet.

Liqueur
Sherbet

COMBINE 2 cups water and 1 cup sugar, bring the syrup to a boil, and boil it rapidly for 5 minutes. Add 1/4 cup lemon juice and 1/2 cup orange juice and cool. Strain the syrup and freeze it. An hour before serving, make an Italian meringue with 2 egg whites and stir it into the sherbet. Continue to freeze, and at the last moment, just before serving, stir in 1/2 cup rum or any of these liqueurs: anisette, apricot, Bénédictine, blackberry, Chartreuse, cherry, Cognac, crème de menthe, Curaçao, maraschino, or peach.

BOIL 2 cups water and 1 cup sugar with a pinch of salt for 5 minutes. While the syrup is hot, stir into it 2 cups Port and 1/4 cup strained lemon juice. Freeze.

Make an Italian meringue with 4 stiffly beaten egg whites. Stir the meringue into the *spoom* about 1 hour before serving, and finish freezing. Serve in chilled sherbet glasses.

Champagne, Muscat, Frontignan, Sherry, Port, Madeira, Malaga or Marsala may be used to make a *spoom*. Use any one or any combination of them in this master recipe.

Spoom au Porto
PORT WINE SPOOM

DISSOLVE 3/4 cup sugar in the juice of 2 lemons and 1 orange. Add a strip each of lemon and orange peel, bring the mixture to a boil, and boil it rapidly for 5 minutes. Remove the fruit peel and cool the syrup. Add 2 cups Champagne or dry white wine and 1/2 cup strong infusion of tea to the cool syrup. Freeze.

Stir an Italian meringue made with 2 egg whites into the *punch glacé* about 1 hour before serving and at the last moment mix in 1 cup rum, a little at a time. Serve in sherbet or punch glasses.

Punch Glacé à la Romaine
ICED ROMAN PUNCH

CUT off the tops of 6 large tangerines and reserve the tops. With a spoon remove all the pulp from the fruit and save the shells for serving the sherbet Squeeze the tangerine juice from the pulp and add to it the juice of 6 more tangerines and enough orange juice to make 2 cups of juice in all. Carefully remove the rind from 4 of the extra tangerine skins and 2 of the orange skins and cut it into very fine strips.

Boil 2 cups water and 1 cup sugar briskly for 5 minutes. Add the rind to the syrup and cool. Add the fruit juice and, if desired, 1 or 2 drops of red and yellow food coloring. Strain the mixture through a fine sieve and freeze it. When the sherbet is partially frozen, fold in 2 egg whites, stiffly beaten with 2 tablespoons sugar, and continue to freeze until the ice is solid. Fill the tangerine shells with the sherbet, put the tops on them, and put the tangerines in the freezer until serving time.

Mandarines Givrées
FROSTED TANGERINES

BOIL 4 cups water and 1 cup sugar for 5 minutes. Make 4 cups mango purée by forcing ripe fresh mango pulp through a sieve. Stir into the purée 1/4 cup

Mango Sherbet

lemon juice, add the sugar syrup, cool the mixture and freeze it in the usual way.

When the sherbet is partially frozen, stir in 3 egg whites stiffly beaten and finish the freezing.

Neige au Clicquot
CHAMPAGNE SHERBET

BOIL 1 1/4 cups sugar and 1 cup water for 5 minutes. Cool the syrup and stir in 1 1/2 cups sparkling Champagne and the juice of 1 lemon. Freeze the sherbet, using 3 parts ice to 1 part rock salt. When the sherbet is almost frozen, fold in a meringue made by whipping 2 egg whites until they are stiff and stirring in 2 tablespoons fine granulated sugar. Pile the sherbet into sherbet glasses and top each portion with 2 tablespoons Champagne.

Cranberry Sherbet

COOK 2 cups cranberries in 1 1/2 cups water until they are soft and rub them through a fine sieve. Stir in 1 teaspoon gelatin softened in 2 tablespoons cold water, 1 1/4 cups sugar, 1 cup orange juice, and 2 tablespoons lemon juice. Freeze the sherbet to the halfway point. Fold in 2 stiffly beaten egg whites and finish the freezing.

A marquise *is an ice enriched with whipped cream.*

Marquise aux Fraises
STRAWBERRY MARQUISE

CRUSH and strain through a fine sieve 4 cups strawberries. Sweeten the purée to taste and add enough cold water to make 2 cups liquid. Boil 3/4 cup sugar in 1 1/2 cups water for 5 minutes. Cool the syrup and stir it into the strawberry purée. Add the juice of 1 lemon and mix thoroughly. Freeze the ice.

Just before serving, stir in 2 cups heavy cream, whipped, and 1 cup kirsch.

Marquise au Champagne

BOIL 1 1/2 cups water and 3/4 cup sugar for 5 minutes. Add the grated rind of 1/2 orange, the juice of 2 lemons and 2 oranges, and 1/4 teaspoon salt. Cool the syrup, add 1 pint chilled Champagne, and strain the mixture into a refrigerator tray. Freeze the ice.

Just before serving, stir in 2 cups heavy cream, beaten until fairly stiff, and 1 1/2 tablespoons brandy. Pile the *marquise* in sherbet or Champagne glasses and pour 2 tablespoons Champagne over each serving.

Or spoon the *marquise* over wild strawberries steeped in Champagne and a little sugar.

GRATE enough fresh pineapple to make 1 1/2 cups. Put the pineapple in a saucepan with 1 cup pineapple juice, the grated rind of 1 lemon, and 1 cup each of water and sugar. Bring the liquid to a boil and boil it for 5 minutes. Strain, add the juice of 1 lemon, and a little confectioners' sugar if necessary, and freeze the ice. When the mixture is frozen, fold in 1 cup whipped cream and 3 tablespoons kirsch and serve immediately.

Marquise à l'Ananas
PINEAPPLE MARQUISE

Mousses, parfaits, and their ilk should freeze without stirring. In the trays of the refrigerator, make your mousse in fluted paper cups or small soufflé dishes or individual ice cream molds. In the home freezer, there is room for bombe *molds and large decorative forms of various sorts. Ice cream molds large and small may be buried in a mixture of 3 parts ice to 1 part rock salt, providing that the covers are adjusted tightly and sealed with a buttered cloth to prevent the salty water from seeping into the cream. Allow from 2 to 4 hours for the freezing, depending upon the size of the mold and the efficiency of the freezing mechanism.*

BOIL 1 1/2 cups sugar and 1 cup water rapidly for 5 minutes. Cool. Beat 8 egg yolks in the top of a double boiler and whip in the syrup gradually. Add some seeds from the inside of a vanilla bean for flavoring and cook the custard over very hot but not boiling water, stirring constantly, until it becomes creamy and thick. Rub the custard through a fine sieve and stir it over cracked ice until it cools. Whip 1 quart heavy cream until it is stiff enough to hold a shape, add vanilla extract to taste, and fold the cream into the cooled custard. Freeze without stirring.

Mousse Vanille

This basic recipe may be varied to taste with extracts, liqueurs, or puréed fruits. It is used as a *pâte à bombe*, a filling for a decorative *bombe* mold that is lined with ice cream.

Pâte à Bombe
BOMBE FILLING

Follow the directions for vanilla mousse. Omit the vanilla, flavor the mousse with 1 tablespoon apricot brandy and add 1 cup apricot purée sweetened to taste.

Mousse aux Abricots
APRICOT MOUSSE

MASH and press through a fine sieve enough fresh peeled peaches to make 2 cups purée. Soften 1 tablespoon gelatin in 1/4 cup cold water for 5 minutes and stir it over boiling water until it is thoroughly dissolved. Add the gelatin,

Peach Mousse

661

2 tablespoons lemon juice, and 3/4 cup sugar to the peach purée, and chill thoroughly. Fold in 2 cups heavy cream, whipped, and freeze without stirring.

Pineapple Rum Mousse   PEEL and core a large pineapple. Cut half the pineapple into 1/2-inch-thick slices. Put the slices in a bowl and sprinkle them with 2 1/2 tablespoons sugar and 1 tablespoon dark rum. Grate the rest of the pineapple into a bowl and stir in sugar to taste. Add 2 tablespoons rum, fold the fruit mixture into 4 cups heavy cream, whipped, and freeze without stirring. Serve garnished with the marinated pineapple slices.

Raspberry Mousse   WASH and hull 2 quarts raspberries. Crush them with a fork, sprinkle them with 2 cups fine granulated sugar, and let them stand for 1 hour. Rub the raspberries through a fine sieve to remove the seeds and stir 1 tablespoon lemon juice into the purée. Whip 2 quarts heavy cream and fold it into the purée. Turn the mixture into two 1 1/2-quart molds and freeze without stirring. Serve garnished with whole raspberries.

Berry Mousses   Other berries may be used in the same way.

Frozen Rum Cream   BEAT 8 egg yolks and 1/2 cup sugar until the mixture is thick and pale in color. Fold in 6 egg whites, stiffly beaten, and 3 cups whipped cream, and stir in very gradually 1 cup rum. Turn the cream into a deep refrigerator tray and freeze without stirring for 8 hours. Serve in sherbet glasses garnished with rum-flavored whipped cream, if desired.

Sour Cream Mousse   MIX 2 cups thick sour cream thoroughly with 1 tablespoon rum, 1/4 cup each of macaroon crumbs and melted sweet chocolate, 1/2 cup sugar, and 1 teaspoon vanilla. Turn the mixture into a mold and freeze without stirring.

Frozen Cheese   BEAT 2 cups cottage cheese as smooth as possible in an electric mixer. Add gradually 3 cups sour cream and continue to beat. Add 2 cups confectioners' sugar and 1 teaspoon vanilla and beat until the sugar is dissolved. Freeze without stirring.

Serve with sour cream and a tart jelly on the side. Or garnish with candied fruits or fresh fruits or berries.

The parfait, which like the mousse requires no stirring as it freezes, always begins with a sugar syrup.

BOIL 2/3 cup sugar and 1 1/2 cups water rapidly for 5 minutes. Cool the syrup and stir in 2 teaspoons vanilla extract and 2 cups grated fresh coconut. Mix well, fold in 2 cups heavy cream, whipped, and turn the mixture into a parfait mold. Seal the mold and freeze without stirring. *Coconut Parfait*

BOIL 1 1/2 cups sugar and 1/2 cup water rapidly for 5 minutes. Gradually beat the syrup into 6 egg yolks and cook the mixture over very low heat, stirring constantly, until it is thick and smooth. Do not let it boil. Strain the cream through a fine sieve and stir it over cracked ice until it is cold. *Parfait Grand Marnier*

    Stir into the cream 2 tablespoons Grand Marnier and fold in 1 cup heavy cream, whipped. Turn the mixture into a parfait mold, seal the mold, and freeze without stirring.

BRING to a boil 3/4 cup maple syrup and cook it without stirring until it spins a light thread, or registers 228° F. on a candy thermometer. Beat the syrup gradually into 2 stiffly beaten egg whites and continue to beat until the meringue is cool and very thick. Stir in 1 teaspoon vanilla and fold in 1 cup heavy cream, whipped, and 1/2 cup chopped pecans. Spoon the mixture into 6 individual fluted paper cups, sprinkle with chopped pecans, and freeze without stirring for about 2 hours, or until the parfait is frozen hard. *Maple Pecan Parfait*

BOIL 1 cup each of sugar and water rapidly for 5 minutes. Pour the hot syrup over 1 cup chopped mint leaves and let it stand for 1 hour. Strain the syrup through a sieve lined with two layers of cheesecloth and bring it again to the boiling point. Pour the syrup in a fine stream into 3 stiffly beaten egg whites, beating constantly, and continue to beat until the meringue is thick and cool. Add a pinch of salt and a few drops of green food coloring. Fold in 2 cups heavy cream, whipped, and freeze without stirring. *Mint Parfait*

BOIL 1 cup sugar and 1/3 cup water until the syrup spins a light thread, or registers 228° F. on a candy thermometer. Pour the hot syrup in a fine stream *Pistachio Parfait*

Strawberry Parfait

into 3 stiffly beaten egg whites, beating constantly, and continue to beat until the meringue is cool. Stir in 2 teaspoons vanilla and a few drops of green food coloring, fold in 2 cups heavy cream, whipped, and 1 cup coarsely ground pistachio nuts, and freeze without stirring.

BOIL 2/3 cup sugar and 1/4 cup water for 5 minutes. Beat 6 egg yolks until *Prune Parfait* they are fluffy and gradually add the syrup, beating constantly. Cook the cream over hot water, stirring constantly, until it thickens. Remove from the heat, beat until cool, and chill.

    Stir 1 cup prune purée and 2 tablespoons Mirabelle or brandy into the cooled cream and fold in 2 cups heavy cream, whipped until stiff. Turn into a refrigerator tray and freeze without stirring.

WASH, hull, and crush 1 quart strawberries and press them through a fine *Strawberry* sieve to remove the seeds. Boil 1 cup sugar and 3/4 cup water for 5 minutes. *Parfait* Beat 3 egg whites and 1/4 teaspoon salt until stiff. Pour the hot syrup into the egg whites in a fine stream, beating constantly, and continue to beat until the meringue is thick and cool. Fold in the strawberry purée and 2 cups heavy cream, whipped, and freeze without stirring.

    Granités, *like mousses and parfaits, are not stirred during the freezing.*

BOIL 4 cups water and 2 cups sugar for 5 minutes. Add the grated rind of *Lime Granité* 1 lime and from 1/2 to 1 cup lime juice, according to taste. Cool the mixture and strain it into a refrigerator tray. Freeze without stirring until it forms a granular mass. Serve in sherbet glasses.

FOLLOW the recipe for lime granité, substituting lemon rind and juice for *Lemon Granité* the lime. Pour 2 tablespoons crème de menthe over each serving, if desired, or garnish with sprays of fresh mint.

BOIL 1 cup each of water and sugar for 5 minutes. Cool the syrup and mix *Tea Granité* it with 3 cups chilled double-strength tea. Pour the mixture into a refrigerator tray and freeze it without stirring, until it forms a granular mass. Serve in sherbet glasses with 1 tablespoon rum over each serving.

Bombes The first bombes *were spherical, whence their name; today's* bombes *may be molded in any desired shape. The only requirement is that the mold be fitted with a cover. Chill the mold well before filling it. Line it with a 3/4-inch-thick layer of ice cream, sherbet, or water ice, spreading it as evenly as possible. If the shell should soften during this operation, cover the mold and set it in the freezer to harden. Add the filling by spoonfuls until the mold all but overflows. Cover the cream with buttered wax paper and adjust the lid. A thin coat of butter will seal the seam and make the mold waterproof. Then, lacking a freezer, the mold may be packed in a mixture of 3 or 4 parts ice to 1 part rock salt. Allow several hours for the* bombe *to freeze and mellow before serving time. To unmold a* bombe, *dip the mold quickly in very hot water, dry it, and invert it on a chilled serving platter. Garnish the* bombe *quickly and slice it with a silver knife dipped in hot water.*

Bombe Line a *bombe* mold with orange ice and fill the center with a mousse flavored
Fleurs d'Oranger with Curaçao instead of with vanilla.

Bombe Andalouse Line a *bombe* mold with vanilla mousse and fill it with apricot ice flavored with apricot liqueur or brandy.

Bombe Line a *bombe* mold with apricot ice and fill the center with vanilla mousse.
Marie Antoinette

Bombe Alhambra Line a *bombe* mold with vanilla ice cream and fill the center with strawberry ice cream. Freeze. Unmold the *bombe* and surround it with strawberries marinated in kirsch.

Bombe Traviata Line a *bombe* mold with strawberry ice cream and fill the center with lemon ice mixed with a small quantity of slivered crystallized fruits marinated in kirsch.

Bombe Georgette Line a *bombe* mold with praline ice cream and fill the center with pine-apple ice.

Bombe Arlésienne Line a *bombe* mold with lemon ice and fill the center with raspberry ice.

Bombe Fédora Line a *bombe* mold with orange ice and fill the center with praline ice cream.

Line a *bombe* mold with pistachio ice cream and fill the center with apricot mousse.

Line a *bombe* mold with chocolate ice cream and fill the center with praline ice cream.

Line a *bombe* mold with praline ice cream and fill the center with strawberry ice cream.

Line a *bombe* mold with rum-flavored pineapple ice and fill the center with orange ice.

Line a *bombe* mold with strawberry ice and fill the center with vanilla mousse.

CUT enough candied fruits such as cherries, pineapple, and citron into small dice to measure 3/4 cup and mix them with 1/4 cup white raisins. Marinate the fruit in 1/4 cup kirsch for 1 hour, stirring frequently, and then mix the fruit and liqueur with 1 quart vanilla ice cream. Put the mixture into a spherical *bombe* mold and freeze it until the cream is solid.

Boule de Neige
SNOWBALL

Unmold the *boule* onto a chilled platter to garnish. Put whipped cream, sweetened to taste and flavored with vanilla, into a pastry tube fitted with a fluted nozzle and make small pointed rosettes all over and close enough together to mask the ice cream completely. Decorate with crystallized violets.

LINE long curved molds or narrow tin boxes with wax paper. Spread the bottom and sides with a thick layer of pistachio ice cream—vanilla ice cream mixed with 1 cup ground pistachios, flavored with 1 teaspoon almond extract, and tinted pale green with food coloring. Sprinkle generously with sultana raisins that have been soaked for 1 hour in brandy. Fill the center of the molds with vanilla ice cream or whipped cream and cover the center filling with a top layer of pistachio ice cream. Freeze.

Sultana Mold

Pistachio Ice Cream

Boil 1 cup sugar dissolved in 1/4 cup water with a few drops of lemon juice, for 8 minutes. Cool slightly and stir in 1/3 cup claret. Cool the sauce and serve it with the unmolded sultana mold.

BEAT 6 egg yolks with 1/2 cup sugar until the mixture is very thick and pale in color. Flavor with vanilla extract or add the seeds from the inside of a 1-inch piece of vanilla bean. Fold in 3 cups whipped cream. Fill a heart-shaped mold and place it in the freezer. Macaroons or ladyfingers

Heart of Cream with Strawberries

sprinkled with a liqueur may be put in the center of the cream in the mold.

To serve, dip the mold for an instant in hot water, turn out the cream into a rather deep serving plate, and decorate it with chocolate leaves. Surround the cream with strawberries, washed, hulled, and sprinkled with kirsch, and pour a vanilla sauce over them.

Spumoni
Gourmet

IN a saucepan beat 5 egg yolks and 3/4 cup sugar until the mixture is thick and pale in color. Stir in 2 cups milk, add a 1-inch piece of vanilla bean, and cook over very low heat, stirring constantly, until the custard is thick. Be careful not to let it boil. Discard the vanilla bean and cool the custard. Turn it into a refrigerator tray and freeze it for about 2 hours, or until it is firm, but soft enough to be molded easily.

Whip 1 cup heavy cream until it is stiff, fold in 1/4 cup sugar and 1 tablespoon each of chopped maraschino cherries, shredded candied orange peel, and slivered blanched almonds and chill the mixture.

Chill a 1-quart jelly or *spumoni* mold and line the inside of the mold with the frozen custard. Fill the center of the mold with the chilled whipped cream mixture, cover the top of the mold with wax paper, and freeze the *spumoni* without stirring.

The marriage of ice cream and fruit was made in gourmets' heaven. The fruit and ice cream desserts that follow are typical of haute cuisine.

Abricots
Flambés

APRICOTS BLAZED
WITH KIRSCH

HEAT 1 cup apricot sauce with 1/4 cup kirsch. Add 2 cups drained cooked apricots and heat them well in the sauce. Sprinkle with 1/4 cup warmed kirsch and ignite the spirit. Serve the sauce flaming over hard frozen vanilla or coffee ice cream.

Cherries
with Kirsch

PIT 2 pounds cherries. Crack 2 dozen of the pits and tie them in a cheese-cloth bag. In a saucepan put 2 cups dry red wine, 1 cup sugar, and the bag of pits, bring the liquid to a boil, and boil it for 5 minutes. Add the cherries, cover the pan, and simmer them for 8 to 10 minutes. Remove the cherries with a skimmer to a serving bowl and cool. Cook the syrup until it is reduced to 1 1/2 cups and strain it through a fine sieve. Cool. Add 3 tablespoons kirsch to the sauce and pour it over the cherries. Top each serving with a scoop of vanilla ice cream.

PUT fresh figs on apricot ice and cover with apricot sauce flavored with kirsch. Decorate with sweetened whipped cream forced through a pastry bag fitted with a fancy tube and veil with spun sugar.

    Other fruits or berries may be substituted for the figs.

Figs
Santa Clara

REMOVE the pits from poached peaches and stuff the fruit with vanilla ice cream. Set them on raspberry ice and cover with whipped cream. Sprinkle with chopped praline and veil with spun sugar.

Peaches Frisson

MAKE a light syrup by boiling 2 cups water and 3/4 cup sugar for 5 minutes. Put 6 firm ripe peaches, peeled, in a saucepan, pour the syrup over them, and add either a piece of vanilla bean or a slice of lemon. Bring the syrup to a boil and simmer gently for 10 to 15 minutes, or until the peaches are tender. Cool the peaches in the syrup. To serve, drain the peaches and place them on individual servings of coffee ice cream or arrange them around a mold of ice cream or in the center of an ice cream ring. Cover with kirsch-flavored *sauce riche*. Garnish with crystallized violets, if available, and mask with spun sugar.

Pêches Annette
PEACHES ANNETTE

DRAIN and dry 3 poached, halved peaches. Fill the peach halves with vanilla ice cream, rounding the cream to make the fruit look whole. Coat the peach side with some stiff apricot sauce and sprinkle the ice cream with slivered almonds.

    Serve each peach on a round of *génoise* that has been saturated with kirsch, maraschino, or Cointreau and coated with raspberry glaze.

*Pêches
Eléonore*

PEEL, halve, and discard the pits from 6 large peaches. Poach the peaches in sugar syrup flavored with ginger. Cool the fruit and chill it.

    Arrange two peach halves on a plate, fill the centers with ice cream, and sprinkle with chopped walnuts and chopped preserved or candied ginger.

*Peaches
Celestial*

SPRINKLE 1 cup fresh peaches, peeled and sliced, with a little sugar, pour over them 1/4 cup kirsch, Curaçao, or Cointreau, and let the fruit marinate in the liqueur for 30 minutes. Garnish 6 glasses with a large spoonful of

*Ice Cream
with Peaches*

the marinated fruit and cover the fruit with a scoop of peach ice cream. Put half a fresh peach, peeled, on top of the ice cream and sprinkle it with a little of the same liqueur used to marinate the peach slices.

Ice Cream with Fruits

Other fruits may used in the same way.

Peach Alaska

ARRANGE 1 quart molded raspberry ice on a layer of *génoise* that is cut 1 inch larger all the way around than the ice. Drain 6 poached, halved peaches and place them, rounded side up, on top of the ice. Cover cake, ice, and fruit with a thick layer of *meringue suisse*, sprinkle with fine granulated sugar, and bake the Alaska in a very hot oven (450° F.) for about 5 minutes, or until the meringue is delicately browned. Serve at once.

Poires Belle Dijonnaise

PEARS DIJON

PACK a ring mold with raspberry ice and put it in the freezer. At serving time, unmold the ice and in the center of the ring arrange 6 poached pears that have been chilled. Coat with *sauce riche* flavored with prunelle liqueur.

Pineapple Melba

SELECT 3 small ripe pineapples and cut them in half lengthwise, leaving on the green top. With a fork, scrape out the flesh, discarding the hard core and being careful not to break through the shell. Sprinkle the inside of the shells with a little sugar and set them in the refrigerator until they are very cold. Use the shredded flesh to make pineapple ice cream. To serve, place half a pineapple shell on each serving plate. Fill the shells with the pineapple ice cream and pour over them some raspberry purée.

Raisins Jubilee

RINSE 1 cup seedless raisins, cover with boiling water, and let them stand for 5 minutes. Drain them well, add 1/4 teaspoon grated lemon rind, 1 tablespoon lemon juice, 3 generous tablespoons brown sugar, and 3 tablespoons brandy. Mix well, cover, and marinate the raisins in the liquid for at least 1 hour.

Just before serving, add 2 more tablespoons brandy and heat the mixture to the boiling point in a chafing dish or saucepan. Ignite the liquid and stir gently, spooning the liquid over the raisins until the flame dies. Serve at once over hard-frozen vanilla ice cream.

Fill a large sherbet glass almost to the top with hard-frozen vanilla ice cream. Cover the ice cream with a thick layer of ground freshly roasted peanuts and decorate the whole with thin slices of preserved quince. In Mallorca, where this dessert originated, the nuts are mixed with an equal quantity of ground *chufa* root, obtainable in Spanish grocery stores.

Helado
Edna May
PEANUT QUINCE
SUNDAE

Combine 3/4 cup each of clear honey and cold water and cook for several minutes until well blended. Remove the syrup from the heat and pour it over 2 dozen ripe green-colored figs that have been carefully peeled and sectioned in quarters. Cool the fruit mixture before refrigerating it for several hours. Serve over firm vanilla ice cream.

Figs in Honey

Squeeze and strain enough fresh orange juice to measure 1 1/4 cups. Stir into it the finely grated rind of 2 small oranges and set the mixture aside. Peel 6 navel oranges, removing the white pulp and membrane. Section the oranges and put the sections in a serving bowl. Chill until needed.

Beat the yolks of 5 eggs with a rotary beater until they are light and creamy. Gradually beat in 1 cup sugar and continue beating until the mixture is smooth. Stir in the orange juice thoroughly and transfer it to the top of a double boiler over boiling water. Cook the mixture for about 5 minutes, beating constantly with a rotary beater until the sauce froths up and is well thickened. Remove it from the heat, cool it, and chill it. To serve, fold 1 pint soft vanilla ice cream into the sauce, pour it over the orange slices, and serve at once.

Oranges
in Iced Orange
Cream

Peel 6 medium pears of uniform size and leave them whole with their stems attached. As they are peeled, drop them in a bowl of cold water acidulated with the juice of 1 lemon.

Combine in a saucepan 2 cups light brown sugar and 3 cups water. Bring the mixture to a boil, lower the heat, and cook the syrup for 3 to 4 minutes. Drain the pears thoroughly, add them to the hot syrup, and simmer them gently until they are tender. The pears must be firm enough to stand upright in the serving dish.

Pour several inches of Cointreau into a small bowl. Dip each pear into the Cointreau, rotating it several times until the fruit is saturated. Arrange the pears upright in a serving dish. Cook the syrup until it is moderately thick and pour in the remaining Cointreau in which the pears were dipped. Cool. Pour the syrup over the pears and chill until serving time. Spoon softened vanilla ice cream into a serving bowl and pass it separately.

Pears
with Ice Cream

671

Soufflé Infante SLICE off the tops of 6 small thick-skinned oranges and with a grape-fruit knife cut the fruit from the skin. Cut the fruit into sections and lift them out. Reserve the fruit for another use. Chill the orange shells thoroughly and fill them with orange sherbet. Store the filled shells in the freezer until serving time.

Beat 3 egg whites until they are stiff, adding gradually 1/2 cup sugar. Fold in 3 egg yolks, beaten until light, and 1/4 teaspoon vanilla. Cover the sherbet with this mixture, piling it high and being sure that it touches the shell all around and seals the sherbet in completely. Bake the oranges in a very hot oven (450° F.) for a few minutes to brown the topping.

Mexican TOP a scoop of coffee ice cream with a brandied chestnut and pour over
Coffee Kahlúa it 2 tablespoons Kahlúa.

There are those who believe that dessert sauces serve the doubtfully useful function of gilding the lily. We are not among them, and the sauces that follow argue for us.

Sauce Vanille IN the top of a double boiler scald 1 cup each of milk and cream with
à l'Anglaise half a vanilla bean. Whip 4 egg yolks with 1/2 cup sugar and 1/4 tea-spoon flour until the mixture is very light. Add the hot milk and cream
VANILLA SAUCE OR slowly, stirring vigorously, and return the custard to the top of the double
SOFT CUSTARD boiler. Cook the custard over simmering water, stirring constantly, until the mixture is thick enough to coat the back of a spoon. Strain the custard through a fine sieve and cool it, stirring from time to time. This sauce can be kept in the refrigerator for two or three days. Flavor the sauce further, if desired, with any cordial or liqueur.

Sauce Riche Fold 1 cup heavy cream, whipped, into 1/2 cup vanilla sauce, and flavor the sauce with 1/4 cup Grand Marnier or another liqueur.

Chocolate Stir into 2 cups vanilla sauce 4 ounces sweet chocolate, or 2 ounces bitter
Cream Sauce chocolate and 2 tablespoons sugar, melted with 3 tablespoons water.

Coffee Sauce Omit the vanilla from vanilla sauce. Add to 2 cups of the sauce 1/4 cup double-strength coffee.

Soufflé Infante

Rum *Coffee Sauce*	To 2 cups coffee sauce add 2 tablespoons rum. Cool the sauce and just before serving, fold in 1/4 cup cream, whipped.

Rum Sauce Mix 1/2 cup vanilla sauce with 1/4 cup dark rum and fold in 1/2 cup heavy cream, whipped. Serve cold.

Fruit Sauce COMBINE 1 cup unsweetened fruit juice—cherry, plum, strawberry, or raspberry, for instance—with 1/4 cup sugar and the juice of 1/2 lemon. Bring the mixture to a boil. Mix 1 teaspoon cornstarch or arrowroot with 2 tablespoons cold fruit juice and add it to the boiling juice. Cook the sauce until it is clear and slightly thickened. Serve hot or cold.

Glacéed
Fruit Sauce COMBINE 1 cup orange juice, 1/4 cup lemon juice, and 1/2 cup pineapple juice with 2 cups sugar, and cook the mixture for about 10 minutes, or until it is syrupy. Add 1 tablespoon corn syrup and 1/2 cup finely chopped mixed glacéed fruits. Simmer the sauce slowly for 20 minutes. Cool. Fold in 2 tablespoons slivered toasted almonds. Serve cold.

Apricot Sauce WASH 1/2 pound dried apricots, soak them in water to cover for several hours, and simmer them in the same water until they are soft. Rub the fruit through a sieve or purée it in a blender, add 1/2 cup sugar, and stir the purée over heat for a few minutes. Flavor the sauce to taste with kirsch or another liqueur. This sauce will keep indefinitely in the refrigerator if it is packed in a sterile jar and a little rum or Cognac is poured over it.

Berry Sauce RUB 2 cups fresh berries through a fine sieve. Bring 1/2 cup each of sugar and water to a boil and simmer gently for 5 minutes. Combine the sieved berries with the syrup and flavor the sauce to taste with kirsch or another liqueur. Serve cold.

Berry
Jelly Sauce BRING to a boil 1/2 cup each of strained raspberry or other berry juice and currant jelly. Mix 1 teaspoon cornstarch with 2 tablespoons of the cold berry juice and add it to the boiling liquid. Cook the sauce until it is clear and slightly thickened. Serve cold.

IN a saucepan mix 1/2 cup sugar with 1 tablespoon cornstarch. Add 1 cup water slowly and cook the mixture over low heat for about 5 minutes, or until it has thickened. Stir the mixture constantly while it cooks. Stir in 3 tablespoons each of lemon juice and butter, 1 teaspoon grated lemon rind, and 1/8 teaspoon salt. Serve hot or cold with cake or with hot or cold puddings.

Clear
Lemon Sauce

SUBSTITUTE strained orange juice for the water in clear lemon sauce.

Clear
Orange Sauce

MAKE clear lemon sauce, cool it, and fold in 1 cup cream, whipped. Serve with cake or with cold desserts.

Lemon
Mousseline
Sauce

CREAM 1/2 cup sweet butter well and gradually beat in 1 1/2 cups confectioners' sugar and 2 tablespoons or more brandy, rum, or any liqueur, or combinations thereof, to taste.

Hard Sauce

CREAM 1/2 cup sweet butter and beat in gradually 1 1/2 cups dark-brown sugar. This mixture requires longer beating than the white sugar mixtures. Add slowly 3 to 4 tablespoons strong black coffee or coffee extract and a generous pinch of nutmeg.

Coffee
Hard Sauce

CREAM together until the mixture is light and fluffy 6 tablespoons sweet butter and 3 tablespoons sugar. Add slowly 3 tablespoons well-flavored cider or Calvados and blend well. Use instead of the usual hard sauce with hot puddings, or with mincement or apple pie.

Cider
Hard Sauce

IN the top of a double boiler over hot water melt 4 ounces unsweetened chocolate with 1 tablespoon Cointreau and stir until smooth. Add a pinch of salt and stir in 10 tablespoons strained honey. Cook the mixture over hot water, stirring frequently, until it is thoroughly blended and smooth, then stir in 1/3 cup blanched, shredded, toasted almonds. Cover the pan, remove it from the heat and let the sauce steam for 15 minutes, stirring it occasionally. Serve lukewarm.

Honey
Chocolate
Sauce

675

Chocolate Sauce

ADD 2 cups water to 1 pound grated sweet chocolate. Bring the mixture to a boil and cook it over hot water until the sauce is smooth. The sauce will be thin. Rub it through a fine sieve, flavor it to taste with rum or with coffee extract, and serve warm.

Chocolate Sauce

MIX equal parts of sugar and water in a heavy skillet and cook the mixture, stirring, until it forms a golden syrup. To coat molds, use the syrup hot. To make a less brittle coating that is easier to handle, add a little more water and cook the caramel, stirring, until the water is completely incorporated. Caramel syrup can be stored in the refrigerator.

Caramel Syrup

MELT 3 cups sugar in a heavy skillet over low heat, stirring constantly. If a strong caramel flavor is desired, allow the sugar to burn slightly. Slowly stir into the melted sugar 3 cups boiling water and cook the syrup until it reaches the consistency desired. It should be as thick as maple syrup. Flavor the sauce with 2 tablespoons rum and serve it hot or cold, with cake or with hot or cold desserts. Add nuts, if desired.

Rum Caramel Sauce

WHIP together in the top of a double boiler 6 egg yolks and 2/3 cup sugar. Add 1 cup Marsala, stirring constantly. Put the pan over cold water and cook the mixture until the water reaches the boiling point and the sauce is thick and creamy. Add 1 tablespoon kirsch. Serve hot with hot or cold desserts.

Sauce Sabayon

PUT 1 1/2 cups coffee, ground as finely as possible, in a glass jar equipped with a tightly fitting lid. Add as much cold water as the coffee will absorb, cover the jar, and set it in a cold place for 24 hours. Strain the liquid through a fine muslin cloth. There should be about 1 cup very strong coffee extract to use as a flavoring.

Coffee Extract

IN the top of a double boiler blend together well 1 cup sugar, 1 tablespoon quick-cooking tapioca, and 1/4 teaspoon salt. Gradually add 1 1/2 cups boiling water, stirring constantly. Beat 1 egg until it is light and

Foamy Brandy Sauce

foamy, add a little of the hot mixture, then stir both into the sauce. Cook the sauce over hot water for 3 to 5 minutes, or until it is slightly thickened, stirring constantly. Remove it from the heat and stir in 1 1/2 tablespoons butter and 1/4 cup brandy. Serve hot, with hot puddings.

The sauce may be flavored with fruit juice, Sherry, or a liqueur in place of the brandy.

Hot Wine Sauce   COMBINE 1 1/2 cups red wine, 1/2 cup sugar, the grated rind of 1/2 lemon, 2 cloves, crushed, and a piece of cinnamon and simmer the mixture for 5 minutes. Strain the wine and serve it hot, with hot puddings.

Sour Cream Orange Sauce   CREAM 3/4 cup confectioners' sugar and 3 tablespoons butter until the mixture is very light and fluffy. Add 1 cup sour cream, 1 teaspoon grated orange rind, and 3 tablespoons orange juice. Mix all together well and serve cold, with warm cake or hot puddings.

Banana Sauce   PEEL and scrape a large ripe banana and rub it through a sieve. Add 1/4 cup sugar and 1 tablespoon Curaçao or maraschino liqueur and bring the mixture to the boiling point. Chill the banana mixture thoroughly and fold in 1/2 cup whipped heavy cream.

Grand Marnier Sauce   SCALD 1 cup milk with a 1-inch piece of vanilla bean. Beat 4 eggs until they are light and add gradually, beating constantly, 1/2 cup sugar and 3/4 cup heavy cream. Add gradually 1/3 teaspoon salt and the scalded milk, beating briskly. Cook the sauce in the top of a double boiler over hot water, stirring it constantly until it is thick enough to coat the spoon. Beat in 3 tablespoons Grand Marnier and serve the sauce hot or cold.

Pâtisserie

Cake need not defend its historical position as the most sociable of foods. The fabled *Gemütlichkeit* of Central Europe is largely a matter of many cups of coffee and many platters of cake. In the Scandinavian countries, where the coffeepot forever murmurs hospitably at the back of the stove, the aromas of yeast and spice permeate every honest kitchen. Trays of dainty pastries, in an array that would do credit to the imagination of an artist, crown many a cordial dinner *à la française*; in the Near East hours spent in conversation over the coffee cups are inevitably bolstered by cakes. In our own country, no evening among friends is complete without the traditional cup of coffee and piece of cake or of pie.

Some of the more elaborately decorated confections, we feel, may be logically left to the skilled hands of the professional pastry chef. But it is true that almost all cakes (and it should be recorded that even the most complicated pastry *pièce montée* is nothing more than a combination of certain simple basic preparations that are within the reach of any amateur's skill) can be, should be, made at home.

We have collected here for your American kitchen a repertory of pastries in the French manner; this section is as complete as space will allow. For lagniappe, we include our choice of pastries from the corners of the earth and a hearty bonus of typically American pies, cakes, and cookies.

By definition—our definition—a coffeecake is a cake to enjoy with coffee. It is not so sweet as a gâteau, nor so plain as a bread; it is a particularly felicitous combination of both.

Savarin SOFTEN 1 cake compressed yeast in 1/2 cup milk at temperature given on page 573. Or sprinkle 1 package granular yeast into 1/4 cup water at temperature given on page 573, let the yeast soften for 5 minutes, add 1/4 cup lukewarm milk, and stir.

Sift 2 cups flour into a mixing bowl. Make a well in the center and into it pour the yeast and 4 lightly beaten eggs. Mix the flour into the liquid. Add a little more lukewarm milk if necessary to make a soft, sticky dough, since the amount of liquid needed depends on the size of the eggs used. Beat the dough for 2 minutes, preferably with the hand, raising it up with the fingers and letting it fall back into the bowl.

Cover the bowl lightly with a towel and put it in a warm place for about 45 minutes, or until the dough doubles in bulk. Punch down the dough and sprinkle over it 1/2 teaspoon salt and 1 tablespoon sugar. Spread the dough with 2/3 cup softened sweet butter and again beat the dough with the hand for 3 or 4 minutes. Half fill a buttered ring mold with the dough and keep the mold in a warm place until the dough rises to the top. Bake the cake in a hot oven (400° F.) for 10 minutes, reduce the temperature to moderate (350° F.), and bake the cake for 30 minutes longer, or until it tests done. The baking time will vary with the size of the mold. To serve, sprinkle with confectioners' sugar and, if desired, fill the center of the ring with fresh fruits marinated in brandy or liqueur.

Savarin PEEL, quarter, and core 2 pounds fresh ripe pears. Put them in a bowl and *aux Poires* sprinkle over them 1 1/2 cups sugar. Let them stand overnight, covered.
PEAR SAVARIN Add 4 to 6 tablespoons kirsch and cook the pears slowly for 5 to 10 minutes. Spoon the syrup from the pears over a savarin until it is saturated. Cool the pears and turn them into the center of the cake, reserving enough to encircle the cake. Cover the pears with whipped cream, piling it high in the center. Serve at once.

Fruit Savarin Other fruits, such as apricots, cherries, or peaches, may be used instead of the pears.

Savarin SOAK a savarin in syrup for *babas* flavored with kirsch. Coat the top with *Chantilly* apricot glaze and fill the center with whipped cream, piling it high in the center. Garnish the border of the cake with whipped cream forced through a fluted pastry tube.

SOAK a savarin in syrup for *babas* flavored with rum or with a liqueur and fill the center with *crème pâtissière.*

Savarin à la Crème

FOLLOW the recipe for savarin. With the softened butter work into the batter 1 1/2 tablespoons sultana raisins and 1 tablespoon currants. The baba is baked in a high round mold, often fluted.

Baba

THE baked *baba* may be simply soaked in a rum syrup and flambéed at the table with more rum. Or it may be filled with ice cream and fruit.

Individual *babas* baked in small molds with high, decorated sides may be effectively blazed at table in a chafing dish.

Rum Baba

BOIL 1 cup sugar and 1 1/2 cups water rapidly for 5 minutes, until the syrup registers 218° F. on a candy thermometer. Remove the saucepan from the heat and stir in 1/2 cup rum or kirsch.

Syrup for Babas

BOIL 1 1/2 cups sugar and 3 cups apricot juice rapidly for 10 minutes. Remove the saucepan from the heat and stir in 3 teaspoons lemon juice and 3/4 cup rum.

Apricot Syrup for Babas

HALF fill a buttered ring mold with savarin dough and keep the mold in a warm place until the dough rises to the top. Bake the cake in a hot oven (400° F.) for 10 minutes, reduce the temperature to moderate (350° F.), and bake it for 30 minutes longer, or until it tests done. The baking time will vary with the size of the mold.

Baba Savoureux

Pound 1 cup blanched almonds with 1 cup sugar in a mortar until the mixture is a smooth paste and add, little by little, 2 cups water. Strain this almond milk through a fine sieve.

Soak the baba in the almond milk. Fill the hollowed-out center of the cake with whipped cream, sweetened and flavored with vanilla extract. Adjust the top slice and spread the cake with confectioners' sugar icing flavored with almond extract. Sprinkle with toasted slivered almonds.

Pomponnettes au Kirsch   HALF fill small round molds shaped like charlotte molds with *baba* dough. Let the dough rise to the top of the molds and bake them in a hot oven (425° F.) for 7 to 8 minutes. Remove the cakes from the molds and dip them in a syrup for *babas* flavored with kirsch. Drain them on a rack, sprinkle them with a little kirsch, and glaze them with confectioners' sugar icing, half white and half pink.

Marignans   FILL small boat-shaped molds half full with savarin dough. Set them in a warm place until the dough rises to the top. Bake the cakes in a hot oven (400° F.) for 15 to 20 minutes. Unmold them and saturate them in syrup for *babas*.

To serve, split the *marignans* lengthwise and in the pocket thus formed, insert small fluted meringues made with Italian meringue. Glaze the *marignans* with apricot glaze.

Gâteau Manon   HALF fill a *brioche mousseline* mold or a timbale mold, well-buttered, with savarin dough. Let the dough rise to the top of the mold. Tie a band of buttered heavy paper around the top of the mold and extending about 2 inches above it. Bake the *gâteau* in a hot oven (400° F.) for 10 minutes, reduce the temperature to moderate (350° F.), and bake the *gâteau* for 20 to 30 minutes longer. Remove the paper.

When the savarin is cool, unmold it, and cut it crosswise into 5 slices. Soak the slices lightly in syrup for *babas* flavored with kirsch and reconstruct the cake, spreading each slice with a layer of *crème pâtissière*. Spread the top and sides of the *gâteau* with apricot glaze and cover thickly with blanched almonds, slivered and lightly browned in butter. Sprinkle with confectioners' sugar.

Gorenflot   BUTTER a hexagonal tubular mold and sprinkle the bottom with 1/2 cup blanched chopped almonds. Bake savarin dough in the mold in the usual fashion. Turn out the cake onto a rack. Combine 1/2 cup orgeat syrup, or almond-and-orange-flavored corn syrup, with 1/3 cup boiling water, prick the cake well with a fork and spoon the syrup over the cake until it is all absorbed. Mix together 2 tablespoons Pernod and 1 tablespoon anisette and spoon the liqueurs over the cake. Cover the cake with apricot glaze and fill the center with whipped cream sweetened and flavored with Pernod or anisette.

The basic sweet yeast dough for rolls, given on page 575, serves as foundation for a group of international coffeecakes.

PUT in the bottom of buttered muffin cups 1 teaspoon brown sugar, 1/2 teaspoon each of butter and water, and a few pecan halves. Roll out basic sweet yeast dough into a long rectangle 1/2 inch thick and about 8 inches wide. Brush the dough with melted butter, sprinkle it generously with 1/2 cup brown sugar, and roll it up like a jelly roll. Cut it into 1-inch slices and put the slices, cut side down, in the muffin tins. Let the rolls rise in a warm place, covered, for about 45 minutes, or until they double in bulk, and bake them in a moderate oven (350° F.) for 25 minutes. Remove the rolls from the oven, let them stand for 1 minute, then transfer them quickly from the tins to a cake rack.

Butterscotch Pecan Rolls

PUT 1 teaspoon honey and 1/2 teaspoon orange juice into each cup of well-buttered muffin tins. Roll out basic sweet yeast dough into a large rectangle and spread it with a mixture of 1/4 cup each of softened butter and sugar and 1 tablespoon grated orange rind. Roll the dough up like a jelly roll and cut it into slices 1 inch thick. Place the slices, cut side down, in the prepared tins and put them in a warm place to rise, covered, for 45 minutes, or until they double in bulk. Bake them in a moderately hot oven (375° F.) for 20 minutes. Remove the buns from the oven, let them stand for 1 minute, then transfer them quickly from the tins to a cake rack.

Honey Orange Buns

ROLL out basic sweet yeast dough into a rectangle 1/2 inch thick and brush it with melted butter. Cover the dough thickly with a combination of fruit and nuts, brown sugar and cinnamon, roll it up like a jelly roll, and cut it into 1-inch slices. Put the rolls, cut side down, close together in a generously buttered high-sided pan on a 1/4-inch-thick layer of honey. Let the buns rise in a warm spot, covered, for about 45 minutes, or until they double in bulk, and bake them in a moderately hot oven (375° F.) for 25 minutes. Remove the rolls from the oven, let them stand in the pan for 25 minutes, then turn them out on a cake rack.

Fruit and Nut Buns

DIVIDE basic sweet yeast dough into three parts. Roll each part into a rectangle about 1/2 inch thick and 8 inches wide. Brush them with melted butter, sprinkle them with 1/2 cup brown sugar, 1/2 cup raisins, and 2 teaspoons cinnamon, and roll each one up like a jelly roll, sealing the edges with water. Place the rolls, making one circle, on a buttered baking

Swedish Coffee Ring

sheet with the sealed edges down, moisten the ends slightly, and join them securely to form a ring. With kitchen scissors, make deep slantwise cuts in the ring about two-thirds through and at intervals of 1 inch. Turn each slice partly on its side to give a petallike appearance. To make a double ring, swing every other cut slice toward the center of the ring. Brush the ring with melted butter, cover it with a towel, and place it in a warm spot to rise for about 45 minutes, or until it doubles in bulk.

Bake the coffee ring in a moderate oven (350 F.) for 30 to 35 minutes. While it is still warm, frost it with 1 cup confectioners' sugar mixed to a spreading paste with 3 tablespoons light cream. Sprinkle with 1/2 cup chopped nutmeats and decorate with colorful bits of candied fruit.

French Crumb Cake

SCALD 1 cup milk or equal parts of milk and cream. Add 2/3 cup sweet butter, 2 teaspoons salt, and 1/2 cup sugar. Mix well. Cool the mixture, stirring occasionally to prevent a film from forming over the surface. Soften 2 cakes compressed yeast or 2 packages granular yeast in 1/4 cup water at temperature given on page 573. Stir in 1 tablespoon grated orange rind and add 4 eggs, one at a time, beating vigorously after each addition. Stir in the milk and butter mixture and add gradually about 4 1/2 cups twice-sifted cake flour, or enough to make a soft dough. Cover the dough with a light cloth and set it to rise in a warm place for about 4 hours, or until it has more than doubled in bulk.

Fill well-buttered shallow pans about one-third full with the dough. Brush with melted butter and sprinkle with a crumb mixture made as follows: Mix 1/2 cup cake flour, 1/4 cup confectioners' sugar, and 1/2 teaspoon ground cinnamon. Rub in 1/2 cup sweet butter and a generous pinch of salt.

Let the dough rise again for 30 to 35 minutes, and bake the cakes in a hot oven (425° F.) for 20 to 25 minutes, or until the tops are well browned and the cakes leave the sides of the pans.

Honey Twist Coffeecake

SCALD 1 cup milk, add 6 tablespoons butter, 1/4 cup honey, and 1 teaspoon salt and cool to lukewarm. Add 2 cakes compressed yeast or 2 packages granular yeast softened in 1/4 cup water at temperature given on page 573 and 2 eggs, well beaten. Beat in 4 to 5 cups sifted flour, or enough to make a soft dough. Knead the dough on a floured board until it is smooth, form it into a ball, and place in a buttered bowl. Cover the bowl and let the dough rise in warm spot until it doubles in bulk.

Punch down the dough and form it into a long roll about 1 inch in diameter. Coil the dough loosely in a round buttered cake pan, beginning at the center and working toward the outer edge. Spread the dough with 6 tablespoons butter creamed with 1/4 cup sugar, 1 egg white, and 3 tablespoons honey. Sprinkle with 1/2 cup chopped nuts and bake in a moderately hot oven (375° F.) for 25 to 30 minutes.

SOFTEN 1 cake compressed yeast or 1 package granular yeast in 1/4 cup water at temperature given on page 573. Scald 1 cup milk, stir in 1 cup butter, 1/4 cup sugar, and 1 teaspoon salt, and cool to lukewarm. Add the softened yeast, 2 eggs beaten with 1 egg yolk, and about 3 cups flour, or enough to make a stiff batter. Beat the batter vigorously with a wooden spoon until it begins to blister. With the hands, knead in more flour until the dough is soft but not sticky. Turn out the dough on a floured board and knead it for about 5 minutes until it is smooth and satiny. Cover it and let it rise in a warm place for about 1 1/2 hours, or until it doubles in bulk. Punch down the dough with a floured fist and let it rise to double its bulk again. The second rising will take about 45 minutes.

Punch down the dough and let it rest for 10 minutes. Roll it out on a lightly floured board into a rectangle about 1 inch thick. Brush the dough with melted butter, roll it tightly like a jelly roll, and put it in a buttered loaf pan. Let it rise in a warm spot for about 1 hour, or until it doubles in bulk, and bake it in a moderate oven (350° F.) for 45 minutes.

Kuchen

PUNCH down *Kuchen* dough and let it rest for the last 10 minutes. Roll it out into a rectangle 1 inch thick and spread it generously with soft butter. Sprinkle over it 1 cup raisins, 1/2 cup each of ground walnuts, pecans, or blanched almonds and sugar, white or brown, and 2 teaspoons cinnamon. Roll up the dough tightly and put it in a large buttered tube pan. Let it rise again for about 1 hour, or until it doubles in bulk, and bake it in a moderate oven (350° F.) for 50 minutes.

Any of the fillings for coffeecake may be used for the filled *Kuchen*.

Filled Kuchen

SCALD 2 1/2 cups milk and let it cool to lukewarm. Soften 2 cakes compressed yeast or 2 packages granular yeast in 1/2 cup of the milk at temperature given on page 573. Mix the remaining milk with 1 cup each of sugar and melted butter, 2 teaspoons ground cardamom, and 1/2 teaspoon

Swedish Cardamom Buns

salt. Add 2 cups flour and beat the mixture until it is smooth. Add the yeast and about 6 more cups flour, beating with a wooden spoon until the dough is smooth and firm.

Sprinkle the dough with a small amount of flour, cover it lightly with a towel, and let it rise in a warm place until it is double in bulk. Turn it out on a lightly floured baking board and knead until smooth. Roll out the dough 1/2 inch thick and cut it into strips 1/2 inch wide. Twist two and two together and shape the twisted strips into rings or figure eights. Place them on a buttered baking sheet, cover, and let them rise until they double in bulk. Brush with slightly beaten egg and sprinkle with sugar and finely chopped almonds. Bake the buns in a hot oven (400° F.) for 10 to 15 minutes. Serve warm.

Hot Cross Buns   SOFTEN 2 cakes compressed yeast or 2 packages granular yeast in 1/2 cup water at temperature given on page 573. Mix together 1 cup warm milk, 3/4 cup currants, 1/2 cup each of butter, sugar, and raisins, 3 eggs, 1/2 teaspoon salt, and a little rum or vanilla. Add the yeast and 5 cups flour. Knead the dough and place it in a buttered warm bowl, sprinkle the dough with a little flour, cover it with a towel and put it in a warm place to rise for about 2 hours, or until it doubles in bulk. Punch down the dough and let it rise for another 30 minutes. Shape it into small round buns. Arrange the buns slightly apart in a buttered baking pan; they will spread as they rise. Let the buns rise until they are double in bulk and bake them in a moderate oven (350° F.) until they are brown. Decorate with a cross of icing, made by mixing confectioners' sugar to a paste with a little cream, or sprinkle them with confectioners' sugar.

Kolacky   DIVIDE basic sweet yeast dough into pieces about the size of walnuts and form each piece into a smooth ball. Put the balls 2 inches apart on a buttered baking sheet and let them rise, covered, in a warm place for 30 minutes. Press down the center of each roll with the thumb, making a hollow 1/4 inch deep. Brush the hollows with melted butter and fill them with marmalade, jam, or with any of the fillings suggested for coffeecake. Put them in a warm place for another 30 minutes to double in bulk and bake them in a moderate oven (350° F.) for 20 minutes. When the *kolacky* are cool, sprinkle them generously with confectioners' sugar, or ice them with confectioners' sugar mixed to a paste with a little cream.

SOFTEN 1 cake compressed yeast or 1 package granular yeast in 1/4 cup water at temperature given on page 573. Sift 2 1/2 cups flour into a mixing bowl and with the finger tips or a pastry blender work in 1/2 cup butter until it is evenly distributed. Add the yeast, 2 beaten eggs, 1/2 cup sugar, 1 teaspoon salt, and 1 cup sour cream and beat the mixture vigorously. Cover the bowl and put the dough in the refrigerator to rest overnight.

Schnecken

Next day, put the dough in a warm place to rise for about 3 hours, or until it doubles in bulk. Punch down the dough, turn it out on a lightly floured board, and knead for about 5 minutes, adding if necessary a little more flour to make a dough that is soft but not sticky. Roll out the dough on a lightly floured board into a thin sheet, sprinkle thickly with sugar, cinnamon, chopped nuts, and raisins, and roll it up like a jelly roll. Cut the roll into slices 1/2 inch thick and place the slices on a buttered baking sheet. Let the *Schnecken* rise in a warm place for about 45 minutes, or until they double in bulk, and bake them in a moderate oven (350° F.) for 25 to 30 minutes.

Danish Pastry

SIFT 1/3 cup flour over 3/4 pound cold sweet butter and work the flour into the butter thoroughly. Wrap the butter dough in wax paper and chill it until firm.

Soften 2 cakes compressed yeast or 2 packages granular yeast in 1/4 cup water at temperature given on page 573 with 1 tablespoon sugar. Stir in 1 beaten egg, 1/4 cup sugar, and 1 cup cold milk. Add gradually about 3 1/2 cups flour, beating with a wooden spoon after each addition until the dough is smooth and glossy. The dough should be firm and not sticky. Roll it out on a well-floured board into a 14-inch square. Roll out the butter dough into a rectangle about 6 by 12 inches and place it over half the dough. Fold the other half of the dough over this and press the edges together.

Roll out the folded dough into a long rectangle about 1/2 inch thick. Fold one third of the dough over the center third and fold the remaining third of the dough on top, making three layers. Turn the folded dough so that one of the open ends faces front. Roll out again into a long rectangle, fold over as before, and turn. Repeat the rolling, folding, and turning once more and then chill the dough for at least 1 hour or overnight. Repeat the turning operation three times more and chill the dough for 1 hour. It is then ready to be rolled out, cut into various shapes for crescents, envelopes, cockscombs, or pinwheels, and filled.

Place prepared rolls on buttered baking sheets, cover lightly with a towel, and chill for at least 2 hours before baking. Bake them immediately on taking them from the refrigerator in a hot oven (400° F.) for 5 minutes. Reduce the temperature to moderate (350° F.) and bake them for 10 minutes longer, or until they are delicately browned. Be careful not to overbake. The surface of each pastry may be brushed with a little beaten egg before baking.

Frost the hot pastries with confectioners' sugar mixed to a paste with a little cream. This recipe makes about 40 small pastries, but the filled and shaped pastries may be kept in the refrigerator on baking sheets, covered, for several days and baked as they are needed.

Crescents   Roll out Danish pastry dough 1/8 inch thick and cut it into long strips 5 inches wide. Cut the strips crosswise into triangles 3 inches wide at the base. Place 1 teaspoon of filling on the base and roll up, curving the ends to form a crescent. Or roll the dough without filling to make buttery breakfast crescents.

Envelopes   Roll out Danish pastry dough 1/8 inch thick and cut it into 4-inch squares. Spread the squares with 1 tablespoon of filling and fold the corners into the center, pressing down the edges firmly.

Cockscombs   Roll out Danish pastry dough 1/8 inch thick and cut it into long strips 5 inches wide. Spread each strip lightly with filling and fold one third over the center third. Fold the remaining third over to make three layers. Slice across the folds 1/2 inch thick and cut 5 deep gashes in the side of each slice.

Pinwheels   Roll out Danish pastry dough into a rectangle 1/4 inch thick and spread the surface with filling. Roll the dough up like a jelly roll and cut it into slices 1/2 inch thick. Or roll the dough up without a filling, slice it, and put a tablespoon of cherry preserves on each slice. Sprinkle the preserves with sugar syrup to help prevent burning.

Elephant Ears   Roll the pastry into a rectangle 12 inches wide and spread it with filling. Fold 2 inches of each side in toward the middle, then fold the sides in again, so that the folded edges meet. Fold once more, in half. Cut the folded pastry into slices 1/2 inch thick and lay them, cut side down, on a baking sheet. They will spread in baking and form ears, or *palmiers*, as they are sometimes called.

Variations of Danish Pastry

The difference between a bread and a coffeecake may be simply its filling. Vive la différence!

Almond Paste Put 1 cup blanched almonds through a food chopper or blend them in a blender and stir in 1/2 cup sugar. Add 1 beaten egg and beat until the paste is smooth.

Pecan Paste Put 1 cup pecan meats through a food chopper or blend them in a blender and stir in 1/2 cup brown sugar. Add 1 beaten egg and a pinch of cinnamon and beat until the paste is smooth.

Chopped Dates and Nuts Mix together 1/2 cup each of chopped nuts and pitted dates, 1/4 cup each of chopped candied fruit and sugar, 1/2 teaspoon nutmeg, and the grated rind of 1 lemon.

Fruits and Nuts Mix together 1/2 cup each of ground cooked prunes or apricots, seedless raisins, and brown sugar, 1/4 cup chopped nuts, 3 tablespoons each of chopped fruit peel and chopped citron, and 1 teaspoon cinnamon.

Prunes or Apricots Mix together 1 cup chopped cooked prunes or apricots, 1/4 cup sugar, 2 tablespoons prune or apricot juice, 1 tablespoon lemon juice, 1/2 teaspoon cinnamon, and a pinch of ground cloves.

Date and Nut Paste Pit and cook 1 cup dates in 1/4 cup water with 1 teaspoon grated orange rind for 15 minutes. Remove them from the heat and beat in 1 tablespoon brown sugar and 1/4 cup chopped nuts.

Poppy Seeds Cook 1 cup ground poppy seeds in 1/4 cup milk with 2 tablespoons honey and 1 tablespoon sugar for about 5 minutes. Beat in 1 tablespoon butter and 1/2 teaspoon cinnamon.

Raisins Bring 1 cup each of sugar and water to a boil. Add 1 cup each of chopped raisins and nuts, the grated rind of 1 lemon, and 1 teaspoon cinnamon and cook for about 8 minutes, stirring constantly until the mixture is thick.

In France, a butter cake of unsurpassed lightness and delicacy is made without any leavening except the air beaten into many eggs. This is the Genoa cake, the génoise, *the butter cake which is the basis for so many grand* gâteaux *and for the fanciful iced dainties of the petits fours tray.*

IN a bowl combine 4 eggs, 1/2 cup plus 1 tablespoon sugar, and 1/2 teaspoon vanilla extract. Set the bowl in a second bowl filled with fairly hot water and beat the mixture until it is lukewarm, very light and fluffy, and has doubled in bulk. This will take about 20 minutes with a hand whip or 5 minutes with an electric beater. Remove the bowl from the hot water and continue to beat the mixture until it is cool. Measure 1 cup less 2 tablespoons sifted cake flour and cut and fold it into the mixture in 3 portions with a spatula. Fold in 7 tablespoons butter melted over low heat and cooled. Pour the batter into a buttered and floured pan to a depth of 3/4 inch to 2 inches, depending upon how the cake is to be used. Bake the cake in a moderate oven (350° F.) for 25 to 35 minutes, until it tests done. Turn the cake out on a wire rack to cool. This recipe makes one 10-inch square cake or two very thin 8-inch layers or an 8-inch round high cake. If you wish to cut the cake into small fancy shapes and ice them to make petits fours, bake the cake in a 10- by 12-inch sheet. In France, layer cakes are frequently constructed by slicing a large cake horizontally into as many layers as desired.

Génoise
LIGHT
BUTTER CAKE

*French
Layer Cakes*

SPLIT a cooled *génoise* into two or three layers. Reshape the cake with a filling of marmalade, butter cream, or pastry cream between the layers. Spread the top and sides with a thin coating of apricot glaze and ice it smoothly with *glace royale* or with fondant flavored with vanilla, rum, kirsch, or any other appropriate spirit or liqueur. Complete the décor with a sprinkling of finely chopped pistachios or grilled almonds or garnish it gaily with candied fruits.

*Génoise
Fourrée*
FILLED GÉNOISE

SPLIT a cooled *génoise* in half and sprinkle the cut surfaces with Calvados. Spread the bottom slice with thick, sweetened applesauce and cover this with a thick layer of *crème pâtissière* flavored with Calvados. Top with the second layer of cake and brush top and sides with apricot glaze. Ice top and sides with pink fondant flavored with Calvados and decorate the top with apple quarters cooked in syrup, halved almonds, and diamonds of angelica.

*Gâteau
Normand*

BAKE a *génoise* in a buttered flan ring placed on a buttered and floured baking sheet or in a springform pan. Cool the cake, cut it into 2 thin layers, and spread the layers with kirsch-flavored *crème au beurre* about 1/2 inch thick.

Rub sugar with a speck of green food coloring between the palms

*Fromage
de Brie
en Surprise*
BRIE CHEESE
SURPRISE

of the hands, and sprinkle the sugar generously over the top of the cake. Sprinkle confectioners' sugar heavily over the green sugar. The cake will resemble a whole Brie cheese.

Gâteau Ambassadeur

BAKE and cool a *génoise*. Slice off the top of the cake and scoop out the inside, leaving a shell about 3/4 inch thick on the sides and 1/2 inch thick on the bottom. Prepare a macédoine of mixed diced fresh fruits, including some strawberries, sweeten it with a little confectioners' sugar and flavor it with 1 or 2 tablespoons kirsch. Fill the hollowed-out cake with this mixture and replace the top. Brush the cake with apricot jam and sprinkle it with chopped toasted almonds.

L'Exotique
COCONUT CAKE

MAKE a *génoise*, reducing the flour to 3/4 cup and adding 1/2 cup finely grated coconut to the batter. Bake it on a buttered and floured baking sheet. Cool and cut the cake in half. Stir 1/4 cup grated coconut into 1 cup rum-flavored *crème au beurre* and fill the cake with this cream. Frost the top and sides of the cake with Italian meringue, decorate the sides with triangles of candied orange rind and angelica, and sprinkle the top with grated coconut.

Gâteau Régent aux Marrons
CHESTNUT CAKE

PUT three layers of cooled *génoise* together with *crème au beurre aux marrons*.

Spread the top and sides of the cake with apricot glaze. In the center, put a thin slice of candied green cherry and surround it with blanched almond halves to imitate the petals of a daisy.

Warm 2 cups of rum fondant over boiling water and add hot water to thin. Pour the warm fondant over the cake, spreading it quickly with a spatula around the sides and covering cake and decorations with a thin veil of icing.

Crème au Beurre aux Marrons
CHESTNUT BUTTER CREAM

Mix 4 cups finely chopped glacéed chestnuts with 3/4 cup soft sweet butter. Whip in gradually 1 cup sugar syrup—equal parts of sugar and water—cooked until it spins a thread, and flavor with rum, kirsch, or vanilla.

Le Baquet de Macaroni
MACARONI BASKET

BAKE a *génoise* in a buttered flan ring placed on a buttered and floured baking sheet or in a springform pan. When the cake is cool, spread the top and sides with *crème au beurre*.

Cut 15 *langues de chat* in half crosswise and arrange them close together around the sides of the cake, cut side down, to imitate the staves of a basket. Fill the basket thus formed with *crème au Beurre*, pressed from a pastry bag fitted with a small round tube and allowed to fall lightly at random to simulate macaroni. Sprinkle with finely chopped toasted almonds to represent bread crumbs.

Langues de Chat
CATS' TONGUES

Cream 1/2 cup each of butter and sugar, and 1 teaspoon vanilla extract until the mixture is light and fluffy. Add 4 egg whites, one at a time, mixing well after each addition. Sift 1/2 cup flour, a little at a time, over the surface and carefully fold it in. Press the batter through a pastry bag fitted with a plain tube onto a buttered and floured baking sheet, making tubular strips about 4 inches long and of the diameter of a pencil. Bake the cats' tongues in a hot oven (450° F.) for 4 to 5 minutes, or until the edges are golden. Remove them from the baking sheet and cool them on absorbent paper.

Gâteau
Sans-Gêne
PRALINE CAKE

BAKE a *génoise* in a buttered and floured 8-inch round cake pan, 2 inches deep. When the cake is cool, split it, and put the layers together with *crème au beurre pralinée*. Frost the top and sides smoothly with the cream and press finely chopped toasted almonds around the sides. On top, arrange 6 *petits cornets*, filled with *crème au beurre pralinée*, pointed ends together in the center, open ends out. Place a large rosette of cream in the center over the pointed ends of the *cornets* and insert the pointed end of another *cornet* into the top of the rosette.

Petits Cornets
LITTLE CONES

Beat 1 egg white until it is stiff. Fold in gently 2 tablespoons each of sugar and finely ground almonds and 1 tablespoon flour. Fold in 2 table-spoons butter, melted and cooled, a pinch of salt, and a few drops of vanilla extract.

Drop the batter by teaspoons onto a buttered and floured baking sheet about 2 inches apart and bake the circles in a hot oven (400° F.) for 4 to 5 minutes, or until they are lightly browned. While they are still warm, form them quickly into cones. *Petits cornets* also appear on the petits fours tray.

La Lutèce
CHESTNUT WALNUT
CAKE

BAKE a *génoise* in an 8-inch round cake pan, buttered and floured, 2 inches deep. When the cake is cool, split it into 3 layers, and put the layers together with walnut butter cream.

Spread the top and sides with a thin coating of apricot glaze and ice the cake with chocolate fondant.

Fill a pastry cone, fitted with a small round tube, with vanilla chestnut purée and press out the purée, allowing it to fall at random in the center of the cake to form a nest. Decorate the mound of chestnut purée and the sides of the cake with a ring of perfect walnut halves.

Walnut Butter Cream

Moisten 1 1/4 cups finely ground walnuts with 2 tablespoons rum. Beat 1 egg white and 1/4 cup sugar over boiling water until a meringue of the consistency of heavy cream is formed. Stir the walnuts into the meringue and beat in gradually 3/4 cup soft sweet butter.

Vanilla Chestnut Purée

Simmer 1 pound peeled chestnuts in milk flavored with a piece of vanilla bean for about 20 minutes or until the nuts are soft. Drain the chestnuts and rub them through a fine sieve.

Combine in a heavy saucepan 2/3 cup sugar, 1/4 cup water, and a 1-inch stick of vanilla bean. Cook the syrup until it will form a soft ball when dropped into cold water. Discard the vanilla bean and blend the syrup with the chestnut purée, working the mixture thoroughly until it forms a thick paste. Cool to lukewarm and stir in 1 tablespoon soft butter.

Gâteau Bourdaloue
ALMOND CREAM CAKE

BAKE a *génoise* in a buttered and floured deep 7-inch round cake pan. When the cake is cool, cut a slice from the top and hollow out the center. Fill the hollow with *crème bourdaloue* and replace the top. Spread the top and sides of the cake with a thin layer of apricot glaze and ice the cake smoothly with chocolate fondant or chocolate butter cream.

Crème Bourdaloue
ALMOND CREAM

Make almond milk: Blanch 1/3 pound almonds and dry them in a slow oven (300° F.) for 20 to 30 minutes. Put them through a food chopper, adding 1 1/2 cups water gradually. Pound water and chopped nuts together in a mortar until the liquid becomes milky in appearance and is almond flavored. Strain the milk through a sieve lined with cheesecloth.

Combine 3/4 cup sugar, 1 whole egg, 2 egg yolks, and 3 tablespoons rice flour in a saucepan. Scald the almond milk and stir it into the egg mixture, little by little. Cook over low heat, stirring constantly, until the cream is thick and smooth, but do not allow it to boil. Remove the pan from the heat and stir in 2 tablespoons butter and 1 tablespoon kirsch.

L'Envoi de Nice
BASKET FROM NICE

SPLIT and fill a 10-inch rectangular *génoise* with mocha butter cream. Cover the top and sides with a thin layer of mocha cream, which will later serve as an adhesive. Cut from a sheet of warm Parisian nougat 5 rectangles of the dimensions of the sides and the top of the *génoise*. Decorate these pieces in a basket weave with coffee butter cream and chocolate butter cream in this way: Use a pastry bag fitted with a round tube for the chocolate cream, a bag fitted with a flat tube for the coffee cream.

Starting at the left end of the first nougat rectangle, press out a perpendicular "rope" of chocolate cream. With coffee cream make little horizontal crosspieces, or bands, across the rope, leaving between the bands spaces as wide as the bands. Make a second chocolate-cream rope just to the right of the ends of the bands. With coffee cream, press out across the second rope horizontal bands that begin in the spaces left between the first bands. Now press out a third chocolate-cream rope and press a third set of bands across it, filling the spaces left between the second bands. (The third bands will thus seem to be continuations of the first, and will seem to have emerged from under the second rope, like strips of caning weaving in and out of the stakes of a basket.) Proceed in this manner across each of the nougat rectangles.

Press the nougat pieces against the sides and top of the cake, thus giving it the appearance of a wicker basket. With a pastry tube, decorate the top of the cake with butter cream flowers and leaves suggestive of the Nice region, or use the crystallized leaves, violets, mimosa flowers, and rose petals that are imported from France and sold at fine food shops.

COMBINE in the top of a double boiler 3/4 cup sugar, 4 whole eggs, and 2 egg yolks. Beat the mixture with a whip over hot water for 15 minutes, or until the eggs are lukewarm, light, and fluffy. Remove the pan from the hot water and beat the mixture until it is cool and has reached the ribbon stage.

Add a scant 1/2 cup each of flour and potato flour, sifting it over the surface and folding it in gently with a spatula. Fold in 1/3 cup ground almonds in the same way. Fold in 2 tablespoons Curaçao and 1/3 cup melted and cooled butter, being careful not to include the sediment that collects at the bottom of the pan.

Butter a deep round cake pan and sprinkle it with finely chopped blanched almonds and with sugar. Pour into the pan one half the batter and sprinkle with 1/3 cup finely diced preserved fruits. Add the remaining batter and bake the cake in a moderate oven (350° F.) for 45 to 50 minutes. Remove the cake immediately from the pan to a cake rack to cool and serve it sprinkled generously with confectioners' sugar.

Gâteau Financier

PUT 12 ounces, or 1 1/2 cups, almond paste in a mixing bowl. Add 3/4 cup sugar and a little water to soften the paste and blend thoroughly. Mix in gradually 6 beaten egg yolks and beat until the mixture is smooth and

Gâteau Montpensier

fluffy. Add 1/4 cup mixed candied fruits, finely chopped, 1 teaspoon lemon juice, 1 generous tablespoon rum, and 1/2 cup flour and mix until all the ingredients are combined. Beat 6 egg whites until stiff but not dry and fold them into the batter, along with a pinch of salt and 1/4 cup butter, melted and cooled.

Turn the batter into a paper-lined, buttered pan, sprinkle it with slivered blanched almonds, and bake in a slow oven (300° F.) for about 1 hour.

Pain de Gênes
ALMOND CAKE

CRUSH 1/2 pound almonds to a powder. Combine the powder with 6 table-spoons fine granulated sugar and 2 eggs, and beat the mixture well with a hand whip or an electric beater. Add 6 tablespoons sugar and another egg, and continue to beat until the mixture is very light and fluffy. Put 6 tablespoons butter, cut in small pieces, into a warm bowl and work it with a wooden spoon until it is very creamy, but not oily. With a metal spatula cut and fold the softened butter into the first mixture. Fold in 1/2 cup cake flour sifted with 1/4 teaspoon salt, and 1 tablespoon kirsch.

Pour the batter into a shallow 8- or 9-inch pan that has been lined with heavy wax paper and well buttered. Bake the cake in a slow oven (300° F.) for 35 to 40 minutes. Turn it out on a rack to cool. Remove the paper and serve the cake plain or with a sprinkling of confectioners' sugar.

A second basic butter cake has something of the texture of spongecake. Like the génoise, *it is used to make a variety of decorated cakes.*

Pâte à Biscuit au Beurre
BUTTER SPONGECAKE

BEAT 4 egg yolks and 1/2 cup sugar in a warm bowl with a hand whip or electric beater until the mixture is very light and fluffy and almost white. Beat in 1 teaspoon vanilla extract. Measure 1 cup less 2 tablespoons sifted cake flour and fold it into the mixture in 3 portions with a spatula. Beat 4 egg whites until they are stiff and cut and fold them into the batter with the spatula. Add 1/4 cup butter, melted over low heat and cooled, gradually cutting and folding it in with the spatula.

Pour the batter into an 8- or 9-inch pan that has been buttered and sprinkled with flour. Fill the pan to a depth of 3/4 inch to 2 inches, depending upon how the cake is to be used. Bake the cake in a moderate oven (350° F.) for 25 to 40 minutes, or until it tests done. Turn it out on a wire rack to cool. Split it to make 2 or 3 layers and spread pastry cream or jam between the layers. Spread apricot jam or purée very thinly over the top and sides and then cover the cake with fondant icing. Decorate it with glazed fruit.

BAKE *pâte à biscuit au beurre* in an 8-inch round cake pan, buttered and floured, about 1 1/2 inches deep, in a moderate oven (350° F.) for 40 minutes, or until a cake tester comes out clean. Remove the cake from the pan to a cake rack to cool, split it into 2 or 3 layers, and sandwich the layers with *crème au beurre moka*.

Gâteau Moka

Frost the top and sides smoothly with mocha butter cream and press crystallized sugar or chopped toasted almonds around the sides. Decorate the top with scrolls and rosettes of more of the same cream, pressed through a pastry bag fitted with a large fluted tube.

FLAVOR *pâte à biscuit au beurre* with vanilla and divide the batter in half. Fold into one half 1 1/2 tablespoons cocoa. Spoon the batters, alternating the colors, into an 8- or 9-inch round cake pan, buttered and floured, about 1 1/2 inches deep. Bake in a moderate oven (350° F.) for 40 minutes, or until the cake tests done. Remove the cake from the pan to a rack to cool, split it, and sandwich the layers with a marble butter cream made by lightly combining but not blending equal parts of vanilla and chocolate butter cream. Ice the cake with equal parts of white and chocolate fondant lightly mixed so that the colors do not merge.

Gâteau Marbre
MARBLE CAKE

FOLD 1/2 cup almond powder into the batter for *pâte à biscuit au beurre* and bake the cake in the usual way. Cool it on a rack before frosting it.

Gâteau Manqué

Mix together 1 egg white, 1/2 cup confectioners' sugar and 3 tablespoons almond powder. The mixture should be just soft enough to spread easily. If necessary, add more sugar. Spread the icing over the cake and sprinkle it with a little confectioners' sugar. Return the cake to a very slow oven (225° F.) until the icing forms a light crust. The *gâteau manqué* may be garnished with candied cherries and citron.

BAKE *pâte à biscuit au beurre* in an 8-inch round cake pan, buttered and floured, about 2 1/2 inches deep, in a moderate oven (350° F.) for 40 minutes, or until a cake tester comes out clean. Remove the cake from the pan to a rack to cool. Frost the top and sides smoothly with chocolate or

Gâteau Panaché
CAKE OF MANY COLORS

697

coffee butter cream and press finely chopped toasted almonds around the sides.

With the back of a knife score the top of the cake into quarters and cover each section with tiny rosettes of differently colored and flavored butter creams, pressed through pastry bags or cones fitted with small fluted tubes.

Gâteau
Petit Duc

FOLD 1/2 cup finely ground toasted hazelnuts into *pâte à biscuit au beurre* and turn the batter into an 8- or 9-inch round cake pan, buttered and floured. Bake the cake in a moderate oven (350° F.) for 40 minutes, or until it tests done. Cool it on a rack, split it, and sandwich the layers with *crème au beurre aux noisettes.* Frost the top and sides smoothly with more of the same cream and cover the cream with small round flat cookies, *petites galettes.* The *petites galettes* are made from the same cookie dough used for the little *cornets* for *gâteau Sans-Gêne,* but they are cooled on the baking sheet and not rolled into cones. Between the cookies and around the base of the cake, make small rosettes of hazelnut butter cream, pressed through a pastry bag fitted with a small fluted tube.

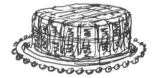

Gâteau
Mexicain

BEAT 5 egg yolks until they are light and fluffy. Add gradually 1/2 cup sugar and continue to beat until the mixture is thick and pale in color. Sift 3/4 cup sifted flour mixed with 3 tablespoons cocoa over the surface, a little at a time, and fold it in gently with a spatula. Fold in the stiffly beaten whites of 4 eggs in the same manner and finally fold in 5 tablespoons butter, melted and cooled, being careful not to include the sediment that has collected at the bottom of the pan.

Turn the batter into a round cake pan, buttered and floured, about 1 1/2 inches deep, and bake it in a moderate oven (350° F.) for 40 minutes, or until a cake tester comes out clean. Cool the cake on a rack, split it, and put the layers together with *crème au beurre chocolat.* Spread the top and sides with a thin layer of apricot glaze and ice the cake with chocolate fondant.

Put 3/4 cup royal icing into a pastry bag or cone fitted with a small round tube and press out a series of parallel lines of the royal icing 3/4 inch apart across the top of the cake. A very pretty decoration can be easily made by very lightly drawing the point of a knife across the lines at intervals.

The distinguishing characteristics of a spongecake are its lack of short-ening and its illusion of richness.

IN a warm bowl beat 1/2 cup fine granulated sugar, 1 teaspoon finely grated orange rind, and 4 egg yolks until the mixture is very fluffy and runs off a spoon in ribbons. Fold in 1/2 cup sifted cake flour a little at a time with a spatula. Fold in 3 stiffly beaten egg whites. Butter and flour an 8- or 9-inch pan about 2 or 2 1/2 inches deep. Bake the *mousseline* in a moderate oven (350° F.) for 40 minutes, or until it tests done.

    Turn the cake out on a cake rack to cool. Ice it with fondant flavored with orange extract and decorate it with candied orange peel cut in small dice.

Mousseline à l'Orange
ORANGE SPONGECAKE

MAKE the batter for *mousseline à l'orange*, but omit the grated orange rind. Fold into the batter 3 tablespoons ground, lightly toasted hazelnuts. Bake the cake, cool it, and ice it with vanilla fondant. Sprinkle heavily with confectioners' sugar.

Mousseline aux Noisettes
HAZELNUT SPONGECAKE

MIX 1 cup diced preserved orange peel with 1/4 cup apricot purée. Stir in 3 tablespoons rum and let the peel marinate for half an hour, stirring it occasionally.

    Make the batter for *mousseline à l'orange*. Turn half the batter into a square cake pan, buttered and floured, about 2 inches deep, and cover it with half the rum-soaked peel. Pour in the remaining batter and bake the cake in a moderate oven (350° F.) for about 40 minutes, or until it tests done. Cool the cake on a rack, split it, and reshape it with the remaining rum-soaked peel spread between the layers.

    Spread the top and sides of the *mousseline* with orange marmalade, thinned to spreading consistency with a little warm water, and ice the cake with fondant flavored with rum and tinted with a drop of yellow food coloring. Garnish the sides of the cake with small circles or diamonds of preserved orange rind.

Gâteau Valencia

OIL a baking sheet 15 by 10 inches, line it with wax paper, and oil the paper. Add 1/4 cup sugar to 5 egg yolks and beat until the mixture is thick and pale in color. Carefully fold in 3 tablespoons cake flour, 1 teaspoon vanilla, and the stiffly beaten whites of 5 eggs.

    Spread the batter evenly on the baking sheet and bake it in a moderate oven (350° F.) for about 12 minutes, or until a knife inserted in the center comes out clean. Sprinkle the cake with fine granulated sugar and invert

Biscuit Roulé
SPONGE ROLL

Chocolate Roll

the baking sheet on a sheet of wax paper. With the help of a spatula gently remove the pan and then the wax paper from the bottom of the cake. Sprinkle the cake again with fine granulated sugar and spread it with crushed and sweetened strawberries, with any desired jam or jelly, or with pastry cream. Roll up the cake lengthwise with the help of the wax paper.

When the roll is thoroughly cool, frost it with a thick layer of whipped cream, sweetened and flavored to taste, and garnish with whole berries or with appropriate sliced fruit.

BUTTER a large baking sheet, line it with wax paper, and butter the paper.
Beat 5 egg yolks until they are light and fluffy. Add gradually 1 cup fine granulated sugar and beat until the mixture is very thick and pale in color. Stir in 6 ounces of dark sweet chocolate, melted over low heat with 3 tablespoons coffee and cooled, and finally fold in 5 stiffly beaten egg whites.

Spread the batter evenly over the prepared sheet and bake in a moderate oven (350° F.) for 15 minutes, or until the cake tests done. Be careful not to overbake. Cover the cake with a damp towel for half an hour, until it is cool. Loosen it from the baking sheet and dust the surface generously with cocoa. Turn the cake over onto a sheet of wax paper and gently remove the paper from the bottom. Spread the cake with 2 cups heavy cream, whipped, sweetened, and flavored to taste, and roll it lengthwise into a long slim roll.

To roll this delicate cake, lift up two corners of the wax paper and flip over about 2 inches of the cake onto itself. Continue to roll by lifting the wax paper. The last flip should deposit the cake on a long wooden board or platter. Dust the top with a little more cocoa.

Biscuit Roulé au Chocolat
CHOCOLATE ROLL

BAKE a *biscuit roulé*. At serving time whip 2 cups heavy cream and add 1 teaspoon coffee extract. Fold in 1/4 cup confectioners' sugar and 1 cup black walnuts, chopped. Unroll the cooled cake, spread it with the whipped cream mixture, and roll it again. Slice and serve with rum caramel sauce.

Nut Sponge Roll

BEAT 9 egg yolks until they are very light and fluffy, and gradually beat in 1 2/3 cups sugar. Beat in the grated rind and the juice of 1 medium lemon. Stir in slowly 1 scant cup potato starch and fold in carefully 9 egg whites, beaten until stiff but not dry. Pour the batter into a large tube pan with a removable bottom. The pan should not be buttered. Bake the cake in a slow oven (300° F.) for about 50 minutes, or until it is nicely browned.

Potato Starch Spongecake

Rum Cream Cake

BEAT 3 eggs until they are light, gradually add 1 cup sugar, and beat the mixture until it is thick and pale in color. Stir in 3 tablespoons cold water and 1 cup flour, sifted 3 times with 1 teaspoon double-action baking powder and a pinch of salt. Add 1 tablespoon vanilla, pour the batter into a 9-inch springform pan, and bake the cake in a moderate oven (350° F.) for 25 minutes. Cool it in the pan. Top it with the following rum cream: In a saucepan soften 2 tablespoons gelatin in 1/4 cup cold water for 5 minutes. Pour over this 2 cups scalded milk, stir well, and add 3/4 cup sugar. Heat but do not boil the milk mixture and pour it over 4 beaten egg yolks, stirring constantly. Stir in gradually 1/4 cup Jamaica rum and set aside to cool. When the gelatin begins to set, add 1 cup cream, whipped, and pour the mixture over the cake. Put it in the refrigerator to set.

Remove the springform pan, sprinkle the cake with chopped pistachio nuts or almonds, and serve on a large cake plate.

Kaiser-schmaren
THE KAISER'S NONSENSE

BEAT 1/4 cup sugar with 5 egg yolks until the mixture is foamy. Stir in 1 1/2 cups flour, sifted with a dash of salt, alternately with 1 cup milk and fold in the stiffly beaten whites of 5 eggs. Spread the batter in a buttered and floured baking pan and bake in a hot oven (400° F.) for about 8 minutes, or until lightly browned.

Tear the baked cake into small pieces with 2 forks. Mix the broken cake with 1/2 cup sultana raisins, softened in hot water and well drained, and turn cake and raisins into a small baking dish. Add 1/4 cup melted butter and bake in a hot oven (425° F.) for 3 or 4 minutes. Serve very hot, sprinkled generously with confectioners' sugar.

Golden Angel Food Cake

IN a saucepan combine 1 1/4 cups sugar, 1/2 cup water, and 1/4 teaspoon cream of tartar, bring to a boil, and cook the syrup until it spins a light thread. Beat 8 egg yolks until they are fluffy, gradually beat in the syrup, and continue to beat until the mixture is thick and cool. Sift 1 cup sifted cake flour with 1/4 teaspoon salt 6 times and fold the flour gently into the egg yolks. Beat 8 egg whites until they are frothy, add 3/4 teaspoon cream of tartar, and continue to beat until the egg whites are stiff but not dry. Fold in the egg whites and 1 teaspoon lemon juice, orange juice, or vanilla.

Bake the cake in a dry tube pan in a slow oven (300° F.) for about 1 1/2 hours, or until it tests done. Invert the pan and let the cake cool before removing it.

Although there is little semantic justification for the label, certain elaborate cakes are called tortes. Most of them are rich with nuts and eggs and sparse of flour and butter.

BEAT together 8 egg yolks and 1 cup confectioners' sugar until the mixture is thick and lemon colored, using a hand whip or an electric beater at low speed. Add 1 cup filberts, finely chopped.

    Moisten 1 cup fine dry bread crumbs with 2 tablespoons rum and add the crumbs to the batter. Fold in 6 egg whites, stiffly beaten but not dry. Pour the batter into a buttered springform pan sprinkled with fine bread crumbs, and bake the torte in a moderate oven (350° F.) for about 40 minutes, or until it tests done. Cool the torte, remove it to a serving platter, split the cake in half, and spread the bottom half with raspberry jam. Replace the top layer and decorate the cake with orange-flavored fondant icing.

Nusstorte
NUT TORTE

CREAM together 2 cups sugar and 10 egg yolks. Stir in 4 cups zwieback crumbs, 1 cup each of blanched almonds, chopped, and mixed candied citron, lemon, and orange peel, chopped, 1 teaspoon each of baking powder and vanilla extract, the juice of 1/2 lemon, and 1/2 cup rum. Fold in the stiffly beaten whites of 10 eggs. Butter an 11-inch springform pan generously and pour the batter into it. Bake the torte for 1 hour in a slow oven (300° F.). When the cake is cool split it into three layers. Sprinkle each layer with 2 tablespoons rum and sandwich the layers with 1 cup cream, whipped.

Rum Nut Torte

BEAT 6 egg yolks until they are light, gradually add 1 cup sugar, and beat until the mixture is thick and pale in color. Stir in 1 cup finely ground walnuts, 1 cup dry spongecake or ladyfinger crumbs, the grated rind of 1 orange, 2 tablespoons orange juice, and a pinch of salt. Beat 6 egg whites until they are stiff but not dry and fold them in gently but thoroughly. Divide the batter between two 9-inch layer-cake pans, buttered and sprinkled with fine bread crumbs. Bake the layers in a moderate oven (350° F.) for 30 to 35 minutes and cool them on a cake rack. Sandwich them with apricot or pineapple jam and frost top and sides with whipped cream flavored to taste with a few drops of an orange-based liqueur.

Orange Walnut Torte

BEAT 5 egg yolks until they are light and add gradually 1 cup fine granulated sugar. Fold in 1 cup fine dry bread crumbs soaked in 2 tablespoons Sherry and 3 tablespoons lemon juice. Blanch and shred 1 cup almonds

Jägertorte
HUNTER'S TORTE

and fold in 3/4 cup, reserving the rest. Sprinkle the mixture with 1/2 teaspoon baking powder and fold in 5 egg whites, beaten until stiff but not dry with a pinch of salt. Pour the batter into a buttered shallow pan and bake the torte in a moderate oven (350° F.) for about 25 minutes, or until it browns and tests done. Cool the cake and spread it with any tart jam or jelly. Beat 4 egg whites until they are stiff with 1/2 teaspoon cream of tartar and add gradually 1/2 cup sugar, beating constantly until the meringue is thick and smooth. Cover the cake with the meringue, sprinkle it with the reserved almonds, and bake it in a slow oven (300° F.) for about 15 minutes, until the meringue browns.

Mohntorte
POPPY SEED TORTE

BEAT 12 egg yolks with 2 1/4 cups sugar until they are thick and pale in color. Stir in 3/4 cup sultana raisins, soaked in white wine and drained, 1 1/2 cups finely ground poppy seeds, the grated rind of 1 lemon, 1 teaspoon cinnamon, and 1/2 teaspoon ground cloves and mix well. Fold in the 12 egg whites, beaten until they are stiff but not dry. Butter two 9-inch springform pans and sprinkle them with fine dry bread crumbs. Bake the batter in the two pans in a moderate oven (350° F.) for 50 to 60 minutes. Remove the layers from the pans to a rack and cool. Sprinkle each layer with 1/4 cup rum.

Sandwich the layers with apricot jam and top with whipped cream.

Danish
Applesauce
Torte

IN a buttered baking dish put 2 cups thick, lightly sweetened applesauce. Combine 1 1/3 cups finely ground blanched almonds with 1/2 cup confectioners' sugar and beat in 3 yolks, one at a time. Fold in 3 egg whites, stiffly beaten, and spread this mixture over the applesauce. The mixture may be forced through a pastry tube to make a decorative topping for the torte. Set the dish in a shallow pan of hot water and bake the torte in a moderate oven (350° F.) for 15 minutes, until the almond meringue is set and lightly browned. Serve warm, with whipped cream.

Panforte
di Siena

COMBINE 3/4 cup each of almonds, blanched, and hazelnuts, lightly toasted, 1/3 cup cocoa, 1/2 cup flour, 1 1/2 teaspoons cinnamon, 1/4 teaspoon allspice, and 3/4 cup each of finely cut candied orange peel, citron, and lemon peel. In a large saucepan combine 3/4 cup each of honey and sugar, bring to a boil, and simmer until a little of the syrup dropped into cold water forms a soft ball. Add the fruit and nut mixture, and mix well.

Turn the mixture into a 9-inch springform pan lined with buttered paper and bake in a slow oven (300° F.) for 30 minutes. Loosen the sides of the pan slightly and remove the bottom. Cool the cake before removing the sides. Sprinkle with 2 tablespoons confectioners' sugar mixed with 1 tablespoon cinnamon.

Nut Roll

BEAT 6 egg yolks with 3/4 cup sugar until the mixture is very thick and pale in color. Fold in 1 1/2 cups ground nuts, 2 teaspoons vanilla, 1 teaspoon baking powder, and the stiffly beaten whites of 6 eggs.

Oil a large baking sheet, line it with wax paper, and oil the paper. Spread the batter on the sheet and bake it in a moderate oven (350° F.) for 15 to 20 minutes. Cover the cake in the baking sheet with a towel wrung out of cold water and let it cool.

Remove the towel and sprinkle the cake generously with sifted confectioners' sugar. Loosen it from the sides of the pan, turn it out, sugared side down, on wax paper and remove the wax paper adhering to the bottom. Spread the cake with 2 cups heavy cream, whipped and flavored with sugar and vanilla, and roll it up lengthwise.

Punschtorte
PUNCH TORTE

BEAT 2 whole eggs and 7 egg yolks until they are fluffy. Add 1 1/4 cups sugar and continue to beat until the mixture is thick and pale in color. Stir in the juice and grated rind of 1 lemon and 1 3/4 cups sifted cake flour. Beat the 7 egg whites until they are stiff but not dry and fold them gently into the batter. Butter and flour 2 springform pans, divide the batter evenly between them, and bake them in a moderate oven (350° F.) for 30 to 35 minutes, or until a straw inserted in the center comes out clean. Remove the cakes from the pans to a cake rack and cool them.

Moisten both layers with 1/4 cup rum sweetened with 1 tablespoon sugar and diluted with 1/2 cup water. Sandwich the soaked layers with a thin layer of raspberry or strawberry jam and ice the top and sides of the torte with a thin coating of rum glaze.

Operatårta

BEAT together 3 egg yolks, 1 whole egg, and 2/3 cup sugar, until the mixture is very pale and light. Sift 1 tablespoon flour with 1/4 cup potato flour and fold the flour into the egg mixture. Beat 3 egg whites until they are stiff and fold them in carefully. Pour the batter into a deep round cake pan that has been buttered and sprinkled with bread crumbs.

Bake the cake in a moderate oven (350° F.) for about 30 minutes, or until it is brown and tests done.

Combine 2 egg yolks, 1 tablespoon sugar, 2 teaspoons potato flour, and 1 cup cream in the top of a double boiler, and cook, stirring constantly, until the custard is smooth and thick. Add 1/2 tablespoon gelatin softened in a little water, 1/2 teaspoon vanilla extract, and stir, off the heat, until the gelatin is thoroughly dissolved. Cool the cream over cracked ice, stirring it occasionally, and chill it. Fold in 1 cup heavy cream, whipped until stiff.

Divide the cooled cake into three or four layers and fill it with the cream. Spread a little of the cream on top.

Put 1 cup blanched almonds twice through a food chopper, and pound the almonds as finely as possible with a pestle and mortar. Slowly work in 2/3 cup confectioners' sugar and 1 egg white, unbeaten, to make a smooth, firm paste. Roll the paste out on wax paper and cut a circle the size of the cake. Lay it on the cake and sprinkle with sugar.

The ethereal meringue shell, made principally of egg whites and sugar, inspires another group of exquisite confections.

Meringue
Suisse

BEAT 4 egg whites with a pinch of salt until they are stiff but not dry. Beat in 1/2 teaspoon lemon juice or vinegar and gradually add 3/4 cup fine granulated sugar, about 1 tablespoon at a time, beating constantly until the meringue is thick and very satiny. Fold in 1/4 cup sugar and 1 teaspoon vanilla.

Meringue
Shells

FIT a pastry bag with a large round tube and fill the bag with *meringue suisse.* Press out ovals of the meringue, an inch apart, onto a baking sheet covered with wax paper; push the pastry bag gently backwards several times while the meringue is being forced out to give the ovals a wavy surface.

Sprinkle the shells with fine granulated sugar and bake them in a very slow oven (200° F.) for about 1 hour without letting them color. Remove the meringues from the paper and, while they are still warm, scoop out the soft part from the under surface. Put the shells upside down on the baking sheet and dry them in the slack oven with the heat off.

PRESS a meringue shell on each side of a scoop of ice cream. Decorate the edge of the shells with sweetened whipped cream pressed through a pastry bag fitted with a small fluted tube.

LINE 2 baking sheets with buttered wax paper and trace 2 circles on each, 8 inches in diameter and 1 inch apart. Spread the circles thinly and evenly with *meringue suisse* and bake in a very slow oven (250° F.) for about 20 minutes, being careful that the meringues do not color. Remove the meringue circles with a spatula, while they are still pliable, to cake racks to cool and crisp.

Whip 2 cups heavy cream until it is stiff and reserve 1 cup of it for decorating the cake. Into the remaining cream fold 2 cups sliced and sugared peaches, strawberries, or raspberries.

When ready to serve, put the 4 meringue circles together with layers of the fruit and cream mixture. Color the reserved whipped cream with a drop of red or yellow food coloring to harmonize with the fruit in the filling, if desired. Spread the sides of the cake smoothly with the colored cream and cover the top with small rosettes of the cream pressed through a pastry bag fitted with a small fluted tube. Or spread the top evenly with the whipped cream and sprinkle with finely chopped grilled almonds or thin shavings of chocolate, or garnish the cake with sliced peaches or whole berries.

BEAT 5 egg whites with a pinch of salt until they are stiff but not dry. Beat in gradually 3/4 cup fine granulated sugar, about 1 tablespoon at a time, and continue to beat until the meringue is thick and smooth. Fold in gently 1/4 cup sugar, 1 teaspoon vanilla, and 3/4 cup grated almonds.

BAKE three circles of *pâte à meringue aux amandes*, cool them, and sandwich them with mocha butter cream. Sprinkle the top generously with sifted confectioners' sugar.

BRUSH 2 baking sheets with oil and dust them lightly with flour. Using a 9-inch cake pan as a guide, trace 2 circles on each baking sheet and spread them evenly with *pâte à meringue aux amandes* and bake them in a very slow oven (250° F.) for about 30 minutes, or until they are set. Remove the circles to a flat surface to cool and crisp.

Stir 1/2 cup praline powder into chocolate butter cream and sandwich the layers with the *crème au beurre chocolat pralinée*. Frost top and sides smoothly with more chocolate praline butter cream, press chopped toasted almonds around the sides of the *gateâu*, and sprinkle the top with confectioners' sugar.

Gâteau
Succès
Pyramide
CHOCOLATE
HAZELNUT CAKE

SPREAD *pâte à meringue aux amandes* in thin layers on the bottoms of 4 springform pans or on circles traced on buttered and floured baking sheets. Bake them in a very slow oven (250° F.) for about 30 minutes, or until the meringue is set.

While the meringue is cooling, cook 1/2 cup sugar, 3 tablespoons water, and a pinch of cream of tartar until it spins a thread. Beat the syrup gradually into 2 beaten eggs. Beat in gradually 3/4 cup sweet butter. Divide the cream in half and to one half add 1 ounce semisweet chocolate melted with 1 tablespoon coffee and a dash of dark rum. Fold 1/4 cup praline powder made with hazelnuts into the other half.

Put a circle of the meringue on a platter and spread it with the chocolate cream. Place another circle of meringue on the chocolate cream and spread it with whipped cream. Place a third circle on the whipped cream and spread it with the hazelnut praline cream. Top with the last meringue circle. Spread the sides of the cake with whipped cream and sprinkle with finely chopped hazelnuts. Sprinkle the top with sifted confectioners' sugar.

Gâteau
Sans Rival

MAKE a *pâte à meringue aux amandes*, substituting ground hazelnuts for the almonds. Spread the batter 1/3 inch thick on rectangles 8 by 5 inches traced on wax paper and bake it in a very slow oven (250° F.) for about 30 minutes, or until it sets. Remove the rectangles to a flat surface to cool and crisp. Sandwich them with nut butter cream. Frost the top of the cake smoothly with more hazelnut butter cream and sprinkle with chopped almonds.

Gâteau
Dacquoise

SPREAD *pâte à meringue aux amandes* on two 9-inch circles traced on oiled and floured baking sheets. Bake them in a very slow oven (250° F.) for about 30 minutes, or until they are set. Remove them to a flat surface to cool and crisp. Sandwich them with a 1 1/2-inch-thick layer of butter cream—vanilla, coffee, pistachio, or chocolate—and through a pastry bag fitted with a fluted tube press out a circle of butter-cream rosettes around the sides between the 2 layers. Sprinkle the top generously with sifted confectioners' sugar.

Gâteau Dacquoise

Gâteau
Triomphe

COMBINE 1/2 cup grated blanched almonds and 1/3 cup sugar. Add 3 egg whites, one at a time, beating vigorously after each addition. Stir in 2 1/2 tablespoons cornstarch and 1 teaspoon vanilla and fold in 3 egg whites, stiffly beaten. Spread the batter on two 9-inch circles traced on an oiled and floured baking sheet, sprinkle them with sugar, and bake them in a very slow oven (250° F.) for about 30 minutes, or until they are set. Remove them to a flat surface to cool. Sandwich them with butter cream flavored to taste and sprinkle the cake with confectioners' sugar.

Gâteau
Fanny

SPREAD the batter for *gâteau triomphe* on 3 circles instead of 2. Sandwich the baked and cooled layers with *crème au beurre au chocolat*. Frost top and sides with chocolate butter cream and sprinkle with chopped blanched almonds or praline powder. Chill overnight before serving.

Himmeltorte
SOUR CREAM CAKE

CREAM together 1 1/2 cups butter and 1/4 cup sugar until the mixture is very light and fluffy. Add 4 large egg yolks, one at a time, beating well after each addition. Stir in the grated rind of 1 lemon and work in gradually 4 cups sifted flour. Pat the dough into 3 buttered and floured oblong pans about 7 by 11 inches. Beat 1 egg white until it is stiff, beat in 1/4 cup sugar and 1 teaspoon cinnamon, and fold in 1/2 cup chopped blanched almonds. Spread the meringue on the dough and bake the layers in a hot oven (450° F.) for 10 to 12 minutes. Reduce the oven temperature to moderate (350° F.) and continue to bake for about 15 minutes longer, or until the cake is done.

Sour Cream
Filling

Mix 1/4 cup sugar with 1 tablespoon cornstarch and stir in 2 cups sour cream. Cook, stirring constantly, until the cream coats the spoon. Pour the cream gradually over 2 beaten egg yolks, beating vigorously. Return the mixture to the heat and cook, stirring, for 1 minute longer. Cool the cream.

Cool the layers on a cake rack and sandwich them with raspberry jam and a little of the sour cream filling. Frost the entire cake with the remaining sour cream filling.

Schaumtorte
STRAWBERRY
MERINGUE TORTE

BEAT 8 egg whites until they are stiff enough to stand in soft peaks. Continue beating, adding gradually 1 1/2 cups fine granulated sugar, 2 tablespoons at a time. Beat in 1 tablespoon each of vinegar and vanilla and fold in gently another 1/2 cup fine granulated sugar, to make a meringue.

Oil and flour 2 baking sheets and on each trace 2 circles 8 inches in diameter. Spread one circle evenly with a layer of the meringue about 1/4 inch thick. Put the remaining meringue into a large pastry bag fitted with a large fluted tube. On two of the circles form rings of meringue about 1 inch high and 1 1/2 inches wide. On the fourth circle press out a ring of large meringue kisses, each touching the next, to make a wreath of kisses. Bake the meringues in a slow oven (250° F.) for 30 to 40 minutes, or until they are crisp but not colored. Remove them to a cake rack to cool and dry. Additional kisses may be made to garnish the base of the shell.

To serve, place the solid meringue circle on a serving platter and put the two rings on top of it. Fold 2 cups strawberries, sliced and sweetened, into 1 pint heavy cream, whipped, and fill the shell. Arrange the wreath of kisses on the top and garnish the torte with a sprig of holly.

Here are some variations on the cake beloved of country kitchens in every country, the leavened butter cake. The pans for these cakes may be buttered and floured, or the bottoms may be lined with wax paper. The cake will rise, brown, and shrink from the sides of the pan when it is baked, and a tester—skewer, straw, or knife—inserted in the center will come out clean and dry.

CREAM 1/2 cup butter and 2 cups sugar until the mixture is fluffy and beat in 3 eggs, one at a time. Sift together 3 cups sifted cake flour, 3 teaspoons baking powder, and a pinch of salt. Stir the dry ingredients into the butter-sugar mixture alternately with 1 cup milk. Add 1/2 teaspoon grated lime rind and turn the batter into 4 prepared 8-inch layer cake pans. Bake the layers in a moderately hot oven (375° F.) for about 30 minutes, or until they test done. Cool them on cake racks.

Lime Cream Cake

In a saucepan combine the juice of 4 limes, 2 cups sugar, 2 eggs, beaten, 1 cup cold water, and 2 tablespoons each of butter and cornstarch. Cook the cream over simmering water, stirring constantly, until it is thickened. Let it cool.

Sandwich the layers with the lime cream and let it set for several hours. Just before serving, top the cake with 1 cup cream, whipped.

CREAM 1/2 cup butter. Sift in gradually 2 cups brown sugar and beat the mixture until it is light and creamy. Beat in 4 egg yolks, one at a time. Sift together 1 1/2 cups sifted cake flour and 1 1/2 teaspoons baking pow-

Caramel Cake

der. Beat these sifted ingredients into the butter mixture alternately with 1/4 cup milk. Add 2 teaspoons vanilla and, if desired, 1 cup chopped nut meats. Whip 4 egg whites until they are stiff but not dry, beat into them 1/2 teaspoon salt, and fold them gently into the cake batter.

Bake the cake in 2 prepared 8-inch layer cake pans in a moderately hot oven (375° F.) for about 20 minutes. Remove the layers from the pans to a cake rack to cool. Fill and frost the layers with caramel nut

Caramel Nut Frosting frosting. Combine 2 cups brown sugar and 1 cup light cream. Stir until the sugar is dissolved and boil the mixture, without stirring, to the soft-ball stage, 238° F. on a candy thermometer. Add 3 tablespoons butter, remove the syrup from the heat, and let it cool. Then add 1 teaspoon vanilla and beat the frosting until it is thick and creamy. Should it become too heavy for easy spreading, thin it with a little cream. Stir in 1/4 cup chopped nut meats.

Black Walnut Cake CREAM 1/2 cup butter and add gradually 1 1/4 cups confectioners' sugar, beating until the mixture is very light. Add 1/2 cup milk, 1 teaspoon vanilla extract, and a few drops of almond extract. Mix in 2 cups flour sifted with 2 1/2 teaspoons baking powder. Beat 5 egg whites with a pinch of salt until they are stiff but not dry, fold them into the mixture carefully, and then fold in very lightly 1/2 cup well-floured broken black walnut meats. Pour the batter into a buttered oblong cake pan and bake the cake in a moderately hot oven (375° F.) for about 20 minutes. Let the cake cool, and frost it with water icing.

Ambrosia Cake CREAM 3/4 cup butter, add to it gradually 1 1/2 cups sugar, and cream them thoroughly together. Add 3 eggs, one at a time, beating vigorously after each addition. Sift together 3 cups sifted cake flour, 3 teaspoons baking powder, and 1/2 teaspoon salt.

Add these dry ingredients to the egg mixture alternately with 1 cup milk, stirring after each addition to blend thoroughly. Stir in 2 teaspoons vanilla and pour the mixture into 2 prepared 9-inch layer cake pans. Bake the layers in a moderately hot oven (375° F.) for about 30 minutes. Cool. Sandwich the layers with orange coconut filling and frost the cake with uncooked marshmallow frosting.

Orange Coconut Filling In a saucepan combine 1 cup sugar, 3 1/2 tablespoons cornstarch, the grated rind of 1 orange, 1/2 cup orange juice, 3 tablespoons lemon juice,

1 egg, slightly beaten, and 2 tablespoons each of butter and water. Cook the mixture over low heat for about 10 minutes, stirring constantly, until it is thick and clear, but do not let it boil. Cool and stir in 3/4 cup grated coconut.

Rinse a small bowl with hot water. Add 3/4 cup sugar, 1/8 teaspoon cream of tartar, 1 egg white, and 1/3 cup boiling water. Beat vigorously with an electric beater until the mixture is very thick and fluffy and will hold its shape. Flavor with 1 teaspoon vanilla and cover the cake. Sprinkle the frosting with shredded coconut. Serve within a few hours; this frosting will not stand up for long periods.

Marshmallow Frosting

MIX thoroughly 2 tablespoons each of soft butter and molasses, spread the mixture in a 9-inch ring mold and sprinkle generously with finely chopped nuts.

Cream 1/2 cup butter with 1/2 cup sugar and 3 tablespoons molasses. Stir in 1/2 teaspoon each of ginger and cinnamon and 1 egg, beaten, and beat the mixture until it is very light. Stir in 2 cups sifted cake flour sifted with 2 teaspoons baking powder, 1/2 teaspon salt, and 1/4 teaspoon soda, alternately with 1 cup sour cream. Turn the batter into the prepared pan and bake the cake in a moderate oven (350° F.) for about 45 minutes, or until a cake tester comes out clean. Turn the cake immediately onto a cake rack to cool and sprinkle it generously with sifted confectioners' sugar.

Sour Cream Spice Cake

SIFT together 2 cups sifted cake flour, 2 tablespoons baking powder, and 1 teaspoon salt. Cream 1 cup sugar and 1/2 cup butter until the mixture is light and fluffy. Add 2 well-beaten eggs and beat the mixture thoroughly. Add the sifted dry ingredients alternately with 2/3 cup milk, mixing well after each addition.

Divide the batter into 2 parts. To one part add 2 tablespoons molasses, 1 teaspoon cinnamon, and 1/2 teaspoon each of cloves and nutmeg. Drop the batters by tablespoons into a prepared 8-inch-square cake pan, alternating the light and dark. Bake the cake in a moderate oven (350° F.) for about 1 hour, or until it tests done.

Spice Marble Cake

CREAM 3/4 cup butter, stir in gradually 1 1/3 cups sugar, and beat the mixture until it is light and fluffy. Stir in 3 beaten egg yolks. Sift 2 cups sifted cake flour twice with 1 teaspoon each of baking powder, freshly grated nutmeg, and cinnamon, and 1/2 teaspoon each of soda, cloves, and

Spice Cake

salt. Add the dry ingredients alternately with 1 scant cup sour milk or buttermilk, beating the batter until it is smooth after each addition. Fold in 3 egg whites, beaten until stiff but not dry. Turn the batter into a prepared 9-inch tube pan and bake the cake in a moderate oven (350° F.) for 1 hour, or until a cake tester comes out clean. Turn the cake onto a serving platter, sprinkle it with sifted confectioners' sugar, and serve hot.

Westphalian Cherry Cake   CREAM 3 tablespoons butter, add 2/3 cup sugar and blend the two thoroughly. Beat in 2 beaten egg yolks. Sift together 3 times 1 1/4 cups sifted flour, 1/4 teaspoon salt, and 2 1/2 teaspoons baking powder. Add the flour alternately with 1/2 cup milk. Add 1 teaspoon vanilla extract and fold in 2 egg whites, beaten until stiff but not dry. Put 1 1/2 cups cooked, pitted black cherries in the bottom of a prepared 8-inch springform cake pan and pour the batter over the fruit. Swirl a fork through the batter. Bake the cake in a moderately hot oven (375° F.) for 35 minutes, or until it tests done. This cake may be made with fresh apricots or cooked blue plums.

Swedish Apple Cake   PEEL, core, and cut in half 10 tart apples. Combine 1 cup each of sugar and water, 1/2 cup white wine, 1/2 teaspoon cinnamon, and the rind of 1 lemon, and cook the syrup for 5 minutes. Poach the apples in the syrup until they are tender. Turn apples and syrup into a buttered deep baking dish.

Beat 5 egg yolks until they are light and fluffy and add 3/4 cup cream and 3 tablespoons melted butter. Sift 1 cup flour with 1/2 cup sugar and 1 teaspoon baking powder and fold this lightly but thoroughly into the egg yolk mixture. Fold in 5 egg whites, beaten until stiff. Pour the batter over the apples and sprinkle it lightly with confectioners' sugar. Set the dish in a shallow pan of hot water and bake the cake in a hot oven (425° F.) for about 30 minutes, until the topping is golden brown. Serve at room temperature, with the following sauce: Sift 3/4 cup confectioners' sugar, add 3 tablespoons butter, and cook the mixture over hot water, stirring constantly, until it is smooth and creamy. Beat in 3 egg yolks and add slowly, stirring constantly, 1/2 cup boiling water. Stir the sauce over boiling water until it thickens. Add 1 teaspoon each of vanilla extract, grated lemon rind, and 1 or 2 tablespoons Cointreau, Calvados, or rum to taste. Serve hot or chilled.

SIFT 2 3/4 cups sifted flour with 1 teaspoon cinnamon, 3/4 teaspoon each of nutmeg, cream of tartar, and soda, 1/2 teaspoon ground cardamom seeds, and 1/4 teaspoon salt. Melt 2/3 cup butter and 1 1/2 tablespoons lard and stir in 3 tablespoons dark-brown sugar and 1 tablespoon white sugar. Beat 3 eggs until they are very fluffy and add gradually 1 1/2 cups honey, 3/4 cup sour cream, and the butter-sugar mixture, stirring vigorously. Gradually stir in the sifted dry ingredients.

Estonian Honey Cake

Turn the batter into a buttered and floured square cake pan about 2 inches deep and cover the top at regular intervals with blanched halved almonds. Bake the cake in a moderate oven (350° F.) for about 35 minutes, or until it tests done. Remove the cake from the pan to a rack to cool, then put it in a tightly closed container to ripen for at least two days. It will keep for weeks.

SIFT 2 1/4 cups cake flour with 2 teaspoons baking powder, 1 teaspoon soda, 1/2 teaspoon each of cinnamon and allspice, and 1/4 teaspoon cloves. Cream 1/2 cup butter well with 1 1/2 cups sugar. Beat in 2 eggs and beat until the mixture is light and fluffy. Stir in 1/2 teaspoon vanilla extract and 1/2 cup strained pumpkin.

Pumpkin Cake

Add 1/2 cup sour milk alternately with the sifted dry ingredients to make a smooth batter. Pour the batter into 2 buttered and floured layer-cake pans or into a fluted mold and bake the cake in a moderate oven (350° F.) until it tests done.

IN a saucepan combine 1 1/2 cups dark beer, 1 cup molasses, and 1/2 cup butter and bring the mixture to a boil, stirring until the butter is melted. Add 1 1/2 cups seeded raisins and cool the mixture.

German Beer Cake

Sift together 3 cups sifted cake flour, 1 teaspoon each of salt and cinnamon, 3 teaspoons baking powder, and 1/4 teaspoon each of soda, nutmeg, and cloves. Stir the dry ingredients gradually into the beer mixture. Stir in 1/2 cup chopped nuts and turn the batter into a large buttered and lightly floured tube pan. Bake the cake in a moderate oven (350° F.) for about 1 hour, or until it tests done.

OVER low heat melt 4 squares or ounces of semisweet chocolate with 1/2 cup strong coffee, stirring until the chocolate is melted and the mixture is smooth. Cream 1/2 cup butter with 1 cup sugar until the mixture is light and fluffy and stir in 2 eggs, lightly beaten, and the melted chocolate.

Egyptian Cake

Sift together 1 3/4 cups sifted flour, 2 teaspoons baking powder, 1 teaspoon cinnamon, and 1/4 teaspoon cloves. Stir the sifted dry ingredients into the butter mixture alternately with 1/2 cup milk. Stir in 1 teaspoon vanilla and turn the batter into 2 buttered and lightly floured 8-inch layer cake pans. Bake the layers in a moderate oven (350° F.) for 25 minutes, or until they are done. Turn the layers onto cake racks to cool, and sandwich them with whipped cream sweetened to taste and flavored with a little cinnamon.

Brandied Fruitcake

CREAM 2 cups butter, add 2 cups brown sugar gradually, and cream the mixture until it is light and fluffy. Stir in 9 eggs, well beaten. Sift 6 cups flour with 1 1/2 tablespoons baking powder and 1 tablespoon mixed cinnamon, allspice, cloves, and nutmeg, and stir the dry ingredients into the batter alternately with 2 cups brandy. Fold in 2 pounds currants, 1 pound Malaga raisins, 1/2 pound each of candied cherries and blanched almonds, and 1/4 pound mixed orange and lemon peel, sliced, all tossed lightly with 1/2 cup flour.

Turn the batter into 2 large loaf pans lined with buttered, heavy brown paper. Bake the cakes in a very slow oven (250° F.) for about 2 hours, or until they test done.

White Fruitcake

CREAM 1 cup butter with 1 1/2 cups sugar. Sift 4 cups flour with 3 teaspoons baking powder, 1 teaspoon salt, and 1/2 teaspoon grated nutmeg. Mix the flour with 1 pound sultana raisins and 1/2 pound each of candied citron, candied lemon peel, candied orange peel, candied pineapple, and slivered almonds. Combine the floured fruit with the butter-sugar mixture, alternately with 1 cup Sherry, or enough to moisten the mixture. Fold in the whites of 10 eggs, beaten until stiff. Line three 2-pound cake tins with buttered paper, pour in the batter, and bake the cakes in a very slow oven (250° F.) for 2 1/2 hours. Increase the oven temperature to slow (300° F.) and continue to bake the cakes for 15 minutes, or until they test done.

Honey Fruitcake

CUT 1 pound each of citron, candied apricots, and candied pineapple and 2 ounces each of candied orange peel, and candied lemon peel into small pieces and mix them with 3 pounds seeded raisins, 1 1/2 pounds currants and 1 pound candied cherries. Put the mixed fruit in a large dish and sift over it 1 1/2 cups flour, mixing thoroughly. Sift 2 teaspoons soda with another 1 1/2 cups flour. Bring to a boil 1 cup butter mixed with 3 1/2 cups honey, remove the pan from the heat, and stir in 3 teaspoons ground cardamon seeds, 2 teaspoons each of cinnamon and ginger, and 1/2 teaspoon ground cloves. Cool the mixture before stirring it gradually into 6 well-beaten egg yolks. Stir in the sifted flour mixture and 1/2 cup tart jelly and fold in 6 stiffly beaten egg whites. Finally fold in the fruits.

Divide the batter among 4 buttered loaf pans, tie buttered paper over the pans, and steam the cakes for 5 hours in a covered kettle in hot water that comes halfway up the sides of the pans. Remove the paper covers and bake the cakes in a slow oven (300° F.) for about 1 hour.

Plum Cake

Cut 1 cup butter into small pieces and work it in a warm bowl with a wooden spoon until it is soft and creamy. Gradually beat in 1 cup sugar. Add 5 eggs, one at a time, beating well after each. Fold in little by little 1 3/4 cups sifted cake flour sifted with 1/2 teaspoon baking powder. Dredge lightly with flour 1/2 cup each of California and sultana raisins and 1/4 cup candied cherries and fold the fruit lightly into the batter. Fold in the grated rind of 1 lemon and 2 tablespoons rum. Line 2 loaf pans with white paper, butter the paper well, and fill the pans two-thirds full. Bake the cakes in a slow oven (300° F.) for about 1 1/4 hours, or until they are golden brown and test done.

Fruitcake in Sugared Grapefruit Shells

Remove the pulp and membrane from 6 grapefruit halves, cover the shells with boiling water, and cook them for 20 minutes, or until they are tender.

Combine and bring to a boil 2 cups sugar and 1 cup each of light corn syrup and water. Cook the grapefruit skins in this syrup for about 10 minutes, or until a candy thermometer registers 230° F. Invert the shells on a cookie sheet to drain, roll them in sugar, and put them over cups to dry.

Fill the shells to within a half inch of the top with any fruitcake batter. Bake them on a buttered cookie sheet in a very slow oven (250° F.) for about 1 hour, or until the fruitcake tests done.

Cheesecake stands second only to apple pie in national popularity. Here are some of the most popular versions of this popular dessert.

Soufflé Cheesecake

Line the bottom of a springform pan with tart dough and the sides of the pan with a band of the same dough. Bake the shell in a hot oven (400° F.) for about 15 minutes, or until it is browned.

Beat 6 egg yolks until they are light and beat in gradually 1 3/4 cups sugar mixed with 3 tablespoons flour. Add 3 tablespoons melted butter and 2 teaspoons grated orange rind. Add 1 tablespoon Cointreau and beat in gradually 2 pounds softened cream cheese and 1 cup cream. Fold in the 6 egg whites beaten until stiff. Pour the mixture into the prepared pan and bake the cake in a very hot oven (500° F.) for 10 minutes. Reduce the oven temperature to very slow (225° F.) and continue to bake the cake for about an hour. Turn off the heat, open the oven door, and let the cake cool in the oven. Chill it before serving. Soufflé-type cheesecakes require a light and skillful hand; fortunately, even if the cake falls its taste is unimpaired!

Sour Cream Cheesecake BEAT 2 eggs thoroughly, add 1/2 cup sugar, 6 ounces each of cottage cheese and cream cheese, and 1/2 teaspoon vanilla, and beat well. Pour the batter into a springform pan lined with a graham cracker crumb shell and bake in a moderate oven (350° F.) for 20 minutes. Cool for 5 minutes. Pour over the cake 1 1/2 cups sour cream sweetened with 2 tablespoons sugar and flavored with 1/2 teaspoon vanilla extract. Bake the cake in a very hot oven (475° F.) for 5 minutes. Chill before serving.

Fruit Cheesecake LINE the bottom and sides of buttered 10-inch springform pan with tart dough. Bake the shell in a slow oven (300° F.) for about 15 minutes, or until it is a light golden color.

Combine 1/2 pound each of dry pot cheese and cream cheese, 1/4 cup flour, 1/2 teaspoon each of salt, vanilla, and grated lemon rind, and 2 whole eggs. Mix these well in an electric mixer. Add 1/4 cup melted sweet butter and continue beating. Add 1 cup hot milk and blend thoroughly. Fold in 4 egg whites beaten until stiff with 3/4 cup sugar.

Spread 3/4 cup drained crushed pineapple, cherries, or other fruit over the baked crust and cover with the cheese filling. Bake the cake in a slow oven (300° F.) for 45 minutes. Let the cake cool, and chill it before serving.

Strawberry Cheese Pie LINE the bottom of a springform pan with tart dough and the sides with a band of the dough. Bake the dough in a hot oven (400° F.) for about 15 minutes, or until it is lightly browned. Mix 2 1/2 pounds cream cheese, 1 3/4 cups sugar, 3 tablespoons flour, and 1 1/2 teaspoons each of grated orange rind and lemon rind. Add 5 whole eggs and 3 egg yolks, one at a time, beating lightly after each addition. Fold in 1/4 cup heavy cream.

Turn the cheese filling into the baked crust and return the pie to a very hot oven (500° F.) for 12 minutes. Reduce the temperature to very slow (200° F.) and bake the pie for 1 hour. Let the pie cool completely and garnish it generously with large perfect strawberries.

Mash 1/2 cup berries and combine them with 1 cup each of sugar and water. Bring the mixture to a boil, force it through a fine sieve, and boil it again. Stir in 2 tablespoons cornstarch mixed to a paste with 1/4 cup cold water. Boil the mixture, stirring it constantly for a minute or two, until it is clear. Let the glaze cool and pour it over the pie. Cherries or berries of other kinds may be substituted for strawberries.

COMBINE 1 1/4 pounds ricotta cheese, 2 cups sugar, 1 teaspoon vanilla, and 2 tablespoons crème de cacao and beat vigorously until the mixture is smooth and fluffy. Add 2 tablespoons each of sweet chocolate and candied fruit, finely chopped, and mix well.

Cassata alla Siciliana

Cut a moist spongecake into 1-inch slices and line the bottom and sides of a casserole with them. Pour the filling into the casserole, cover with more cake slices, and chill in the refrigerator overnight. Decorate the top with candied fruit and sprinkle with confectioners' sugar.

DRAIN a can of crushed pineapple. Add 2 tablespoons gelatin to 3/4 cup of the pineapple syrup in a saucepan and let the gelatin soften. Add 1/2 cup sugar and a pinch of salt. Stir until the sugar is dissolved, then stir in 2 egg yolks, well beaten. Cook the mixture over simmering water for about 5 minutes, or until the gelatin is dissolved and the mixture thickens slightly. Remove from the heat and stir in 2 tablespoons lemon juice, 1 teaspoon grated lemon rind, and 1 cup of the crushed pineapple. Cool.

Pineapple Cheesecake

Press 3 cups creamed cottage cheese through a fine sieve into a large mixing bowl and stir in the gelatin mixture. Stir over cracked ice until the mixture begins to set. Beat 2 egg whites until they are stiff but not dry and fold in 1/4 cup sugar. Fold this meringue into the cheese mixture, and lastly fold in 1 cup heavy cream, whipped.

Line a springform pan with graham cracker crumb crust. Turn the batter into the pan and chill the cake thoroughly.

SOFTEN 2 tablespoons gelatin in 3 tablespoons cold water. Add 1/4 cup boiling water and stir until the gelatin is thoroughly dissolved. Rub 1/2 pound creamy cottage cheese through a fine sieve and beat into it gradually

Orange Cheese Pie

Paskha

1/4 cup sugar, 1/2 cup orange juice, and the grated rind of 1 orange. Add the dissolved gelatin and beat thoroughly. Fold in the stiffly beaten whites of 3 eggs, turn the mixture into a baked 9-inch pie shell, and chill it until it is set. Decorate the pie with orange sections, free of pith and membrane.

Bring to a boil 1 cup each of sugar and orange juice. Stir 1 tablespoon cornstarch to a smooth paste with 1/4 cup water and add it to the boiling juice. Cook for 1 minute, stirring constantly, until the glaze is clear, and cool it slightly. Cover the pie carefully with this orange glaze, and serve it well chilled.

Pot Cheese Cake

PRESS 1 pound dry pot cheese through a fine sieve. Cream 3 tablespoons butter until soft and fluffy, add the sieved cheese, 1 teaspoon salt, and 1/3 cup flour and beat thoroughly. Add 3 egg yolks, one at a time, beating well after each addition, and stir in the juice and grated rind of 1 lemon. Beat 3 egg whites until they are stiff but not dry, and gradually fold in 12 tablespoons sugar. Fold this meringue lightly into the cheese mixture, then stir in 1 cup milk. Line an oblong pan with rich pie dough and pour in the filling. Bake in a moderate oven (350° F.) for 45 to 60 minutes.

Paskha

PUT 1 1/2 pounds dry pot cheese through a very fine sieve and blend it well with 1/2 pound sweet butter and 3 ounces cream cheese, to make a smooth mixture. Beat 4 egg yolks with 1 1/2 cups sugar and combine this mixture with the cheese. Add 1 cup heavy cream and mix well. Add 2/3 cup each of chopped blanched almonds and mixed candied fruits and raisins. Flavor with the seeds scraped from 1 vanilla bean and mix until the fruits are evenly distributed. Line a pyramidal *paskha* form with cheesecloth wrung out of cold water. Pour the mixture into the form and fold the cheesecloth to cover the bottom of the cake. Weight the cheese down well and allow it to drip for 24 hours. A deep flowerpot with a hole in the bottom for drainage makes a satisfactory *paskha* mold. Unmold the *paskha* and decorate it as you wish. *Paskha* is traditionally served with *kulich*, the Russian Easter bread.

Cream puffs, eclairs, and their ilk are made with pâte à chou. *These light, dry shells may be split and filled with whipped cream,* crème pâtissière, *or any compatible mixture, and frosted to taste with fondant icing in any flavor. Garnishings such as nuts and fruits are a matter of choice.*

Pâte à Chou
CREAM PUFF PASTE

IN a small saucepan, bring to a boil 1 cup water, 1/2 cup butter, 1/2 teaspoon salt, and 1 teaspoon sugar. Add all at once 1 cup flour and cook the paste over low heat, beating it briskly and constantly until the ingredients are thoroughly combined and the mixture cleanly leaves the sides of the pan and forms a ball. Remove the pan from the heat and beat in 4 eggs, one at a time. If the eggs are unusually small, add an extra one.

Choux
CREAM PUFFS

DROP cream puff paste from a teaspoon or tablespoon, or force it through a pastry bag onto a greased baking sheet, allowing space for expansion. To form éclairs, use a pastry bag with a plain round tube. Force the mixture through the bag to make strips 3 1/2 to 4 inches long and 1 inch wide or 2 inches long and 1/2 inch wide, depending upon the size desired. To make a ring, shape the paste on a baking sheet with a spoon. To glaze the top of the puffs, brush them with *dorure*. Bake them in a hot oven (425° F.) for 15 to 18 minutes, reduce the temperature to moderately hot (375° F.) and bake them until they are brown and feel light in the hand. If the puffs start to brown too quickly, cover them with a piece of paper.

Profiteroles au Chocolat

Bake small cream puffs, fill them with *crème pâtissière*, whipped cream, or ice cream, and serve with hot chocolate or other dessert sauce.

Choux Glacés à la Crème
FROSTED CREAM PUFFS

DROP *pâte à chou* from a tablespoon onto a buttered and floured baking sheet. Shape the mounds into thick rectangles. Brush each rectangle with a mixture of 1 egg yolk beaten with 1 teaspoon water. Bake the puffs in the usual way and cool them on a wire rack.

Cut a slit in the center of the top of each puff and with a pastry tube fill the puffs with pastry cream flavored with rum. Frost with confectioners' sugar frosting tinted pale green and flavored with rum. Sprinkle lightly with grated chocolate.

Polka Tart

ROLL out tart dough about 1/8 inch thick and cut a round about 8 inches in diameter. Place the round on a buttered baking sheet. With a pastry bag fitted with a round tube, make a rim of *pâte à chou* around the edge. Brush the tart shell with *dorure* and bake it in a hot oven (425° F.) for 10 to 12 minutes, or until it is brown.

Cool the shell and fill it with *crème pâtissière*. Sprinkle the cream with confectioners' sugar put through a fine sieve, then caramelize the sugar by passing a red hot iron rod above it.

BUTTER and flour a baking sheet and trace on it a circle 8 inches in diameter. Press out a circle of *pâte à chou* about 1 1/2 inches thick through a pastry bag fitted with a large plain tube. Brush the paste with an egg yolk beaten with a little milk and sprinkle generously with blanched shredded almonds. Bake the paste in a hot oven (400° F.) for 15 minutes, reduce the temperature to moderately slow (325° F.), and bake it for 30 to 35 minutes longer, or until the crown is golden and dry. Cool, carefully split the ring horizontally, and sandwich the halves with whipped cream, sweetened and flavored to taste, *crème Saint-Honoré*, or *crème pralinée*. Sprinkle the Paris-Brest with confectioners' sugar.

Paris-Brest

WITH a pastry bag form a large round of *pâte à chou* paste on a greased baking sheet, starting at the center and going around in a spiral. Sprinkle the round with sugar and bake it in a hot oven (400° F.) for 15 minutes, lower the temperature to moderately slow (325° F.), and bake it until it is brown and light in the hand. Cool the cake, split it, and fill it with whipped cream, *crème Saint-Honore* or preserved fruit.

Pain de la Mecque
MECCA CAKE

PREPARE Parisian nougat as follows: Blanch, chop finely, and toast 1 1/4 pounds shelled almonds. Over low heat in a heavy saucepan cook 2 cups fine granulated sugar with the juice of 1/2 lemon, stirring constantly, until the syrup is golden brown. Stir in the warm almonds, mix well, and spread the mixture thinly on an oiled marble slab or a large platter. Keep the nougat warm in a very slow oven (250° F.).

To make the base of the *croquembouche*, oil a 7- or 8-inch round layer-cake pan. Cut a circle of nougat large enough to line the bottom and sides of the pan and press it in firmly. Let the nougat cool and harden and turn it out of the pan, upside down.

With an oiled knife, cut small triangles from the sheet of warm nougat— enough to go around the base and "hat"—and lay them over an oiled rolling pin to cool and harden. Dip the bottoms of the triangles into caramel syrup, made by cooking 1/3 cup water and 1 cup sugar to a golden syrup,

Croquembouche

Parisian Nougat

and press them onto the bottom edge of the inverted nougat base, their tips fanning outward and down, like a fountain.

To make the "hat," lay a circle of nougat over the back of a small oiled muffin cup. With caramel syrup fix 4 triangles to the bottom edge of this nougat cup, their tips curling upward.

Cut a circle of nougat and lay it over a small inverted oiled bowl to cool and harden. Place the smaller nougat cup, with the triangles, on top of the larger one.

Cut 1 1/2-inch crescents of the nougat and let them cool. Shape a small stick of nougat, like a pencil, 1 1/2 inches long. Dip a bit of the convex edge of each crescent into the caramel syrup and fix them around the stick one by one, making a circle of crescents standing on end.

Cut out of nougat, and let harden, shapes like squat M's—or like two saw teeth—about 1 1/2 inches wide. Dip the straight edges in the caramel syrup and fix the shapes together, standing on end in a circle, with the saw teeth pointing out.

Fix this decoration on top of the crescents with a little caramel syrup and set the crescent decoration on the smaller nougat cup. This "hat" goes on the completed *croquembouche*. Finish all the edges of the base and "hat" with dots made by pressing fondant through a pastry tube.

To make the body of the *croquembouche*, bake about 60 cream puffs about the size of walnuts. Cool them and fill them with *crème pâtissière* or *crème Saint-Honoré*. Dip one cream puff at a time into the hot caramel syrup and set a circle of them around the outer edge of the nougat base. Place a second, smaller circle of cream puffs on top of the first layer, in the crevices between them. Continue to build a pyramid in this fashion, in five decreasing circles. Set the prepared nougat "hat" on the last circle.

Every nation has its own version of the fried cake; in France fried cakes are made with pâte à chou. *Some other examples of this kind of cake cookery are listed here.*

French Doughnuts   MAKE *pâte à chou*. Heat fat in a deep kettle to 365° F. Cut a round of heavy paper the same diameter as the kettle and spread it lightly with fat or shortening. Spoon the paste into a pastry bag fitted with a large star tube and press it out on the paper in rings about 2 inches in diameter, keeping the rings well apart. Take the paper in both hands and invert it over the hot deep fat; the rings will drop. Fry them on both sides to a golden brown and drain them on absorbent paper.

The doughnuts may be split and filled with jam, whipped cream, or custard, or they may be simply iced with confectioners' sugar mixed to a spreading consistency with a little hot milk or cream.

Beignets soufflés, or puffed fritters, may be made with the same dough. These are served hot, with fruit sauces or with sugar and cinnamon or preserves. To shape them, use two tablespoons and push the dough directly into the hot deep fat.

Beignets Soufflés for Dessert

SOFTEN 1/2 cake compressed yeast or 1/2 package granular yeast in 3 tablespoons water at temperature given on page 573. Add 1/4 cup lukewarm milk and then 1 cup flour, and beat all together well. Cover the sponge with a towel and put it in a warm place to rise until it is light and bubbly. Sift 3 cups flour into a bowl, make a well in the center, and in the well put 2 tablespoons sugar, 1/2 teaspoon salt, 3/4 cup soft butter, 3 eggs, and the grated rind of 1 lemon. Gradually pull the flour into the center with the hands or a heavy wooden spoon and add 1 cup warm milk little by little to make a soft dough. Add the yeast mixture and work the dough until it is smooth and elastic. Cut off small pieces of the dough, flatten them in the hands, and put 1 teaspoon jam in the center of each. Form the dough into balls around the jam. Let the *beignets* rise in a warm place until they double in bulk and fry them to a golden brown in hot deep fat (375° F.). Drain them on absorbent paper and sprinkle them with confectioners' sugar.

Beignets d'Orléans

SOFTEN 1 cake compressed yeast or 1 envelope granular yeast in 1/2 cup water at temperature given on page 573 and combine this liquid with 1 cup flour to make a ball of dough. Cut a cross on the top of the ball, drop the ball into a deep bowl filled with warm water, and let it stand until it rises to the surface. Sift together in a bowl 3 cups flour, 1/2 teaspoon salt, and 2 tablespoons sugar. Add 6 eggs, a generous 1/2 cup well-kneaded butter and 2 tablespoons Cognac or rum and work them well into the dough. Continue to work all together until the mixture is very elastic. When the sponge rises to the surface of the water, add it to the dough in the bowl, cutting and folding it in without working the mixture any further. Cover the dough with a towel and let it rise at room temperature until it doubles

Bugnes
RAISED DOUGHNUTS

in bulk. Punch it down, forming it into a large ball. Break off pieces the size of small eggs and shape them into balls. Arrange the balls on a floured baking sheet and let them rise until they double in bulk. Fry them until they are brown in hot deep fat (375° F.). Drain them on absorbent paper.

To make jelly doughnuts, use a pastry tube to force a tart jelly into the doughnut. The same dough may be used to shape sticks, twists, or other forms. The cakes may then be dusted with sugar and cinnamon, or iced with confectioners' sugar icing.

Sopaipillas   SIFT together 4 cups flour, 1 teaspoon baking powder, and 3/4 teaspoon salt. Beat 2 eggs well, add 1 cup milk, and stir in the dry ingredients, adding a little more flour if necessary to make a soft dough.

Roll out the dough very thinly on a lightly floured board and cut it into small squares. Fry the squares, a few at a time, in hot deep fat (375° F.) to a delicate golden brown. Drain the *sopaipillas* on absorbent paper and sprinkle them with confectioners' sugar.

Cenci
ITALIAN FRIED
TWISTS

BEAT 3 eggs until they are frothy with 2 tablespoons sugar, a pinch of salt, and 1 tablespoon Curaçao. Add gradually 2 cups flour sifted with 1 1/2 teaspoons baking powder and work in a generous teaspoon soft butter. The dough should be soft, but if necessary, add a little more flour to make it stiff enough to knead. Knead the dough on a lightly floured board until it is smooth, cover it, and let it rest for an hour. Divide the dough in half and roll out each half into a thin rectangle. Cut the dough into strips less than 1 inch wide and about 5 inches long. Twist the strips and set them aside for about 10 minutes. Fry the twists a few at a time in hot deep fat (370° F.) Drain them on absorbent paper and sprinkle them lightly with confectioners' sugar.

Rosettes   COMBINE 1 cup each of flour and milk, 1 tablespoon sugar, 2 beaten eggs, and a pinch of salt and beat with a rotary beater until the batter is smooth. Dip a *rosette* iron into hot deep fat (370° F.) and dip it into the batter up to but not over the edge of the iron. Lower the iron gently into the hot fat and fry the *rosette* for 1 1/2 minutes, or until it is golden. Loosen the *rosette* from the iron with a fork. Drain it on absorbent paper.

Store *rosettes* in a tight container and they will keep fresh and crisp for weeks. Serve them sprinkled generously with confectioners' sugar.

SIFT 2 cups flour with 2 teaspoons baking powder, a pinch each of nutmeg and cloves, and 1/2 teaspoon salt. Work in lightly with a fork 1 egg beaten with 1/2 cup each of sugar and cream, to make a soft dough which can be handled. Chill the dough for about 30 minutes, knead it briefly, roll it out 1/4 inch thick on a lightly floured pastry board, and cut out the doughnuts. Let the doughnuts rest for 10 minutes. Fry them in hot deep fat (370° F.) a few at a time, turning them once when they brown on the under side. Drain them on absorbent paper and dredge them with confectioners' sugar or with granulated sugar flavored with cinnamon.

*Cake
Doughnuts*

BEAT 3 eggs thoroughly. Add slowly 1 1/4 cups sugar, beating constantly. Melt 1 1/2 ounces bitter chocolate with 2 tablespoons butter and cool. Stir the chocolate into the eggs and sugar and add 1 cup sour milk. Sift 3 3/4 cups sifted flour with 2 teaspoons baking powder, 1 teaspoon soda, 1/2 teaspoon salt and, if desired, 1/4 teaspoon cinnamon or 1/2 teaspoon nutmeg. Stir the sifted ingredients into the egg mixture, blend well, and chill the dough to make it easier to handle.

*Devil's Food
Doughnuts*

Turn the chilled dough onto a lightly floured board, roll it out 1 inch thick, handling it as little as possible, and cut it into rounds with a floured doughnut cutter. Fry the doughnuts, a few at a time, in hot deep fat (370° F.), turning them as they brown and rise to the top of the fat and turning them again, once or more during the frying, until they are evenly browned. Drain the doughnuts on absorbent paper, cool, and sprinkle with sugar.

To make *cannoli*, you will need tapered tin tubes about 3/4 inch in diameter and 6 inches in length, or a reasonable facsimile.

*Cannoli alla
Siciliana*

On a pastry board make a well in the center of 1 1/3 cups flour. In the well put 2 tablespoons shortening, a pinch of salt, and 1/2 teaspoon sugar. Work the center ingredients to a smooth paste and combine it with the flour, adding water or a little wine to make a rather firm dough. Form the dough into a ball, cover it with a napkin, and let it rest for about 1 hour.

Roll out the dough 1/16 inch thick and cut it into 4-inch squares. Place one of the tin tubes diagonally across a square and wrap the dough around the tube, overlapping the two points and pressing them a little with the fingers to close the *cannoli*. Wrap all the squares in the same way and fry them, one or two at a time, in hot deep fat (370° F.) until they are brown and crisp. Let them drain and cool a little on absorbent paper and then remove the *cannoli* carefully from the tubes. Let them cool thoroughly before filling them with the following sweetened cheese:

Combine thoroughly 1 pound ricotta cheese and 1 cup fine granulated sugar and press the mixture through a sieve two or three times to make a smooth paste. To this may be added, according to taste, a little orange flower water, a little melted chocolate, or some finely chopped nuts or candied fruits. Fill the *cannoli* and sprinkle them generously with confectioners' sugar. This recipe makes 12 *cannoli*.

The sine qua non *of* la pâtisserie française *is the marvelously light and delicate pastry of a thousand layers,* pâte feuilletée. *This puff paste, as we call it in English, has more uses in French cuisine than has any other* pâte. *You will find reference to it in recipes for pastries, for hors-d'oeuvre, and for* pièces montées *of every description. Like most pastry doughs, it freezes magnificently; you will find it as accommodating as it is versatile.*

Pâte
Feuilletée
PUFF PASTE

KNEAD 1 pound sweet butter in ice water until it has the consistency of soft dough and is free of lumps. Remove the washed butter from the water and squeeze it to extract any pockets of water. Wrap the butter in wax paper and chill it until it is firm.

Measure 4 cups flour, shaking it down in the measuring cup to make approximately 1 pound flour. Wash a tabletop with ice water, dry it well, and sift the measured flour onto it in a mound. Sprinkle the flour with 1/2 teaspoon salt. Gradually work into the flour about 1 1/2 cups ice water, or enough to make a dough that is very firm. Work quickly, rubbing the flour and water together until the dough cleans the table. Do not knead the dough. Kneading would make the dough elastic, and this must be avoided.

This dough is called the *détrempe*, and in countries where the ingredients that go into fine pastries are weighed rather than measured, the weight of the *détrempe* should be twice the weight of the washed butter, or about 2 pounds. Both the butter and the *détrempe* should have the same firm consistency.

Form the dough into a ball and chill it for 30 minutes. Put the dough on a floured board and roll it into a long rectangle 1/2 inch thick. Turn the rectangle so that it is horizontal on the board. Flatten the butter into a cake 1/2 inch thick and put it in the center of the dough. Fold the flap of dough on the right to cover the butter, then fold the flap of dough on the left over the right flap. Press the edges of the dough firmly together to enclose the butter. Chill the dough for 20 minutes.

Place the dough on the floured board in exactly the same position as it was before it was chilled and again roll it out into a long rectangle about 1/2 inch thick. Roll lightly to within half an inch of each end. Be careful not to let the butter break through the dough or the air trapped between the layers of dough will be lost, and it is this air that will expand in the oven heat and cause the paste to rise. If the *détrempe* is firm enough, and both the washed butter and the *détrempe* have the same firmness, the butter will not break through. Turn the dough so that it is horizontal on the board and fold as before—right side to center, left side over the right side, making three layers of dough. This rolling, turning, and folding is called a "turn." Make another turn and chill the dough in the refrigerator for 20 minutes. Make two more turns, always being certain that the dough is placed in the same position after chilling as it was before, and chill the dough for 20 minutes.

Two more turns must be made to complete the paste. If the paste is to be used immediately, make the last two turns, chill the dough again, then roll it out, cut and bake. The first four turns, however, may be made several days before the paste is needed. Put the dough in a bowl, cover it with a damp cloth, and store in the refrigerator. Make the last two turns just before cutting and baking the paste. Chill the dough for 20 minutes after the last two turns before rolling it out.

This amount of puff paste will make 1 large *gâteau* or 24 small *gâteaux*. Leftover scraps of puff paste can be gathered together and rerolled for cookies or hors-d'oeuvre. They cannot be used for the most delicate of puff paste pastries.

Puff Paste Shell
VOL-AU-VENT

ROLL out puff paste 3/8 inch thick and cut out a 7-inch circle. Moisten a baking sheet with water and lay the pastry on it, top side down. Roll out puff paste to the same thickness and cut another 7-inch circle. Cut out and reserve the center of this circle, leaving a 1-inch rim. Moisten the first circle for an inch in from the edge and on it lay the cutout rim, top side down. Press the borders firmly together and cut small scallops each about 1/2 inch wide to make a decorative edging. Lay the reserved circle lightly inside the rim and chill the pastry for about 15 minutes, or until very cold.

Brush the top with 1 egg beaten with a little milk and bake the shell in a very hot oven (450° F.) for about 10 minutes, or until it is well puffed and lightly browned. Reduce the temperature to moderately hot (375° F.) and bake the shell for 25 to 30 minutes longer. Remove it from the oven and with a sharp knife gently lift out the center circle, which will serve as a cover for the filled shell.

Patty Shells
For individual patty shells, follow the procedure above but cut small circles of the desired size.

Gâteau
Mille-Feuille
ROLL out puff paste 1/8 inch thick on a lightly floured board and cut it into 4 circles, 8 inches in diameter. Cut centers 4 inches in diameter from two of the circles to make rings. Place the rings and circles on moistened baking sheets and chill them for 20 minutes. Sprinkle them with sugar and prick the tops in several places with the tines of a fork. Bake them in a very hot oven (450° F.) for 15 minutes, reduce the temperature to moderate (350° F.), and bake them for another 15 minutes, or until the pastry is golden brown and dry.

Sandwich the pastry with apricot marmalade or red currant jelly, using the circles for the top and bottom of the *gâteau*. Spread the sides with apricot glaze and cover with finely chopped toasted almonds. On the top of the cake arrange 20 fluted rings of puff paste 2 inches in diameter, baked in a very hot oven (450° F.) for about 20 minutes, or until they are well puffed but not brown. Sprinkle generously with confectioners' sugar.

Although it is not traditional, there is no reason why the hollow center of the *gâteau* cannot be filled with pastry cream or whipped cream before the top circle is put in place.

Mille-Feuille
Puff paste may be cut into rectangles 5 inches by 12 inches and baked as above. Spread 2 of the rectangles thickly with sweetened whipped cream. Lay them one on the other and top with the third. With a pastry tube, pipe around the edges rosettes of whipped cream. Sprinkle with confectioners' sugar.

Dartois
ROLL out puff paste 1/4 inch thick on a lightly floured board and cut a strip 20 inches long and 8 inches wide. Put the strip on a baking sheet lined with heavy paper and spread the strip 1/2 inch thick with *crème pâtissière*, leaving a 1/2-inch border all round. Moisten the border with water.

Roll out another piece of puff paste 1/3 inch thick, cut another strip of the same dimensions as the first, and place this strip over the filling. Brush the top with beaten egg, cut shallow diagonal lines on top with a sharp knife, and press the edges together firmly. Bake the paste in a very hot oven (450° F.) for 15 minutes, or until the paste is puffed. Reduce the temperature to moderate (350° F.) and bake the paste for 25 minutes, or until it is golden. Sprinkle with confectioners' sugar and bake for another 5 minutes, or until the sugar is caramelized. Serve the *dartois* whole or cut 1-inch slices to make *petits dartois*.

ROLL out puff paste 1/8 inch thick on a lightly floured board and cut it into 3 circles, 8 inches in diameter. Spread almond cream 1/2 inch thick on one of the circles, leaving a 1/2-inch border free of cream. Cut the center 7 1/2 inches in diameter from the second circle, making a ring 1/2 inch wide. Moisten the edge of the first round and place the ring over the cream. Moisten the ring and cover it and the cream with the third circle. Press firmly with the thumb all the way around the edge to seal the layers of paste, brush the top with an egg beaten with 2 tablespoons milk, and score the top with a sharp knife, making lines curving out from the center, like a pinwheel.

Pithiviers
PITHIVIERS CAKE

Place the *gâteau* on a baking sheet lined with heavy paper and chill it for 20 minutes. Bake it in a very hot oven (450° F.) for 15 to 20 minutes, or until the paste is puffed. Reduce the temperature to moderate (350° F.) and bake the *gâteau* for 25 minutes, or until it is golden. Sprinkle with confectioners' sugar and bake for 5 minutes longer, or until the sugar is caramelized.

ROLL out 2 oblongs of puff paste 12 inches long and 4 1/2 to 5 inches wide, one piece 1/8 inch thick, the other 1/4 inch thick. Lay the 1/8-inch-thick layer on a moistened baking sheet. Spread the center with red currant jelly or raspberry jam (or a mixture of the two), leaving a border of about 3/4 inch all around the rectangle. Fold the thicker rectangle in half lengthwise and, starting 1 1/2 inches from each end, make parallel cuts, 1/4 inch apart, from the fold to within 1 1/2 inches of the top edges. Moisten the edges of the bottom layer, unfold the cut layer and cover the bottom layer with it. Seal the edges well. With a sharp knife make tiny decorative nicks, 1/2 inch apart, along the edges to make a scalloped effect. Brush the top of the cake with *dorure* and prick the edges in a few places with a fork. Bake in a hot oven (400° F.) for about 20 minutes. Brush the top with thick apricot purée and sprinkle the edges with sugar or chopped almonds. The *gâteau jalousie* may be served whole or it may be cut crosswise into 1 1/2-inch slices.

*Gâteau
Jalousie*

ROLL out 2 separate sheets of puff paste, one piece 1/8 inch thick and the other 1/4 inch thick. Cut them into 8-inch circles, using a plate as a guide. Turn the thinner layer onto a moistened baking sheet. Spread the center with *crème pâtissière* leaving a clear border of about 1 1/2 inches around the edge. Moisten the edge with water, place the other layer on top, and press the two edges together to seal them. Make tiny nicks with a small knife around the

Conversation
CREAM CAKE

edge to give a decorative scalloped effect. Make a smooth paste with confectioners' sugar and 1 egg white and spread this over the top. Cut very narrow strips of puff paste, brush them with *dorure*, and arrange them in a pattern on top of the cake. Bake it in a hot oven (400° F.) for 25 to 30 minutes.

To make individual *conversations*, line individual tart molds with puff paste, prick the bottoms and fill the molds just to the top with pastry cream. Moisten the edge of the pastry with water and cover the tarts with circles of puff paste. Trim the edges and seal them. Finish the tarts as you would the large *conversation* and bake them for 15 to 18 minutes, until they are golden brown.

Palmiers ROLL out puff paste 1/8 inch thick, 10 to 15 inches long and 4 1/4 inches wide. Sprinkle the strip with sugar. Fold over the long sides so that they meet in the center and sprinkle the strip again with sugar. Fold over the long sides again so that they meet in the center. You now have a long folded strip 1 inch wide and 1/2 inch thick. Cut the strip crosswise into slices 1/4 to 1/2 inch wide. Lay the slices, cut side down, on a buttered baking sheet and spread them open to make a small V. Bake the *palmiers* in a hot oven (400° F.) until the bottom is caramelized and brown, then turn them over to caramelize and brown the other side.

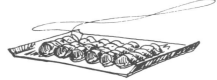

Cornets ROLL out puff paste on a lightly floured board 1/8 inch thick. Cut the paste
Feuilletés into strips 10 inches long and 1 inch wide. Wind each strip around a buttered
à la Crème slender metal cone, or "lady lock," overlapping the edges slightly. Start at
LADY LOCKS the wide part of the cone and roll almost to the end. Fasten the end securely. Place the tubes 1 inch apart on a baking sheet lined with heavy paper and bake the cornets in a very hot oven (450° F.) for 15 minutes, or until puffed and golden. Slip the cornets off the tubes, cool them, and fill them with *crème pâtissière*.

Sacristains ROLL out puff paste on a lightly floured board into a long band 1/4 inch thick. Brush the surface with beaten egg and sprinkle it with finely chopped, blanched almonds and confectioners' sugar. Cut the band crosswise into 1/2-inch strips and twist each strip several times like a corkscrew. Put the corkscrews on a moistened baking sheet 1 inch apart and bake them in a hot oven (450° F.) for 10 to 15 minutes, or until they are puffed and golden.

ROLL out puff paste 1/4 inch thick and cut it into strips 4 inches wide. Add enough confectioners' sugar to 1 egg white to make a smooth paste and spread the paste over the top of the puff paste strips. Cut the strips crosswise into pieces 1 1/2 inches wide and lay them on a moistened pan. Bake the *allumettes* in a hot oven (400° F.) for 10 to 12 minutes.

Allumettes Glacées

LINE 6 small, fluted *baba* molds with puff paste or plain tart dough, prick the paste with a fork and put 1/2 teaspoon butter in each. Fill the molds three-quarters full with this mixture: Beat 2 eggs with 1/2 cup sugar until they are light and add 2 tablespoons flour, 1 cup cold milk, and a little orange flower water. Bake the *darioles* in a hot oven (400° F.) for 15 minutes.

Darioles

LINE 12 individual deep tart molds with puff paste and prick the paste well with a fork. Put 1/2 teaspoon apricot jam in each mold and fill the shells with the following mixture: Beat 2 eggs with 1/2 cup sugar until they are light and fluffy, flavor with a little vanilla extract and add 4 or 5 dry macaroons, crushed to make very fine crumbs. Sprinkle the tarts lightly with chopped almonds and bake them in a hot oven (400° F.) for 12 to 15 minutes.

Mirlitons

ROLL out puff paste 1/4 inch thick and cut out an 8- or 9-inch circle, using a plate as a guide. Peel, core, and grate 5 large sour apples. Sauté the apples in 1/4 cup melted butter until they are tender. Add sugar to taste (1/2 cup or more), 1 teaspoon vanilla extract, 1 tablespoon rum or Cognac, and a dash of pepper. Cool the mixture and spread it on the dough, leaving clear a 1 1/2-inch border. Moisten the edge of the dough, fold the circle in half, pinch the edges securely together, and then turn up the edge. Brush the turnover lightly with egg beaten with a little milk, prick it well with a fork, and bake it in a very hot oven (450° F.) for about 30 minutes, or until the crust is delicately browned. About 5 minutes before taking the *chausson* from the oven, sprinkle it with confectioners' sugar, to glaze it.

Chausson aux Pommes
APPLE TURNOVER

FOLLOW the recipe for *chausson aux pommes*, but make tiny individual turnovers. Fill them with the apple mixture or with jam or pastry cream and bake them for 12 to 15 minutes in a hot oven (400° F.).

Petits Chaussons

Chausson aux Fraises
STRAWBERRY TURNOVER

FOLLOW the directions for *chausson aux pommes*, but instead of using apples for the filling, spread 3 or 4 crushed macaroons or ladyfingers over the paste and over these put 1 cup strawberries, washed and thoroughly dried, and 2 teaspoons red currant jelly.

Fig Turnovers

FILL large dried figs with hard sauce. Put each fig in a circle of puff paste or any pastry dough, fold the dough over the fig and seal the edges. Prick the turnovers with a fork and bake them in a hot oven (400° F.) until the crust is delicately browned.

The ineffable delicacy of the many-leaved pastries of the Near East is not easily attained by the inexperienced hand. Fortunately, these thin sheets of dough, made by the baker's special equipment, can be purchased in Syrian, Armenian, Turkish, and Greek neighborhood shops. The recipe is given here for the benefit of the intrepid tyro.

Baklava

IN a mixing bowl combine 5 cups sifted flour, 1/4 teaspoon double-action baking powder, and 1 teaspoon salt. Add 5 beaten eggs and 5 tablespoons vegetable oil and knead for 15 minutes, adding gradually about 3/4 cup lukewarm water and forcing the dough from the edges to the center of the bowl. Keep the hands slightly oiled while kneading.

Sprinkle a little cornstarch on a pastry board. Divide the dough into 4 equal parts. Shape each part into a long roll and divide each roll into 5 parts, making 20 pieces of dough. Form the pieces of dough into balls, roll them in oil, and place them in an oiled pan. Cover them with a towel, place another pan over the dough pan, and let the dough rest for 2 hours, before attempting to stretch it.

Cover a table top at least 4 feet square with oilcloth. Sift cornstarch lightly over this and place on it one of the balls of dough. Roll out the dough to 9 inches in diameter. Stretch and work it over a wooden rod 3/4 inch thick and almost 4 feet long, pressing the dough out lightly with the hands until it is a very thin circle about 2 feet in diameter. Keep the oilcloth sprinkled with cornstarch to prevent the dough from sticking. Fold the circle in half and then in half again and set it aside, covered with a towel. Continue until all the 20 balls are rolled and folded and placed one on top of the other beneath the towel.

Open and spread out 5 of the folded circles, one on top of the other.

Place a large square pan in the center of these and cut the dough around it. Place each flat, square piece in the pan with all the trimmings. Repeat with 5 more sheets of dough and sprinkle with 2 cups finely chopped walnuts. Place the remaining 10 sheets of dough in the pan in the same way until they have all been cut and added, placing the last cuttings beneath the last square sheet. With a sharp knife, cut the dough into 5 sections diagonally in both directions, making 25 diamond-shaped cakes. Let the dough rest in the pan for 2 hours before baking.

Melt 1 1/2 pounds butter in a saucepan, sprinkle into it 1/2 teaspoon flour, and simmer the butter over very low heat for about 20 minutes, or until it forms a white foam. Skim off the foam and pour the butter into another saucepan very carefully to avoid disturbing the sediment that has settled to the bottom. Add 2 1/4 cups melted vegetable shortening and keep this mixture at the simmering point while the *baklava* is baking.

Preheat the oven to very hot (450° F.) and lower the temperature to moderate (350° F.). Pour 1 1/2 cups of the butter-shortening mixture over the pastry, place it in the oven, and bake it for 7 minutes. Pour over it another 1 1/2 cups of the fat mixture, reduce the temperature to moderately slow (325° F.), and bake it for 7 minutes longer. Pour in the remainder of the fat, reduce the oven temperature to slow (300° F.), and bake it for 20 minutes longer. Remove the *baklava* from the oven, drain off all the fat possible through a fine sieve, return the pan to the oven, and bake the *baklava* for another 5 minutes. Drain off any remaining fat and cool the pastry in the pan.

Bring to a boil 1 1/2 cups honey, 1/2 cup water, 1 tablespoon lemon juice, *Honey Syrup* and a thin slice of lemon. Boil the mixture until it has the consistency of a thick syrup and cool it. To serve the *baklava*, pour the honey syrup around the edge of the pan and between the slices, sprinkle a few drops on top, and serve immediately.

Melt 1 pound butter slowly and skim the foam from the top. Put 1 pound *Baklava* unsalted pistachio nuts through the coarsest blade of a food chopper, and mix *Syrian Style* them thoroughly with 1/4 cup sugar and 1 tablespoon rosewater.

Butter a round 9-inch cake pan generously with some of the melted butter. Place 2 layers of *baklava* dough on it and brush them well with melted butter. Repeat until half the dough is used. Squeeze the overhanging edges of dough into the sides of the pan and spread a thick layer of the nut mixture over the dough. Cover the nuts with more layers of dough as before. Cut the *baklava* diagonally into diamonds, butter the top well, and bake it in a very hot oven (500° F.) for 10 minutes. Lower the temperature to slow (300° F.), and bake the *baklava* for about an hour, or until the pastry is golden brown, basting occasionally with the remaining butter. Remove the *baklava* from the oven and pour immediately over it 1/2 cup cold sugar syrup, lightly flavored with rosewater.

Bird's Nest STACK 5 sheets of thin Near Eastern pastry dough and cut out 5-inch circles. In the center of each circle put a spoonful of chopped pistachio nuts and fold the sides of the circle partly over the filling. Baste the pastries generously with sweet butter and bake them in a moderate oven (350° F.) for about 30 minutes, until they are well browned. Pour over the nests a little rosewater-flavored syrup. Cool and serve with more rosewater syrup and with *kaymak*.

Saragli
WALNUT ROLLS

TRIM a sheet of *baklava* dough to a rectangular shape. Along one short end spread a row of chopped walnuts, using about 3 tablespoons. Roll up the sheet like a thin jelly roll and put it in a baking pan, trimming the ends to fit if necessary. Trim and roll up similarly all the stretched sheets of *baklava* dough, placing them side by side in the pan. Bake as for *baklava* and cool. When ready to serve, pour honey syrup or the rosewater-flavored syrup used for the Syrian pastries around the edges of the pan and between the pastry rolls, and on top. Serve with *kaymak*.

Kadaifi Roll KADAIFI is a pastry dough that resembles shredded wheat, but is soft and fresh, and not at all dry. Buy it by the pound at a shop that sells Near Eastern delicacies. Flatten the shredded dough into a narrow rectangle, cover it with chopped walnuts, pistachios, or almonds, and roll it up. Or use the nut filling for *baklava*. Bake the roll in a moderate oven (350° F.) for about 30 minutes. Remove it from the oven and baste it generously with sugar syrup flavored with rosewater, lemon, or orange. Cover the pan while the *kadaifi* cools. To serve, cut the roll into 2-inch lengths.

Ekmek
Kadayif

SOAK 8 slices of zwieback in 2 cups hot water mixed with the juice of 2 lemons. When they are puffed and soft, remove them from the water and place them in a flat round pan. Pour over them 2 cups honey and bake them in a moderate oven (350° F.) for about 45 minutes, or until they are lightly browned. Chill and serve cold with *kaymak*.

BOIL 2 cups sugar with 3 cups water for 5 minutes. Flavor the syrup with a few drops rosewater or with lemon or orange rind and a clove.

Flavored Sugar Syrup

CREAM 1 1/2 cups sweet butter with 1/2 cup sugar and 1 egg. Stir in 1 1/2 cups chopped walnuts or almonds and flavor the filling with 1 teaspoon cinnamon. Use this filling with the prepared thin sheets of Near Eastern pastry dough.

Nut Filling for Near Eastern Pastries

SWEETEN ricotta, well drained, with a little sugar, to taste, and cream it slightly. This filling may be used to make pastries of any shape, providing that the cheese is well covered and contained so that it cannot run out.

Cheese Filling for Near Eastern Pastries

THIS delicacy adds richness to the rich Near Eastern pastries with which it is served.

Bring 1 quart heavy cream to a boil in a large kettle, over very low heat. Lift a ladleful of the cream out of the kettle and pour it back from a height, to make as many bubbles as possible. Continue this process for 30 minutes to 1 hour, until the pan is full of cream bubbles. Put the kettle in a warm place for 2 hours, then chill the cream well. The cream that sets on top of the liquid is the *kaymak*; it may be spooned off or cut off with a sharp knife and served in slices.

Kaymak
CLOTTED CREAM

Like the dough for the pastries of the Near East, the dough for strudel, the pastry of Middle Europe, requires expert technique. Unfortunately, and unlike the baklava *dough, it cannot be purchased. Fortunately, and unlike the* baklava *dough, it can be produced acceptably, if not perfectly, by the earnest amateur.*

SIFT 2 1/2 cups sifted flour onto a pastry board and make a well in the center. In the well put 1 egg, lightly beaten, 3 tablespoons oil, and 1/2 teaspoon salt. Gradually work in the flour, adding about 2/3 cup warm water, or just enough water to make a soft and rather sticky dough.

The dough must be worked vigorously to make it elastic. Lift the dough

Strudel Dough

in one hand and crash it down on the table. Repeat the lifting and crashing of the dough about 100 times, or until the dough no longer sticks to hands or table. Form the dough into a ball and brush the surface with oil. Cover the dough with a warm bowl and let it rest for 30 minutes.

Spread a cloth on a table about 3 feet wide and 5 feet long. Sprinkle the cloth lightly with flour. Place the dough in the center, sprinkle it lightly with flour, and roll it into a large circle, turning it several times to prevent it from sticking to the cloth. Roll the outer edges as thinly as possible.

Flour both hands, tuck in the thumbs, and reach under the dough. With the backs of the hands, begin gently stretching the dough from the center to the outer edge. Use a hand-over-hand motion, being careful not to tear the dough, for it cannot be mended. Move around the table and stretch the dough until it hangs over the edges of the table in a sheet as thin as tissue paper.

The edges of the dough that overhang the table will be thicker than the rest of the dough. Cut the edges off with kitchen scissors and let the sheet of dough dry for 10 minutes. Do not let it become brittle.

Melt 3/4 cup butter and with a pastry brush, coat the entire surface of the dough with some of the butter. Cover from half to two-thirds of the dough with any of the fillings that follow, fold the overhanging flaps of dough over the filling, and brush the flaps with the melted butter.

Pick up the tablecloth and turn the end of the dough covered with filling over onto itself. Continue to roll the dough loosely in jelly-roll fashion, pulling the cloth and dough toward you as the strudel is rolled. The last flip of the cloth should deposit the strudel on a buttered baking sheet.

Another method of filling the strudel is perhaps easier for the amateur; cut the dough into rectangles, pile 2 or 3 layers together, spread half the dough with the filling, and roll the dough in jelly-roll fashion.

Brush the strudel well with melted butter and bake it in a moderately hot oven (375° F.) for 45 to 50 minutes, or until it is golden, basting several times with the remaining melted butter. Sprinkle generously with confectioners' sugar and serve the strudel warm with sweetened or unsweetened whipped cream.

Cherry Strudel   Make and stretch the strudel dough. Brush the dough with melted butter and sprinkle two-thirds of the surface with 1/2 cup fine dry bread crumbs and 2 cups sweet cherries. Sprinkle the fruit with 1 cup sugar mixed with 1/2 teaspoon each of cloves and nutmeg, and with 1 cup each of raisins and chopped almonds. Roll the strudel, brush it generously with melted butter, and bake it in the usual way. Other fresh fruits, such as apples, peaches, the less juicy plums and the like, may be used in the same way.

Make and stretch the strudel dough and brush it with melted butter. Sprinkle two-thirds of the surface with 1/2 cup fine dry bread crumbs and 1 cup sugar mixed with 1 teaspoon cinnamon. Spread on this 2 cups finely diced pineapple and 1 1/2 cups each of seeded raisins, walnuts, and maraschino cherries, all finely chopped. Roll the strudel, brush it generously with melted butter, and bake it in the usual way. Cut it into very thin slices to serve. *Fruit Nut Strudel*

Make and stretch the strudel dough. Chop 2 cups dried white figs, 1 cup each of almonds, lightly toasted, and white raisins, and 1/2 cup candied cherries. Toss the mixture with 1/2 cup each of apricot jam and sugar, 1 teaspoon cinnamon, and the grated rind of 1 lemon. *Fruit Strudel*

Sprinkle the prepared dough for strudel with melted butter. Spread the fruit mixture over two-thirds of the dough and roll up the strudel like a jelly roll, starting with the end that is filled, pulling the cloth toward you and flipping the dough over. Cut the strudel in lengths to fit a baking sheet and arrange them side by side on it, or shape the strudel into a large crescent on the baking sheet. Brush the top of the strudel with melted butter and bake it in the usual way.

Make and stretch the strudel dough and brush it with butter. Combine in a heavy saucepan 8 ounces semisweet chocolate, grated, and 1/4 cup butter. Cook together over low heat until the chocolate is melted. Stir frequently. Blend into the mixture 3/4 cup sugar, 8 egg yolks, lightly beaten, 1 cup fine bread crumbs, toasted until they are brown, 1/4 cup finely ground almonds, and 1/2 teaspoon vanilla. *Chocolate Strudel*

Beat 8 egg whites until they hold a shape and fold them into the chocolate mixture gently but thoroughly. Spread the filling over two-thirds of the dough, roll up the pastry, and cut little slits in the top of the strudel. Brush the surface with melted butter and bake in the usual way. Sprinkle the strudel with fine granulated sugar immediately it is taken out of the oven.

Make and stretch the strudel dough and brush it with butter. Sprinkle two-thirds of the surface with 2 cups rhubarb, cut into 1/2-inch pieces, 1 cup sugar mixed with 1 teaspoon cinnamon, and 1/2 cup fine dry bread crumbs. Roll up the pastry, brush it generously with melted butter, and bake it in the usual way. *Rhubarb Strudel*

When the strudel is golden brown, sprinkle it liberally with fine granulated sugar.

Cream Cheese Strudel Make and stretch the strudel dough and brush it with melted butter. Cream together 2/3 cup each of butter and sugar until the mixture is light and fluffy. Beat 6 egg yolks well and stir them into the butter and sugar with a pinch of salt, the grated rind of 1 lemon, and 1 2/3 cups sour cream. Cream 1 pound cream cheese until it is soft and smooth and press it through a fine sieve. Mix the cream cheese with the egg yolk mixture and press through the sieve to assure smoothness. Fold in 6 egg whites, stiffly beaten.

Spread the filling about 1 inch thick over two-thirds of the strudel, not too close to the edge. Sprinkle the filling with 1 cup sultana raisins. Roll the strudel very loosely, brush it with melted butter, and bake it in the usual fashion.

Tyrolese Strudel Make and stretch the strudel dough and brush it with melted butter. Cream together until the mixture is light and fluffy 2/3 cup butter and 1/2 cup sugar. Add 6 egg yolks, well beaten, 2/3 cup chopped walnuts or almonds, 1 cup chopped raisins, 1/4 cup each of sliced dates and figs, the grated rind of 1 lemon, and 1/2 teaspoon cinnamon. Fold in 6 egg whites, beaten until stiff. Spread this filling over half the surface of the dough, roll the strudel, brush it with melted butter, and bake it in the usual fashion.

The secrets of successful pie crust are two: cold ingredients, minimum handling. Chill the crust before adding the filling and again before baking. Pie dough put into the oven directly from the home freezer is particularly good. When a recipe calls for a prepared pie shell, any of the following doughs may be used, with discretion.

Basic Pie Dough SIFT 2 cups flour into a mixing bowl with 1 teaspoon salt. With two knives or a pastry blender, cut into the flour 2/3 cup cold, firm vegetable shortening. The particles should be as big as peas. Sprinkle with 1/4 cup ice water and toss with a fork until the mixture holds together. Work quickly and gently. If more water is needed, add a very little at a time. Chill the dough thoroughly before attempting to roll it out. Divide the dough in half and roll each half lightly and quickly into a circle. Fit the bottom crust into the pie pan and trim. Chill the crust before filling it. Add the prepared filling and cover with the top crust, which should be slightly larger all around than the pan. Moisten the edge of the lower crust, tuck the upper crust under the lower, and seal by

Tyrolese Strudel

crimping with a fork or by fluting the rim with the fingers. Cut several slits in the top crust and bake as indicated in the individual recipe.

A little sugar may be added to the ingredients for pie crust, and orange or grapefruit juice or other fruit juices may be substituted for the water.

Flaky Pie Dough   SIFT 2 cups flour and 1 teaspoon salt into a chilled mixing bowl. With two knives, or a pastry blender, blend 1/3 cup cold butter into the flour. Cut in another 1/3 cup cold butter, until the lumps are the size of small peas. Sprinkle ice water, at little at a time, over the flour-butter mixture and work it in quickly and gently until the dough can be gathered together with a fork and cleans the bowl. Use as little water as possible—4 to 6 tablespoons should be enough. Form the dough into a ball, wrap it in wax paper, and chill it for 30 minutes. Roll out the dough into a rectangle about 1/3 inch thick and cover it with 3 tablespoons hard butter cut in thin shavings. Fold the upper third of the dough over the center and fold the lower third of dough over the upper flap, making 3 layers of dough. Give the dough a quarter turn, roll it out thinly into a rectangle and fold it again into thirds. Chill the dough well.

Baked Diamond Lattice Crust   THE bottom layer of dough must hang 1/2 inch over the edge of the pie plate. Roll out the second half of the dough thinly and cut it into strips 1/2 inch wide with a floured knife or pastry wheel. Place strips of dough 1 inch apart over the filling. Place other strips diagonally across them to make diamond-shaped openings. Or weave the strips in and out, beginning with the center strip and working out to both sides. Trim the ends of the strips. Moisten the overhanging edge with cold water, turn it over the strips, and flute the edge or crimp it with the tines of a fork.

Pie Shell   ROLL out pie dough 1/8 inch thick and line a pie plate. Trim, leaving a 1/2-inch margin all round. Fold the edge and flute it with the fingers to make a standing rim. Chill for at least 30 minutes before baking. Prick the dough with a fork, line the shell with wax paper, and fill it with rice or beans to prevent the dough from puffing. Bake in a very hot oven (450° F.) for about 15 minutes, or until the shell is golden. Discard rice or beans and paper and cool the shell before filling it.

Brazil Nut Pie Shell   GRIND 2 cups Brazil nuts and mix them with 1/4 cup sugar. Press the sweetened nuts firmly on the bottom and sides of a pie plate and chill before adding the filling.

CRUSH zwieback or vanilla, chocolate, or ginger wafers, or graham crackers *Crumb Shell*
with a rolling pin and press the crumbs through a sieve to make 1 1/2 cups
fine crumbs. Mix the crumbs with 1/4 cup each of sugar and melted sweet
butter. Butter a pie plate generously and pat the cookie crumbs thickly
over the bottom and sides. Chill before filling. Zwieback crumbs may be
flavored with cinnamon or a little grated lemon rind, depending upon the
filling that is used. The crust may be toasted for 5 minutes in a very hot
oven (450° F.) and cooled.

BEAT 3 egg whites with a pinch of salt until they are foamy. Add 1/4 *Meringue*
teaspoon cream of tartar or 1 teaspoon lemon juice and continue to beat *Nest*
until the egg whites stand in soft peaks when the beater is withdrawn.
Gradually beat in 3/4 cup fine granulated sugar, a little at a time, and
continue to beat until all the sugar is added and the meringue is thick and
glossy. Stir in 1 teaspoon vanilla extract. Spread the meringue thickly over
the bottom and sides of a pie plate, building it up half an inch above the
edge of the plate to form a nest. Bake the shell in a very slow oven (250° F.)
for 30 to 45 minutes, or until the surface of the nest is crusty, but still
pure white. Loosen the meringue from the pan while it is still warm and
cool it before adding the filling.

 *Deep glass pie plates are particularly suitable for double-crusted fruit
pies; depth helps to hold in the juices and the glass allows the cook to
make sure of a crisply browned bottom crust. Fruit pies taste best warm;
reheating at serving time improves their flavor.*

LINE a pie plate with rich pastry and fill it with 1 quart very thinly sliced *Sour Cream*
or grated tart apples, piling them up high in the center. Sprinkle over the *Apple Pie*
apples 1 scant cup sugar, white or brown, mixed with 1/2 teaspoon cinnamon.
Pour over all 1 cup sour cream and bake the pie in a very hot oven
(450° F) for 10 minutes. Reduce the temperature to moderate (350° F.)
and bake the pie for another 20 minutes, or until the apples are tender The
pie may be covered with strips of pastry, lattice fashion, before baking.

LINE a 9-inch pie plate with pie dough and fill it with about 5 cups sliced *Honey*
tart apples. Sprinkle over the apples 1 teaspoon flour mixed with 1/2 tea- *Apple Pie*

spoon cinnamon, 1 tablespoon lemon juice, and 1 teaspoon grated lemon rind. Dot the surface with 2 tablespoons butter and cover with a latticework of pastry. Bake the pie in a very hot oven (450° F.) for 10 minutes, reduce the temperature to moderate (350° F.), and bake for another 30 minutes, or until the apples are tender and the crust is lightly browned. Remove the pie from the oven and pour 2/3 cup honey through the openings in the top crust. Let the pie stand for at least 30 minutes and serve it sprinkled with confectioners' sugar.

Pecan Raisin Apple Pie

PEEL, core, and slice thinly 6 to 9 cooking apples, depending on their size. Mix with 1/4 cup chopped pecans, 3 tablespoons dry red wine, a pinch of salt, 1/2 cup sugar (more if the apples are very tart), 1/2 cup seedless raisins, 1 teaspoon grated orange peel, and 3 tablespoons cherry jam or preserves. Cook gently for 15 minutes, stirring frequently to prevent the mixture from scorching.

Line a 9-inch pie plate with dough, fill it with the apple mixture and cover with a top crust pierced to allow the steam to escape. Bake the pie for 10 minutes in a very hot oven (450° F.), reduce the temperature to moderate (350° F.), and bake the pie for 30 minutes longer.

Deep Dish Apple Pie

PEEL, core, and slice 8 large tart apples. Put the slices in a deep baking dish, sprinkle them with 1 cup sugar and the juice and grated rind of 1 orange, and dot with 1/4 cup butter.

Roll out pie dough 1/8 inch thick and cut a small round hole in the center. Place the dough over the apples, press it firmly against the edge of the baking dish, and trim. Bake the pie in a very hot oven (450° F.) for 15 minutes, reduce the temperature to moderate (350° F.), and bake the pie for about 45 minutes longer, or until the crust is golden and the apples are tender.

Remove the pie from the oven and pour 1/4 cup rum through a small funnel into the hole in the crust. Serve the pie warm, with a pitcher of heavy cream.

Blackberry Pie

SIFT 3 tablespoons flour with 1 cup sugar and mix lightly with 1 tablespoon grated orange rind and 3 cups blackberries. Fill a pie plate lined with pie dough with the fruit and dot the surface with 2 tablespoons butter.

Cover the fruit with a diamond lattice. Bake the pie in a hot oven (400° F.) for 15 minutes, reduce the temperature to moderately slow (325° F.) and bake the pie for 20 minutes more, until the crust is well browned. Pour 2 tablespoons blackberry brandy into the apertures and serve the pie hot, with a pitcher of heavy cream.

Blueberry Pie

MAKE a rich pie pastry, using 3 cups flour, and use a little more than half of this to line a 9-inch pie pan. The crust should be thicker than it is for other pies.

Mix 1 scant cup sugar, 1/8 teaspoon salt, and 1/4 cup flour. Sprinkle a few tablespoons of this mixture evenly over the bottom crust. Toss the remainder with 4 cups washed and well-drained blueberries and pour the fruit into the pie shell. A little ground cloves, cardamom, or nutmeg may be added, if you like. Dot the fruit with 1 1/2 tablespoons butter in pea-sized pieces, adjust the top crust, seal the edges, and cut several slashes for the escape of steam. Bake the pie for 10 minutes in a very hot oven (450° F.), reduce the temperature to moderate (350° F.), and bake the pie for 30 minutes longer.

Date Pie

COMBINE 1 1/2 cups chopped dates, 1 beaten egg, 1 cup sour cream, 3/4 cup brown sugar, 1/2 cup chopped walnuts, 2 tablespoons brandy, and a pinch each of salt and nutmeg, and beat thoroughly. Turn the mixture into a 9-inch pie plate lined with pie dough and cover it with a lattice topping. Bake the pie in a hot oven (425° F.) for 10 minutes, reduce the temperature to moderately slow (325° F.), and bake the pie for about 30 minutes longer, or until the crust is browned and the filling is set. Serve with unsweetened whipped cream.

Cherry Pie

PUT 1 quart pitted, sour cherries and their juice in a saucepan. Add 1 cup sugar mixed with 1 tablespoon cornstarch and cook, stirring, until the juice is slightly thickened. Add a few drops of almond extract and more sugar, if necessary. Cool the mixture.

Line a 9-inch pie plate with flaky pie dough, fill it with the fruit, and cover the fruit with a lattice topping. Bake the pie in a moderate oven (350° F.) for about 45 minutes, or until the crust is golden.

Nectarine Pie

LINE a deep pie dish or casserole with pie dough and fill it with sliced nectarines. Sprinkle the fruit with 1 tablespoon lemon juice, 1/2 teaspoon

745

cinnamon, and 1/4 teaspoon salt. Cover the filling with a layer of pie dough cut to fit and prick this pastry lid with the tines of a fork.

Bake the pie in a very hot oven (450° F.) for 10 minutes. Reduce the temperature to moderate (350° F.) and bake the pie for about 30 minutes longer, or until the nectarines are tender and the crust is golden. Remove the pie from the oven, carefully lift the top crust, and sweeten the hot fruit liberally with sugar. Sprinkle the fruit with 2 tablespoons brandy and 1 tablespoon melted butter and mix gently but thoroughly. Replace the crust and serve the pie hot with a brandy hard sauce or cold with heavy cream, plain or whipped.

Peach Skillet Pie

ROLL out pie dough into a large square 1/8 inch thick. Arrange the dough in a large heavy skillet, letting the corners hang over the edge. Fill the skillet with sliced peaches and sprinkle the peaches with 1/2 cup sugar, 1/2 teaspoon nutmeg, 1 tablespoon lemon juice, and a pinch of salt. Dot the fruit with 2 tablespoons butter and fold the overhanging corners of dough into the center of the pie. Bake the pie in a very hot oven (450° F.) for 10 minutes. Reduce the temperature to moderately hot (375° F.), and bake the pie for 30 minutes longer. Serve hot, with heavy cream.

Sour Cream Peach Pie

TOSS 5 cups sliced, fresh peaches lightly with 1/2 cup brown sugar, 1 tablespoon cornstarch, 1/2 teaspoon cinnamon, 1/4 teaspoon nutmeg, and a pinch of salt. Turn the fruit into a pie plate lined with rich pie dough, pour 1 1/2 cups sour cream over the fruit, and bake the pie in a hot oven (400° F.) for about 25 minutes, or until the crust is golden. Serve hot or cold, topped with sour cream.

Pear Pie

LINE a 9-inch pie plate with pie dough. Peel and core 8 large cooking pears and slice them into the plate. Sprinkle the slices with 1/2 cup sugar, 1 tablespoon lemon juice, the grated rind of half a lemon, 1/2 teaspoon vanilla, and a sprinkling of nutmeg. Cover the filling with a lattice topping and bake the pie in a very hot oven (450° F.) for 10 minutes. Reduce the temperature to moderate (350° F.) and bake the pie for about 30 minutes longer, or until the crust is golden brown.

Raisin Pie

IN a saucepan combine 1/3 cup lemon juice, 1/2 cup orange juice, 1 teaspoon grated lemon rind, 2 teaspoons grated orange rind, 1 cup light-brown sugar, a pinch of salt, 2 cups seeded raisins, and 1 1/2 cups water and bring the mixture to a boil. Mix 4 1/2 tablespoons flour to a paste with 1/4 cup cold water and stir it gradually into the hot mixture. Cook, stirring, for about 5 minutes, or until the mixture is thickened.

Line a pie plate with dough, pour in the filling, and cover with a lattice topping. Bake the pie in a very hot oven (450° F.) for 10 minutes, reduce the temperature to moderate (350° F.), and bake the pie for about 30 minutes longer.

IN a large bowl combine 1 pound each of currants, Malaga raisins, sultana raisins, candied cherries, suet, finely chopped, brown sugar, and apples, peeled, cored, and finely chopped. Stir in about 1 tablespoon mixed ground nutmeg, cloves, and cinnamon, or spice to taste, and moisten the mixture with 2 cups each of brandy and ale. Store the mincemeat, covered, in the refrigerator for 1 week, stirring thoroughly every day.

Brandied Mincemeat Pie

Line two 10-inch pie plates with flaky dough and fill them with mincemeat. Cover the mincemeat with a thin layer of dough, flute the edges, and make several slits in the top. Bake the pies in a very hot oven (450° F.) for about 10 minutes, reduce the temperature to moderate (350° F.), and bake the pies for about 35 minutes, or until the crusts are golden. While the pies are hot, pour 1/4 cup brandy through the slits in the crust into each pie. Serve warm.

Any leftover mincemeat may be stored, covered, in the refrigerator for several months.

CUT 2 pounds tender rhubarb stalks into 1-inch pieces. There should be 4 cups fruit. Mix the rhubarb with 1 1/2 cups sugar, the grated rind of 1 lemon, and 2 tablespoons flour, and put the mixture in a deep pie dish, with an egg cup or custard cup inverted in the center to draw up the juice and prevent the crust from sagging. Cover the dish with pie dough and press the edges to the dish with the tines of a fork.

Deep Dish Rhubarb Pie

Slash the dough in several places for the steam to escape and bake the pie in a very hot oven (450° F.) for 10 minutes. Reduce the temperature to moderate (350° F.) and bake the pie for 25 minutes longer. Sprinkle the crust with sugar and bake for another 10 minutes, or until the sugar is melted.

Custard pies, a designation that here includes all pie mixtures made with eggs, are baked without a top covering. Put them in a hot oven for 10 to 15 minutes to set the pastry crust; reduce the heat and continue to bake at the lower temperature suitable for egg cookery until the custard is cooked. Insert the testing knife near the center of the pie, not at the center. Custards continue to bake on their retained heat for several minutes after they are removed from the oven.

Creole Pecan Pie

CREAM 1/4 cup butter with 1/2 cup sugar and beat in 3 eggs, 1 cup dark corn syrup, and 1 1/4 cups coarsely chopped pecans. Pour the custard into an unbaked pie shell and bake the pie for 10 minutes in a hot oven (400° F.). Reduce the temperature to slow (300° F.) and bake the pie for 35 to 40 minutes longer, or until the crust is browned and the filling is set.

Maple Walnut Pie

SUBSTITUTE maple syrup for the corn syrup specified for Creole pecan pie, and use walnuts instead of pecans.

Tyler Pudding Pie

IN a saucepan combine 1 1/2 cups each of brown sugar and white sugar and 1 cup each of butter and heavy cream. Place the saucepan over boiling water and cook the mixture, stirring occasionally, until the sugar is dissolved. Beat 5 eggs until they are thick and pale in color. Gradually beat the hot cream-sugar mixture into the eggs, and stir in 1 teaspoon vanilla extract.

Pour the filling into a 9-inch pie plate lined with flaky pastry dough and dust it with freshly grated nutmeg. Bake the pie in a very hot oven (450° F.) for 10 minutes. Reduce the temperature to moderately slow (325° F.) and bake the pie for 30 minutes longer.

Vinegar Pie

BEAT together 4 eggs and 1/2 cup sugar. Add 1/2 teaspoon salt, 2 teaspoons vinegar, and 1/4 teaspoon grated nutmeg. Add gradually, stirring constantly, 3 cups hot milk and pour the mixture into a pie plate lined with pie dough. Bake the pie in a very hot oven (450° F.) for 10 minutes, reduce the temperature to moderate (350° F.) and bake the pie for about 25 minutes longer, or until the crust is brown and the filling is set.

CREAM 1/4 cup butter and stir in 3 cups brown sugar and 2 tablespoons flour. Mix well and beat in 3 well-beaten eggs, 1/2 cup cream, 1/8 teaspoon salt, and 1/2 teaspoon vanilla. Pour the mixture into a 9-inch pie plate lined with pastry and bake the pie in a hot oven (400° F.) for 5 minutes. Reduce the temperature to moderate (350° F.) and bake the pie for 20 to 25 minutes, or until the filling is just set. Serve cold, with unsweetened whipped cream flavored with vanilla extract.

Chess Pie

BEAT 4 eggs until they are very light, add 1 1/2 cups boiled, mashed sweet potatoes and 1/3 cup sugar, and beat all together. Stir in 2 tablespoons honey, 1/2 cup crushed black walnuts or pecans, 2/3 cup milk, 1/3 cup orange juice, 1 teaspoon vanilla extract and a pinch of salt. Pour the mixture into an unbaked pie shell and bake the pie in a very hot oven (450° F.) for 10 minutes. Reduce the temperature to moderate (350° F.) and bake the pie for 30 minutes longer, or until a silver knife inserted near the center comes out clean. Cool the pie and spread it with whipped cream flavored with 1 tablespoon grated orange peel and 1/2 teaspoon nutmeg.

Sweet Potato Pie

HEAT 1 cup sour cream in the top of a double boiler. In a mixing bowl mix together 1/2 cup sour cream, 1 1/2 cups pumpkin purée, the beaten yolks of 3 eggs, 1 cup brown sugar, 3/4 teaspoon cinnamon and 1/4 teaspoon each of nutmeg, ground ginger, and salt. Add the seasoned purée slowly to the hot cream and cook the mixture over hot water, stirring constantly, until it is thick. Cool the custard and fold into it the stiffly beaten whites of 3 eggs. Pour the custard into a lightly baked 9-inch pie shell. Bake the pie in a moderate oven (350° F.) for 20 minutes, or until the top is nicely browned. Serve with whipped cream.

Pumpkin Sour Cream Pie

BEAT 8 egg yolks and 3/4 cup sugar until the mixture is very thick, creamy, and light in color. Stir in the juice of 3 lemons and 1 teaspoon grated lemon rind and cook the mixture over simmering water until it is thickened. Cool slightly and fold in the stiffly beaten whites of 8 eggs. Turn the filling into a baked 9-inch pie shell, piling it high in swirls, and bake the pie in a moderate oven (350° F.) for about 15 minutes, or until the filling is set and golden brown. Cool, and sprinkle with confectioners' sugar.

Lemon Mousse Pie

BEAT 3 egg yolks until they are light and lemon colored and add 1/2 cup freshly squeezed lime juice and 1 teaspoon grated lime rind. Beat in the

Key Lime Pie

contents of a 15-ounce can of sweetened condensed milk and a drop or two of green food coloring to attain a natural lime tint. Pour the custard into a baked pie shell with a fluted standing rim. Beat 4 egg whites until they are stiff but not dry and beat in gradually 1/2 cup fine granulated sugar and 1 teaspoon lime juice. Spread the meringue thickly over the filling, bringing it to the crust all around and pulling it into irregular peaks. Bake the pie in a moderate oven (350° F.) for about 15 minutes, until the meringue is delicately browned. Serve the pie well chilled. This unusual recipe originated in the Florida Keys.

Prune Pie   WASH and soak 1 pound dried prunes in hot water for 2 hours. Cook the prunes for about 25 minutes, until they are tender, drain them, and force the flesh through a fine sieve to make 1 cup prune purée.

Beat 4 egg whites with a pinch of salt until they are stiff but not dry. Gradually beat in 1/2 cup sugar and continue to beat until the meringue is thick and glossy. Stir 1 tablespoon lemon juice into the prune purée and fold the purée into the meringue. Turn the mixture into a 9-inch baked pie shell and bake it in a moderate oven (350° F.) for about 20 minutes, or until it is golden brown.

A fairly recent addition to the pie family is the cream pie. In all of its versions, the prepared filling is turned into a prepared pie shell. These pies are assembled, rather than baked.

Curaçao   IN the top of a double boiler combine 2 cups hot milk and 1/4 cup each
Custard Pie   of sugar and Curaçao. Add 8 egg yolks beaten with 1/4 cup heavy cream and cook the mixture over boiling water, stirring constantly, until the custard thickens. Pour the custard into a bowl set in another bowl of cracked ice and stir it until it cools. Turn the cooled cream into a baked pie shell and sprinkle it with 1 tablespoon each of finely grated orange rind and chopped pistachio nuts. Chill well before serving.

Fresh Coconut   IN the top of a double boiler, combine 1/3 cup sifted flour, 1/3 teaspoon
Meringue Pie   salt, and 1/4 cup sugar, and stir in 1/2 cup milk. Add 1 1/2 cups hot milk, stirring constantly. Cook the mixture over hot water until it thickens, stirring constantly. Beat 3 or 4 egg yolks until they are light and lemon

colored. Blend a little of the mixture from the double boiler with the egg yolks, and return the egg mixture to the pan. Add 1 cup grated fresh coconut and cook for 3 or 4 minutes longer. Stir the cream over cracked ice until it is cool. Add 1 teaspoon vanilla. Pour the mixture into a baked pie shell and top it with a meringue made of 3 stiffly beaten egg whites sweetened with 6 tablespoons sugar. Bake the pie in a moderately slow oven (325° F.) for 15 minutes, or until the meringue is delicately browned. Chill well before serving.

PEEL and slice ripe persimmons, discard the seeds and press the pulp through a fine sieve. Mix 2 cups of this persimmon purée with an equal amount of whipped cream. Add a dash of lemon juice, and sugar to taste. Chill well and pour the filling into a baked pie shell or into tart shells. Serve at once.

Persimmon Pie

Other fresh fruits may be puréed and used in the same way.

Fruit Purée Cream Pie

HEAT 1/2 cup prune juice and dissolve in it 1 tablespoon gelatin soaked in 1/4 cup water. Stir in 1/2 cup sugar, a pinch of salt, 1 tablespoon brandy, and 1 1/2 cups purée of cooked prunes. Cool the mixture and fold in 1 cup heavy cream, whipped. Pour the filling into a baked pie shell and garnish the surface of the pie with whipped cream and toasted almond slivers.

Prune Cream Pie

Dried apricots may be substituted for the prunes.

Apricot Cream Pie

BEAT 4 egg yolks and 1/4 cup sugar until the mixture is thick and pale in color. Stir in gradually 1 cup hot milk and cook the mixture over boiling water, stirring constantly, until the custard thickens. Remove the saucepan from the heat, flavor it with 1 teaspoon vanilla extract, and stir it over cracked ice until it is well chilled.

Strawberry Cream Pie

Beat 4 egg whites until they are stiff and fold them into 2 cups heavy cream, whipped and sweetened to taste. Fold in the cold custard and 2 cups sliced strawberries. If frozen, sugared strawberries are used, adjust the sweetening to taste. Turn the filling into a baked pie shell and serve the pie at once.

Other berries and fruits, such as peaches, chopped, may be used in the same way.

Berry or Fruit Cream Pie

Butterscotch Pie

COOK 1 1/2 cups brown sugar and 1/2 cup butter in the top of a double boiler over low heat, stirring gently, until the butter is melted and the mixture is well blended. Beat 4 egg yolks with 4 1/2 tablespoons flour and add 1 1/2 cups warm milk. Add this mixture slowly to the butter-sugar mixture and cook over low direct heat, stirring until the custard is thick. Put the pan over boiling water and cook, stirring occasionally, for 10 minutes. Stir in 2 teaspoons vanilla and 1/2 cup crushed pecans and pour the filling into a baked pie shell.

Beat 3 egg whites with a pinch of salt until they are stiff. Gradually add 6 tablespoons sugar and continue to beat the meringue until it is thick and glossy. Spread the meringue over the filling and brown it in a moderate oven (350° F.)

The meringue may be omitted and the cooled pie spread with whipped cream.

Eggnog Pie

IN the top of a double boiler beat 3 egg yolks and 1/3 cup sugar until the mixture is thick and pale in color. Stir in 1 tablespoon gelatin, softened in 1/4 cup water, and 1 cup hot milk, and cook over boiling water, stirring constantly, until the cream is smooth. Stir the cream over cracked ice until it is cool and begins to set. Fold in 3 egg whites, stiffly beaten, 1 cup heavy cream, whipped, and 2 tablespoons dark rum and turn the mixture into a baked pie shell. Decorate with whipped cream, sprinkle with nutmeg, and chill until serving time.

Black Bottom Pie

IN the top of a double boiler combine 4 egg yolks, 1/2 cup sugar mixed with 1 1/4 tablespoons cornstarch, and 2 cups scalded milk. Cook the mixture over boiling water, stirring, until it is thick enough to coat a spoon. Stir into the custard 1 tablespoon gelatin softened in 1/4 cup water. Divide the custard in half.

To one part, add 2 squares unsweetened chocolate, melted and cooled, and 1 teaspoon vanilla. Pour it into a cooled baked 9-inch pastry shell or a chocolate- or ginger-wafer crumb shell. Chill the chocolate custard until it is firm.

Beat 4 egg whites with 1/4 teaspoon cream of tartar, add gradually 1/2 cup sugar, and continue to beat the meringue until it holds its shape. Cool the vanilla custard, add 3 tablespoons rum, and fold in the meringue. Spread the rum custard over the chocolate, piping a ribbon of custard around the edge with a pastry bag, if desired. At serving time, spread the pie with sweetened whipped cream and sprinkle it with shaved or grated semisweet chocolate.

COMBINE 1 cup almond paste and 2 cups milk and stir over low heat until the almond milk is hot and smooth. Stir the almond milk gradually into 4 beaten egg yolks and cook the mixture over boiling water, stirring constantly, until the custard coats the spoon. Stir in 1 tablespoon gelatin softened in 1/4 cup water, then stir the cream over cracked ice until it is cool and begins to set. Stir in 1 teaspoon vanilla or 1/2 teaspoon almond extract, fold in 2 cups heavy cream, whipped, and turn the filling into a baked pie shell. Sprinkle with grated chocolate and chill before serving.

Almond Cream Pie

BEAT a large egg with 2 tablespoons sugar until the mixture is very thick and pale. Fold in 6 tablespoons sifted flour and 2 tablespoons melted butter. Bake the spongecake batter in a buttered pie plate in a moderate oven (350° F.) for about 30 minutes, or until the cake tests done. Turn the cake out on a rack to cool and split it into 2 layers.

Rum Cake Pie

Beat 3 eggs with 5 tablespoons sugar and 6 tablespoons sifted flour. Add gradually 2 cups hot milk and cook over boiling water, stirring constantly, for about 10 minutes, until the custard is thick and smooth. Cool over cracked ice, stirring occasionally, and fold in 1 1/2 cups heavy cream, whipped, and 2 tablespoons or more dark rum.

Fill a baked pie shell half full of the cooled custard and top it with a layer of cake. Add the rest of the cream and the second cake layer. Sprinkle the cake generously with rum, decorate it with whipped cream, and sprinkle it with shavings of dark sweet chocolate.

Chiffon pies get their name from their light and airy texture; they get their texture from stiffly beaten egg whites. The shells for chiffon pies may be made of any pie or tart dough, of sweetened crumbs, or of meringue.

SOAK the grated rind of 1 lime in 2/3 cup strained lime juice for 1 hour.

Lime Chiffon Pie

Beat 5 egg yolks vigorously, adding gradually 1 cup sugar. Stir in the lime juice, strained through a fine sieve to remove the rind, and cook over simmering water, stirring constantly, for about 5 minutes, or until the custard is thickened. Stir in 4 teaspoons gelatin softened in 1/4 cup cold water. Cool until the filling begins to set. Beat 5 egg whites until they are stiff and beat in gradually 1/2 cup sugar. Fold the meringue into the lime filling and pile the filling into a baked graham cracker crumb shell.

753

Chocolate Rum
Chiffon Pie

MELT 2 ounces unsweetened chocolate over boiling water with 1 tablespoon strong black coffee, stirring until the chocolate is melted and smooth. Stir in 2/3 cup sugar, a pinch of salt, and 1/2 cup hot milk and cook for 3 minutes, stirring constantly. Stir in 1 tablespoon gelatin softened in 1/4 cup water. Stir the cream over cracked ice until it is cool and thickened. Beat in 2 tablespoons rum, fold in 1 1/2 cups heavy cream, whipped, and pile the mixture into a baked pie shell. Decorate the top with 1/2 cup heavy cream, whipped and pressed through a pastry bag fitted with a fluted tube, and sprinkle with paper-thin shavings of bitter chocolate.

Coffee
Chiffon Pie

IN the top of a double boiler combine 4 egg yolks, 1/2 cup sugar, a pinch of salt, and 1/2 cup strong black coffee. Cook over boiling water, stirring constantly, until the custard coats the spoon. Stir in 1 tablespoon gelatin, softened in 1/4 cup water, and 2 tablespoons Cognac or Armagnac and stir over cracked ice until the custard is cool and thickened. Beat 4 egg whites until they are stiff, gradually beat in 1/2 cup sugar, and fold the meringue into the coffee custard. Turn the filling into a baked pie shell, chill, and top with whipped cream.

Apricot
Chiffon Pie

HEAT 1/2 cup apricot juice and stir in 1 tablespoon gelatin softened in 1/4 cup water. Stir in 1/2 cup sugar, a pinch of salt, 2 tablespoons lemon juice, and 1 1/2 cups cooked apricot purée. Cool, fold in 1 cup heavy cream, whipped, and turn the filling into a baked pie shell. Garnish with whipped cream and sprinkle with pistachios.

Cranberry
Chiffon Pie

COOK 2 cups cranberries in 1/2 cup water until the skins burst, and press the fruit through a fine sieve. Bring the cranberry purée to a boil, add 1/4 cup orange juice, 1/2 cup sugar, and 1 tablespoon gelatin softened in 1/4 cup cold water, and stir until the sugar is dissolved. Cool.

Beat 3 egg whites until they are stiff and gradually beat in 6 tablespoons sugar. Fold the meringue and 3/4 cup heavy cream, whipped, into the cranberry mixture and turn the filling into a baked pie shell. Chill until firm.

Raspberry
Chiffon Pie

SOFTEN 1 tablespoon gelatin in 1/4 cup Sherry and dissolve it over hot water. Beat 3 egg yolks with 2/3 cup sugar and a pinch of salt until they are pale and light and add 1 1/2 tablespoons lemon juice. Crush enough raspberries to make 1/2 cup pulp and juice, strain the purée, and add it to the egg. Cook the mixture in the top of a double boiler over hot water, stirring constantly, until it thickens slightly. Add the gelatin mixture and stir the cream over cracked ice until it is cool. Chill the mixture until it is thick and fold in 1 1/2 cups fresh raspberries and 3 stiffly beaten egg whites. Pour the mixture into a meringue nest or baked pie shell and chill it well before serving.

SOFTEN 2 teaspoons gelatin in 3 tablespoons water. In a double boiler combine 2 beaten egg yolks, 3/4 cup warm milk, 1/4 cup sugar, and a pinch of salt and cook over hot water, stirring constantly, until the custard coats the spoon. Stir in the softened gelatin and 2 tablespoons green Chartreuse or Curaçao and cool.

Fresh Fig Chiffon Pie

Fold into the custard 1 1/2 cups diced fresh figs and 1 cup heavy cream, whipped. Beat 2 egg whites until they are stiff and beat in 2 tablespoons sugar. Fold the meringue into the filling, turn the filling into a baked pie shell, and chill the pie until it is firm. Sprinkle lightly with nutmeg before serving.

Tart doughs are always made with butter, they sometimes include eggs, and are usually sweetened.

SIFT 2 cups flour onto a pastry board and make a well in the center. In the well put 3/4 cup soft sweet butter, 1 1/2 tablespoons sugar, and 1/2 teaspoon salt. Work these to a smooth paste, then quickly work in the flour, adding gradually about 5 to 6 tablespoons water, or enough to make a firm dough that just cleans the board. Do not handle the dough unnecessarily. Mix it well but lightly. Wrap the dough in wax paper and chill it for 2 hours.

Pâte à Foncer
PLAIN TART DOUGH

SIFT 1 cup flour onto a pastry board and make a well in the center. In the well put 1/3 cup soft sweet butter, 1 egg, 1/4 cup sugar, and a pinch of salt. The grated rind of 1 lemon or a few drops of vanilla extract may also be added. Mix the center ingredients to a smooth paste, then quickly work in the flour, adding a very little cold water, if necessary, to make a firm dough that cleans the board. Wrap the dough in wax paper and chill it for at least 1 hour. Use to line one 8-inch pie plate or flan ring.

Pâte Sucrée
SWEET TART DOUGH

Mürbteig
RICH TART DOUGH

SIFT 1 cup flour onto a pastry board and make a well in the center. In the well put 1/2 cup soft sweet butter, 1 tablespoon sugar, 1 egg yolk, and a pinch of salt. The grated rind of 1 lemon may be added. Mix the center ingredients to a smooth paste, then quickly work in the flour, adding a very little cold water if needed to make a firm dough that just cleans the board. Wrap the dough in wax paper and chill it for at least 1 hour. Use to line one 8-inch pie plate or flan ring.

Flan Shell

ON a lightly floured board roll chilled tart dough into a circle to 1/4 inch thick. Slip the dough over a buttered flan ring on a buttered baking sheet and press it gently but firmly against the inner side of the ring. Make a small fold of the dough around the inner top edge of the ring and cut away the dough above the fold. Then raise the fold to make a standing border and flute the border with thumb and index finger, or pinch it all around with a pastry pincher. Prick the dough with the tines of a fork and chill it for 30 minutes.

To bake an unfilled flan shell, cover the dough with wax paper and weight the paper down with 1 cup dry rice or beans. Bake the shell in a hot oven (400° F.) for 10 minutes, reduce the temperature to moderate (350° F.) and bake the shell for 15 minutes longer, or until the crust is a pale gold. Discard the rice or beans and paper, cool, and fill with a prepared filling.

If the dough is to be baked with the filling, the shell should be chilled for 30 minutes, filled with fruit, sugar, and spices, and baked as indicated in the individual recipe.

Individual
Tart Shells

ROLL any tart dough into a sheet 1/4 inch thick. Cut rounds of dough to line tart pans or the backs of muffin tins. Fit the dough into the pans and prick it well with a fork. A little rice in foil or in wax paper in each pan will help the shells to keep their shape. Rounds of dough may be fitted over the backs of muffin tins by pinching the excess dough at regular intervals to shape the shells. Tart shells should be baked in a very hot oven (450° F.) for about 15 minutes, or until they are delicately browned.

The tart recipes that follow are typical of the many sorts of fruit pastry that appear on the French pastry tray; infinite variations are possible.

PARE, core, and quarter 6 cooking apples and put them in a saucepan with 1/2 cup each of water and sugar and 2 tablespoons butter. Cover the saucepan tightly and cook the apples over moderate heat until they are tender. Press the apples through a fine sieve or purée them in a blender and let the purée cool.

Line a flan ring with tart dough and fill it halfway with the apple purée. Peel, core, and slice 4 small cooking apples and arrange the slices over the apple purée in a spiral, starting at the center and working out, the slices overlapping. Sprinkle the fruit with sugar and bake the tart in a hot oven (400° F.) for 25 to 30 minutes, or until the apples are tender and the crust is golden. Glaze the hot tart with apricot jam melted and thinned with a little hot water to spreading consistency.

*Tarte aux
Pommes*
APPLE TART

BUTTER an 8-inch pie plate thickly and cover the bottom with 3/4 cup fine granulated sugar. Over the sugar arrange about 6 tart apples, peeled, quartered, and cored. Sprinkle the apples with 1/2 teaspoon nutmeg, and the grated rind and juice of half a lemon, and dot with 2 tablespoons butter.

Roll tart dough 1/8 inch thick, cut out a circle 8 inches in diameter, and lay the circle over the apples. Bake the tart in a moderately hot oven (375° F.) for about 30 minutes, or until the apples are tender, the crust is golden, and the sugar is well caramelized in the bottom of the plate. Invert the tart on a serving dish and serve it warm, with whipped cream sugared and flavored to taste.

*Tarte des
Demoiselles
Tatin*
UPSIDE-DOWN
APPLE TART

Peaches, apricots, or pears may be used instead of the apples.

*Upside-Down
Peach, Apricot,
or Pear Tart*

LINE a flan ring with a tart dough and fill it with 1 pound dark, sweet, pitted cherries. Combine 1/2 cup flour and 2 tablespoons sugar. Stir in 1 egg lightly beaten with 2 cups milk, 2 tablespoons Cognac, and 3 tablespoons melted butter and pour the batter over the cherries. Bake the tart in a moderate oven (350° F.) for 35 to 40 minutes, or until the crust is golden. Serve warm, sprinkled with sugar.

Clafouti
CHERRY TART

FILL a baked tart shell with about 2 cups washed, dried, and chilled blueberries. Pour over them the following glaze: Bring slowly to a boil 1 cup blueberries and 2 tablespoons water. Cover the pan and simmer the berries

*Blueberry
Tart*

until they are soft, then put them through a sieve into a double boiler. Stir in 2 tablespoons sugar and 1 1/2 tablespoons cornstarch mixed with a little cold water or lemon juice to taste. Cook the glaze and stir it over hot water until it is thick and clear. Let the glaze cool for 15 minutes and pour it over the blueberries in the shell. Chill the tart well before serving it.

Tarte aux Groseilles Vertes
GOOSEBERRY TART

LINE a flan ring with tart dough and fill it with 1 quart gooseberries, washed and tailed. Sprinkle 1 cup sugar over the gooseberries and bake the tart in a moderate oven (350° F.) for 20 minutes. Drip over the berries 1 egg yolk lightly beaten with 3 tablespoons heavy cream and continue to bake for 15 minutes longer, or until the crust is lightly browned.

Tarte aux Raisins
GREEN GRAPE TART

LINE a flan ring with tart pastry and fill it with 2 cups seedless green grapes.
Make a batter by combining 3 tablespoons flour, 1 egg, slightly beaten, 1 tablespoon sugar, a pinch of salt, and 1/2 cup milk and pour it over the grapes. Bake the tart in a moderately hot oven (375° F.) for 40 minutes, or until the grapes are tender and the top is delicately browned.

Tarte aux Pêches Chantilly
WHIPPED CREAM PEACH TART

FILL a baked and cooled flan shell with whipped cream sweetened to taste and flavored with vanilla. Cover the cream with ripe peaches, peeled and halved, cut side down, and glaze the peaches with 2 tablespoons peach or apricot jam melted with 2 tablespoons boiling water and pressed through a fine sieve. Sprinkle the tart with shredded blanched almonds, toasted to a golden brown, and chill it before serving.

Whipped Cream Nectarine Tart

Nectarines may be substituted for the peaches.

Tarte aux Pêches
PEACH TART

LINE a flan ring with tart dough and sprinkle the dough with 1/2 cup sugar. Cover the sugar with fresh peaches, peeled, pitted, and halved, cut side down, in a spiral from the center, the halves overlapping. Bake the tart in a moderate oven (350° F.) for 15 minutes. Drip over the fruit 1 egg yolk beaten with 3 tablespoons heavy cream and continue to bake for 15 minutes longer, or until the fruit is tender and the crust is a golden brown.

Tarte aux Prunes
PLUM TART

LINE a flan ring with a tart dough and sprinkle it with dry cake crumbs. Halve and stone 3 pounds plums and arrange them cut side down on the cake crumbs. Sprinkle the plums generously with sugar and bake the tart in a hot oven (400° F.) for 25 to 30 minutes, or until the crust is golden and the fruit is tender. If the plums are blue or red, glaze them with melted currant jelly. If they are yellow plums, glaze them with apricot jam thinned with a little boiling water and pressed through a fine sieve.

COOK 12 to 15 prunes until they are tender in 1 1/2 cups red wine to which a scant 1/2 cup sugar and 1 or 2 slices of lemon have been added. Remove the pits and cool the prunes. Line a buttered tart pan with tart dough, building up the edge to hold in fruit and juice. Fill it with the fruit and cover the top with strips of the pastry. Brush the latticework with a mixture of 1 egg beaten with a little milk. Bake the tart in a very hot oven (450° F.) for about 15 minutes, or until the pastry is browned.

Tarte aux Pruneaux
PRUNE TART

IN a saucepan beat 1 whole egg, 1 egg yolk, and 3 tablespoons each of sugar and flour until the mixture is light and fluffy. Soften 2 teaspoons gelatin in 1 tablespoon cold water and dissolve it in 3/4 cup hot milk. Add the milk to the egg mixture and cook over moderate heat, stirring constantly, until the cream is hot and thick, but be careful not to let it boil. Stir the cream over cracked ice to cool it quickly and fold in 2 egg whites, beaten until stiff, 1/2 cup heavy cream, whipped, and 2 tablespoons Jamaica rum.

Turn the pastry cream into a baked tart shell and arrange large ripe strawberries attractively over the cream. Glaze the strawberries with 3 tablespoons red currant jelly, melted and thinned with 1 tablespoon boiling water.

Tarte aux Fraises
STRAWBERRY TART

When the matter is considered dispassionately, it appears that the myriad small mysteries of the pastry tray add up to nothing more than miniature versions of full-size tarts and cakes. For instance, any tart recipe may be adapted for use with individual tart shells, and the meringue shell, custom tailored, serves as a vehicle for any pastry cream.

DROP *meringue suisse* by tablespoons onto a baking sheet lined with wax paper, or press it out into small mounds through a pastry bag fitted with a large round tube. Bake the meringues for 30 minutes in a slow oven (300° F.), until they are dry, but not colored. Strip the meringues from the paper and scoop them out to make hollow shells. Cool the shells. To serve, put 2 shells together with a spoonful of slightly crushed, sweetened

Meringues aux Framboises
RASPBERRY MERINGUES

Lime Meringues

raspberries between them, and pipe a fluted border of whipped cream around the meringues where they join.

TURN *meringue suisse* into a pastry bag fitted with a large open-star tube. Line a baking sheet with wax paper and draw on it circles about 2 inches in diameter. Fill in the circles with the meringue pressed through the pastry tube, then build up a rim around the circles about 1 inch thick and 1 inch high. Sprinkle the meringue nests with fine granulated sugar and bake them in a slow oven (250° F.) for 30 minutes, watching them carefully. Remove them from the paper to a cake rack with a spatula while they are still moist in the center and before they color.

Combine 4 egg yolks, beaten, 1/4 cup lime juice, 1/2 cup sugar, a very few drops of food coloring, and a pinch of salt. Cook over simmering water, stirring constantly, until the custard is thick. Cool and fold in 2 cups heavy cream, whipped. Fill the dry, cool meringue nests with the custard and chill well before serving. Top with whipped cream, if desired.

LINE individual tart pans with any tart paste and prick the paste well. Line the pans with wax paper and fill them with dried beans. Bake the shells in a hot oven (425° F.) for 15 minutes, until the crust is golden brown. Discard beans and paper and cool the shells. Fill with strawberries, bananas, sliced peaches or nectarines, pitted cherries, grapes or plums, or blueberries. Glaze red fruits with tart currant jelly or light colored fruits with apricot jam melted over hot water and stirred to a smooth, thick syrup.

IN a saucepan melt 1/2 cup butter and stir in the juice of 3 lemons, the grated rind of 1 lemon, a pinch of salt, 1 1/2 cups sugar, and 3 egg yolks beaten with 3 whole eggs. Cook over simmering water, whisking constantly, until the mixture is thickened, and let it cool. Fill baked tart shells with the lemon butter and top with a dollop of sour cream.

TOAST 1 1/2 cups shredded fresh coconut in a moderate oven (350° F.) for about 15 minutes, or until it is a delicate brown. Stir the coconut frequently.

In the top of a double boiler combine 1/3 cup sifted flour, 1/4 teaspoon salt, 1/4 cup sugar, and 1/2 cup milk. Stir in 1 1/2 cups hot light cream and cook the mixture over boiling water, stirring frequently, until the sauce is smooth and thick. Beat 4 egg yolks with a little of the hot sauce and return this combination to the sauce. Add 1 cup of the toasted coconut and cook, stirring, for 3 minutes longer. Remove the cream from the heat, cool it, and flavor it with 2 teaspoons triple sec. Turn the cream into baked tart shells. Beat 4 egg whites until they are stiff, add 1 teaspoon lemon juice, gradually beat in 1/2 cup fine granulated sugar, and continue beating the meringue until it is thick and glossy. Pile it in thick swirls on the tarts and bake them in a moderate oven (350° F.) for 15 minutes, or until the meringue is golden. Sprinkle with the rest of the toasted coconut.

The icings and fillings that follow are most versatile and therefore most widely used for pastries, desserts, and confections in haute cuisine.

Crème Chantilly
WHIPPED CREAM

Vanilla Sugar

WHIP heavy cream in a chilled bowl until it is thick but still light. The cream should not be too stiff and heavy. Into each cup of whipped cream fold 1 to 1 1/2 tablespoons vanilla sugar.

To make vanilla sugar, split a piece of vanilla bean and scrape out the little seeds with a small knife. Combine the seeds with confectioners' sugar and crush together well.

Crème Pâtissière
PASTRY CREAM

SCALD 1 1/2 cups milk with a piece of vanilla bean. If vanilla extract is used, it must be added at the last. Mix in a saucepan 1/2 cup sugar and 4 egg yolks, working them together with a spoon until creamy and light in color. Add 1/4 cup flour, mixing just enough to blend. Add the scalded milk gradually, stirring until well combined. Cook over low heat, stirring vigorously, until the cream reaches the boiling point, but do not let it boil. Remove the vanilla bean or add a few drops of vanilla extract and strain the cream through a fine sieve. Stir the cream occasionally as it cools to prevent a crust from forming.

Crème Pâtissière au Chocolat

Follow the directions for making *crème pâtissière*, but add to the scalded milk 2 ounces melted and cooled unsweetened chocolate.

Crème Pâtissière Variée

Flavor *crème pâtissière* with coffee, chocolate and coffee, or with any liqueur.

Crème Saint-Honoré

Soften 1 tablespoon gelatin in 2 tablespoons cold water and stir it into 3 cups hot *crème pâtissière*. Beat 6 egg whites until they are stiff but not dry and beat in gradually 1/3 cup sugar. Fold this meringue into the *crème*.

IN a saucepan combine 1/3 cup flour, 3/4 cup sugar, and a pinch of salt. Add 1 egg and 1 egg yolk and mix thoroughly. Stir in another egg and another egg yolk.

Crème Frangipane
FRANGIPANE CREAM

Scald 2 cups milk with a 1-inch piece of vanilla bean and add it, little by little, to the cream, stirring until combined. Cook, stirring vigorously, until the cream almost reaches the boiling point and continue to cook gently, still stirring, for 2 minutes.

Remove the pan from the heat, discard the vanilla bean, and stir in 2 tablespoons butter and 4 macaroons, crushed. Cool the cream, stirring it occasionally to prevent a crust from forming.

STIR 9 tablespoons sugar, 1/4 cup water, and 1/8 teaspoon cream of tartar over low heat until the sugar is dissolved. Raise the heat and cook the syrup rapidly until it spins a light thread.

Crème au Beurre au Sirop
WHIPPED BUTTER CREAM

Beat the syrup gradually into 5 beaten egg yolks and continue to whip until the cream is thick and cool.

Whip 1 cup soft sweet butter until it is light and fluffy and beat it gradually into the cream. Chill the butter cream until it reaches spreading consistency. This icing is sometimes called simply butter cream, or *crème au beurre.*

Flavor the cream with vanilla or almond extract, or rum, brandy, or kirsch, or with Cointreau, Curaçao, Bénédictine, or a similar liqueur.

Melt 3 ounces of chocolate with 1 tablespoon water, cool the chocolate, and add it to butter cream.

Chocolate Butter Cream

Substitute very strong coffee for water in making the syrup for butter cream and flavor the cream with coffee essence.

Coffee Butter Cream

Stir 1/3 cup finely chopped or grated pistachios or hazelnuts into butter cream.

Nut Butter Cream

Stir 1/4 cup praline powder into butter cream.

Praline Butter Cream

CREAM 1/2 pound sweet butter and work in 1/2 cup sugar. Blend well and add 2 teaspoons triple-strength coffee and 1 tablespoon cocoa. Use to decorate elaborate *gâteaux.*

Mocha Butter Cream

Fondant   IN a heavy 2-quart saucepan, combine 3 cups sugar, 1 cup hot water, and 1/8 teaspoon cream of tartar. Stir steadily over low heat until the sugar is completely dissolved. Increase the heat and cook rapidly, without further stirring, until a candy thermometer registers 238° F., or until a few drops of the hot syrup form a soft ball in cold water. During the cooking, wash down the crystals that form on the sides of the saucepan with a brush moistened with water or with a fork wrapped in a damp cloth.

When the syrup reaches 238° F., pour it at once onto a marble slab or an enamel-top table or a large, flat, smooth platter to cool to lukewarm. When the center of the batch of fondant is lukewarm to the hand (about 110° F.) work the fondant vigorously with a spatula until it becomes white and solid. Let the fondant rest for a few minutes and knead until soft and creamy. Store in a tightly covered jar at room temperature for two days before using.

Fondant Icing   Add 1 teaspoon vanilla extract to 1 cup fondant in a saucepan and stir over very low heat until the fondant is just warm to the touch. Be careful not to overheat it or it will be dull when cool instead of shiny.

If the fondant is too thick, add a little warm water to bring it to the right spreading consistency. It should be thick enough to mask the cake, yet soft enough for easy spreading.

The vanilla flavoring may be replaced by almond or coffee extract or rum, kirsch, brandy, anisette, Curaçao, or Bénédictine.

Chocolate Fondant   Add 2 squares of chocolate melted and cooled to lukewarm to 1 cup fondant and stir over low heat until the fondant is warm to the finger. Thin with water to the right consistency.

Quick Fondant   SIFT 1 1/2 cups confectioners' sugar and add 1/2 teaspoon lemon juice and, very gradually, enough water to make a thick mixture that will spread. To use the fondant, heat it to lukewarm by placing the pan or bowl over hot water. Add any desired flavoring.

Confectioners' Sugar Icing   BEAT 3/4 cup confectioners' sugar with 2 tablespoons hot milk until the icing is smooth. Flavor with rum or vanilla.

Royal Icing   To 1 egg white add enough confectioners' sugar to make a thick, smooth paste, stirring constantly. Keep the icing covered with a damp cloth at all times.

Fondant

Transparent Icing MAKE a thick syrup by boiling 1 cup sugar in 1/2 cup water, without stirring, until the syrup spins a thread or the candy thermometer registers 220° F. Pour the syrup slowly in a thin stream into a bowl, working it constantly with a wooden spoon until it becomes white and thick. Add 1 teaspoon rum and continue to work the cream until it is lukewarm. Pour the icing over a cake decorated with nuts and fruits.

Water Icing MIX 1 cup sifted confectioner's sugar with 1 tablespoon warm water, or enough to make a paste that will be soft enough to spread lightly. If desired, the icing may be tinted with a drop of food coloring or flavored with coffee extract.

Confectioners' Sugar Glaze SIFT 1 cup confectioners' sugar into a bowl. Add gradually about 2 tablespoons cream or milk, fruit juice, brandy or rum, or any favorite liqueur to make a smooth paste of a good spreading consistency.

Raspberry Glaze COMBINE 3/4 cup raspberry juice and 1 tablespoon cornstarch and strain the mixture into the top of a double boiler. Add 2 tablespoons sugar and cook over boiling water, stirring constantly, until the glaze is thick and clear.

Orange Glaze BRING to a boil 1 cup each of sugar and orange juice. Dissolve 1 tablespoon cornstarch in 1/4 cup cold water and stir into the boiling juice. Cook and stir the glaze for 1 minute and cool it before using.

Peach Glaze MASH enough peeled and sliced peaches to measure 1/2 cup and combine these with 1 cup each of sugar and water. Bring the mixture to a boil and press it through a fine sieve. Bring it again to a boil. Dissolve 2 teaspoons cornstarch in 1/4 cup cold water and stir it into the peach syrup. Boil for 1 minute, stirring, and cool the glaze before using.

Rum Glaze SIFT 1 cup confectioners' sugar into a small, heavy saucepan. Add 1 tablespoon water and stir the sugar over low heat until it is completely dissolved. Add, drop by drop, about 2 tablespoons rum, continuing to stir until the syrup coats the spoon.

WASH 1/2 pound dried apricots, cover them with 2 cups water, and soak them for several hours. Bring to a boil and simmer until the apricots are soft. Rub fruit and water together through a sieve and add 1/2 cup sugar. Cook the purée until the sugar is dissolved, stirring constantly to prevent scorching. Pour the glaze into a jar, cover, and cool. To use, thin the glaze to the desired consistency with a little hot water. *Apricot Glaze*

COMBINE 1/2 cup each of grated blanched almonds and sugar, 1/4 cup soft butter, 2 egg yolks, 1/4 cup rum, and a drop of almond extract. Beat these with a wooden spoon until the cream is well blended. *Almond Cream*

BLANCH almonds as follows: Soak shelled almonds in boiling water for 2 or 3 minutes, until the skins loosen. Drain the nuts, plunge them into cold water, and rub off the skins. Chop the nuts, spread them on a shallow pan, and dry them thoroughly in a very slow oven (250° F.). Cool the nuts and put them through a food chopper, using the finest blade. The almonds may take on a little color during the drying, but they should not be allowed to darken. *Almond Powder*

GRIND blanched almonds and pound them to a smooth paste, using a pestle and mortar. To sweeten the paste, use half granulated sugar and half confectioners' sugar, to taste. *Almond Paste*

IN a heavy-bottomed saucepan combine 3/4 cup sugar, 1/4 cup water, and 1/4 teaspoon cream of tartar and bring to a boil. Add 1/2 cup shredded blanched almonds and cook without stirring until the syrup turns a rich amber. Pour the syrup into a lightly buttered, shallow pan to cool. Pulverize the praline in a mortar and store the powder in the refrigerator. *Praline Powder*

Iced Petits Fours

$\mathcal{P}$etits $\mathcal{F}$ours

Some of the fancifully iced cakes on the pastry tray are miniatures of the classic *gâteaux*. Others, made of *génoise* or another basic cake *pâte*, are decorated in a variety of ways limited only by the cook's ingenuity.

CUT tiny rectangles, squares, diamonds, or circles from a *génoise* about 3/4 inch thick. Spread the tops with any butter cream or split the cakes and put them together with butter cream, and chill for 2 hours.

Dip the little cakes into melted fondant, colored and flavored to taste. The fondant should be just warm to the touch. If it is overheated, the icing will be dull instead of shiny when it cools. Many variations are possible:

Spread small circles of *génoise* with coffee butter cream. Chill and dip them in coffee fondant.

Spread small circles of *génoise* with kirsch-flavored butter cream. Chill and dip them in rose-colored fondant flavored with kirsch. Place a drop of chocolate fondant on top of each.

Spread diamond-shaped pieces of *génoise* with chocolate butter cream. Chill, dip them in chocolate fondant, and sprinkle with a pinch of finely chopped toasted almonds.

Split circles of *génoise* and put them together with chestnut or hazelnut butter cream. Chill and dip them in white fondant flavored with vanilla.

Petits Fours à la Crème Glacés
ICED PETITS FOURS

769

Make a spiral around each little cake with chocolate fondant pressed through a pastry bag fitted with a tiny round tube.

Spread circles of *génoise* with butter cream flavored with kirsch. Top each cake with half a candied cherry and chill. Dip the circles in fondant flavored with kirsch.

Spread circles of *génoise* with coffee butter cream. Sprinkle with chopped hazelnuts and chill. Dip the circles in coffee fondant and top each with a grilled hazelnut.

Fill rectangles of *génoise* with butter cream flavored with anisette. Chill and dip them in fondant flavored with anisette and decorate each with three thin bands of chocolate fondant pressed through a pastry bag fitted with a tiny round tube.

Fill squares of *génoise* with coffee butter cream mixed with grated blanched almonds and flavored with rum. Chill and dip each cake into coffee fondant flavored with rum.

Petits Fours aux Confitures CUT a 3/4-inch-thick *génoise* into different shapes. Split the little cakes and put them together with jam or marmalade. Dip them into fondant colored and flavored to taste, and decorate them.

Put rectangles of *génoise* together with raspberry jam. Dip them into rose-colored fondant flavored with *eau-de-vie de framboise* instead of vanilla and decorate with two thin lines of chocolate fondant pressed through a pastry bag fitted with a very small round tube.

Sandwich triangles of *génoise* with marmalade. Dip them into pale green fondant flavored with kümmel and put a drop of chocolate fondant on each.

Profiteroles MAKE tiny puffs of *pâte à chou*. Cool them, make a small hole in the side of each, and using a pastry bag with a small tube, force into them a filling of *crème pâtissière* or butter cream. Frost the tops with fondant of a compatible flavor. Finely chopped nuts may be used as a final garnish.

Éclairs SHAPE the *pâte à chou* into finger-size éclairs. Bake and cool them. Slit the éclairs and fill and frost them as above.

Ruriks IN a mortar grind 1/2 cup dry blanched almonds to a powder. Add gradually 1/2 cup confectioners' sugar and grind and pound until the almonds and sugar are thoroughly blended. Moisten the mixture with enough rum to make a firm paste. Divide the paste into pieces the size of walnuts and form each piece into a small square 1 inch thick. Dip the squares in rum-flavored fondant and decorate each with half a candied cherry.

The fondant must be stirred over very low heat until it is just warm to the touch. If the fondant is too thick, add a little warm water to bring it to the right spreading consistency.

SUBSTITUTE kirsch for the rum in the recipe for Ruriks. Form the paste into balls the size of walnuts and dip them in fondant mixed with finely chopped pistachios and colored green. Top each ball with half a pistachio.

Siciliens

ADD to the paste in the recipe for Ruriks 1/4 cup finely chopped candied orange peel. Form the paste into round cakes about 1 inch thick and dip them in orange-flavored fondant. Top each *maltais* with a small round of candied orange peel.

Maltais

BEAT 3 egg whites until they are stiff but not dry. Fold in a scant 1/2 cup each of grated blanched almonds and fine granulated sugar. Press the meringue through a pastry bag fitted with a plain round tube onto a buttered and floured baking sheet in round or oval mounds. Gently press a hollow in the center of each mound with a wet silver spoon. Sprinkle the mounds with grated almonds and fill the center with a paste made by mixing thoroughly a scant 1/2 cup each of grated blanched almonds and sugar with 1 egg, 1 egg yolk, 1/4 cup melted butter, and 1 tablespoon rum.

Miroirs

Bake the meringues in a moderate oven (350° F.) for 10 to 12 minutes, or until lightly browned. Cool, brush the filling with melted apricot marmalade, and cover the glaze with a thin layer of fondant flavored with rum.

The petits fours secs *that follow are grouped according to the ingredients that they include or omit. Some of them are designed to accompany the dessert course of an elaborate dinner; others are destined to go quickly into and out of the family cookie jar.*

SIFT 1 cup sifted flour, 1/4 cup sugar, and 1/4 teaspoon salt into a bowl. Add 1/4 cup soft butter, 2 egg yolks, and 1 teaspoon vanilla extract and knead until the dough is well blended. Chill it for 2 hours.

Navettes Sucrées
SUGAR SHUTTLES

Divide the dough into portions the size of a small walnut. Roll each piece of dough with the palm of the hand on a lightly floured board to give it the shape of a sewing-machine shuttle. Dip each in egg white and roll in sugar. Bake on a lightly buttered baking sheet in a moderate oven (350° F.) for about 8 minutes, or until the little cookies are lightly browned.

Kourabiedes
GREEK CAKES

CREAM together thoroughly 1 pound sweet butter, the yolk of 1 egg, and 2 tablespoons confectioners' sugar. Gradually work in 4 cups sifted flour to make a soft dough. Roll out the dough 3/4 inch thick on a lightly floured board and cut it into diamond shapes. Bake the diamonds on a buttered baking sheet in a moderate oven (325° F.) for 25 to 30 minutes. Let them cool on the sheet for 10 minutes and sprinkle them with confectioners' sugar.

Gâteaux de Milan

SIFT into a mixing bowl 1 1/4 cups flour, a scant 1/2 cup sugar, and a pinch of salt. Add 3/4 cup butter, the grated rind of half a lemon, 1 tablespoon Cognac or rum, and 2 or 3 egg yolks. Mix all the ingredients to a firm dough, wrap the dough in wax paper, and chill it for 1 hour.

Roll out the dough 3/8 inch thick on a lightly floured board and cut it into rounds with a floured cookie cutter. Brush the rounds with beaten egg and bake them on a buttered baking sheet in a hot oven (450° F.) for 10 to 12 minutes.

Haman's Hats

MIX together 1/2 cup each of vegetable oil and sugar, 1 well-beaten egg, and 1/4 cup milk. Sift in 2 1/2 cups flour sifted with 3 teaspoons baking powder and 1/2 teaspoon salt, and knead the dough well. Roll out the dough thinly on a lightly floured board and cut out 4-inch circles. Put a spoonful of poppy seed or prune filling in the center of each round and fold up the edges to meet in the center and form a tricorn. Pinch well to seal. Bake the Haman's hats on an oiled baking sheet in a moderate oven (350° F.) for about 20 minutes, or until they are nicely browned.

Chocolate Wafers

CREAM 3/4 cup butter, add gradually 1 1/4 cups sugar, and cream together until light and fluffy. Add 1 tablespoon rum extract and 1 egg and beat thoroughly. Sift together 1 1/2 cups sifted flour, 3/4 cup cocoa, 1 1/2 teaspoons baking powder, and 1/4 teaspoon salt. Add the sifted dry ingredients gradually, mixing well after each addition to make a light dough. Roll out the dough 1/8 inch thick on a lightly floured board and cut it with a floured cookie cutter into rounds about 2 1/2 inches in diameter. Bake the rounds on an ungreased baking sheet in a hot oven (400° F.) for 8 minutes.

CREAM together 1/2 cup sugar and 1/4 cup butter, and beat in 4 eggs, one at a time. Sift 1 cup flour with 2 teaspoons cinnamon and add the flour alternately with 1/4 cup Sherry. Drop the dough by teaspoons 2 inches apart on a buttered baking sheet. Bake the wafers in a very hot oven (450° F.) for about 8 minutes, sprinkle them with sugar, and remove them from the pan with a spatula. While they are still warm, they may be shaped into tubes or cones.

Sherry Wafers

BEAT 1 whole egg and 1 egg yolk with 2/3 cup sugar until the mixture is thick and pale in color. Stir in 1 teaspoon vanilla and 1 1/4 cups sifted flour. Spoon the dough into a pastry bag fitted with a small round tube and press out strips as thick as the little finger and twice as long. Sprinkle the batons with chopped almonds and bake in a moderate oven (350° F.) for 8 minutes.

Baguettes Flamandes
FLEMISH BATONS

BEAT 4 egg whites until they are stiff and beat in gradually 1 cup confectioners' sugar to make a stiff meringue. Fold in 1 ounce baking chocolate, grated, 1/2 cup flour sifted with 1/2 teaspoon baking powder, and 1/2 teaspoon vanilla extract. Drop the batter by teaspoons 2 inches apart on a buttered baking sheet. Bake the cookies for about 10 minutes in a moderate oven (350° F.).

Chocolate Snaps

IN a bowl combine 2 1/2 cups flour, 1/4 cup finely chopped candied orange peel, 1 tablespoon powdered aniseeds, 1/2 teaspoon cinnamon, and 1/2 cup chopped walnuts.

In a saucepan dissolve 1 1/2 cups sugar in 1/3 cup water, bring to a boil, and cook until the syrup forms a soft ball when a little is dropped into cold water. Add the flour and nut mixture, remove the saucepan from the heat, and stir the mixture vigorously. Pour the thick paste on a lightly floured board to cool a little. When the paste is cool enough to handle, knead it thoroughly and roll it out 1/3 inch thick. Cut the paste into rounds about 2 inches in diameter and bake them on a buttered and floured baking sheet in a very slow oven (250° F.) for about 30 minutes.

Cavallucci di Siena

Blidas   BEAT 3 egg whites until they are stiff but not dry. Fold in 1/2 cup each of sugar and grated blanched almonds, 3 tablespoons sifted flour, the grated rind of 2 oranges, and a few drops of orange food coloring. Drop the batter onto a buttered and floured baking sheet by tablespoons or press it into oval cakes through a pastry bag fitted with a plain round tube. Sprinkle with sugar and bake in a moderate oven (350° F.) for 12 to 15 minutes.

Nuts are worked into the cookie dough, they are sprinkled on the cookie, they are used decoratively, and all to the good.

Almond Wafers   MIX together 5 egg whites, 3/4 cup confectioners' sugar, and a little salt, and beat the mixture until it is very light. Stir in 5 tablespoons flour, 6 tablespoons melted butter, and 2 tablespoons milk. Add 1/4 cup almond paste and beat until the batter is smooth. Add 1/2 cup blanched, slivered almonds. Drop the batter by spoonfuls onto a buttered baking sheet, leaving room for the wafers to spread, and bake in a very hot oven (450° F.) for 5 to 8 minutes, or until golden. Remove the wafers with a spatula. If desired, the wafers may be twisted into cones or tubes over a wooden spoon handle while they are still warm.

Sablés aux Amandes   IN a mixing bowl combine 1 1/4 cups sifted flour, 1/4 cup grated blanched almonds, 1/3 cup sugar, 1/2 teaspoon salt, and 1/2 cup soft butter. Add 2 lightly beaten egg yolks and 1 teaspoon lemon juice and knead the mixture until the dough forms a firm ball. Wrap the dough in wax paper and chill it for 2 hours.

Roll out the dough 1/4 inch thick on a lightly floured board and cut it into circles 6 inches in diameter. Cut each circle into 4 pie-shaped wedges and make a simple design on each wedge with a pointed knife or the tines of a fork. Brush the wedges with beaten egg, sprinkle with confectioners' sugar, and bake on a buttered and floured baking sheet in a hot oven (425° F.) for 6 to 8 minutes.

Amandines   CREAM 2/3 cup butter and 1/2 cup sugar until the mixture is light and fluffy. Stir in 2 cups sifted flour sifted with 1/2 teaspoon baking powder, 2 eggs, lightly beaten, and 1 teaspoon vanilla extract and mix well. Form the dough into a ball, wrap it in wax paper, and chill it for 1 hour.

Roll out the dough 1/4 inch thick on a lightly floured board and cut it into strips 1 inch wide. Put the strips on a buttered and floured baking sheet and brush them with a little beaten egg. Combine 1/2 cup finely chopped blanched almonds and 1/4 cup sugar, sprinkle the mixture over the strips, and score them at intervals of 1 inch. Bake the amandines in a moderately hot oven (375° F.) for about 15 minutes, or until they are delicately browned. Cool and cut the strips as they were scored.

Galettes Suisses
SWISS ALMOND COOKIES

MIX together thoroughly 3/4 cup grated blanched almonds, 2/3 cup sugar, and 3 egg yolks. Sift 1 1/4 cups flour into a bowl and make a well in the center. Turn the almond mixture into the well with 2 tablespoons soft butter, 1/2 teaspoon salt, and 1 teaspoon vanilla extract. Work all the ingredients into a firm dough and chill it for at least 1 hour.

Roll out the dough 1/8 inch thick on a lightly floured board and cut it into small rounds or ovals with a floured cookie cutter. Brush them with 1 egg yolk beaten with 1 teaspoon water, sprinkle with shredded blanched almonds and fine granulated sugar, and bake in a hot oven (400° F.) for 8 to 10 minutes.

Nut Sandwiches

CREAM 1/4 cup butter with 3/4 cup sugar and beat in 2 eggs. Work in 2 cups flour sifted with 1/2 teaspoon baking powder, and chill the dough well. Divide the dough in half and roll each half into a thin rectangle. Put one rectangle on a buttered baking sheet, brush it with melted butter, and sprinkle it thickly with 1 cup finely chopped nuts mixed with 1/2 cup sugar. Cover with the second layer of dough, and press the edges together. Brush the top with melted butter and sprinkle it lightly with sugar. Bake the cake in a moderate oven (350° F.) for about 15 minutes, or until it is nicely browned. Cool it slightly and cut it with a sharp knife into uniform fingers.

Benne Wafers

CREAM together 1 1/2 tablespoons butter and 1 cup light brown sugar until light and smooth. Add 1 beaten egg, 2 tablespoons flour, 1/4 teaspoon salt, 1 teaspoon vanilla, and 1/2 cup parched benne seeds. Mix all together and drop from a teaspoon onto a buttered cookie sheet. Flatten the wafers with a knife dipped in ice water and bake them in a moderate oven (350° F.) for 6 minutes.

Molded cookies are particularly decorative, and have the further advantage of eliminating one step in preparation, since they shape themselves.

Friandises aux Amandes MIX together thoroughly 1/2 cup grated blanched almonds and a scant 1/2 cup fine granulated sugar. Add 4 egg whites, a little at a time, beating well after each addition. Stir in 3 tablespoons flour, 1/2 teaspoon vanilla, and a scant 1/2 cup cooled *beurre noisette*—butter cooked slowly until slightly browned. Turn the batter into small buttered and floured molds and bake in a moderate oven (350° F.) for 8 to 10 minutes, depending on the size of the molds. Remove the *friands* from the molds to a rack to cool.

Visitandines IN a mixing bowl combine 3/4 cup grated blanched almonds and 1 cup sugar. Work in little by little 4 egg whites and beat the mixture vigorously for 6 minutes. Stir in 1 teaspoon vanilla, 3/4 cup sifted flour, and 1 cup cooled *beurre noisette*—butter cooked slowly until slightly browned.

Fill small oval or round molds, buttered and floured, three-fourths full with batter and bake in a moderate oven (350° F.) for about 15 minutes, or until the *visitandines* are browned.

Coconut Macaroon Cups IN a saucepan combine 3 cups flaked or freshly grated coconut, 1/3 cup sugar, and 1 egg white and heat the mixture over boiling water, stirring occasionally. Remove from the heat and stir in 6 tablespoons cake flour sifted with 1/2 teaspoon baking powder. Add 1/2 teaspoon almond extract and mix well.

Beat 1 egg white until it is stiff. Add 1/3 cup sugar a little at a time, beating well after each addition. Fold the meringue into the coconut mixture and fill tiny paper cups in muffin tins two-thirds full with the batter. Bake the cups in a moderately slow oven (325° F.) for about 25 minutes.

Cocoa Bars MELT 2/3 cup butter and stir in 2/3 cup cocoa. Turn the mixture into a mixing bowl and stir in 2 cups sugar and 4 eggs, well beaten. Stir in 1 cup flour sifted with 1 teaspoon each of baking powder and salt. Add 2 teaspoons vanilla extract and fold in 1 cup coarsely chopped nut meats. Spread the batter 1/2 inch thick in a buttered shallow pan. Bake for about 35 minutes in a moderately slow oven (325° F.), until a shiny brown crust forms. Cut the cake into small bars with a sharp knife and cool on a cake rack.

Nut Bars BEAT 4 eggs and 2 cups brown sugar until the mixture is very light. Fold in 1 1/3 cups sifted flour sifted with 1 teaspoon soda and 1/2 teaspoon salt,

Friandises aux Amandes

and stir in 2 cups chopped pecans or walnuts. Spread the mixture on a buttered shallow pan and bake it in a moderate oven (350° F.) for about 25 minutes. Cut the cake into bars, roll the bars in confectioners' sugar, and cool them.

Coconut Bars   CREAM 1/2 cup butter. Add gradually 1/2 cup brown sugar and beat until smooth. Stir in 1 cup sifted flour and spread the batter in the bottom of an 8-inch-square cake pan. Bake it in a moderately hot oven (375° F.) for 20 minutes.

Beat 2 eggs and 1 cup brown sugar until smooth. Stir in 1 teaspoon vanilla, 1 cup chopped walnuts, and 1/2 cup shredded coconut tossed with 2 tablespoons flour and a pinch of salt. Spread this batter over the baked crust and continue to bake for 20 minutes longer. Cool the cake, sprinkle it with confectioners' sugar, and cut it into squares or bars.

Croquets   SIFT into a mixing bowl 1 1/4 cups sifted flour, 1/3 cup sugar, and a
aux Amandes   pinch of salt. Add 1/3 cup butter, 1/2 cup unblanched almonds, the grated rind of 1 lemon or 1 orange, and 1 egg and mix all the ingredients to a firm dough. Chop the dough with a heavy knife to cut the almonds a little and form it into a long slim loaf slightly thicker in the center than at the ends. Score the loaf in crisscross lines with a sharp knife, brush it with beaten egg, and bake on a buttered and floured baking sheet in a moderately hot oven (375° F.) for 18 to 20 minutes. Cool and slice.

Biscotti   IN a bowl beat 2 eggs and a generous 1/2 cup sugar very thoroughly. Add
al Anice   gradually 1 1/4 cups sifted flour, blending gently and thoroughly. Add
ANISE BISCUITS   1 teaspoon aniseeds. Butter and flour a shallow 4-inch-wide pan, pour in the batter, and bake it in a moderately hot oven (375° F.) for 20 minutes.

Remove the cake from the pan, and cut it into 1-inch slices. Place the slices on a buttered baking dish and bake them for about 5 minutes, or until they are brown. Turn the slices and bake them for 5 minutes longer, or until the other side is brown.

Mandelbrot   BEAT 3 eggs with 1 cup sugar and stir in 1/3 cup vegetable oil, 1 teaspoon
ALMOND SLICES   lemon juice, 1/2 teaspoon almond extract, and the grated rind of 1 lemon. Sift 3 cups sifted flour with 3 teaspoons baking powder and 1/4 tea-

spoon salt. Add the flour gradually with 1/2 cup coarsely cut blanched almonds, to make a rather firm dough. Knead the dough lightly and form it into loaves about 3 inches wide and 1 inch thick. Bake the loaves on an oiled baking sheet in a moderate oven (350° F.) for about 45 minutes, until they are lightly browned. Slice the loaves 1/2 inch thick while they are still warm and return the slices to the oven to crisp and brown on both sides.

Spices, fruits, and honey are the distinguishing ingredients of this group of cookies.

Applesauce Cookies

CREAM 3/4 cup butter and 1 cup sugar until the mixture is light and fluffy. Stir in 1 egg, lightly beaten. Sift together 2 1/2 cups sifted flour, 1/2 teaspoon each of soda and cinnamon, and 1/4 teaspoon each of salt and cloves. Stir 1/2 cup chopped nuts into the dry ingredients and mix all into the creamed mixture alternately with 1/2 cup applesauce. Shape the dough into long rolls and chill for easy handling. Slice the rolls thinly and bake the cookies on buttered baking sheets in a moderate oven (350° F.) for 12 minutes, or until they are lightly browned.

Gingerbread Men

INTO a bowl sift 2 3/4 cups cake flour. Add 3 teaspoons baking powder, 1/4 teaspoon baking soda, 1 teaspoon each of powdered cloves and ginger, 1 scant tablespoon cinnamon, and 1/2 teaspoon salt and sift again. In another bowl combine 1 beaten egg, 1/4 teaspoon allspice, 1 cup brown sugar, 2/3 cup dark molasses and 1/2 cup butter and mix these together well. Stir the liquid into the flour-spice mixture and, using both hands, mix the dough until all the flour has been worked in. Divide the dough and roll half at a time into a sheet 1/3 inch thick. Cut the gingerbread men with a floured cutter. Transfer the men to a buttered baking sheet and use pieces of seedless raisins, candied fruits, or nuts to make eyes, nose and mouth. Bake the gingerbread men in a moderately hot oven (375° F.) for about 12 minutes, or until they are lightly browned.

Ginger Creams

CREAM 1/2 cup butter, add 1 cup sugar gradually, and cream until light and fluffy. Add 1 egg and 1 cup molasses and mix thoroughly. Sift together 4 cups sifted flour, 2 teaspoons each of soda and cinnamon, 1/2 teaspoon salt, and 1 teaspoon each of powdered nutmeg and cloves. Add the sifted

Pumpkin Cookies

dry ingredients alternately with 1 cup hot water. Stir in 1/2 cup finely ground crystallized ginger.

Drop the batter by teaspoons onto a buttered baking sheet and bake the cookies in a hot oven (400° F.) for about 8 minutes. Cover the still slightly warm cookies with confectioners' sugar icing.

CREAM together 1/2 cup soft butter and 1 1/4 cups brown sugar until the mixture is light and fluffy and add 2 well-beaten eggs and 1 1/2 cups pumpkin purée. Sift together 2 1/2 cups sifted flour, 3 teaspoons baking powder, 1 teaspoon cinnamon, 1/2 teaspoon each of nutmeg and salt, and 1/4 teaspoon powdered ginger. Add the dry ingredients to the pumpkin mixture, stirring until well blended. Add 1 cup seeded raisins and 1 cup chopped pecans. Drop the batter by teaspoons onto a buttered baking sheet. Bake the cookies in a hot oven (400° F.) for 15 minutes, or until they are lightly browned.

Pumpkin Cookies

IN a mixing bowl cream 1 1/2 cups shaved maple sugar and 1 cup butter. Mix in 3 eggs, lightly beaten, and stir in 3 cups flour sifted with 1 teaspoon baking powder alternately with 1 teaspoon soda dissolved in 1/2 cup hot water. Add 1 cup chopped walnuts and 1 1/2 cups chopped, pitted dates and mix well. Drop the batter by teaspoons onto a buttered baking sheet and bake the cookies in a moderately hot oven (375° F.) for about 15 minutes, or until they are golden.

Maple Date Cookies

SIFT 1 cup flour onto a pastry board and make a well in the center. In the well put 1/4 cup each of sugar and soft butter, a pinch of salt, and 2 egg yolks. Work the center ingredients into a smooth paste and then work in the flour to make a soft dough. Mix in 1 cup finely chopped candied fruits, wrap the dough in wax paper, and chill it for 3 hours.

On a lightly floured board roll out the dough less than 1/8 inch thick and cut into fluted rounds about 4 inches in diameter. Bake the biscuits on a buttered baking sheet in a moderate oven (350° F.) for 6 minutes, or until they are tinged with brown.

Cool the *fourrés* and sandwich them in pairs with honey as a filling. Sprinkle the tops with confectioners' sugar.

Honey-Filled Biscuits

CREAM 1/2 cup butter until it is light and cream it with 1/3 cup sugar until the mixture is fluffy. Add 1 egg and beat well. Stir in 1 cup warm honey,

Honey Squares

2 tablespoons lemon juice, and about 3 1/2 cups flour, sifted with 2 teaspoons baking powder and a pinch of salt. Stir in 2/3 cup blanched, chopped almonds and chill the dough for at least 1 hour.

Roll out the dough 1/4 inch thick and cut it into strips or squares. Bake the cookies on a buttered cookie sheet in a moderate oven (350° F.) for 10 to 12 minutes.

Meringue cookies achieve their unique qualities of lightness and frothiness by omitting both flour and butter.

Amygthalota
ALMOND COOKIES

Mix together 1 1/2 cups sugar and 2 pounds almonds, blanched and finely chopped. Beat 4 egg whites until they are frothy with a pinch of salt. Add 1/2 teaspoon lemon juice and continue to beat until the whites are very stiff, but not dry. Fold in the almonds and sugar and add 2 tablespoons rosewater. Drop the batter by teaspoons onto a buttered and floured baking sheet and bake in a slow oven (300° F.) for about 20 minutes.

Patriciens

In a saucepan combine 2 cups sugar, 2/3 cup water, and a pinch of cream of tartar. Bring to a boil and cook rapidly until the syrup spins a light thread. Pour the syrup gradually into 3 stiffly beaten egg whites, beating constantly. Fold into the meringue a scant 1/2 cup each of fine granulated sugar and ground almonds and 1 teaspoon vanilla extract.

Press the meringue through a pastry bag fitted with a plain round tube onto a buttered and floured baking sheet in small rounds or ovals. Put the meringues in a warm place to dry for 3 hours and bake them in a slow oven (300° F.) for 15 to 20 minutes, or until they are delicately browned. Cool. Sandwich them in pairs with vanilla butter cream mixed with sieved meringue crumbs. Sprinkle with confectioners' sugar.

Suspiros

Blanch 1 1/2 cups almonds and cut them into lengthwise slivers. Dry the nuts and mix them with 1 teaspoon grated orange peel.

Beat 3 egg whites until they are stiff but not dry.

Boil together in a saucepan 1 1/2 cups sugar and 1/2 cup water until a drop of the syrup forms a soft ball in cold water. Beat this syrup gradually into the egg whites. Stir in 1 teaspoon rum and the almonds and drop the meringue by teaspoons, well spaced, on a baking sheet covered with oiled paper. Bake the cookies in a moderate oven (350° F.) until they are lightly browned.

Homemade candies lack professional perfection but they have a fascination of their own. The basic recipe for fondant will be found on page 764.

MAKE fondant and store it in a covered jar to ripen at room temperature for two days before using it to make bonbons.

Heat the fondant to lukewarm, stir in any desired food coloring, a drop at a time, and flavor to taste with peppermint, almond, or vanilla extract, or brandy, rum, or any preferred flavoring. Cool the fondant and knead it until it is soft and smooth. Break the fondant into pieces the size of walnuts and shape the pieces into rounds or ovals. For instance, shape fondant into an oval and press a Brazil nut firmly into the center; form it into smooth balls and press a walnut or a pecan half or an almond on either side like wings.

Let the bonbons stand for 2 hours to form a crust, then brush them with 1/4 cup light corn syrup mixed with 1 tablespoon hot water. Serve the bonbons in small individual paper cups.

Fondant Bonbons

PUT ripened fondant in the top of a double boiler over cold water, and slowly bring the water to a boil. Lower the heat, add a few drops of peppermint extract and a drop of green food coloring, and stir the fondant gently until it is completely melted and has reached 170° F. on a candy thermometer. Drop the fondant from the tip of a teaspoon onto a lightly oiled baking sheet or onto wax paper.

Fondant patties may be colored and flavored to taste.

Mint Patties

COVER a cookie sheet with wax paper and place it over a tray of ice. Put 3 or 4 generous tablespoons of fondant in the top of a small double boiler over hot, but not boiling, water. Add a drop or two of vanilla and a little food coloring and stir until the fondant is melted. Hold whole perfect dry strawberries by their stems, dip them into the melted fondant more than halfway and turn them fruit end up so that the fondant runs down to the stem. Lay the berries on the cold cookie sheet to harden the coating.

Strawberries in Fondant

Cherries
in Fondant

FOLLOW the procedure above, holding the cherries by their stems and coating them completely with the fondant.

Pâte
d'Amandes
ALMOND PASTE

BLANCH 1 cup almonds and remove the skins. Dry the nuts overnight in a warm place or in a very slow oven (250° F.) for about 30 minutes. Chill the nuts and pound them to a paste in a mortar. Add 1 tablespoon ice water, a few drops at a time, and knead back in the oil that has been forced out by the pounding. The paste must be very smooth and free of hard particles. Stir in 1 egg white, a pinch of salt, and 1 teaspoon lemon juice, or kirsch. Beat in little by little about 1 cup confectioners' sugar until the paste becomes too stiff to beat. Turn it out on a pastry board and knead in another 1/2 cup confectioners' sugar, or more if needed to make a soft, sweet paste. Store the *pâte d'amandes* in a tightly covered container to ripen for several hours before coloring it and forming it into fancy shapes.

Pâte
d'Amandes
Fondante

WARM 1 cup ripened fondant over hot water and work it into a smooth cream, adding a few drops of water if needed. Combine the warm fondant with 1 cup almonds, blanched, ground, and pounded to a paste in a mortar, and 1 cup confectioners' sugar, or enough to make a smooth, firm paste. Let the *pâte d'amandes fondante* ripen for several hours in a bowl, covered with a damp cloth, before molding it into various shapes.

Marzipan
Shapes

MARZIPAN shapes are molded in the palm of the hand. If one has a flair for sculpturing, very beautiful roses, gardenias, and more complicated flowers may be fashioned. Lacking artistic talent, one can, with a little practice, become proficient in making little fruits and vegetables and the simpler flowers.

The finished shapes may be realistically painted with food colors diluted with water, or the almond paste may be colored before it is molded. To color the paste, knead a small quantity of either *pâte d'amandes* or *pâte d'amandes fondante* on a pastry board until it is perfectly smooth. Add food coloring drop by drop, kneading until the color is evenly distributed through the paste.

Marzipan may be brushed with a light syrup to give it a shine, particularly attractive for marzipan fruits such as cherries, oranges, or apples. Let the marzipan stand for 2 to 3 hours before brushing it with a syrup made by combining 1/2 cup light corn syrup and 2 tablespoons hot water.

PEACHES, pears, and bananas are all made from yellow-tinted *pâte d'amandes*. The top and bottom of the peach are slightly flattened. Paint the cheek pink. The pear is broad at the base and tapers to the small top. Use currants or cloves for the blossom ends and insert in the tops small stems with a leaf attached. *Marzipan Fruits*

A little cocoa dissolved in hot water may be brushed on bananas to make the characteristic markings on the skin. Tint the ends with diluted green food coloring. Use deep yellow paste for lemons, orange for oranges, brilliant orange-red for tomatoes, and brush them with syrup.

COMBINE in a saucepan 1 cup grated hazelnuts, 1/2 cup sugar, and 2 ounces semisweet chocolate. Gradually blend in 1/2 cup water. Cook the mixture over very low heat, stirring it constantly, until the chocolate melts and the sugar dissolves. Cool the mixture, form it into small balls and coat the balls well with cocoa. Store in a cool place. *Chocolate Hazelnut Truffles*

SIFT together 2 tablespoons cocoa and 1 cup confectioners' sugar. Stir in 1/4 cup bourbon combined with 2 tablespoons light corn syrup. Add 2 1/2 cups crushed vanilla wafers and 1 cup broken pecans and mix. Roll the mixture into small balls and dredge with 1/2 cup confectioners' sugar. *Bourbon Balls*

Rum balls may be made in the same way. *Rum Balls*

BLANCH 1 pound almonds and dry them well in a warm place. In a heavy saucepan dissolve 2 cups sugar in 1 cup hot water with a pinch of cream of tartar. Bring to a boil and cook, without stirring, for about 15 minutes, or until the syrup begins to turn amber. Set the saucepan immediately into a shallow pan of cold water to prevent further cooking of the syrup, then place it over hot water to keep the glaze soft while it is being used. Dip the almonds one at a time in the hot glaze and put them on wax paper to dry and harden. If desired, the tips of the almonds may be then dipped in melted chocolate. *Glacéed Almonds*

Other nuts may be glazed in the same way. *Glacéed Nuts*

Memo to the Cook

The recipes in this book are seasoned to GOURMET's taste. Taste is a matter for the individual, for the cook, in short, for you. To season is not difficult. If we suggest one seasoning and you prefer another—substitute at will.

In this section we have gathered together the basic preparations that belong equally to all branches of gourmet cookery; basic preparations that apply particularly, or even primarily to the recipes in a single chapter are given therein.

As stated in GOURMET Magazine all these years, all recipes, unless otherwise noted, are for six persons.

Brown sauce, also called sauce espagnole, *is the basic sauce from which most dark sauces are derived.*

Brown Sauce
SAUCE ESPAGNOLE

MELT 1/2 cup beef, veal, or pork drippings in a heavy saucepan. Add 1 small carrot and 2 onions, coarsely chopped, and cook them until the onions just start to turn golden, shaking the pan to ensure even cooking. Add 1/2 cup flour and cook, stirring frequently, until flour, carrots, and onions are a rich brown. Add 3 cups hot brown stock and 1 stalk of celery, 3 sprigs of parsley, 1 small bay leaf, 1 garlic clove, and a pinch of thyme, all chopped. Cook, stirring, until the mixture thickens.

Add 3 more cups stock and simmer slowly over very low heat, stirring occasionally, for 1 to 1 1/2 hours, or until the mixture is reduced to about 3 cups. As it cooks, skim off the fat which rises to the surface. Add 1/4 cup tomato sauce or 1/2 cup tomato purée. Cook the sauce for a few minutes longer and strain it through a fine sieve. Add 2 more cups stock and continue to cook slowly for about 1 hour, skimming occasionally, until the sauce is reduced to about 4 cups. Cool, stirring occasionally. Store it, covered, in the refrigerator. If not used within a week, reheat.

IN a saucepan brown very lightly 1 finely chopped onion in 2 tablespoons fat. Add 2 tablespoons flour and cook, stirring, until the *roux* is brown. Add 2 cups brown stock and 3 tablespoons tomato purée and cook, stirring, until the sauce thickens. Continue to cook the sauce until it is reduced to about 1 cup. Season to taste. *Simple Brown Sauce*

Add 1 tablespoon *glace de viande* to 2 cups brown sauce. Cook 1/3 cup dry Sherry with the chopped stems and peelings of 5 or 6 mushrooms until the moisture is reduced to half. Combine the two mixtures and simmer the sauce for 15 minutes. *Demi-Glace Sauce*

Cook 2 cups brown sauce until it is reduced to about 1 cup. Add 1/3 cup Madeira. Heat the sauce well but do not let it boil or the flavor of the wine will be lost. *Madeira Sauce*

Cook 2 shallots, finely chopped, in 1/2 cup red wine until the wine is reduced by three-fourths. Add 1 cup brown sauce and simmer gently for 10 minutes. Remove the marrow from a split beef bone, cut it into small dice, poach it in boiling salted water for no more than 1 or 2 minutes, and drain it. Just before serving the sauce, add to it 2 tablespoons beef marrow and 1/2 teaspoon chopped parsley. *Bordelaise Sauce*

Poached Beef Marrow

Cook 1 teaspoon chopped shallots and 2 tomatoes, peeled, seeded, and chopped, in 3/4 cup Marsala wine until the tomatoes are soft and the mixture is reduced by half. Add 1/2 cup brown sauce, 2 tablespoons finely diced mushrooms sautéed in a little butter and seasoned with a little lemon juice and salt to taste, and 2 tablespoons very finely chopped cooked ham. Boil the sauce for 5 minutes and add 1 teaspoon finely chopped parsley. *Sauce Italienne*

787

Sauce
Périgourdine

To 1 cup brown sauce add 3 tablespoons Madeira, 1 tablespoon chopped truffles, a little of the liquid from the truffle can, and the juices, free of fat, from a pan in which poultry was roasted. Heat all together, swirl in 1 tablespoon butter, and remove the sauce from the heat as soon as the butter is melted. The sauce should not boil after the butter is added.

Sauce Romaine

Cook 2 tablespoons sugar in a heavy saucepan until it is a light golden color. Add 1/2 cup vinegar and cook the mixture until it is reduced to almost nothing. Stir in 1 cup brown sauce, bring the sauce to a boil, and add 2 tablespoons raisins, Smyrna or Corinth if possible. Simmer the sauce for 10 minutes longer. Use for veal, beef, tongue, and venison.

The basic white sauce is the béchamel, *but in an emergency ordinary cream sauce and judicious seasoning may take its place.*

Béchamel
Sauce

IN a saucepan heat 1/4 cup butter and cook in it over low heat 1/2 onion, finely minced, without letting the onion take on color. Stir in 1/2 cup flour and gradually add 1 quart milk heated to the boiling point. Cook, stirring constantly, until the mixture is smooth.

In another saucepan simmer 1/4 pound chopped lean veal in 2 tablespoons butter over very low heat. Season with a sprig of thyme or a tiny pinch of thyme leaves—powdered thyme will discolor the sauce—a pinch of white pepper, and a pinch of freshly grated nutmeg. Cook the mixture for 5 minutes, stirring to keep the veal from browning. Add the veal to the sauce and blend thoroughly. Add salt to taste.

Cook the sauce over hot water for about 1 hour, stirring from time to time. Strain the sauce through a fine sieve and dot it with tiny flecks of butter, which will melt and prevent the forming of a film on the surface. This recipe makes 4 cups of sauce.

Mornay Sauce

Heat 2 cups béchamel sauce over low heat, stirring constantly. When the boiling point is reached, add 1 tablespoon grated Parmesan cheese and 1 tablespoon grated Gruyère. Stir constantly with a small whisk until the sauce is smooth and thickened. Remove it from the heat and finish it with 2 tablespoons butter, added gradually.

Velouté

MELT 1/4 cup butter in a saucepan, add 1/4 cup flour, mix well, and cook for a few minutes without letting the flour take on color. Add 6 cups boiling white stock, 2 cups at a time, stirring the mixture vigorously with a wire whip. Add 1 cup chopped mushrooms or mushroom peelings and stems, 3 white peppercorns, a little salt if necessary, and 1 sprig of parsley. Cook the sauce, stirring frequently, for about 1 hour, skimming it from time to time, until it is reduced by one-third and has the consistency of heavy cream. Strain the sauce through a fine sieve. If it is to be stored, stir it occasionally with the whip as it cools and dot it with bits of butter. If it is too thick, add more stock.

When *velouté* is made with chicken stock it is called chicken *velouté*

Chicken Velouté

Cook 1 onion, finely chopped, in a saucepan in 1 tablespoon butter until it is soft but not brown. Add 1 small bay leaf, a little thyme, and 1 table-spoon curry powder and mix well. Add 1/4 cup fish or chicken stock, depending on the way the sauce is to be used, and bring to a boil. Add 1 1/2 cups *velouté*, made with fish or chicken stock, boil the sauce for 15 minutes and strain it through a fine sieve. Finish with 1/2 cup cream.

Velouté au Cari
CURRIED CREAM SAUCE

Cook 2 cups chicken stock with 3 sliced mushrooms, or an equivalent amount of mushroom stems and peelings, until it is reduced by two-thirds the original quantity. Combine the stock with 1 cup *sauce velouté*. Bring the sauce to a boil, reduce it to about 1 cup, and gradually add 1 cup sweet cream, stirring constantly. Correct the seasoning with salt and a little cayenne pepper and strain the sauce through a fine sieve. If the sauce is not to be used immediately, fleck the surface with butter.

Sauce Suprême

MELT 2 tablespoons butter, stir in gradually 2 tablespoons flour, and stir the *roux* over low heat for about 5 minutes. It should not be allowed to take on color. Stir in slowly 1 cup scalded milk and continue to cook, still stirring, until the sauce is smooth and thick. Season to taste.

For a thin cream sauce, reduce the amount of the butter and flour to 1 tablespoon each.

For a thick sauce, use 3 tablespoons each of butter and flour.

Cream Sauce or White Sauce

A rich cream sauce is made by adding to the cream sauce 2 egg yolks, beaten and then warmed by the addition of a little of the sauce. The rich cream sauce should not be allowed to boil after the egg yolks are added.

Rich Cream Sauce

Hollandaise Sauce

DIVIDE 1/2 cup butter into 3 parts. In the top of a double boiler, or in a heatproof bowl over hot water, put 4 egg yolks and 1 part of the butter. Stir the mixture rapidly and constantly over hot but not boiling water until the butter is melted. Add the second piece of butter. As the mixture thickens and the butter melts, add the third part, stirring constantly from the bottom of the pan. Do not allow the water over which the sauce is cooking to come to a boil.

When the butter is melted and all is well mixed, remove the saucepan from the heat and continue to beat the sauce for at least 2 minutes longer. Add 2 teaspoons lemon juice or vinegar and a pinch each of white pepper and salt. Replace the saucepan over the hot but not boiling water for 2 minutes, beating constantly.

Should the mixture curdle, immediately beat in 1 to 2 tablespoons boiling water, beating constantly, in order to rebind the emulsion.

Sauce Mousseline

Stir equal parts of hollandaise sauce and whipped cream over hot water until the sauce is hot.

Béarnaise Sauce

DIVIDE 1 cup butter at room temperature into 3 parts. Combine 3 sprigs of tarragon, 3 sprigs of chervil, 2 shallots, all finely chopped, 4 crushed peppercorns, and 1/4 cup each of tarragon vinegar and white wine in the top of a double boiler. Cook these ingredients over direct heat until they are reduced to a thick paste. Cool slightly. Put the pan over hot water and add 3 egg yolks and 1 tablespoon water. Stir briskly with a small wire whisk until the mixture is light and fluffy. Add the first portion of butter and stir constantly until the mixture is thick and smooth. Add the second and third parts, stirring briskly after each addition. Season the sauce to taste with salt and a pinch of cayenne, strain it through a fine sieve, and add 3 sprigs each of tarragon and chervil, both finely chopped. For grilled meats and grilled fish.

Sauce à l'Indienne
CURRY SAUCE

COOK 1/2 cup finely chopped onion in 3 tablespoons butter, together with 1 cup cubed green apple, until the apples are tender and the onions transparent, stirring frequently with a wooden spoon. Remove the pan from the heat and sprinkle the apple mixture with 2 tablespoons flour sifted with 2 teaspoons curry powder, 1/2 teaspoon salt, and a few grains of nutmeg and cayenne. Blend well.

Add 1 slice of garlic, 1 small bay leaf, 4 sprigs of parsley, and 6 thin slices of onion to 1 1/2 cups chicken stock, simmer the stock until it is somewhat reduced, and strain it. Gradually stir the reduced stock into the apple mixture.

Bring the sauce to a boil, and cook, stirring constantly from the bottom of the saucepan, until it thickens and bubbles. Place the pan over hot water and simmer the sauce for 5 or 6 minutes, stirring occasionally. Taste for seasoning and serve very hot.

SAUTÉ 1 small onion, finely chopped, in 1/4 cup butter until the onion is transparent but not brown. Stir in 2 tablespoons flour and 1 tablespoon paprika and cook, stirring, until the mixture is well blended. Add gradually, stirring, 1 cup well-seasoned chicken stock and 1/2 cup dry white wine. Continue to cook, stirring, until the sauce is thickened and smooth. Place it over boiling water and cook for 15 minutes. Season to taste with salt and finish with 1/4 cup heavy cream.

Hungarian Sauce

IN 1 1/2 tablespoons butter sauté 2 small onions, finely minced, until they are soft but not brown. Moisten them with 1/2 cup dry white wine, stir well, and reduce the liquid over high heat to almost nothing, stirring occasionally. Pour in 1 generous cup scalded sour cream, stirring constantly, and continue to stir until the mixture is thoroughly blended. Simmer the sauce very gently for 5 minutes. Strain it through a fine sieve or cheesecloth and season with salt and pepper to taste. Just before serving add 1 teaspoon strained lemon juice. Serve with chicken, veal, or game.

Sauce Smitane

BROWN lightly 2 shallots, chopped, and 1/2 onion, thinly sliced, in 1 generous tablespoon goose fat, pork fat, or butter. In another saucepan heat 3/4 cup white wine. Ignite 1 tablespoon brandy and add it to the wine, or add 1 tablespoon Madeira.

Add 1 teaspoon flour to the shallots and onion and brown the *roux* lightly. Moisten with a little bouillon and add the wine. Cover the sauce and simmer it over very low heat, stirring often, for 20 minutes. Strain the sauce, add a truffle, finely diced, and cook for 2 or 3 minutes.

Sauce Périgueux

IN a heavy saucepan melt 3 tablespoons butter. Add 1 small carrot and 1 small onion, both coarsely chopped, and cook until the onion is soft but not brown. Stir in 1/4 cup flour and cook until the *roux* turns golden. Add 2 to 2 1/2 cups cooked tomatoes or chopped fresh tomatoes, 1 1/2 cups

Tomato Sauce

brown stock or water, 2 garlic cloves, crushed, 1/2 teaspoon salt, 1 teaspoon sugar, a pinch of thyme, a little pepper, and a *bouquet garni* of 4 sprays of parsley, 1 stalk of celery with the leaves, and half a bay leaf tied together.

Bring the sauce to a boil, stirring constantly until it thickens, and continue to cook, stirring occasionally and skimming the surface when necessary, for 1 to 1 1/2 hours, or until the sauce is reduced to about 2 cups. Discard the *bouquet garni* and rub the sauce through a fine sieve. Bring the sauce again to a boil and cook for 5 minutes, stirring.

Pan Gravy PAN gravy is made simply with the drippings of roasted beef, veal, pork, or fowl. Remove the meat to a heated platter, skim the excess fat from the drippings, and add a little stock to the remaining pan juices, stirring to incorporate all the brown bits that adhere to the pan. This gravy may be thickened with *beurre manié*—equal parts of flour and butter kneaded together—in the proportion of 2 tablespoons to 1 cup liquid. It should be cooked for a few minutes after the *beurre manié* is added.

Meunière Butter MELT 1/2 cup butter in a small saucepan and cook it slowly until it turns hazelnut brown in color. Add the juice of 1/2 lemon, 1 tablespoon chopped parsley, and salt and pepper to taste.

Butter Caper Sauce MELT 1/2 cup butter over low heat and skim off the foam. Add 1 tablespoon lemon juice, 1/4 cup capers, and salt to taste.

Maître d'Hôtel Butter CREAM 1/2 cup butter with 1 tablespoon chopped parsley, the juice of half a lemon, and salt and pepper to taste.

Homemade mayonnaise is well worth the effort it takes and takes far less effort than one would think.

Mayonnaise RINSE a mixing bowl with hot water and dry it well. In it beat 2 egg yolks with a rotary beater. Add 1/2 teaspoon salt, a little white pepper, 1/2 teaspoon dry mustard, and 1 teaspoon vinegar. Mix well. Add 1 cup light olive, or part olive and part peanut, oil drop by drop at first, beating continually, until a little more than 1/4 cup has been added. Add 1/2 teaspoon vinegar, still beating, and then pour in the rest of the oil in a thin stream. Beat continually and stop adding the oil from time to time to make sure the mixture is well combined. When the oil has been added and the mayonnaise is thick, finish with 1/2 teaspoon vinegar, or use lemon or lime juice. If the mayonnaise should curdle, wash the beater, beat 1 egg yolk in another bowl and very slowly add the curdled mayonnaise to the fresh egg yolk, beating constantly to form a new emulsion.

If you use an electric beater, set it at medium speed.

Add a nugget of anchovy paste the size of a pea and 1 hard-cooked egg white, finely chopped, to 1 cup freshly made mayonnaise. Cook together 2 tablespoons each of capers, chervil, parsley, shallots, and onion, all chopped, for 15 minutes in 1/4 cup dry white wine and 1 tablespoon lemon juice. Cool and combine with the mayonnaise. Chill well before serving with eggs or shellfish. *Ravigote Mayonnaise*

To 2 cups mayonnaise add 1/2 cup finely chopped sour pickles and 2 tablespoons finely chopped capers, both carefully drained and dried, 1 tablespoon each of prepared mustard and mixed chopped parsley, tarragon, and chervil. For celeriac salad and shrimps. *Sauce Rémoulade*

To 1 cup freshly made mayonnaise add 3 tablespoons chili sauce and 1 teaspoon each of finely chopped pimientos and chives. For fish, egg, and vegetable salads. *Russian Dressing*

To 1/2 cup good vinegar—wine, cider, or malt vinegar—add 3/4 teaspoon salt and 1/4 teaspoon ground white pepper. Stir well with a fork and add 1 1/2 cups olive oil. Beat the mixture with a fork until it thickens. *French Dressing*

For a thicker, creamier dressing, put an ice cube into the mixing bowl and stir the dressing for a minute or two longer. Or set the mixing bowl into another bowl filled with ice while the dressing is being stirred. The dressing may be made in a bottle and shaken vigorously.

To this basic dressing can be added, singly or in combination, as your imagination and your purpose dictate, capers, Tabasco, chopped mixed herbs, curry powder, horseradish, paprika, tomato ketchup, chili sauce, Roquefort or blue cheese, or tarragon—to cite only a few possibilities. *French Dressing Variations*

CRUSH 6 to 8 garlic cloves very thoroughly in a mortar and pound in 1/4 teaspoon salt. Put the mixture in a bowl with 2 egg yolks and mix thoroughly. Add a few drops of olive oil and beat vigorously. Continue adding oil, *Aioli Sauce* GARLIC MAYONNAISE a very little at a time, until about 2 tablespoons have been added, then in a thin stream until 1 cup has been added, beating constantly. If the mixture seems too thick add 1/2 teaspoon or more of water. Add the juice of 1/2 lemon. Serve on hot or cold fish or vegetables, or with boiled beef.

Certain classical garnishes are used over and over again in haute cuisine.

Cockscombs for Garnish

SELECT 12 cockscombs from fresh, young fowl. Scrape away the outside skin, make small incisions in the points, and chill the combs, covered with cold water, for several hours, changing the water two or three times.

Drain and cover the combs with 2 cups salted cold water mixed with 1 tablespoon flour and the juice of 1 lemon. Bring to a boil and cook gently for 20 to 30 minutes, or until the combs are tender. Drain before using.

Mousseline Forcemeat of Chicken or Veal

REMOVE the skin and sinews from 1/2 pound breast of chicken. Cut the meat into small pieces, add 1/4 teaspoon salt and a little white pepper, and pound it in a mortar or put it through the finest blade of a food chopper, gradually adding 1 egg white. Rub the mixture through a fine sieve into a saucepan. Put the pan on a bed of ice, work the mixture with a wooden spoon until it is chilled, and add gradually about 1 cup heavy cream, working it in a little at a time. Lean veal may be used in place of the chicken in this recipe.

Mousselines

For garnishing, *mousseline* forcemeat is shaped with 2 tablespoons into small *mousselines quenelles*, called simply *mousselines*. Heap the forcemeat in one spoon and press another spoon over it to form an olive shape. Dip the second spoon into warm water, slip it under the forcemeat, and slide the *mousseline* into a buttered pan. When the *mousselines* are all formed, add a little salted water or chicken stock to the pan, bring the liquid just to a boil, and poach the *mousselines* very gently over low heat for 10 to 15 minutes, until they are firm. Do not let the liquid boil or they will split. Skim them carefully from the pan with a perforated spoon and dry them on a towel. When *mousselines* are used for garnishing elaborate dishes, they are usually decorated with pieces of truffle cut in flowershapes. These pieces must be carefully pressed into the tops of the *mousselines* and great care must be taken in poaching, or the decoration will fall off.

Other quenelles for garnishing may be made by shaping forcemeat on a floured board to form small balls or ovals. Poach these as described above.

Quenelles

SELECT 12 firm, fresh white mushrooms, remove the stems, and soak the caps in cold water for a short time. With a small, sharp knife, carve the top of each cap into a pinwheel-like design, turning the cap in the left hand while working with the knife in the right. Cook the turned mushrooms in 1/2 cup slightly salted water with 1 tablespoon butter and the juice of 1/2 lemon for 5 minutes. Let the mushrooms cool in the liquid.

Turned Mushrooms

WASH sprigs of parsley and dry them well. Drop them into hot deep fat (390° F.) and fry them for a few seconds, or until they rise to the surface of the fat and begin to crisp. Drain on absorbent paper and sprinkle with salt.

Fried Parsley

PEEL tomatoes and cut off the tops and reserve them. Squeeze very gently to remove seeds and juice. Slice 1 or 2 cucumbers very thin, sprinkle with salt and let stand 10 to 15 minutes. Drain and dry the cucumbers in a towel. Dress the cucumbers with vinaigrette sauce and sprinkle them with a little chopped parsley. Fill the tomatoes with the cucumber mixture and replace the tops. Use to garnish fish platters.

Tomatoes Filled with Cucumber Salad

Tomatoes may be stuffed with any salad mixture of raw or cooked vegetables bound with a suitable dressing.

Stuffed Tomatoes

ANY cooked or preserved fruit may be used to garnish meat or poultry. To the syrup in which the fruit was poached, add half as much vinegar. Tie in a cheesecloth bag a piece of stick cinnamon and 12 cloves. Put the spice bag in the syrup and simmer the syrup until it achieves the desired spicy flavor. Discard the bag and pour the boiling syrup over the cooked fruit. Let it cool in the syrup. Serve cold, sprinkled with a little freshly grated nutmeg.

Spiced Fruit Garnish

REMOVE the almond shells, cover the nuts with boiling water, and let them stand for 1 minute. Drain away the hot water, rinse the nuts in cold water, and slip off the skins.

To Blanch Almonds

Before the blanched almonds can be slivered, grated, ground, or otherwise processed for future use, they must be thoroughly dried. Spread them in a pan in a moderate oven (350° F.). Shake the pan frequently for even heating. The nuts will be dry and ready to use within 15 minutes.

In the following alphabetical listing are the accessories to gourmet cookery to which reference is frequently made throughout this volume. Other preparations mentioned within the recipes are listed in the index.

Bar Syrup	Boil together for 5 minutes 3 cups sugar and 1 cup water. Store in a tightly closed container and use to sweeten drinks.
Beurre Manié	Knead together 2 parts butter and 1 part flour, and use this kneaded butter to thicken sauces or soups.
Clarified Butter	Melt butter in a small pot and carefully pour the clear fat off the milky sediment that will settle to the bottom of the pot.
Bouquet Garni or Faggot	Tie together an assortment of fresh herbs, usually including celery, parsley, thyme, and bay leaf, and sometimes fennel, leek, marjoram, and tarragon. This bunch of seasoning herbs may be easily removed from the pot and discarded.
Dorure	Mix 1 tablespoon milk with 1 egg and brush the mixture on bread or cake or other foods that are to be baked in the oven.
Fines Herbes	Combine minced fresh chives, chervil, tarragon, and basil in any desired proportions.
Flour and Baking Powder	Use all-purpose flour and double-action baking powder unless otherwise indicated.
Foie Gras	*Foie gras* is the liver of a force-fed goose. Whole *foie gras* is imported from France in cans, cooked. The seasoned loaf of ground and mashed goose liver, also available in cans, is called *pâté de purée de foie gras en bloc*. When *pâté de foie gras* is called for, use slices of this loaf. *Purée de foie gras* is a portion of the *bloc* mashed or put through a sieve.
Glace de Viande and Meat Extract	*Glace de viande* is a gelatinous, highly concentrated flavoring essence achieved by long, slow cooking of meats, bones, and vegetables. It is available at some specialty shops as *glace de viande* or as meat glaze. Meat extract, using about one-third the quantity called for, usually makes an acceptable substitute.
Mirepoix	Cook until soft in a little butter 1 carrot, 1 onion, and 1 stalk of celery, all finely chopped, with a bay leaf, a pinch of thyme, and salt and pepper to taste. A little chopped ham or bacon may be added to the *mirepoix*.

Weights and Means

This table of measurements and equivalents is compiled for the special convenience of the thousands of owners of THE GOURMET COOKBOOK, VOLUMES I *and* II, *who speak British English, rather than American English, in their kitchens.*

American

British

American	British
1 cup	an 8-ounce measuring cup or a teacup that will hold 8 fluid ounces
1 cup liquid	8 fluid ounces
1 cup all-purpose flour	5 ounces plain flour
1 cup cake flour	3 1/2 ounces self-raising flour (omit baking powder and salt in recipe)
2 cups butter	1 pound
2 cups sugar	1 pound
3 1/2 cups confectioners' sugar	1 pound icing sugar
3 cups brown sugar	1 pound brown sugar
2 cups rice	1 pound
1 square baking chocolate	1 ounce
1 cake or envelope yeast	1/4 ounce bakers' yeast
1 envelope or tablespoon granulated gelatin	3 to 4 sheets (4″×9″), enough to jelly 2 cups liquid

Approximate oven temperatures:

	STANDARD GAS SETTINGS	REGULO
250° F.	1/4	5
300° F.	1	6
350° F.	4	7
400° F.	6	8
450° F.	8	9

Special Acknowledgments

We wish to express our appreciation to the many firms, all in New York City, who made available the beautiful accessories that appear in the color photographs of this book. Articles not credited are privately owned.

Frontispiece
   antique salt box—Richard V. Hare; *egg basket*—Soupçon Gift & Food Shop; *butter crock*—The Stone House; *glass jar, basket, wooden bowl with spoon, cream pitcher*—Merrill Ames Gift Shop; *antique copper ladle*—Pampered Kitchens, Inc.

21, *Toulouse-Lautrec poster:* "Jane Avril" —Old Print Center of Phyllis Lucas.

24, no special acknowledgments.

46, *wine rack*—Sherry Wine & Spirits Co., Inc. *glass*—Baccarat, Inc.

55, *cruet*—America House; *plates*—Ginori Fifth Avenue.

61, *fabric, red enamel dish, mortar*—America House.

64, *pewter plate, china dish*—Vito Giallo Antiques.

73, *fabric*—Brunschwig & Fils Inc.; *plate*—Mayhew.

76, *vermeil basket, plate*—Tiffany & Co.; *fabric*—J. H. Thorp & Co., Inc.

89, *crock*—La Cuisinière, Inc.

100, *chessmen, antique chessboard*—Wakefield-Young Books; *glass and bowls*—Baccarat, Inc.

109, *brass serving plate, picture*—Leigh Hammond; *soup bowl, flower container*—Mayhew.

120, *fur rug*—Leigh Hammond; *tureen*—Ginori Fifth Avenue.

125, *earthenware dinner plate, soup plate*—Ginori Fifth Avenue; *pewter spoon*—Leigh Hammond.

135, no special acknowledgments.

138, no special acknowledgments.

148, *copper baking dish*—La Cuisinière, Inc.

157, *print*—Old Print Center of Phyllis Lucas.

160, *Italian pottery platter*—Mayhew.

177, *bust of Admiral Dewey, antique toy battleship*—F. A. O. Schwarz.

180, *copper pan*—D/R International Inc.; *flower containers*—Mayhew; *scale*—La Cuisinière, Inc.; *fabric*—Cohama Fabrics.

193, *baking dish*—La Cuisinière, Inc.

204, *bowl, plate, spoon*—Bonniers, Inc.; *poster*—Nassau Bahamas Development Board.

217, no special acknowledgments.

220, *tray*—Ginori Fifth Avenue; *fork and spoon*—Mayhew.

229, *casserole*—Ginori Fifth Avenue; *antique toy*—F. A. O. Schwarz.

232, no special acknowledgments.

241, *cork picture*—Belgravia House; *platter, salt dish*—Cartier.

244, *platter*—Ginori Fifth Avenue.

257, *platter*—Mayhew.

268, *copper dish*—Bazar Français; *serving fork and spoon*—Christofle silver at Plummer McCutcheon; *fabric*—Boussac of France, Inc.

277, *spice box and spice holder*—Lar; *earthenware platter*—Stuart's Gifts; *spoon*—Mayhew.

288, *pewter platter*—Harry Hirsch.

293, *antique Cretan throw, casserole, pepper grinder, pitcher*—Greek Island, Ltd.

296, *chafing dish, painted wood rooster*—Bonniers, Inc.

301, *platter, flower holders, picture*—David Barrett; *cloth*— La Grande Maison de Blanc.

304, *sterling platter, sauceboat, ladle*—Ginori Fifth Avenue; *wooden cachepot*—David Barrett; *carving set*—Gorham at Frank McCormack.

313, *plate, pitcher and glasses*—Ginori Fifth Avenue.

316, *platter and plate*—Soupçon Gift & Food Shop; *metal flower holder*—The Noisy Oyster.

321, *platter and sauce bowl*—The Noisy Oyster; *silver spoon and cruet set*—Plummer McCutcheon; *fabric*—Cohama Fabrics.

324, *platter*—The Noisy Oyster; *silver inkwell*—Past and Present; *fabric*—Cohama Fabrics.

345, *platter*—Tiffany & Co.

356, *platter, crystal bowl, quail figurine*—Tiffany & Co.

361, *carving knife and fork, tray, sauceboat*—Plummer McCutcheon.

364, *pitcher, kitchen fork, bowl*—La Cuisinière, Inc.

381, *platter, lace cloth*—Plummer McCutcheon; *sauceboat*—Vito Giallo Antiques.

384, *doll*—Lar; *platter*—Mayhew.

389, *hibachi*—Azuma.

392, *platter*—Bonniers, Inc.; *spoon*—Harry Hirsch.

401, *pot*—La Cuisinière Inc.; *figurine*—Belgravia House; *plate, platter*—Bonniers, Inc.

404, *plates*—Mayhew; *basket*—Vito Giallo Antiques.

413, *platter, serving spoon and fork*—Ginori Fifth Avenue; *serving dish, beaded flower arrangement*—Bonwit Teller.

416, *oyster forks*—Reed & Barton.

425, *serving plate*—B. Altman & Co.; *serving fork*—Cartier; *flock wallpaper*—Brunschwig & Fils.

428, *platter*—James Robinson, Inc.; *18th century boxes, flower holder*—Jansen Shop, Inc.; *candelabra*—Carole Stupell.

437, *meat block*—B. Altman & Co.; *terrine*—Bazar Français.

448, *platter*—Plummer McCutcheon; *antique faïence letter holder*—Chodoff Antiques; *fabric*—Cohama Fabrics.

457, *casserole, artichoke salt and pepper shakers*—Soupçon Gift & Food Shop.

468, *plate*—Soupçon Gift & Food Shop; *ticking*—Brunschwig & Fils, Inc.

473, *platter, server*—Christofle Silver, Inc.; *tablecloth*—D. Porthault, Inc.; *tureen*—Ceralene, Inc.; *flower arrangement*—Bouquets à la Carte.

483, *plates, wineglass*—Soupçon Gift & Food Shop.

486, *silver frying pan servers, salt and pepper shakers*—Tiffany & Co.

496, *spoon*—Christofle Silver, Inc.

513, *candlestick, wax portrait*—Vito Giallo Antiques; *platter, knife*—S. Wyler, Inc.

523, *glasses*—Mayhew.

526, no special acknowledgments.

536, no special acknowledgments.

545, *pewter bowl*—Harry Hirsch; *bull*—Stuart's Gifts.

548, *platter, flower holder*—D/R International, Inc.; *toast rack*—Cardel Ltd.; *fabric*—Cohama Fabrics.

565, no special acknowledgment.

568, *platter, cheese dish, butter dish, flatware*—Ginori Fifth Avenue.

581, *throw, candies, doll*—Paprikas Weiss Importers.

584, *plate, pitcher, pot, and cornstick pan*—La Cuisinière, Inc.

593, *Edwardian custard cups*—La Cuisinière, Inc.

596, *soufflé dishes*—Soupçon Gift & Food Shop; *clock*—Timepieces Clock Shop; *fabric*—Brunschwig & Fils, Inc.

605, *faïence flower holder*—Red Shutters; *spoon*—Harry Hirsch.

616, *bowl*—Mayhew; *spoon*—H. Nils Danish Silver, Inc.; *silver pail*—Chodoff Antiques; *background fabric*—Brunschwig & Fils, Inc.

621, *plate, glass, napkin*—Mediterranean Shop.

624, *bowl*—Baccarat, Inc.; *spoon*—Christofle Silver, Inc.; *cloth*—D. Porthault, Inc.

633, oil painting by Bernard Lamotte, privately owned; no other special acknowledgments.

636, *platter, serving spoons, swan and ladle*—Plummer McCutcheon; *coffee pot and cup*—Mayhew; *fabric*—Cohama Fabrics.

645, *soufflé dish*—La Cuisinière, Inc.; *sauceboat*—Cartier, Inc.; *marble*—Niccolini, Inc.; *linen*—Léron, Inc.

664, *glasses*—Fostoria Glass Corporation; *spoons*—Plummer McCutcheon; *poodle*—Bonwit Teller; *background fabric*—Boussac of France, Inc.

673, *plate, finger bowl and plate, box*—Bonwit Teller; *fork and spoon*—Gorham at Plummer McCutcheon.

676, *compote*—Carole Stupell; *fabric*—Cohama Fabrics.

689, no special acknowledgments.

700, *glass containers*—Bonniers, Inc.; *board, wire whip*—Bazar Français.

709, *platter*—Carole Stupell; *flower holder*—Mayhew; *plates*—Malmaison.

720, *silver gilt pineapple, plate, glass box, brocade*—Malmaison.

741, no special acknowledgments.

760, *platter*—Christofle Silver Inc.; *server*—Cartier; *flower basket*—Soupçon Gift & Food Shop; *bamboo flower holder*—Chodoff Antiques; *silk flowers*—Richard V. Hare.

765, no special acknowledgments.

768, *two-tiered tray*—Carole Stupell; *flower holder*—Mayhew; *mirror*—Jansen Shop, Inc.

777, *cake stand, vermeil obelisks*—Tiffany & Co.

780, *pitcher and tumblers*—America House; *ironstone plate*—Vito Giallo Antiques; *fabric*—Brunschwig & Fils, Inc.

Index

807